Technology–Supported Environments for Personalized Learning:
Methods and Case Studies

John O'Donoghue
University of Central Lancashire, UK

INFORMATION SCIENCE REFERENCE

Hershey · New York

Director of Editorial Content:	Kristin Klinger
Senior Managing Editor:	Jamie Snavely
Assistant Managing Editor:	Michael Brehm
Publishing Assistant:	Sean Woznicki
Typesetter:	Mike Killian, Kurt Smith, Sean Woznicki
Cover Design:	Lisa Tosheff
Printed at:	Yurchak Printing Inc.

Published in the United States of America by
Information Science Reference (an imprint of IGI Global)
701 E. Chocolate Avenue
Hershey PA 17033
Tel: 717-533-8845
Fax: 717-533-8661
E-mail: cust@igi-global.com
Web site: http://www.igi-global.com/reference

Library of Congress Cataloging-in-Publication Data

Technology-supported environments for personalized learning : methods and case studies / John O'Donoghue, editor.
    p. cm.

  Includes bibliographical references and index.
  Summary: "This book explores the metaphor of anytime and anywhere individual education as well as the idea of tailoring instruction to meet individual needs"--Provided by publisher.

  ISBN 978-1-60566-884-0 (hardcover) -- ISBN 978-1-60566-885-7 (ebook) 1.
Computer-assisted instruction. 2. Individualized instruction. I. O'Donoghue,
John, 1959-
  LB1028.5.T426 2010
  371.33'4--dc22

                        2009035434

British Cataloguing in Publication Data
A Cataloguing in Publication record for this book is available from the British Library.

All work contributed to this book is new, previously-unpublished material. The views expressed in this book are those of the authors, but not necessarily of the publisher.

Dedication

There is a before and there is an after. There is a day, a moment when, abruptly, one life ends and another begins. In the blink of an eye, you are where you never desired yourself to be, people unrecognisable to yourselves, transformed beyond your own understanding. With no going back. This is what happened to me.

In May I received the news that we all must fear and dread. Without any signs or symptoms I was diagnosed with cancer. This devastating news is traumatic for the individual, but the effect on my family is difficult to comprehend.

This book is dedicated to Carole, my beloved wife, who has been my strength, salvation, nurse, mentor and eternal soul mate. Life would have been very different for me without her at this present time. I thank her for her love and loyalty under such difficult times.

Words are insufficient to express my love and affection. Many tears have been shed over the intervening weeks, but with Carole and my children Hannah and Alice we look positively forward. At such moments, I understood the importance of saying "I LOVE YOU" in time and to give our loved ones the time that they deserve.

Nothing in life is more important than your family. Give them the time they deserve, because these things cannot be put off till "some other time."

Value always what we all too often take for granted, especially as time passes.

John O'Donoghue

Table of Contents

Section 3
Technological Issues

Detailed Table of Contents

Chapter 1

Gráinne Conole, Open University, UK

This introductory chapter considers the discourse of the concept of personalisation and how it can be supported through technology-enhanced learning. It looks at the policy rhetoric and considers to what extent it is realised in practice. The chapter describes a range of illustrative examples of how technologies are being used to meet the personalised learning agenda.

Section 1
Infrastructural and Cultural Issues

Chapter 2

Beth Granter, University of Sussex, UK

This chapter, inspired by direct experience from working on the development of the University of Sussex's Student Personal Learning and Social Homepages (SPLASH) project, discusses how 'Web 2.0' technologies can be used to make institutional websites more democratic. The SPLASH mashup project was non-typical in that it intended to create an environment which would be fully customisable by the learner, so that no content was obligatory. Examples from working on this project are used to illustrate benefits which can be gained from, and barriers to the uptake of, more open publishing methods and an organically structured site architecture. Issues affecting learners, tutors, the institution as a whole, and how the power dynamic between all three may change, are discussed. Parallels are drawn between teaching methods online and those offline, both traditional and modern.

Chapter 3

Sabrina Leone, Università Politecnica delle Marche, Italy

The attainment of lifelong learning objectives is being mediated by a complex process of innovation in education and society, by the integration of institutional actions and by the major role of coordination that university has assumed. The revolution that technology has engendered in every field has flowed into a rethinking of knowledge, knowledge management, teaching and learning, networks and the individual. The knowledge society requires new roles and skills, new forms of communication and a new awareness as "active citizens". Consequently, the shifting role of education systems in networked organizations is decisive in order to support learners in forming diverse personal learning networks to deeply understand complex fields. This chapter aims to discuss consistency (i.e. solidity and reliability) and effectiveness (i.e. success, usefulness and value) of a personal learning environment as a new learning space and to highlight its contribution and relevance to lifelong learning. PLE critical points and approaches will be discussed exploiting three case studies.

Chapter 4

This chapter details the implementation of a university-wide social networking platform "Community@ Brighton" – using the open source Elgg platform and describes the technical, institutional and educational issues arising from the two years of experience in running the platform. The strategic vision of providing a social network platform alongside an institutional VLE to provide an integrated Shared Learning Environment is also explored, including key case studies and discussion on the challenges such technologies place on existing models of online learning and teaching.

Chapter 5

Students who have grown up in the digital age have certain expectations for learning in Higher Education (HE). "Using a complex mix of virtual and face-to-face environments, personal and institutional technologies, learners of all ages are developing new working practices around the technologies available to them. Increasingly, they look for flexibility and openness in the institutional policies and provision that support their learning." (JISC, 2007). The divide between the institutional eLearning provision and the expectations of students who have grown up in a digital world was highlighted through the UK eLearning benchmarking exercise. Institutional eLearning provision and processes within the HE sector were investigated and analysed through this exercise, which was led by the Higher Education Academy (HEA) in collaboration with the Joint Information Systems Committee (JISC). This paper presents the experience of two UK Universities, Bournemouth and Reading, whose participation in the benchmarking exercise provides examples of institutional provision. Subsequent Pathfinder funding enabled them to build on their strengths with projects aimed at narrowing the divide between student expectations of eLearning and institutional provision. The eRes: Innovative eLearning with e-Resources project (Bournemouth) encourages students to use quality e-resources in their learning. The "Driving Institutional Reform: Exploring Change with Technology" (DIRECT) project (Reading) has developed a framework to transform its internal quality management processes.

Kevin Burden, The University of Hull, UK

Simon Atkinson, Massey University, New Zealand

This chapter describes the ways in which individual academics have sought to realise a degree of personalisation in their teaching practice through their engagement with the DiAL-e Framework (Digital Artefacts for Learner Engagement). The DiAL-e Framework (www.dial-e.net) is a new conceptual model, articulated as a paper-based and web-based tool, for designing learning engagements. The policy and theoretical context, evolution of the framework and the methodology used to utilise the framework with academic staff seeking to personalise the learning experience is outlined. Details of three case studies resulting from this early work are described and conclusions drawn as to how such frameworks might assist staff in thinking about personalised learning scenarios.

Elfneh Udessa Bariso, College of North East London, UK

Electronic media can contribute to personalisation of learning both in formal and informal contexts. Efforts are made both at individual and organisational levels in Further Education to harness new technologies to enhance personal learning experiences. Personalised eLearning supports contents, activities and collaboration aimed at meeting the needs and wants of the learner (Hill, 2004 & 2008; Coryell & Chlup, 2007). However, some technology critics argue that there is very little research to support whether eLearning is an effective approach to minimise the exclusion of disadvantaged groups in society, e.g. learners of English for Speakers of Other Languages (ESOL) (Webb, 2006). The author contends that use of technology could act as a barrier to participation in learning. This study was conducted to assess the extent to which eLearning resources promote integrative/explorative learner-centred Computer Assisted Language Learning (CALL). This chapter reports on the findings of a qualitative action research project involving one-to-one interviews with learners (n=12) at the College of North East London (CONEL) on their deployment of various new technologies (virtual and personal learning environments) in ESOL studies during the academic year 2007/8. Additionally, three focus group interviews were held including six learner interviewees each (n=18). Semi-structured interviews were conducted with four colleagues who actively integrated CALL into delivery of their ESOL sessions. Data was also collected from programme reviews, course evaluation reports and a research diary. The results of the study suggest that new technologies promote personalised learning when applied with careful planning even among learners who appear to be technophobic or are reluctant to use e-resources. Barriers hindering the integration of e-resources into the curriculum are discussed and possible solutions are also suggested.

Section 2
Pedagogical Issues

Chapter 8

    Richard Hall, De Montfort University, UK
    Steve Mackenzie, De Montfort University, UK
    Melanie Hall, Staffordshire University, UK

The adoption across higher education of participatory, collaborative and connective 'read/write web' tools and synchronous classrooms has the potential to extend learner engagement and motivation. Embedding these user-centred tools within curriculum practices offers the possibility for a sixth-generation iteration of distance learning that frames a learner-focused pedagogy. This pedagogy is underpinned by problem-based activities that pivot around a cycle of needing/wanting, doing, digesting and feedback. They are supported by a facilitating tutor taking a connectivist approach to stimulate learning. This chapter highlights both the drivers for this sixth-generation iteration and the subsequent development of a model know as SCORE 2.0, or *Synchronous Community Orientated Reflective and Experiential 2.0*. The impact of this model on two cohorts of adult distance learners is discussed, in order to evaluate opportunities for future pedagogical development.

Chapter 9

    Paul Lowe, University of the Arts London, UK
    Margo Blythman, University of the Arts London, UK

In a context of mass higher education it can be a challenge to build a reasonable level of personalised learning into the student experience. This chapter explores the relationship between personalised learning, reflection and the use of blogs in the building of a collaborative learning community through opportunities to build professional identity. The authors outline how the postgraduate programme in the Media school at the London College of Communication, University of the Arts London uses web 2.0 tools on the photography programme, in particular blogs, in developing reflective practitioners within a collaborative community of practice. The unique opportunities presented by live blogs in opening up the process of articulating experience into learning, enhance what the authors characterise as the 'E-flective practitioner'.

Chapter 10

    Ruth Pilkington, University of Central Lancashire, UK

The chapter suggests the implementation of personalised learning within Higher Education raises fundamental issues and challenges when developing academic staff to support this form of learning and explores some of the challenges raised. It discusses the value of personalised learning for professional development in particular within the context of UK Professional Standards for HE staff. The chapter uses a case study to illustrate the issues and solutions offered by personalised eLearning and identifies particular issues of literacy, prior learning and comfort with respect to online delivery that need to be recognised for both developers and professional learners. The case study draws on a Joint Informations Systems Committee (JISC) funded project under the RePRODUCE banner and compares findings with existing traditional means of developing staff, as well as discussing the processes represented and the contributions that can be made when personalising learning more widely within HE.

Chapter 11

Susi Peacock, Queen Margaret University, UK
Kate Morss, Queen Margaret University, UK
Alison Scott, Queen Margaret University, UK
Jane Hislop, Queen Margaret University, UK
Lindesay Irvine, Queen Margaret University, UK
Sue Murray, Queen Margaret University, UK
Simon T Girdler, Queen Margaret University, UK

Personalisation, with its emphasis on learner choice and lifelong learning, challenges educators to provide an innovative, student-centric educational experience. New technologies have great potential to support personalisation; however, institutions must review their approaches to assessment and feedback and their strategies to learning and teaching as well as increasing opportunities for collaborative learning and extending their external partnerships. This is a significant agenda for any institution. In this chapter, through the authors' four case studies drawn from different subject areas in a higher educational institution, they illustrate how ePortfolios when integrated into the curriculum and combined with reflection can support personalised learning. The authors' also discuss the challenges of such an approach including lack of learner engagement with the reflective process, an increase in tutor time, restricted learner access to technology and the need for dynamic ePersonalisation. They offer suggestions for educators in addressing such issues in order to provide a truly personalised learning experience.

Chapter 12

Iain Doherty, University of Auckland, New Zealand
Adam Blake, University of Auckland, New Zealand

The authors consider personalised learning in the context of delivering a specialist postgraduate course – ClinEd 711, ELearning and Clinical Education – at the Faculty of Medical and Health Sciences, University of Auckland. They describe the pedagogical theory underlying the course design and our experience of delivering ClinEd 711 with particular reference to the personalised learning process that the course design facilitated. They present their research results for the student experience of ClinEd 711 and discuss changes made to the course as a result of student feedback. They make reference to the introduction of student-led modules to further personalise the students' learning experience. ClinEd 711 is a specialist postgraduate course with low student numbers; with this in mind the authors discuss the implications of their pedagogical approach for those educators involved in teaching larger classes. They conclude their paper with a discussion of the role of the educator in personalised learning.

Chapter 13
    Len Webster, Monash University, Australia
    Patricie Mertova, Monash University, Australia
    Kim Styles, Monash University, Australia
    Lindsay Smith, Monash University, Australia

This chapter provides a case study outlining strategies which represent a starting point in the development of a personalised learning environment (PLE). The initial strategies focus on student engagement in two units run by the Faculty of Information Technology at Monash University, Australia. The case study looks at changing the approach to a more personalised learning environment in the respective IT units, and it also outlines how the changes were made based on a meta-analysis research of the Australian Course Experience Questionnaire (CEQ).

Chapter 14
    Alberto Ramírez Martinell, Lancaster University, UK
    Julie-Ann Sime, Lancaster University, UK

To close the gap between formal education and professional practice, Higher Education (HE) practitioners need to be aware of the importance of offering realistic learning scenarios where students can profit from personalised learning opportunities and meaningful learning. In this chapter, the authors study the extent to which viewing video recordings of the individual performances of dance and music students benefited the learning process. Evidence was gathered from two groups of undergraduate performing arts students at a HE institution in the United Kingdom, and from their corresponding teachers, who independently offered their students a personalised way of accessing visually relevant feedback on their performances via a virtual learning environment. Results suggest that this access to personalised learning facilitated critical reflection and learning from experience. It enabled the students to reposition themselves in relation to their actual performance, fostered their will to learn, and reaffirmed them as potential professional performers.

Chapter 15
    Neil Andrew Gordon, University of Hull, UK

This chapter considers some ways in which personalised learning can potentially be delivered by means of appropriate assessment and the use of associated technologies. Recognising that for many students, learning is driven by summative assessment, the chapter considers how by blending summative and formative assessment, students can be encouraged to develop and take responsibility for their own learning along with ways in which technology can make this assessment be tailored to the individual student. The approaches described can support and encourage self-regulated learning – itself an effective way of providing the more general concept of student-centred learning. The framework of learning that is engendered – with the use of technology – has the potential to allow an educational pathway which reflects individual students' needs and aptitudes, and which can thus provide a form of personalised learning. This chapter describes some of the relevant theory – which forms the context within which this work is based and has developed - before then describing two case studies where this blend of formative and summative assessment is described and analysed. This is followed by a discussion of some of the more general issues.

Section 3
Technological Issues

  Debbie Holley, London Metropolitan University Business School, UK
  Lyn Greaves, Thames Valley University, UK
  Claire Bradley, London Metropolitan University, UK
  John Cook, London Metropolitan University, UK

This chapter shows how a suite of learning objects were developed by the Centre for Excellence in Teaching and Learning for Reusable Learning Objects (www.RLO-CETL.ac.uk), one of 74 CETLs being funded by the UK's Higher Education Funding Council for England. The learning objects were used to support students within a blended learning context. It shows student personalised learning: learning that can be any time (in the 24 hour digital world), any place (the university experienced in the home or workplace), any where (limited only by the students choice and internet access – trains, boats, planes, global learning). It focuses on two case studies at UK Higher Education institutions that demonstrate any time, any place learning. London Metropolitan University (London Met) and Thames Valley University (TVU), have both used and reused learning objects in different contexts. In each case study the background and the resulting blended learning design is outlined, followed by evaluation data illustrating the student experience and how the learning design and the learning objects have encouraged personalised learning. The chapter concludes with the start of the third iteration of use – to facilitate informal learning 'any where', through the incorporation of learning objects that can be used on mobile phones.

  Dirk Thißen, IMC (UK) Learning, UK
  Volker Zimmermann, IMC AG, Germany
  Tilman Küchler, IMC AG, Germany

Personalisation is a key requirement to motivate learners to use learning technology and self-paced content. Whereas most research and technologies focus on personalisation of content, this paper focuses on the personalisation of the tools and platform technologies for learning. When designing a learning environment, most organisations worked in the past on their internal business processes and content but did not focus on what the learner really does with the learning tools the organisation provided to them. Changing the perspective to the user shows, that they create today "around the organisational solutions" their own technology-enhanced learning world using a whole set of technologies: Learning management system (LMS) of the company, learning management system of a further education institution or of a university, different social network platforms, search engines, open web services in the internet like blogs or wikis, and a lot more other applications. Therefore the challenge for organisations today is how they can manage this variety of technologies by also enforcing the creativity and motivation of the users to personalise and individualise their learning environment. This paper proposes a solution by describing an architecture for a responsive and open learning environment. It delivers examples and a procedure how such a solution can be built step-by-step. The approach can be used in schools, higher education institutions, corporations or further education institutions.

Chapter 18

This chapter describes two tools for personalised learning that were outcomes of projects led by the author for use in educational settings. These are the Virtual Resources for Online Research Training (V-ResORT) and the Virtual Interactive Platform (ViP) learning tools. The former was designed to support post graduate research students to develop an understanding of educational research through an exploration of researcher video narratives. The latter was designed to support online communities in sharing and critiquing videos of practice. These tools support the development of a learner identity characterized by proactive participation in construction and reconstruction of knowledge rather than pure consumption. This involves an engagement with communities of practice which it is argued is central to personalised learning.

This chapter illustrates a curricular intervention carried out at Coventry University (UK) with undergraduate students reading English. It explores how the students maximised their use of the tools available within the ePortfolio software PebblePad. It discusses how the software tools were used to enhance and personalise the students' learning experience and engage in the discourse of 'becoming researchers' in the second year module *Dissertation Methods and Approaches*. It proposes that the use of some ePortfolio tools helped many students to become critical and to actively engage in their ontological journey of transition to becoming independent thinkers. However it also reports that some problematic issues surfaced following the implementation of the curricular action: some students find active learning and active engagement in the scholarship of research 'troublesome'. Finally this chapter gives consideration to how to integrate the lessons learned from this experience into the curriculum for the next cohort of students.

Chapter 20

Stuart Nolan, Hex Induction, UK

LEGO Serious Play is a business development process where users build metaphorical models from LEGO bricks in order to explore and share their perceptions of various aspects of their working lives. They model important symbolic elements of their personality, emotions, working practices, organization, and the relationships between these elements in order to share stories that aid the construction of organizational knowledge. This chapter reports on trials using LEGO Serious Play with HE students from a range of subject areas who used metaphorical modelling to articulate their learning autobiographies, current situations, orientations to learning, and aspirations. The models helped students make informed choices and helped staff to understand their needs and personalise the learning provision appropriately.

Chapter 21

Samantha Osborne, University of Kent, UK
Ruben Martin, University of Kent, UK
Louise Frith, University of Kent, UK

The University of Kent is piloting the use of ePortfolios in a number of departments; the School of Social Policy, Sociology and Social Research took the opportunity to pilot ePortfolios to investigate whether ePortfolios could improve communication and collaboration between student, placement supervisor and academic tutors whilst Social Work students are out on work-based placement. Social Work students are required to complete two reflective practice documents during each of their two placements during Years 2 and 3 of their degree to assess their competence against a set of National Standards. The chapter will discuss the adoption of a Personalised Learning Environment for recording assessed practice and how the tools provided can enhance the different categories of users' experiences both in terms of reflective practice and personal development. The chapter gives a background to the pilot and describes the different profiles of each user group which are students, academic staff, practitioners, and other stakeholders. It will also examine to what extent the pilot is in line with government initiatives such as the Leitch Review and Burgess Report and research into the use of ePortfolios for reflection; the issues surrounding the introduction of new technology to non-traditional students and outside organizations; how technology has changed student and practitioner's perceptions and expectations in the production of a collaborative body of evidence; and the future pedagogical implications of using technology with Social Work students and practitioners.

Chapter 22

Anne Nortcliffe, Sheffield Hallam University, UK
Andrew Middleton, Sheffield Hallam University, UK

Audio feedback is a method that can provide rich, personal and detailed feedback that can convey more than the written word. This is particularly achieved through the capturing of the expressive quality of the speaker's voice. Audio feedback has the potential to promote student engagement in the feedback process, as it is not associated with the negative connotations of written feedback. This chapter will draw upon the growing literature base and recent research. It will indicate how different approaches to using audio technology can enhance the learning experience and the feedback process through its personal and timely qualities. The chapter will conclude with guidelines for best practice for implementation of audio feedback.

Five billion songs, and counting, have been downloaded (completely legally) through Apple Computer's online iTunes Store. The iTunes University links free educational content from over seventy tertiary institutions worldwide, and is now available to New Zealand tertiary institutions. The Internet has revolutionised the delivery and access of media and education – making access to a worldwide audience or market merely a Google (or iTunes Store) search away! But, what are the real-world practicalities of this for contemporary music students and teachers today? How can these tools be utilised to facilitate personalised learning environments. Within this context, this chapter presents and evaluates a mobile learning case study at Unitec in the Diploma of Contemporary Music on the Waitakere campus.

Preface

Technology catalyses changes not only in what we do but in how we think. It changes people's awareness of themselves, of one another, of their relationship with the world.[1]

Personalised learning seems to have been adopted as the new mantra in education. This is in part due to the widespread availability of software which purports to support honourable aspects of learning, reflection, consolidation and extension…. to name but a few. The environment for learning has also radically changed from didactic taught classroom or lecture based delivery to an environment which empowers learners to take responsibility for their own learning. Such backgrounds as VLEs, MLEs, LMS and Web 2.0 tools, blogs, WIKIS, social networks all have changed the engagement between learner and teacher, as well as between learner and learner. This is within a variety of contexts both formal and informal.

The political dimension is also attributable. The UK government is keen that children, pupils and students will 'enjoy and benefit from a personal learning experience'. Surely, learning has always been personal? The way I learn is not the way you learn. This is true of how I experience and assimilate the learning occurrence in the lecture hall. How I use a blog or social network site as my preferred learning platform is inevitably and fundamentally different to any other user. The depth and meaning of reflection on my experience may be due to the rigours of my course and the often imposed assessment pattern or personal as I want to 'see' how and how much I have learnt, understood, or can apply in a variety of alternative scenarios. Personalisation, learner, pupil or student centredness advocate the use of the learner's own predilection, behaviour and activities.

The tension is between the formal institutional assessment regime and methods which are often incoherently mapped against the personal, individual learning strategies advocated by misaligned curriculum ideologies which advocate personalised learning and independent activity based engagement. These do not nestle comfortably within many institutions who feel it necessary to have generic examinations which 'test' against what was learned and remembered during a specific course, module or learning episode. This is often to the detriment of utilising skills, knowledge and personal learning attributes which can be assimilated within a future scenario or domain.

The content of this publication highlights the many areas in which practitioners are attempting to implement learning technologies and reflects themes of current topical interest. Personalising learning and the learner experience can be supported, enhanced and encouraged by the application and intervention of technology. However, this must be carefully considered within the realms of what is both possible and desirable. Internal and external factors also make a significant difference i.e. the institutional impediments and often unsalable network access, the culture of the institution or environment, the engagement with and by the students in formal, informal and situated learning. Finally technology, Web 2.0 and increasingly social networks provide an opportunity to delve into additional learning experiences, but these do need careful consideration if we are not to dilute the value, nature and experience of learning itself.

The book has three main sections: Infrastructural and Cultural Issues, Pedagogical Issues and Technological Issues. The first section on infrastructure considers aspects related to the major infrastructural, cultural and organisational changes required, if innovation is going to effect any change in the institutional regime. It will focus on the role of the student and the tutor in the personalisation of the learning process. The section on pedagogical issues presents descriptions of the different cases and ways in which practitioners have attempted to use learning technologies and give personal examples which illustrate both the potential and dangers of personalised learning technologies. The section on technological issues will present descriptions of the "tools" that practitioners are using, outline their strengths and weaknesses and highlight issues that need to be considered when planning to implement new personalised learning environments.

Whilst the chapters are located within a section, the nature of technological use cannot be so compartmentalised - so many of the studies and topics reported here cut across many boundaries, infrastructural and cultural, pedagogic and technological. The key issues highlighted and discussed include widening access and participation, student-centred and collaborative learning and the changing role of the tutor/ pupil/ student.

CHAPTER DESCRIPTIONS

This book consists of 23 chapters, written by 47 authors, loosely grouped into the three sections as follows.

Introduction/ Chapter 1: *Personalisation through Technology-Enhanced Learning.* Gráinne Conole. This introductory chapter considers the discourse of the concept of personalisation and how it can be supported through technology-enhanced learning. It looks at the policy rhetoric and considers to what extent it is realised in practice. The chapter describes a range of illustrative examples of how technologies are being used to meet the personalised learning agenda.

Section I: Infrastructural and Cultural Issues

Chapter 2: Breaking the Hierarchy: Democratising the Institutional Webspace. Beth Granter. This chapter, inspired by direct experience from working on the development of the University of Sussex's Student Personal Learning and Social Homepages (SPLASH) project, discusses how 'Web 2.0' technologies can be used to make institutional websites more democratic. The SPLASH project was non-typical in that it intended to create an environment which would be fully customisable by the learner, so that no content was obligatory. Examples from working on this project are used to illustrate benefits which can be gained from, and barriers to the uptake of, more open publishing methods and an organically structured site architecture. Issues affecting learners, tutors, the institution as a whole, and how the power dynamic between all three may change, are discussed. Parallels are drawn between teaching methods online and those offline, both traditional and modern.

Chapter 3: *PLE: A Brick in the Construction of a Lifelong Learning Society.* Sabrina Leone. The attainment of lifelong learning objectives is being mediated by a complex process of innovation in education and society, by the integration of institutional actions and by the major role of coordination that university has assumed. The revolution that technology has engendered in every field has flowed into a rethinking of knowledge, knowledge management, teaching and learning, networks and the individual. The knowledge society requires new roles and skills, new forms of communication and a new awareness as 'active citizens'. Consequently, the shifting role of education systems in networked organisations is decisive in order to support learners in forming diverse personal learning networks to deeply understand complex fields. This chapter aims to discuss consistency and effectiveness of a personal learning environment as a new learning space and to highlight its contribution and relevance to lifelong learning. PLE critical points and approaches will be discussed exploiting three case studies.

Chapter 4: *Community@Brighton: The Development of an Institutional Shared Learning Environment.* Stan Stanier. This chapter details the implementation of a university-wide social networking platform 'Community@Brighton' - using the open source Elgg platform and describes the technical, institutional and educational issues arising from the two years of experience in running the platform. The strategic vision of providing a social network platform alongside an institutional VLE to provide an integrated Shared Learning Environment is also explored, including key case studies and discussion on the challenges such technologies place on existing models of online learning and teaching.

Chapter 5: *ELearning: Institutional Provision and Student Expectations.* Barbara Newland and Maria-Christiana Papaefthimiou. Students who have grown up in the digital age have certain expectations for learning in Higher Education. The divide between the institutional eLearning provision and the expectations of students (who have grown up in a digital world) was highlighted through the UK eLearning benchmarking exercise. Institutional eLearning provision and processes within the HE sector are investigated and analysed through this exercise, which was led by the Higher Education Academy in collaboration with the Joint Information Systems Committee. This chapter presents the experience of two UK Universities, Bournemouth and Reading, whose participation in the benchmarking exercise provides examples of institutional provision. Subsequent Pathfinder funding enabled them to build on their strengths with projects aimed at narrowing the divide between student expectations of eLearning and institutional provision.

Chapter 6: *Personalising Teaching and Learning with Digital Resources: DiAL-e Framework Case Studies.* Kevin Burden and Simon Atkinson. This chapter describes the ways in which individual academics have sought to realise a degree of personalisation in their teaching practice through their engagement with the DiAL-e Framework (Digital Artefacts for Learner Engagement). The DiAL-e Framework is a new conceptual model, articulated as a paper-based and web-based tool, for designing learning engagements. The policy and theoretical context, evolution of the framework and the methodology used to utilise the framework with academic staff seeking to personalise the learning experience is outlined. Details of three case studies resulting from this early work are described and conclusions drawn as to how such frameworks might assist staff in thinking about personalised learning scenarios.

Chapter 7: *Personalised eLearning in Further Education.* Elfneh Udessa Bariso. Electronic media can contribute to personalisation of learning both in formal and informal contexts. Efforts are made both at individual and organisational levels in Further Education to harness new technologies to enhance personal learning experiences. This study was conducted to assess the extent to which eLearning resources promote integrative/explorative learner-centred Computer Assisted Language Learning (CALL). This chapter reports on the findings of a qualitative action research project involving one-to-one interviews with learners at the College of North East London on their deployment of various new technologies in ESOL studies during the academic year 2007/8. The results of the study suggest that new technologies promote personalised learning when applied with careful planning even among learners who appear to be technophobic or are reluctant to use e-resources. Barriers hindering the integration of e-resources into the curriculum are discussed and possible solutions are also suggested.

Section II: Pedagogical Issues

Chapter 8: *The Impact of Interactive and Collaborative Learning Activities on the Personalised Learning of Adult Distance Learners.* Richard Hall, Steve Mackenzie and Melanie Hall. The adoption across higher education of participatory, collaborative and connective 'read/write web' tools and synchronous classrooms has the potential to extend learner engagement and motivation. Embedding these user-centred tools within curriculum practices offers the possibility for a sixth-generation iteration of distance learning that frames a learner-focused pedagogy. This pedagogy is underpinned by problem-based activities that pivot around a cycle of needing/wanting, doing, digesting and feedback. They are supported by a facilitating tutor taking a connectivist approach to stimulate learning. This chapter highlights both the drivers for this sixth-generation iteration and the subsequent development of a model know as SCORE 2.0, or *Synchronous Community Orientated Reflective and Experiential 2.0.* The impact of this model on two cohorts of adult distance learners is discussed, in order to evaluate opportunities for future pedagogical development.

Chapter 9: *Blogs and the e-Flective Practitioner: Professional not Confessional.* Paul Lowe and Margo Blythman. In a context of mass higher education it can be a challenge to build a reasonable level of personalised learning into the student experience. This chapter explores the relationship between personalised learning, reflection and the use of blogs in the building of a collaborative learning community through opportunities to build professional identity. A postgraduate programme in the media school at the London College of Communication, University of the Arts London uses Web 2.0 tools on the photography programme, in particular blogs, in developing reflective practitioners within a collaborative community of practice. The unique opportunities presented by live blogs in opening up the process of articulating experience into learning, enhance what is characterised as the 'E-flective practitioner'.

Chapter 10: *Building Practitioner Skills in Personalised eLearning: Messages for Professional Development.* Ruth Pilkington. The chapter suggests the implementation of personalised learning within Higher Education (HE), raises fundamental issues and challenges when developing academic staff to support this form of learning and explores some of the challenges raised. It discusses the value of personalised learning for professional development in particular within the context of UK Professional Standards for HE staff. The chapter uses a case study to illustrate the issues and solutions offered by personalised eLearning and identifies particular issues of literacy, prior learning and comfort with respect to online delivery that need to be recognised for both developers and professional learners. The case study draws on a Joint Informations Systems Committee funded project under the RePRODUCE banner and compares findings with existing traditional means of developing staff, as well as discussing the processes represented and the contributions that can be made when personalising learning more widely within HE.

Chapter 11: *Using ePortfolios in Higher Education to Encourage Learner Reflection and Support Personalised Learning.* Susi Peacock, Kate Morss, Alison Scott, Jane Hislop, Lindesay Irvine, Sue Murray and Simon Girdler. Personalisation, with an emphasis on learner choice and lifelong learning, challenges educators to provide an innovative, student-centric educational experience. New technologies have great potential to support personalisation; however, institutions must review their approaches to assessment and feedback and their strategies to learning and teaching as well as increasing opportunities for collaborative learning and extending their external partnerships. This is a significant agenda for any institution. In this chapter, through four case studies drawn from different subject areas in a higher educational institution, ePortfolios are integrated into the curriculum and combined with reflection to support personalised learning. The challenges of such an approach are discussed including lack of learner engagement with the reflective process, an increase in tutor time, restricted learner access to technology and the need for dynamic ePersonalisation. Suggestions are offered for educators in addressing such issues in order to provide a truly personalised learning experience.

Chapter 12: *Personalised Learning: A Case Study in Teaching Clinical Educators Instructional Design Skills.* Iain Doherty and Adam Blake. This chapter considers personalised learning in the context of delivering a specialist postgraduate course. It describes the pedagogical theory underlying the course design and our experience of delivering a course with particular reference to the personalised learning process that this course design facilitated. Research results for the student experience and discuss changes made to the course as a result of student feedback are presented. Reference is made to the introduction of student-led modules to further personalise the students' learning experience. The course ClinEd 711 is a specialist postgraduate course with low student numbers; with this in mind the implications of our pedagogical approach for those educators involved in teaching larger classes is considered. The chapter concludes with a discussion of the role of the educator in personalised learning.

Chapter 13: *Research-Led Curriculum Redesign for Personalised Learning Environments: A Case Study in the Faculty of Information Technology.* Len Webster, Patricie Mertova, Kim Styles and Lindsay Smith. This chapter provides a case study outlining strategies which represent a starting point in the development of a personalised learning environment (PLE). The initial strategies focus on student engagement in two units run by the Faculty of Information Technology at Monash University, Australia. The case study looks at changing the approach to a more personalised learning environment in the respective IT units, and it also outlines how the changes were made based on a meta-analysis research of the Australian Course Experience Questionnaire (CEQ).

Chapter 14: *Video-Enriched Learning Experiences for Performing Arts Students: Two exploratory Case Studies.* Alberto Ramirez Martinell and Julie-Ann Sime. To close the gap between formal education and professional practice, Higher Education (HE) practitioners need to be aware of the importance of offering realistic learning scenarios where students can profit from personalised learning opportunities and meaningful learning. In this chapter, the extent to which viewing video recordings of the individual performances of dance and music students benefited the learning process are studied. Evidence is gathered from two groups of undergraduate performing arts students at a HE institution in the UK, and from their corresponding teachers, who independently offered their students a personalised way of accessing visually relevant feedback on their performances via a virtual learning environment. Results suggest that this access to personalised learning facilitated critical reflection and learning from experience. It has enabled the students to reposition themselves in relation to their actual performance, fostered their will to learn, and reaffirmed them as potential professional performers.

Chapter 15: *Enabling Personalised Learning through Formative and Summative Assessment.* Neil Gordon. This chapter considers some ways in which personalised learning can potentially be delivered by means of appropriate assessment and the use of associated technologies. Recognising that for many students, learning is driven by summative assessment, the chapter considers how by blending summative and formative assessment, students can be encouraged to develop and take responsibility for their own learning along with ways in which technology can make this assessment tailored to the individual student. The approaches described can support and encourage self-regulated learning - itself an effective way of providing the more general concept of student-centred learning. The framework of learning that is engendered - with the use of technology - has the potential to allow an educational pathway which reflects individual students' needs and aptitudes, and which can thus provide a form of personalised learning. This chapter describes some of the relevant theory, which forms the context within which this work is based and has developed, then illustrates two case studies where this blend of formative and summative assessment is described and analysed. This is followed by a discussion of some of the more general issues.

Section III: Technological Issues

Chapter 16: *"You Can Take Out of it What You Want": How Learning Objects within Blended Learning Designs Encourage Personalised Learning.* Debbie Holley, Lyn Greaves, Claire Bradley and John Cook. This chapter shows how a suite of learning objects were developed by the Centre for Excellence in Teaching and Learning for Reusable Learning Objects, one of 74 CETLs being funded by the UK's Higher Education Funding Council for England. The learning objects were used to support students within a blended learning context. It focuses on two case studies at UK Higher Education institutions that demonstrate any time, any place learning. London Metropolitan University and Thames Valley University, have both used and reused learning objects in different contexts. In each case study the background and the resulting blended learning design is outlined, followed by evaluation data illustrating the student experience and how the learning design and the learning objects have encouraged personalised learning. The chapter concludes with the start of the third iteration of use - to facilitate informal learning 'anywhere', through the incorporation of learning objects that can be used on mobile phones.

Chapter 17: *Into the Great Wide Open: Responsive Learning Environments for Personalised Learning.* Dirk Thissen, Volker Zimmermannn and Tilman Küchler. Personalisation is a key requirement to motivate learners to use learning technology and self-paced content. Whereas most research and technologies focus on personalisation of content, this chapter focuses on the personalisation of the tools and platform technologies for learning. When designing a learning environment, most organisations worked in the past on their internal business processes and content but did not focus on what the learner really does with the learning tools the organisation provided to them. Changing the perspective to the user shows, that they create today 'around the organisational solutions' their own technology-enhanced learning world using a whole set of technologies: Learning management system (LMS) of the company, of a further education institution or of a university, different social network platforms, search engines, open web services in the internet like blogs or wikis, and a lot more other applications. Therefore the challenge for organisations today is how they can manage this variety of technologies by also enforcing the creativity and motivation of the users to personalise and individualise their learning environment.

Chapter 18: *Personalisation and the Online Video Narrative Learning Tools V-ResORT and the ViP.* Gordon Joyes. This chapter describes two tools for personalised learning that were outcomes of projects led by the author for use in educational settings. These are the Virtual Resources for Online Research Training (V-ResORT) and the Virtual Interactive Platform (ViP) learning tools. The former was designed to support post graduate research students to develop an understanding of educational research through an exploration of researcher video narratives. The latter was designed to support online communities in sharing and critiquing videos of practice. These tools support the development of a learner identity characterized by proactive participation in construction and reconstruction of knowledge rather than pure consumption. This involves an engagement with communities of practice which it is argued is central to personalised learning.

Chapter 19: *Shared Spaces and 'Secret Gardens': The Troublesome Journey from Undergraduate Students To Undergraduate Scholars via PebblePad.* Marina Orsini-Jones. This chapter illustrates a curricular intervention carried out at Coventry University (UK) with undergraduate students reading English. It explores how the students maximised their use of the tools available within the ePortfolio software PebblePad. It discusses how the software tools were used to enhance and personalise the students' learning experience and engage in the discourse of 'becoming researchers'. It proposes that the use of some ePortfolio tools helped many students to become critical and to actively engage in their ontological journey of transition to becoming independent thinkers. However it also reports that some problematic issues surfaced following the implementation of the curricular action: some students find active learning and active engagement in the scholarship of research 'troublesome'. Finally this chapter gives consideration to how to integrate the lessons learned from this experience into the curriculum for students.

Chapter 20: *Physical Metaphorical Modelling with LEGO as a Technology for Collaborative Personalised Learning.* Stuart Nolan. LEGO Serious Play is a business development process where users build metaphorical models from LEGO bricks in order to explore and share their perceptions of various aspects of their working lives. They model important symbolic elements of their personality, emotions, working practices, organization, and the relationships between these elements in order to share stories that aid the construction of organizational knowledge. This chapter reports on trials using LEGO Serious Play with HE students from a range of subject areas who used metaphorical modelling to articulate their learning autobiographies, current situations, orientations to learning, and aspirations. The models helped students make informed choices and helped staff to understand their needs and personalise the learning provision appropriately.

Chapter 21: *Using ePortfolios to Evidence Practice Learning for Social Work Students.* Samantha Osborne, Ruben Martin and Louise Frith. The University of Kent is piloting the use of ePortfolios in a number of departments and took the opportunity to investigate whether they could improve communication and collaboration between student, placement supervisor and academic tutors whilst students are out on work-based placement. The chapter discusses the adoption of a Personalised Learning Environment for recording assessed practice and how the tools provided can enhance the different categories of users' experiences both in terms of reflective practice and personal development. The chapter gives a background to the pilot and describes the different profiles of each user group which are students, academic staff, practitioners, and other stakeholders. It examines to what extent the pilot is in line with UK government initiatives such as the Leitch Review and Burgess Report and research into the use of ePortfolios for reflection; the issues surrounding the introduction of new technology to non-traditional students and outside organizations; how technology has changed student and practitioner's perceptions and expectations in the production of a collaborative body of evidence; and the future pedagogical implications of using technology with Social Work students and practitioners.

Chapter 22: *Effective Assignment Feedback through Timely and Personal Digital Audio Engagement.* Anne Nortcliffe and Andrew Middleton. Audio feedback is a method which can provide rich, personal and detailed feedback that can convey more than the written word. This is particularly achieved through the capturing of the expressive quality of the speaker's voice. Audio feedback has the potential to promote student engagement in the feedback process, as it is not associated with the negative connotations of written feedback. This chapter draws upon the growing literature base and recent research. It indicates how different approaches to using audio technology can enhance the learning experience and the feedback process through its personal and timely qualities. The chapter concludes with guidelines and suggestions for best practice for the implementation of audio feedback.

Chapter 23: *Contemporary Music Students and Mobile Technology.* Thomas Cochrane. Five billion songs, and counting, have been downloaded (completely legally) through Apple Computer's online iTunes Store. The iTunes University links free educational content from over seventy tertiary institutions worldwide, and is now available to New Zealand tertiary institutions. The Internet has revolutionised the delivery and access of media and education - making access to a worldwide audience or market merely a Google (or iTunes Store) search away! But, what are the real-world practicalities of this for contemporary music students and teachers today? How can these tools be utilised to facilitate personalised learning environments. Within this context, this chapter presents and evaluates a mobile learning case study at Unitec in the Diploma of Contemporary Music on the Waitakere campus.

CONCLUSION

Technology and the Web are valuable resources, enriching the educational resources we provide already. The key is providing appropriate environments and then reinforcing the experiences with concrete activities. It is important that eLearning is recognised as a supplement to the personal interaction provided by lecturers, teachers, parents and peers, not a replacement.

Technology provides opportunities never before available - such as remote global communication and file sharing, reflection, consolidation, collaboration and exploration, simulation and active independent individualised learning. Yet school, college and university departments are in danger of sabotaging - through incomplete and, in some cases, detrimental implementation plans - the power of technology to transform the teaching and learning process.

The twenty-three chapters included in this book were selected from a large number of submissions. They cover vastly different subjects, group sizes and institutional types - music to social, whole class to individual delivery and engagement, large universities to small departments, undergraduate to post graduate. They are driven by the passion of the staff involved to 'make a difference', not by simply using technology, but by applying technology in an innovative way to enhance, enrich and extend the learning in which our students are involved.

The book presents case studies, research findings, developments and interventions which will provide guidelines and benchmarks with which the reader will be able to see how, why and where their own implementation of technology is either struggling or 'not making a difference' within the context of personalised learning.

My fervent hope is that this book will make a difference to the many classrooms of computers and technology which increasing pervade and saturate our educational institutions and the lack of 'real' or meaningful learner engagement provided by this intrusion.

John O'Donoghue
2009

ENDNOTE

[1]   Turkle, S. (1984). *The Second Self: Computers and the Human Spirit.* New York: Simon and Schuster.

Acknowledgment

I would like to thank IGI Global for affording me this opportunity to edit this book. It has reinforced my concerns for the intransigence of educational communities to change. Equally it has reassured me that change is possible, driven by the passion, enthusiasm and excitement of an increasing band of innovators. Forty seven of them present their findings here in twenty three chapters. I thank them all.

I also thank all the referees who provided constructive and comprehensive reviews of all the chapters. They work anonymously in the background, but their tireless effort is much appreciated.

Many thanks to the team at IGI Global, in particular Joel Gamon and Kristin Roth, who have answered my queries, provided advice, guidance and support and patiently tolerated my inability to always keep to the schedule.

Finally I must again thank all the authors for the excellent contributions. They have shared their work, failures and successes. Email is wonderful and this publication would not have been possible without it. The disadvantage of such a medium is that it does not provide me with the personal opportunity to thank you all for contributing to a book which will hopefully enlighten, support and encourage colleagues to venture into the technology supported learning and teaching arena.

John O'Donoghue
2009

Chapter 1
Personalisation through Technology–Enhanced Learning

Gráinne Conole
Open University, UK

INTRODUCTION

There is a growing awareness that one-size-fits-all approaches to school knowledge and organisation are ill-adapted both to individuals' needs and to the knowledge society at large. To move beyond uniform, mass provision can be described as "personalisation" of education and of public services more widely.[1]

This quote is the introduction to an OECD (Organisation for Economic Cooperation and Development) publication (OECD, 2006) that illustrates the growing importance being placed on the concept of personalised learning. This is evident in the increasing reference to this and related terms in national and international policy documents

DOI: 10.4018/978-1-60566-884-0.ch001

(NSF, 2008; DfES, 2006; Becta, 2008; European Commission, 2008). This chapter will consider the discourse of the concept of personalisation and how it can be supported through technology-enhanced learning. This introduction will look at the policy rhetoric and consider to what extent it is realised in practice. It will describe a range of illustrative examples of how technologies are being used to meet the personalised learning agenda.

A Starter for Ten… Definitions of Personalisation

What is personalisation? Although this seems to be a deceptively simple and common term, its usage in an educational context is complex and subtle. Dictionary definitions of the word 'personalise' include 'to endow with personal or individual qualities of characteristics',[2] or 'design or produce (something) to meet someone's individual requirements.'[3] It means many different things.

Indeed the personalisation agenda (like the technology-enhanced learning agenda) raises profound questions about the nature of education. This chapter will consider the ways in which personalisation and personalised learning are referenced from three perspectives: in policy discourse, in terms of technical developments and pedagogically. It will provide a general, yet comprehensive, overview of the field; looking both at the vision and the challenges that attempting to adopt a personalised approach raise.

The increased interest in the concept of personalised learning can in part be attributed to the fact that policy makers and educationalists have come to realise that a 'one-size-fits-all' approach to education is inappropriate and won't meet either individual or societal needs. It aligns closely with related policy agendas around the development of the information society and the concept of lifelong learning and the broader agenda concerned with living and working in a complex, modern context.

Policy documents provide a useful rarefied view of how the notion of personalisation is being seen in an educational context. The policy document 'Harnessing Technology: Transforming Learning and Children's Services' sets out the UK Government's plans for using Information and Communication Technologies, and has recently been updated by Becta (Becta, 2008). The concept of personalization is a strong theme throughout the document:

Critically, learners are making use of technology to support flexible learning stimulated by their personal use of technology. [pg. 3] Used well, technology enables more effective and more personalised teaching and learning [pg. 11] Making such [digital] resources more easily accessible to both learners and practitioners will help to ensure that learners have greater choice and control over their learning programmes, where appropriate

enabling learners to adapt the pace and depth of study. [pg. 26]

A key role of learning professionals is to ensure that programmes of learning are geared to the needs of individuals and provide the right level of challenge. Technology-based tools can improve assessment for learning by providing ways in which learners can demonstrate and share their achievements, as well as providing information on progress. Combined with tailored content and resources, there are greater opportunities for a more differentiated learning experience where learners' needs are better understood and met. [pg.26] … an understanding of how the use of technology supports more personalised approaches to learning. [pg. 30]

And the learner entitlement framework includes the following statement:

Personalised learning which reflects learners' interests, preferred approaches, abilities and choices, and tailored access to materials and content. [pg. 33]

Similarly an EU document on Framework Seven technology-enhanced learning activities has numerous references to personalisation. Accommodate personalisation to respond to specific learning needs and contexts (mass- individualisation) pg 3 [The project 80days] will integrate models of adaptive personalised learning and adaptive interactive storytelling in gaming environments. Pg 6 [The project Grapple] aims at delivering a technology-enhanced learning environment for life-long learning, able to automatically adapt to personal preferences, prior knowledge, skills and competences, learning goals and the personal or social context in which the learning takes place. Pg 7

And finally one of the core research questions cited in the National Science Foundation (NSF) report on 'cyberlearning' is;

Figure 1. Putting personalised learning at the centre of policy directives

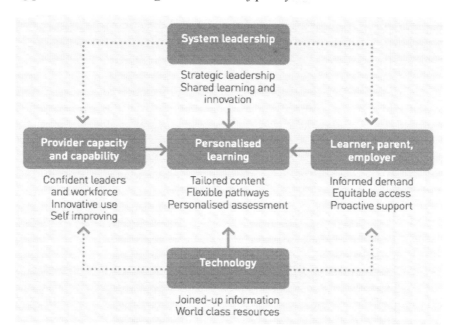

How can cyberlearning infrastructure be used to mediate personalized learning across all the context in which it happens? Pg 38

The power of technology to provide personalisation will become greater and greater as we improve the quality of the instructional aspect of the Web-based course. Pg 42

Such powerful statements about personalisation point to a vision of an education system of tomorrow which utilise technologies in innovative ways to customise and personalise learning, to equip today's learners with the range of competences and skills they will need to face the challenges of living and working in an increasingly complex societal context.

The Context of Modern Education

The reasons for the emergence of the concept of personalised learning are multifaceted. In part it is a response to addressing the challenges of liv-

ing and working in modern society; in part it is capitalising on the affordances of new technologies and how they can be individually appropriated and enable learners to be part of a global, connected distributed intelligence and in part it is due to a recognition that current educational provision is too narrow and restrictive and is not meeting either the needs of individuals or society as a whole. This section provides an overview of some of these factors.

Society

Giddens, Beck and others point to the radical changes which have occurred in society in the last few decades. We live in an increasingly connected, 'Networked Society' (Castells, 2000). Giddens (2000) outlines the impact of globalisation on all aspects of our lives – from changing societal norms and values to the blurring of national boundaries and identities. Globalisation feels very real with to-day's international concerns over global warming and the domino effect of the credit crunch around the world. Beck (1992) warns of the unintended consequences of technologies, whilst Virilio (2005) warns of our over reliance on technology and outlines a nightmare dystopian future.

These wider societal forces and trends are having a profound impact on education. They raise fundamental questions about what is education in a modern context and how should it be delivered. We are seeing a diversification of life trajectories with individuals having multiple career paths. Traditional high status professions such as lawyers and doctors are no longer valued to the same extend. Some are choosing alternative lifestyles, shunning the traditional career path. In a world where content is essentially free (OECD, 2007; Atkins et al., 2007) and where expertise is a click away via a google search or a twitter query, what is the role of educational establishments? Is formal learning and associated accreditation increasingly loosing currency?

Technologies

The pace of technological change and its associated impact on society is phenomenal, as a scan of the NCM horizon reports[4] that forecast future technological development testifies. The relentless drive towards ubiquitous and mobile technologies continues, the next stage beyond social networking and web 2.0 practices is emerging through the power of cloud computing, alternative realities through virtual worlds and gaming technologies offer new forms of social practices and interactions. As Pea and Wallis assert users and technologies are co-evolving and new practices are emerging that could not have been envisaged (cited in NSF, 2008: 13).

The affordances of new technologies in terms of access to rich, multiple representations of information and in terms of new forms of communication and collaboration seem to offer exciting possibilities for education and in particular offer a variety of means of achieving personalised learning.

However, although new technologies are being taken up and used in education, it might be argued that the impact across the sector is still relatively marginal with a significant amount of teaching practice predominantly occurring through traditional approaches. The barriers for this lack of uptake are complex and are both technical and pedagogical. The challenge for the personalisation agenda is how to identify and address these barriers.

Changing Learners and the Implications for Educational Institutions

Within the wider societal context, recent research looking at learners and in particular their use of technologies, suggests that their patterns of learning and their attitudes to learning are changing (see for example ECAR, 2007; Kennedy et al., 2008; Conole et al., 2008). Although some of the ideas attributed to the so called 'net generation' discourse don't bear close scrutiny, there is an emerging pattern of changing behaviours. Today's learners see technology as core to their learning (Conole et al., 2008); computer and mobile ownership is high (ECAR, 2007). They use the Internet routinely to support their learning; to find information and to discuss work with peers and teachers. They are comfortable working with multiple representations, are digitally literate, adopt an experiential and outcomes-focused approach to their learning. However it is less clear to what extent they are able to make academic judgements about the material they find. It is not clear to what extent, if at all, they have improved higher order skills such as critical analysis and evaluation. Indeed immersion in such a technologically rich environment may well lead to confusion for many students and a need for scaffolding and support to guide them appropriately in the use of these tools.

Technologies have also had an increasing impact on teachers and others who support learning and teaching processes. Conole (forthcoming) provides a summary of some of the ways in which the role of teaching has changed in recent decades and how technological developments have impacted teaching and educational institutions. She argues that the teaching role is changing and that many teachers lack the necessary skills to harness the potential of new technologies and that they are confused by the bewildering array of technologies and the possible ways in which they can be used to support learners.

The teacher-student nexus is also under threat; in an information-rich, web 2.0 world where the focus is on user-generated content, peer dialogue and co-construction of knowledge, the notion of teacher as 'expert' and student as 'receiver' makes little sense.

She also argues that educational institutions are ill equipped to capitalise on the potential of new technologies; working with legacy systems, unable (or unwilling) to undertake the radical restructuring that is likely to be needed.

Perspectives on Personalising Education

I want to return to the OECD document on personalising learning referenced at the beginning (OECD, 2006), as it provides a valuable summary of both the historical development of the concept of personalised learning, along with some critical reflections from key researchers in the field.

Hopkins (2006) provides a review of the foundations of personalisation, arguing that they are partly historical and partly social. The concept reflects the growing appetite for learning, and links to the moral purpose driving personalisation. He describes how the concept is in part a reaction against the traditional educational context: with the limitations of physical space, the lack of innovative uses of technology, the constraints arising from the rigid nature of the curriculum, the problems associated with teaching large classes, and the conservative nature of many educational institutions. For Hopkins the challenge is to connect the possibility of truly personalised pedagogy

with the promise of more flexible, responsive, and transparent systems of organisation. (OECD, 2006:18)

Providing a Government perspective, Miliband (2006) outlines three challenges in realising the personalisation agenda: excellence and equality, flexibility with accountability, and the need to have a personal focus. He stresses that personalised learning is not about returning to child-centred theories of learning, but a more holistic approach to education. He then articulates five components of personalised learning to guide policy development:

1. based on the strengths and weakness of individual students, through effective use of assessment and data
2. through development of competences and confidence of learners
3. by providing appropriate curriculum choice
4. through adopting a radical approach to the organisation of learning and teaching – with a shift towards a focus on student progress
5. by developing an appropriate infrastructure of support – both technical and personal.

Järvelä (2006) reviews the research evidence associated with personalised learning. She also distinguishes personalisation from individualisation and from social learning and sees it as an approach in educational practice and policy where every learner matters. She outlines seven key dimensions for achieving personalised learning.

1. The development of key skills. What kind of knowledge will future learning and work situations need? Knowledge construction and knowledge sharing form the core processes of learning, higher order skills (such as the ability to evaluate, classify, make inferences, define problems and reflect) are becoming increasingly important.

Through personalised learning, students are taught to use conceptual and factual knowledge in purposeful activities in authentic environments.

2. The improvement of student learner skills. The increasing importance of teaching learners how to analyse, critique, judge, compare and evaluate.
3. Encouraging learning through building motivation. By providing them with motivated learning schemas and opportunities to work in different learning environments so they can participate in the type of learning activities that promote learning and understanding
4. Designing new learning environments for collaborative learning. Key in a rapidly changing society is the need to prepare learners to participate in socially organised activities.

How could the collaborative process in personalised learning be regulated in order to favour the emergence of these types of interactions? How can technology be designed to enhance personalised learning environments in ways that increase the possibilities that such rich interactions occur? OCDE, 2006: 35

5. Devising new models of assessment. Realising a truly personalised learning agenda will require radically different forms of assessment with a great emphasis on the process of learning rather than products.
6. The use of technology as a personal cognitive and social tool. The need to develop models that use technology to support individual and social learning activities. ICT can increase authenticity and interest, can build virtual communities, can help share perspectives, can facilitate use of TEL inquiry and PBL approaches, can provide innovative ways of integrating just in time support and interaction in different learning contexts.

7. Remembering that teachers are key. New learning environments require complex design. Teachers will need to develop new pedagogical reflective thinking skills in mentoring learning, mediating values and social skills as well as evaluating student and their own activities.

Creating opportunities for sharing expertise and discourse around shared texts and data about student learning. (OCED, 2006: 42)

She concludes by echoing the arguments made earlier in this chapter; that we live in a constantly changing world; on a daily basis we need to make sense of a complex set of symbolic information and diverse cultural products. This places a heavy cognitive load on individuals; ongoing, lifelong learning is a critical means of tackling this.

Paludan (2006) postulates on the future of education, he argues there is something both politically correct and inherently redundant about the concept of personalised learning (OECD, 2006: 83) and cautions that in reality we are still a long way from a personalised education system and that the inertia of current educational systems is a major barrier to achieving the vision.

Leadbeater (2006) concludes by contextualising personalised learning in the wider UK agenda of personalisation. He argues that the approach assumes that learners should be actively engaged in setting their own targets, devising their own learning plans and choosing from a range of ways to learn.

Realising Personalisation through Technology-Enhanced Learning Environments

There have been many good examples over the last decade of the use of technology to foster particular pedagogical approaches. Scardamalia and Bereiter (2006) through their knowledge forum,[5] developed a innovative system for collective shared knowledge building. How could such a system be enhanced now to incorporate new web 2.0 practices and support personalisation? Dillenbourg and others (see for example Dillenbourg, 1999; Dillenbourg et al., 1996) have developed a range of collaborative learning environments, which blur the boundaries between physical and virtual spaces. How might this be extended to realise personalised learning – across different devices and in different contexts? A number of researchers have designed learning environments to foster a particular pedagogical approach. For example the work of Jonassen, Grabinger and others (see for example Jonassen et al., 1995; Grabinger and Dunlop, 1996) on the development of constructivist learning environments and authentic environments for support problem-based or scenario learning, such as Stagestruck (Harper et al., 2000) and SBL interactive (Stewart and Brown, 2008).

The question is what do we now need to do to build on this – to harness new technologies to foster personalised learning? What new models do we need that combine the capacities that are needed to adopt a personalised learning approach with the affordances of new technologies?

As part of the broader personalisation agenda the term Personal Learning Environments (PLEs) has gained currency over the last decade. The wikipedia entry[6] traces the emergence of the term, from early socio-constructivist systems such as Colloquia through to today's more commonly accepted notion of loosely coupled tools, foregrounding the social dimensions of learning.

This section will consider some recent examples of initiatives that are attempting to leverage technologies to foster personalised learning. The examples demonstrate how different initiatives are adopting different approaches to enabling personalisation – some offer holistic, but learner-centred learning environments, others focus on particular aspects – such as aggregating learning opportunities via an e-portfolio. This provides a valuable snapshot of how teachers and learners are beginning to utilise technologies in different ways to support personalised learning.

Appropriating Individual Tools for Personalised Learning

A number of web 2.0 tools have been used in ways that foster personalised learning. The website for Pebblepad[7] argues that it is much more than an ePortfolio. It is a Personal Learning System being used in learning contexts as diverse as schools, colleges, universities and professional bodies; by learners, teachers and assessors; for PDP, CPD and L&T. PebblePad has been designed with the learner at the centre of the system. It provides scaffolding to help users create records of learning, achievement and aspiration and has a reflective structure underpinning all of its core elements.

Hirst (2008) has been exploring the notion of an 'uncourse' as the antithesis to tradition OU courses where everything that a student needs is provided for them. He has experimented with this notion by teaching a course via a blog. His central argument is that research shows students are engaged in a multitude of activities whilst studying and therefore courses should be designed to foster and enable this, rather than constrain students to a single, linear, teacher-directed narrative.

Individually Constructed PLEs

Atwell (2007) argues that a PLE is not an application, but more of a new approach to using technologies for learning. In other words it is comprised of all the different tools we use in our everyday life for learning. Leslie (2009) provides a link to a collection of representations of different PLEs. Looking at the figures what is striking is the diversity of tools being used and the ways in which individuals choose to represent their PLEs. Martin (2007) categorises her tools into three areas: gathering information, processing information and acting on learning. In contrast, Delgrado (2007) using ELGG as his central focus, with all the links to the tools linked into his personal profile. Leslie categorises these into one of four types: tool-orientated (where the representation emphasises the tools being used), use/action-orientated (where what the tools are being used for in terms of learning is emphasised), people-orientated (where the people involved in the network are highlighted) and hybrid/abstract or other (which is a mixture of other representations). Leslie's list illustrates the multitude of different ways that individuals are appropriating technologies to suit their own preferred way of learning. It is also evident that PLEs are not static; as users and tools co-evolve so individual PLEs will change. For example, two years after his PLE post, Atwell reflects that the PLE he described in 2007 had changed (Atwell, 2008) arguing that it was not so much the shift in technologies that was significant but the way in which he is using them.

So whilst before my PLE comprised of a series of tools for managing learning, for consumption and for creation, and tools for communication - today the communication tools are central in managing my networked and collaborative learning.

Extending Openness: From Open Content to Open Courses

In 2008 Siemens and Downes ran a twelve-week course '- Connectivism and Connective Knowledge Online Course'.[8] They described the course as a MOOG (Massive Open Online Course). The content, delivery and support for the course was totally free, anyone could join and an impressive 2400 did, although the actual number of very active participants was smaller (ca. 200). The course provides a nice example of an extension of the open movement, moving a step beyond the Open Educational Resource movement to providing a totally free course. Although designed in a fairly conventional format – divided into topics and spread over a number of weeks, the course exploited a range of technologies and provided

a mechanism for participants to connect with leading experts in the field. Because the course used a range of technologies, participants were able to personalise the course to suit their own learning needs and to customised the learning materials to suit their own preferred learning approaches. The course offered an interesting blend of synchronous and asynchronous tools to support different aspects of learning; opportunities to discuss and reflect via blogs and forums, exploration of alternative communicative channels such as second life, content aggregation via tagging through delicious. Reflecting on the experience Siemens concludes:

Did we change the world? No. Not yet. But we (and I mean all course participants, not just Stephen and I) managed to explore what is possible online. People self-organized in their preferred spaces. They etched away at the hallowed plaque of "what it means to be an expert". They learned in transparent environments, and in the process, became teachers to others. Those that observed (or lurked as is the more common term), hopefully found value in the course as well. Perhaps life circumstances, personal schedule, motivation for participating, confidence, familiarity with the online environment, or numerous other factors, impacted their ability to contribute. While we can't "measure them" the way I've tried to do with blog and moodle participants, their continued subscription to The Daily and the comments encountered in F2F conferences suggest they also found some value in the course. http://ltc.umanitoba.ca/connectivism/?p=182

Adopting a Web 2.0 Approach to Learning: SocialLearn

What would a new university look like if we started with a blank sheet of paper, capitalising on the very best of what we know about good pedagogy coupled with harnessing the potential of new technologies? This is the question that has underpinned the development of a new initiative at the Open University, UK. The SocialLearn project is exploring how web 2.0 technologies can be harnessed for learning. SocialLearn expresses the University's aspiration to develop a new web-based educational offering with the potential to achieve significant business growth globally in ways that are consistent with OU values, which is responsive to future conditions, and which is cost-effective and scaleable (Walton et al., 2008). There are four main aspects to SocialLearn. Firstly, each learner will have a learner profile, which records their learning progress and can be used as a mechanism to share goals, resources and activities. Secondly, the project is adopting an open API (Applications Programming Interface) approach allowing developers to integrate with SocialLearn to allow the creation of loosely-coupled customized personal learning environments. Thirdly, the project is developing a range of specialized learning applications that aim to facilitate and foster web 2.0 learning approaches. Fourthly, a proof of concept site. Walton et al. (2008) conclude:

SocialLearn is not a proposal to develop yet another web-based platform for learning. The vision is much broader than that; we see it as an organisational pedagogical and technical platform for experimenting with disruptive technologies.

New Models of Learning for Personalisation

The previous section has described some of the ways in which technologies are being used to foster personalised learning. However, these practical examples are not grounded theoretically, there are no specific learning theories for personalisation. Nonetheless, there is a wide body of research generally on what constitutes good learning; from more didactic instructionally focused theories through to those emphasising a socio-cultural perspective. Conole (2008) argues that in essence good learning is a combination of four things, i.e. learning through:

- thinking and reflection
- conversation and interaction
- experience and activity
- evidence and demonstration (see Figure 2)

She goes on to describe a schema which using this framework as a means of mapping learning principles and argues can such schema can be used by teachers as a means of designing learning activities and in particular effective use of technologies.

The previous section describing a range of different examples of how technologies are being appropriated to support personalisation offer a starting point to begin to develop new pedagogical models for personalisation. Is it possible to distil from these the essence of personalisation and how the affordances of technologies can be mapped to create a technology-enhanced personalised learning environment? As Conole (2008) argues, this is part of a wider problem in terms of capitalising on the opportunities of new technologies for learning. The closest we have so far are theories that attempt to take account of the ubiquitous and connected nature of new technologies; such as connectivism. Siemens argues:

The starting point of connectivism is the individual. Personal knowledge is comprised of a network, which feeds into organizations and institutions, which in turn feed back into the network, and then continue to provide learning to individual. This cycle of knowledge development (personal to network to organization) allows learners to remain current in their field through the connections they have formed.

There is a need to re-conceptualise learning for the mobile age, to recognise the essential role of mobility and communication in the process of

Figure 2.

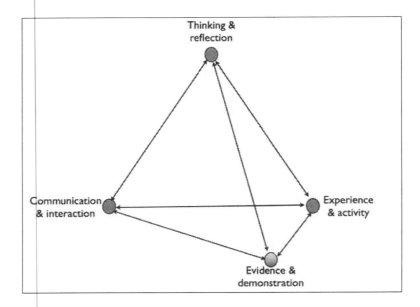

learning, and also to indicate the importance of context in establishing meaning, and the transformative effect of digital networks in supporting virtual communities that transcend barriers of age and culture.

Although it can be argued that both of these theories contain elements of personalisation, as yet there is no unifying theory specifically around personalised learning. Until we have such theories our designs of learning environments that attempt to foster personalisation are likely to be atheoretical; there is a danger that they will be technological deterministic. As Järvelä argues – 'models are needed for the effective use of technology to support individual and social learning' (OECD, 2006: 11)

Counter Arguments and the Challenges of Realising the Vision

Despite the widespread enthusiasm and support for the concept of personalisation and personalised learning, there are those who are sceptical of some of the current discourse (see for example

Ledda, 2007; Campbell et al., 2007; Johnson, 2004; Guldberg, 2004). Fraser (2006) writing about a policy document for the FE sector in the UK (DfES, 2006) highlights the following phrase in the report:

Increasing personalisation so that individual needs and circumstances are built into the design and delivery of education and training.

I'd argue that it is precisely this kind of misguided assurance - that the scope of individual needs and circumstances can be anticipated to the extent that they can be built in to provision and delivered to learners - that leads to exclusionary practice.

In a TLRP commentary Pollard referring to the UK Government's Personalised Learning welcomes the vision but highlights four particular challenges (Pollard, 2004). The first is conceptual – what are the theoretical and empirical foundations for the concept of personalised learning? The second is authenticity – is this really still more about teaching and curriculum delivery than learning? The third questions how realistic and achievable are the plans? And finally, what are the risks involved and how can they be managed?

Realising the vision inherent in much of the policy statements on personalisation brings with it a set of challenges; many of which are not exclusive to utilising technologies for personalised learning, but are equally relevant to the uptake of technology in educational generally:

- What does personalisation mean in a technology-enhanced environment?
- How do we take account of a digital divide that is ever narrower but deeper?
- What new digital literacy skills will learners and teachers need to capitalise on the potential of new technologies to support personalised learning?
- True personalisation will require a radical rethinking of the curriculum, the inertia of existing educational systems and cultures may be one of the biggest barriers to change.
- Personalisation challenges existing norms about assessment, what should be assessed, how can learners demonstrate what and how they have learnt? How can we shift from a focus on the products of learning to more on the processes of learning?
- How can we ensure approaches to personalisation are theoretically informed and how do we avoid adopting a technologically deterministic approach?
- A key challenge is to produce new pedagogical models which marry the affordances of personalisation with the best affordances of technologies
- There is a blurring of the boundaries of formal and informal education; what is the role of personalised learning across these contexts?
- There is a need for new business models – in a world where content and support is potentially free, where formal, traditional

accreditations schemes increasingly have less meaning and individual portfolios gain prominence - what is the purpose of traditional educational institutions?
- There is a mismatch between the policy directives on personalisation and actual practice, how do we bridge the gap?

We would like you to reflect on the issues raised in this introductory chapter as you read through the case studies, examples and reflections in the remainder of the book. The concept of personalised learning offers an exciting vision of a future of learning that is truly tailored to individual needs, abilities and interests. Technologies have much to offer in terms of unlocking this potential, but their use will need to be pedagogical informed. The chapters in this book give a glimpse of what is possible and a taster of future developments.

REFERENCES

Atkins, D., Seely Brown, J., & Hammond, A. L. (2007). *A review of the Open Educational Resource movement: achievements, challenges and new opportunities.* Report to the William and Flora Hewlett Foundation. Retrieved February 8, 2009 from http://www.hewlett.org/NR/rdonlyres/5D2E3386-3974-4314-8F67-5C2F22EC4F9B/0/AReviewoftheOpenEducationalResourcesOERMovement_BlogLink.pdf

Beck, U. (1992). *Risk society towards a new modernity.* London: Sage.

Becta (2008). *Harnessing technology: next generation learning 2008-14.* Retrieved February 8, 2009 from http://publications.becta.org.uk/display.cfm?resID=37348&page=1835

Campbell, R. J., Robinson, W., Neelands, J., Hewston, R., & Mazzoli, L. (2007). Personalised learning: ambiguities in theory and practice. *British Journal of Educational Studies, 55*(2), 135–154. doi:10.1111/j.1467-8527.2007.00370.x

Castells, M. (2000). *The rise of the network society.* Oxford: Blackwell.

Conole, G. (2008). New schemas for mapping pedagogies and technologies. [Retrieved from http://www.ariadne.ac.uk/]. *Ariadne*, (July): 2008.

Conole, G. (forthcoming). Stepping over the edge: the implications of new technologies for education. In M. Lee & C. McLouglin (eds.), *Web 2.0-based e-learning: applying social informatics for tertiary teaching.* Hershey, PA: ICI Global.

Conole, G., De Laat, M., Dillon, T., & Darby, J. (2008, February). 'Disruptive technologies', 'pedagogical innovation': What's new? Findings from an in-depth study of students' use and perception of technology.' . *Computers & Education, 50*(2), 511–524. doi:10.1016/j.compedu.2007.09.009

Delgado, D. (2007). *My Personal Learning Environment (PLE)* [blog posting]. Retrieved from http://eduspaces.net/davidds/weblog/193197.html

DfES. (2006). *Personalising further education, developing a vision.* Department for Education and Skills white paper. Retrieved February 8, 2009 from http://www.dcsf.gov.uk/consultations/downloadableDocs/DfES%20Personalisation.pdf

Dillenbourg, P. (1999). What do you mean by collaborative learning? In P. Dillenbourg (Ed) *Collaborative-learning: Cognitive and Computational Approaches* (pp.1-19). Oxford, UK: Elsevier.

Dillenbourg, P., Baker, M., Blaye, A., & O'Malley, C. (1996). The evolution of research on collaborative learning. In E. Spada & P. Reiman (Eds) *Learning in Humans and Machine: Towards an interdisciplinary learning science* (pp. 189-211). Oxford, UK: Elsevier.

ECAR. (2007). The ECAR study of undergraduate students and Information Technology. *Educause report, 6.* Retrieved from http://connect.educause.edu/library/abstract/TheECARStudyofUnderg/45075

European Commission. (2008). *An updated strategic framework for European cooperation in education and training.* Communication from the Commission to the European Parliament, the Council, the European Economic and Social Committee and the Committee of the Regions. Retrieved February 8, 2009 from http://ec.europa.eu/education/lifelong-learning-policy/doc28_en.htm

Fraser, J. (2006, October 12th). *Personalisation: customization - is it enough* [blog post]. Retrieved February 8, 2009 from http://fraser.typepad.com/edtechuk/2006/10/personalisation.html

Giddens, A. (2000). *Runaway World: How Globalization is Reshaping Our Lives.* New York: Routledge.

Grabinger, R. S., & Dunlop, J. C. (1996). Rich environments for active learning. *Association for Learning Technology Journal, 3*(2), 5–34.

Green, H., Facer, K., Rudd, T., Dillon, P., & Humphreys, T. (2005). *Personalisation and digital technologies.* Bristol, UK: Futurelab. Retrieved February 5, 2009 from http://www.futurelab.org.uk/resources/documents/opening_education/Personalisation_report.pdf

Guldberg, H. (2004, July 21st). *Class divisions – who benefits from the 'personalised learning' strategy of dividing school pupils into sub-sets?* [blog posting]. Retrieved from http://www.spiked-online.co.uk/Articles/0000000CA60E.htm

Harper, B., Hedberg, J., & Wright, R. (2000). Who benefits from virtuality? *Computers & Education, 34*(3-4), 163–176. doi:10.1016/S0360-1315(99)00043-3

Hirst, T. (2008, December 23). *So what else are you doing at the moment?* [blog posting]. Retrieved February 9, 2009 from http://ouseful.wordpress.com/2008/12/23/so-what-else-are-you-doing-at-the-moment/

Hopkins, D. (2006). Choice and voice in personalised learning. In *Personalised Learning: schooling for tomorrow*, (pp. 1-22). Paris: OECD publication, Centre for educational research and innovation. Retrieved February 5th, 2009 http://www.oecd.org/document/49/0,3343,en_2649_35845581_36168625_1_1_1_1,00.html

Järvelä, S. (2006). Personalised Learning and Changing Conceptions of Childhood and Youth. In *Personalised Learning: schooling for tomorrow*, (pp. 35-52). Paris: OECD publication, Centre for educational research and innovation. Retrieved February 5th, 2009 http://www.oecd.org/document/49/0,3343,en_2649_35845581_36168625_1_1_1_1,00.html

Johnson, M. (2004). *Personalised learning? An emperor's outfit?* London: Institute for Public Policy Research. Retrieved February 8, 2009 from https://www.ippr.org/uploadedFiles/research/projects/Education/Personalised%20Learning.pdf

Jonassen, D., Davidson, M., Collins, M., Campbell, J., & Banna Haag, B. (1995). Constructivism and computer-mediated communication in distance education. *American Journal of Distance Education*. Retrieved February 9, 2009 from http://www.uni-oldenburg.de/zef/cde/media/readings/jonassen95.pdf, 9/2/09.

Kennedy, G., Judd, T. S., Churchward, A., Gray, K., & Krause, K. L. (2008). First year students' experiences with technology: are they really digital natives? *Australiasian Journal of Educational Technology*, 24(1), 108–122.

Leadbeater, C. (2006). Personalisation: getting the questions right. In *Personalised Learning: schooling for tomorrow*, (pp. 95-110). Paris: OECD publication, Centre for educational research and innovation. Retrieved February 5, 2009 from http://www.oecd.org/document/49/0,3343,en_2649_35845581_36168625_1_1_1_1,00.html

Ledda, M. (2007). Personalised politics – how 'personalisation' devalues education and diminishes citizenship, blog posting 25th June 2007, http://www.culturewars.org.uk/2007-06/personalised.htm, last accessed 8/2/09.

Leslie, S. (2009). *A collection of PLE diagrams*. Retrieved from http://edtechpost.wikispaces.com/PLE+Diagrams

Martin, M. (2007). *My personal learning environment* [blog posting]. Retrieved from http://michelemartin.typepad.com/thebambooproject-blog/2007/04/my_personal_lea.html

McLoughlin, C., & Lee, M. (2008). The three P's of pedagogy for the networked society: personalization, participation and productivity. *International Journal of Teaching and Learning in Higher Education*, 20(1), 10–27.

Millband, D. (2006). "Personalised learning" New insights into fostering. In *Personalised Learning: schooling for tomorrow*. (23-34). Paris: OECD publication, Centre for educational research and innovation. Retrieved February, 5, 2009, from http://www.oecd.org/document/49/0,3343,en_2649_35845581_36168625_1_1_1_1,00.html

NSF task force on cyberlearning (2008). *Fostering learning in the networked world: learning opportunity and challenge. A 21st Century agenda for the National Science Foundation*. Report of the NSF task force on cyberlearning. Retrieved February 8, 2009 from http://www.nsf.gov/publications/pub_summ.jsp?ods_key=nsf08204

OECD. (2006). *Personalising education: Schooling for tomorrow.* OECD report. Paris: OECD. Retrieved February 5, from http://www.oecd.org/document/49/0,3343,en_2649_35845581_36168625_1_1_1_1,00.html

OECD. (2007). *Giving knowledge for free – the emergence of open educational resources, Centre for educational research and innovation,* Paris: OECD. Retrieved February 5, 2009 from http://www.oecd.org/dataoecd/35/7/38654317.pdf

Paludan, J. P. (2006). Personalised learning in 2025. In *Personalised Learning: schooling for tomorrow,* (pp. 71-84). Paris: OECD publication. Retrieved February 5, 2009 from http://www.oecd.org/document/49/0,3343,en_2649_35845581_36168625_1_1_1_1,00.html

Pollard, A. (2004). *Personalised learning – a commentary by the teaching and learning research programme.* Retrieved February 8, 2009 from http://www.tlrp.org/documents/personalised_learning.pdf

Scardamalia, M., & Bereiter, C. (2006). Knowledge building: Theory, pedagogy, and technology. In K. Sawyer (Ed.), *Cambridge Handbook of the Learning Sciences* (pp. 97-118). New York: Cambridge University Press.

Sharples, M., Taylor, J., & Vavoula, G. (2005). Towards a theory of mobile learning, in R. Andrews & C. Haythornthwaite (eds.) *The Sage Handbook of Elearning Research.* London: Sage, pp. 221-47.

Stewart. T. & Brown, M. (2008). Developing interactive scenarios: the value of good planning, whiteboards and table-based schemas. In *Proceedings of Ascilite 2008,* Melbourne. Retrieved February 9, 2009 from http://www.ascilite.org.au/conferences/melbourne08/procs/stewart.pdf

Virilio, P. (2005). *The information bomb.* London: Verso.

Walton, A.J., Weller, M. & Conole, G. (forthcoming). *SocialLearn – widening participation and sustainability of higher education, in EDEN book.*

ENDNOTES

[1] http://www.oecd.org/document/49/0,3343,en_2649_35845581_36168625_1_1_1_1,00.html

[2] http://dictionary.reverso.net/english-definitions/personalisation

[3] http://www.askoxford.com/concise_oed/personalize?view=uk

[4] http://www.nmc.org/horizon

[5] http://www.knowledgeforum.com/

[6] http://en.wikipedia.org/wiki/Personal_Learning_Environment

[7] http://www.pebblelearning.co.uk/

[8] http://ltc.umanitoba.ca/wiki/Connectivism

Section 1
Infrastructural and Cultural Issues

Chapter 2
Breaking the Hierarchy:
Democratising the Institutional Web Space

Beth Granter
University of Sussex, UK

ABSTRACT

This chapter, inspired by direct experience from working on the development of the University of Sussex's Student Personal Learning and Social Homepages (SPLASH) project, discusses how 'Web 2.0' technologies can be used to make institutional websites more democratic. The SPLASH mashup project was non-typical in that it intended to create an environment which would be fully customisable by the learner, so that no content was obligatory. Examples from working on this project are used to illustrate benefits which can be gained from, and barriers to the uptake of, more open publishing methods and an organically structured site architecture. Issues affecting learners, tutors, the institution as a whole, and how the power dynamic between all three may change, are discussed. Parallels are drawn between teaching methods online and those offline, both traditional and modern.

INTRODUCTION

Learning culture is but a slice of culture overall, and people are becoming more important than institutions in all facets of life. Command and control of organizational structures are giving way to democratizing networks. Learners, workers, all of us make decisions we previously would have taken to authorities for approval. (Cross, 2008)

This chapter will draw on experience gained through the development of the Student Personal Learning and Social Homepages (SPLASH) project at the University of Sussex, which was funded by JISC under the User-owned technology demonstrators strand (Granter, 2008). Challenges faced by the project included managing negative institutional attitudes towards critical content being published by students against the University, misconceptions such as improved online communication being thought to increase plagiarism, fears of defamation, fears that personalisation of the learning environ-

DOI: 10.4018/978-1-60566-884-0.ch002

ment would damage institutional branding and fears of certain students' viewpoints offending other students.

This chapter hopes to address these concerns and to deliver logical reasoning around how the benefits of incorporating social media into an institutional website outweigh the risks, and how in spite of any newly visible criticism, moving towards a more open publishing policy online will improve the reputation of the institution, as it will eventually be seen to be more honest and more trustworthy than those with closed publishing policies who operate under a hierarchy of strict editorial control. Allowing students a voice will add to the identity of the institution as one with confidence in its ability to provide a high standard of education and support and as an institution with a 'nothing to hide' attitude.

Personalisation of the learning environment addresses the power imbalance in education, improving the ability of students to learn from each other, thereby putting some power into the hands of the students. Giving students more choice over the content they receive from the institution in turn puts extra pressures on the institution to provide useful and interesting content; furthermore, the feedback available in the form of usage statistics will put major pressures on different institutional units to perform to a high level as they compete for attention and space. Thus, within the context of a history of corporate control of information, projects aiming to create democratic personalised learning environments are likely to find conflict within the institution itself.

Although the term 'Web 2.0' is already beginning to be regarded as a dated term, its use here is appropriate because Web 2.0 describes succinctly a number of theories and tools aligned with a more democratic use of the internet. In the scope of this chapter, Web 2.0 is used to describe blogging, wikis, forums, user generated content, online communities and social media. 'Social media' here refers to any online tool or space which allows communication and/or collaboration between a number of people, often in a networked environment (Wikipedia, 2008).

Openness and Utopia

Openness is associated with values such as tolerance, individual freedom, lifelong learning, participation, empowerment and cooperation, as opposed to typical closed-world values of command and control, top-down management, centralized and bureaucratic governance, over-regulation. (Straub, 2008)

Web 2.0 technologies are creating a more democratic web by allowing anyone to publish content, in comparison to the traditional unidirectional flow of information from corporation to user. University websites have previously consisted of institutional information being presented for the consumption of their students, potential students, businesses and all other audiences. A typical University website currently consists of reading lists and lecture notes posted by tutors, promotional information written by its press and communications division, and departmental web content written by authorised web editors. The offline version of this content would be traditional printed prospectus', standard format lectures and the mainstream press.

While collaborative group work and student discussion has been increasingly encouraged in modern teaching, in the form of seminars etc. (Terenzini et al, 2001), it is only in the last few years that the tools have been available which could mirror this more democratic style of learning online. The mainstream press has been opening up its websites via user generated content in the form of blogs and forums (and more recently, rich media (Plesser, 2006)) since the very beginning of the twenty first century - allowing the public to have a voice (Jenny, 2003). University websites seem to have limited the use of Web 2.0 tools to the domain of eLearning, conveniently maintaining complete institutional control over public facing content. Initially conceived as a *social* networking mashup space, the SPLASH project was intended to create more than just an eLearning space – the blogging aspect can be used as a public publishing platform for any purpose within reason. However, creating a very democratic space within an otherwise closed website is not changing the central system, but is the equivalent of creating a co-operative commune in the woods in a city which remains essentially capitalist, when I believe we should be taking steps to build the online equivalent of an anarcho-syndicalist society;

Anarcho-syndicalists view labour unions as a potential force for revolutionary social change, replacing capitalism and the State with a new society democratically self-managed by workers. (Wikipedia, 2008 (my emphasis))

Instead of mirroring existing societal structures when building the web, we can choose to build it as a new utopia. It is my view that when the utopian model is working online, we are one step closer to achieving utopia offline.

Reputation and Citizen Journalism

Currently, open publishing platforms such as Wikipedia, citizen journalism sites such as Indymedia and online social networking sites such as Facebook are flourishing, but there are institutional concerns over adopting similar open publishing policies within the context of a university website. Educational institutions in general put a great deal of resources into maintaining their online reputation as a professional institution. New social media sites which allow users to publish their own opinions of products and services, such as GetSatisfaction.com, are seen by businesses to be threatening as they provide the space for criticism which could damage their reputation (Bowles, 2006). ELearning projects hoping to harness the educational benefits of Web 2.0 technology through wikis, blogs etc., are likely to be confronted with barriers to their progress as a result

of institutional fears such as these. Individual academics have raised concerns about defamation, which they feared a university-endorsed open publishing platform might facilitate. They understood that the tools on the web could already be (and sometimes were being) used to discuss a tutor negatively – but it was when these same tools were brought within a university website that the content published through them would have to be recognised and dealt with. The only consolation we were able to give was that they could use these public feedback areas to gain knowledge of how they might improve their teaching practice, and in turn respond to dissatisfied students and help them with their issues. Of course this will not be a satisfactory response to tutors who are aware of being unpopular amongst their students.

Folksonomy

Political centralization… is a relic belonging to the social condition marked by industrial capitalism: a myriad of interdependent industrial productions that require homogeneity in order for there to be the predictability that is necessary for the various manufacturing outputs to be interoperable with one another. (Cole, 2008)

A strategy similar to political centralisation is generally employed when designing, building and managing traditional university websites. Hence, departmental sections of the whole website must each have a homogeneous semantic structure, not only to ensure that usability is good across the site for the end user, but perhaps because we are currently comfortable with this level of structure and control as it mirrors the structure we see in our institutions, and in our society.

When considering the offline organisation of higher educational institutions, there is often conflict between the opinions of students, lecturers and central administrative teams – each being under different pressures and having different needs from the organisation. Hence, the University of Sussex has had four restructures in seven years, much to the frustration of many staff and students, who feel their needs are not being met (Hodges, 2008). Since the structure of an institutional website is likely to mirror that of the institution itself, restructures inevitably create a massive workload for web teams, who may be positioned by association as having some responsibility for a new, unpopular, institutional structure, because of their technical responsibility to control the website structure. As with many universities, the relationship between the University of Sussex as an institution and the University of Sussex Student Union (USSU) has historically been less than perfect. As a university famous for direct action and its constituency of politically active students, there is often a feeling of scepticism still held by USSU members towards 'The Administration'. Protest marches on Sussex House, which houses Student Recruitment, the Press and Communications Division, Student Accounts and the Vice Chancellor's Office, are not uncommon. Increases in fees at a national level, and questions over University finances and management practices at a local level, are often the main causes for protest. In such a time of unrest, and particularly in the culture of protest that Sussex remains in today, it should be seen as courageous of the University to open up any of its public facing web space to its students and staff via post-moderation (ability to moderate *after* content has gone 'live' on the site). It is yet to be seen how any moderation will be handled by those authorised, and how those being moderated will respond. The Student Union's Communications Officer was regularly consulted throughout the development of the SPLASH project, and the concerns he voiced were mainly around issues of moderation, privacy and control. Ensuring that the student body felt comfortable using the system we were building was of course very important to the project, which had to balance the desire for the opportunity for free-speech and public debate, with concerns over the potential for bullying and invasion of privacy.

Within any large organisation, there are likely to be recurring disagreements between the central administration and departmental staff over how information on the institution's website is organised, i.e. the information architecture of a site. Locally, those closest to a particular area of study with specialist knowledge will naturally want to have as much control as possible over their content, as they feel they are most qualified to organise it. However, central teams have the understanding that organising content in a uniform manner across departments makes browsing easier and is vital for good usability of a website (Tidwell, 2005). There is generally no dynamic interaction between related items of content housed on separate departmental web pages, that is, inter-departmental links where topics or research cross boundaries of categorisation rely on the web editors entering manual links which relies on the web editor being aware of related content elsewhere on the site. There is no opportunity for comment, no automated track-backs for referenced content, no ability to create new links across subjects through tagging. A hierarchy of editorial control operates where trained content creators are guided by web editors who operate under the control of a PR and Communications division.

Traditional hierarchies with their burgeoning bureaucracies and disconnected silos are typical manifestations [of the closed world]. The rise of social networking sites, virtual worlds, blogs, wikis and 3D Internet give us a first idea of the potential of the "interactive and collaborative web" dubbed Web 2.0. Now we have the infrastructure and tools to operate in new ways in open systems. (Straub, 2008)

To overcome any power struggle between departments and central teams over information architecture, it is possible to provide multiple ways of navigating content. A consistent top level and secondary level navigation system is certainly necessary, and after consulting departments the central team should be able to create this navigation, the main site map and traditional user journeys. Subject specific content can then be placed into the most relevant areas and categories, using the institutional taxonomy, as is standard with current web Content Management Systems. In addition, to create a parallel and organic navigation option, feedback on the information architecture of a site could come through the use of tagging. The content could be tagged by any individual, which would generate tag clouds made up of subject-specific folksonomies. People within departments may then find it easier to navigate content via these tags rather than the institutionally defined categories. This more flexible and open approach to content structure could also account for changes over time if this affects the way that the information needs to be organised. Fears of abuse of such a system could be reduced via a log-in system so the person tagging is identifiable. Abuses could also be flagged by other users so the system could be self-policing.

In addition, the learning effect on students and staff alike of the opportunity to reorder and recategorise the content they are learning from will not only be through the benefit of awareness of new connections between topics, therefore enhancing the solidification of the contents' meanings in the mind, but will also be through the benefit of rethinking the learning experience itself – to think of it not as an experience requiring institutional *schooling*, but one which can come from oneself and one's community. Attempts at re-educating our society into this frame of mind, where learning outside the framework of the traditional institutional schooling system is validated by all, echoes Illich's calls for "deschooling society", which is based on the theory that, "Most learning happens casually, and even most intentional learning is not the result of programmed instruction" (Illich, 1970). Returning to the topic of folksonomies and tagging, then, Illich states that,

The majority cannot and should not be rallied for discussion around a slogan, a word, or a picture. But the idea remains the same: they should be able to meet around a problem chosen and defined by their own initiative. Creative, exploratory learning requires peers currently puzzled about the same terms or problems. Large universities make the futile attempt to match them by multiplying their courses, and they generally fail since they are bound to curriculum, course structure, and bureaucratic administration.

Illich goes on to envisage a solution in the form of a system which did not yet exist at the time of his writing – a computer network where individuals make contact for the purpose of discussion around a topic chosen by themselves.

The Knowledge Economy

A great deal has been written about e-government and democracy, mainly with regard to American politics. These studies suggest ways in which Web 2.0 tools could be used to democratise government processes via online referendums and increased discourse between governing councils and the public. In an article on the website Midwest Populist America, Cole uses the well known example of Nature's experiment, which proved the equivalence in reliability of the social knowledge platform Wikipedia to the traditionally produced Encyclopaedia Britannica (Giles, 2005), to support his argument that "radical democracy – a state that is, oftentimes, embodied by Web 2.0 communities – is not only a deontological ideal – a social condition that we should strive to foster, because it is inherently desirable – but a form of social organization that is pragmatically endowed." He goes on to say that "social knowledge produces knowledge constructs on a scale that supersedes in volume and quality the knowledge built from traditional social institutions, such as the Academe" (Cole, 2008). Although more research is needed to conclusively prove this statement, the initial studies do seem to support this theory, which is of great concern to those making a career out of their expertise. Historically, science is considered to be closely aligned to a 'pure truth' and proven facts, distanced from opinion and unauthorised or unapproved research. While there should be no reason why theories and hypothesis cannot be created more collaboratively and internationally, using Web 2.0 technologies as a tool to aide this process, the whole culture of academia has grown around peer review, citation scores, and getting published in respectable journals (Henneberg, 1997). When anyone can self publish and non-traditional open publishing spaces become respected, the knowledge economy itself becomes unstable.

In the field of pharmaceutical research for example, open publishing is likely to pose a problem with regard to patents and sponsorships. Where huge finances are required to carry out practical research, methods of production will need to remain under strict ownership of the sponsor. Where there are great financial gains to be made from finding a solution to a problem, collaboration amongst strangers towards a common goal will be rare. In Wallis' review of the SAPIENS project (which was set up to provide electronic versions of Scottish periodicals) he concludes that electronic publishing is "not cost free and a subscription model is necessary to sustain such a service" (Wallis, 2004). Although this is a review of the practice of open *access* to traditional publications and not specifically about *open publishing*, the two are directly related because all or almost all open publishing platforms are used to create freely available (open access) intellectual property (Wikipedia, 2008).

In Web 2.0 culture, original content may be considered more trustworthy than that which has been rewritten by copywriters and editors. In order to self-publish such original content, researchers need tools and training for online publishing, guidance on the different tones of writing to use in different online spaces, and a definitive place to publish to be provided for them. Increasing numbers of researchers are likely to have their own blog or homepage already and this may reduce the likelihood of some institutions recognising the need to provide these services to its staff and students. However, aggregation of up-to-date content (e.g. via RSS) could be seen as a valid method of supporting this content. The opportunity to publish alongside other researchers from the same institution is the benefit, not specifically the provision of a blogging platform itself. Indeed, many researchers will value the opportunity to choose a platform for themselves that suits their needs or is familiar to them. On the other hand, less experienced users may need a platform to be provided by the institution before they feel they can 'trust' the software. Additionally, when an institution aggregates the content of its researchers, it is providing a recognisable badge of approval and authority to the work that a previously independent, self-published researcher's blog could not achieve.

Student Personal Learning and Social Homepages (SPLASH)

The SPLASH project provides a simple blogging platform to users, alongside an RSS feed output display where external blogs can be imported and displayed on a user's SPLASH Profile. A major concern throughout the project was that the user should keep total control and ownership of all of their content, even outside the lifetime of their university membership. To achieve this, the SPLASH project took a very different shape to other Personal Learning Environment (PLE) and ePortfolio projects, by insisting that all content created by the user, except blog posts, would be hosted externally. In the case of blog posts which constituted the only university hosted, user-generated content, a large factor in the project plan was that the blog should be easily exportable into external blogging systems which allow content import such as Wordpress or Blogger.

Keeping as much content external as possible means that the user has choice over where their content is held, which goes some way towards giving them complete ownership over their content (notwithstanding external host company terms and conditions – users would still need to ensure that when agreeing to these terms, their ownership rights to their content are not infringed upon). In addition, when the user moves between institutions, although the presentation of aggregated content within SPLASH will be lost, the content itself remains.

The main concept behind SPLASH was that it would have a function similar to an iGoogle dashboard or a NetVibes page, with fully customisable drag-and-drop widgets to bring in information chosen by the user. This constituted the SPLASH 'Dashboard'. The SPLASH user's profile page would also function in this way, but the user would probably choose to put different information here, presumably information about, or created by, themselves – or useful resources they wished to share. They would then be able to choose privacy settings on a per-widget basis, ranging from totally private, to certain classmates, tutors or contacts only, to totally public. This means that the information visible on an individual's profile would vary depending on who is looking at it, and whether they are logged in.

Throughout the development of SPLASH, University members – students, academics and support staff, were invited to give their input into the project's functionality specification. This was done via the student newspaper, the university website, and existing internal eLearning interest group email lists. Although the number of people coming forward to offer their opinion was scarce, through various recommendations, a working group was formed consisting of three academics, each offering access to students in one of their classes, and also one student union group – the Gender Society. It was important to involve the Student Union and academics in order to have the support of the students and tutors when the

project launched – so that they knew they had had opportunities for input and therefore felt some ownership of the project. These 'case study groups' were called upon during initial meetings when determining functionality and design, and again to test the usability of the system when development began. They were also chosen to beta test the system when it initially launched. In addition, open forum presentations occurred across campus at various stages of development of the SPLASH project, some targeted specifically at academics, some at IT support staff and some at students. During these presentations, the progress of the project was discussed and feedback received.

The groups of students chosen to beta test the project were specifically chosen to test a range of different learning situations in order to consider a range of students' needs. Product Design undergraduates were considered likely to benefit from sharing multimedia online, Social Work students spent a lot of time off campus and many were part-time, so we were interested in how SPLASH might help build social ties between students in that group who had fewer opportunities to meet each other offline, Human-Computer Interaction students were expected to embrace the technology and to provide useful insight into what could be possible, and the Gender Society were thought to challenge any preconceptions of identity representation, choice, and privacy, as well as to offer ideas on how they wanted to use SPLASH for organising and promoting a group which was not course-specific.

Although I finished working as Project Manager/Developer on the SPLASH project three months before it launched in October 2008, my successor Hesan Yousif has diligently kept the project blog up to date (Yousif et. al., 2009) so I have been able to follow the progress and launch of SPLASH from outside the institution. However, at the time of writing, SPLASH is still very much in beta mode, having been live for only four months, so it has certainly not yet reached the critical mass of users necessary to test it to its full potential.

Although all first year students have been given access to SPLASH this year, extensive marketing and promotion of the system on campus and online is still necessary to engage students until the critical mass of active users is reached. For this reason, my analyses in this essay remain based on the experiences I had first-hand with the planning and development stages of the project, including the varied attitudes to the project that I encountered whilst working towards its launch. In the future, a discussion of the techniques employed in recruiting membership and use of the system, and how successful the system was found after launch, including any effect on learning outcomes, will indeed be useful.

Editorial Control

When editorial control of departmental websites is handed to the departments themselves via Content Management Systems (CMS), there can be tensions between the lecturers and departmental administrators who are publishing to a live University website, and between the central administrators and communications teams. Tensions are likely to arise around quality control, tone of voice used online, and branding, as central teams are forced to accept a certain level of loss of control over the University image that is portrayed publicly. Most University websites' content is managed mainly by CMS which allow authorised web editors to maintain areas of the website that are related to their work. This system is still not fully democratic or open because there is often a hierarchy of editorial control over content; becoming a web editor requires training (even when using a CMS) and brings with it responsibilities that many university staff do not wish to take on, and the unidirectional flow of content from the institution to the reader remains. Although this is a step in the right direction in that it transforms the one-to-many model website into a few-to-many model website, the structure of a CMS driven website is still essentially the equivalent of a brochure or prospectus.

For a true many-to-many democratic site to exist, live feedback mechanisms must be embedded throughout the site. In addition, feedback that is submitted and the responses to such feedback should be fully public so that readers can track how each others' complaints and suggestions are handled. Such transparency of customer service via sites such as Getsatisfaction.com has been successful in boosting consumer confidence in a brand for many companies in the private sector. Lessons could also be learnt from the community news voting site Digg.com when developing editorial tools used to promote items as featured articles on a website, i.e. we should consider allowing users to choose homepage content themselves. Not everyone wants to be a content producer, some might just want some degree of editorial influence.

I suggest that on an individual level, the essence of personalised learning is in the autonomous behaviour it facilitates for its users, or else it is not truly personal. However, on an institutional scale, all structure and organisation need not be lost to anarchy. Gannon-Leary & Fontainha (2007) point to the need for leadership, in the form of a moderator for example, in order for a community of practice to be sustained successfully: "Stuckey and Smith (2004) argue that there are identifiable features to a successful CoP, and most importantly the ability to sustain the community, the chief of which is the need for 'leadership' which, in the case of a CoP, may be a moderator, facilitator or list owner". This indicates that ongoing support (in the form of a community moderator) is needed from the institution if an online community is to be successful. How this moderation is put into practice can be a very sensitive issue. It is worth noting that the Student Union Communications Officer who was the SPLASH project's main student representative was, for the first year of the project, also active in the Student Union Autonomous Society (which was not an official society, but was a politically active association of students on campus), and this individual was passionately concerned about the potential abuse of power that the University could have if all students were communicating within a University controlled system. Luckily, that student's successor was considerably more positive about the opportunities that SPLASH could provide for union groups to organise and promote themselves. It is clear from this situation that the political stance of stakeholders can have a dramatic effect on their buy-in to a Personalised Learning Environment.

Personalisation and Identity

The need to allow a mixture of social interaction alongside instructional teaching in the same environment, as well as the need for strong identity representation in virtual communities, has been explained by Gannon-Leary & Fontainha in relation to how a lack of opportunity for socialising in a virtual community of practice, and hidden or multiple identities, may negatively affect users' sense of 'trust' in that community:

A fifth barrier involves trust. The virtual CoP lacks the opportunity for face-to face interaction and socialising which can consolidate group membership. Consequently individuals may fail to engage in the CoP, preferring to work autonomously. Trust building is vital for sharing (Jarvenpaa & Leidner, 1999; Kirkup, 2002; Gibson & Manuel, 2003; Ellis et al 2004) and trust primarily develops through face-to-face interactions. In the virtual environment, identities can remain hidden and members may adopt different personas (Tomes, 2001; Turkle, 1997). (Gannon-Leary & Fontainha, 2007)

This would indicate that seemingly frivolous attempts to facilitate self expression through an online profile within the community (such as personal profile design themes, avatar choice etc.) are indeed important to facilitating sharing, and therefore learning, within the community, via their effect on solidifying identities online,

which in turn should encourage sociability and therefore learning.

The SPLASH project was based around the concept of a wholly customisable networked mash-up. Users have a personal dashboard composed of widgets that they choose – none are obligatory. Of the widgets on offer, some are explicitly learning related, containing information specific to that user's academic courses, whilst others may keep the user updated on their personal and social life, for example via a Facebook widget (not excluding the possibility that the user uses Facebook for academic learning). As well as a dashboard, the user has a profile with widget-specific privacy settings, and is automatically networked with course-mates as well as having a user-created network of contacts. When we discuss a personalised learning environment, we are not only suggesting that the user be able to customise layout and design, but that they should be able to choose what content they receive, what content they share, and with whom. In Designing for Change: Mash-Up Personal Learning Environments (Wild, Modritscher & Sigurdarson, 2008), the assumption is made that "establishing a learning environment, i.e. a network of people, artefacts, and tools (consciously or unconsciously) involved in learning activities, is part of the learning outcomes, not an instructional condition". That is, the process of customising one's learning experience, for example through choosing what widgets to put on your dashboard, and by researching and adding contacts, defines these as useful and relevant in the learner's mind – it is an editing and organisational process having a learning outcome in itself.

When it was proposed that users would be able to fully personalise their learning environment, there were fears from some departments that information that they deemed to be important would not reach the students if the students were able to choose the sources of information they receive. At the University of Sussex, different units across the University were eager to push their content at the students via a widget in the SPLASH project, and became uneasy when confronted with the concept that a student would be able to choose to remove their information feed from their online learning space. Indeed, projects which create personalised learning environments such as this will create an extra pressure on institutional units, which will be forced to make their content more engaging and useful for their audience or risk their content being removed by the user. It is assumed by some that extra work will be required to make their content desirable, so staff may be unsupportive of such projects. This indicates a lack of confidence in the value of the content that the unit is providing to the user. If there is a genuine need for this content, then the unit should be producing a high quality resource anyway, so its staff should have nothing to fear. Once implemented though, the result will be higher quality content delivered to the student, as units compete to prove their value.

Another potential effect of allowing such customisation lies in how the attitude to learning will vary amongst students. Students' reasons for being at university will not always include the simple desire to learn. They may be delaying the task of finding employment, or may have been pressured into attending by their parents. They may also simply be there to gain a qualification to improve their chances in the job market. Many students are likely to be at university due to a mixture of any of these reasons. So, the desire of the student to learn will vary, and as such their selection of information that they choose to receive via customisable systems will vary to the extent that it is relevant to (academic, course based) learning. Where previously the content they receive via university web pages would always contain a uniform amount of course based learning material, irrelevant of how interested the student was, giving the student a choice about whether they receive this information at all is likely to result in an exaggerated division between those who are learning (academically) and those who are not, dependent on the customisations they have made. So, whilst those with an existing tendency to be

interested in the course-based learning materials are likely to benefit by the customisations and become more engaged with the content they have chosen, those who are not already interested in their course may make customisations likely to further remove themselves from learning materials, becoming further disengaged from their course content. I have based the above hypothesis on theories around new digital technology's effects on the 'reinforcement of existing patterns of political engagement and participation' (Barney, 2008).

Far from mobilizing the general public, the Internet may thereby function to increase divisions between the actives and apathetics within societies...it is difficult to know how the Internet per se can ever reach the civically disengaged. (Norris, 2001 in Barney, 2008)

If this applies to the *learning* disengaged as I have suggested, it could result in a polarisation of students into those who are successful and those who are struggling.

Informal Learning

Rethinking the educational experience as something that can happen in any context, not only within the institution, but through other life experiences including work and leisure, is a change in thought demanded from society by Illich in his book, Deschooling Society (1970). In Deschooling Society, Illich explains how a change of attitude towards education and learning to one which values equally learning experiences outside of the context of the institution, where no certificates or grades are awarded, would deeply challenge the power of the school (or university), and in turn, challenge the power of the whole of modern society. Perhaps it is for this reason that mixing what we might call 'informal learning', e.g. learning via social interaction between peers rather than by direct tuition from lecturer to student, remains a revolutionary concept to many within the institution, something which may unsettle lecturers and others in positions of authority within a university.

Whilst researching user and tutor needs for the SPLASH project, it became apparent that modern learners felt comfortable mixing the expression of their social online persona with their learning/ professional online persona, whilst some lecturers who were attempting to be pioneers of eLearning, were not yet comfortable with navigating these mixed use environments. For example, one tutor came to us with concerns that her students were using a class forum, which she had set up in Moodle for her course, to organise their social activities. For her, this was an inappropriate use of the space and she felt uncomfortable being included in such conversations. However, such use by the students is an indicator that they felt enough ownership of that space to use it for social *as well as* distinctly learning oriented activities, and feeling ownership of the space will have a positive impact on their learning outcomes from that space.

Lave and Wenger (1991) discuss learning as participation in a social world describing how people learn better in social settings and through social interaction. Virtual CoPs [Communities of Practice] encompass this concept in that they establish a networked environment where the necessary interactions that improve learning can occur (Wenger et al., 2002). (Gannon-Leary & Fontainha, 2007)

It is possible that when the line between a learning space and a social space is unclear, as in many Web 2.0 environments, those tradition-ally in a position of authority over the learning space (the tutors) might feel threatened due to the altered power dynamic. In this case, the tu-tor, in expressing her concern over the explicitly social aspects of the SPLASH project, a 'Personal Learning Environment', was basing these feelings on the discomfort she had felt when having to navigate through social behaviour within Moodle,

a 'Virtual Learning Environment'. However, "the PLE approach is based on a learner-centred view of learning and differs fundamentally from the alternative Learning Management Systems or Virtual Learning Environments approach, both of which are based on an institution or course-centred view of learning. …Important concepts in PLEs include the integration of both formal and infor-mal learning episodes into a single experience" (Attwell, 2008). Therefore, tutors' expectations of appropriate behaviour within a PLE need to be adjusted, which they might find difficult when they are only just starting to be comfortable with the different dynamics within VLEs.

CONCLUSION

Clearly, it is not only the tools that are used on a University website that must change, but the entire mindset of the education system. This is likely to happen in a staggered process because many successful case studies of the use of demo-cratic web tools are needed to gain support for an institutional strategy of open publishing. Whilst an initial amount of support is needed to fund projects to develop tools for democratic learn-ing, when the initial tools are deployed, they will struggle to achieve their optimum results because the number of users of the tools has not yet reached the required critical mass – this is the 'network effect'.

The network effect dictates that the value of being in the network increases exponentially with the number of participants, or connected nodes to the network. (Wild, Modritscher & Sigurdarson, 2008)

This is based on the original interpretation of Metcalf's Law. Although this theory has received criticism in its application to social networks (Briscoe et. al., 2006), Metcalf has revisited his theory to state that the current model best suited for understanding the value of social networks in relation to their size, has to take into account the *affinity* of members within that network, which would result in a model closer to Chris Anderson's theory of The Long Tail (Metcalfe, 2006). That means that once the critical mass of *valuable* connections has been reached, there is likely to be a 'long tail' dropoff of value added per member as the overall size of the network continues to grow, and also means that the critical mass required for the value of the network to surpass the cost of the network, would be reached more quickly if the network is modelled in a way that maximises opportunities for members to have affinity with one another, for example through socialising, self expression and informal learning activity.

I believe that projects such as the SPLASH project, are working towards providing these opportunities through new social media tools, in institutional web spaces which previously were not open to such social activity. Currently we are in the difficult period where the technology is becoming available yet it is hard to prove its worth to the unconverted without mainstream acceptance and use. One solution might be for pioneering institutions to take the necessary risks and provide the resources needed for such projects to flourish, and to embrace informal learning activity within such systems. The University of Sussex with its SPLASH project, and related projects in the field of personalised learning, have taken the first steps towards implementing these new systems. It is too early to evaluate the effect that the SPLASH project will have on learning outcomes, so this chapter can only hope to inspire further research.

Now that the SPLASH project has been launched and the initial project funding has come to an end, it remains to be seen how well supported the continuation of the project will be by the University itself. These kinds of project need support not only through the technological development, but throughout ongoing maintenance, for community development and moderation. As a

forester is required to plant saplings and to prune hedges, so also a manager is needed to ensure a healthy ecology in the ongoing evolution of an online community.

In conclusion, educational institutions need not stop at using Web 2.0 tools within designated online learning environments, as their use throughout an institutional website will benefit the institution as a whole, by improving internal communications and relations. While the move towards an open publishing environment will have to overcome barriers to uptake because of fears of defamation and loss of control, the overall result will be positive as all members of the institution will have ownership of the content and joint responsibility for creating the best possible representation of the organisation, which is in everybody's interests. Whilst the ideal scenario might involve site-wide opportunities for instantly publicly visible user feedback on information architecture, feedback on 'official' content as well as the ability to create user generated content, more people will need to become comfortable with the concepts of a democratic, non-hierarchical authorship model, and this can only come through time and experience with these kinds of environments.

Note: In accordance with the policy of open publishing and democracy discussed in this chapter, I intend to publish this text on my blog (accessible via http://bethgranter.com) which allows public commenting.

More information on the SPLASH project: http://sussex.ac.uk/splash

REFERENCES

Attwell, G. (2008). Personal Learning Environments – a new learning concept or a new learning system? In V. Homung-Prahauser, M. Luckman, & M. Kalz, (Ed.), *Selbstorganisiertes Lernen im Internet – Edumedia Proceeding*. Retrieved October 29, 2008, from http://edumedia.salzburgresearch.at/images/stories/4_EduMedia_Konferenz/Praesentationen/edumedia_proceeding.pdf

Barney, D. (2008). *The Network Society*. Cambridge, UK: Polity Press Ltd.

Bowles, J. (2006). Why CEOs Are Afraid Of Social Media. *Enterprise Web 2.0*. Retrieved October 16, 2008, from http://www.enterpriseweb2.com/?p=77

Briscoe, B., Odlyzko, A., & Tilly, B. (2006). Metcalfe's Law is Wrong. *Ieee Spectrum Online*. Retrieved February 22, 2009, from http://spectrum.ieee.org/jul06/4109

Cole, R. (2008). Review of "Bad for Democracy," by Professor Dana D. Nelson. *Midwest Populist America*. Retrieved October 18, 2008, from http://www.midwest-populistamerica.com/articles/review-of-bad-for-democracy-by-professor-dana-d-nelson

Cross, J. (2008). From Content to Context. In V. Hornung-Prahauser, M. Luckman, & M. Kalz (Ed.). *Selbstorganisiertes Lernen im Internet – Edumedia Proceeding*. Retrieved October 29, 2008, from http://edumedia.salzburgresearch.at/images/stories/4_EduMedia_Konferenz/Praesentationen/edumedia_proceeding.pdf

Gannon-Leary, P., & Fontainha, E. (2007). Communities of Practice and virtual learning communities: benefits, barriers and success factors. *eLearning Papers, 5*, September 2007. Retrieved October 16, 2008 from http://www.elearningeuropa.info

Giles, J. (2005, December 15). Special Report Internet encyclopaedias go head to head. *Nature, 438*, 900–901. doi:10.1038/438900a

Granter, B. (2008). Student Personal Learning and Social Homepages. *University of Sussex website*. Retrieved October 26, 2008, from http://sussex.ac.uk/splash

Henneberg, M. (1997). Peer review: the Holy Office of modern science. *naturalSCIENCE, 1*(2). Retrieved October 24, 2008, from http://natural-science.com/ns/articles/01-02/ns_mh.html

Hodges, L. (2008). Conflict on campus. *The Independent*, October 2, 2008, 2.

Illich, I. (1970). *Deschooling Society*. Retrieved October 20, 2008, from http://www.davidtinapple.com/illich/1970_deschooling.html.

Jenny (2003). Eric Zorn Now Blogging on Chicago Tribune site. *The Shifted Librarian*. Retrieved October 20, 2008, from http://www.theshiftedlibrarian.com/2003/08/19.html#a4463

Metcalfe, B. (2006). Metcalfe's Law Recurses Down the Long Tail of Social Networking. *VCMike's Blog*. Retrieved February 22, 2009, from http://vcmike.wordpress.com/2006/08/18/metcalfe-social-networks/

Plesser, A. (2006). Mainstream Media To Embrace Homegrown Video Uploads: New York Times Newspapers, Conde Nast and Others Take the Plunge. *Beet.TV*. Retrieved October 22, 2008, from http://www.beet.tv/2006/12/mainstream_medi.html.

Straub, R. (2008). Is the world open? *Global Focus, 2*(1). Retrieved October 22, 2008, from http://www.efmd.org

Terenzini, P., Cabrera, A., Colbeck, C., Parente, J., & Bjorklund, S. (2001). Collaborative learning vs. lecture/discussion: Students' reported learning gains . *Journal of Engineering Education, 90*(1), 123–130.

Tidwell, J. (2005). *Designing Interfaces: Patterns for Effective Interaction Design*. Sebastopol, CA: O'Reilly Media Inc.

Wallis, J. (2004). Facilitating Scottish cultural publishing online. *Library Review, 53*(5), 265. doi:10.1108/00242530410538409

Wikipedia (2008). Anarcho-syndicalism. *Wikipedia*. Retrieved February 21, 2009, http://en.wikipedia.org/wiki/Anarcho-syndicalism

Wikipedia (2008). Open publishing. *Wikipedia*. Retrieved October 17, 2008, http://en.wikipedia.org/wiki/Open_publishing

Wikipedia (2008). Social media. *Wikipedia*. Retrieved February 21, 2009, http://en.wikipedia.org/wiki/Social_media

Wild, F., Modritscher, F., & Sigurdarson, S. (2008). Designing for Change: Mash-Up Personal Learning Environments. *eLearning Papers, 9*, July 2008. Retrieved October 16, 2008 from http://www.elearningeuropa.info

Yousif, H., et al. (2009). *SPLASH Blog*. Retrieved February 28, 2009, http://splashproject.blogspot.com/

Chapter 3
PLE:
A Brick in the Construction of a Lifelong Learning Society

Sabrina Leone
Università Politecnica delle Marche, Italy

ABSTRACT

The attainment of lifelong learning objectives is being mediated by a complex process of innovation in education and society, by the integration of institutional actions and by the major role of coordination that university has assumed. The revolution that technology has engendered in every field has flowed into a rethinking of knowledge, knowledge management, teaching and learning, networks and the individual. The knowledge society requires new roles and skills, new forms of communication and a new awareness as "active citizens". Consequently, the shifting role of education systems in networked organizations is decisive in order to support learners in forming diverse personal learning networks to deeply understand complex fields. This chapter aims to discuss consistency (i.e. solidity and reliability) and effectiveness (i.e. success, usefulness and value) of a personal learning environment as a new learning space and to highlight its contribution and relevance to lifelong learning. PLE critical points and approaches will be discussed exploiting three case studies.

INTRODUCTION

The only man who is educated is the man who has learned how to learn [...] how to adapt and change [...]. Changingness, a reliance on process rather than upon static knowledge, is the only thing that makes any sense as a goal for education in the modern world. (Kirschenbaum & Henderson, 2002, p. 304)

DOI: 10.4018/978-1-60566-884-0.ch003

The introduction of lifelong learning objectives and policies has poised us on the threshold of major change in education and society. By now, learning to learn and learning have become the first motivation towards development, empowerment, continuity and generation of value, with the help of Web 2.0 tools.

The implications of the adoption of a lifelong learning paradigm, which is strongly supported by the use of new technologies, are profound and they have already impacted on all aspects of educational institutions. Undoubtedly these are exciting, but challenging times. The revolution that technology has engendered in every field has flowed into a re-thinking of knowledge, knowledge management, teaching and learning, networks and the individual. The knowledge society requires new roles and skills, new forms of communication and a new awareness as "active citizens". Consequently, the shifting role of education systems in networked organizations is decisive in order to support learners in forming diverse personal learning networks to deeply understand complex fields.

This process is catalyzed by two dimensions: the learner's awareness of the importance of a personal approach to knowledge, beyond fixed educational paths; secondly, the learner's interaction with a learning community capable of stimulating, negotiating and validating personal modes of knowledge management in a knowledge-sharing environment. In this perspective, education in general and eLearning in particular have become strategic. But which eLearning? Today designing online adult education means being able to build modules or courses which favour generative learning, a personalised and shared construction of knowledge: the learner needs to interact, together with his/her peers, with a system in which he/she can act as a co-protagonist in the construction of his/her knowledge. New teaching strategies have to be adopted to achieve this aim. Accordingly, it is necessary to move from a trans-missive approach to a constructivist one, from a linear learning system to a networked one, from an individual vision to a cooperative one, from a fixed programme to a project to be organized.

All this is possible if to the two levels of planning, teaching planning of modular learning objects and technological planning of the communication environment, a third level is added, that is informal eLearning. The adoption of online learning tools and methods should be preceded by the distinction between formal teaching spaces and the spaces agreed in the learning communities. Formal teaching spaces are defined within LMSs. Spaces agreed in the learning communities, instead, are to be used by social software (dynamic platforms, blogs, wikis, e-mails). They are aimed to build networks of virtual identities and to define personal learning environments of dynamic contents, based on continuous accesses, validations, dialogic exchanges. As a consequence, the process by which technologies, used by communication experts, impose learning within prescribed interactions is inverted; social software allows the learner to the fundamental use of technologies as means to represent, connect and express his/her knowledge.

In my experience as a teacher, a student and an individual, lifelong learning paradigm and social constructivism respond effectively and coherently to the need for greater emphasis to be put upon flexibility, transferability, individualisation, modularisation and mobility in education. However, are teaching and learning developing to make these changes possible? Can we really speak of "new" learning environments? Are learning tools and support adequate (availability of technology-based tools, open and distance learning methods access, teachers/trainers trained)? How does the teacher's role change when technology is used? How does the learner's way of working change? Which learning strategies are useful in technology-enhanced environments? What are the changes and the expectations when conventional class activities are, partially or completely, shifted into a technology-rich learning environment? How should the learner's efforts in personalised learning be supported? To what extent can we speak of "personalised learning environments" coherently? Can PLE be considered as a brick in the construction of a lifelong learning society?

This chapter aims to discuss consistency (i.e. solidity and reliability) and effectiveness (i.e. success, usefulness and value) of a personal learning environment as a new learning space and to highlight its contribution and relevance to lifelong learning.

The first section will analyse the theoretical framework of the new learning paradigm for a lifelong learning approach, the synergy of new technologies and person-centred teaching and learning and, finally, the progression from Virtual Learning Environments (VLE) to Personal Learning Environments (PLE). The current definitions of personal learning environment within research literature will allow for the exploration of models, approaches and theories implied, to define the evolution of personalised learning. In particular, the differences and peculiarities of the two learning paradigms of VLE and PLE will be highlighted, also in order to point out the progression from Web 1.0 – "the original web"-, Web 2.0 – the web of blog, forum and wiki – and Web 3.0 – a future web, Tim Berners-Lee's "Semantic" Web – and their continuities.

In the second section, PLE critical points and approaches will be discussed exploiting three case studies:

1. a recent experience of introduction to the construction of personalised learning environments that I have carried out at the University of Wollongong, Australia, with my students of third year of Italian Language and Culture. I have designed and implemented a blended learning system which has allowed me to have the students introduced gradually to a technology-enhanced learning environment and to acquire the necessary skills to become creative and effective designers of their own learning space;

2. a personal experience of formal learning in a blended environment that I carried out in 2002 at the University of Florence, Italy, within a postgraduate course for eLearning designers. Beyond the extremely useful and positive practice of online cooperative learning, it gave to me the opportunity to realize the creation of a personal learning environment within a formal setting;

3. the third case study is my personalised learning space. I do believe in lifelong learning as the fundamental tool to contribute and participate in the global society, and being a student helps me to improve myself as a teacher/facilitator. After an acceptable period of "dependence" (Hochswender, Martin & Morino, 2006), my personal and learning goals have been "independence" and "collaboration" at the same time. I'm still working to achieve pure "interdependence".

THEORETICAL FRAMEWORK

A New Learning Paradigm for a Lifelong Learning Approach

"Lifelong learning is a cultural term denoting a new paradigm. It is a shift away from the notion of provider-driven 'education' toward individualised learning." (UNESCO, 1999). Furthermore, it includes "all learning activity undertaken throughout life, with the aim of improving knowledge, skills and competencies within a personal, civic, social and/or employment-related perspective." (*European Report on Quality Indicators of Lifelong Learning,* 2002). The Italian National Strategic Plan 2007-2013 (*Quadro Strategico Nazionale 2007-2013,* 2006) defines lifelong learning as a system that aims to contribute to the employability of active population and the qualification of human resources promoting the process of modernization and innovation of education, training and work systems. As a result, learning to learn is the key competence for lifelong learning, the basic one to be developed within a suitable learning environment for all citizens, including persons with fewer chances (those with special needs and school dropouts), throughout the whole lifetime (from pre-school to adult learners) and through formal, non-formal and informal learning environments (Fredriksson and Hoskins, 2007). Learning to learn consists in acquiring the necessary skills to organise one's own knowledge and learning, finding, choosing and using various sources and modalities of information and education. A learner can search among those formal, non-formal and informal environments which offer adequate flexibility and response to the his/her time available, personal strategies and methods of study and work.

Starting from 1996, in Europe lifelong learning policies have brought awareness and promotion of "lifelong learning for all", thus supporting attentiveness to an active citizenship (Demetrio, 2002) in the knowledge society (in terms of information, participation and training). These guiding principles have induced new interpretations of teaching and learning, new approaches which consider the variety of needs, education systems, issues related to the social organization and to the level of technological development of a country. Ever since, lifelong learning has been very much debated and has become the central concern in most European education and training policies and conference agendas.

In this regard, over recent years research literature has urged a new theoretical framework of teaching and learning methods in tertiary education (Alberici, 2007; Avallone, 2006; Catarsi, 2007; Colapietro, 2007; Cusmai, 2007; Grimaldi & Quaglino, 2004; Marconato, 2003) to sustain the new educational models that are being introduced. The traditional instruction paradigm, in which the time of learning is held constant and learning varies, is being progressively replaced by the learning paradigm (Barr & Tagg, 1995; Jonassen & Land, 2000; von Glasersfeld, 1998), which allows to give emphasis to the learner's needs and to the learning process, rather than to the teacher as a repository of knowledge and to teaching itself. Accordingly, the trainer is increasingly becoming a facilitator and an interpreter of strategic aims; his/her professionalism is widening from knowledge transfer towards an overall view of organizational development and human resources (Avallone, 2006; Frigo, 1993; Grimaldi

& Quaglino, 2004). The teacher's new mission is to produce learning, to create powerful learning environments and to elicit students' discovery and construction of knowledge (Grimaldi & Quaglino, 2004; Loiodice, 2007). Success is measured by students' learning and achievement outcomes, learning growth and the quality of arousing students' interest and engagement (Leone, 2008a). A large number of researches (Alberici, Catarsi, Colapietro & Loiodice, 2007; Varisco, 2002) have foregrounded the necessity to regard the learning paradigm as the suitable framework to support an effective implementation of lifelong learning policies. The result of this synergy can be summed up in the following key elements of a lifelong learning approach:

- flexible delivery, with a modular approach (multiple options for scheduling, location and modes of learning);
- increasing self-directed learning, to suit individual learning goals and needs;
- constructivist learning methods, including experiential learning and problem based learning;
- the teacher acting as an expert and a facilitator, providing a well-designed learning environment to promote active and involving learning experiences;
- acknowledgement and assessment of prior (experiential) learning, which includes the various skills and competencies (non-formal and informal learning) that learners bring, in addition to the traditional formal qualifications earned upon completion of secondary school;
- provision of services needed by adults (career and academic advise prior to enrolment, assistance with financing education, childcare and transportation, revision of academic skills as needed prior to the course, and learning support while participating in higher education) (Leone, 2008b).

Although this outline is emerging in response to a new model in knowledge construction, it nonetheless engenders new issues related to the combination of blocks of knowledge, to the design of well-constructed education plans and training projects on the part of the individual (Frigo, 2000; Avallone, 2006). Undoubtedly, new learning environments are focused on the individual and on small communities (Avallone, 2006), enhanced by new data communication and the Internet. ICT is increasing interaction in learning and teaching processes and a new psychological approach is being developed (Annacontini, 2007) as a result - connessionism.

The Synergy of New Technologies and Person-Centred Teaching and Learning

The decisive effects of new technologies and the Internet on the world of communication and education are evident by now. The widespread embracing of ICTs in education has brought about multifaceted benefits: more flexible, personalized and self-paced learning environments; the capacity to reinforce students' engagement, to enhance critical analysis and to encourage the social construction of knowledge as well as the creation of virtual collaborative learning spaces; efficiency in managing contents, people and communication (Leone, 2008a).

If technology undoubtedly betters the learning experience and makes it more authentic, nevertheless, the point of departure has to be a revised teaching and learning approach. The benefits arising from a technology-enhanced learning environment have to be evaluated within the learning experience, the usefulness of learning and its enhancements. A simple access to contents does not make students learn. The shifting role of education systems in networked organizations is crucial in order to sustain learners in creating assorted personal learning networks to deeply understand complex fields. This process is conditioned by two major points: the learner's awareness of the importance of a personal approach to knowledge, beyond fixed educational contents; secondly, the learner's interaction with a learning community capable of stimulating, negotiating and validating personal modes of knowledge management in a knowledge-sharing environment. In this perspective, education in general and eLearning in particular have become strategic. But which eLearning? Pushed by the deep change that the so called "Web 2.0" is effecting on the numerous services present in the Net, users are assuming a more and more active role in the production of contents – for example through blogs and video (YouTube), image (Flickr) and slide (SlideShare) sharing. This evolution is overshadowing all the hard work that has been carried out over recent years on formal eLearning, namely platforms and Virtual Learning Environments. These organization-centred spaces are now being brought into question by the driving Personal Learning Environments, which are person-centred settings (Bonaiuti, 2007). Person-Centred Teaching and Learning theory has been elaborated by the famous American psychologist Carl Rogers as a totally new approach to education that is valid for learners of all age groups independent of their social background (Rogers, 1983). In Roger's view, human beings are constructive in nature and make every effort to realise and express their "experiencing organism". Individuals' constructive tendency can expand better in a setting that is characterized by the three requisites known as "Rogers's variables": realness (in terms of congruence, genuineness, authenticity), acceptance (in terms of respect, positive regard, caring manners) and empathic understanding. Although the American psychologist's approach could seem incompatible with traditional curricula, as a teacher I have found that person-centred teaching/learning, combined with the use of new ICT tools, is a really successful and motivating approach (Leone, 2008a), which Motschnig-Pitrik & Mallich (2004) refer to as PCeL (Person-Centred eLearning).

The framework of the learner-centred new alternative to traditional VLE consists of the following elements (Giovannella, 2008):

- connessionism and situationism as dominant pedagogic visions;
- the web is used as a platform or an environment, rather than a medium, where various services (like Flickr, De.licio.us, ePortfolio) and contents can be aggregated for the construction of a PLE, according to the needs of the moment; the space can work off-line as well, thanks to the application of suitable widgets;
- educational materials are socially produced (all the participants play an active role) and symmetric relations develop among the various parties involved in the education path;
- open source, open content and open society which, as a result, foresee the adoption of open "machine-readable" standards (not only specific for education) and the interconnection with proprietary ones;
- working life as a workflow; the learning process is included only at specific steps of the workflow and contextualised collaboration is preferred;
- the learner's capability of managing learning processes aiming to social interaction, as a means to learn to produce and communicate;
- ePortfolio as main tool to communicate one's own aggregation of knowledge and competences.

Indeed, over recent times the debate of researchers on eLearning has progressively moved towards the potential of informal learning (Bonaiuti, 2007). This approach is based on "informal" interactions, networked ones and in the Net, which aim to mutual learning (Trentin, 2004). Acquisition and development of new contents are mainly linked to learning how to exploit the knowledge which can be functional to one's own professional or personal life. The "2.0 age" demands that education becomes more person-centred and more attentive to the uniqueness of the person's learning experience. Consequently, systems of selective access to knowledge in the right moment need to be promoted and fixed. An extraordinary support to these processes is offered by the synergy of knowledge management/sharing technologies and those centred on the semantic connotation of information, like the "Semantic Web" (Berners-Lee, Handler & Lassila, 2001), with the technologies of group and interpersonal interaction between the members of a distributed professional community, like net technologies in general and groupware technologies in particular (Trentin, 2005). On the whole, eLearning 2.0 foregrounds the possible exploitation of social networking and of the tools for informal cooperation to improve and enrich formal eLearning as well.

The Progression from the "Original Web" to the "Semantic Web", from VLE To PLE

The progression from the network as information provider (Web 1.0) to the network as platform (Web 2.0), introduced by O'Reilly (2005), has brought about a new technological paradigm (Gaballo, 2007). The shift from Web 1.0, "the original web", to Web 2.0, the web of social networking tools, such as blogs, forums, wikis and podcasts, has created unique and powerful information sharing and collaboration features. We have witnessed the evolution from simple web sites that were largely read-only to read-write ones, from centralization of information to decentralization and spreading of knowledge. Contents and competences are no more delivered through a top-down education process, but they are created and used through a bottom-up procedure, through symmetric interaction and real-time information, through the millions of blogs which are present in the universe of bits of the World Wide Web.

Over these years the extremely rapid transformation in social relationships that are established in the web is definitely influencing the planning and the delivery of blended or pure online learning environments. Communication in the Net is undergoing the following major changes (Giovannella, 2008):

a) a generalised tendency towards a more limited use of e-mail, which is replaced by more and more popular instant communication tools like Messenger and Skype;
b) a highlight of blogs and personal sites that meet the participants' need to turn into the protagonists of the Net;
c) the driving growth of peer-to-peer systems, that are becoming real mutual assistance and knowledge-sharing communities;
d) the evolution of social sharing and publication tools for links (De.licio.us), images (Flickr) and videos (YouTube);
e) the diffusion of shots of news which are easily collected by suitable aggregators that allow for their circulation and social sharing;
f) the broad use of folksonomies as a valid alternative to traditional ontologies in the development of semantic or relational search engines.

Folksonomies themselves can become the key factor for the development of a future web, Web 3.0, Tim Berners-Lee's "Semantic" Web: it is not "a separate Web", it is "an extension of the current one" where information is attributed "well-defined meaning, better enabling computers and people to work in cooperation" (Berners-Lee & Handler & Lassila, 2001). In Berners-Lee's vision, the Web is a universal catalyst for data, information and knowledge exchange. Consequently, in his view the Semantic Web represents the Web's evolution into an environment where the documents published (html pages, files, images, etc.) are associated to information and data (metadata) able to define the semantic context of the documents

in a suitable format for search, interpretation, and automatic processing in general. In the near future, this will lead to refined searches thanks to the introduction of intelligent agents in the text, and to the construction of networks of relations and connections between documents, far beyond the current simple hypertextual links. In brief, while the Web 2.0 is people-oriented and users develop and exploit it to communicate, the Semantic Web is machine-oriented and users structure data to have the machines communicate among themselves (Ankolekar et al., 2007). The evolution of the Semantic Web will proceed if new actors will be involved and new applications will be designed for generic users. Moreover, processors for semantic data, services based on semantic technologies, revolutionary collaborative applications are necessary to start the real sharing of semantic notations.

A step further is the Social Semantic Web, the combination of technologies, strategies and methodologies from the Web 2.0 and the Semantic Web. While the Semantic Web will provide means for businesses to interoperate across domains, the Social Semantic Web will encompass the creation of explicit and semantically rich knowledge representations as a result of developments in social interactions, opening up for a more social interface to the semantics of businesses. As a whole, the Social Semantic Web can be considered as a Web of collective knowledge systems, a Web which aims to integrate the formal frame of the Semantic Web with a pragmatic approach based on description codes for semantic browsing using heuristic classification and semiotic ontologies. The core of a social semantic system is a continuous process of eliciting key knowledge of a field through semi-formal ontologies, taxonomies or folksonomies.

An evident parallel effect of the evolution of the Web through the three stages described above (and in Table 1) is increasing questioning about the standards which have been applied to uselessly delimit learning and teaching processes in

Table 1. From Web 1.0 to Semantic Web

Web 1.0	Web 2.0	Semantic Web
Personal websites	Blogs	Semantic blogs
Content management systems	Wikis	Semantic wikis
Altavista, Google	Google personalised, dumbfind	Semantic search
Citeseer, project Gutenberg	Google scholar, book search	Semantic digital libraries
Message boards	Community portals	Semantic forums and community portals
Buddy lists, address books	Online social networks	Semantic social networks
		Semantic social information spaces

the name of interoperability of contents (Learning Objects). Current discussion about the pedagogical vision of technology-enhanced learning is focusing on the validity and the adequateness of online learning environments of Web 1.0 age, namely Virtual Learning Environments (VLE). At the same time, researchers (Calvani, 2005; Downes, 2005; Trentin, 2004; Wilson, 2005; Attwell, 2006; Buonaiuti, 2007; Fini e Vanni, 2004; Ranieri 2005) are debating on the adoption of Personal Learning Environments (PLE) as the new generation of learning settings - Learning 2.0 (Downes, 2005) -, capable of interpreting present and upcoming trends and behaviours and based on the aggregation of Web 2.0 services (Wilson, 2005).

Giovannella (2008) proposes a third alternative between organization/product-centred VLE and, with a vision which swings from open market to open society, user-centred PLE: Learning Places (LP), settings that are opened to the interaction with the outside and attentive to the development of individuals' virtual identity.

The main criticism to traditional VLE regards:

- the focus on the creation on rigid schemes, blocks and platforms, which engenders the lack of sharing and common spaces;
- asymmetric relations, and the consequent limited production of contents according to the participants' roles (teachers/learners);

- the lack of adoption of open and simple standards, like for example RSS;
- a poor interaction with the community external to the learning environment, in terms of visibility of the outcomes of the learning process, lack of access to the contents – not even to the alumni. Dequalification of the learning community and scanty interrelation among different education contexts are the evident consequences.

In particular, in view of a lifelong learning approach, traditional VLE shows insufficient consideration of learning as a social practice strongly centred on dialogic exchange (including constructivist school's collaborative and cooperative model). As a result, knowledge tends to be frustrated within the restricted space of a specific learning process. Furthermore, this closeness of traditional VLE impedes the construction of the individual's virtual identity, which is, instead, a crucial aim in lifelong learning policies. The comparison between VLE and PLE points out how the latter is more adherent to the users' expectations of flexibility, active participation and individualisation of a learning environment (Calvani, Buonaiuti, Fini & Ranieri, 2007; Downes, 2005). A Personal Learning Environment is an open system, interconnected with other PLEs and with other external services; it is an activity-based learning environment, user-managed and learner-centred. In Downes's view (2006), a PLE is a tool that allows anyone to "engage in a distributed environment" made up of "a network of people, services and resources". It does not consist of "just Web 2.0, but it is certainly Web 2.0" since "it is a read-write application" (in the broadest sense possible). A PLE is a concept rather than specific software, a group of techniques and a variety of tools to gather information, explore and develop relationships between pieces of information. A PLE helps to view the subject as a landscape as well as individual pieces of information; to create a personal repository of materials and relationships clustered around a unifying topic or concept; to document, reflect, communicate, collaborate. Information and knowledge reside in electronic sources (locally produced files and notes, Internet/Intranet, eLearning courses, reference sites, text/audio/video/graphics files, shared presentations, RSS feeds) and in non-electronic sources (books and journals, classroom based courses, professional meetings, live interaction with colleagues). A PLE, at the same time, develops and is fed by autonomy, pragmatic, relevance, building on prior knowledge, goal-directed approach. A PLE facilitates the access to and the aggregation, the configuration and the management of the individual's learning experiences (Lubesky, 2006). In this sense, a VLE is much less flexible than a PLE; however, the two settings can be interconnected through sharing-knowledge technologies, like RSS.

Anderson (2006) concurs that VLEs may survive if they will adopt the learner-centred model. Attwell (2007) sets out from the assumption that ePortfolio, a basic tool of PLE, is the future of learning systems to state that PLE is the new learning setting to look at. Buonaiuti (2007) outlines hypothetical scenarios for the school of the future in which learning has the informal features of PLE.

Finally, the passage from the current to the emerging eLearning paradigm has been promoted by users, later followed by institutions. In Italy, two universities are experimenting a PLE for their students: the University of Siena with the "3_is PLE 0.2" and the University of Florence with "LTEver", that will be presented and analysed as case study in the second section of this chapter.

CASE STUDIES OF PERSONAL LEARNING ENVIRONMENTS

This second section aims to examine three case studies illustrating different contexts of adoption of the learner-centred approach and of creation of a personal learning environment. The following discussion aims to evaluate solidity, usefulness and value of a personal learning environment as a new learning space and to highlight its contribution and relevance to lifelong learning. All the three examples come from my background as a teacher, a student and an individual.

Case Study 1: An Experience of PLE for the Students of Italian Language and Culture at the University of Wollongong, Australia

This case study reports a recent experience of blended learning and of introduction to the construction of personalised learning environments that I have carried out at the University of Wollongong with my students of second and third year – 26 and 7 students respectively - of Italian Language and Culture. The students were between 20 and 25 years old; 30 girls and 3 boys. The experience has aimed at enhancing students' language skills through a more aware and active learning process .

While I was preparing this environment, I wondered continuously if I was really going to provide the students with the crucial skills and tools to support their increasing awareness as active learners: they should have been able to identify their needs and preferences in learning, to acquire a "personal learner's know-how", like basic tools of interaction and research, online and offline (Siemens, 2008). Brain storming and problem solving have been used to analyse the students' learning method, their learning goals in the view of their personal goals, how they choose their learning contents, how they interact with a network (learning by doing). Metacognitive tasks have been central in the development of the work.

All the students were already familiar with the Internet, a few were already aware of the use of technologies in a different manner and context (podcasts, forums and communities), but, still, some didn't feel self-confident and preferred not to use technology before this course. Only two of the seven students in third year had worked previously (none in second year) in a technology-enhanced learning environment (WebCT), which they had lived as positive, even though they lamented a lack of communication because many participants hadn't made use of the forum. Most of the students were unfamiliar with cooperative learning and with social interaction, and they were at their very first experience of online community. This has required a thorough and sensitive construction of an emotionally favourable learning environment to reduce their affective barriers and support learning, through scaffolding, mediation, focus on achievements, positive reinforcement, peer assessment and self assessment.

I have designed and implemented a blended learning system (Motschnig-Pitrik & Mallich, 2004; Cusmai, 2007) because it would have allowed me to have the students introduced gradually to a technology-enhanced learning environment and to acquire the necessary skills to become later creative and effective designers of their own learning space. Major issues during our classes have been: approach to knowledge and to knowledge management (Gaballo, 2007), collaboration and cooperation, time management concerns in learning. The blended learning pedagogical model was implemented on two compulsory face-to-face weekly two-hour classes in second year, and on a compulsory face-to-face weekly three-hour lecture in third year, on additional optional e-tutoring for an average of two hours per week and on an average of four hours per week of self-learning, online and offline, employing the personalised learning environment that they would have built step by step along the formal eLearning course. The blended learning pedagogical model has combined:

1. learners' independent work with CALL (Computer-Assisted Language Learning) tasks and materials for developing language skills in an online web-based interactive multimedia environment;
2. online and face-to-face tutoring by the Italian teacher-tutor;
3. face-to-face classes with the Italian teacher-tutor, as an opportunity to check learning outcomes, to provide feedback and to emotionally support learners helping them build their personal confidence and fix learning objectives.

The web-based interactive multimedia gathered all the CALL materials, task-based activities, and ICT tools learners were provided with at the beginning of the semester (Autumn 2008). Each module included language learning activities and tasks which provided the students with opportunities to learn by doing, to develop autonomy, to work at their pace exploiting multimedia contents and online synchronous (chat) and asynchronous communication (one-to-one emails, mailing lists, forums) (Absalom & Marden Pais, 2004). Learners were exposed to foreign language input through audiovisual material depicting real characters which allowed for multimodal content delivery to reach heterogeneous learning styles. Students interacted with Italian communities in communicative tasks which engaged them in socio-cognitive processes and gave them opportunities to be in touch with a real audience (Barr & Tagg, 1995; Ellis, 1999; Jonassen & Land, 2000; Varisco, 2002; von Glasersfeld, 1998). Special attention was given to issues of online pedagogy (Calvani & Rotta, 2000), such as providing a more human-like dimension for positive and corrective feedback, giving students the sense of belonging to a learning community, and helping them develop their self-confidence as they worked on their language skills through individual practice, communication - both through CMC and face-to-face- and collaboration.

Only half of the 26 second year students affectively participated in the activities. As a matter of fact, most of the learners showed strong barriers to the use of new technologies, but while half of them were curious and motivated by the challenge, the rest manifested resistance and frustration which ended in a global loss of enthusiasm. The third year students' initial frustrating impact with an intense use of new technologies was overcome and in the following steps they appeared to be involved and motivated. At the end of the course, a survey was submitted to the students to have their feedback about the impact of the use of new technologies in Italian classes (overall impact on the participants, difficulties and advantages, outcomes in terms of creation of networks and cooperative learning). Second year students' global view was affected by the strong initial barriers to new technologies and an insufficient closeness in and between work groups. Third year students' overall perception appeared to be extremely positive, despite initial difficulties (a software incompatibility and poor Internet connection on campus).

On the whole, learners defined as "challenging" learning how to use new technologies, but definitely worth it for the "very useful know-how" they acquired: "a broader perspective on topics, an easier way to communicate and collaborate ideas and points of view". In their opinion, "it was just a matter of getting used to a different way of learning". "It was an interactive experience, and enabled us to learn in varied ways which kept our interest. It introduced us to new things and widened our ideas of what is available and useful in a classroom. We were provided with an op-portunity to interact with not only our classmates, but with other people around the globe. It was also accessible at home and you could submit it with the click of a finger. The technologies were a great idea!"

Case Study 2: The Creation of a Personal Learning Environment within a Formal Learning Experience at the University of Florence, Italy

ELearning offers a wide range of scenarios simultaneously characterised by different approaches. In this sense, formal and informal eLearning can interoperate. The border line between the two systems is not always well defined and it gives space to a continuity which allows the individual to identify the most suitable mix of learning tools and contexts. Formal eLearning is one of the possible means that the members of a professional community have to acquire new knowledge, and knowledge management/sharing methods and technologies (informal learning) can be added progressively to complete institution-driven learning spaces with the opportunity for the individual to personalise learning solutions (Trentin, 2005).

The learning experience described below represents an example of possible coexistence of formal and informal learning. It involved me as a student within a post-graduate course on eLearning (specialization in planning of online education), delivered in a blended environment, that I attended in 2002 at the University of Florence.

The course aimed to provide the participants with the fundamental planning, organizational and relational skills to effectively exploit the Internet in an educational project, in terms of access to and employ of remote educational resources, in terms of new communication, cooperation and management opportunities, both for the education system and for companies interested in eLearning. Particular attention was reserved to the evaluation of all the necessary key factors during the design of an online educational path: needs, costs, technological platform, tutors, assessment, quality standards. The course lasted five months over an average of 150 hours of work and it encompassed three face-to-face classes. The participants admitted were 250; most of them were secondary school experienced teachers, some were VET trainers and some were human resources managers in private companies. The course was later subdivided into ten sub-areas of specialization and within each area work groups of eight to ten people were formed to carry out cooperative activities (last phase). The organization in small groups was the fundamental premise to promote collaborative activities in which the learners could experience debate and negotiation in the construction of the project work, for which cohesion and interdependence are necessary. (Calvani, 2005).

The tutor-supervisor coordinated and scheduled activities, answered to technical and organizational doubts, emotionally supported the tutors of sub-groups in their challenging role. The tutors of the sub-groups supplied technical, pedagogical, methodological, organizational and social support to the learners. Books, educational materials and guide-lines were delivered to the participants at the very beginning. The course was articulated on four steps: individual technological warm-up, personal documentation (an introduction to contents and general issues related to the themes), sharing and socialization activities, cooperative project work. Online activity was developed in three stages: documentation (individual), sharing (tutor-groups) and collaboration/cooperation (collaborative/cooperative groups).

The environment drew its theoretical framework from the constructivist model of dispersed learning, according to which knowledge has to be situated in a context and in a social space, collaboratively constructed through sharing. Consequently, this learning experience showed adherence to the engaged learning approach, namely those situations in which at least three key elements summed up in the formula "relate-create-donate" are present (Calvani & Rotta, 2000). The basic assumption of this model is that learning is enhanced in collaborative groups, through project works and if the result is authentic and "spend-able". The general theoretical background of the course can be expressed by the following key factors. In relation to the adoption of technologies in teaching and learning, ICTs are used as a tool to support the development of a learning community, rather than as a means to deliver contents. Basic technological facilities and tools were proposed to make the interaction between participants simpler. From the methodological point of view, the global approach was centred on the collaborative group and on the consequent highlight of relational dynamics. The course was metacognitive and oriented to favour the learners' reflection on the methodologies used and on the crucial factors in online activities, rather than being centred on the output and on specific contents. Great importance was attributed to the project work (project oriented approach). Contents were targeted on adult learners with prior expertise and available to collaborate and share their knowledge, namely teachers and professionals. Emphasis was on textuality (sending, presentation of written messages/texts, discussion, text production), with a consequent increase of the participants' involvement. The guide-lines provided at the beginning were modular and included possible integrations by the participants (co-authoring). The organizers chose not to adopt groupware platforms nor proprietary environments. The technologies employed were gradually introduced: web pages in the documentation phase, emails for support and communication with the tutor, web forum and mailing-list in the phases of sharing and collaboration.

Area forum and mailing-list were used for the collection of materials and tasks assigned by the tutor supervisor, for discussions about general questions and for interaction between sub-groups. Later, each sub-group adopted a platform for autonomous communication (for example a Ya-hooGroups mailing-list) and other tools (Nicenet) for collaborative work.

Considering that the course was addressed to teachers and professionals, the experience was hands-on to provide the participants with a repeatable experience in their work place (meta-course). In this sense, strengths were: the use of a basic technological framework (absence of installation procedures, free access, transparency of the server); the punctual focus on reflection on operative methodologies and on the recurrent organizational and management issues related to the work carried out.

At the end of the course, the participants were individually interviewed about the contents developed and the outcomes of their personal experience online. Some of the participants pointed out their uneasiness with the learning team-centred model adopted within the course. In their opinion, a deeper explanation of the numerous issues related to designing an online learning environment would have let the learners better exploit the following hands-on phases. Moreover, the large number of persons enrolled in the course, their different background and levels of knowledge were the main reasons for unsatisfactory interaction. Finally, time constraints were an issue along the whole course.

My sub-group's and my personal point of view were nearly opposite to our colleagues'. We, too, felt pressed by time constraints and deadlines, nevertheless we appreciated the usefulness of metacognitiveness and the challenge of being for most of the time involved in hands-on activities. We realized how productive and gratifying working collaboratively and cooperatively can be. Furthermore, we rated social and professional communication strongly motivating and enriching. In the end, I didn't expect such a positive and flexible experience from a formal environment and, beyond this, I had underestimated the opportunity of exploiting between-the-lines communication to develop a personal learning space. I was glad to find out, a few years later, that the University of Florence had started out an informal continuation of its formal learning

environments: LTEver, which is illustrated in the following case study.

Case Study 3: My Personalised Learning Space from "Dependence" to "Interdependence"

On one occasion, a Buddhist monk explained that there are three stages in the development of human beings: dependence, independence and collaboration. Unfortunately the majority of people is completely unaware of the third stage, collaboration (or interdependence), and they consider only two options, dependence or independence. (Hochswender, Martin & Morino, 2006, p.130)

This third case study aims to report an example of personal learning environment started out by an Italian University, as a bridge from the formal to the informal learning environments active within its organization. As an alumna, I was invited to join the space.

In January 2007 the *Laboratorio di Tecnologie dell'Educazione* (Laboratory of Technologies for Education) (LTE) of the University of Florence set out a virtual community for staff, teachers, students, alumni and contributors: LTEver (http://lte-unifi.it/elgg), with the suffix "ever" (for ever) to indicate continuity.

As a rule, at the end of courses, virtual classrooms, forums and other environments lose their interest and end, too. Alumni's and teachers' recurrent intention to keep in touch and build a community is seldom put into practice. Inadequate technological support tools chiefly account for this: traditional platforms (LMSs) are limited in flexibility, personalization and control elements. As a result, recently researchers (Attwell, 2007; Calvani *et al.*, 2007; Downes, 2006; Wilson, 2005) have been promoting the diffusion of Personal Learning Environment (PLE) as a suitable learner-centred setting to support both formal and informal learning.

LTEver is based on Elgg (http://elgg.org), an open source system that its authors (Tosh &

Werdmüller, 2004) have defined as "learning landscape", explicitly a system that, starting with basic elements such as blogs, ePortfolio and social networking, is able to encourage reflection and socialization in learning communities. LTEver was designed to provide members with a totally self-managed personal space fit to support activities like blogs, file sharing, creation of communities and social networking through tags automatically obtained from the users' contents and profiles. Besides, this system is a connection to the courses that members have attended and attend within Moodle, where students can find, in their virtual classrooms, links to the recent activities in LTEver. The compatibility between Elgg and Moodle allowed the implementation of an ePortfolio for current students. This outcome is an example of interoperability between "personal" and "institutional" systems, in view of the new eLearning 2.0 paradigm (Calvani *et al.*, 2007). Freedom of action and symmetric relations characterize Elgg and are vital for the development of LTEver. Once users are logged in, they can freely configure their personal space by completing or updating their profile, adding RSS feeds from other sites, building communities, sharing files and inviting new users to join the community. Furthermore, attention to privacy and confidentiality is ensured through a simple control of the allowed level of access, which can be determined by the user. (Fini, 2008)

A certain number of studies are being carried out on LTEver, and some weaknesses and strengths have already been stressed. The system shows some information overload, mainly due to the originally muddled aggregation of the informal blogs; secondly, some problems of usability of the system arose (Rigutti *et al.*, 2008); finally, active participation seems to be restricted to a relatively small number of users, a threat in the case of a small and highly focused professional context (Calvani *et al.*, 2007), although the majority of social media have evidenced this trend. On the other hand, positive elements are: high quality of

contributions, so effectively filtered information, assessed on the basis of the significantly lower "level of noise" (i.e., the quantity of not pertinent posts) in comparison to the generality of the blogosphere; steady trend of growth of users and posts; the take-up of some spontaneous initiatives (for example the participation in the online course "Introduction to Open Education"), principally within consolidated communities (Fini, 2008). This finding highlights 2.0 communities' potential as future active promoters of more structured activities.

DISCUSSION

Nowadays, central objective of all education systems should be orienting learners towards a lifelong learning vision of their knowledge and of the world. Educational institutions' current challenge consists in a rethinking of their interactions with learners. Rapid information growth, enhanced learner control of knowledge creation and diffusion, and the increasing reference to network models to interpret and support complex social changes are trends that impact more and more society (Siemens, 2008).

In my opinion, reframing the transmission and the management of knowledge means reflecting on far beyond its access, rather on its construction and reproduction, on social active participation, on new roles and relations. In my experience as a teacher, a student and an individual, illustrated in the case studies above, lifelong learning paradigm and social constructivism respond effectively and coherently to the need for greater emphasis to be put upon flexibility, transferability, individualisation, modularisation and mobility in education. However, are teaching and learning developing to make these changes possible? Can we really speak of "new" learning environments? Are learning tools and support adequate (availability of technology-based tools, open and distance learning methods access, teachers/trainers trained)? How does the teacher's role change when technology is used? How does the learner's way of working change? Which learning strategies are useful in technology-enhanced environments? What are the changes and the expectations when conventional class activities are, partially or completely, shifted into a technology-rich learning environment? How should the learner's efforts in personalised learning be supported?

Undoubtedly, the adoption of a lifelong learning paradigm has to be embedded in a highly technology-enhanced educational setting to respond adequately to the pressure of these times. I can only partially agree with the many voices sustaining that technology is the only solution to a still partially rigid and remote education system. Actually, I concur that the systematic use of new technologies should be accompanied by preliminary research, testing, training and top-down support. The embracing of the latest technology cannot alone carry any durable, regular and efficient improvement to teaching and learning to turn current learning environments into "new" ones. Noticeably the use of emerging technologies needs to be supported by a marked pedagogical change in which teachers' skills and role need to be redefined. Teachers need to develop pedagogical background and technological skills that represent a sizeable change to the more traditional teaching and learning system and that allow the instructional designer to keep up with the critical role of educator to educators.

Moreover, the construction of technology-oriented learning environments (ICT, eLearning) must be modulated on the basis of concrete cognitive and cultural pre-requisites and objectives, strictly related to the participants and to the context. The shifting role of education systems in networked organizations is a crucial change to facilitate learners to develop and participate in diverse personal learning networks.

In my view, this process is catalyzed by two dimensions: the learner's awareness of the importance of a personal approach to knowledge ("learn to learn"); secondly, the learner's interaction with a learning community capable of stimulating, negotiating and validating personal modes of knowledge management in a knowledge-sharing environment. The space between these two dimensions has to ensure participation in a shared context, but also the opportunity to react creatively and autonomously to it. An integrated vision of a learning environment has to modulate the varied modalities of transmission of knowledge: from traditional to intentional trans-generational transmission to a self-directed and metareflective one. At this point, the univocity of the roles adult-teacher and teenager-learner has turned off.

The three case studies that I have proposed in the second section aimed to highlight how important the modulation of learning strategies and tools, according to the learner's needs, expectations and background, is to successfully feed a personal learning environment intended in the broadest sense. Besides, I am convinced that the synergy of formal and informal learning environments, VLEs and PLEs, offers a complete and powerful learning landscape. While the second case study reported my experience as a student within a VLE (a post-graduate course on eLearning) at the University of Florence, the third case study illustrated how the two spaces can effectively interoperate if they are supported by a suitable technological system (LTEver). As a member of LTEver, I regret of not having enough time to be more active. As an alumna, I have found this informal environment very interesting and useful, even though I sustain that complex fields need more than PLEs to be understood and acquired; they need in-depth and continuous engagement in "learning places" (Giovannella, 2008). In relation to this, I have wondered to what extent we can speak of personalised learning environments coherently and if a PLE is a solid, consistent and effective learning environment. Certainly, third generation eLearning models aim to produce knowledge and to optimize its fruition, at the same time. They mean to ensure the development of personal skills of contents analysis and aggregation to be applied within shared learning programmes. Nevertheless, designing PLEs based on services and contents aggregators could lead to the development of weak aggregations in which the risk would be a reduction of the solidity of the educational and pedagogical experience as a result of the reduction of cultural stratification. Apart from this, in technology-oriented settings the possibility to express individual epistemic models and make them accessible, represents a chance of great expressive value and an opportunity of relational exchange.

The adoption of online learning tools and methods should be preceded by the distinction between formal teaching spaces and the spaces agreed in the learning communities. Formal teaching spaces are defined within LMSs. Spaces agreed in the learning communities, instead, are to be used by social software (dynamic platforms, blogs, wikis, e-mails). They are aimed to build networks of virtual identities and to define personal learning environments of dynamic contents, based on continuous accesses, validations, dialogic exchanges. However, I insist on the usefulness of the identification of modes of continuity and coordination between formal and informal spaces. In this way, the process by which technologies, used by communication experts, impose learning within prescribed interactions is inverted; social software allows the learner to the fundamental use of technologies as means to represent, connect and express his/her knowledge (Vitali, 2007), previously deepened within formal learning environments.

Finally, can PLE be considered as a brick in the construction of a lifelong learning society? It certainly can, as a brick. A brick is not a whole construction, but a bricklayer can't do without it to make a building. Starting from Stephen Downes's (2006) definition, my personal learning environment is a concept, a variety of techniques and tools which allow me to engage in a distributed environment, made up of a network of people,

services and electronic and non-electronic resources, to gather information, explore and develop relationships between pieces of information; to document, reflect, interact, collaborate, cooperate. My personal learning environment, at the same time, develops and is fed by autonomy, pragmatic, active participation, building on prior knowledge, goal-directed approach. It draws from formal, non-formal and informal learning environments. I do believe in lifelong learning as the fundamental tool to contribute and participate in the global society, and being a student helps me to improve myself as a teacher/facilitator. After an acceptable period of "dependence" (Hochswender, Martin & Morino, 2006), my personal and learning goals have been "independence" and "collaboration" at the same time. I'm still working to achieve pure "interdependence".

FUTURE DIRECTIONS

The evolution of technology has accelerated the production and the diffusion of information, and it has engendered a continuous knowledge turnover. Our knowledge becomes inadequate rapidly, our life styles change, our professional profiles change; however our working life gets longer and longer and we have a growing need of acquiring new knowledge, competences and skills.

The new educational challenge is integrating formal eLearning with the informal tools provided by Web 2.0 and by social software. Net surfers can choose among a very large number of tools to aggregate, manage, organise and share their knowledge. Anyhow, the results of researches and reflections have to be systematized again to keep the flexibility that Web 2.0 offers and the coordination and the validation that an institution can grant. Education cannot be confined within imposed learning spaces; it has to evolve towards various forms of social software and integrate formal and informal. The challenge is a reconsideration of teaching methodologies as a result of new learning needs and Web 2.0 communicative and technological innovation.

CONCLUSION

The introduction of lifelong learning objectives and policies has poised us on the threshold of major change in education and society. By now, learning to learn and learning have become the first motivation towards development, empowerment, continuity and generation of value, with the help of Web 2.0 tools. The revolution that technology has engendered in every field has flowed into a rethinking of knowledge, knowledge management, teaching and learning, networks and the individual. The knowledge society requires new roles and skills, new forms of communication and a new awareness as "active citizens". In this perspective, education in general and eLearning in particular have become strategic. But which eLearning? Formal eLearning, through Virtual Learning Environments, or informal eLearning 2.0, through Personal Learning Environments? Attention has moved from LMSs and e-content, to professional experience added to knowledge sharing and learning communities. From learning to learn to learning through others, the importance of informal learning is an evidence at the end of this study, informal eLearning in particular. PLE can certainly be considered as a brick in the construction of a lifelong learning society. A brick is not a whole construction, but a bricklayer can't do without it to make a building.

REFERENCES

Absalom, M., & Marden Pais, M. (2004). Email Communication and Language Learning at University - an Australian Case Study. *Computer Assisted Language Learning*, *17*(3-4), 403–440. doi:10.1080/0958822042000319647

Alberici, A. (2007). Una nuova popolazione universitaria. In A. Alberici (Ed.), *Adulti e Università. Sfide ed innovazioni nella formazione universitaria e continua*. Milano, Italy: Franco Angeli.

Alberici, A., Catarsi, C., Colapietro, V., & Loiodice, I. (2007). *Adulti e Università. Sfide ed innovazioni nella formazione universitaria e continua*. Milano, Italy: Franco Angeli.

Anderson, P. (2006). What is Web 2.0? Ideas, technologies and implications for education. *JISC*. Retrieved May 12, 2007, from http://www.ukoln.ac.uk/terminolgy/JISC-review2006.html

Ankolekar, A., Krötzsch, M., Tran, T., & Vr, D. (2007). *The Two Cultures - Mashing up Web 2.0 and the Semantic Web*. Retrieved May 18, 2008 from http://www.aifb.uni-karlsruhe.de/WBS/aan/resources/papers/www-07-tc.pdf

Annacontini, G. (2007). Adulti in rete: tecnologie didattiche e formazione universitaria. In A. Alberici (Ed.), *Adulti e Università. Sfide ed innovazioni nella formazione universitaria e continua*. Milano, Italy: Franco Angeli

Attwell, G. (2006). Personal Learning Environments. *The Wales Wide Web*. Retrieved June 30, 2008, from http://www.knownet.com/writing/weblogs/Graham_Attwell/entries/6521819364

Avallone, F. (Ed.). (2006). *Tutor. Manuale teorico-pratico per migliorare l'efficacia dei sistemi formativi*. Milano, Italy: Guerini.

Barr, R., & Tagg, J. (1995). From Teaching to Learning: A New Paradigm for Undergraduate Education. *Change Magazine, 2*(12), 8-12. Retrieved January 11, 2008, from www.cic.uiuc.edu/resources/deo/paradigm.html

Berners-Lee, T., Handler, J., & Lassila, O. (2001). The Semantic Web. *Scientific American*. Retrieved September 23, 2008 from http://www.ryerson.ca/~dgrimsha/courses/cps720_02/resources/Scientific%20American%20The%20Semantic%20Web.htm

Bonaiuti, G. (2007). I learning object nella prospettiva dell'eLearning 2.0. In *Atti del IV congresso Sie-l*. Macerata: EUM.

Calvani, A. (2005). Rete, comunità e conoscenza. *Costruire e gestire dinamiche collaborative.* Trento: Erickson.

Calvani, A., Buonaiuti, G., Fini, A. & Ranieri, M. (2007). I Personal Learning Environment: una chiave di volta per il Lifelong Learning? *Atti del IV congresso* Sie-l. Macerata: EUM.

Calvani, A., & Rotta, M. (2000). *Fare formazione in internet.* Trento: Erickson.

Catarsi, C. (2007). La formazione di terza generazione: necessaria rifinitura di un paradigma". In A. Alberici (Ed.), *Adulti e Università. Sfide ed innovazioni nella formazione universitaria e continua.* Milano, Italy: Franco Angeli.

Colapietro, V. (2007). Studenti adulti all'università: il peso dell'esperienza. In A. Alberici (Ed.), *Adulti e Università. Sfide ed innovazioni nella formazione universitaria e continua.* Milano, Italy: Franco Angeli.

Cusmai, M. (2007). L'allestimento di ambienti di apprendimento costruttivisti nella formazione blended. *Formazione e Cambiamento, 7*(48). Retrieved December 10, 2007, from http://db.formez.it/ArchivioNews.nsf/F&C

Demetrio, D. (2002). Cittadini in formazione. In Baratelli M. et al (Ed.), *F.A.Re. Formazione con gli adulti. Esperienze a confronto.* Milano: Franco Angeli.

Downes, S. (2005). ELearning 2.0. *eLearn Magazine*, October 17, 2005. Retrieved September 23, 2008 from http://elearnmag.org/subpage.cfm?section=articles&article=29-1

Downes, S. (2006). Learning Networks and Connective Knowledge. *eLearn Magazine*, October 16, 2006. Retrieved September 23, 2008 from http://it.coe.uga.edu/itforum/paper92/paper92.html

Ellis, R. (1999). *Learning a second language through interaction.* Amsterdam: John Benjamins Publishing Company.

European Commission. (2002). *European Report on Quality Indicators of Lifelong Learning.* Brussels: European Commission.

Fini, A. (2008). ELearning 2.0. A case study on a growing community. *Journal of eLearning and Knowledge Society, 4*(3), 167 - 175.

Fini, A., & Vanni, L. (2004), Learning Objects e metadati. *I quaderni di Form@re*, n. 2. Trento: Erickson.

Fredriksson, U., & Hoskins, B. (2007). The development of learning to learn in a European context. *Curriculum Journal, 18*(2), 127–134. doi:10.1080/09585170701445921

Frigo, F. (1993). La formazione per le Piccole Imprese: le condizioni per lo sviluppo. Ruolo degli organismi e fabbisogni dei formatori. *Osservatorio ISFOL, 5*, 15–23.

Frigo, F. (2000). *La formazione continua in Italia: l'esperienza della legge 236/93.* Milano, Italy: Franco Angeli.

Gaballo, V. (2007). Web 2.0 Educational eLearning and knowledge management in higher education. *Atti del IV congresso* Sie-l. Macerata, Italy: EUM.

Giovannella, C. (2008). Learning 2.0? *Atti del V congresso* Sie-l. Macerata, Italy: EUM.

Grimaldi, A., & Quaglino, G. P. (Eds.). (2004). *Tra orientamento e auto-orientamento tra formazione e autoformazione*. Roma: ISFOL

Hochswender, W., Martin, G., & Morino, T. (2006). *Il Budda nello specchio*. Milano: Esperia.

Jonassen, D. H., & Land, S. M. (2000). *Theoretical Foundations of Learning Environment*. Mahwah, NJ: Lawrence Erlbaum Associates.

Kirschenbaum, H., & Henderson, L. V. (2002). The Interpersonal Relationship in the Facilitation of Learning. In *The Carl Rogers Reader*. London: Constable.

Leone, S. (2008a). The use of new technologies in advanced Italian classes. In I. Olney, G. Lefoe, J. Mantei, & J. Herrington (Eds.), *Proceedings of the Second Emerging Technologies Conference 2008*, (pp. 120-129). Wollongong, Australia: University of Wollongong.

Leone, S. (2008b). Lifelong learning and tertiary education in Italy. *The International Journal of Interdisciplinary Social Sciences*, 3(2), 7–14.

Loiodice, I. (2007). Formazione e orientamento degli adulti: il ruolo dell'università. In A. Alberici (Ed.), *Adulti e Università. Sfide ed innovazioni nella formazione universitaria e continua*. Milano: Franco Angeli.

Lubesky, R. (2006). The present and future of Personal Learning Environments (PLE). *Optusnet*. Retrieved June 14, 2008 from http://members.optusnet.com.au/rlubensky/2006/12/present-and-future-ofpersonal-learning.html

Marconato, G. (2003). Oltre l'eLearning. *Sviluppo & Organizzazione*, 200(12), 7–11.

Motschnig-Pitrik, R., & Mallich, K. (2004). Effects of Person-Centered Attitudes on Professional and Social Competence in a Blended Learning Paradigm. *Educational Technology & Society*, 7(4), 176–192.

O'Reilly, T. (2005). *What Is Web 2.0. Design Patterns and Business Models for the Next Generation of Software*. Retrieved September 18, 2007 from http://www.oreillynet.com/pub/a/oreilly/tim/news/2005/09/30/what-is-web-20.html?page=1

Ranieri, M. (2005). *ELearning: modelli e strategie didattiche*. Trento, Italy: Erickson.

Rigutti, S., Paletti, G. & Morandini, A. (2008). Lifelong Learning eLearning 2.0: il contributo degli studi sull'usabilità. *Je-LKS - Journal of eLearning and Knowledge Society, 4*(1), 91-100.

Rogers, C. R. (1983). *Freedom to Learn for the 80's*. Columbus, OH: Charles E. Merrill Publishing.

Siemens, G. (2008). *Learning and Knowing in Networks: Changing roles for Educators and Designer*. Retrieved October 10, 2008 from http://it.coe.uga.edu/itforum/Paper105/Siemens.pdf

Tosh, D., & Werdmuller, B. (2004). *Creation of a learning landscape: weblogging and social networking in the context of ePortfolios*. Retrieved September 24, 2008 from http://elgg.net/bwerdmuller/files/61/179/Learning_landscape.pdf

Trentin, G. (2004). *Apprendimento in rete e condivisione delle conoscenze: ruolo, dinamiche e tecnologie delle comunità professionali online*. Milano, Italy: Franco Angeli.

Trentin, G. (2005). From "formal" to "informal" eLearning through knowledge management and sharing. *Journal of eLearning and Knowledge Society, 1*(2), 209-217.

UNESCO Institute for Education. (1999). *Glossary of Adult Learning in Europe*. Hamburg, Germany: UNESCO.

Varisco, B. M. (2002). *Costruttivismo socio-culturale. Genesi filosofiche, sviluppi psico-pedagogici, applicazioni didattiche*. Roma: Carocci.

Vitali, G. (2007). Relazione di gruppo e metacognizione in apprendimento nei modelli eLearning di terza generazione. *Atti del IV congresso* Sie-l. Macerata, Italy: EUM.

von Glasersfeld, E. (1998). *Il costruttivismo radicale. Una via per conoscere ed apprendere.* Roma: Società Stampa Sportiva.

Wilson, S. (2005). *Future VLE – The Visual Vision.* Retrieved September 18, 2008 from http://www.cetis.ac.uk/members/scott/blogview?entry=20050125170206

Chapter 4
Community@Brighton:
The Development of an Institutional Shared Learning Environment

Stan Stanier
University of Brighton, UK

ABSTRACT

This chapter details the implementation of a university-wide social networking platform "Community@ Brighton" – using the open source Elgg platform and describes the technical, institutional and educational issues arising from the two years of experience in running the platform. The strategic vision of providing a social network platform alongside an institutional VLE to provide an integrated Shared Learning Environment is also explored, including key case studies and discussion on the challenges such technologies place on existing models of online learning and teaching.

INTRODUCTION

In 2006 the University of Brighton launched Community@Brighton, an institutionally hosted social network using Elgg (http://elgg.org) as the underlying technical platform. Community@Brighton is currently believed to be the World's largest HE-based social network with some 36,000 registered users comprising students, staff and associates of the university.

Whilst part of the remit of this service was to provide an online social arena for students based on geographically disparate campuses to communicate and socialise, it's implementation was also part of a wider strategy of evolution towards a Shared Learning Environment (SLE) aimed at extending the learning, teaching and research opportunities of the institutional VLE and realising the potential of Web 2.0 technologies to support and enhance learning and research.

This chapter will outline the strategic and theoretical background to the development of an SLE, present the technical framework used for implementation, describe, by way of key case studies, the experiences of users so far and discuss the issues and challenges that have arisen over the first two years of service.

DOI: 10.4018/978-1-60566-884-0.ch004

BACKGROUND

Since the mid 1990's, eLearning within HE has been largely underpinned by the use of the Virtual Learning Environment (VLE). During this period, the VLE product market has seen the emergence of just a handful of key products, leaving little choice or variance in the services provided and the dominance of these key players in the market, combined with a lack of competition between products, has resulted in a virtually uniform set of features and, consequently, little variation in use across institutions. Virtually all VLEs provide facilities for structuring information according to existing curricula structures – providing areas dedicated for each school, course, module or other unit of study. Within these areas, tutors can be allocated control, students can be registered and tools are provided to support learning – including document upload, online testing, discussion fora and other communication mechanisms. In effect, most VLEs model themselves on "traditional" teaching environments, offering almost total control of the teaching output to recognised tutors, absolute privacy within units of study and protection of the institution's intellectual copyright. It could be argued that the success of VLEs has, in large part, been due to the fact that they represent a mirror of teaching practice in the real world and thus a comfortable metaphor for academics to adopt who otherwise might be reluctant to use technologies within their teaching. There is little doubt that VLEs have played a significant role in enhancing the learning experience within HE, even if only at the level of information delivery to learners. However, an understandable emphasis on ease of use has led to inflexibility, it could be argued that a lack of market competition has resulted in a lack of innovation and creative development of new facilities and, by continuing to model "traditional" practices, VLEs have erected artificial barriers that actually limit learning opportunities and artificially enforce learning models that would otherwise be easy to extend and adapt given the

technological developments that have taken place since their inception.

In short, VLEs erect barriers across a number of key perspectives of learning:

*   Institutional ring-fencing – the majority of VLEs require an institutional account for access – i.e., participation from external users is largely barred
*   Absolute tutor control – whilst VLEs do allow learners to be given various levels of control, the implementation model most commonly adopted is one where the tutor is god and frequently the only type of user who can post learning materials, provide access to tools and determine what is learned and the routes through that learning
*   Course-specific – students can only engage in the courses/modules they are registered on – participation across courses or subject areas is generally prohibited.
*   Limited learner participation – at a most general level, the only facility available within a standard VLE toolset that allows learner participation is the discussion board and even these rarely allow learners to do anything other than make comments and add file attachments. In short, the VLE model reinforces a didactic approach to learning & teaching.

Even amongst early adopters of VLEs, concerns over the model leading to passive rather than active learner engagement were being raised:

Using Virtual Learning Environments (VLEs) poses important educational issues for Universities. Without addressing the issues of effective learning, their use can compound the mistakes of the past and leave the learner with a passive, unengaging experience leading to surface learning. Educators need to recognise that learning is a social process and that providing an effective learning environment which facilitates the active acquisition of subject-specific and general expertise, and addresses the need to adopt a specific subject or professional culture, requires more than electronically delivered course notes and email discussion. (Styles, 2000).

In stark contrast, the world outside education has seen a massive leap in technological development since the turn of the millennium. The evolution of Web 2.0 and the emergence of massive social networks has, without doubt, changed the face of both technology and society itself. No longer are "ordinary" individuals dependent upon a few information suppliers for knowledge – they have become the information providers, the arbiters of access to information and the repurposers of information. Today our students can upload photos, videos and other documents, post their views, comment on the contribution of others and keep in immediate contact with friends on a myriad of free external services and yet be in a position where virtually none of these services is available to them within their formal studies. As O'Hear (2005) argues "It is this level of integration and participation that is driving the web 2.0 revolution - a phenomenon offering a very different approach to eLearning."

Social networks have become virtually ubiquitous and, combined with the equal ubiquity of networked devices and the power of personal computing to access, edit and combine media, have resulted in the emergence of a new concept – that of a Personal Learning Environment (PLE). For example, Attwell (2007) argues that PLEs "might be useful or indeed central to learning in the future". Put simply, a PLE is the sum of the facilities we all have at our disposal which allow us, as learners, to access, manage and share the knowledge, resources and people that contribute to our learning. These two worldviews have, up to now, been almost mutually exclusive and, at the very least, represent different ends of the learning spectrum. Indeed, Wilson (2005) has predicted that the VLE of the future will be far more PLE

in shape than the traditional VLE model. VLEs represent controlled learning, PLEs represent informal, to some extent chaotic learning. In a VLE, the institution and tutors have control, learners take rather than give. In a PLE, the learner has full control, taking from and giving to a variety of sources, their university or college being just one node in a network that can extend around the world. As Dron (2006) argues – control in all it's manifestations is a significant factor in the development of learning and Web 2.0 technologies offer new models for control that may sit alongside and augment more traditional VLE platforms:

the social technologies underpinning Web 2.0 are fundamentally different in their dynamics of control and, consequently, when designed and used with care, offer benefits that significantly exceed the promise of their forebears. Dron (2006)

Indeed, such has been the impact of these technologies, that new theories of learning have emerged to take into account the connected state of being that we experience today:

Connectivism is the integration of principles explored by chaos, network, and complexity and self-organization theories. Learning is a process that occurs within nebulous environments of shifting core elements – not entirely under the control of the individual. Learning (defined as actionable knowledge) can reside outside of ourselves (within an organization or a database), is focused on connecting specialized information sets, and the connections that enable us to learn more are more important than our current state of knowing. Siemens (2004).

Such new ways of learning are beginning to challenge existing methodologies – as Eijkman argues:

Web 2.0's privileging of non-foundational knowledge construction challenges conventional thinking about the nature of knowledge, learning, and academia's role as the supreme arbiter of "true" and "valid" knowledge. Conventional foundational ideas about learning work against the grain when applied to Web 2.0 and its architecture of participatory knowledge construction. Eijkman (2008).

So why should these diverse approaches be mutually exclusive? Why shouldn't they be combined to harness the value of both the VLE AND the PLE models? Might such a combination actually yield something more powerful than the sum of those parts?

It was with this in mind that the University of Brighton began work on Community@Brighton in 2006.

IMPLEMENTING A SHARED LEARNING ENVIRONMENT: OUR EXPERIENCES SO FAR

Initially, the project remit was simply to provide a blogging service to allow all staff and students a personal blog but, following extensive evaluation of products available at the time, it became clear that Elgg both satisfied the technical requirements for providing a blogging service and also offered the opportunity to provide an institutionally hosted PLE platform integrated with the university's VLE – allowing a combination of course-structured, tutor-led teaching, management and sharing of personal learning resources and the breaking of barriers across institutions and courses allowing far greater learner participation, collaboration and sharing of knowledge, materials and opinion and the possible development of a new kind of learning environment – a Shared Learning Environment (see Figure 1). At this point, it should be made clear that, in considering Elgg as an institutional PLE platform, we are not disregarding some of the core concepts of a PLE – i.e. that it is the sum of all the components available to an individual

to manage their learning – including facilities on personal computers and those available via external networks. However, we do view Elgg as providing facilities at an institutional level that better enable personal learning and provide a university-wide platform for all learners to store, manage and share personal learning materials and experiences.

Our vision was one of at least a 5-year implementation, recognising that the adoption of these new technologies and a comprehensive understanding of how they might work together with the VLE would take considerable time. Not only do these new technologies represent a challenge to approaches to online learning, they also represent challenges to the student/ tutor relationship, the perception of how social and academic activities might interrelate and how technologies need to adapt to best meet the needs of education.

Technical Requirements

As mentioned above, the original requirement of this project was simply to provide a blogging service for all staff and students at the university. With this in mind, the original technical requirements of the project were:

- Provide possible integration with the Blackboard VLE used within the university.
- Be able to use our central LDAP server for authentication (hence allowing for common usernames and passwords across systems).
- Have the ability for users to be registered using the same data feeds used to populate our VLE (these feeds being derived from other central systems such as the student record system).
- Provide a mechanism for single-sign on between the VLE and the new service, preventing users form having to log in twice.

- Have sufficient security and access levels to ensure data could be maintained privately and ensure users had a choice of who they wished to share information with
- That the system should be able to both aggregate incoming RSS feeds and publish its own, public RSS feeds
- That it should have the potential to be customised to meet our specific educational needs
- Needed to be able to scale to use by several thousand users (in our case 36,000)
- Preferably open source

Why Elgg?

Following an extensive evaluation of the blogging products available at the time, it became clear that Elgg was the only platform that satisfied all the above technical requirements. In addition, Elgg offered far more than just a simple blogging tool – providing facilities for a far more fully-fledged PLE platform as well as community or group-based facilities that allowed participation at multiple levels and for multiple purposes. In this respect, Elgg is a true social network application rather than a single-functionality Web 2.0 tool. Elgg is relatively unique in offering such a combination of services and represented a far great opportunity for the

Figure 1. The shared learning environment model

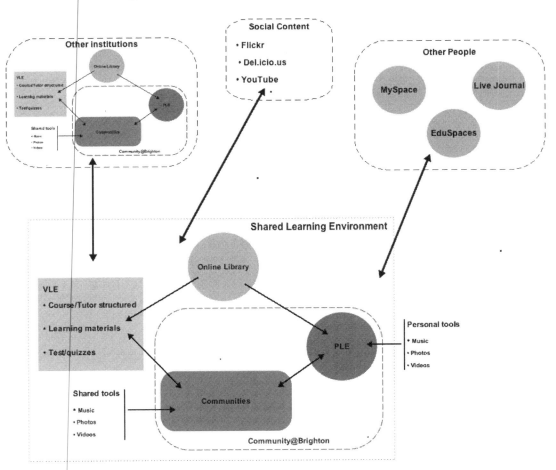

university to implement a service that combined common social networking tools with the tools already available within our VLE. In particular, the following features were considered to be of particular importance in developing the concept of an SLE in combination with our VLE:

- By default, Elgg provides tools for blogging, aggregating RSS feeds, storing files and bookmarks
- It operates at two levels – personal and group/community. The above tool set is available for both personal and community participation
- All users have equality of participation – the only hierarchy amongst users that exists is the notion of a community or group owner who has the rights to set specific details for a community. Any user can create a community and determine who can join and participate
- Elgg provides mechanisms for creating personal access control groups – allowing each individual user to create groups and determine precisely who they wish to share their information with. Other access control groups are created automatically (e.g. all members of each community).
- The provision of APIs to allow the core code to be extended using a plugin architecture means additional functionality can be relatively easily added

Finally, Elgg was one of the few services we evaluated that actually began life within HE and had been developed specifically for educational use. At the time of our evaluation, Elgg was already in use in a small number of UK universities and others in the US and Europe. Perhaps more interestingly, it was also being used as the hosting platform for one of the world's largest eLearning networks (http://eduspaces.net) bringing eLearning practitioners together to explore and discuss new approaches to eLearning.

The Institutional Perspective

Clearly, there were considerations beyond the pure technical and functional requirements that the university needed to make and need to continue to monitor:

Security and Reputation

In 2005, the university's Information Strategy Committee considered the original proposal for implementing a university-wide blogging service. Chief amongst the issues discussed by this committee were those of ensuring data security – particularly given that the proposal explicitly recommended that the service have a public-facing element (i.e. users could make contributions visible to the public at large if they wished). A second consideration was one of risk to the university's reputation. At the time of submitting the proposal there had been a number of high-profile cases of disgruntled staff airing their grievances about their employers via public blogs. Clearly, implementing any tool that allows all staff and students to voice opinion publically carries with it some risk of damage to the institution's reputation should someone choose to use the service to defame the university in some way. With respect to the former consideration, the committee was happy to defer judgement to the expertise of staff within its central Information Services department in considering the security facilities within any of the products being evaluated. In terms of the latter consideration, the proposed scale of implementation and the staffing resources available, made any options for active policing/vetting of contributions unfeasible and the committee decided that the university's conditions of use for its computing facilities were sufficiently robust enough to mitigate any potential risk and simply asked that two facilities should be available within the service. The first of these was the requirement that the conditions of use for computing facilities be linked to on every page of the service, the second that the service have a facility to allow users to report offensive content.

The Implications of the Use of External Networks

Whilst not a significant concern at the time of considering the original proposal, the use of external networks for learning and teaching has become a key area for discussion in many universities over the last two years. The emergence of massive, free social networks such as Facebook, MySpace, Flickr and YouTube and their wide-scale use outside the educational arena have led many academics to consider using such services to deliver components of their teaching. The rationales for using such services are many and various including:

- If all students on a course use Facebook then why not use it to communicate with them – it is, after all, probably a more relevant tool for students than most VLEs.
- Few VLEs offer facilities for uploading and sharing images or video so why not use Flickr or YouTube as they cost nothing?
- Other free, hosted social networks (e.g. Ning) offer wide toolsets and the facility for staff to build their own social network specifically for their courses
- Given the lag in development of similar features within the leading VLE products and an often similar lag in provision of such services within universities, these free external networks offer academics their only chance to experiment with these new technologies and consider their potential in learning, teaching and research.

Such arguments may well seem compelling – these services come at no cost, are often underpinned by financially stable companies such as Google and have significantly greater resources to dedicate to research and development than any university. As a sector, how can we possibly compete with the multi-billion dollar budgets of these major web 2.0 players? Why bother to invest in local attempts at replicating such services when they exist already and are free to use?

The reality is there are many risks associated with such activities including:

- If an academic or student posts material to an external network who owns the data? How does a university preserve intellectual copyright in such circumstances? Close inspection of the data policies of many of these social networks reveals a common model that data ownership transfers to the network once it is published within it.
- Will the network be there tomorrow? Whilst the most popular networks generate significant profit, their financial success is totally dependent upon their popularity. Use of these networks has proven to be fickle with users frequently using multiple networks and migrating from one to another according to the flow of popularity. Consider the apparent dominance of MySpace 3 years ago and its current position compared to Facebook now. Even given the current dominance of Facebook, its audience is largely confined to specific age groups – Beebo is currently a more popular service amongst teenagers.
- Who are you speaking to? – If a university hosts a service it can, largely, guarantee that the online users a tutor interacts with are actually their students. Is this the case for external networks? How do we know whether we are talking to our students or others hoping to learn without paying fees to our institution?
- Can we adapt the service to meet our specific needs? In some cases the answer is yes – Ning (http://www.ning.com/) allows users to configure their network from a choice of tools, themes and other facilities but, in the

case of others, such modifications are often superficial and rarely of great relevance to education. Facebook may be the current choice of social network for our students but does an emphasis on throwing virtual custard pies at your friends and other purely social activities foster or support online learning and would it be in Facebook's interest to develop educationally focussed facilities? Admittedly, one of Facebook's success factors has been its ability to allow others to develop applications for it and there are numerous examples of attempts to develop educational functionality via these applications but does the general context of the service foster study or learning?

- Can the external network be integrated in any way with other university systems? When considering the scale of even our smallest universities, there is usually a need to automate registration processes to ensure several thousands of students have quick and equal access to services. Another reason for integrating with existing services is to make accessing services and information easy – everything can be accessed from one place rather than data and communications being fragmented across numerous external networks and relying on learners to use aggregating tools to assimilate and manage all the information.

Gaining Experience of Emerging Technologies

The potential of Web 2.0 technologies for enhancing online learning has received significant coverage in the academic press of late. As Alexander argues:

Web 2.0's lowered barrier to entry may influence a variety of cultural forms with powerful implications for education, from storytelling to classroom teaching to individual learning. It is *much simpler to set up a del.icio.us tag for a topic one wants to pursue or to spin off a blog or blog departmental topic than it is to physically meet co-learners and experts in a classroom or even to track down a professor. Starting a wiki-level text entry is far easier than beginning an article or book. What new, natively digital textual forms are impending as small-scale production scales up? "Web 1.0" has already demonstrated immense powers for connecting learners, teachers, and materials. How much more broadly will this connective matrix grow under the impact of the openness, ease of entry, and social nature of Web 2.0? How can higher education respond, when it offers a complex, contradictory mix of openness and restriction, public engagement and cloistering?* Alexander (2006).

From an institutional perspective, such technologies represent significant future challenges, both in terms of delivering the technologies and in their apparent paradigm shifts in approaches to teaching & learning. Such challenges are not easy to plan for or simulate at a large-scale level and, given the risks associated with using external networks stated above, there are many good reasons why universities need to begin to dip their toes in the water and consider all the various challenges that providing such services may pose.

Developing an Escape Strategy

As has already been stated, a key element to the strategy behind Community@Brighton was to provide a service that augmented the existing VLE service by providing tools and mechanisms that are not currently available within the VLE. However, another institutional consideration that all universities who have wide-scale VLE implementation face is that of lock-in to the VLE product. Currently, there are virtually no tools available to allow migration of data between the main VLE products and those that do exist are intended for small-scale migration rather than the wholesale migration of data from many thousands of users and courses. In this respect, universities that have implemented VLEs at a full institutional level are, to some extent, locked in to their particular product or, at least, face a significant technical challenge in moving to a different product (and this does not take into consideration other challenges such as staff development). Add to this the relative lack of differences in features between the main products and the equation begins to point to potential stagnation. If we can't change products are we not at the mercy of the VLE vendors to determine the characteristics of our educational technologies? So, from an institutional perspective, what are the escape routes? How does an institution plan an appropriate exit strategy when faced with such lock-in? In our planning for Community@ Brighton a number of issues were considered that related to such an exit strategy:

1. There is little doubt that the various features of Web 2.0 technologies will play a significant role in future technology enhanced learning platforms – consequently, implementing these at an early stage will help prepare our academic community for the challenges to traditional teaching methodologies discussed by Eijkman (2008) and the potential new approaches to learning envisioned in Connectivism theory by Siemens (2004).

2. If the stagnation in VLE feature sets is to continue, then adding Web 2.0 services alongside and integrated with our VLE would at least provide room for expansion of facilities.

3. By implementing an open source and extensible architecture such as that available with Elgg, we effectively open the door for a gradual migration from VLE lock-in, rather than being forced in to a "big bang" migration scenario. In addition, using a product that is easy to develop and customise may well allow for a gradual development of a new

service – one that is both modern in technological approach and customised to meet the specific needs of the user community.

Add to this the potential power of the VLE and PLE services working together and allowing the two ends of the spectrum to interrelate, for all users to access, share and participate in an SLE, and perhaps we actually negate any future need for an exit strategy – rather we have built the foundations for a completely new generation of learning platforms that encompass the best of both worlds?

Delivering the Service

So far we have considered the theoretical and strategic issues surrounding the development of Community@Brighton, but what of the implementation itself? The following section outlines the key elements to delivering the service and details how the service is delivered to users.

Levels of Integration

One of the key technical requirements of this project was to integrate it with existing registration processes and with our existing VLE service. This involved integration at three levels:

1. Making use of existing data feeds from our student record system. With 36,000 users, manual registration of users and adding them to course groups was out of the question. At the time of implementation, we already had a robust mechanism for populating our VLE both with user accounts and their registrations on course/module areas and adopting the same processes for Community@Brighton was considered essential. Consequently we commissioned a customisation from the Elgg developers that allowed us to use the same data feeds to populate our new service. These processes

run as a scheduled task and currently add, update, disable and delete user accounts as well as adding and removing users from Elgg communities that represent course or module areas. This therefore guarantees that when a student is added to our systems they are automatically added to both our VLE and Community@Brighton.

2. Single authentication and sign-on. One of our aims for this service was to have it fit within an existing student portal umbrella. In 2001 when we initially introduced our VLE service we decided to clearly brand the service as "studentcentral". One of the rationale for this was to avoid associating the service with the underlying product (Blackboard) thus ensuring we could change products or add services under a single umbrella that students would be familiar with an ensure they had a single portal to use for all their university materials. As the university uses a central LDAP service for authentication and both Elgg and Blackboard support LDAP, using this central authentication service required no additional work or customisation. However, whilst the two services could authenticate against a common database, this did not remove the need for users to login to each service separately. To enable users to login once for both services we deployed a commercially available plugin for our VLE that allows single-sign with a variety of external services and simply required 5 lines of additional code within Elgg to enable this. This also meant that the main route into Community@Brighton would be through the student portal and therefore reinforce both it's status as a component of the wider service (studentcentral) and also strengthen it's perception by academics as an additional tools set of the university's eLearning platform.

3. Linking to Community@Brighton from within the VLE. Figure 2 & Figure 3 shows

screen shots of the service as seen both from the student portal and from within a course/module area within the VLE. As can be seen, the student portal presents tabs for key services such as the user's VLE home page, the online library, and access to personal administrative information. As a result of the single-sign plugin we were also able to present Community@Brighton as a tab within the portal. This is also augmented by a portal module on all user homepages that display the main RSS feed from Community@Brighton - allowing everyone to see immediately the latest posts and news from the service. As well as linking from the portal, it is also relatively simple to link directly from course areas within the VLE to specific areas within Community@Brighton. So, for example, if a course has a shared area on Community@Brighton a tutor can link to the course blog, filestore, photos or bookmarks directly from within their parallel area in the VLE therefore allowing these new tools to be used in conjunction with, and in the same context as, the tools available within the VLE.

Phased Introduction

As our view was that the effective implementation of Community@Brighton and a thorough understanding of how it would work alongside the VLE to form a nascent SLE would take at least 5 years, we were careful not to impose the new service on academics early on. To this end, we focussed our initial efforts at selling the new service at two levels: first, as a purely social network to foster communication amongst students across our different campuses, second to work with enthusiastic early adopter staff who wished to explore the potential of these new technologies within their teaching and research. At the time of writing we are moving into a second phase of implementation – involving two core elements:

Figure 2. Presenting Community@Brighton from a tab in the student portal (studentcentral)

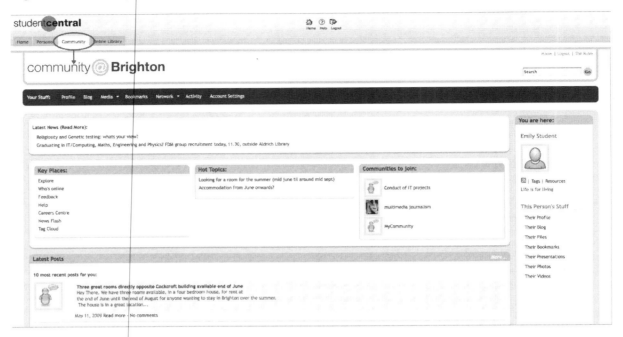

Figure 3. Presenting Community@Brighton via a link within a VLE course area

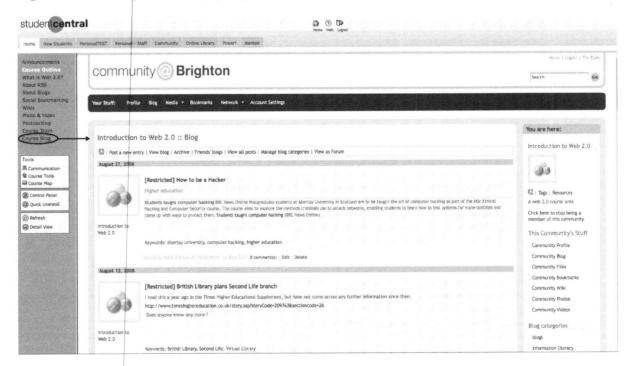

1. Gather experience from the early phase, complete customisations recommended by early adopters and disseminate that experience to other staff and use our experiences to develop a comprehensive staff development programme

2. Attempt to widen use by investigating how best to allow external participants such as subject experts, business and industry partners and research collaborators to use the service and realise one of the key potential benefits of Web 2.0 technologies – to forge relationships and collaboration across institutional barriers.

Customisations

One of the key elements of our implementation was to ensure the service adapted to meet the specific needs of the user community and to learn from the experiences of early adopters as to the requirements for allowing these new facilities to fully support learning and teaching. To date, the following represent the main customisations that have been made:

- **Presentation tool** – one of the potential areas of use of a service such as Community@Brighton is in the development of ePortfolios. The ability for all students to maintain a reflective blog, upload files, images and other materials and contribute to group discussions goes a long way to developing an institutional PLE platform. The natural outlet of such a platform is the ability for students to create ePortfolios of their contributions for access by others. Whilst students can make any of their contributions visible to specific groups, all logged in users or the public at large, there was no easy mechanism for them to draw together key materials in a coherent way for presentation to, e.g. a tutor or prospective employer. Consequently, we commissioned the development of a presentation tool which allows students to create presentations by using a "pick'n'mix" approach from their contributions to the service – allowing them to create pages, add text annotations, choose which blogs posts and files they wish to include and decide whether or not to include associated comments. Components of each presentation are then frozen in time (i.e. if they include a blog post and then change the original, the copy in the presentation does not change). Once a presentation is completed, the student can choose who to share it with – whether this is a fellow member of Community@Brighton, or a specific external individual (in this case they are able to email a URL to the prospective reader who can then gain access without needing to login to the service).

- **Media sharing** – whilst initially the service allowed users to upload images and videos alongside other document types, we very quickly began receiving requests from both staff and students to provide services similar to those offered by Flickr and YouTube – i.e. photo galleries and automatic conversion of video content to flash format to allow videos to be played directly within Communtiy@Brighton pages. We therefore commissioned the development of a "mediastream" plugin for Elgg that differentiated between file types as they were uploaded. All images that are uploaded now get added to the user and site "photostream" – allowing an image gallery display of these files and the development of a site-wide image resource which has now grown to in excess of 2000 photos shared across the community since it's introduction 1 year ago. With the same plugin, if a video is uploaded, it is automatically converted to FLV format and wrapped in a video player embedded within Community@

Brighton pages, allowing any reader with the Flash browser plugin to watch uploaded videos and avoiding the early pitfalls seen whereby users were reliant on having either the correct versions of QuickTime, Windows Media Player or other proprietary software installed in order to view uploaded video content.

- **Staff administration facilities** – it became clear quite early on that staff requiring students to use their personal blogs to contribute to their course encountered issues with managing these contributions. If a tutor was working with 20 students, then they effectively had to scan 20 blogs to monitor and assess contributions. Even if such contributions were made to a shared course area, managing contributions from individuals was challenging. As a result we have developed a number of additional interfaces for staff that allow relatively immediate viewing of student contributions – presenting lists of their students, indicating the number of posts made by each student and allowing staff to filer the lists by date, name and whether they have commented on the contribution.

- **Community notifications** – another issue raised by teaching staff was the extent to which they, and their students, were alerted to contributions to their course areas on Community@Brighton. Whilst Elgg provides RSS feeds that can be subscribed to, it became clear that few users actually understand or use RSS as a mechanism for being alerted to new information. It was therefore important to determine a more effective mechanism for users to receive notifications of new material. As Elgg already has a built-in email notification mechanism, it appeared a logical step to extend this facility. By default, Elgg's notification mechanism allows each use to mark specific blog posts as "interesting" and therefore receive

an email notification should someone comment on that post. However, this does not extend to alerts when a new post is made to that blog and this was seen as particularly important for shared blogs within course communities to ensure that all members were alerted to new posting and to encourage participation. We therefore extended the notifications system to automatically send email notifications to all members of a community if the community owner chose to use this facility.

- **Institutional news feeds** – one of the advantages of using Web 2.0 service is its ability to share information with other services. Prior to implementing Community@Brighton, the university had no central way of publishing news items across multiple web services. By using the RSS feeds from Community@Brighton we were able to push news items from the service out to a number of other platforms including the VLE, staff intranet, public website and various plasma screen placed in key positions around our campuses.

- **Deleting users** – as with many other systems, when a user is deleted in Elgg, their contributions are deleted as well. Within our VLE, the only contributions made by students are generally posts to discussion boards and we encourage all staff to back-up and export their VLE course areas every semester (as well as our standard central backups). Given the numerous possibilities for students to contribute to individual and shared learning across the Community@Brighton service, it is very difficult to provide a mechanism to backup individual contributions (we do, of course backup the whole system daily). Equally, a user's contribution may well be of value to future learners well beyond the point they leave the university. Consequently, we were faced with the issue of how to

Table 1.

N° of Blog Posts	27413
N° of comments	9714
N° of files shared	5715
N° of communities created	423
% students that have used the service	79%

deal with user deletions once they were fed to us from our student records system – to delete everything, or try to preserve and make anonymous contributions for future value. We have adopted the latter approach, customising the user deletion routines so the user account and their contributions do not get deleted – rather the user's name and username are changed (their name is changed to "This person has now left the university" and their old details stored should there ever be a need to resurrect contributions from a previous student. The result of this customisation is that all contributions are preserved once a user is deleted – it is simply the case that the user's identity is removed from their contributions.

Usage

A summary of activity and usage of Community@ Brighton over the 2 years of operation is shown in Table 1.

Usage can generally be split into three main areas:

- **Social** – there has been considerable use of Community@Brighton for purely social purposes ranging from general discussions on topical issues to student groups using the service to arrange social events. Given the split-campus nature of our university this has helped draw what were relatively separate student communities on each campus

together and build a sense of a more global online community.

- **Academic** – as discussed in more detail below, we have had many early-adopter projects investigating the use of Community@ Brighton for educational purposes. Whilst these are difficult to quantify in terms of overall use, approximately half the 423 communities that have been created have been for academic purposes.

- **Support** – one of the uses that has been both pleasing and surprising has been the use of the service for mutual support. Several students have used the service to highlight problems with student life or difficulties with their courses. Not only have these been quickly taken up by the relevant student support service, they have also been responded to by many students – offering sympathy, exchanging similar experiences, offering help and clearly acting as a source of comfort and support for the students concerned. On a wider scale, we have provided a specific community for new students – providing access to this 4 months prior to their arrival. In the 4 months leading up to the start of the 2008/9 academic year, this community received 139 posts and 438 comments – a mix of students introducing themselves and raising issues about the courses, how to prepare for student life and how to sort out accommodation.

Perhaps a more interesting perspective of usage is to compare the use of blogs within Com-

Table 2.

Blog posts vs Discussion Board posts	2006/7	2007/8
Discussion Board Posts	8828	9134
Blog Posts (inc comments)	18993	18304

munity@Brighton with the use of discussion boards within the VLE as these are the closest facilities which can be directly compared (Table 2 and Figure 4)

CASE STUDIES

In the two years of operation of the service there have been numerous examples of using the service to support learning, teaching and research. The case studies that follow hopefully represent examples of the different types of use.

Case Study 1: Personal Development Planning in Electrical Engineering

Problem addressed: Managing 70 personal tutees, allocating sufficient time for meetings, discussion and feedback. Could the technologies available help support these processes? In this case study, the course tutor was already involved in a pilot project looking at personal development planning (PDP) within their course and wished to take this one step further by using Community@ Brighton to support student reflection, allow the tutor to comment privately on student contributions and for the students to produce a final ePortfolio presentation summarising their PDP activities. As most of the contributions were seen as being personal, rather than contributions to a shared community, it was decided to ask students to post to their personal blogs, including posting a fortnightly video diary. Private access control groups were set up for each student to allow them to make their posts only available to the tutor thus allowing for a private dialog between student and

tutor. In all, 70 level 1 students from an Electrical Engineering course took part in the project and their contributions did not form part of the overall assessment for the module within which the project was embedded. This generated 207 blog posts over the course of a single semester from 46 students. Subsequent discussion with the students revealed the following observations:

- A significant proportion of the students failed to understand why they were being asked to contribute blog postings and appeared not to see the point of reflecting on their studies
- Those students that did understand, valued the experience and particularly valued the comments from their tutor – as reflected in

Figure 4.

Discussion Board Posts vs Blog Posts

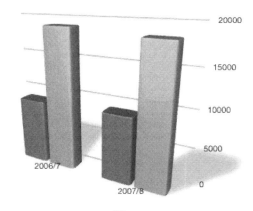

the fact that 21 of the students posted four or more blog posts.

- Some students found the use of Community@Brighton in communicating with each other very helpful and actually created a separate community for their colleagues to discuss issues and arrange social events.

From the tutor perspective, there was clear value in using the technologies – particularly given that prior to the project they had to arrange separate personal tutorial time for every student – now they could communicate with them at times that were convenient to them. However, what became readily apparent early on in the project was the difficulty in managing the flow of information. The tutor found themselves having to scan across 70 blogs to check for new posts, make comments and try to record contributions. Whilst Elgg provides a friends list, which made it relatively easy for the tutor to list all their students on a single page, they still had to visit each student blog in turn to check for new activity. As a result, a separate interface page was created for the tutor that listed all their students on a single page, together with the number of posts each had made and various ways of sorting this information. This allowed the tutor to maintain a single "register" of contributions, get a clear picture of who was contributing and identify those students who were not engaging in the activity. This demonstrates one of the key issues with social technology design vs VLE design in that many social technologies have few, if any, concepts of user management beyond system administration. In this respect, one of the perceived strengths of the VLE model, that of learner management, is missing yet still needed in social networks where they are to be used within an education context.

Support required: This tutor worked closely with support staff to ensure all students received an introductory session on general use of Elgg, understanding access controls, blogging and cre-

ating video diaries. A separate session was also arranged towards the end of the project to show students how to use the presentation tool to draw their contributions together into a single presentation for the tutor to provide feedback on.

Case Study 2: Sharing Photographs

Problem addressed: Our VLE has minimal facilities for students to upload their own work and share with others. From an academic point of view, one of the appealing aspects of Community@Brighton that has become apparent is its ability to allow students to share media. Indeed this is reflected in both this case study and the one that follows. Our VLE has no facility to allow students to share images or other media with each other apart from adding attachments to a discussion board where media is not displayed embedded within the page and is difficult to view and comment on at the same time. A tutor teaching a level 1 photography course decided that Community@Brighton offered the possibility both for their students to upload their work and for their peers to view and comment on it, but also for the students to make their work more widely available to the rest of the university community. To enable this, a course community was created and linked to from their course area within the VLE – effectively being presented as an additional facility within the VLE. Students were asked to post their photographs from a number of assignments to the photo area within this community. In total, 70 photos were posted by 18 students from a total group size of 39. As with the previous case study, the student group appeared split as to the extent they understood the point of engaging in the task with those that did, contributing regularly. What was particularly interesting about this study was the fact that nobody commented on any of the uploaded work. There are a number of reasons why this might have been the case. First, the comments facility within the photo area did not present a text field to add comments to by default (unlike blogs and other file types) – users are required to click a link to expand the view and reveal the comments box. This may have led to participants simply not realising they could post comments. Secondly, it was difficult to gauge from conversations with the tutor the extent to which students commented on each other's work during tutorial and seminar sessions and therefore it may be that students simply were not familiar with the concept of commenting/criticising each other. Finally, the tutor made no comments so there were no precedents set for students to follow.

Support required: The students on this module were given a 2 hour session introducing them to Community@Brighton and specifically how to upload and share photographs within their course community area. No further support was requested.

Case Study 3: Cross-Course Collaboration

Problem addressed: The current structure of our VLE makes cross-course collaboration cumbersome and a lack of facilities for sharing student work make cross-course collaboration on video production difficult. As discussed elsewhere, one of the key aims of introducing these new technologies was to break artificial barriers erected by the VLE and encourage sharing of learning and materials across courses. Two courses whose curricular studies focus on the made and collected object, (History of Decorative Arts and Design from the school of Arts and Communication and 3D Design and Materials Practice from the school of Architecture and Design) looked for a contemporary method of sharing their common interests. The tutors from these courses felt students would benefit from collaborating with each other and understanding the different perspectives each brought to the field of visual research through film. Students were paired, one from each course, and set a number of assignments requiring them to produce short video films of specific topics, post

them to a shared blog, write a short explanation about what inspired each piece and to comment on each others work. 24 students participated in the project with a total of 59 blog posts (all including videos) being contributed. (Figure 5)

Both tutors and students saw the benefits of such collaboration and the use of the technologies to support this. In a follow-up survey of students 58% of the students stated that they felt the ability to share work encouraged personal reflection and critical analysis. The tutors also found unexpected benefits in the use of the technologies beyond those of encouraging reflection and different perspectives on the subject:

In bringing students together in pairs to work in a medium that neither were specialists in, we observed an unexpected learning outcome. Through their engagement with the imaginative and technical learning process, students began emulating each others' newly acquired skills, especially in the use of language to describe technical details… by week three of the project, students were talking confidently in a highly technical, descriptive language. Letschka & Seddon (2007).

Support required: Staff & students were given an introductory session on using Community@Brighton and uploading/sharing videos. A custom elgg plugin was developed allowing students to upload a variety of video formats which were converted automatically to Flash video format to ensure uploaded videos were visible to a wide audience.

Case Study 4: Cross-Institutional Collaboration

Problem addressed: Screen Archive South East wanted to make available elements of its video archive for students to download, edit and re-upload, making a dynamic and constantly growing resource of video. Prior to the introduction of Community@Brighton, there were no facilities to enable this.

Figure 5.

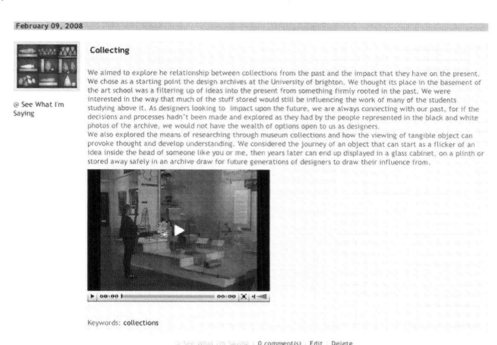

Following the success of the video sharing project described in case study 3, colleagues from the Screen Archive South East (SASE) (http://www. brighton.ac.uk/screenarchive/) and the university's school of Education began the filmbank project – a pilot scheme to offer a selection of Brighton films from the screen archive collection as materials for learning & teaching. A partnership was established with colleagues in the Education Faculty, researchers from SASE and with Access to HE students at Varndean school. A community area was set up for this project and colleagues from SASE uploaded a selection of historical films about Brighton to the video area of this community. Students from both the school of Education and Varndean were asked to work in small groups, download one of the films of their choice and edit it, adding new sound tracks, voice-overs or additional footage to create new material which could then be uploaded to the resource – thus creating an ever-expanding resource of materials for future participants. (Figure 6)

In all 29 films were re-edited and uploaded to the community area with both students and staff commenting positively on the experience including:

This is the best thing I've seen ever!

It is clear from the level of participation and the lack of technical support required from students that they found the process easy, engaging and enjoyable and it will be interesting to see how this resource develops over time and how it might extended to other areas to further support learning and teaching.

Support required: Students participating in this project were not given introductory sessions and no issues were raised with the use of the technologies. A minor customisation of the video plugin (see above) was required to allow students to download the original versions of the videos rather than the converted flash files to allow them to be editable.

Figure 6.

Case Study 5: A Course Portal

Problem addressed: The tutor on this module was a long-standing advocate of the use of Web 2.0 technologies in learning & teaching. However, the university VLE provided minimal facilities to draw together contributions from learners and resources from external services. This final case study outlines the construction of a course area that combined both facilities within the VLE, a shared course community and student personal blogs into a single course portal. The course was a level 3 module called "Developments in Learning Technologies" and was run by one of the key early adopters of the new technologies. The tutor embedded the course community profile page as the course home page within the VLE – thus providing a single point of entry for all their course materials. As the community profile page can be adapted to add a variety of information and widgets (blocks that

bring information in from a variety of sources), this was used as a single point of access to a variety of supporting information including links to student blogs, tags used within the course, latest posts to the course community, course files and videos from the tutor (see Figure 7)

In all, 233 posts were made to this course alongside numerous files, comments, shared bookmarks and other materials. Such activity goes way beyond the usage of discussion boards within course areas previously observed within the VLE alone and demonstrates the extent to which, given the opportunity, students will engage, participate and contribute to a course. During these early phases of implementation, this represents the first real moves towards the vision of a shared learning environment. In addition, a key factor of this course was that many of the participants made their blog posts visible to the whole university community – thus encouraging comment and discussion with others sharing interests in the subject

Figure 7.

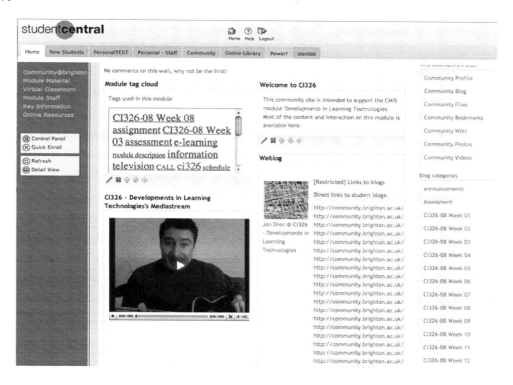

area (including the central learning technologies support team) and therefore representing the first steps towards sharing of knowledge and learning across the university.

Support required: None – tutor was able to build the course portal themselves using Elgg's widget tools.

FUTURE RESEARCH DIRECTIONS

There is little doubt that the introduction of Community@Brighton has significantly augmented the facilities that were already available within our VLE, increasing opportunities for learner participation, information sharing and collaboration across traditional barriers. Along the way issues and benefits have been identified that have helped us identify areas requiring further modifications and future phases of research and staff development.

Crossing Institutional Barriers

Whilst it is relatively easy to encourage people to use technologies to collaborate across traditional course structures, one of the central aims of our vision was also to extend learning and collaboration beyond the institution – to allow participation from external contributors. The benefits of this are many – from inviting external experts to join in discussions on course blogs to establishing links with external business partners and drawing upon external information resources. Unfortunately, this aim has yet to be realised to any significant extent – largely due to the understandable considerations of data security and protection of intellectual copyright. However, recent technical developments, including OpenID (http://openid.net) and shibboleth (http://shibboleth.internet2.edu) now make trusted collaboration with external bodies a very real possibility. Implicit within both of these systems is the concept of trust between organisations and the ability for each organisation to develop lists of trusted partners that allow users of each organisation to access and contribute to the services of others. One of our next steps will be to assess the implications of adopting these technologies (Blackboard supports Shibboleth whereas Elgg supports OpenID), monitor the extent to which either of them become the dominant standard and evaluate the extent to which the two can be used together to provide a controlled and secure mechanism for trusted external participation within our emerging SLE.

Staff Understanding and the Cultural Shift

It has become clear from discussions with many staff over the last two years that there is a considerable lack of understanding of Web 2.0 technologies and their potential to support learning and teaching. As might be anticipated, there appears to be a significant generational factor both in understanding and preparedness to use these new technologies with staff under 30 generally being better informed and more prepared to try out the new services. Terms commonplace in Web 2.0 services such as tags, RSS, blogs etc are generally unfamiliar to many staff and common misconceptions such as "blogs are always public" predominate. Equally, staff are often conservative in approach to teaching styles and reluctant to consider the new more flexible and participative forms of learning Web 2.0 technologies enable. In many cases this is not necessarily a reluctance to improve teaching and learning but a lack of time and resources to dedicate to experimentation and learning such new approaches. Indeed, a key conclusion of our findings so far is that use of these new technologies does involve additional work and time (albeit allowing greater flexibility as to when this happens) for teaching staff. Encouraging greater participation from learners and sharing of knowledge from a wide variety of sources, requires more work to asses that greater

participation and validate the resources. This represents a significant departure from the tightly structured and student-management facilities available within most VLEs towards a merger of these two worlds – a model that includes equality of participation and contribution for the learner as well as facilities for tutors to manage those contributions. It is clear that if the use of social networks such as Community@Brighton within education is to be successful, then there is a need to develop interfaces that allow staff quick and simple access to student management facilities and reduce the potential information overload these new approaches may incur. This will be our main focus of development efforts over the next phase of implementation. A key question here is how much emphasis should we place in embedding extended administration facilities in Community@Brighton within the VLE and further emphasise an integrated service? Most staff are familiar with the control panel interface provided by our VLE and expect to be able to configure eLearning tools from this interface so it would make sense from an ease of use perspective to locate Community@Brighton administration within the same context. However, would such an approach detract from breaking mindsets away from the comfort zone of the VLE and opening minds to a wider set of services with completely different approaches to learning & teaching?

Support Requirements

As well as extending administrative facilities within Community@Brighton, a key focus will be on staff development. Until the introduction of Community@Brighton, most of our staff development focus was on how to use the tools available within the VLE with only a small component focussing on application and pedagogy. This was, in part, due to the nature of our training program at the time (combinations of formal workshops and one-to-one support sessions) and, in part, due to the fact that the VLE mirrored standard practices to such an extent that there was very little explanation required for staff to understand how to apply tools that were available. Since the introduction of Community@Brighton, it has become clear that simply informing staff how to operate the facilities available is not sufficient for them to fully understand how to apply them. The differences in approaches to learning and teaching need to be explained, as does the potential for greater student participation and reach to external organisations and individuals. As a result, we have now moved our efforts away from traditional workshops to intensive course design programs run over 2 or 3 days and providing opportunities for staff to learn about the new technologies available, see how others are using them and consider how to plan and redesign their courses to incorporate their use. Such events require far greater resources both in organisation and in follow-up support and we will be monitoring their success carefully in order to try to identify the best approaches to staff development in these areas.

Understanding Student Attitudes

Given the widespread use of networks such as Facebook, Flickr and YouTube by our students, it is unsurprising that students draw comparisons between these networks and Community@Brighton. Whilst we have had many comments comparing features across networks and requests to enable features present on popular external networks, a possibly more interesting issue is that of student perception of the purpose of these technologies and their relevance to education. Discussions with many students have revealed a general opinion that social networks form part of their social life and are entirely separate from their university activities. This is exemplified by a poll undertaken with our students asking them whether they would see any value in us developing a Facebook application that would feed new information from studentcentral into their Facebook accounts. The answer was a resounding "no" – and many commented that

they wished to keep their university and social activities completely separate. Such findings are echoed elsewhere including Creanor et al (2006) and Acar (2008) This presents a dilemma to anyone wishing to implement social networking technologies within an educational context – how to provide tools commonly available in external social networks without them being branded as pure social tools – i.e. how do we reinforce the educational value of these tools amongst our students and avoid them being simply regarded as the university Facebook? Whilst still early days in our implementation, a common finding from many of the courses that have made use of these tools is that, approximately half of most student groups, when given the opportunity to more fully participate in their courses online, often quickly understand the value of sharing knowledge and make frequent use of the services for these purposes. Our next steps need to be to attempt to understand why the other half don't engage and how we can provide a clear message that explains this fusion of social and academic that Community@Brighton represents.

CONCLUSION

It is difficult to summarise all the various conclusions we have reached as a result of our experiences so far. Considering usage statistics alone, it would appear that introducing Community@Brighton has significantly increased online activity – particularly from students. Whilst adding new tools and features to an online learning environment can rarely be said to be a bad thing, many tools often remain little used or only applicable to niche areas. For tools or services to be used extensively they must have relevance to their users and clear application in their learning and teaching. It is interesting then, to see the extent of activity within Community@Brighton – over the last two years the service has seen an average of 59 contributions per day (blog posts, comments and files) compared to 26 contributions to discussion boards within the VLE per day over the same time period. It is also interesting to consider the use of the discussion boards prior to the introduction of Community@Brighton.In 2005/6 the discussion boards received 11489 posts. This was the 5th year of operation of the VLE and, at the time, included several open discussion boards used for social purposes by students. The usage of Community@Brighton has exceeded even this earlier figure from the VLE in each year of operation. Unfortunately, there is little empirical evidence to help us understand the exact reasons for this – it is extremely difficult to separate social from academic activity within Community@Brighton and so the proportional use is unclear. However, it is fairly obvious that students have voted with their feet and adopted a service that is, hopefully, more relevant to them, certainly more familiar in terms of the technologies they use outside their studies and hopefully augments their online learning experience.

For staff, to some extent, the converse is true. These technologies represent challenges on at least two fronts – familiarity with the technologies themselves and understanding the expanding pedagogic horizons they might represent. Age and perception of technologies play a significant role – many staff feel they've missed the boat or that these are technologies for their children's generation and the time required to experiment and change is in short supply. It was for these reasons that we foresaw our implementation as taking at least 5 years…for staff to be given time to consider the potential, to dip their toes in the water, for early adopters to plough ahead and lay the foundations we can all build upon and for the technologies to mature and adapt to the specific needs of education. We are not yet half way through this period yet it is clear one of our key foci for future work will be in staff development and, in particular, a paradigm shift away from teaching the "hows" to greater emphasis on the "whys" and far more thorough discussion and collabora-

tion amongst colleagues on the nature of these emerging pedagogies.

It is interesting then, that one of our earliest more general observations has been the greater relevance this new service has to colleagues in our faculty of Art & Design. Over the 6 years we have run our VLE, courses based within our Faculty of Art & Design consistently showed lowest take up with many staff citing the facilities and structure of the VLE as being too inflexible and inappropriate for their modes of teaching. Since introducing Community@Brighton, we have seen substantial interest from this faculty with the ability for students to share media, engage in dialog and critique each other's work seen as having particular value within these subjects which tend to rely more heavily on student participation and analysis than many other subject areas. What of our vision of the Shared Learning Environment? We have, without doubt, augmented our existing provision with tools that enable a more flexible, participative and collaborative approach to learning and teaching and they have been heavily used in a variety of ways. However, our experiences so far suggest there is still a long way to go before we either realise or abandon this vision of learners, teachers and researchers actively and regularly sharing information and collaborating across course and institutional barriers. Institutions are understandably conservative in their approach to sharing, and the usage figures suggest this is also the case for staff and students – consider the number of comments to blog posts (9722: 27575) – suggesting a relatively low proportion of posts actually become "conversations". To move closer to this vision we need to understand what the barriers are to people sharing learning, when such sharing & collaboration is appropriate across traditional barriers and how we might help foster a culture that is prepared to engage in such activities in ways that really improve the learning experience.

REFERENCES

Acar, A. (2008). Antecedents and Consequences of Online Social Networking Behavior: The Case of Facebook. *Journal of Website Promotion, 3*(1), 62–83. doi:10.1080/15533610802052654

Alexander, B. (2006). Web 2.0: A New Wave of Innovation for Teaching and Learning? *EDUCAUSE Review, 41*(2), 32–44.

Attwell, G. (2007). The Personal Learning Environments - the future of eLearning? *eLearning Papers, 2*(1). Retrieved September 16, 2008, from http://www.elearningpapers.eu/index.php?page=doc&doc_id=8553&doclng=6

Creanor, L., Trinder, K., Gowan, D., & Howells, C. (2006). *LEX: The Learner Experience of eLearning – Final project report*. Retrieved September 16, 2008, from http://www.jisc.ac.uk/elp_learneroutcomes

Dron, J. (2006). *Control and Constraint in ELearning: Choosing When to Choose*. Hershey, PA: IGI Global.

Eijkman, H. (2008). Web 2.0 as a non-foundational network-centric learning space. *Campus-Wide Information Systems, 25*(2), 93–104. doi:10.1108/10650740810866567

Letschka, P., & Seddon, G. (2007). *See What I'm Saying?* Project report to Centre for Excellence in Learning & Teaching through Design. Retrieved September 18, 2008, from http://cetld.brighton.ac.uk/projects/completed-projects/see-what-i-m-saying/see-what-i-m-saying-results

O'Hear, S. (2005). *Seconds out, round two*. Retrieved September 18, 2008, from http://www.guardian.co.uk/education/2005/nov/15/elearning.technology3

Siemens, G. (2004). Connectivism: A Learning Theory of the Digital Age. *Elearnspace*. Retrieved September 16, 2008, from http://wwwelearnspace.org/Articles/connectivism.htm

Wilson, S. (2005). *The VLE of the Future*. Retrieved September 16, 2008, from http://zope.cetis.ac.uk/members/scott/blogview?entry=20050117150356

Chapter 5
eLearning:
Institutional Provision and Student Expectations

Barbara Newland
Bournemouth University, UK

Maria-Christiana Papaefthimiou
University of Reading, UK

ABSTRACT

Students who have grown up in the digital age have certain expectations for learning in Higher Education (HE). "Using a complex mix of virtual and face-to-face environments, personal and institutional technologies, learners of all ages are developing new working practices around the technologies available to them. Increasingly, they look for flexibility and openness in the institutional policies and provision that support their learning." (JISC, 2007). The divide between the institutional eLearning provision and the expectations of students who have grown up in a digital world was highlighted through the UK eLearning benchmarking exercise. Institutional eLearning provision and processes within the HE sector were investigated and analysed through this exercise, which was led by the Higher Education Academy (HEA) in collaboration with the Joint Information Systems Committee (JISC). This paper presents the experience of two UK Universities, Bournemouth and Reading, whose participation in the benchmarking exercise provides examples of institutional provision. Subsequent Pathfinder funding enabled them to build on their strengths with projects aimed at narrowing the divide between student expectations of eLearning and institutional provision. The eRes: Innovative eLearning with e-Resources project (Bournemouth) encourages students to use quality e-resources in their learning. The "Driving Institutional Reform: Exploring Change with Technology" (DIRECT) project (Reading) has developed a framework to transform its internal quality management processes.

DOI: 10.4018/978-1-60566-884-0.ch005

INTRODUCTION

There is a digital divide between institutional provision and individual student expectations of eLearning in Higher Education (HE). This has been highlighted by the eLearning benchmarking exercise that has investigated and analysed institutional eLearning provision and processes within the UK HE sector. This major UK initiative has been led by the Higher Education Academy (HEA) in collaboration with the Joint Information Systems Committee (JISC). Five methodologies were used for the exercise with most institutions selecting the Association of Commonwealth Universities Observatory on Borderless Higher Education (ACU/OBHE) methodology. The ACU/OBHE process is presented here through the experience of two UK Universities, Bournemouth and Reading and its outcomes provide examples of institutional provision by identifying areas of strengths and the level at which eLearning is embedded.

Students who have grown up in the digital age have expectations for their learning experience in HE. "Using a complex mix of virtual and face-to-face environments, personal and institutional technologies, learners of all ages are developing new working practices around the technologies available to them. Increasingly, they look for flexibility and openness in the institutional policies and provision that support their learning."(JISC, 2007) However, there seems to be a digital divide between the institutional provision and use of eLearning and the expectations of students who have grown up in a digital world. Funding through the Pathfinder Programme has enabled both Bournemouth and Reading Universities to implement projects which attempt to align institutional provision and student expectations.

Bournemouth and Reading Universities are both situated in southern England and have a similar number of undergraduate students. The University of Reading has more postgraduate students and academic staff. Bournemouth has

been going through a period of great change with a new Vice-Chancellor, new Pro Vice-Chancellors and three out of six Schools have new Deans. The new Corporate Plan 2006 – 2012 states "Our student-centred learning environment emphasises both intellectual achievement and employability" (Bournemouth, 2006). Reading is a research focused University and is also going through change with a review of the Centre for Development of Teaching and Learning (CDoTL), the establishment of the Enhancement Committee as well as a review of the Directorates and a new Teaching and Learning Strategy. Both Bournemouth and Reading use Blackboard for their Virtual Learning Environment (VLE). Bournemouth has been using Blackboard Basic since 2002 and the full Blackboard Academic Suite since 2006. There was major change in eLearning at Bournemouth as the University moved from four VLEs to one during 2006 and 2007. Reading has been using Blackboard since 2001 and moved to a pilot phase of the Blackboard Academic Suite in 2006. In both Universities the VLE provides a personalised student learning environment as the students see the modules in which they are enrolled. This environment usually includes resources such as lecture materials handouts and PowerPoint slides and communication through the use of announcements and email. Collaboration is possible through discussion forum, blogs and wikis within whole module or group areas. Assessment may be through e-assessments such as multiple-choice quizzes or through assessment of contributions to collaborative work.

STUDENT EXPECTATIONS: LEARNERS IN THE DIGITAL AGE

Student expectations of their learning experience in HE have changed. Students in different age ranges, such as the Baby Boomers and Net Generation, have different attitudes towards using computers for learning (Tapscott, 1997). Tapscott identifies generations of learners as the Baby Boom from 1946–1964, which became the TV generation, the Baby Bust from 1965–1977, sometimes called Generation X, and the Baby Boom Echo from 1977–1997. The extensive use of email started in 1994, along with the rapid growth of use of the Internet and mobile phones. Eighteen year old students starting university in 2008 will have been born in 1989/90. These students have grown up in a world in which computers are part of life and they like to multi-task and are used to continuous communication, through texting, phone calls and email, and instant access to information via the Internet (Oblinger, 2003). Net Generation learners are students who were born in the 1980s and later and "They all use computers in their class work and in their hobbies. They have a wide range of interests, outside their chosen area of study. They are not locked into one thing, although all are highly motivated and pursue their interests with passion. They use the latest in technology, whether cell phones, computers, PDAs, MP3 players, or digital cameras. They expect things to work properly and work fast." (McNeely, 2005) Brown suggests that "laptops are viewed more as a kind of dinosauric technology" due to recent developments with mobile phones in their use of multimedia and internet. (Brown, 2006)

Themes identified from the Net Generation (N-Gen) use of digital media include fierce independence, a culture of innovation, investigation and immediacy. N-Geners have "high independence and autonomy, growing from their experience as initiators of communication and information handling activity." Their "unprecedented access to information also gives them the power to acquire the knowledge necessary to confront information they feel may not be correct". (Tapscott, 1997) "N-Geners live and breathe innovation, constantly looking for ways to do things better." With their culture of investigation "when it comes to technology, N-Gen's initial focus is not how it works but how to work it." In terms of immediacy "Interactivity and the speed of the Net have greatly

increased the process of communicating. What used to take days or weeks, now takes seconds." (Tapscott, 1997) Therefore the learners of the digital age have expectations of things happening quickly.

Tapscott outlines a shift from broadcast to interactive learning, as instruction changes to construction and discovery with learning becoming a social activity facilitated by the teacher (Tapscott, 1997). Brown also states that "today's students learn in ways different from how we learn" as they are always 'multiprocessing' – they do several things simultaneously – listen to music, talk on the cell phone, and use computers, all at the same time." (Brown, 2000) He identifies three dimensions to describe the digital age. The first dimension relates to the literacy of today, which involves image and screen literacy as well as text, and the ability to navigate through it. The second dimension is discovery based learning. The third is reasoning and the ability to find and use material to build something deemed important to the finder and this requires critical judgment and has a bias towards action. These dimensions combine so that "learning becomes situated in action; it becomes as much social as cognitive, it is concrete rather than abstract, and it becomes intertwined with judgment and exploration." (Brown, 2000) Understandings are socially constructed online and learning becomes part of action and knowledge creation, as Brown sees a "shift between using technology to support the individual to using technology to support the relationships between individuals." (Brown, 2000)

Oblinger asks "If the Net Generation values experiential learning, working in teams, and social networking, what are the implications for classrooms and the overall learning environment?" (Oblinger, 2005) McNeely states that these students "get bored if not challenged properly, but when challenged, they excel in creative and innovative ways. They learn by doing, not by reading the instruction manual or listening to lectures. These are the learners that faculty must reach." For these students "learning through social interaction is important. Feedback from the professor is vital, and working in groups is the norm." (McNeely, 2005)

In 2007, a JISC study in the UK of student expectations found "65% 'regularly' use social networking sites" and "over a quarter 'regularly' use wikis, blogs or online networks." Also, "62% agreed with the statement 'I expect IT to play a much bigger role in my learning than it does now'" (JISCb, 2007). The annual American Horizon Report "seeks to identify and describe emerging technologies likely to have a large impact on teaching, learning, or creative expression within learning-focussed organizations." (NMC/ELI, 2008) In 2008, it found "the gap between students' perceptions of technology and that of faculty continues to widen." Faculty were either unaware of tools or "have difficulty integrating them into educational processes." (NMC/ELI, 2008) The ECAR study also found that one of the areas for optimizing technology effectiveness for learning is through training academics "how to effectively integrate technology and pedagogy." (Caruso, 2007).

In terms of Social Networking Sites (SNS), "half of SNS users have integrated SNSs into their academic life as a mechanism for communicating with classmates about course-related topics. Only 5.5%, however, extend their use of SNS to communicate with instructors about course related matters." (Salaway, 2008) A widespread attitude is that IT resources are best situated in learning environments where technology is balanced with other learning activities, especially face to face interactions with faculty and students in the classroom." (Salaway, 2008)

INSTITUTIONAL PROVISION

Higher Education Academy eLearning Benchmarking Exercise

The current state of institutional provision in relation to eLearning has been identified through the HEA eLearning benchmarking exercise. The HEA led this exercise in collaboration with JISC as part of the Higher Education Funding Council for England's (HEFCE) ten-year eLearning strategy. This strategy aims "to help the sector use new technology as effectively as they can, so that it becomes a 'normal' or embedded part of their activities." (HEFCE, 2005) It also supports institutions in their visions for using eLearning to transform learning and teaching.

The HEA states that the aims of the eLearning benchmarking exercise are:

- "to provide institutions with an opportunity to participate in an externally-driven process of reflection and analysis of their current eLearning provision and processes using a recognised methodology. Institutions can use this process to inform their internal decision-making and planning, and compare their practice with other institutions involved in the exercise
- to help identify areas of strategic importance arising from the institutional reflections and analyses that inform the work of JISC, the Academy and the Funding Councils." (HEA, 2008)

HE institutions were invited to participate in the benchmarking exercise in a phased approach. The funding available took the form of support provided by the HEA through five days consultancy to each of the institutions. Table 1 shows the start and end dates with the number of universities that participated for each phase of the benchmarking exercise. (Morrison, 2007)

Table 1. Benchmarking dates

Phase	Start date	End date	Number of institutions
Pilot	January 2006	July 2006	12
Phase 1	October 2006	May 2007	38
Phase 2	May 2007	December 2007	27
Total			77

ELEARNING BENCHMARKING METHODOLOGIES

The five methodologies used in the eLearning benchmarking exercise are ACU/OBHE, Embedding Learning Technologies Institutionally (ELTI), eLearning Maturity Model (eMM), MIT90s and Pick and Mix (HEA, 2008). Table 2 shows the number of universities which used each methodology in each phase. (Morrison, 2007)

The ACU/OBHE methodology has been applied to Higher Education in many different countries. The OBHE's primary purpose is "to provide strategic information to enable policy-makers and institutional-organisational leaders to make informed decisions relevant to their existing and/or future transnational higher education initiatives." (OBHE, 2008). The Observatory accomplishes its mission through "extensive collaboration with global higher education, government, and private sector organisations that are key stakeholders in the global higher education arena. The Observatory is also committed to bringing together international faculty to conduct scholarly research in various areas of transnational higher education." (OBHE, 2008) Currently, the Observatory has organisational subscribers representing fifty countries worldwide engaged in various aspects of transnational higher education and international co-operation.

The ELTI model was originally developed as a JISC project at the University of Bristol. It focuses on "three general areas of exploration: Culture, Infrastructure and Expertise" (HEA, 2008). The eMM methodology was developed in New Zealand and is "based on the principle that an organisation's processes mature along a five step model of capability from "ad-hoc" to a "culture of continuous improvement" (HEA, 2008).

The MIT90s framework was developed at MIT in the early 1990s. It is based on the idea that the use of IT passes through five levels from evolutionary to revolutionary (HEA, 2008). The Pick and Mix methodology was developed from work at Manchester University in 2005. It incorporates a range of criteria from other methodologies which are "a mix of 'process' criteria and 'metric' output criteria; covering student-facing and staff-facing

Table 2. Elearning benchmarking methodologies (Heac, 2008)

Methodology	Pilot	Phase 1	Phase 2	Total
ACU/OBHE	4	21	10	35
ELTI	3	6	0	9
eMM	1	0	7	8
MIT90s	1	4	0	5
Pick and Mix	3	7	10	20
Total				77

issues as well as strategy, structure and IT topics" (HEA, 2008).

Each participating institution was invited to select a methodology that was appropriate to their context. Although the outcomes from the exercise were never intended to be published in the form of league tables, it was possible for institutions to compare themselves with others using the same methodology.

Examples of Institutional Provision

Examples of institutional provision are given by the experience of two UK Universities, Bournemouth and Reading, which participated in the benchmarking exercise. Both universities chose the ACU/OBHE as the most appropriate methodology for their institutional context because of its structured approach and international reputation. The methodology focuses on rigorous institutional self-review based on how the institution operates at present. The process of self-review requires completion of an Institutional Review Document (IRD) using questions prepared by the ACU/OBHE. The IRD includes contextual information including mission and drivers, key processes in strategic development, resources and management plus an overall summary with a single institutional viewpoint. Following completion of the IRD, universities participate in a two-day workshop to share findings and construct the basis of sector comparison. Finally, each institution develops their own action plan.

Both universities established project management structures led by the authors. These structures consisted of Strategy Steering Committees and Project Groups with detailed project plans. Existing committees such as the ELearning Strategy Committee acted as the Benchmarking Strategy Steering Committee. The Project Groups were chaired by the authors with academic representatives from across the University and from Professional Services. The completion of the IRD required a range of mechanisms for collecting

data from academics and students through focus groups, blogs and surveys as well as from internal resources. The timescale for participating in the exercise was very tight as the whole exercise lasted for only six months. Therefore, both institutions employed temporary research assistants to help with focus groups and analyse data from surveys. All the information provided to the OBHE is on a confidential basis. This confidentiality was vital to ensure the benchmarking exercise was known to be an internal process and not an external audit or league table.

Outcomes from Benchmarking to Inform Institutional Changes

Bournemouth and Reading Universities decided to share their experiences of engaging with the benchmarking exercise. The Manager of Educational Development Services from Bournemouth University and the eLearning Manager from the University of Reading had worked together previously and both participated in national workshops organised as part of the benchmarking processes. Informal discussions regarding our experiences of engaging in such a rigorous process in such a short timescale led to the decision to disseminate the comparison of their experiences.

The eLearning benchmarking exercise showed that there is "a sense of growing confidence about the use of technology for learning and teaching, and a much deeper understanding of the issues for institutional policy." (HEAc) It identified both strengths and areas for further development in each institution. It highlighted the divide between the institutional eLearning provision and the expectations of students who have grown up in a digital world.

The University of Reading has supported processes and structures with a robust technical infrastructure which has encouraged and sustained enthusiasm for eLearning innovations among staff. A community of practice has developed with academics having a sense of ownership and control over their innovations within an evolutionary, non-directive and flexible approach appropriate to a research intensive university culture. Areas for further development in embedding eLearning include the alignment of the Teaching and Learning and eLearning strategies; the need to provide sustainable resources for eLearning; moving beyond the "champions" in order to embed eLearning across the institution, developing mechanisms to evaluate eLearning activities and more importantly, monitoring the student expectations of eLearning to improve their learning experience.

The strengths identified at Bournemouth University are its strong central support for academic staff from the Educational Development Services (EDS) and its investment in e-resources. The EDS enhances the practice of learning and teaching through encouraging innovation in the curriculum and promoting scholarship and research. It supports and develops the use of the University's VLE by promoting the appropriate use of eLearning through resources, communication, collaboration and assessment tools. EDS has a Centre for Academic Practice which supports scholarship and pedagogical research. (EDS, 2007) The Library strategy of supporting flexible, independent student learning by providing easy access to quality materials has resulted in an investment of over 50% on e-resources (Newland, 2007). The areas of eLearning for further development include encouraging staff to use the potential of the VLE to engage more actively in eLearning with their students.

Both Bournemouth and Reading found that their VLE, which provides a personalised learning environment, is vital to the student learning experience. ELearning is no longer just supplementary to the student learning experience but has become an integral part of learning. Both universities had strong central institutional provision for eLearning.

Participation in the benchmarking exercise has benefited both institutions. First, the completion of the IRD provided the opportunity to discover and reflect on the exploitation and embedding of eLearning in their institutional processes and practices, and the development of action plans for the future. Secondly, the impact of learning technologies on learning and teaching and implications for institutional resourcing were highlighted. Thirdly, it enabled the institutions to make comparisons between themselves and other institutions in the UK to inform future developments (Papaefthimiou, 2008). The results of the benchmarking exercise are confidential to an institution but comparisons were possible as the OBHE collated and anonymised the institutional results. Finally, the exercise had enabled the identification of strengths and universities could bid for funding through the Pathfinder Programme to build on these strengths and implement changes following from their action plans. Both Bournemouth and Reading were successful in their bids for Pathfinder funding.

NARROWING THE DIVIDE: CULTURAL ISSUES

The Pathfinder Programme helped Bournemouth and Reading Universities to narrow the divide between student expectations of a personalised learning environment and institutional provision, which was identified in the benchmarking exercise. Both universities provide a personalised environment through their VLEs and institutional provision which includes strong central support for eLearning. However, further developments were identified which could narrow the divide between student expectations and the institutional provision. The Pathfinder Programme provided the opportunity for these developments by building on institutional strengths identified in the benchmarking. The Programme was led by the HEA as "a transformation initiative which has organisational change, development and dissemination as its core aims. The goals of the Programme are focussed on exploiting and developing synergies to enhance and change practice where necessary." (HEAb, 2008) Twenty-eight universities participated in the Programme, which ended in May 2008. Bournemouth and Reading's Pathfinder projects aimed to support recommendations from the JISC Learner Experience studies which included "promoting active learning methods that go beyond a 'filing cabinet' use of a VLE" and "developing strategies to respond to the digital divide." (JISC, 2007)

During the Pathfinder Programme the twenty-eight participating Universities were divided into clusters of four. Bournemouth and Reading had expressed an interest in developing synergies in their bids for funding but they were placed in different clusters. However, the Manager of EDS at Bournemouth and the eLearning Manager at Reading decided to continue to collaborate during their projects. This collaboration enabled sharing of project methodologies and emerging developments as well as final outcomes.

CHANGING THE STUDENT ENVIRONMENT

To bring the student expectations and the academic world closer together Bournemouth's Pathfinder project "Innovative eLearning with e-Resources" (eRes) encourages the academic to use a range of quality e-resources in their teaching and the student to go beyond Google in their learning. Learners prefer to use Internet search engines rather than libraries for information retrieval (JISC, 2007). eRes has developed pedagogical frameworks which bring together learning activities and academically led quality e-resources within the unit of study. Most academics are making their lecture materials available to students through a VLE, and students find this helpful in their learning and the flexibility it provides (Newland, 2003). At the same time there has been a widespread introduction of linking to digital libraries from within VLEs

following JISC-funded projects (JISC, 2003). This potential has radically increased from 2007 with changes to the Copyright Licensing Agency scanning licence. This change has enabled short loan materials, which previously could only be used by one student at a time, to be scanned and made available simultaneously to groups of students. This enabled greater collaborative learning through group work either face-to-face or online with discussion forum and Web 2.0 technologies such as blogs, wikis and social bookmarking. Thus providing the learning experience expected by Net Generation students.

The range of pedagogical frameworks developed by the eRes project are illustrated in Figure 1: Student Learning Experience. These frameworks are embedded in the student learning experience and focus on learning with quality e-resources. These e-resources, such as scanned short loan items, e-journals and e-books, are at the centre as the project aims to encourage students to engage with other electronic resources apart from Google. All of the e-resources are available within the unit of study to give the student a personalised learning experience. The pedagogical activities using e-resources range from assessing, collaborative learning to the social construction of knowledge. Further details of some of these learning activities are given later in the chapter.

As part of its Pathfinder project "Driving Institutional Reform: Exploring Change with Technology" (DIRECT), the University of Reading has developed a framework to transform its internal quality management processes. This project has contributed to a change in the institution's Periodic Review process, shifting the focus on assurance and review of past provision to a focus on enhancement and continuous development, where the role of eLearning and student representation play a key role. This has led to Schools rethinking their programmes and ways of planning for the future. The aims of the University of Reading Pathfinder DIRECT Programme are a) to develop a process that will enable Schools

Figure 1. Student learning experience (Newland Et Al, 2008a)

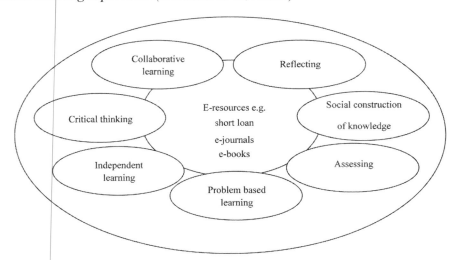

to drive enhancement strategically; b) to develop more proactive institutional support for Schools which will help staff engage with eLearning and the wider teaching and learning enhancement agenda; and c) to ensure that the student voice and experience is central to the design, redesign and review of programmes.

The Pathfinder DIRECT project has developed a process which supports academic Schools to consider their portfolio of programmes and to develop a culture of forward-looking improvement and enhancement using the harnessing power of technology.

Figure 2 shows a visual map of stages and processes involved in the framework. The rationale for the framework was based on our need for the methodology to be accessible, practical, flexible and transferable across the sector. The use of a visual map allows us to provide academic teams with a simple overview of the process and enables us to enter into discussion about their own objectives in engaging with it. The visual map represents the process as a journey and a cycle, to emphasise both the forward progression and the recursive nature of enhancement, and this reflects the 'messy, multifaceted and iterative' process of curriculum design (Conole, forthcoming). The framework allows different Schools to

engage with the process according to their own criteria. In a recent review of curriculum design tools (Conole, forthcoming), it was found that comprehensive guides existed, but most lacked a directive element. Thus a key objective in designing our framework was to represent the ongoing nature of enhancement. This allows different Schools to engage with the process according to their own criteria, their own subject and culture, and is also a journey which aids development and enhancement for academic teams using a series of resources developed for the purpose.

The Pathfinder process has two phases. The first phase supports Schools in the lead up to Periodic Review; this is followed by the second phase which is the longer term and ongoing process of enhancement. The framework is divided into the following stages: consultation, data gathering and review, reflection, consolidation, enhancement (Phase 1), the Periodic Review event, enhancement and evaluation (Phase 2).

Consultation

The aim of the consultation stage is to identify criteria, a schedule and timeline that will enable the School to clarify key objectives for the review.

Figure 2. The process developed at the University Of Reading

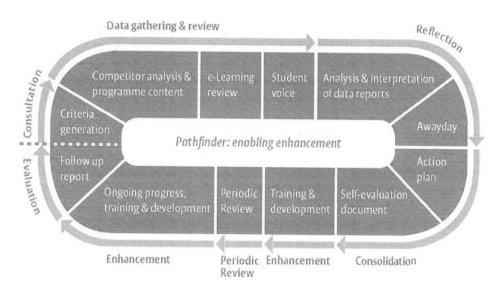

Data Gathering and Review

This stage provides an objective overview of the programmes in the School – a snapshot of 'where they are now', drawing upon: competitor analysis and programme context, eLearning review and inclusion of the student voice. The result of this process is a Contextual Review report, written for the School by the Pathfinder team, and which forms part of the documentation for the Periodic Review event.

Competitor Analysis and Programme Context

Using the criteria generated in the consultation process, information is collected about competitors, recruitment and admissions, student profile, student progression and graduate destinations. The process involves the extraction of the relevant data from sources both internal and external to the University.

eLearning Review

This section consists of an eLearning audit regarding staff skills and attitudes, an audit of online activity, and feedback from students. It seeks to identify how eLearning might be better exploited to address issues arising from data gathering and the review process.

Student Voice

The collection and analysis of student feedback is captured from existing sources such as the National Student Survey, minutes from Student-Staff Liaison Committee meetings and Schools' module evaluation forms. This data is complemented by detailed student reflection on programme provision captured through a student experience survey and focus group sessions, both of which are specially designed for the School in collaboration with the Pathfinder team.

Reflection

The reflection process has two sub-stages: the analysis and interpretation of data, and the School Awayday. During the Awayday discussions are held around the Contextual Review document and an action plan for the future is developed.

Analysis and Interpretation of Data

Data is analysed, triangulated and presented within the Contextual Review report. Information is presented not as final conclusions by the Pathfinder team, but as initial observations which inform discussions, and lead to the School's own interpretations.

School Awayday

A major milestone in the Pathfinder process is the School Awayday, which is facilitated by an external consultant, and the Pathfinder team. The aim is to arrive at a shared understanding through a collaborative process, which challenges assumptions, identifies strengths and weaknesses and develops a shared vision for the future.

Consolidation

This process is undertaken within the School, during which the academic team reflect on the process so far and develop a detailed action plan of enhancements to be achieved, how and in what timescales. This becomes part of the Self-Evaluation Document drawn up by the School and submitted to the Periodic Review panel.

Enhancement

The enhancement process can start immediately following the Awayday to address any immediate concerns. These are the short term needs that are addressed through training sessions and workshops tailored to the Schools' specific needs to cover eLearning, assessment, etc. The longer term needs relate to the creation of new programmes, and ongoing support for enhancement including the use of eLearning. The enhancement process offers an invaluable opportunity for teaching and learning support teams to work with the School at a more strategic level, and this is achieved by a process of ongoing engagement, where the Pathfinder team can draw upon other internal expertise and resources within the University, when required.

Evaluation

Evaluation occurs a year after the Periodic Review process when the School will be given the opportunity to evaluate progress and report on actions and progress to date.

The rationale for the change was to align programme provision with the student learning experience by effectively using student feedback and expectations in programme and curriculum design. This was the result of a number of initiatives, including an internal review of institutional processes, and actions arising from our involvement in the eLearning Benchmarking Exercise as mentioned above. Student participation is now strengthened by the inclusion of student feedback on programme provision; a student submission document commenting on the School's Periodic Review Documentation, and Students' Union support for students involved in the Periodic Review Panel. This level of student participation in a core quality management process represents a step change in its purpose, and reflects a real commitment to enabling enhancement that is aiming to bridge the divide between institutional provision and student expectations.

The principle behind the student data collection methodology used by the project is to move beyond the standard student satisfaction questions, and to capture a more holistic view of the student experience, including the development of their learning, the activities they engage with, and their perception of the quality of learning. Existing student data is captured from sources such as the National Student Survey, minutes from Student-Staff Liaison Committee meetings and Schools' module evaluation forms. Further data is collected using a Student Experience Survey developed as part of the Pathfinder project, and focus groups that include a section on eLearning.

The value of capturing the student voice is that it is subject specific, and is collected independently of the Schools. Previously, academics were responsible for data collection in preparation for Periodic Review. Now, student data is collected independently, analysed, cross-referenced and consolidated with other data to build a rich picture, provide objectivity and strengthen the analysis fed back to Schools.

CHANGING ACADEMIC PRACTICE

To help academics move closer to narrowing the divide between their teaching and student ways of learning, the eRes project aims to enable the majority of academics to take the next step forward by building on their current use of e-resources. Academics are now exploiting the new opportunities of accessing e-resources in the form of digitised library books and journals in constructivist learning activities. For example, encouraging collaborative learning with Web 2.0 technologies was made possible through multiple simultaneous access to e-books, e-journals and scanned short-loan materials. Students can study in groups using quality e-resources in a way that was not possible through traditional library lending to individual users. Students expect to work in groups so this is bringing the individual expectations and institution provision closer together. (McNeely, 2005)

Examples of case studies with a range of pedagogic approaches in different subject areas are shown in the Table 3: Case Studies. These case studies along with briefing papers on reading

strategies and staff development guidelines are available from the eRes web site (eRes, 2008).

In each case EDS worked with the academic to develop a project plan and support the project development and implementation. Student and academic feedback was obtained from a range of methods including surveys and interviews with academics.

An example of personalising the student learning experience is given by the case study on "Assessing Large Cohorts: The Evolution of an e-Assessment" (Newland, 2008). In this case study the Accounting students were able to check their own understanding and review their progress by the use of timed e-assessments on the topics being studied. This not only supported personalised learning but also made students aware of their own responsibility to manage their learning independently. One student commented that it was "Really useful being able to complete the tests in our own time. Takes the pressure off us." By analysing the results of the e-assessment the academics were able to monitor student progression and identify areas of weakness which could then be addressed. The academics initially invested time in creating the questions but these can be re-used each year. They also required support from a learning technologist to learn how to use the e-assessment tool. This case study is an example of narrowing the gap between student expectations and institutional provision through academics providing opportunities for online, independent learning with the support of EDS.

Another example showing how the use of quality e-resources can personalise the student learning experience is the case study on "Online Publisher Resources – An Integrated Approach to Enhance Student Engagement." These e-resources were online materials from Pearson Publishing integrated within the University VLE in a module in Business Studies. They included learning materials and online activities which were made available each week after the lecture in a "Learning Pack" using time-release functionality within the

Table 3. Case studies (Newland, 2008)

Pedagogy	Title	Subject
Assessing	A New Revision Format for CPE and LLB Students Studying the Law of Torts	Law
	Assessing Large Cohorts – The Evolution of an e-Assessment	Accounting
	Effect of CPS on Learning	Nursing
	Online Publisher Resources – An Integrated Approach to Enhance Student Engagement	Human Resources Management
Collaborative learning/ Social construction of knowledge	Collaborative Learning in a First-Year Occupational Therapy Skills Unit	Occupational Therapy
	Evaluating Wikis in Group Work	Archaeology
	Online Seminar Discussions	Psychology and Computing
	The UNICEF UK Baby-Friendly Initiative – Exploring and Sharing the Evidence	Midwifery
	Using Blogs to Encourage an Awareness of Current Developments and Issues in Services Marketing	Services Marketing
Critical thinking	Social Construction of Knowledge and Development of Critical Thinking Through Collaborative Distance Learning	Business and Management
Independent learning	A Virtual Infection Control Simulation - the Development of a Serious Game in the Healthcare Sector	Health and Social Care
	Introducing Blended Learning into a Biomechanics Unit	Biomechanics
Problem-based learning	e-Resources in Problem-Based Learning	Design Engineering

VLE. Using these activities the academic hoped that the students "would deepen their knowledge and understanding, encourage them to read more widely and develop their time management and independent learning skills." The online resources included e-assessments so the academic could monitor student progress. The feedback from students was generally positive. For example, one student commented "the Learning Packs were well-structured, and I believe they did help with my learning as when I missed a lecture or seminar I was able to use the Learning Pack to help with catching up, they helped a lot specifically with revising." Academic time was required to evaluate the e-resources and support from the learning technologist was vital. This support was particularly required at the start of the project to work with the publisher to ensure the online materials functioned correctly. (Newland, 2008).

The case study on "Evaluating Wikis in Group Work" illustrates the use of Web 2.0 technologies with quality e-resources in group work. Net Generation students expect to engage in collaborative learning. In this example, closed group wikis and discussion boards were used to facilitate the creation of group-based presentation materials. The academic hoped to increase student understanding of theoretical topics in a module in Archaeology by encouraging students to engage with quality e-resources. These e-resources, such as e-journals and e-books, were located by the students to encourage their engagement and to improve their skills in finding quality resources. The academic commented that "What I've done is given them the skills to be able to go out and get the papers and the subject information and process that." The closed-group wiki and associated discussion forum enabled the students to collaborate in a "safe" environment to prepare group materials for seminars. Some students required support in using the wiki as not all students have the same level of confidence with Web 2.0 technologies.

Some students were also initially apprehensive about editing each others' work. The academic is able to monitor individual contributions to the wiki and discussion forum and hence is able to view the process as well as assess the final product of the group work. The academic found an improvement in module results through an increase in student understanding of key concepts. (Newland, 2008).

These case studies show that bridging the gap between student expectations and institutional provision does require support from learning technologists, librarians and staff developers. At Bournemouth support from EDS was identified as a strength in the eLearning benchmarking exercise and this strength has been key to the success of the eRes Pathfinder project. Other institutions wishing to develop a more personalised learning environment to meet student expectations will have to provide this type of support.

Academic practice was changed at the University of Reading through academic staff reflecting on student feedback. Academic staff reflected on the findings, thereby using their time more efficiently and effectively to focus on the issues raised by students and consider how to plan the content and delivery of their programmes to cater for student expectations. This process has also enabled the University to provide proactive support to academic staff through assisting them to appropriately incorporate new teaching methods and technologies in the curriculum. This approach has already being used with three academic Schools. In one case student feedback has enacted plans to review the School's assessment strategy, and in another to use technology to enhance the teaching of a particular programme of study.

NARROWING THE DIVIDE: INFRASTRUCTURAL CHANGES

Strategic changes to narrow the divide include the new eRes e-reading strategy. This helps redefine the traditional concept of "reading for a degree" and builds on previous studies which focussed on enabling access to e-resources and information literacy. It develops further a recommendation from the JISC Learner Experience studies to assist "learners to develop skills of selection, evaluation and appropriate use of information" (JISC, 2007). By considering Brown's definition of student literacy described above it should help to narrow the digital divide (eRes, 2008). eRes also identified the support required by academics from librarians, staff developers and learning technologists so that other institutions could implement the required support structure.

At the University of Reading, the process developed has been embedded within the Quality Management Processes and more specifically the Periodic Review Process. The result was a shift from quality assurance to quality enhancement where the student voice plays a significant role.

Both initiatives followed the Pathfinder Programme focus "on the design, planning, implementation, and evaluation of transformation processes and activities which are intended to lead, ultimately, to the full and effective embedding of eLearning into the learning and teaching processes of the entire institution." (HEAc, 2008)

CONCLUSION

Students who have grown up in the digital age have new expectations for their learning experience in HE and there is a divide between these expectations and institutional provision. The eLearning Benchmarking Exercise enabled HEIs in the UK to identify their levels of provision and support for eLearning and to benchmark themselves with others within the sector. Following this exercise both Bournemouth and Reading Universities were funded to implement Pathfinder projects (eRes and DIRECT respectively) which attempt to address this digital divide.

The key outcome of the Benchmarking and Pathfinder programme was "building relationships" and the transforming theme was "directly empowering people to use technology to enhance practice, processes and provision." It "focused on eLearning, but has achieved a broader significance for quality enhancement and continuous improvement in all aspects of provision. There is increasing strategic recognition that technology-based solutions are integral to all aspects of the sector's business, with particular reference to the core activities of learning, teaching and assessment." (HEAc, 2008)

The eRes project is supporting academic staff and students in their use of quality e-resources for teaching and learning using Web 2.0 technologies. The DIRECT project's multi-dimensional approach of gathering and using student feedback has resulted in Schools revising teaching strategies and designing enhanced programmes to meet student expectations by embedding the use of eLearning. This partnership between the Schools and their students has provided the University with a genuine opportunity to become more proactive in integrating student feedback in planning and enhancing programme provision through the Periodic Review process. Both projects have challenged staff perceptions about student expectations and experience; and engaged them in development activities where the student voice is central

The gap in new technology adoption between school-leavers and the generation teaching them will continue to exist for universities in the future. Students in the future will continue to have new expectations for their learning experience. Therefore, institutions need to establish processes and continue to support educational development services that encourage institutional reflection and support appropriate adaptation and change.

REFERENCES

Bournemouth University. (2006). *Corporate Plan 2006 – 2012*. Retrieved 18 February, 2008, from http://www.bournemouth.ac.uk/about/introduction_to_bu/corporate_plan/downloads/corporate_plan.pdf

Brown, J. S. (2000). *New Learning Environments for the 21st Century*. Retrieved 29 October, 2008, from http://www.johnseelybrown.com/newlearning.pdf

Brown, J. S. (2006). Growing up Digital: How the Web Changes the Work, Education and the Ways People Learn. *Change, 32*, March/April. Retrieved 29 October, 2008, from http://www.johnseelybrown.com/Growing_up_digital.pdf

Caruso, J. B., & Salaway, G. (2007). *The ECAR Study of Undergraduate Students and Information Technology*. Boulder, CO: EDUCAUSE.

Conole, G. (forthcoming). Using Compendium as a tool to support the design of learning activities. In A. Okada, S. Buckingham Shum, & T. Sherborne (Eds.), *Knowledge Cartography – software tools and mapping techniques*. Retrieved December 14, 2007, from http://kmi.open.ac.uk/projects/kc-book

Educational Development Services (EDS). (2008). Retrieved October 29, 2008, from http://www.bournemouth.ac.uk/eds/

eRes, Innovative eLearning with e-Resources, (2008). Retrieved October 29, 2008, from http://www.bournemouth.ac.uk/eds/eres/

HEA. Higher Education Academy, (2008). *ELearning Benchmarking Exercise*. Retrieved 20 February, 2008, from http://www.heacademy.ac.uk/ourwork/learning/elearning/benchmarking

HEAb, Higher Education Academy, (2008). *Pathfinder*. Retrieved 20 February, 2008, from http://www.heacademy.ac.uk/ourwork/learning/elearning/Pathfinder

HEAc, Higher Education Academy Evaluation and Dissemination Support Team. (2008). *Challenges and Realisations from the Higher Education Academy/JISC Benchmarking and Pathfinder Programme: An End of Programme Review.* HEA/JISC

Higher Education Funding Council for England (HEFCE). (2005). *HEFCE Strategy for ELearning.* Retrieved October 29, 2008, from http://www.hefce.ac.uk/pubs/hefce/2005/05_12/#exec

JISC. (2003). *Practical Exploitation of Linking Digital Libraries and VLEs.* Retrieved 29 October, 2008, from http://www.jisc.ac.uk/whatwedo/programmes/programme_divle/mle_divle_final_reports.aspx

JISC. (2007). *In Their Own Words: Exploring the Learner's Perspective on ELearning,* HEFCE

JISCb. (2007). *Student Expectations Study.* Retrieved October 29, 2008, from http://www.jisc.ac.uk/publications/publications/studentexpectations

McNeely, B. (2005). *Using Technology as a Learning Tool, Not Just the Cool New Thing, Educating the Net Generation,* EDUCAUSE. Retrieved 29 October, 2008, from http://www.educause.edu/UsingTechnologyasaLearningTool%2CNotJusttheCoolNewThing/6060

Morrison, D. (2007). *The Benchmarking and Pathfinder Programme: a 'Basic Essentials Briefing."* Retrieved February 20, 2008, from http://elearning.heacademy.ac.uk/weblogs/Pathfinder/wp-content/uploads/2007/11/BenchPathfinderEssentialsBriefing.pdf

New Media Consortium (NMC), & the EDUCAUSE Learning Initiative (ELI), (2008). *2008 Horizon Report.* New Media Consortium.

Newland, B. (2003). Evaluating the Impact of a VLE on Learning and Teaching. In *Proceedings of World Conference on Educational Multimedia, Hypermedia and Telecommunications,* USA.

Newland, B. (2008). *eRes: Innovative eLearning with e-Resources.* Bournemouth, UK.

Newland, B., Beard, J., Byles, L., Cheshir, K., Dale, P., & Callard, S. (2008a). *Bournemouth University Pathfinder Phase 1: The Pathfinder Journey.* Higher Education Academy. Retrieved October 29, 2008, from http://elearning.heacademy.ac.uk/weblogs/pathfinder/

Newland, B., & Papaefthimiou, M. (2007). *Learning from the HEA ELearning Benchmarking Exercise.* Paper presented at the Blackboard European Conference, Nice.

OBHE. (2008). *Observatory on Borderless Higher Education.* Retrieved October 29, 2008, from http://www.obhe.ac.uk/

Oblinger, D. (2003). Boomers, Gen-Xers and Millennials, Understanding the New Students. *EDUCAUSE Review, July/August.*

Oblinger, D., & Oblinger, J. (2005). *Educating the Net Generation.* EDUCAUSE. Retrieved October 29, 2008, from http://www.educause.edu/EducatingtheNetGeneration/5989

Papaefthimiou, M., & Newland, B. (2008) How Embedded is ELearning? Benchmarking ELearning in the UK HE Sector. In *Proceedings of World Conference on Educational Multimedia, Hypermedia and Telecommunications,* Vienna.

Papaefthimiou, M., Newland, B., & Callard, S. (2007). *Lessons Learnt from Implementing the Blackboard Content System.* Paper presented at the Blackboard European Conference, Nice.

Salaway, G., & Caruso, J. B. (2008). *The ECAR Study of Undergraduate Students and Information Technology*. EDUCAUSE. Retrieved October 29, 2008, from http://net.educause.edu/ir/library/pdf/ers0808/rs/ers08081.pdf

Tapscott, P. (1997). *Growing Up Digital: the Rise of the Net Generation*. New York: McGraw Hill.

Chapter 6
Personalising Teaching and Learning with Digital Resources:
DiAL-e Framework Case Studies

Kevin Burden
The University of Hull, UK

Simon Atkinson
Massey University, New Zealand

ABSTRACT

This chapter describes the ways in which individual academics have sought to realise a degree of personalisation in their teaching practice through their engagement with the DiAL-e Framework (Digital Artefacts for Learner Engagement). The DiAL-e Framework (www.dial-e.net) is a new conceptual model, articulated as a paper-based and web-based tool, for designing learning engagements. The policy and theoretical context, evolution of the framework and the methodology used to utilise the framework with academic staff seeking to personalise the learning experience is outlined. Details of three case studies resulting from this early work are described and conclusions drawn as to how such frameworks might assist staff in thinking about personalised learning scenarios.

INTRODUCTION

Teaching in tertiary education has long been challenged for the endurance of a mass produced, content-driven transmission model of learning, unsuitable for the needs of the individual learner, and indeed the wider society it serves (Daniel, 1996). This has led some practitioners to explore the virtues of its antithesis, an entirely student-centred mode of learning based on an individualised or atomised notion of the learner with a minimum of teacher

direction or interference (Brandes & Ginnes, 1996). For some institutions and students the pendulum has swung completely from a prevailing transmission model towards an entirely student-centred, individualised model. The role of the teacher in each of these extreme caricatures is deeply unsatisfactory and ill defined. In the content driven paradigm, the teacher is centre stage in terms of the classroom dynamics but is often uncertain about what their role should be beyond the transmission of an established body of knowledge or perceived wisdom. Conversely, in the student-centred model the teacher is often disenfranchised and may feel left without a role

DOI: 10.4018/978-1-60566-884-0.ch006

as the emphasis switches almost entirely to the individual learner dynamic.

In the 1990s and 2000s a range of emerging research and policy priorities have impacted on this pendulum swing, between the teacher-focused and learner-centred conceptualisations of teaching delivery models. The adoption of Internet delivery mechanisms challenged the design of essentially print-based distance education materials, but has arguably fallen short in revolutionising the learner experience. Policy and practice driven initiative such as the UK Open University's CURVE (CoUrse Reuse & VErsioning) project from 2001-2004 (http://kn.open.ac.uk/public/workspace.cfm?wpid=5391) sought to refocus content design issues around contextualisation and presentation issues, emphasising rapid redevelopment and redeployment of resources. MIT OpenCourseWare (http://ocw.mit.edu) and the Open University's OpenLearn projects (http://openlearn.open.ac.uk/), building on earlier work by the CopyLeft movement (http://www.gnu.org/copyleft/copyleft.html) have made 'content', but not the learning experience, freely available, and have had a significant impact on senior managers and policy makers in Higher Education who have been left wondering what constitutes an 'asset'. UK government funding for the Centres for Excellence in Teaching & Learning (CETLs), such as that for Re-Usable Learning Objects (http://www.rlo-cetl.ac.uk/), have also provided momentum to the Open Educational Resources (OER) movement and increasingly impacts on 'frontline' academics' perceptions of the primacy of specialist subject content. Along with this growing acceptance that 'content is NOT king', there is a parallel and complementary development exploring the reuse and re-contextualisation not of content but of the 'learning design' or 'learner engagement activity' itself. Recent funding from the United Kingdom's Teaching & Learning Research Project (TLRP) for 'A Learning Design Support Environment (LDSE) for Teachers and Lecturers' (http://www.tlrp.org/proj/tel/laurillard.html) suggest a

recognition of the importance of this endeavour (Laurillard, 2008). Other innovations such as the Open University's 'Cloudworks' project (www.cloudworks.ac.uk), through which a community of teaching practitioners exchange ideas for practical learning situations, and the Digital Artefacts for Learner Engagement Framework (DiAL-e) described here, are attempts to see not just the content as malleable and versatile, but the patterns and practicum of learner engagement as equally flexible and transferable between levels and disciplines. Content and learning designs may be reusable and available for re-contextualisation, but how does one make them relevant to the individual learner?

What is 'Personalisation'?

Put simply, personalising learning and teaching means taking a highly structured and responsive approach to each child's and young person's learning, in order that all are able to progress, achieve and participate. (Gilbert, 2006, p.12)

The literature on personalisation is complex. In education, the definitions for personalisation are often synonymous with individualisation. Many commentators have noted the obvious problems such a definition poses and the impracticalities of achieving such an outcome in a mass education system outside institutions such as Cambridge, where the one-to-one tutorial system seems enshrined (Steffens & Underwood, 2008). However, terms such as individualisation, self-regulation, meta-cognition and personalisation are often seen to be aspects of the same notion, and it is important to establish a working definition along with some criteria, before attempting to establish and illustrate the relationship between personalisation and technology in this chapter.

Steffens & Underwood (2008) offer an interesting take on this debate noting the inter-relationships that exist between important core ideas such as self-regulation, meta-cognition and personalisation. Personalisation, they argue, is the current political vogue for policy-makers, emerging as it does from the literature around policy debate. The related notions of self-regulation and meta-cognition have emerged largely from a body of literature in psychology, inter-related with concepts such as forethought, performance control and self-reflection (Steffens & Underwood, 2008, p. 167). They contrast these features, which are largely learner orientated, with personalisation, which they characterise as largely environment centred, attempting to modify the environment to fit student characteristics. In the final analysis, it may well be argued that this is a largely semantic debate as personalisation, self-regulation, and meta-cognition are all part of the same issue:

...here our opening position will be to assume that the personalisation of learning and self-regulated learning are overlapping concepts. While the former act at the operational level in that it is concerned with providing opportunities for the learner, self-regulation and meta-cognitive awareness are subsumed under the individual's ability to take advantage of those opportunities. (Underwood & Banyan, 2008 p. 234)

However, this is not a definition that would meet with universal approval. Some authors have noted the dangers of accepting a definition of personalisation that re-arranges the deck-chairs but leaves the underlying structures and behaviours largely unaltered; "…personalised learning is not a matter of tailoring curriculum, teaching and assessment to 'fit' the individual, but is a question of developing social practices that enable people to become all that they are capable of becoming…" (Pollard and James, 2004, p. 6)

Here then lies an apparent dichotomy between proponents of personalisation who advocate a largely environment focused perspective, and adherents to a more individual approach who argue for self-regulation and meta-cognition. In effect, one position argues that the environment around the learner should be modified to fit the individual, whilst the other argues for strategies which will enable the learner themselves to become more flexible in their outlook and methodology when approaching a task of learning. Some defining characteristics or constructs of these alternative positions are listed in the table below.

These semantic discussions have influenced the policy debate around personalisation. Persistent gaps in attainment in compulsory education, and challenges in retention and completion in post-compulsory education, make the discrepancies in achievement and opportunity a matter of social justice. In many respects, our current education systems are failing. Clearly one size does not fit all in education and so the notion that each individual should have the opportunity to have a personalised learning experience has gained significant adherents. The 2020 Teaching and Learning Review Group (Gilbert, 2006) goes on to suggest that personalised learning is learner-centred, knowledge-centred and assessment-centred. As with contemporary politics, it seems, the centre ground appears rather crowded.

The political context is an important one. At the time of its writing in 2004, Charles Leadbeater, in his consultation report 'Learning about Personalisation' (Leadbeater, 2004), reflected the concern felt in many liberal democracies, equating personalisation with the ideal of 'consumer choice'. In this context, he described personalisation in terms of a response to choice. Leadbeater advocates the student's choice of how to learn, what to learn and how they are assessed, calling on schools to develop the necessarily flexible policies and processes to enable such choice. The need to recognise that significant proportions of learning take place outside the classroom, and that individuals have different social support mechanisms and access to technology are all features of the report.

The solution advocated is one in which teachers in compulsory education become 'brokers' and schools 'solution assemblers'. The focus is very much on institutional transformations, recognising the impact that such personalisation will have on policy and practice from national curriculum to funding regimes. The impact on staff is acknowledged, though doubtless inadequately, in the minds of those affected. Significantly, Leadbeater's report was subtitled 'teachers transforming teaching'. In subsequent work, David Hargreaves and colleagues at iNet (2008) have developed a descriptor of the 'means' by which personalisation is achievable, these being:

- Student Voice
- Assessment for Learning
- Learning to Learn
- New Technologies
- Curriculum
- Advice & Guidance
- Mentoring & Coaching
- Workforce reform
- Design & Organisation

These nine 'gateways' to personalisation are further grouped into four areas of 'deep learning, experience, support and leadership'. FutureLab research has focused on the role that learning technologies might play in developing a deep level of engagement on the part of learners. This is the level at which the learner has significant control of all aspects of their learning and so is empowered to:

- Make choices
- Initiate dialogue
- Develop equitable relationship with instructors
- Participate in systemic change

These concepts might be further characterised as personalisation enabled through:

- Choice
- Engagement
- Participation

- Responsiveness
- Flexibility
- Tailored experience
- Adaptability
- Learner Independence (BECTA, 2007)

It is notable that BECTA (2007, p. 1) warns "Personalising learning is not the same as individualised learning although it contains elements of individualised learning and one-to-one tuition. Nor is it letting learners work at their own slowest pace or a return to child-centred education".

The Significance of Personalisation in Tertiary Education

In Further and Higher Education there has been very little debate concerning professional transformation as a result of changes in the availability, mutability and reusability of digital resources. Indeed, much of the debate concerning personalisation in higher education has been linked with customisation of virtual learning environments, the development of personal development planning policies and the associated adoption of ePortfolio for personal development, and in some instances, assessment. These largely environment focused characteristics are identified in the right hand column of Table 1.

The apparent lack of willingness of much of post-compulsory education to engage with the systemic change to teaching practices advocated in the compulsory sector is regrettable, and rather surprising, given the imperatives of widening participation. The focus on personalisation in most universities has been limited to the responsiveness of facilitation technologies. Teaching practice and institutions (timetabling, room structures, environments, and flexible curricula) have been very slow to respond. Whilst we advocate a more radical reappraisal of the learning context in higher education, we also believe that there is value in addressing opportunities that digital

Table 1. Characteristics of learner-centred and environment centred constructs (adapted from Steffens and Underwood, 2008)

Learner-orientated constructs (self-regulation and meta-cognition)	Environment-orientated constructs (*individualisation*)
• Emphasises the development of self-regulating strategies • Forethought • Performance control • Self-reflection	• Focuses on modifying the 'environment' to fit learner needs
• Focuses on the development of personal meta-cognition strategies • Knowledge and awareness of one's own cognitive processes • Ability to monitor and regulate cognitive processes	• Emphasises choice but from a predetermined set of options (e.g. pupil voice) • Providing opportunities for learners to engage in pre-defined activity
• Promoting self-regulating tasks • (developing the capacity to chose what, where, when and how to learn)	• Freedom to self-regulate means of achieving a given task, but not the nature of the task itself
• Pro-activity: developing social practices and tasks to encourage the individual to take up the opportunities on offer	• Providing variety of choice to maximise potential (e.g. different pedagogies, teaching styles, learning opportunities) but the onus is left to the individual to make effective use of the choices

technologies offer in post compulsory education. To do so effectively will open up opportunities to engage in a wider sectorial discussion regarding change. Indeed, we would concur with FutureLab colleagues who suggested that:

Our focus in this paper on the role of digital technologies is not driven by a naïve or interested desire to extend the use of technology in schools for its own sake. Instead it is driven by, on the one hand, an urgent sense that without the use of these resources, it is hard to conceive how the systemic change needed to reshape the education system around the learner can be achieved; and on the other, an awareness that many learners today are already creating personalised learning environments for themselves outside school using digital resources. (Green, et al, 2005, p. 4)

These new resources and the tools associated with them will require the learning and teaching professions, at all levels, to adjust their outlooks and pedagogical models. James Marcum (2002, p. 202) suggests that the library profession must "expand its definitions of librarianship to include new forms of expertise — as happened for archivists and systems librarians — to encompass

the skills of presentation, content management, and visualization, and must recast the model of information literacy to embrace multiple illiteracies and socio-technical competencies". It will be necessary for educators in post-compulsory education to reconsider the definition of their role in the same shifting context.

A key consideration in this reappraisal of our role lies in recognising that the digital media and its presentational mode are intrinsically linked and that they should be seen as belonging to socio-technical networks, rather than just seen as tools. The result of this redefinition is that lecturers are not simply appending digital content to their established delivery model, but are changing the dynamics of a socio-technical network. They do this regardless of whether they do it consciously, but to be conscious of it affords new opportunities (Kling, 2000). This links back to the discussion about physical spaces above. Kling & Courtright explain this different conception of spaces in the context of an analysis of a high school, which could be:

wholly social, and focus on such behaviours as the formations of informal student cliques. Or the ensemble could be seen as wholly technical. The high school could be the subject of a technical analysis of its structures: the likelihood that it would collapse in an earthquake. A socio-technical analysis of behaviour in the high school would focus on a mix of social and technical elements. For example, if the classroom chairs are bolted to the floor in some rooms and not in others, one may examine different kinds of class organization and communication in these rooms with different physical capabilities. The structuring of spaces, such as rooms that are assigned to student clubs, may influence the ways that cliques form and how they manage their social boundaries with technologies (i.e., closed doors). High schools are neither completely social entities nor completely technological entities, even though social psychologists and structural engineers may analyze them as if they were. (Kling & Courtright, 2003, p. 222)

A socio-technical analysis of digital artefacts deployed into a learning context must take account of the social behaviour and the organisation of artefacts, from physical buildings or virtual learning spaces, from personal dynamics amongst learners to perceptions of lecturing staff in a thoroughly integrative manner. In recognising this complex network, one can suggest that personalisation is acknowledging the individual nature of the learning experience.

Case Studies: Spaces, Places and Personalisation

In 2006, a team from The University of Hull was commissioned by the Joint Information Services Committee (JISC) to develop learning and teaching support materials for one of the phase I digitisation projects, the NewsFilm Online archive (www.nfo.ac.uk). This is one of six projects sponsored by the JISC in the first phase of digitisation projects, which aim to make available to the academic community teaching and learning resources, which might otherwise be inaccessible.

In the case of the NewsFilm Online archive, the project has digitised 3,000 hours of Independent Television News (ITN) news archive materials stretching back to the early part of the twentieth century. These resources have been segmented into 60,000 clips that are freely available to the FE and HE community through an online repository. The role of The University of Hull team was two-fold in this process:

- To produce a set of exemplar learning and teaching resources and exemplars that would assist take-up of the NewsFilm Online archive amongst lecturers, students and researchers in Further and Higher education
- To develop a generic template for the use of digital media resources that could be deployed to support the take-up of other the JISC digitisation collections, both in phase I and phase II

The DiAL-e Framework is the practical manifestation of this second outcome. As a conceptual model for designing learning engagements it is a practical framework. In both its paper-based form and online manifestations (http://213.133.67.199/JISC/index.php) it is populated with authentic exemplars, which enable users to identify learning designs for the use of digital artefacts. The designs are cross-referenced to various learning spaces enabling users to identify learning designs by context (space), learning activity, or a combination of both.

Development of the DiAL-e Framework

No a priori theories or assumptions were used to develop the original iteration of the DiAL-e Framework. Indeed, there was little or no firm evidence to indicate how people might choose to work with the final NewsFilm online archive when it was originally conceived. Whilst it was felt that certain learning theories and their subsequent constructs were more important than others, no predetermined strategy as to how to develop the exemplar materials required for the project existed. It was strongly suspected (subsequently borne out in field trials) that users would probably revert to a certain default position in terms of how they set about searching for, and subsequently using, the archives they found. This might be expressed as the 'content default', in which practitioners identify a topic they are interested in (for example, the Korea War) and use a simple search facility to locate clips relating to this topic. They typically find a huge mass of vaguely related materials on their chosen default – in which case they probably spend a large amount of time unnecessarily filtering out the good from the bad – or find hardly anything and quickly become depressed and frustrated with the entire operation. Either way, it was hypothesised, practitioners would not see the full value of the archive or use it effectively without a more refined set of strategies with which to approach it. These strategies would become the basis of a toolkit, which was constructed early in the life of the project.

From a very early stage in the project, the development exemplars were primarily driven by learning designs or activities rather than epistemological considerations alone. This is not to deny the importance or relevance of such considerations, rather to recognise from the beginning that content alone should not be the driving force. Since the archive with which the project was concerned was considered by many to be an essentially social sciences collection (for example, news items from the ITN news collection) it was considered important to demonstrate that such materials could be used in a wide range of discipline areas. It was also considered important that the focus should not be limited to the content nature of the artefact alone.

The emerging framework tool was based around learning designs that academic practitioners could understand and use, whilst also recognising a valid theoretical underpinning. To achieve this, a number of principles were developed for the framework designs, these included:

- **Transferability:** the need to design a tool that could apply to any video archive, and indeed most digitised media assets
- **Content independent:** focused on learning designs and activities rather than the inherent subject matter of the asset itself
- Underpinned by an active or constructivist pedagogy
- Designed to facilitate a collaborative and community-based approach (as exemplified by YouTube)

Spaces and Learning Designs

The resulting DiAL-e Framework is effectively a toolkit consisting of a matrix made up of two axes, each relating to the different decisions educators need to consider before they engage with digital resources of this nature (see horizontal axis Table 2). A number of different learning spaces are identified (vertical axis), ranging from large (e.g. lecture theatre) through to small (e.g. tutorial), and including virtual spaces (e.g. online), practical spaces (e.g. a workshop), independent spaces (e.g. the library), along with mobile learning spaces (e.g. handheld and mobile telephone devices). These are the spaces in which learners will engage with the resources through the learning designs.

The other axis of the DiAL-e matrix identifies ten discrete, though related, learning designs. The ten learning designs identified to date are not exclusive and feedback from user testing suggests there is a significant degree of mutuality between the various designs. However, each design has a specific focus and relates to a set of activities, which will develop a particular skill or set of understandings, and is transferable to other contexts. This means that practitioners should be able to apply the learning design to other digital

Table 2. The DiAL-e framework in its simplest, unpopulated, paper-based form

Stimulation						
Narrative						
Collaboration						
Conceptualisation						
Inquiry						
Authoring						
Empathising						
Research						
Representations						
Figurative						
	Large	Small	Practical	Independent	Virtual	Mobile

resources and other contexts. The ten learning designs, described in further detail at www.dial-e. net form the vertical axis of the matrix illustrated in Table 2.

The matrix or framework tool is intended to be an iterative device allowing users to identify exemplars by a combination of the learning design and the spaces in which that design might operate. In the interactive web-based version of the tool, developed for the JISC Assisted Take-Up materials website for the NewsFilm Online archive (http://213.133.67.199/JISC/index.php), exemplars illustrating each of the learning designs are richly illustrated. These can be ranked by users in a YouTube type rating interface. Additionally, an upload facility exists, allowing practitioners and students to submit their own exemplars or re-purposing existing exemplars (along with appropriate commentary), which will eventually populate the matrix with more ideas and illustrations.

The Case Studies: Context and Background

The context for the case studies which follow, is a national project funded through the Quality Improvement Agency (QIA) to develop a set of digital resources for use in their educational online portal, The Excellence Gateway, as part of a professional development package for Further Education lecturers (http://excellence.qia. org.uk/). The project was designed to develop a set of exemplar materials for professional development purposes to encourage lecturers to extend their teaching repertoire using media rich digital resources. These included the NewsFilm Online archive, referred to above, and also the other phase I digitisation projects, which feature Nineteenth century newspapers, British Library sound archives, digital census returns, Eighteenth century Parliamentary papers and medical back journals from the Welcome Trust. The University of Hull coordinated the project, which involved participants from nine Further Education colleges across the Yorkshire and Humber Regional Support Centre (RSC) region, and staff from the RSC itself.

Colleges from across the Yorkshire and Humber region were invited to participate in the project by selecting up to five members of staff to undertake training and development. Funding was made available to cover up to five days of staff time. Three of these days consisted of a residential event to share the philosophy and approach of the DiAL-e Framework and to cover some of the skills and techniques required to re-purpose the resources. The rest of the time was available

Table 3. Evaluation criteria for learning engagement (derived from BECTA, 2007)

Learner choice
Depth of engagement
Degree of participation
Responsiveness of resource to learner needs
Flexibility of resources (across disciplines and learning designs)
Ability to tailor an experience for the individual
Adaptability of resources to context
Affordances of resources to promote learner independence

for participants to use flexibly, which included in-house support and coaching if required.

Although there were no restrictions attached to the original invitation, it was encouraging to read the successful bids, which covered a wide cross section of discipline areas and phases, including both academic and vocational subjects. The final colleges selected to participate in the project included staff from the following discipline areas: archaeology & history; modern foreign languages; media arts; photography; staff development; sports science; geography and adult education. The outcomes of the project itself are reported elsewhere (Burden & Atkinson, 2008).

Each of the selected colleges worked to a common brief to produce a set of personalised teaching and learning materials incorporating digitised resources from the collections described above. It was anticipated that the resources would be modelled around the learning designs that had been shared with participants during the workshop sessions, based on the DiAL-e Framework. The term 'personalisation' was operationalised with reference to the evaluation criteria for learning engagement (see Table 3). The project team has sought to explore how the DiAL-e Framework has impacted on the complementary roles of learner and instructor in their engagement with digital resources. Evaluating this impact in terms of 'learning engagement', the product of both parties' activity, has used the following categories for reflection (many of which relate to those advocated by the personalisation agenda):

Case Studies: Methodology

Given the iterative and developmental nature of the DiAL-e Framework itself, a grounded methodology was adopted to collect data and inform future developments, including the development of emerging theoretical models (Glaser & Strauss, 1967). Each of the residential workshops and seminars were filmed and individual participants were interviewed at regular intervals during the process of developing resources. Twenty individual interviews with participants were recorded in addition to all of the plenary sessions in the workshops and seminars. Additionally, each college allowed the research team to film an interview with participants at the end of the project in the college itself. The individual interviews explored the process of developing the resources and the influence of the DiAL-e Framework itself on participants. At the end of the process, the interviews also explored the impact of the learning packages in situ and, additionally, some interviews were conducted with students using the learning packages.

All of the filmed interviews and the plenary sessions were professionally transcribed and the qualitative analysis software, NVivo8, was used to enable coding of the transcripts along with the accompanying video records. The transcripts were examined carefully using an open coding system. These codes, and the associated family trees, which they were ultimately grouped under, form the basis for the descriptive and analytical accounts below.

However, other than introducing these evaluation criteria, the brief was left for the individual participants to interpret. In particular, the concept of personalisation, which has been discussed in the early part of this chapter, was explored in quite different ways by each college. In some cases, the approach was to personalise the environment by providing greater choice of resources within the Personalised Learning Environment (PLE). In other cases, participants chose to explore how media rich resources could be made more accessible to students themselves and explored the notion of self-regulated learning. These themes are explored more fully in the case studies and the discussion, which follow.

Case Studies: Analysis

For the purposes of illustration three case studies have been selected from the nine colleges which participated in the project. These have been chosen to illustrate the different approaches undertaken by participants in the use of the DiAL-e Framework and the digital resources themselves. The case studies are analysed through the personalisation constructs outlined in Table 1. They include an example situated at the environment-orientated end of the continuum, one at the learner-orientated end of the continuum and one that combines elements of each.

The case studies are situated in contrasting learning spaces. One is framed in a largely independent, self-study space or mode, one is located in a highly managed and controlled personal learning space, and one features a more traditional classroom learning space. Various technological affordances are fore-grounded in each of these case studies, but all three use the same set of digital media resources, mediated to varying degrees, through the DiAL-e Framework.

Case Study 1: Using NewsFilm Online Archives to Develop Listening Skills in Modern Foreign Languages

Background

This case study is characterised by an approach to personalisation, which is situated towards the environment-orientated end of the continuum featured in Table 1. It is located in a large sixth-form college in the North East of England, and features a highly structured learning package designed to develop listening skills as part of the A/S modern foreign language syllabus. Staff in the college had identified listening skills as a particular weakness amongst their students and noted a general lack of specific language resources designed to allow students to listen to authentic French accents. Video resources were felt to be particularly beneficial as they made listening more accessible for second language speakers, providing valuable visual cues, such as body gestures and lip movement, generally missing in audio artefacts alone.

The project appealed to members of the modern foreign language faculty because of the opportunity to locate authentic news stories in the NewsFilm Online archive exploiting news reports and stories featuring native French speakers. However, this proved to be more problematic than first imagined, as many of the native accents were described as 'too thick' for students to use effectively. The staff member involved therefore spent considerable time identifying stories and events containing native accents of a suitable quality. This would appear to be a strongly environment centred approach to personalisation with the teacher making considerable effort to modify the learning environment itself by selecting a very narrow range of highly specialised digital resources, rather than attempting to encourage the learners to widen their repertoire of listening skills in order to develop a more sustainable set of learning tools.

The final learning package incorporated a number of different digital video clips based around the football superstar, Eric Cantona, following his suspension from football for violent conduct in 1995. The subject matter was itself highly motivating and realistic for students, and featured a number of different French speakers, such as Cantona's lawyers, speaking entirely in their native language. The clips were re-packaged along with commentary and text provided by the teacher to produce a stand alone learning object which was authored in one of the CELT generative learning object tools (GLO: http://www.ucel.ac.uk/glos/default.htm). This produced a flexible, self-paced learning package that was hosted on the college virtual learning environment allowing students to access it at any time and from any location.

How was the Resource Used?

The approach of building a tightly integrated, self-paced learning package for students, exemplifies a number of the constructs typical of the environment centred approach to personalisation. Learners are able to select, for example, from a variety of tasks set at different levels of difficulty within the package itself. This is achieved by offering additional text prompts at various points in the audio commentary and by providing the option to read an English transcript of the story alongside the spoken French narrative. They are able to navigate both forwards and backwards in the package to retrieve information or clues from earlier sections. However, they have little or no choice over the task itself. These are fixed, and in many cases, answers are predetermined with multiple choice type answers. The resource emphasises learner choice – a construct emphasised in the learner-orientated column – but from a largely predetermined set of options.

Interestingly, the teacher was not inclined to allow the students to access and identify other video materials even though the college has a subscription to a French television service. Instead, she conceptualised the learning package she had produced as a tool to direct students through a series of predetermined tasks and resources in order to develop their listening skills. No data could be identified in this entire case study to support any of the more learner centred constructs of personalisation. Students were engaged in a variety of response type activities such as multiple-choice questions, drag and drop exercises and re-sequencing statements, which served to reinforce their basic listening skills through repetition and reinforcement. The resource does not encourage them to reflect upon their listening strategies nor does it attempt to broaden their capacity to 'hear' different native speakers outside of the range that has been pre-selected for them.

In terms of the DiAL-e Framework, this case study does not suggest it has been used as a flexible vehicle for student engagement (as it was designed). However, some of the learning designs do appear to have been adopted, and indeed adapted, to provide a greater degree of differentiation for students.

...I wanted to create something that was a bit more visual for them, and something that was differentiated so that they could all work at their own pace and at their own levels.

This is also an environment-orientated perspective on personalisation seen as 'differentiation'. It is the teacher who plays the central role in creating varied pathways for learners (e.g. by adding optional English scripts for those weaker listeners), but nonetheless the pathways are all fixed. There is little if any opportunity in this case study for students to identify and follow their own pathways.

True or false statements, multi choice comprehension, comprehension where they write an answer, gap fill exercise – from my point of view that's a good grammar exercise because they have to manipulate the language and the gaps would mean that they couldn't copy stuff straight off what they'd heard, they'd have to prove they can handle the language.

Although the resource was designed to support learners' work independently, the approach that seems to have developed provides few opportunities for learners to exercise, refine or self regulate their own performance, with little freedom to alter what is learned, where it is learned and how it is learned. Even given the rich learning resources that form the basis of this learning package, the students are highly directed by the teacher. There is a sense in which the technology is used to improve their existing listening skill set rather than to develop the capacity for more sustained growth in terms of listening skills that could be used in different contexts.

Case Study 2: Media Moral Panics and Youth Cultures

Background

Despite some similarities with the first example above, this case study exemplifies a more mixed approach to personalisation, combining elements of both the learner-orientated and environment-orientated approaches or constructs to the use of digital technologies.

Set in a large rural college serving a diverse range of communities across North Yorkshire, the participants produced a Flash authored multimedia teaching and learning package based around the theme of media moral panics and youth cultures from the 1950s to the present day. Students are able to select video clips easily within a visually stimulating interface. Using a wide selection of carefully selected newsreel clips and television news stories, the authors fashioned a highly flexible resource which can be used in a wide variety of different formats and spaces. Unlike the first example, users are able to navigate through the

resources in a non-linear fashion selecting a variety of open-ended resources and flexible tasks to reinforce their understanding of issues around moral panics and youth cultures.

The resource was produced by three lecturers from the media and journalism department in the college to support a BTEC (Business & Technology Education Council) national media award. They initially adopted a very subject focused approach seeking to identify a rather narrow range of resources from the archive to support a rather prescriptive range of teaching activities, all characteristics of the more environment centred approach to personalisation described in Table 1.

The motivation to produce the learning package arose from staff curiosity and the exploration of how to engage students with digital resources when teaching a demanding or abstract topic such as 'moral panics'. The regular reoccurrence in the media of this topic, and the nature of how it is usually represented, is not one that the students find straightforward. Yet this is an essential requirement for successful completion of the award.

The NewsFilm Online resources and the British Library Nineteenth Century Newspaper collections both contain rich and engaging content, which could be used to contextualise the abstract concept of 'moral panics'. Starting with news stories of Teddy Boys in the 1950s, Mods and Rockers in the 1960s and Punk Rockers in the 1970s/80s, the project team were able to assemble an impressive collection of illustrative resources with which to engage students in thinking about how the media represents this perennial theme or topic. The original intention of the project had been to use some complementary resources from popular sitcom shows of the time to contrast how the media reports these types of stories, compared to fictional television soaps. Unfortunately, due to licensing issues, this was not possible and the project concentrated instead on those resources from the JISC collection where the rights had already been cleared.

During the course of the production, the intended audience and purpose of the learning package altered quite significantly. Following one of the workshops held at the start of the project, a decision was taken to broaden the scope of the resource by making it available as a tutor-based resource for all colleagues across all subject areas in the college, rather than just a media department resource. This coincided with the decision to produce the resource in a more accessible format (Flash) rather than a proprietary one, which would limit access for students, especially off campus and via the college intranet. This was an important shift in many respects. It suggests that the influence of the DiAL-e Framework, which emphasises a non-discipline approach to the use of media resources in this way, was beginning to have an impact in terms of participants' thinking about and around engagement:

...we've looked at how this can be linked into Every Child Matters and other tutorial possible topics, which can be used across college and also more specifically for some areas, perhaps, history, sociology, English, perhaps, looking at how language has developed and different colloquial ways of expressing in the news reports that the young people have.

It also indicates (and this is apparent in the above quotation) a shifting perspective around the role of the learner with an implicit acknowledgement that technology, such as digital resources, can be used to engage thinking in a range of subject disciplines if the focus is centred on cognitive activity, rather than content alone. This is a central principle behind the DiAL-e Framework itself and one more inclined towards the learner-orientated constructs in Table 1.

As the project neared completion, the participants became ever more thoughtful about how they could customise or personalise the resource for different learners in different contexts. Indeed, they ended up producing two versions of the final

resource. What they termed the 'lite' version and the 'full' version. The lite version was intended for use by tutors across the college as a stimulus for discussion and debate. The full version was intended for media and journalist students and was constructed in such a way as to encourage greater student interaction, including the option to edit and re-purpose the materials in order for students to improve their own skills in production, interviewing, and research. In both versions, students were able freely to select stimulating and thoughtful short video clips around a theme or topic selected using a simple interface. The resource was open-ended in this way, rather than prescriptive as in the first case study.

Whilst this case study still emphasises many of the environment-orientated constructs around personalisation (for example, it provides a variety of choices for the learner and contains resources which have been very carefully pre-selected form a much larger archive – a feature of a modified environment), it is not entirely environment-orientated. The approach adapted by the teaching staff in the way they used the resource echoes many of the characteristics highlighted in the learner-orientated constructs. In addition to providing opportunities to self-regulate where, when and how the learning might take place with a resource such as this – all features of the environment-orientated constructs – it also promoted self-regulation of the task itself, a feature of the learner-centred constructs. Students are free to use the resource as a starting point for a variety of different learning tasks and staff often invited students to identify their own research questions that the resource might, or might not, support. Critically, in terms of personalisation and the debate central to this chapter, students were supported in moving towards personal meta-cognitive strategies using the resource as a stimulus. They self reported in their own learning logs, and in feedback to the authors, several strategies they had been encouraged to develop in order to reflect upon the resources and to examine further their thinking processes through the resources.

Case Study 3: Teaching Staff to Teach Using Digital Resources

Background

The final case study in this series reflects upon a very different use of digital resources and one located more clearly in the learner-orientated column of constructs.

This example is based in a large further education college in the East Riding of Yorkshire. The focus of the learning package was a staff development resource to support lecturers undertaking the college's in-house Postgraduate Certificate in Further Education. The member of staff responsible for teaching the certificate attended the initial workshops largely out of curiosity, interested to explore how digital media resources, such as the NewsFilm collection and the Nineteenth Century Newspapers might be adapted to support his programme. His primary motivation was to use the digital resources described above to enrich and stimulate students undertaking the accredited certificate. However, it is worth noting that his focus and perspective shifted quite considerably as he engaged with the philosophy and strategies inherent to the DiAL-e Framework itself, and in doing so moved towards a more learner centred approach to personalisation, which is the focus of this chapter.

This is one of the more complex learning packages to describe and one of the most ambitious attempted by any participant during the project. It was designed to illustrate to students how digital resources can be used to develop 'differentiated teaching strategies' whilst also modelling to the students themselves what this approach might look like in the classroom. Behind all of this, the author also aimed to encourage the users to become more reflective in their approach to teaching with these resources, setting them a number

of metacognitive tasks through the course of the learning package.

The actual learning package was a loosely structured 'model lesson', which trainees could adapt and use to structure their own lessons and teaching sessions. It consisted of various digital artefacts re-purposed from the various collections, including a selection of silent clips from the First World War (re-purposed from Remembrance day new-reels of the 1920s), various images of commemoration services taken from the 1920s through to the present day, and a selection of original audio commentaries featuring veterans talking about their experiences in the two world wars. Such sombre representations of Remembrance Day were then contrasted with a selection of nineteenth century newspaper stories reporting a more celebratory commemoration of Trafalgar Day (21st October). These re-purposed resources were made available to students as freestanding materials that they could use in a variety of different ways according to their objectives and needs. In this case, the member of staff involved was already very proficient in the use of multimedia for teaching and learning purposes and was himself, a lead instructor for other colleagues in the college, who were interested in using multimedia for teaching purposes. However, he was very interested in exploring the DiAL-e Framework itself, which he saw as having tremendous potential as a framework with which to support his trainee students in structuring and differentiating their lessons using media rich resources. His intention, therefore, was to produce a set of learning materials that would exemplify what a differentiated or personalised learning experience might look like from the point of view of learners. This was a very student focused approach with trainees adopting the role of students as the trainer modelled good practice through the use of the technology that he had developed for this project.

The resource itself concentrated on the theme of remembrance and commemoration. Although these were clearly valuable resources for a subject such as history, the participant involved was careful to avoid labelling them as such. To this extent, he linked his learning objectives for the teaching session to transferable skills, rather than content outcomes, and demonstrated how a resource of this nature could be used across a range of different discipline areas including not only religion, philosophy, humanities, politics, but also media studies, English and even sciences.

Most of the focus for students using these resources centres on the DiAL-e learning designs called 'Collaboration' and 'Authorship'. In each of these learning designs, students are required to answer a question or solve a problem using the digital media resources as a tool and resource around which to construct knowledge and understanding. The 'authorship' design differs slightly from the collaborative design in that it requires students actually to use and re-purpose the media itself, although this obviously requires access to certain time-based technologies in specific learning spaces or contexts. Students are also encouraged to demonstrate their understanding and grasp of the topics they have prepared by teaching somebody else. The emphasis on micro-teaching of this nature amplifies many of the learning designs we have incorporated into the DiAL-e Framework, which is itself predicated on engaging students in meaningful, authentic and challenging exercises.

The DiAL-e Framework played an important role in each of the case studies outlined above, in providing for a professional development conversation about aspects of personalisation. The case studies can be seen as examples of socio-technical activity represented by conversations in which it was clearly acknowledged that:

- learners are best engaged by carefully thought out, imaginative learning experiences, not by content per se;
- the teacher/educator has a central role to play in mediating the quality of the learner experience when technology is employed;

- the value of digital resources as a tool for engaging learners rests in the dialogical experience which is created around the experience (Laurillard, 2002);
- learners need the opportunity to reflect critically on their learning experiences in order to encourage them to change or alter their perspectives (Mezirow, 1978);
- the issue of space is critical, but largely unexplored: space is not defined solely by its physical elements, but rather by the user's perceptions of learning within a space.

In these case studies, three different approaches to providing learners with personalised experiences have been identified. The different ways in which each case study chose to 'personalise' the learning experience is evaluated against the criteria set up in Table 3 and is summarised in Table 4.

FUTURE RESEARCH

Learning Design models or matrices which aim to support educators to engage learners in meaningful, challenging and deep learning activities, in effect to personalise their learning, are set to become increasingly important. In the case studies above, we have seen evidence that supports the proposition that the DiAL-e Framework in seeking to meet this design need also has transformative learning potential for staff. In particular, the role of critical reflection and rational discourse is seen to bring about significant perspective transformations. These were tested in our workshops around the DiAL-e Framework, despite involving much briefer engagements than Mezirow (1978) might have advocated. We believe the framework tool has potential as a professional development device in contexts such as these, and we continue to develop it as an instrument for professional development support. The framework is currently underpinning the development and testing of an

Table 4. Case studies evaluated for learning engagement

Evaluation Criteria for Learning Engagement	Case Study One	Case Study Two	Case Study Three
Learner choice	Choice of when	Time-line access to selected resources	Wide selection of freestanding resource
Depth of engagement	Response activities	Choice of reuse options	Free digital manipulation of resource
Degree of participation	Structured and regulated – classroom engagement	Resource made 'open' via intranet	Open resource
Responsiveness of resource to learner needs	Need for visual cues in language learning	Curriculum alignment – media rich in line with expectations	Exemplar materials chosen for generic interest
Flexibility of resources (across disciplines and learning designs)	Use of GLO tool advocates re-use	Recognition of multi-disciplinary applications	Resources linked to transferable skills activity
Ability to tailor an experience for the individual	Self-paced materials – differentiated engagement	Individual free to manipulate resources	Individual repurposing freestanding materials
Adaptability of resources to context	Digital resources edited to fit delivery mode	Two versions of resource emerged to suit contexts	Open ended and unstructured resource
Affordances of resources to promote learner independence	Ability to replay, retry and reuse	Student resource designed for reuse and repurposing	Emphasis on individual response to resources

online taught postgraduate module for the JISC, which explores the issues in using and re-using digital content to support teaching and learning in tertiary education (http://www.hull.ac.uk/dial/). It is also being adapted to provide a pedagogical framework for a new European funded project exploring the use of digital video in schools (http://www.educational-concepts.de/projects/edutube.html). Further iterations of the framework are likely in the United Kingdom and New Zealand, as other digital collections begin to explore the potential of using the framework to support the take-up of their resources in a similar fashion to that described above for the ITN NewsFilm Online archive.

CONCLUSION

The DiAL-e Framework developed from a desire to encourage academic staff in post-compulsory settings to focus on pedagogical activities that utilised digital artefacts that would effectively engage students. Given a stereotypical large lecture situation as being representative of a traditional,

didactic, information-delivery, or presentational, approach to teaching and learning, the project sought to develop a range of learning designs that challenged this paradigm. An attempt to articulate Laurillard's conversational framework (Laurillard, 2002) in the light of the growing availability of digitised resources developed into a framework to support practitioners to move from their 'default' position, their preconceived notion, in relation to identifying, in a content-specific mode, what they regard as suitable resources. What has emerged has been a radical re-conceptualising of teaching strategies, borne of the transformative nature, not just of the digital resources themselves, but also of the process of engaging with a challenging conceptual framework, a disorientating dilemma.

The Digital Artefacts for Learner Engagement Framework (DiAL-e) and the case studies illustrated here suggests one approach to redress the imbalance between a whole student-centred approach and the traditional teacher-centred approach. This learning design framework does not advocate the use of technology to improve the efficiency by which teachers 'deliver' content, nor to legitimise entirely autonomous, individualised learning paradigms by the exploitation of Web 2.0 based technologies. Rather, it offers a rationale that emphasises the importance of the role of the educator based on the principles of 'dialogical conversation' (Laurillard, 2002), critical self-reflection and rational discourse (Mezirow, 1978). In doing so, it provides educators with a practical tool or instrument through which to structure engaging learning experiences and meaningful deep personalisation strategies, supporting independent yet collaborative learner engagement.

REFERENCES

BECTA. (2007). *Personalising Learning: The Opportunities Offered by Technology*. Retrieved October 28, 2008, from http://feandskills.becta. org.uk/display.cfm?resID=31571

Brandes, D., & Ginnes, P. (1996). *A Guide to Student-Centred*. Oxford, UK: Basil Blackwell.

Burden, K., & Atkinson, S. (2008). The Transformative Potential of the DiAL-e Framework: Crossing Boundaries, Pushing Frontiers. *Where are you in the digital landscape? Proceedings ascilite, Melbourne, 2008.*

Daniel, J. S. (1996). *The mega-universities and knowledge media: technology strategies for higher education*. London: Kogan Page.

Gilbert, C. (2006). *2020 Vision: Report of the teaching and learning in 2020 review group*. Nottingham, UK: Department for Education and Skills.

Glaser, B. G., & Strauss, A. (1967). Discovery of Grounded Theory. *Strategies for Qualitative Research*. Chicago: Aldine.

Green, H., Facer, K., Rudd, T., Dillon, P., & Humphreys, P. (2005). *Personalisation and Digital Technologies*. Bristol: FutureLab.

Hargreaves, D. (2008). *Personalising learning*. Retrieved October 28, 2008, from http://www.ssat-inet.net/whatwedo/personalisinglearning.aspx

Kling, R. (2000). Learning About Information Technologies and Social Change: The Contribution of Social Informatics. *The Information Society, 16*(3), 217–232. doi:10.1080/01972240050133661

Kling, R., & Courtright, C. (2003). Group Behavior and Learning in Electronic Forums: A Sociotechnical Approach. *The Information Society, 19*(3), 221–235. doi:10.1080/01972240309465

Laurillard, D. (2002). *Rethinking university teaching: a conversational framework for the effective use of learning*. London: Routledge.

Laurillard, D. (2008). The teacher as action researcher: Using technology to capture pedagogic form. *Studies in Higher Education, 33*(2), 139–154. doi:10.1080/03075070801915908

Leadbeater, C. (2004). *Learning about personalisation*. London: Demos.

Marcum, J. (2002). Beyond Visual Culture: The Challenge of Visual Ecology. *portal. Libraries and the Academy, 2*(2), 2189–2206.

Mezirow, J. (1978). Perspective Transformation. *Adult Education Quarterly, 28*(2), 100–110. doi:10.1177/074171367802800202

Pollard, A., & James, M. (Eds.). (2004). *Personalised Learning: a commentary by the teaching and learning research programme*. Teaching and Learning Research programme. Swindon, UK: Economic and Social Research Council.

Steffens, K., & Underwood, J. (2008). Self-regulated learning in a digital world. *Technology, Pedagogy and Education, 17*(3).

Underwood, J., & Banyard, P. (2008). Managers', teachers', and learners' perceptions of personalised learning: evidence from Impact 2007. *Technology, Pedagogy and Education, 17*(3). doi:10.1080/14759390802383850

Chapter 7
Personalised eLearning in Further Education

Elfneh Udessa Bariso
College of North East London, UK

ABSTRACT

Electronic media can contribute to personalisation of learning both in formal and informal contexts. Efforts are made both at individual and organisational levels in Further Education to harness new technologies to enhance personal learning experiences. Personalised eLearning supports contents, activities and collaboration aimed at meeting the needs and wants of the learner (Hill, 2004 & 2008; Coryell & Chlup, 2007). However, some technology critics argue that there is very little research to support whether eLearning is an effective approach to minimise the exclusion of disadvantaged groups in society, e.g. learners of English for Speakers of Other Languages (ESOL) (Webb, 2006). The author contends that use of technology could act as a barrier to participation in learning. This study was conducted to assess the extent to which eLearning resources promote integrative/explorative learner-centred Computer Assisted Language Learning (CALL). This chapter reports on the findings of a qualitative action research project involving one-to-one interviews with learners (n=12) at the College of North East London (CONEL) on their deployment of various new technologies (virtual and personal learning environments) in ESOL studies during the academic year 2007/8. Additionally, three focus group interviews were held including six learner interviewees each (n=18). Semi-structured interviews were conducted with four colleagues who actively integrated CALL into delivery of their ESOL sessions. Data was also collected from programme reviews, course evaluation reports and a research diary. The results of the study suggest that new technologies promote personalised learning when applied with careful planning even among learners who appear to be technophobic or are reluctant to use e-resources. Barriers hindering the integration of e-resources into the curriculum are discussed and possible solutions are also suggested.

DOI: 10.4018/978-1-60566-884-0.ch007

INTRODUCTION

This chapter tackles two main research questions: 1) To what extent can Computer Assisted Language Learning (**CALL**) promote personalised learning among low level English for Speakers of Other Languages (ESOL) learners in Further Education (FE)? 2) What factors can impact upon the use of CALL by these learners? The chapter critically scrutinises a number of new technologies applied in The College of North East London (CONEL) ESOL programmes and assesses their effectiveness in personalising learning to draw lessons for improved practice in the future. For example, out of necessity the CONEL ESOL programmes relied heavily on using the College **Virtual Learning Environment** (VLE), Moodle. As Wilson et al (2006, p. 10) observe that the hegemony of VLE "…is being challenged, partly from within education by the desire to bridge the worlds of formal and informal learning and to realize the goals of lifelong learning, and partly from outside education by the increasingly prevalent forms of social software and the new paradigms of the web as technology platform". The ESOL programme reported here employed non-VLE resources as well to compensate for the limitations of VLE to personalise learning.

The chapter is divided into four parts. The first part provides the background to the study and its context – FE and CONEL. This part also gives an over view of personalised learning initiatives and the use of new technologies in learning, more specifically, CALL. Part two presents the research methodology. The research findings are presented in part three, with an analysis of the types of new technologies (both hardware and software packages) applied and factors affected learners' use of CALL. In part four the lessons learnt from the deployment of new technologies in an ESOL programme are discussed. Finally conclusions from the processes of applying new technologies to personalise learning and the ac-

tion research process are drawn. Directions for future research also suggested.

BACKGROUND: WIDENING PARTICIPATION, PERSONALISED LEARNING AND USE OF NEW TECHNOLOGIES IN FE

In an attempt to widen participation in learning, the UK Government is aiming for 100% attendance in schools, FE or training until age of 19. The UK Government defines widening participation as "helping more people from under-represented groups, particularly low socioeconomic groups, to participate successfully in higher education" (Department for Education and Skills (DfES), 2006a, p.5). The Government is also aiming to achieve a 50% participation rate of under-30-year-olds who will have participated in some form of higher education by 2010.

One way of promoting widening participation is to personalise learning. The UK Government has launched various consultations and policy documents focusing on individual learners or potential learners to address non-participation, underachievement and skills gap at all levels. For instance, the FE white paper, Further Education: Raising Skills, Improving Life Chances (DfES, 2006a) argues that when learners participate in decisions affecting their learning experience, they are likely to participate more and play a more active role in the provider's quality improvement process. The sector wide consultation paper, Personalising Further Education: Developing a Vision (DfES, 2006b), aimed to establish a shared vision as to what **personalisation** means in the FE sector and how the full benefits of personalised learning can be reaped by learners, providers, employers and the country as a whole. The document defined personalisation in an educational setting as "… working in partnership with the learner and employer – to tailor their learning experience and pathways, according to their needs and personal objectives – in a way which delivers success" (DfES, 2006b, p. 7). In this study personalisation is perceived, as a task of providing every learner with fulfilling learning opportunities to meet legitimate individual learning needs supported by appropriate resources that promote choice, tackle barriers and advance learner autonomy.

The Government in its e-Strategy stated its ambition to harness digital and interactive technologies to achieve a more personalised approach within all areas of education and children's services, covering all sectors for five years and beyond (DfES, 2005). The Government also believes that personalising learning has an integral role in enhancing quality provision (DfES, 2006b & c). The central characteristic of such a new [education] system will be personalisation – so that the system fits to the individual rather than the individual having to fit to the system. In the FE context, "there is evidence that some colleges use ICT [Information and Communications Technology] to personalise learning. Some learning platforms offer basic personalisation features, and some colleges make use of ePortfolios for managing evidence of learning. However, the use of ICT to support personalisation is at an early stage and still has a long way to go" (British Educational Communications and Technology Agency (BECTA), 2006, p. 1). Whalley, Welch & Williamson (2006) and Hill (2004; 2008) contend that FE learners now live in a technology-rich information society in which they have to negotiate their place; so by not integrating new technologies into the curriculum, colleges run the risk of alienating learners from education and acting as if technology is irrelevant to them.

Computers have been introduced to the field of language learning since the 1960s. Warschauer (1996) classified the development of CALL into three stages: Behaviouristic CALL, Communicative CALL and Integrative CALL (Multimedia and the Internet). Bax (2003) also divided the three phases as Restricted, Open and Integrated

CALL, which correspond with Warschauer's three categories. Each stage relates to a certain level of technological advancement and pedagogical theories at a given time. Behavouralist/Restricted theory of language learning, viewed repetitive use of learning material as vital in gaining language skills. Thus, computers were seen as ideal tools since the machines could present the same task as many times as the learner wanted it to do so. The learner could practise at his/her own pace and the drills could be adapted to the level of the learner's language competence. At this stage, CALL programs were designed to provide a stimulus to which the learner provided a response.

The prominence of the **Communicative** in the late 1970's and 1980's reflected in the way CALL programs were used, leading to the so-called Communicative/Open approach CALL. In the Communicative language learning/teaching approach, the focus is on using the language, i.e. teaching/learning grammar implicitly rather than explicitly. Originality and flexibility in learners' output of language was more accepted than in the earlier approach. In this phase, computers provided contexts for the learner to use the language. These contexts could be asking for directions to a place or applying for a job. Nonetheless, Communicative/Open CALL was criticised that it used the computer in a disorganised and disconnected manner. The Communicative/Open approach was also blamed for the use of computer for trivial ends rather than essential aims of language teaching/learning. Although it overcame drills, skills such as reading and listening were still taught in a compartmentalized fashion.

To address the above criticisms, **Integrated** (ive) / explorative / CALL began from the 1990's by integrating the teaching of language skills into tasks to provide direction and coherence. This stage coincided with the development of multimedia technology (providing text, graphics, sound and animation) and computer-mediated communication. With the increased power of new technologies and availability of resources, computers became

Table 1. The three stages of CALL (from Warschauer, 2004, p. 11)

Stage	1970s-1980s: Structural CALL	1980s-1990s: Communicative CALL	21st Century: Integrative CALL
Technology	Mainframe	PCs	Multimedia and Internet
English-Teaching Paradigm	Grammar-Translation & Audio-Lingual	Communicate Language Teaching	Content-Based, ESP/EAP
View of Language	Structural (a formal structural system)	Cognitive (a mentally constructed system)	Socio-cognitive (developed in social interaction)
Principal Use of Computers	Drill and Practice	Communicative Exercises	Authentic Discourse
Principal Objective	Accuracy	Fluency	Agency

tools for extending the learning process and opportunities beyond the classroom. Multimedia / integrative/explorative CALL imitated the real world by integrating listening and viewing/seeing – augmenting the authenticity of learning experiences. The learner has more control on the pace and the manner of their interaction with media and content. Now many CALL programs offer links to clarification on various words, phrases or concepts concurrently. This feature enables the learner to engage in an explorative learning journey. Warschauer (2004) summarises these three stages in CALL development with the underpinning language learning theories and advancement in technology (Table 1).

ICT in education literature has reported numerous advantages of using eLearning, including: with the right resources eLearning can be accessed any time from any location, could widen participation by overcoming institutional low expectation about achievement of some social groups; provide learner autonomy to learn at their own pace; meet different learning styles; can stimulate learner's senses via use of multimedia and interactions (Hill, 2008).

Similarly, CALL literature identifies a number of benefits that CALL can offer. These include meeting a need to promote: (a) experiential learning, (b) motivation, (c) learner achievement, (d) use of authentic learning materials, (e) greater interaction, (f) personalisation or individualisation, (g) independence from a single source of information, and (h) global understanding, i.e. to facilitate the learners' access to and an awareness of the web and promote their active participation in the global community. Davies (2005) asserts that the main advantage of multimedia CALL packages and the Internet is that they enable the integration of all language skills (reading, writing, speaking and listening) into a single activity. Additionally, the learner can have a high degree of control over the path that he/she follows through the learning materials, which can augment personalised learning. These packages promote both asynchronous and synchronous communication between learners and teachers.

Nevertheless, as Lee (2000) points out there are several factors that hinder or promote the use of CALL to personalise eLearning. Some of these barriers and drivers such as attitudinal, situational, labour market and institutional impediments and promoters are discussed below in conjunction with the research findings.

eLearning at CONEL

CONEL is a large FE college in North East London based in the London Borough of Haringey. Its learners come predominantly from Haringey, Hackney, Enfield and other neighbouring Boroughs. The College has about 1000 staff and approximately 15,000 learners enrol per annum. More than 200 basic to advanced level courses are run every year. The curriculum offer covers ten sector subject areas, with a strong focus on vocational specialism. The recent inspection report of the Office for Standards in Education (Ofsted) concludes that **CONEL** is committed to providing the best possible education and training to all its learners, regardless of their prior achievements. Students have access to excellent teaching and first-class facilities (Ofsted, 2008). A 92% achievement rate in the year 2006/7 placed CONEL in the top ten percent of colleges in England.

In terms of **eLearning**, in the academic year 2007/8 CONEL had a number of ICT rooms and other support services such as the library and the Study Skills Centre with Internet connected PCs that could be used by learners and staff. Most of the classrooms were fitted with a PC and an Interactive White Board. For remote access, CONEL provided a single portal solution to create a virtual environment for teaching and learning for its learners and staff thorough its gateway called CONEL Learning Gateway (CLG), which allowed remote access for teaching staff in particular. A host of teaching/learning materials and other documents were made available via CLG (https://clg.CONEL. ac.uk). The College also had a four-member team of eLearning support staff. The team organised group eLearning training sessions and gave one-to-one support to staff, who wanted to integrate e-resources into their lessons. The College used Moodle as its VLE. Mobile laptops and mimio technology (http://www.mimio.com) were deployed where there was no PC.

The ESOL for Work Project

CONEL ran one-year new programme called ESOL for Work from September 2007 to June 2008. The learners on the programme studied English at Entry Level 1 or 2 to improve their English language skills so that they would have a better chance of securing employment. The author of this chapter (tutor/researcher) taught three groups of Entry 2 learners on the programme. The outcomes ESOL for Work are discussed elsewhere by Bariso (2008) and Cramb (2008). The overwhelming majority of the learners on the programme were refugees. Some of them had many years of education and work experience in their home countries. However, the majority of them attended only primary education and had never undertaken paid jobs both in the UK or their home countries. Most of these learners had little or no ICT skills when they started the programme. The course team had regular meetings to discuss schemes of work, learner progression, achievement and retention; whereby they also identified and shared teaching and learning resources. However, each lecturer was autonomous as to what resources and approaches to choose and apply in their classes.

From the outset the tutor/researcher tried to use new technologies in his class and encouraged colleagues to collaborate with him in attempting to deploy ICT facilities and collect data to inform practice and improve the quality of teaching and learning. This proposal was received with different levels of "enthusiasm". Some lecturers utilised new technologies to support personalised learning. Others found the use of new technologies too challenging to support learners with low-level English language skills. However, over the year all lecturers used ICT facilities in varying degrees. This chapter will focus on reporting on the different initiatives the author undertook to promote personalised learning through new technologies.

The claim that eLearning enhances language learning and meet individual needs has to be explored (Coryell & Chlup, 2007). Besides teaching ESOL and integrating use of new technologies into lessons and autonomous learning, the author conducted a piece of action research to document the instructional strategies.

Table 2. Barriers/factors affecting access to eLearning /CALL

ICT in education terms	CALL terms
Dispositional (attitudinal)	Acceptance of the technology
Situational (individual circumstances)	Financial barriers, access to new technologies
Institutional (policies and procedures)	Degree of e-resources provision
Technological (ICT/eLearning skills)	Technical and theoretical knowledge
Labour Market (employment opportunities available)	Availability of computer hardware and software

Research Methodology

This was a qualitative action research project that involved one-to-one interviews with learners (n=12) and lecturers (n=4) at CONEL regarding their deployment of various new technologies in ESOL programmes during the academic year 2007/8. In addition three focus group interviews were held including six learner interviewees each (n=18). Semi-structured interviews were conducted with four colleagues who actively integrated the use of new technologies into delivery of their lessons. As an action research project, this study was planned and implemented by the practitioner-researcher in collaboration with the learners and colleagues. Data was collected from learners during or after participating in technology-supported face-to-face ESOL lessons and follow up eLearning episodes or autonomous learning online. Data was also gathered from programme reviews, course evaluation reports and a research diary.

In this study Cross's (1981) and Bariso's (2004) categories of **dispositional, situational, institutional, technological** and **labour market** barriers/factors were used to examine how these factors affect learners' uptake of new technology. Cross's (1981) taxonomy of barriers to participation has been used and modified by various researchers in the field of ICT in education, including Selwyn & Gorard, 1999; Selwyn, Gorard & Williams, 2002; Bariso, 2004). The latter authors expanded Cross's three barrier categories (dispositional, situational and institutional) by adding technological and

labour market barriers. The framework enables to analyse the data on (potential) learner's learning experience thematically and classifies factors affecting access and use of new technologies under five comprehensive categories. The underpinning assumption based on participation studies is that these five sets of barriers are common factors that can affect access to learning, including eLearning. As stated above, these barriers are similar to the ones which are identified by CALL literature; see Table 2.

USES OF eLEARNING IN ESOL FOR WORK

As stated above, while teaching on the ESOL for Work project, the tutor/researcher used various e-resources with a view to personalising learning based on an assumption that one type of resource or method would not address the needs and wants of all learners. These ICT facilities extended from more basic text-based media to advanced multi-media resources. This section summarises how different resources were utilised to promote learner-centred integrative/explorative CALL or eLearning.

PCs, Laptops and Office Suite

PCs and laptop computers were used in many ways to teach learners both English language and computer skills. As authentic language teaching and learning materials they were popular subjects of discussion and also used to generate various computer/laptop related terms to build learners' vocabulary. The difficulty levels of vocabulary dealt with were dependent on the language level and IT awareness of the learners. Beginners named the main parts of a PC and a laptop and explained some of their major functions; while more advanced learners were engaged in detailed discussions of the hardware and their capabilities. These discussions helped with practising sentence constructions and analysing structures such as imperatives. Learners practised how to give or follow instructions. These interactions were related to the learners' personal lives, experiences, plans and aspirations.

At software level, the ordinary Office Suite packages were exploited to encourage interactive learning episodes. For instance, interactive worksheets applying text boxes were produced by the tutor/researcher. Jumbled up contextualised sentences, which the learners had to put in the right order by moving the text boxes were introduced. The learners also put words in the correct word order to form sentences (i.e. subject + verb + object/compliment). More advance learners put sentences in a sequence to form a paragraph(s) in a given context. Diagrams, e.g. parts of the human body or parts of a computer, were numbered and students were asked to type in the names of the parts or write their functions. These terms and structures linked to issues around personal development and employability skills such as healthy living and health and safety respectively. The learners were regularly encouraged to read, write and speak about issues of interest and personal concern to them.

The Excel package was useful to teach mathematical vocabulary such as rows, columns, cells, charts, numbers and arithmetic to integrate Numeracy into ESOL. The learners created tables, graphs and pie charts from their own project data to give presentations. They talked about their findings and questioned each other on project results presented on PowerPoint slides. The tutor/ researcher used PowerPoint slides with interactive notes and exercises. The "Track Changes" and "Insert comments" tools in Word and PowerPoint packages were useful to mark learners' presentations and other work in electronic format to give personalised feedback. The learners were consistently encouraged to develop the habit of utilising the spell-checker, thesaurus and "Help" function to improve their spelling, range of vocabulary and extend their explorative personalised eLearning journey.

Interactive Whiteboard (IWB)

Almost every CONEL classroom was fitted with an interactive whiteboard, a large interactive display that linked to a computer and projector. A projector projected the computer's desktop onto the board's surface, where the learners and the tutor/researcher controlled the computer using an electronic pen or a mouse. The board was mounted to a wall in front of the class. A learner or a group of learners came to the PC or the interactive displays to engage in eLearning activities or complete exercises.

Voting Pads

A voting system called Activote produced by Promethean http://www.askelite.co.uk/activote. html) was used to boost individual and collective participation in the eLearning process. Activote is an integrated personal response system, which is designed to promote whole class participation and enhance personalised eLearning. The system is meant for administering quizzes at the beginning of a lesson to establish the level of prior knowledge or revise past lessons or test comprehension during and at the end of a session. Each learner voted or responded to questions and debates. It was an instant method for finding out the opinions, thought processes or feelings of a whole class with clear feedback on individual learner's views and performance. The learners were anxious when they were told about using the device. Initially numbers were used to identify the learners. After a few sessions, the learners became more confident and did not mind if their names were used and displayed on the whiteboard with their responses. Everybody seemed to be openly discussing their incorrect responses before moving on. Setting up the Voting System was time consuming at the initial stage. Support from an IT technician from the ELearning Unit minimised technical difficulties. Once launching and running the system (by the learners as well) became an easier and faster process the technician's support was no longer required.

The learners used the voting pads individually to answer questions or vote on issues. The individual responses helped to assess individual performance or views. A pad was also given to a pair or small group to elicit their collective responses or opinions. The pair or group members discussed questions, possible answers or positions before giving an agreed response. Individuals were encouraged to debate and persuade their pair or group members in support of their personal views until an agreement was reached so that vocal partners or group members did not dominate. A time limit per question was specified. These discussions augmented learners' interactions, individual's participation and collective decision making. A spirit of healthy competition among pairs and groups always injected some sense of excitement. The learners commented that using Activote was fun and at the same time helped them to concentrate on general points as well as details in the lessons. "During discussions I learnt many new things from other students," said, Abdi. The tutor/researcher gave feedback on responses and moved onto new materials or revised any issues that the learners did not understand.

Using Activote the answers of each learner could be saved for retrieval later, individually or as the whole class. Results could also be exported to the Excel software package for record keeping and further analysis as necessary. The tutor/researcher and the learners used these results in one-to-one tutorials and review meetings to assess learner progress and negotiate new individual learning targets.

DS-2 Digital Voice Recorder

In order to give the learners opportunities to practise their speaking skills, particularly pronunciation, the tutor/researcher borrowed the DS-2 digital voice recorders from the ELearning Unit. This recorder compresses data and records 22 hours of sound into its 64MB flash memory. The learners recorded their own pronunciation practice or conversations with classmates. They listened to the recordings as many times as they wanted by rewinding and replaying. The learners could delete and re-record their conversations.

Recordings were stored on the DS-2 folders. The folders could be named and each recording was marked with the time and date. The recordings could be easily downloaded to a computer or any digital storage device. The learners also uploaded their recordings to a website and sent it to their email accounts. Pressing the Rec button again while recording, paused the recording – on the one hand giving flexibility, particularly for nervous learners; on the other hand, many learners paused recording by mistake and missed recording important discussions, which often caused a roar of laughter by some and fury and frustration to others depending on their temperament. Furthermore, in noisy classrooms the recording quality was poor. However, the learners could find themselves a quieter corner and utilise the tool. Generally this device supported the learners to experiment with their voices, tones and intonations. Some even recorded themselves singing songs in English as well as other languages.

WORLD WIDE WEB (WWW)

During the course, a number of websites, which are meant to support ESOL or English as a Foreign Language (EFL) learners, were used. The quality of these websites varies; therefore, the tutor/researcher was selective as to what site or which parts of a site were exploited. The majority of the learners found these websites useful as supplementary materials or self study resources. The colleagues whom the tutor/researcher interviewed also confirmed that they used some of these websites listed in Table 3.

Besides referring the learners to websites or asking them to find one to amass information and complete exercises, the tutor/researcher also asked them to undertake webquest whereby the learners both individually and in groups had to visit websites and analyse their formats and contents. While beginner learners focused on simpler or surface level aspects such as the quality of the images and text density, more advanced learners evaluated the design and contents at a deeper level. Part of this exercise was raising learners' web search skills so that they would know how to sift through information overload and be able to locate the right resources. They were encouraged to critically evaluate and triangulate the pieces of information they found before utilising them. Search engines such as Google, Yahoo and Everyclick with search strategies, were utilised to assist learners locate and choose information on the web.

Email

Learners who did not have email accounts were assisted to open Internet-based free accounts on Googlemail, Hotmail or Yahoo. This was also part of their form filling practice. Originally, the tutor/researcher gave his College email account for the learners to correspond with him. However, since this account kept filling up and messages bounced, he opened a new Googlemail account dedicated to this purpose. Email correspondence made the learner-leaner and teacher-learner interactions much easier. The learners and the tutor/ researcher asked each other questions; answered

each other's enquiries; and sent reminders, comments and feedback. The learners sent apologies for absence and requested learning resources to be emailed to them. Although the focus of using this media was communicating a message or idea, some comments were made on inaccuracies and vagueness of email messages both by the learners and tutor/researcher. Shang (2007) reported how using email improved writing skills (syntactic complexity and grammatical accuracy) among EFL learners in Taiwan.

Moodle

CONEL used Moodle as its VLE (https://clg. CONEL.ac.uk/VLE/) Moodle is an open source package meant to help educators create online courses with opportunities for rich interaction (http://moodle.com). The tutor/researcher created notes and activities for classes and uploaded them onto Moodle so that the learners could access the materials while they were at CONEL or off site. Various social course activities on Moodle such as chat rooms, forums, wiki and workshop were beneficial in supporting both individual and social learning. The learners found interactive activities more engaging and motivating than those based on static materials. The former promoted learner-learner and learner-tutor interactions. They enabled the learners and the tutor/researcher to make contributions, share ideas and resources together thus enhancing personal and social learning, which in turn, augmented learners' motivation, participation and satisfaction.

The chat module in Moodle provided a chat room where learners could have real time online chats in a secure environment. Some learners took part in chats regularly while others joined in whenever they could. Past chats were saved and learners could read them at their convenience. The tutor/researcher encouraged the learners to discuss educational issues such as their assignments, the course or future job search plans and current issues that could affect them, such as the economy and

Table 3.

Website	Description
Read and write plus http://www.dcsf.gov.uk/readwriteplus/	The "read.write.plus" website was set up by the Adult Basic Skills Strategy Unit at the Department for Children Schools and Families. It aims to be the main source of information and advice on all aspects of implementing Skills for Life (the national strategy for improving adult literacy and numeracy skills). The site includes an employer kit, which supplies techniques for identifying literacy and numeracy needs within an organisation. There is also information on: publications, events, surveys, research development and planning; policy documents and learning materials.
The NLN materials http://www.nln.ac.uk	The NLN Materials are small, flexible 'bite-sized' episodes of eLearning. They are not whole courses but are designed to support a wide range of subject and topic areas. The materials adopt a range of approaches involving some knowledge acquisition, a chance to practise and absorb and assessment tools to check that the subject learnt has been understood.
Training Adult Literacy, ESOL and Numeracy Teachers (TALENT) www.talent.ac.uk	The talent website is a one-stop-shop for Skills for Life teachers across the UK. It stores teaching/eLearning resources and encourages tutors to contribute eLearning resources to the site and share materials with other practitioners. The site links to interactive multimedia sites such as London online (http://www.talent.ac.uk/londononline/welcome/home/index.htm). It also gives advice on training options.
FERL http://ferl.becta.org.uk/	FERL information service provides resources for supporting the use of ICT and eLearning in the classroom in Further Education. This website contains sample materials and related web links across a range of disciplines.
Skills workshop http://www.skillsworkshop.org/e2esol.htm	Skills workshop provides notes, lesson plans and worksheets mapped against the ESOL/Literacy Core curriculum and set at different levels.
BBC World Service – Learning English http://www.bbc.co.uk/worldservice/learningenglish/index.shtml	The site includes vocabulary in the news explained, 'watch and listen', grammar and vocabulary, business English, English quizzes, pronunciation tips (including audio downloads).
a4esl http://a4esl.org/	a4esl presents quizzes (bilingual, vocabulary, grammar), tests, exercises and crossword puzzles. It has teacher resources and also learner materials for practice.
One Stop English http://www.onestopenglish.com/	This website One Stop English comprises: teacher's letters, "Ask the Authors", teachers questions answered, lesson shares (activities written by teachers for teachers), hundreds of worksheets and a forum; useful resource for teachers.
English Online http://www.english-online.org.uk/index.html	This site includes: free English language courses, English language games, and links to English newspapers. A basic resource with a few handy exercises.
ESL Teacher Resources http://bogglesworldesl.com/	The site publishes, Worksheets, Flashcards and jobs for ESL and TEFL teachers.
British Council English Site http://www.learnenglish.org.uk/	Learn English is a free site from the British Council that helps learners and teachers of English. It contains practice exams, 'Theme Weeks', listening downloads, tips for teachers (articles, lesson plans, teaching tips, support for newly qualified teachers). This is a useful site for both teachers and learners.
BBC RAW http://www.bbc.co.uk/raw/	This website is for the BBC's adult literacy campaign. It has games and quizzes.
At Work http://www.bbc.co.uk/atwork/	It offers a range of free resources targeted at employees who may wish to improve their essential skills. By using an innovative mix of online, CD ROM and magazine resources, employees are expected to brush up on their ICT, financial literacy and essential word and number skills.

politics. The level of participation varied from some learners making very little contribution to others almost dominating the interactions. However, as Loewen & Erlam (2006) found even low level language learners perform communicative tasks in chartrooms, suggesting that this mode of communication will continue to be useful to learners and research at all levels.

The learners and the tutor/researcher also used forums to discuss different topics to follow up discussions from issues raised in class or current affairs that most learners were likely to be aware of. Learners were also persuaded to introduce any topic of common interest to the group.

The wiki module enabled learners to collaborate on book like writing projects. Wiki based documents were easy to use and interactive as they could be created, edited and organised by date. Wiki also served as a tool for informal discussions among the learners, which proved a very helpful means for recording the thoughts and progress of the learners. Wiki could also be searched and helped learners to locate any specific issue they were interested in. Some learners used a single learner wiki as their personal journal, which could be seen by the entire class as opposed to a journal, which can be viewed only by the learner and tutor. Although some learners found accessing Moodle remotely challenging due to security settings and the complexity of the package, generally this VLE supported both individualised and group eLearning.

Some of the difficulties that the learners experienced utilising Moodle included inability to access the package, especially from outside the College, restrictions on what learners could and could not do and a lack of access to Internet connected devices. Consequently, some learners preferred using non VLE or non Moodle based resources. In the interviews, learners stated that they always felt that what they did on the College VLE was more monitored and restricted their freedom to personalise their learning compared to what they could do with what could be called more Personal Learning Environments (PLEs) offered by Web 2.0.

In contrast, the currently dominant designs of VLE are criticised for a number of shortcomings. Generally, the VLE design makes it difficult to share contents among courses even within the same VLE. The subordinate capabilities given to learners can restrict their creativity, participation and responsibility for their own learning, making them more passive consumers rather than being active users or producers of knowledge. The homogeneity of the VLE design forces all learners to experience the same system, contents and functionalities, which can hinder personalised lifelong learning experience consciously aimed at meeting individual needs and addressing personal concerns.

Recognising this limitation in the VLE design the tutor/researcher integrated use of various opportunities provided by Web 2.0 such as wiki, weblog, photo and video galleries. Web design templates and Skype *(*www.skype.com) were also incorporated.

Web 2.0 (Wiki, Weblog, etc.)

As Wilson et al (2006) argue that in the field of education technology there is excessive focus on supporting, improving and applying the technology of the VLE or a Learning Management System (LMS) such as WebCT/Blackboard or open source varieties, e.g. Moodle and Sakai. These writers assert that this focus ignores or even marginalises many other emerging new technologies such as weblogs, wikis and social software packages, which have been widely adopted and utilised by numerous people outside educational contexts. In their view these emerging new technologies the ideals of lifelong learning and personalised learning.

Wiki

The tutor/researcher created wiki specific spaces for each class to overcome the difficulties they had in accessing the Moodle-based wiki remotely. Learners were invited via their email addresses to access the class wiki sites which were created at open sources such as wiki.zoho.com, read guidelines and complete projects. Wiki was mainly used to undertake joint projects where the learners were asked to share their work with classmates or comment on each others' work. The joint project included compiling an international recipe book and the "Global Class" book. The international recipe book was a compilation of recipes from different countries where the learners contributed a recipe or two from their own country. The "Global Class" book was a document created from notes added by the learners about their own countries.

Weblog

Although different weblog sites were tried, blogger.com was the main site exploited. Having created a class weblog site, the tutor/researcher invited the learners to the site via their email addresses to join the class weblog, introduce themselves, answer questions, comment on each others postings and initiate topics for discussion. The learners were also taught how to open their own weblog sites if they wished to do so. Weblog was a useful instrument in supporting learners to publish their own diaries over the Internet, make comments on each other's entries, and initiate new topics for discussion. Weblog was also a good medium for sharing information and resources. Similar to the findings of Ducates & Lomicka (2008) the use of weblog enhanced reading and writing skills, a sense of ownership and creativity among the learners.

Photo/Video Galleries (Ringo, Flickr, YouTube)

A number of learners were introduced to the shared online video/photo galleries such as Flickr and Ringo (the latter is now discontinued) for accessing digital resources relevant to their area of interest. Some learners were already familiar with these sites and helped to persuade others to utilise these sites. YouTube has several video clips on diverse English language lessons presented in rich motivating multimedia. The learners could watch these clips as many times as they wished whenever they had access to an Internet connected PC.

Social Bookmarks (http://delicious. com and http://www.furl.net/)

The tutor/researcher and the learners experimented with the use of social bookmarks such as delicious and furl. Many learners liked these facilities as they allow them to access their 'favourite sites' from wherever they could access the Internet. These sites were seen as a good way to organise all their web links and make notes so that they could recall the relevant contents. The bookmark sites also allowed users to share their links and to discover more links. If they did not want to share their web links with other people they still could keep them private. Although some learners stated in the interviews that typing details of websites and descriptions of their contents were tedious and time consuming, generally the bookmark facilities were seen as good organisational resources.

Freewebs

In order to introduce learners to the concept of web design and also "mashup" or connect various relevant sites, a range of free web design and hosting sites were exploited. Hover, most learners found freewebs (http://members.freewebs.com/) numerous functionalities easy to use. The Freewebs site includes blogs, forums, wikis, calendars, guest books, web store, photo gallery, links, web forms, widgets, games, puzzles, videos and hundreds of designer templates. The learners' websites could also be password protected - one of the features which made it very popular among the learners. Usually the learners produced contents related to personal information, education, entertainment, jobs, family, friends and their countries. To coordinate contents in different locations learners linked their freewebs sites to other sites (e.g. http://flickr.com/, http://www.ringo.com/, delicious (http://www.del.icio.us.com/) and YouTube (http://www.youtube.com/).

Skype

After it was released in 2003, Skype (www.skype.com) has increasingly become a user-friendly, Voice over Internet Protocol (VoIP) software. The software package allows users to make voice calls free anywhere in the world from computer to computer, or for a small fee (for calls to a regular phone or mobile phone). With its free voice, chat, audio conferencing and video conferencing features, Skype can support learners through online tutoring both for one-to-one and group tutorials. The tutor/researcher tried online support with three learners who volunteered to test the facility. The volunteers and the tutor/researcher communicated via voice and text chat to clarify issues, discuss assignments and explore Internet sites with English language lessons. The volunteering learners found Skype cheap and easy to use.

To conclude this section, although the functions of non-Moodle-based wikis and weblogs were similar to that of Moodle, learners found the latter to be easily accessible especially when accessing resources from outside CONEL. Learners also felt that the VLE belonged to the College and they might not be able to access it once they finished their course, whereas they saw the PLE as their own. But this trust was a bit shaken among some learners when Ringo announced that they were discontinuing their free service and the contents on Ring had to be relocated somewhere else.

FACTORS AFFECTING ELEARNING

This section summarises dispositional, situational, institutional, technological and labour market issues encountered while deploying new technologies to personalise eLearning among ESOL learners at CONEL.

Concerning dispositional factors, the overwhelming majority of the learners had positive dispositions to new technologies. Even those who had very low ICT skills were prepared to try learning the skills or learning English via technology. With the support and encouragement they were given, even those who were reluctant at the beginning became more engaged in trying to attain ICT skills and ICT based ESOL. However, a very small minority of learners were very reluctant to learn and use ICT skills. Mostly such learners were older and sceptical about the usefulness of learning in general and eLearning in particular to them. Ahmed said he was too old and did not think that learning English and ICT would help him in anyway to find a job or do something useful with ICT. He summed up his view saying, "I'm just waiting for my retirement". Such learners were usually forced by job centres to attend the programme. Colleagues who were interviewed for this study also reported a similar pattern of the majority of learners showing an interest in embracing new technologies and a very few demonstrating reluctance. Thus generally motivation did not seem to be an obstacle for harnessing new technologies for personalising learning among the target learners.

Regarding situational factors, a number of learners indicated that their personal circumstances affected their ability to learn and use ICT skills or improve their English via technology. They reported that they did not have access to ICT facilities at home or near their home. Some of those who had the facilities at home said that as they had to share them with other family members, their access to ICT was limited. A lack of access to ICT off site made it difficult for the learners to participate in online communication via email, weblog or wiki-based projects. The learners reported that due to their low income they could not purchase the hardware or software they needed to fully exploit new technologies. Again, colleagues reported similar situational barriers experienced by a number of their learners. One teacher commented that now, most learners were willing to use ICT, but most of them could not afford to buy the necessary equipment.

In relation to institutional factors, the learners reported that access to new technologies and staff support to utilise them at CONEL was very good. Learners could use ICT facilities in their scheduled CALL sessions, Centenary Learning Centre, IT Rooms and the Study Skills Centre. A few learners reported that they were frustrated that their usernames and passwords did not work. Nine learners stated that they were not able to access the College Moodle remotely. On many occasions, the freewebs site was blocked by the College IT security system and the learners could not work on their websites. On a few occasions even the BBC English language web pages were blocked by the security system. However, the College ICT Services dealt with the difficulties and resolved them. Most learners did not rely on external ICT access points such as public libraries and Internet cafes, whilst a few did. Quite often libraries were busy and offered a maximum of one hour access a day that had to be booked in advance. Internet cafes charged, which discouraged many low income learners from accessing them.

With reference to technological factors, these appeared to be major issues that determined the level of learners' use of new technologies. Not surprisingly, the learners who had intermediate or advanced ICT skills were able to understand how to operate new resources or more willing to experiment with them. They were more likely to take initiative to work out problems by seeking solutions from the technology itself, e.g. surfing the Internet or referring to other sources other than relying on the tutor/researcher. The capacity or the nature of technology contributed to difficulties experienced by the learners. For example, while it was encouraging to have mobile laptops that could be taken to any classroom in the College, the laptops' slow wireless connection to the Internet was discouraging. Additionally many learners unfamiliar with the inbuilt mouse on the laptops found them very problematic to use. The sluggishness of some Activote also disappointed several learners and the tutor/researcher. A lot of learners had to

open a new email account, website or weblog site many times because their username or password was rejected sometimes for unexplained reasons. Sometimes it took frustratingly a long time to open an email account, specially on Googlemail as the system failed to create one for no obvious reason or explanation. The error message simply read, "This account cannot be created".

Nonetheless, overall the learners felt that new technologies helped them to express themselves and have their own products in cyberspace. Khwame (a middle aged male) said, "Until last week I thought computers and the Internet were too complex for me". Even if they did not understand everything they were doing, learners managed to produce useful work with new technologies. The excitement learners showed when they saw a print out of their first word processed document was memorable. The learners' confidence developed and self esteem grew as they picked up ICT and eLearning skills. Initially, the learners with low ICT skills were anxious about using new facilities, as they were worried about deleting or "messing something up". But, once they understood how to operate new technologies, the learners became more relaxed and adventurous. Sara, a middle aged female, commented that she could not believe that she created her own website so easily. She thought that the tutor/researcher was joking when he offered to teach her how to create a website. Beginner users of ICT found losing their work very demotivating to persist with eLearning. Belo thought he saved his CV, which he had typed for many hours, on his floppy disc but managed to save it somewhere else. He could never find it and had to retype it with anger. Ozgur, a male in his mid twenties, remarked that his website was very helpful as he was keeping relevant links and documents such as his CV on his freewebs site.

As far as labour market factors were concerned, there were mixed views. While commonly the learners held a view that ICT skills were important to function at work and home satisfactorily, some of them were not convinced that these skills would significantly improve their chances of securing a well paid job. They argued that in order to obtain a good job, they would need to improve their English and acquire more advanced ICT skills.

SUMMARY AND CONCLUDING REMARKS

The application of eLearning in ESOL for Work at CONEL demonstrated that technology/CALL has promising potential to promote personalised learning. Over one year period the tutor/researcher used computers, Moodle, wiki, weblog, Skype, various Internet based English language websites, Interactive Whiteboard (IWBs), electronic dicta-phones and voting pads to enhance the teaching/learning of ESOL. The College PCs in IT work-shops and mobile laptops where there was no PC were utilised. PCs and laptops were employed in the sessions for different goals from learning how to word process up to producing CVs and creating learners' websites. Most classrooms in the College were fitted with a data projector and IWBs, which were used almost on a daily basis to demonstrate language learning activities and/or IT skills to individuals or by a group of learners to complete tasks or illustrate their answers. The tutor/researcher distributed dictaphones to the learners so that they could record their own or their classmates' speeches to improve their speaking and listening skills. The learners could record, edit, erase or store their recordings. In order to support learners' reading and writing skills, the CONEL Moodle was also used. Various notes and interactive activities that were completed during sessions or independently at the library, IT workshops or home by the learners were uploaded onto the VLE. Moodle based wiki, weblog and chat facilities were employed to promote personalised and collaborative eLearning among the learners. Voting pads were employed to complete individual, pair and group activities or get feedback from the learners on their views, experiences and progress. Other

wikis and weblogs such as zoho.com and blog-ger.com were also used to advance autonomous personalised eLearning/CALL. Different interactive websites such as bbc.co.uk/wkillswise were exploited. Learners were supported to open email accounts and communicate with each other and the tutor/researcher via these accounts.

Although teaching ESOL and technology skills to mixed ability low skills level learners was a challenging task, it was also a rewarding experience. Observing the learners' activities of one year period and discussing their experience, they found the experience fulfilling. They coped with the innovation, learnt independently and also collaborated with others. The learners increasingly took initiatives and supported each other to solve pedagogical and technological problems.

RECOMMENDATIONS

Based on the research results discussed above the following observations and recommendations are made on deployment of new technologies to personalise eLearning or CALL for ESOL learners in an FE context.

- Quite often learners better engage with new technologies when they are convinced that these resources are relevant to their needs and interests. As Coryell & Chlup, (2007) conclude, identifying learners' needs and interest determines the level success in CALL. A danger of being led by new technologies instead of learners' needs and preferences should be avoided.

- The experience of this project backs a view that with the right attitude, commitment and support, even low level ESOL learners with unfavourable attitude to new technologies could achieve and benefit from ICT skills as well as CALL. Thus, learners' slow progress and initial reluctance to use new technologies should not deter tutors from promoting explorative learner centred CALL.

- Some low level ESOL learners could have intermediate or even advanced ICT skills acquired in their own language. Some learners with good English may have little or no ICT skills. Differentiation of lessons while running such mixed ability class could help to cater for individual language and technological needs.

- Low level learners tend to be "scared" of using new technologies. Some of the learners in this study could not believe that they were encouraged to create a website. It is important to demystify a myth around technological complexity and raise learners' awareness that there are simplified versions of ICT resources that ordinary citizens can use and produce good work.

- Teaching low level learners ICT skills or teaching via ICT is a challenging task, specially in a large class. In such a context, it is advisable to facilitate both social and individualised eLearning whereby learners can learn independently and also learn from each other. Establishing a good rapport among course members creates a conducive and collaborative eLearning environment.

- Application of new technologies encouraged learners' creativity. They used their imagination and produced interesting work using word processing, weblog or wiki. Similar to non ICT based teaching it was motivating for learners' efforts to be recognised and their good practice/achievement was shared with peers. In turn this acted as extrinsic motivation which augmented their determination to persist with (e)learning.

- Some ESOL tutors reported that ICT skills were not their strength. Therefore, they were reluctant to integrate e-resources into their lessons. Tutors have to be prepared to learn the necessary skills from experts, colleagues and even their own learners, who need ESOL but could be IT literate.

- Teaching via new technologies and communicating with learners electronically, e.g. email or weblog, could become overwhelming for the tutor, due to promptness of e-communication and the fact that queries were not just about the main subject, ESOL, but also could be about ICT facilities, employability issues or social welfare. Tutors have to agree with their learners as to what to expect in terms of additional eLearning support outside normal lesson times. Learners have to be trained to deal with each other's queries to promote an online community, rather than the tutor trying to deal with all the issues raised.

- Organisations and individual tutors need to be aware of a number of dispositional, situational, institutional, technological and labour market factors/barriers that can affect learners' use of new technologies. This knowledge could help them deal with individual learner's needs and performance.

- New technologies change at an exponential rate introducing and improving diverse capabilities and improved eLearning opportunities. The tutor/researcher had to learn and teach new skills during the project. Tutors and researchers in the field of new technologies in education in general and CALL in particular need to engage in continuous professional development and reflection on their academic and professional practices or lifelong learning.

FUTURE RESEARCH DIRECTIONS

The more educational establishments realise that 'one size does not fit all', the more efforts will be made to personalise learning to meet individual needs and wants. To some extent new technologies have offered tools that can promote personalisation of learning. New technology-based teaching and eLearning resources have been mainly presented in the dominant design of VLEs. Research in the field of new technologies in education has also reflected this bias. However, over recent years some scholars have questioned the hegemony of the VLE approach and proposed more attention to be paid to explore and expand the potential of PLEs. Besides applying VLE, the current project has attempted to design and harness PLE to further personalise eLearning. PLEs are relatively in their infancy and complex to design and implement. Nevertheless, they seem to be promising in addressing some of the current drawbacks in VLEs identified in this research and similar studies. Future research can examine effective ways in which PLEs could be designed and implemented to personalise eLearning in various formal and informal learning milieu.

REFERENCES

Bariso, B. (2004). *New technologies: Tools for Widening Participation in Lifelong Learning?* Unpublished doctoral dissertation, University of London, London.

Bariso, E. (2008, November). *ESOL for Work: Does it Work?* Paper presented at The AAACE 2008 Conference on the Future of Adult Education/Learning, Denver, CO.

Bax, S. (2003). CALL - past, present and future. *System*, *31*(1), 13–28. doi:10.1016/S0346-251X(02)00071-4

BECTA. (2006). *ICT and e-learning in Further Education*. Retrieved July 26, 2008, from http://partners.becta.org.uk/index.php?section=rh&catcode=_re_rp_ap_03&order=2&rid=13649

CONEL. (2008). *3 Year Development Plan for Transforming E-Learning at CONEL*. London: CONEL.

Coryell, E., & Chlup, T. (2007). Implementing E-Learning Components with Adult English Language Learners: Vital Factors Learned. *Computer Assisted Language Learning*, *20*(3), 263–278. doi:10.1080/09588220701489333

Cramb, M. (2008, July). *ESOL for Work Final Report*. Evaluation report submitted to CONEL, London.

Cross, P. (1981). *Adults as Learners: Increasing Participation in Lifelong Learning*. San Francisco, CA: Jossey-Bass Publishers.

Davies, G. (2005). *Computer Assisted Language Learning: Where are we now and where are we going?* Retrieved March 11, 2007 http://www.camsoftpartners.co.uk/docs/UCALL_Keynote.htm#_Toc142650261

DfES. (2005). *Harnessing Technology Transforming Learning and Children's Services*. Retrieved March 19, 2007, http://www.dfes.gov.uk/publications/e-strategy/docs/e-strategy.pdf

DfES. (2006a). *Education: Raising Skills, Improving Life Chances*. Retrieved January 8, 2008, from http://www.official-documents.gov.uk/document/cm67/6768/6768.pdf

DfES. (2006b). *Personalising Further Education: Developing a Vision*. Retrieved February 20, 2008, from http://www.dfes.gov.uk/consultations/downloadableDocs/DfES%20Personalisation.pdf

DfES. (2006c). *Five Year Strategy for Children and Learners: Putting people at the heart of public services*. Retrieved January 10, 2008, from http://www.dfes.gov.uk/publications/5yearstrategy/docs/DfES5Yearstrategy.pdf

Ducates, C., & Lomicka, L. (2008). Adventures in the blogosphere: from blog readers to blog writers. *Computer Assisted Language Learning*, *21*(1), 9–28. doi:10.1080/09588220701865474

Hill, C. (2004). *Teaching Using Information and Learning Technologies in Further Education.* Exeter, UK: Learning Matters.

Hill, C. (2008) *Teaching with eLearning in the Lifelong Learning Sector.* Exeter, UK: Learning Matters.

Lee, K. (2000). *English Teachers' Barriers to the Use of Computer-assisted Language Learning,* Retrieved March 21, 2008, from http://iteslj.org/Articles/Lee-CALLbarriers.html

Loewen, S., & Erlam, R. (2006). Corrective Feedback in the Chatroom: An Experimental. *Computer Assisted Language Learning, 19*(1), 1–14. doi:10.1080/09588220600803311

Ofsted, (2008). *Transforming learning for student success: A good college with outstanding capacity to improve.* Retrieved December 8, 2008, from http://www.conel.ac.uk/docs/conel_ofsted_web_0.pdf

Selwyn, N., & Gorard, S. (1999). Can Technology Really Widen Participation? *Adults Learning,* (February): 27–29.

Selwyn, N., Gorard, S., & Williams, S. (2002). "We are Guinea Pigs Really": Examining the Realities of ICT-Based Adult Learning. *Studies in the Education of Adults, 34*(1), 23–42.

Shang, F. (2007). An Exploratory Study of E-mail Application on FL Writing Performance. *Computer Assisted Language Learning, 20*(1), 79–96. doi:10.1080/09588220601118479

Warschauer, M. (1996). Computer Assisted Language Learning: an Introduction. In S.Fotos (Ed.) *Multimedia language teaching* (pp. 3-20). Tokyo: Logos International.

Warschauer, M. (2004). Technological change and the future of CALL. In S. Fotos & C. Brown (Eds), *New Perspectives on CALL for Second and Foreign Language Classrooms* (pp. 15-25). Mahwah, NJ: Lawrence Erlbaum Associates.

Webb, S. (2006). ICT Based Learning and Social Inclusion: the case of Adult Speakers of Other Languages. In D. Jary & R. Jones (Eds.), *Perspectives and Practice in Widening Participation in the Social Sciences C-SAP Monograph Series No 3.* (pp.174–204). Birmingham, UK: University of Birmingham.

Whalley, J., Welch, T., & Williamson, L. (2006). *E-Learning in FE.* London: Continuum.

Wilson, S., et al. (2006). *Personal Learning Environments: Challenging the dominant design of educational systems.* Retrieved July 4, 2008, from http://dspace.learningnetworks.org/bitstream/1820/727/1/sw_ectel.pdf

Section 2
Pedagogical Issues

Chapter 8

The Impact of Interactive and Collaborative Learning Activities on the Personalised Learning of Adult Distance Learners

Richard Hall
De Montfort University, UK

Steve Mackenzie
De Montfort University, UK

Melanie Hall
Staffordshire University, UK

ABSTRACT

The adoption across higher education of participatory, collaborative and connective 'read/write web' tools and synchronous classrooms has the potential to extend learner engagement and motivation. Embedding these user-centred tools within curriculum practices offers the possibility for a sixth-generation iteration of distance learning that frames a learner-focused pedagogy. This pedagogy is underpinned by problem-based activities that pivot around a cycle of needing/wanting, doing, digesting and feedback. They are supported by a facilitating tutor taking a connectivist approach to stimulate learning. This chapter highlights both the drivers for this sixth-generation iteration and the subsequent development of a model know as SCORE 2.0, or Synchronous Community Orientated Reflective and Experiential 2.0. The impact of this model on two cohorts of adult distance learners is discussed, in order to evaluate opportunities for future pedagogical development.

INTRODUCTION

Distance learning opportunities for adults, in the form of postgraduate, masters or continuing pro-

fessional development courses, have been given extra impetus through employer engagement and work-based learning courses in UK higher education (Confederation of British Industry, 2008; Higher Education Funding Council for England (HEFCE), 2008). The HEFCE Employer Engagement Strategy

DOI: 10.4018/978-1-60566-884-0.ch008

(2006) has a key objective to "promote flexible, responsive provision, in particular testing the development of the workplace as a site of learning". This move towards flexible delivery in multiple locations supports a more personalised educational experience. Through the integration of connectivist pedagogies and new web-based and mobile technologies, these courses carry with them opportunities for innovative, connectivist practices to emerge (National Institute for Adult and Continuing Education (NIACE), 2008; Siemens, 2008).

The wider adoption of participatory, collaborative and connective 'Web 2.0' or 'read/write web' tools has the potential to change pedagogic dynamics (O'Reilly, 2005; Siemens, 2008). This is especially the case where technologies are fused with an evolving understanding of the different ways in which adults learn. Hence, the acknowledgement that social and active learning has an important influence on the affective and cognitive development of learners is important (Bandura, 1989; Bloom, Krathwohl & Masia, 1964; Franklin & van Harmelen, 2007; Gangadharbatla, 2008). This andragogic approach aligns with recent studies on the student experience in higher education (Conole *et al.*, 2006; Trinder *et al.*, 2008), which suggest that a collection of technologies, including both institutional and non-institutional tools, are crucial in connecting students' informal and formal learning.

In order to model these flexible, learner-focused opportunities in the context of adult, distance learning this chapter focuses upon the development of a sixth generation, integrated model of distance learning that combines online synchronous classes and read/write web tasks, supported by an online, community-orientated learning network. The pedagogic strategy is guided by Garrison and Anderson's (2003) 'community of inquiry' model, which emphasises the importance of social, teaching and cognitive presence, with the aim of enhancing the engagement, motivation and satisfaction of adult distance learners.

This sixth-generation model is entitled SCORE2.0 or *Synchronous Community-Oriented Reflective and Experiential (Web) 2.0*. The model is evaluated through the implementation of integrated tasks with Post-Graduate Certificate in Higher Education (PG Cert HE) participants, academics engaging in informal professional development, and adult learners on a Youth and Community course. As a result strategies are identified for enhancing curriculum design and delivery to support adult distance learning, based upon the model.

BACKGROUND

Adult-Learning, Andragogy and Informal Education

Non-traditional, adult students engaged in learning, generally within further or higher education, have been noted as persons aged 25 and over (Whisnant, Sullivan, & Slayton, 1992). For Knowles (1980, p.46), adulthood is realised at 'the point at which individuals perceive themselves to be essentially self-directing'. Gibbons and Wentworth (2001) argued that non-traditional students learn more from the andragogical, self-directed learning noted by Knowles (1975), than through a traditional, instructional pedagogic approach.

For Knowles (1992), non-traditional, adult learners working online become increasingly autonomous and self-motivated within reflective, problem-based learning contexts. As a result, Gibbons and Wentworth (2001) suggest that online instructor training should be based on andragogical theory, in order to accommodate the nature of the online adult learner. However, critics argue that andragogy is not a descriptive model of how adults learn, rather it is a prescriptive model of how adult learners should learn effectively (Tusting & Barton 2006). Schapiro (2003) takes this issue further:

Andragogy and self directed learning are rooted in notions about autonomy and self reliance, as both an ends and a means of the educational process, which downplay the value of various forms of connected, relational knowing and collaborative learning (p.155).

Issues of self-reliance and autonomy within a learning community are reflected in the contested concept of informal education, which is of growing importance in the discussion of andragogy and adult learning. Informal learning is "owned" and "directed" by the learner and involves independent study that is non-formally timetabled. It also encompasses education using non-institutional technologies that takes place away from traditional, educational contexts. In this view, the potential for the personalisation of emergent web and mobile technologies has bought the interface between traditional and non-traditional spaces for learning into sharp relief (Department for Innovation Universities and Skills (DIUS), 2008).

The development of connections between formal and informal education moves us towards a more complex view of the personalisation and ownership of the learning process for adult learners. For many the key is defining personalisation through accredited frameworks in professional settings. Leadbeater (2000) has argued that:

Schools and universities should become more like hubs of learning, within the community, capable of extending into the community... More learning needs to be done at home, in offices and kitchens, in the contexts where knowledge is deployed to solve problems and add value to people's lives (p. 112).

Therefore, the power of an autonomous, personal learning strategy depends upon the individual's ability to fuse their informal and formal learning opportunities. In turn, this fusion occurs within communities that are socially constructed and connected (Bandura 1977; Siemens, 2008; Vygotsky, 1978).

Social-Constructivism and Connectivism

It has been argued that enhanced approaches to learning are underpinned by both socio-constructivist (Bandura, 1977; Driscoll, 1984; Piaget, 1970; Vygotsky, 1978) and connectivist (Siemens, 2008) learning theories. Socio-constructivism highlights the importance of structured, personalised opportunities for developing mastery in new learning situations. Vygotsky (1962) argued that without social interaction, higher cognitive functioning would not emerge. Bandura (1977) stated that:

Learning would be exceedingly laborious, not to mention hazardous, if people had to rely solely on the effects of their own actions to inform them what to do. Fortunately, most human behaviour is learned observationally through modelling: from observing others, one forms an idea of how new behaviours are performed, and on later occasions this coded information serves as a guide for action (p. 22).

Bandura's (1977) theory emphasises the value of social modelling and reciprocal determinism, where individual behaviours both influence, and are influenced by, personal factors and the social environment. This demands that a learner must be able to identify and replicate the behaviour or action to be learned, although this can be problematic where technologies are novel or difficult to access. Learners must also want to demonstrate what they have learned, and this is linked to their expectations for reinforcement or punishment (for example, in the impact of assignment feedback). At each level personal actions and decision-making are socially constructed.

For adult distance learners the facilitation of social interaction is often accommodated through the creation of a virtual online community, linked to Wenger's (1998) 'communities of practice' model (Brown, 2001; Palloff & Pratt, 1999). Garrison and Anderson (2003) extended this work to develop their 'community of inquiry' model as a problem-based framework for facilitating online learning. They focused upon the three key areas of cognition, socialisation and teaching. These personal, socio-constructivist elements can then be fused through a connectivist model, which is portrayed as a learning theory for the digital age (Siemens, 2008).

Connectivism is a networked learning model that reflects the technological and societal changes of the late twentieth/early twenty-first centuries. It recognises that individuals learn by making connections within their neural networks, and that these can be strengthened by creating networks with other individuals and repositories of knowledge. It is our receptiveness to engage with these connections that enables us to learn. Siemens (2004) argues:

The starting point of connectivism is the individual. Personal knowledge is comprised of a network, which feeds into organizations and institutions, which in turn feed back into the network, and then continue to provide learning to individual. This cycle of knowledge development (personal to network to organization) allows learners to remain current in their field through the connections they have formed.

Therefore, where individuals feel able to act within social networks, then their autonomy and subject-mastery can be enhanced.

Connectivism has attracted criticism as an invalid theory of learning (Kerr, 2007), which simply prescribes the development of learning environments and tasks. Moreover, its practical implementation raises many issues for users to consider, around managing online identity and privacy, developing engagement and overcoming marginalisation, and building technological confidence. Anderson (2007) pinpoints 'the need to explore further the informal, social aspects of the learning that takes place and the many issues concerning participation. We cannot, for example,

assume everyone is happy working in the "self-publish" mode' (p. 53). This is a critical issue for adult distance learners, especially those for whom such technologies are an unknown quantity. Therefore, the deployment of a socially-constructed strategy for adult distance learners needs to scaffold differentiated learning opportunities that are empowering. Moreover, any twenty-first century model for enhancing the autonomy of adult learners must take into account user-generated and participative technologies.

ADULT DISTANCE LEARNERS AND ONLINE COMMUNITIES: THE AFFORDANCES OF TECHNOLOGY

Teaster and Blieszner (1999) argue that 'the term distance learning has been applied to many instructional methods: however, its primary distinction is that the teacher and the learner are separate in space and possibly time' (p. 741). Keegan (1995) concurs noting that distance education and training result from the technological separation of teacher and learner, which frees the student from the necessity of travelling to 'a fixed place, at a fixed time, to meet a fixed person' (p. 7). However, distance learners tend to be isolated from each other geographically, which carries the risk of de-motivation and isolation (Simpson, 2002). Alienation can be overcome through the formation of learning communities that in turn impact student satisfaction, retention and learning. Where adult learners are engaging in part-time, short courses, with flexible starting points, the risk of poor retention and drop-out is increased, and the need for engagement heightened.

Garrison and Anderson (2003) extend this view of participation for distance learners to state that 'a community of learners is an essential core element of an educational experience when higher order learning is the desired learning outcome' (p. 22). Thus, working with others is important at three levels. Firstly, through co-operation participants can meet individual goals and are also prepared to help their peers. Secondly, through co-ordination of effort, participants can work together as a group to achieve a common goal, whilst maintaining individual objectives. Finally, through collaboration, the success of the group is seen to be paramount and all individuals contribute to that success (Hofmann, 2004).

In their 'community of inquiry' model, Garrison and Anderson (2003) identify teaching presence, social presence and cognitive presence as key elements in attaining a collaborative state. This lays the foundations for a self-sustaining community of learners that consists of individuals with shared interests, tasks and activities who forge mutually-supportive relationships and shared practices (Wenger, 1998). Brown (2001) and Garrison and Anderson (2003) see shared practices rooted in the development of asynchronous computer-mediated conferencing. For Garrison and Anderson (2003) the pedagogical advantage of such conferencing 'is its capacity to support reflective text-based interaction, independent of the pressures of time and the constraints of distance' (p. 6).

Synchronous technologies can also enhance the engagement, motivation, connectedness and learning of distance students. Stodel, Thompson & MacDonald (2006) state that 'Technologies, such as web-based audio and video conferencing and application sharing, that do not rely on text might be more effective at establishing social presence and supporting richer communication'. Online synchronous classrooms embed voice as the primary communication medium, alongside tools such as interactive whiteboards, participant panels for feedback, text-chat, document upload/download, breakout rooms for small groups, session recording and the ability to hand control of the classroom to the student. Chen, Ko & Kinshuk (2005) highlight the two key benefits of these tools to be immediate feedback and an increased level of motivation through real-time participation. These tools help distance learners to perceive that they are not alone and that they have learning peers with whom they can validate their thinking and decisions.

Embedding the synchronous advantages of these tools within asynchronous learning networks can extend real-time interactions, especially where read/write web technologies are deployed. Although they are also known as Web 2.0 applications (O'Reilly, 2005), the use of the term 'read/write' emphasises an approach rather than a toolset and stresses the marriage of broadcast and interactive tools within a personalisable environment. These applications deliver opportunities for: social networking; social bookmarking; user-generated content; virtual representation; the syndication of content including multimedia; and innovative approaches to content and application-handling, including mash-ups and aggregation. The impact of these tools has prompted practitioners to re-evaluate curriculum delivery. As McGee and Diaz (2007) note:

applications defined as 'Web 2.0' hold the most promise [for teaching and learning] because they are strictly web based and typically free, support collaboration and interaction and are responsive to the user. These applications have great potential to be used in way that is learner-centred, affordable and accessible for teaching and learning purposes (p. 32).

Whilst staff reported using a few Web 2.0 and social software tools they were generally less familiar with how these could be used to support learning and teaching. There were misconceptions surrounding the affordances of the tools, and fears expressed about security and invasion of personal space. At an institutional level there was reluctance to take up new technologies due to considerations of cost and the time it would take staff to develop their own skills (p. 6).

These legitimate concerns about security, safety, privacy, control of data and plagiarism impact upon the connections that can be made between new, web-based tools and the pedagogies that support adult, distance learners. This is especially important in light of the report that some students are 'frustrated at the misuse or lack of use of [read/write web] tools within their institutions' (Conole *et al.*, 2006, p. 95), and that regardless of the course structures or tutor/facilitator preferences, some students are using social software on their own initiative to support their studies (Kurhila, 2006). Therefore, the influence of the facilitating tutor is pivotal in enhancing the experience of adult distance learners.

The Facilitating Tutor

Colvin Clark and Kwinn (2007) describe proactive virtual classroom communities that are framed by: active, task-driven participation by all members; the development of social presence; engagement with problem-solving; and the use and creation of multimedia. In this environment all participants' needs are accommodated and differentiation is supported. Moreover, co-operation, the formation of new teams or networks, and distributed moderation can emerge across the community.

Building such a learning community requires a blueprint that reflects where the students are, in terms of their prior and preferred learning, and their subject and technological confidence. It also needs to align with the course learning outcomes, so that the choice of technologies is appropriate. In meeting these outcomes, it is the responsibility of tutors and course designers to scaffold meaningful, collaborative spaces. Bellon and Oates (2002, p.14) highlight that 'Interaction with the instructor is necessary to motivate all students'.

For Garrison and Anderson (2003) the tutor-as-facilitator is central to the implementation of a blueprint.

The focus is on the learning, but not just what the learner capriciously decides. An educational experience is intended to focus on learning outcomes that have value for society as well as the learner. A learner centred approach risks marginalizing the teacher and the essential value of the transaction in creating a critical community of inquiry. In an educational experience, both the learner and teacher are part of the larger process of learning (p. 65).

There is a strong sense that an extreme, self-directed, andragogical model of learning may not be the most suitable for levering best value from the distance learning process. Instead, negotiation and co-operation between the learner and the tutor is integral to effective planning and scaffolding of learning tasks. The skilled facilitating tutor will guide the adult learner towards self-direction and autonomy, by extending their social, technical and cognitive knowledge and confidence (Salmon, 2002).

In terms of adult distance learning communities the tutor also needs to provide synchronous and asynchronous mechanisms for all types of learners to flourish, in both affective and cognitive terms (Bloom, Krathwohl & Masia, 1964; Driscoll, 1994). In this way learning differences can be respected. For Palloff & Pratt (2001) this occurs where facilitators create courses with varied approaches and modes of delivery. However, active participation requires a balance between autonomy and facilitation, so that learners can chose the media and communities that suit them most appropriately. One outcome will be a constructivist paradigm through which learners can make and record actions, reflect on those actions, and share decisions and thoughts with others. Making sense of constructivist, tutor-facilitated pedagogical drivers, within networks of emerging web-based technologies, demands a new model for distance learning.

DEVELOPING A NEW APPROACH TO ADULT DISTANCE LEARNING

SCORE 2.0: A Sixth-Generation Model for Distance Learning

The development of interactive and collaborative technologies enabled Taylor (2001) to distinguish between 'generations' of distance learning technologies. His first generation is the correspondence model, whilst his second is characterised by the introduction of instructional multi-media like audiotapes and videotapes. His third generation is called the tele-learning model, and includes the conferencing and broadcasting technologies for pedagogical delivery and support. Taylor's fourth generation, the 'flexible learning' model, includes interactive multimedia, internet-based resources and computer-mediated communications. His final, 'intelligent, flexible learning' generation embedded the use of automated response systems and campus portals like Virtual Learning Environments into curriculum delivery.

However, embedding user-centred, networked 'read/write web' tools, alongside synchronous classrooms, has the potential to frame a sixth-generation iteration of distance learning, which more accurately reflects the different ways in which adults learn. Moreover, such a model would also acknowledge the importance of social and active learning (Bandura, 1989; Franklin & van Harmelen, 2007; Gangadharbatla, 2008). This powerful combination of technology and pedagogy has the potential to remove the barrier of isolation that has impacted distance learners (Galusha, 1997), and to align with Siemens' (2008) connectivist view of personal learning development where learning is no longer an internal, individualistic activity.

In order to frame effective adult distance learning using sixth-generation interactive and collaborative technologies, the *Synchronous Community Orientated Reflective and Experiential 2.0 (SCORE 2.0)* model has been developed. The SCORE 2.0 model (Figure 1) fuses the activity-based online synchronous classroom and read/write web tools. Guiding the implementation is the 'community of inquiry' model (Garrison & Anderson, 2003), which emphasises the importance of teaching presence, social presence and cognitive presence. Underpinning this blueprint is the influence of the facilitating tutor, linked to the social influences that impact learners, and their concomitant cognitive engagement.

The model is framed by formal, community-managed, learning activities that are problem-based. These tasks are socially-constructed and managed, with a clear framework and set of outcomes. Communication and feedback are delivered both formally within synchronous classrooms, and informally via read/write web applications that stimulate learning networks. Conceptually the model is aligned with Race's (2001) 'ripples' model of learning, whereby individual engagements in distinct modes of learning impact on each other over time, like ripples on a pond. In SCORE 2.0, these ripples or modes of learning encompass: structured synchronous classroom activities; asynchronous learning tasks; informal activities in a learning network; and personal reflections on achievement.

The online synchronous classroom is at the core of SCORE 2.0, and is the catalyst that drives the learning in the other modes. The model suggests that doing specific tasks (synchronously and asynchronously) that can be digested in a learning network (using social software) with personal feedback, will motivate learners to reflect on their performance (in a blog), and thereby generate a need or want to extend their learning. Due to the nature of the read/write web technologies deployed there are multiple opportunities for enhanced teacher-student interaction and student-student interaction, and for feedback. With this in mind, a scoping evaluation of this model underpins the rest of this chapter.

Figure 1. The SCORE 2.0 model

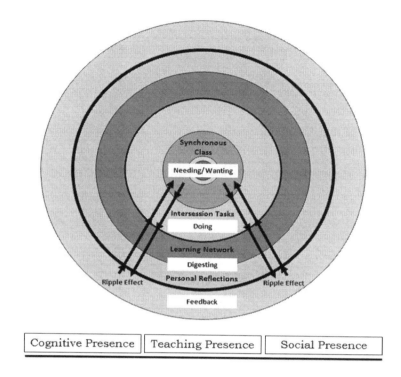

A Note on Context and Evaluation

In order to evaluate the SCORE 2.0 model, convenience sampling was used to select two different types of adult learners. The first was a group of eight PG Cert HE participants (Research Group A) who voluntarily participated in a five week course entitled "*Web 2.0 for Teaching and Learning – the Basics*". Their tasks included analysis, discussion and reflection on the implementation of a range of read/write web tools in the curriculum. The second group consisted of 22 postgraduate distance learning students enrolled on a Masters-level Health and Social Research Methods module at the same institution (Research Group B). It was compulsory for this second group to participate in a three week course entitled '*Internet Research Tools*'. This cohort was split into three sub-groups of eight, eight and seven students. Their tasks included analysis, discussion and reflection on a range of read/write web tools for researching and implementing strategies for youth and community research and development projects. Each research group engaged with three types of technology.

- The 'WebEx' web conferencing software was used to facilitate weekly, online synchronous classroom sessions.
- The read/write web technologies used to facilitate weekly asynchronous learning tasks, feedback and reflection, were blogs (using blogger.com), wikis (using wikispaces.com), social bookmarking (using delicious), and RSS Feeds (using Google Reader).
- The Ning.com social software was the basis for an informal learning network.

The action research strategy relied on three data collection techniques.

1. Online pre- and post-course surveys were designed to gather the perceptions of the participants about the technologies that support their distance learning, both before the course started and after it had finished. Ratings were taken where 0 is low and 10 high. For 'Research Group A', ratings addressed knowledge, ability, inclination and confidence, for each of the four different technologies that the participants analysed. For 'Research Group B', ratings addressed knowledge, ability and inclination, for each of the internet research tools that the participants analysed.

2. An anonymous, end-of-course, online questionnaire was designed to evaluate the impact of the integrated SCORE 2.0 model on engagement, motivation and learning. It enabled participants to rate (where 0 is low and 10 high) the importance of the technologies and tasks in: improving their subject knowledge; building a community of online learners; being motivated to learn more about a subject; and, being motivated to complete the course.

3. Post-delivery, semi-structured interviews were designed to unpick the perceptions and understandings of the participants. The interviews were conducted and a coding scheme was framed and tested by the same evaluator in order to maintain an internal consistency of approach (Boyatzis, 1998; Joffe and Yardley, 2004).

Thus, this latitudinal evaluation examines what adult distance learners say about the impact of both the read/write web and synchronous tasks on their learning experiences. It aims to provide a pragmatic description of their expectations for the use of both these tools and pedagogic approaches in the curriculum. The process was designed to support the critical, reflective, accountable, self-evaluative and participative improvement of practice (Zuber-Skerritt, 1992),

and this aligns with the view of Reason (2003) that the 'fundamental strategy of action research is to 'open communicative space' and help the emergence of "communities of inquiry"' (p. 106). As a result, this stimulates an emergent analysis of the SCORE 2.0 model.

The Pedagogic Value of the SCORE 2.0 Model

For Research Group A, seven questionnaire respondents agreed or strongly agreed that they were satisfied with what they had learnt and that their learning outcomes had been met, whilst for Research Group B this was the case for 19 respondents. For all respondents (n = 29) on both courses, three themes stood out as improving motivation, enjoyment and engagement: 17 highlighted the value of exploring the subjects with others; 11 prioritised the importance of the actual content and learning tasks; and nine saw the influence of the teacher as central. This indicates that the three elements underpinning this model of teaching, social presence (working with others), cognitive presence (subject matter/learning), and teaching presence (the influence of the teacher), were prominent for these participants. Moreover, those students who feel connected, within a structured environment that engages with personally relevant content are likely to be highly motivated.

These three elements were correlated in the interviews. Research Group A raised six themes: the impact of the specific learning tasks; personal motivation; the role of the tutor; interaction with others; practical application; and resource identification. However Research Group B extended this list to include the value of rapid feedback, and the personal importance of having good IT skills. These latter two themes were crucial for these learners who were working toward formal accreditation in the workplace, and at a distance from their tutor.

In order to quantify how their participation and satisfaction with the learning process, all

Table 1. The increases in average participant confidence to deploy specific read/write web tools for Research Group A, based on self-ratings (0 is low and 10 high)

Research Group A	
Blogs perception increase	4.31
Wikis Searching perception increase	4.69
Social Bookmarking perception increase	5.09
Social Networking perception increase	3.25
Overall perception increase	4.33

individuals in Research Group A were asked to assess, at the start and end of their course: their own knowledge about specific tools; their ability to use these tools effectively; their inclination to use them with their own students; and their confidence in deploying these technologies. All individuals in Research Group B were asked to assess, at the start and end of their course: their own knowledge about web-based research; their ability to effectively use specific tools; and their inclination to use them for research. For both groups participants had a low-level of knowledge about the subject matter before they started, and they could all be categorised as beginners.

For Research Group A, whilst knowledge, ability and inclination all saw increases in positive participant assessments, the increases in average participant confidence to deploy specific read/write web tools was as shown in Table 1.

Only two of the eight respondents could be regarded as outliers whose perceptions differed substantially from their peers, with lower scores caused by their lack of confidence with technologies and poor connectivity off-campus. This hampered their access to the synchronous courses. Overall, these academics recognised that tools which could be used to shape meaningful content, namely wikis and social bookmarking, had more potential for academic use than blogs and social networks. These participants also highlighted that they would probably use these tools for pedagogic innovation, sparked by the model of synchronous

classes, asynchronous tasks and structured feedback in a learning network.

For Research Group B, whilst knowledge and ability both saw increases in positive participant assessments, the increase in average participant inclination to use specific web-based research tools was as shown in Table 2.

A priori knowledge about library searching impacted the increase in scores for that strand. However, on inclination to use social bookmarking and RSS only five of 21 questionnaire respondents registered a perception increase between the start and the end of the course of less than 3 points. Moreover, each of the other participants expected to use these tools in their future research.

The Pedagogic Impact of the Synchronous Classes

Participants were asked to rate the influence of the online synchronous classes on four areas, at the end of the classes (Table 3).

These data highlight that participation in the online synchronous classes positively impacted learning, stimulated community-building, and ultimately motivated participants to develop autonomy in learning more about the subject matter. The higher ratings for Research Group A might be attributed to the participants' higher intrinsic motivation, as they enrolled voluntarily on the course and saw it providing continuing professional development opportunities. However, their focus upon structure, motivation and

Table 2. The increases in average participant confidence to deploy specific web tools for Research Group B, based on self-ratings (0 is low and 10 high)

Research Group B	
Social Bookmarking perception increase	3.97
Library Searching perception increase	2.86
RSS perception increase	4.00
Overall perception increase	3.61

engagement was confirmed by the post-course interviews. When asked about the key features that helped with learning, a Research Group A participant noted:

firstly the Preparatory notes and preparing with some basic online skills [were vital]. During the actual class itself, the variety of tasks, working in smaller groups, contributing to analysis of slides, discussing a session, watching videos and the use of a headset to aid the quality of the audio helped me develop.

the synchronous experience was closest to a seminar/tutorial type experience and actually enhanced them because you can do certain things you can't do in a classroom tutorial. So I think it was the best learning experience in this mindset, you cannot just improve on it really.

Of the five interviewees, three also highlighted the importance of feedback alongside an obligation to be present and participate. One argued that the synchronous classrooms enable 'rapid interaction and you can actually direct people to do things and you can see how they are doing it.' Modelling and learning from others was evident.

For Research Group B, the five interviewees focused upon the advantages of synchronous working for building personalised approaches to problem-solving, maintaining learning momentum, and receiving feedback through the social construction of knowledge.

- 'My understanding improved through being able to ask personal questions, [and] be guided through new information/ tools'.
- 'It focused the mind on the subject being taught and therefore forces you to understand the subject or else you will get left behind'.
- 'I could explore things I've never done before but getting immediate feedback and tutoring'.
- 'You can listen to collective views. Listening to different people's ideas and problems with the tasks'.

These participants were then asked 'How do synchronous classes help build a community?'

Table 3. Average participant ratings of the online synchronous classes (0 is low and 10 high)

	Research Group A	Research Group B
Improving understanding of subject	7.75	7.71
Building a community of learners	7.75	6.81
Motivation to learn more about the subject	8.5	7.33
Motivation to complete the course	7.75	7.10

Their answers developed thoughts around social engagement through real-time chat.

- 'There is a certain amount of dedication to classes, like a normal class, so you get the opportunity to catch up with class-mates, and you all go through the same experience'.
- '[Networking was] definitely helped by the group chat because you can directly communicate with people and hear them talking'.
- 'Contact with people regularly helps. You are all going through the same tasks and learning, supporting each other and form-ing [group] norms'.

However, a more negative response focused upon marginalisation and a lack of confidence in online social spaces.

- 'I'm not sure about the community thing… you don't know who you're talk-ing to. For me, it doesn't mean anything. But that might be just me - chat rooms, so-cial networking etc., they just don't work for me.'

For four of the five interviewees, there was recognition of the power of social learning, but some students demonstrated a more individualistic approach. For Research Group B it is possible that longer-term participation in a social network with specific, collaborative tasks would have engaged a community of learners.

Finally, the interviewees from Research Group B were asked 'How do synchronous classes mo-tivate you?' Responses focused upon personal aims and successes and maintaining their learn-ing focus.

- 'I really wanted to try something again af-ter I'd done it once successfully.'
- 'They keep you on track I suppose. As a distance learner - you can go into drift

mode.....it was good for bringing you back'.

- 'Learning is compulsory! Being part of a group that I wouldn't have maybe chosen to join has meant that I have learnt what I wouldn't have done otherwise.'
- 'You know you have to take part or else you will be missing out on something im-portant and when you see other people get-ting it, it makes you more determined to understand as well.'

When asked 'Why do you believe that online synchronous classes for delivering lessons to adult distance learners can be an effective teaching and learning tool?' the interviewees from Research Group A concurred with one of their number who noted 'Because it provides the contact that distance learners need'. This was the primary focus for their belief in the motivating nature of the synchronous classrooms within the SCORE 2.0 model.

Negative issues did arise for participants from both groups, and these focused upon: technical problems (nine participants); difficulties with the fixed routine and time (eight participants); and a preference for face-to-face work (five partici-pants). In part these issues for Research Group B were due to participants logging on from work where they had no control over administration settings and had restricted access to web-based resources. Linked to these problems, conclusions drawn from participant feedback about the live experiences were three-fold.

- A tailored and finely detailed user-guide is critical for the use of conferencing and Voice Over IP (VOIP) technologies.
- If the majority of participants can log-on, view their screen, hear the facilita-tor and other students, use text chat and the whiteboard, then sessions are vi-able even if they cannot use their own microphone.

139

Table 4. Average participant ratings for the influence of the asynchronous learning tasks (0 is low and 10 high)

	Research Group A	Research Group B
Improving understanding of subject	6.25	6.76
Building a community of learners	5.50	5.57
Motivation to learn more about the subject	6.38	6.48
Motivation to complete the course	6.13	6.24

- A mix of VOIP and text-chat are critical, so that no-one is disadvantaged.

Technical problems and IT competency issues can be resolved through preparatory and introductory sessions, in order to promote early diagnoses of problems. However, an analysis of technical constraints within the contexts of work-based learning is critical before tutors decide whether synchronous classes are appropriate.

THE IMPACT OF READ/WRITE WEB TOOLS AND LEARNING TASKS

Read/write web technologies framed spaces for experiential learning that cemented participants' knowledge through specific asynchronous learning tasks. They also provided opportunities for reflection through blogging, collaboration through wikis, and developing associations through social bookmarking, social networking and use of RSS. Participants were asked to rate the influence of the learning tasks on four areas, at the end of the classes (Table 4).

Overall, the tasks rated less favourably than synchronous classrooms in achieving pedagogic aims. Some felt that the online synchronous classes were sufficient to learn about the material, as noted by a participant from Research Group A:

As you get a more and more interactive learning environment it tends to make you less and less

intellectually hard working, you tend to become intellectually lazier, because you can see it on the screen and do it straightaway. So you do not really want to put in the effort and prepare in advance.

because that's when you really get to try things out and learn by trial and error. By doing this you get more of a feel for how you might use the technologies in your work. It all becomes more concrete and less abstract.

On the use of both blogs and wikis, participants from Research Group A felt that the connectedness of the SCORE 2.0 model enabled them to focus upon analysing relevant academic content in a safe environment. One noted that 'I have now signed up to academic blogs in my subject area', whilst a second highlighted that the action research element of the course had empowered her towards a shift in pedagogic practice.

Most of our students again at a lower level are strategic learners, they want to utilise their time gainfully to enhance their exam performance, rather than wider learning, and perhaps that is where wikis and bookmarking might be more useful to them, because wikis allow them to work collaboratively perhaps when they are thinking about a group assignment and social bookmarking let's them quickly share links – so in a sense it is more about the efficiency of input, whereas blogs do require quite a bit of time

These benefits were supported by participants in Research Group B, who reflected upon the portable value of these tools for research, alongside the accessibility of up-to-date materials. On social bookmarking, one interviewee highlighted the importance of portability: 'This was something completely new to me and to be honest it's something that I will use a lot once I start researching on my assignments. It is helpful that I can do it at work and home'. One participant, commenting on the use of RSS for accessing validated, youth workers' blogs noted: 'the RSS feed I've set up for a couple of websites is already paying off. It's great I don't have to keep visiting web sites'. A second focused upon reinforcement and feedback ahead of synchronous sessions: '[it] gave me a chance to practice, to do it for myself... to apply the learning, test out new skills, and highlight any problems.'

The more personal nature of blogging impacts upon the deployment of the SCORE 2.0 model for stimulating participant feedback and reflection. Strategic learning activities and assessments that require more effort from students need to be integrated with tasks that have fewer perceived cognitive overheads. Engagement with informal, reflective and experiential learning may suit those who are more self-directed and autonomous in their study. A useful aspect of blogging is that it allows students to offer opinions and points-of-view, to clarify their understanding and to receive feedback from tutors and peers. Moreover, it also helps with the affective side of learning, as participants can consider the wider motivations of their learning network.

Achieving a Sense of Community?

The synchronous classroom had a major impact in promoting social interaction and a sense of community. The strongest theme to emerge in both research groups was the personally motivating nature of interactions in a network. Additionally participants in Research Group B identified better communication and building community as the most popular benefit, compared with their previous distance learning experience. An interviewee argued that there was 'Some reduction of isolation' and that this was a 'much more efficient way to converse with fellow students, a quicker way of completing tasks and also embedding group work into what can be a lonely student experience'. Asynchronous learning tasks were not perceived to be as useful in building a learning community and more structured tasks may be required to achieve this outcome.

The third component of the SCORE 2.0 Model is a learning network that aggregates all course-related activities within a central, web-based area. Research Group A were asked to rate the effectiveness of their social network (Table 5). (Note that Research Group B did not use the network.)

The ratings suggest that the learning network was a valuable component, both cognitively and affectively. The RSS feeds in this network offered the participants access to a wealth of external information, and are an example of how to extend informal education. One participant stated:

in a sense bringing in external knowledge at a particular point where I was interested in it was useful to me, so perhaps you can say that you know for like-minded people the social network can actually expand the community to even further distance.

In terms of the affective benefits of a learning network a second participant could '*see how social networking really fills a need for students that are away from the campus and want a human contact and learn best with a human contact.*' However, questionnaire respondents from Research Group A shared concerns that major benefits might only be gained by more self-directed adult learners. One argued that 'Ning [the learning network] has got an advantage for higher-level learning where students are self-managing and communicating with each other and learning from that interaction'.

Table 5. The effectiveness of the learning network for Research Group A, based on self-ratings (0 is low and 10 high)

	Research Group A
Improving understanding of subject	7.38
Building a community of learners	7.50
Motivation to learn more about the subject	7.75
Motivation to complete the course	7.50

Despite these concerns the learning network has the advantage of bringing validated information, knowledge and individual opinions to a central location. It has the potential to catalyse on-going relationships and communication, and to stimulate incidental learning. One participant summarised its value as 'enabling you to combine all your learning together'. That said, in terms of maximizing the learning possibilities of this environment, as with the delivery of synchronous classes and the development of asynchronous learning tasks, the facilitating teacher is a critical component.

The Impact of the Facilitating Tutor

The SCORE 2.0 model places the interaction between learner and teacher at the heart of the teaching and learning activities. It highlights that a subset of learners will need explicit direction, in order to develop autonomy. *This means that a range of teaching approaches should be deployed, and that modelling and feedback are critical. The tutor's role goes beyond the delivery of material in a synchronous classroom, and requires careful thinking about structured online learning activities and how best to facilitate a learning network. In the implementation of the SCORE 2.0 model these strands collectively meet the needs of a wide range of adult learners. Additionally the tutor should be available outside synchronous classes and model the behaviours that are expected of the participants.*

In both Research Groups participants noted that the key elements of the facilitating tutor were:

- supporting students outside the synchronous classes;
- giving satisfactory feedback in class; and
- managing the learning activities in a structured way.

From participant ratings there was near universal agreement that the teacher had been successful in laying the foundations for a positive experience by connecting with these three themes. They argued that a structured online presence in the synchronous classes, asynchronous tasks and social networks helped to prepare them for autonomous learning.

However, this role was a graduated one in each of the SCORE 2.0 modes of learning. The tutor was pivotal in the synchronous classes, whilst attempting to leave space in the follow-up tasks and learning network for more informal, participant-led learning opportunities that were semi-structured. Over time the development of autonomous, self-directed learning in each of these areas grew. One participant in Research Group B highlighted that 'the enthusiasm and commitment of session organiser, and input from other participants' scaffolded a developmental learning engagement.

The participants also focused upon the value of the written guides for pre-class preparation and in-class tasks, as well as the role of mentors, or second tutors, during the live synchronous classes.

Bandura, A. (1977). *Social Learning Theory*. New York: General Learning Press.

Bandura, A. (1989). Perceived self-efficacy in the exercise of personal agency. *The Psychologist: Bulletin of the British Psychological Society, 2,* 411–424.

Bellon, T., & Oates, R. (2002). *Best practices in cyberspace. Motivating the online learner.* Harrisburg, PA: Technology-Mediated Learning Resource Center. Retrieved October 28, 2008, from http://168.144.129.112/Articles/Best%20 Practices%20in%20Cyberspace.pdf

Bloom, B. S., Krathwohl, D. R., & Masia, B. B. (1964). *Taxonomy of Educational Objectives: the Classification of Educational Goals. Handbook II: Affective Domain.* New York: McKay.

Boyatzis, R. E. (1998). *Transforming Qualitative Information: Thematic Analysis and Code Development.* Thousand Oaks, CA: Sage.

Brown, R. E. (2001). The process of community building in distance learning classes. *Journal of Asynchronous Learning Networks, 5*(2). Retrieved 28 October, 2008, from http://www.sloan-c.org/ publications/jaln/v5n2/v5n2_brown.asp

Chen, N-S., Ko, H-C., & Kinshuk, L, T. (2005). A model for synchronous learning using the internet. *Innovations in Education and Teaching International, 42*(2), 181–194. doi:10.1080/14703290500062599

Collis, B. (1998). New didactics for university instruction: Why and how. *Computers & Education, 31*(4), 373–395. doi:10.1016/S0360-1315(98)00040-2

Colvin Clark, R., & Kwinn, A. (2007). *The New Virtual Classroom: Evidence-based Guidelines for Synchronous e-Learning.* San Francisco, CA: Pfeiffer.

Confederation Of British Industry. (2008). *CBI Launches New Higher Education Task Force.* Retrieved 28 October, 2008, from http://www. cbi.org.uk/ndbs/press.nsf/0363c1f07c6ca12a80 25671c00381cc7/3f109c6775f30aec802574c60 03a51ce?OpenDocument

Conole, G., de Laat, M., Dillon, T., & Darby, J. (2006). *LXP: Student experience of technologies.* Bristol, UK: Joint Information Systems Committee. Retrieved 28 October, 2008, from http:// www.jisc.ac.uk/whatwedo/programmes/elearning_pedagogy/elp_learneroutcomes.aspx

DIUS. (2008). *Adult Learning – Shaping the Way Ahead.* London: DIUS. Retrieved 28 October, 2008, from http://www.adultlearningconsultation.org.uk/userfiles/DIUS_adu_lea_bro_ an_05.8.pdf

Driscoll, M. P. (1994). *Psychology of learning for instruction.* Boston: Allyn and Bacon.

Franklin, T., & van Harmelen, M. (2007). *Web 2.0 for content for learning and teaching in higher education.* Bristol, UK: Joint Information Systems Committee. Retrieved 28 October, 2008, from http://www.jisc.ac.uk/media/documents/ programmes/digitalrepositories/web2-contentlearning-and-teaching.pdf

Galusha, J. (1997). Barriers to learning in distance education. *Interpersonal Computing and Technology, 5*(4), 6–14. Retrieved 28 October, 2008, from http://www.emoderators.com/ipct-j/1997/ n4/galusha.html

Gangadharbatla, H. (2008). Facebook me: Collective self-esteem, need to belong, and internet self-efficacy as predictors of the iGeneration's attitudes toward social networking sites. *Journal of Interactive Advertising, 8*(2). Retrieved 28 October, 2008, from http://www.jiad.org/article100

Garrison, D. R., & Anderson, T. (2003). *E–Learning in the 21st century: A framework for research and practice.* London, UK: Routledge/Falmer.

Gibbons, H. S., & Wentworth, G. P. (2001). Andrological and Pedagogical Training Differences for Online Instructors. *Online Journal of Distance Learning Administration, 4*(3). Retrieved 28 October, 2008, from http://www.westga.edu/~distance/ojdla/fall43/gibbons_wentworth43.html

Hall, R. (in press, 2009). Towards a fusion of formal and informal learning environments: the impact of the read/write web. *Electronic Journal of eLearning.*

HEFCE. (2006). *Strategy to support links between higher education and employers on skills and lifelong learning.* London, UK: HEFCE. Retrieved 28 October, 2008, from http://www.hefce.ac.uk/econsoc/employer/strat/Board_strategy_plus_annexes.doc

HEFCE. (2008). *Employer engagement.* London, UK: HEFCE. Retrieved 28 October, 2008, from http://www.hefce.ac.uk/econsoc/employer/

Hofmann, J. (2004). *Live and Online! Tips, Techniques, and Ready-to-Use Activities for the Virtual Classroom.* San Francisco, CA: Pfeiffer.

Joffe, H., & Yardley, L. (2004). Content and Thematic Analysis. In L. Yardley, & D. F. Marks (Eds), *Research Methods for Clinical and Health Psychology* (pp. 56-68). London: Sage.

Keegan, D. (1995). *Distance education technology for the new millennium: compressed video teaching* (ZIFF Papiere, Eric Document Reproduction Service No. ED 389 931). Hagen, Germany: Institute for Research into Distance Education.

Kerr, B. (2007, February). *A Challenge to Connectivism.* Paper presented at the Online Connectivism Conference, University of Manitoba, Canada. Retrieved 28 October, 2008, from http://ltc.umanitoba.ca/wiki/Kerr_Presentation

Knowles, M. S. (1975). *Self-Directed Learning. A guide for learners and teachers.* Englewood Cliffs, NJ: Prentice Hall.

Knowles, M. S. (1980). *The Modern Practice of Adult Education. From pedagogy to andragogy* (2nd ed.). Englewood Cliffs, NJ: Prentice Hall.

Knowles, M. S. (1992). Applying principles of adult learning in conference presentations. *Adult Learning, 4*(1), 11–14.

Kurhila, J. (2006). 'Unauthorized' Use of Social Software to Support Formal Higher Education. In T. C. Reeves, & S. F. Yamashita (Eds), *Proceedings of E-Learning 2006* (pp. 2602-2607). Chesapeake, VA: Association for the Advancement of Computing in Education.

Leadbeater, C. (2000). *Living on Thin Air. The new economy.* London: Penguin.

Manchester Metropolitan University. (2007). *The Shock Absorber Project.* Retrieved 28 October, 2008, from http://www.shockabsorber.mmu.ac.uk/

McGee, P., & Diaz, V. (2007). Wikis and Podcasts and Blogs! Oh, My! What Is a Faculty Member Supposed to Do? *EDUCAUSE Review, 42*(5), 28–41. Retrieved 28 October, 2008, from http://connect.educause.edu/Library/EDUCAUSE+Review/WikisandPodcastsandBlogsO/44993

NIACE. (2008). *Mobile Technology – the handheld choice.* Leicester, UK: NIACE. Retrieved 28 October, 2008, from http://www.niace.org.uk/mobiletechnology/

O'Reilly, T. (2005). *What is web 2.0? Design patterns and business models for the next generation of software.* Retrieved 28 October, 2008, from http://www.oreillynet.com/pub/a/oreilly/tim/news/2005/09/30/what-is-web-20.html

Palloff, R. M., & Pratt, K. (1999). *Building learning communities in cyberspace: effective strategies for the online classroom.* San Francisco, CA: Jossey-Bass.

Piaget, J. (1970). *Structuralism.* New York: Harper & Row.

Race, P. (2001). *The lecturer's toolkit - A practical guide to learning, teaching and assessment* (2nd ed.). London: Kogan Page.

Ravensbourne College of Design and Communication. (2008). *Ravensbourne Learner Integration Project.* Retrieved 28 October, 2008, from http://confluence.rave.ac.uk/confluence/display/SCIR-CLINR/Home

Reason, P. (2003). Pragmatist philosophy and action research: Readings and conversation with Richard Rorty. *Action Research, 1,* 103–123. doi:10.1177/14767503030011007

Salmon, G. (2002). *E-moderating: The key to teaching and learning online.* London: Kogan Page.

Schapiro, S. A. (2003). From Andragogy to Collaborative Critical Pedagogy: Learning for Academic, Personal, and Social Empowerment in a Distance-Learning Ph.D. Program. *Journal of Transformative Education, 1*(2), 150-66. Retrieved 28 October, 2008, from http://jtd.sagepub.com/cgi/rapidpdf/1/2/150

Siemens, G. (2004). *Connectivism: A Learning Theory for the Digital Age.* Retrieved 28 October, 2008, from http://www.elearnspace.org/Articles/connectivism.htm

Siemens, G. (2008). *elearnspace: everything elearning.* Retrieved 28 October, 2008, from http://www.elearnspace.org/

Simpson, O. (2002). *Supporting students in online, open, and distance learning.* London: Kogan Page.

Stodel, J., Thompson, T., & Macdonald, C. (2006). Learners' Perspectives on What is Missing from Online Learning: Interpretations through the Community of Inquiry Framework. *International Review of Research on Open and Distance Learning, 7*(3). Retrieved 28 October, 2008, from http://www.irrodl.org/index.php/irrodl/article/view/325/743

Taylor, J. C. (2001, April). *Fifth generation distance education.* Keynote address at International Council for Open and Distance Education, 20th world conference, Dusseldorf, Germany. Retrieved 28 October, 2008, from http://www.usq.edu.au/electpub/ejist/docs/old/vol4no1/2001docs/taylor.html

Teaster, P., & Blieszner, R. (1999). Promises and pitfalls of the interactive television approach to teaching adult development and aging. *Educational Gerontology, 25*(8), 741–754. doi:10.1080/036012799267477

Trinder, K., Guiller, J., Margaryan, A., Littlejohn, A., & Nicol, D. (2008). *Learning from digital natives: bridging formal and informal learning (Final Report).* York, UK: Higher Education Academy. Retrieved 28 October, 2008, from http://www.academy.gcal.ac.uk/ldn/LDNFinalReport.pdf

Tusting, K., & Barton, D. (2006). *Models of adult learning: a literature review.* Leicester: NIACE.

Vygotsky, L. S. (1962). *Thought and language.* Cambridge, MA: MIT Press.

Vygotsky, L. S. (1978). *Mind and society: The development of higher psychological processes.* Cambridge, MA: Harvard University Press.

Wenger, E. (1998). *Communities of Practice. Learning, meaning and identity.* Cambridge, UK: Cambridge University Press.

Whisnant, W. T., & Sullivan, J., C., & Slayton, S. L. (1992). The "old" new resource for education: Student age. *Community Service Catalyst*, *22*(3), 7–11.

Zuber-Skerritt, O. (1992). *Action research in higher education*. London: Kogan Page.

Chapter 9
Blogs and the e–Flective Practitioner:
Professional, not Confessional

Paul Lowe
University of the Arts London, UK

Margo Blythman
University of the Arts London, UK

ABSTRACT

In a context of mass higher education it can be a challenge to build a reasonable level of personalised learning into the student experience. This chapter explores the relationship between personalised learning, reflection and the use of blogs in the building of a collaborative learning community through opportunities to build professional identity. The authors outline how the postgraduate programme in the Media school at the London College of Communication, University of the Arts London uses web 2.0 tools on the photography programme, in particular blogs, in developing reflective practitioners within a collaborative community of practice. The unique opportunities presented by live blogs in opening up the process of articulating experience into learning, enhance what the authors characterise as the 'E-flective practitioner'.

In my opinion, nothing comes closer to a critical assessment of my major project than my almost day-to-day account of my progress with the project (and my studies in general) in the form of this blog. What is more, the blog entries were written in 'real time' while I was working on my project and therefore are, in my opinion, more valuable to analyse my thought processes and my approach to the project than any ex post dissection could be. And in a sense, this blog also reflects – in an unvarnished fashion - my successes, excitement, frustrations and failures along the way without the benefit of hindsight.(Student on MA Photojournalism and Documentary Photography, LCC)

INTRODUCTION AND CONTEXT

Our postgraduate programme at the University of the Arts London is specialist and largely vocational. It aims predominantly at developing the knowledge and skills of professional media practitioners. As

DOI: 10.4018/978-1-60566-884-0.ch009

such, it has implications for any practice-led education where the emphasis is on solving real world problems and developing professional experience. The contemporary world requires a demanding range of skills and attributes from those working in the creative industries. These industries need people who not only have technical skills, but also an aesthetic and creative sensibility, an understanding of ethical issues in a professional context and the capacity to network and market their work. They need to have a sense of themselves in the world. Reich (1992) argues for the need for the education of 'symbolic analysts'. For Reich, symbolic analysts need to refine their skills of 'abstraction; system thinking; experimentation and collaboration' (p229). He argues for a curriculum that is:

fluid and interactive. Instead of emphasising the transmission of information, the focus is on judgement and interpretation..... the student learns to examine reality from many angles, in different lights, and thus to visualise new opportunities and choices.........Rather than teach students how to solve a problem that is presented to them, they are taught to examine why the problem arises and how it is connected to other problems. (230 -1)

Reich's argument clearly connects with 'mode 2 knowledge' which Delanty (2001) outlines as:

a form of knowledge production characterised by reflexivity, transdisciplinarity and heterogeneity (p.102).

Additionally, and this is particularly true of our case study, we are operating in a world where our students come from diverse cultural backgrounds across the globe and are working in a range of physical locations which may well be culturally new to both them and us. Thus we have complex work to do with our students yet we are within the pressures and expectations of contemporary UK higher education. It is a time of increasing student numbers but declining resource where multiple competing demands are made of both staff and students creating a demanding sense of time pressure. (Giddens 1990).

The MA Photojournalism and Documentary Photography course is aimed mostly at mature students who are mid-career professionals looking to deepen and extend their practice, or wishing to gain the skills and methodological toolbox to operate as professional photographers in an editorial and documentary context. Our students are from a wide range of backgrounds and countries. Central to our teaching strategy is the development of critically aware practitioners who are able to combine high levels of technical expertise with compelling aesthetics, underpinned by a strong ethical perspective. There is a high level of interaction with industry, evidenced especially by extensive use of professionals as visiting tutors and mentors. The quotations in this chapter from students all come from participants on this programme; their diversity of age, gender and background means that their experiences are relevant for other courses in other disciplines that involve lifelong learning as well as undergraduate or post graduate education.

Our intention is that students learn through growing into a collaborative learning community, based on professional practice which then enables them to be part of the wider community of practice of photojournalists. For us, legitimate peripheral participation includes:

- Being around those with more expertise
- Story telling that enables the exchange of soft knowledge
- Being present during major activity
- Absorbing, then learning to use the discourse
- Developing attitudes that transform their professional identity
- Building professional identity through multiple, and different forms of, relationships within the community of practice

- Learning the community of practice ways of behaving and underpinning values.
- Developing and maintaining community of practice knowledge

As Lave and Wenger (1991) argue, all three elements, legitimation, peripherality and participation are necessary to further development of a professional identity.

One to one and small group tutorials are central to our teaching method, analogous to Schon's (1987) 'coaching' approach. The students progress in a structured way from small, set assignments to their final major project, thus building a repertoire of skills and methodologies over time. The course has both full-time face to face and two year part-time fully online modes, delivering the same curriculum but in different ways.

We use five interrelated platforms for eLearning on the programme. Firstly we have an industry standard digital image asset management for uploading and interacting with photographs. Secondly we use the Wimba live classroom webconferencing suite for lectures, tutorials and group sessions. Thirdly we employ individual and group blogs for developing reflective practice and collaborative space. Fourthly we use the Ning social networking platform to communicate, host discussion forums and schedule events, and finally we have the Blackboard Virtual Learning Environment for course materials, notes and wikis.

The blogs act as the 'glue' that holds the rest of the eLearning experience together, connecting the synchronous spaces for lectures and tutorials with the asynchronous spaces such as the discussion boards and students' photographs in a real-time environment where posts can be quickly read and reacted upon individually or collectively.

Knowledge for the Contemporary World

Our underpinning aim is to enable our students to operate successfully in the complexity of the contemporary world. How do we prepare our students for this education and this world? 'Soft knowledge' (Kimble et al 2000) and tacit knowledge (Polanyi 1967) are now recognised as key to learning but difficult to codify and pass on through formal transmission methods of education. Kimble et al. (2000) define soft knowledge as knowledge that is 'more subtle, implicit and not so easily articulated.... embedded in the day-to-day working practices of communities' (p221) and is stored in the relationships between members. A social constructivist view of education leads us to recognise the importance of dialogue in learning (Alexander 2008):

Dialogue requires willingness and skill to engage with minds, ideas and ways of thinking, other than your own: it involves the ability to question, listen, reflect, reason, explain, speculate and explore ideas; to analyse problems, frame hypotheses and develop solutions; to discuss, argue, examine evidence, defend, probe and assess arguments; and to see through the rhetorical games that people play in order to disguise their real intentions or deny access to the truth. (p122)

Also key is the encouragement of reflection and reflexivity. Schon's (1983; 1987) theories underpin our teaching methodology, which is based on years of combined practical experience as photographers and journalists as well as academics. The concepts of *reflection-in-action*, and *reflection-on-action* are well established and mirror how photographers operate in the field, making constant decisions on what and how to photograph, but we also see that this process takes place in the planning stage too, what we call *reflection-before-action*. Analysis of the working practices of creative professionals also identifies *knowing-in-action*. Schon (1987) describes this as not depending on 'our being able to describe what we know how to do or even to entertain in conscious thought the knowledge our actions reveal' (p.22). This, like tacit knowledge,

151

recognises that we can do more than we can articulate verbally.

What follows from this is the potential of peer and collaborative learning amongst the student group. We hope our students will collectively generate a 'community of practice' (Wenger 1998) over their time on the course; and that much learning will take place through 'legitimate peripheral participation' (Lave and Wenger 1991). We explore later in this chapter the extent to which this can be achieved in a virtual, as opposed to face to face, community.

The combination of practice based, experiential learning is underpinned by theoretical and contextual studies that locate the practitioner within a professional culture, and locate that community within a broader socio-cultural milieu of the media. The Schonian concept of a 'practicum' forms a key underpinning to the course, providing a 'sandbox' in which the students can develop their professional practice in a controlled environment, as Schon elaborates:

The practicum is a virtual world, relatively free of the pressures, distractions, and risks of the real one, to which, nevertheless it refers. It stands in the intermediate space between the practice world, the 'lay world' of ordinary life, and the esoteric world of the academy (Schon, 1987, p37)

Schon's 'virtual world' maps clearly onto the use of web 2.0 technologies in delivering a rich collaborative experience for the students, and correlates with Eskow & Trevitte's concept of E-E learning, leveraging experiential learning with eLearning so that in the synergy generated by this process students become:

members of two learning communities: the community of practice, where they gather procedural and process knowledge, and the academic community, where they connect their reflections on these experiences to the disciplines. (Eskow & Trevitte, 2007, online reference)

As such, they have the potential to develop into what they describes as 'scholar practitioners', combining real world experiences with deep reflective insights into the role of the practitioner.

The Value of Reflection

Reflection in the context of professional practice essentially seeks to ask four simple questions: where have I been, where am I now, where am I going, and why? In a more formal sense, reflection helps learners to:

- understand what they already know (individual)
- identify what they need to know in order to advance understanding of the subject (contextual)
- make sense of new information and feedback in the context of their own experience (relational)
- guide choices for further learning (developmental) (Higher Education Academy UK Centre for Legal Education, 2008)

By working through a series of set practical assignments which then expand into a self initiated major project of the student's own choice, we seek to build a repertoire of experiences on which the photographer can draw, like a mental image bank of situations that they have resolved photographically that can act as a guide to future projects. As part of this process, we ask students to question constantly what they are doing and why, and to record the journey they are taking whilst studying with us, and on a broader scale to constantly question the media industry they are part of or wish to join. In this, we are thus seeking to develop what Schon (1983;1987) characterises as 'reflective practitioners'.

We see the importance of reflection as contributing not only to students' development of professional practice but also the learning process itself. Boud, Cohen and Walker (1985) argue:

Reflection is an important human activity in which people recapture their experience, think about it, mull it over and evaluate it. It is this working with experience that is important in learning. (p.19)

The Particular Contribution of Blogging

In order to trace this process of continuous self-examination and reflection, we have introduced blogs to the course. Ferdig and Trammel (2004) identify the way in which blogs combine the advantages of more traditional analogue learning journals with the benefits of technology, thereby empowering students with the ability to explore their individual identity:

Blogs allow students to take ownership of their learning and publish authentic artefacts containing their thoughts and understandings. Blogs also provide a way for students to individualize their content; thus, help us rethink using technology to deliver content. (online reference)

In the few years since its inception in the late 1990s, the concept of a blog (Merholz 1999), a shortened version of 'weblog' (Barger 1997), has grown exponentially with an extraordinary array of authors and purposes. The Merriam Webster online Dictionary defines a blog as 'a Web site that contains an online personal journal with reflections, comments, and often hyperlinks provided by the writer'. The 2008 Technorati survey of the blogosphere (Graham 1999) estimates that since 2002 some 133 millions blogs have been established, and that in the year to September 2008 there are some 7.5 million active blogs, with 1.5 million posting on a weekly basis. Technorati characterises this as the 'Active Blogosphere' and defines it as 'The ecosystem of interconnected communities of bloggers and readers at the convergence of journalism and conversation' (Technorati 2008). Blogs are written for all sorts of purposes, but they undoubtedly have the potential to provide a direct

route to an audience unmediated by mainstream media. Technorati acknowledges the impact that this can have on the personal development of the blogger,

The majority of bloggers openly expose their identities on their blogs and recognize the positive impact that blogging has on their personal and professional lives. More than half are now better known in their industry and one in five have been on TV or the radio because of their blog. Blogging has brought many unique opportunities to these bloggers that would not have been available in the pre-blog era. (Technorati 2008)

Seth Goldin, a leading commentator on the blogosphere, maintains that this form of communication will become all pervasive,

The word blog is irrelevant, what's important is that it is now common, and will soon be expected, that every intelligent person (and quite a few unintelligent ones) will have a media platform where they share what they care about with the world. (Goldin 2008)

Within the sector of practice relevant to the concerns of our programme, a substantial number of professionals have established blogs that have significant followings in which they detail their practice and how they navigate the complex and changing world of the photography business; this trend is apparent in many other areas of professional practice too, with educational technologies for example a major area with its own 'Oscars' in the form of the Edublogs awards. The extent of relevant blogs and their significance in terms of generating debate and dialogue within the industry was one of the main drivers in our decision to implement them in our programme, as the participants on the course were already referencing blogs regularly in their studies as sources of cutting edge contemporary industry news and analysis. The personal nature of most blogs clearly allows for significant negotiation of the personal and professional identity of the blogger in relation to an audience. Ferdig and Trammel (2004) note that:

Blogs are useful teaching and learning tools because they provide a space for students to reflect and publish their thoughts and understandings. And because blogs can be commented on, they provide opportunities for feedback and potential scaffolding of new ideas. Blogs also feature hyperlinks, which help students begin to understand the relational and contextual basis of knowledge, knowledge construction and meaning making. (online reference)

We identify several key features of blogs that make them an ideal vehicle to act as a reflective journal. Firstly, blogs serve to map the personal learning journey in real time which, when combined with the depth of personal expression that they allow, generates a level of 'connected knowing' (Brockbank and Mc Gill 2007, p68-9) that is difficult to achieve through more conventional tutorial relationships. Brockbank and McGill characterise connected knowledge as being based on empathy, trust and a willingness to extend or alter one's own perspective. They perceive it as being encouraged through reflective dialogue and a focus on making sense of the other person's experience.

Blogs provide a 'mashable', searchable archive of the student's process and progress, which can include rich media: images, video and links. They give a whole person view as they can include influences and experiences outside the core programme, and thus allow for considerable personal expression, which in turn generates increased interaction with the audience, whether that is tutors, peers or a wider group. Their collaborative nature encourages peer group feedback and commentary, which can lead to new insights at both an individual but also a group level. This sense of the collective intelligence of the group

being leveraged to generate new understandings is elaborated on by Williams and Jacobs (2004), who maintain that:

As a knowledge management tool, blogs provide the potential for relatively undifferentiated articles of information passing through an organisation to be contextualised in a manner that adds value, thus generating 'knowledge' from mere "information". (online reference)

Compared to asynchronous discussion forums such as newsgroups and bulletin boards, Ferdig & Trammel (2004) maintain that blogs are more successful in promoting interactivity that is discussional; a mode of interaction more conducive to improved student and teacher relationships, active learning, higher order thinking, and greater flexibility in teaching and learning more generally. Williams and Jacobs (2004) argue that:

Blogs have the potential, at least, to be a truly transformational technology in that they provide students with a high level of autonomy while simultaneously providing opportunity for greater interaction with peers. (online reference)

This collaborative nature encourages peer group feedback and commentary, and their portability and ease of access and updating means that they can act as 'sandboxes' in real time to explore, develop and record the entire creative professional sphere of the students' endeavours. In this way, by providing a relatively 'safe' area that is monitored by teachers acting as professional mentors, they greatly assist what Schon (1987) has characterised as 'world making', the process by which communities of practitioners:

Through countless acts of attention and inattention, naming, sense making, boundary setting, and control, ...make and maintain the worlds matched to their professional knowledge and know how. (p 36)

In this way blogs sit inside the learning cycle (Kolb 1984), creating a central space where experiences can be reflected on, analysed and acted upon, before reapplying the new paradigms learnt to the repertoire of approaches that characterise the reflective practitioner. Thus the whole process of turning experiences into understanding and generating new insights is documented in real time by the use of blogs. We extend below the concept of the learning cycle, however, as we believe that the blog provides the potential for a new paradigm of describing the learning process in the E-E learning environment.

Learning Clouds

Kolb's (1984) learning cycle has been expanded on and developed by many authors, with Cowan's (2006, p 52) learning spiral development of the concept. However, even though they develop beyond the Kolbian analogy, most of these still suggest a relatively linear progression through the various stages. In contrast, the relationship between experiential learning, reflection, the practitioner's established repertoire and knowledge and the development of new levels of understanding is more fluid and cross-referencing than these models suggest. In many ways, the analogy is with the experience of the web, with hyperlinks connecting different levels of knowledge and information, some of which is very 'hard ' and academic, and some of which is 'softer' and more anecdotal or personal. A learning 'web' suggests more interconnectivity between the various elements of the process, with feedback loops and crossovers operating in addition to more linear unidirectional growth.

However, even this metaphor is essentially two dimensional and flat, and a richer, more expansive and fluid analogy is needed. We therefore suggest the metaphor of a learning 'cloud', where at various points all these different elements are more or less relevant to the progress of understanding, depending on the exact circumstances of each learning experience. Thinking of this in a more three dimensional way, the linkages, connections and cross references that occur are much more complex and interdependent than traditional two-dimensional models as interactions can occur at the soft 'edges' of the process, where several different themes overlap. The 'eureka moment', generated by Schon's concept of 'back talk', (Schon 1987) when apparently unconnected concepts inform each other is more easily explained. This complex process of articulating experience into learning is typical of the 'real world' of work based learning, where problems have to be solved using a wide range of skills, abilities, knowledge and analysis that draws on practical understanding, ethical awareness, emotion, technical ability and intuition.

This is where the blog serves as a place to simultaneously record, reflect, plan, discuss, review and explore one's ideas, testing them out both on oneself and on an invited, closed audience of peers and mentors. The fluid, flexible nature of the blog, with its relatively unstructured hierarchy combined with the ability to search the archive using tags and categories, allows a 'stream of consciousness' style of writing whilst retaining the ability to rapidly and easily cross reference individual posts, reslicing the thoughts of the writer in countless ways depending on the search terms used. This is analogous to the 'double entry' format of journal that Moon (2006) suggests, where entries can be retuned to and revisited in the light of future experiences. Finally, their open-ended and inherently 'unfinished' nature echoes Schon's insight into 'the value of incompleteness' (Schon, 1987, p 272), with the implication that learning is a developmental process, where the journey is as important as the destination.

It is in these ways that blogs sit within the learning cloud, creating the potential for the 'e-flective practitioner', using the unique features of the blog and other web 2.0 platforms to enhance and develop the standpoint of using reflection in learning and practice.

Student Ownership and Engagement with Blogs

In establishing the blogs we give the students full choice over where and how to host their blogs, and on how to set up and design them, following Moon's (2006) advice:

Unless there are reasons for prescribing a particular format, it is desirable that the format of a journal is a matter for personal experiment and choice for the learner because this is a manner through which a sense of ownership – a relation to the writing- is developed. (p 95)

We therefore do not prescribe the hosting service for the blog, nor the layout, format or design. We offer the possibility for students to host their blog on a university provided server, using the wordpress blog farm, but in fact the majority of students choose to host their blogs externally, usually on either wordpress or Google's blogger. com. When asked why, the typical response centres around issues of ownership and portability, with many planning to continue their blogs after they graduate. Indeed a significant proportion of the original group to set up blogs from 2006 are still maintaining their blogs today, and are using them to promote their professional practice, to keep colleagues and friends informed of their progress and to document and record their activities.

For us it is important that the blog represents the whole person in so far as it relates to their professional practice, as Klug (2002) advises:

Write how you really feel and not how you think you should feel. Record what you really think, not what you believe you ought to think. (p.56)

Blogs perform several functions on the course. Their main purpose is to map the individual student's learning journey, thus deepening reflective practice and strengthening their repertoire by articulating experience into learning. In doing so,

they describe and explore issues and problems the students face in their practical assignments. In this extract, for example, a student discusses the thought process by which they analysed a particular situation for its visual potential leading to a radically different approach to the assignment than they first started with, which in turn adds to their 'repertoire' to apply to future situations:

The initial idea was to wait for the 'moment' to reveal itself. It took me about 10 minutes to discover that the moment was revealing itself quite often, but I was looking for 'this moment' the wrong way. Typically we look for the moment when a child leaps, a ball bounces, an arrow strikes the target or a person shouts. As photographers we want to 'freeze' that moment in time. But in this mass of moving people I started discovering it was actually the rare moment when it was the people who were 'freezing' in place - to talk on a phone, get their bearings, meet someone or reverse direction. These moments sometimes lasted a few seconds or a few minutes or a microsecond. So rather than freeze a moment with a fast shutter speed, I slowed down the shutter speed to let the blurred movement of the people help isolate the moments when people 'froze' in place.

The blogs document the process of research and planning on larger projects, essentially creating an instant archive of the creative interaction with the situation. The blogs are vital too in referencing the world outside, providing an arena for the students to explore influences other than the course. This example shows how a student used a writer's insights into a geographical region she was exploring:

I'm currently reading Downriver by Iain Sinclair. He writes beautifully but is also somewhat negative about places along the estuary, '...Canvey Island: a gulag of sinking caravans, overlooked by decommissioned storage tanks.' Yet I sense great passion in his writing. Celebrate might be too strong a word but I want to acknowledge these places for what they are, both good and bad.

As the blogs are open to the whole group, they provide a vital collaborative arena in which to showcase work and get peer group feedback and support. In this dialogue of an initial post and subsequent comments, the support and encouragement that the group provides is clear;

(initial post)

I am finding it hard to put narratives to my stories, my photography over the years has been about my family, friends, life and when put together I can see a narrative but when I have a small amount of time and a short story I tend to panic. I want to be on this course because I want to learn what to do with it. My personal work seems to evolve over years, ...I am confused........

(Comment 1)

Well, I think your confusion, hesitations, fear and whatever else is shared by us all. Don't fret. We're here to help. Don't give up and keep learning. (The tutors)..... are hard on us because they believe in us.

(Comment 2)

I would agree.... While you may be feeling a little confused regarding your progress perhaps, and the occasionally brutal crit sessions that is (tutors name)'s style may sometimes take its toll. I think we all learn more from these short sessions if the tutor is direct yet constructive. Trust their judgment and faith in you and while the technical aspect of photography can be learned relatively easily through practice and reading, having fresh and original ideas is what will make you stand out from your contemporaries.

(Comment from tutor)

Please don't be SCARED. If you are, I will be too.

(Comment 3)

...and whilst you may be worried, the photograph you have here of your daughter tells me you shouldn't.... I was wandering the streets today looking for things to happen and pondering what I need to do to step up a gear in my learning and my skills. Then I look at your photograph and spot the "echoes" that I never used to look for before....when we're pushing so far forwards, we sometimes don't realise how far we've come along.....

They also function as a critical commentary on the course itself, creating a space that maybe less threatening than conventional feedback routes which allows the student body to express its views on both the strengths and weaknesses of the programme, allowing tutors and staff to respond flexibly to students' views in a way difficult to do with other feedback methods.

Informed especially by Moon's work on learning journals, (Moon 2004; 2006), we have used blogs on the course in a staged way, starting out with relatively little formal discussion of reflection in the first term, and using the blogs mainly as a way to enhance interaction and understanding between the cohort and the tutors, and then gradually adding more detailed discussion of reflective practice as the course develops. For example, at the beginning of the programme they are required to write a short 'letter to the world', introducing themselves to their fellow students and tutors and describing their career to date and their reasons for studying the course; and at the end of each phase of the course they write a 'letter to myself' that is essentially a SWOT analysis of where they stand at that moment and what they need to do to advance in their studies. This extract is typical of the reflective nature of these entries:

I feel that this course is making me more focused in my practice. I feel more comfortable with my style of photography and have a more positive outlook of what I potentially can do with it and where it might fit. My approach to photography has pretty much always been related to exploring places, searching for locations that seem to tell a story. I took this same approach to my work this term but I also did portraits of people that I meet along the way. This was a first for me and to my surprise it felt very natural and I think the portraits worked quite well with the landscapes. I'm a bit worried though, that there are not enough stories to my work or that it lacks clarity. I research and read a lot but perhaps the images I take are too general? My ambition is not to create classic photo essays but more trying to give a sense or understanding of a place. At times I feel torn between aesthetics and content....

This process continues throughout the course, culminating in a final critical analysis of their major dissertation project, which draws on the material from the blog in constructing a contextualising statement about the final body of work setting it into a broader context and exploring honestly the successes and failures of the project.

The blogs also perform a vital role in supporting students outside of timetabled sessions, especially in non-teaching weeks when they are engaged in self-directed study. Typically they carry out the bulk of the photographic element of their major project over the summer recess, a period of three months during which there are no formal classes. Being able to keep track of their progress on their projects and give supportive feedback is a major advantage of the blogs. Also, they provide an arena for the student to explore areas outside of the main course structure. In one case, a student who had produced work of only an average standard for the assessed elements of the course posted daily images on their blog that were far more adventurous and exciting than that submitted for course work; images that they may never have seen in a conventional tutorial environment. As a result, the tutorial staff were able to encourage them to direct their work towards the more innovative approach for their final major project,

Enhancing Participation

To promote the collaborative commenting on blogs, we divided the group up into smaller teams of what we call 'blog buddies', where four students would commit themselves to reading and commenting on each other's blogs on a regular basis, as well as trying to respond to other people's blogs where possible. This is based on the concept of the buddy system as used in sporting and safety environments, where 'buddying up' ensures that participants look after each other. This made the process more manageable for students, as they didn't feel the pressure that reading and commenting on a larger number of blogs on a regular basis would entail. Our experience in the first year of using blogs when we didn't use this concept was that students would comment on each others postings, but not in a regular, coherent or systematic way.

However, it must be noted that passive interaction with blogs is not necessarily a symptom of lack of engagement. As Nonnecke & Preece (2001) maintain, 'lurking' is an important aspect of an online community. Reading blogs without commenting on them serves to expand the understanding in the lurker, and also delivers a sense of belonging even if they do not actively engage with the material. Additionally, blogging implies an assumed audience of readers even if they are not visible as commentators, and the semi-public nature of the activity ensures that the blogger is aware of the possibility of disagreement, censure or approval from their readers, enhancing their critical faculties and writing skills.

Perhaps most importantly for personalised learning, tutors use these project descriptions in advance of tutorials to get a sense of what the student's work is about, making tutorials much more effective in delivering exactly the right advice for that particular student. This extract shows how the student worked particularly on the details of body language in her assignment:

I found the shoot quite difficult even though the players remain pretty much in the same position throughout. I looked for small details, like hand movement, concentration on face and eye contact as well as finding a good position to shoot from. I was trying to use the players shoulders to look over, to frame the image, lead the viewer in to the image and create a more exciting perspective. This did not quite work out, I would have to move in closer for such effect but then I was losing faces. I think this would perhaps work out with a wide angle lens.

The blog thus gives tutors greater insights into the individual student. This support can be continued outside of term time and timetabled contact points by giving feedback on ideas and work in progress. Blogs thus give valuable insights into how students deal with the assignments they are set, and how they then convert that experience into knowledge. As such, they greatly assist staff in learning how learners learn. This quote shows how the student has to juggle her academic 'life' with her professional and personal ones, giving an honest and authentic insight into the pressures students face:

Things I have learnt this week

1. *That too much information can overload the brain*
2. *Small girls watching Dr. Who beside you while working is counter productive*
3. *A timetable in order to manage my life is needed*
4. *I know what the word 'meretricious' means*
5. *(our tutor) told us we would have deadlines, what I forgot is that life goes on too, and by some miracle I seem to be getting paid work as well.*

6. *My daughter has nits again...........*
7. *Taking part in this MA is teaching me much more than I thought, the research is really difficult but its really showing me the subject. I am not a writer at all but it is getting my thinking to work on a higher level than before and I am finding those books I found so hard to read just 6 months ago much easier*

Professional Not Confessional: Issues in Using Blogs

A number of issues arise in using blogs mainly as a result of their having wider audience than a single assessing tutor and also the relationship of the blog to assessment.

Ethical Issues

We considered several ethical issues in the use of blogs. The first is that discussion of personal matters generates issues of privacy. Who sees the blog? Is it limited to staff and peers? What about the role of external examiners or family and friends? One student faced a significant dilemma when she realised that people external to the course were making inappropriate comments about images of her family that she had posted on her public facing blog:

Should I stop posting pictures of my kids and life because of this, it kind of gets into a ethical debate about children and photography. The problem is that I photograph my world and kids are part of that right now, but also the web is such a huge unregulated monster that really even if I put privacy barriers on my pictures, who knows how easy they are to get through.

She subsequently decided to make her blog private and only available to her peers and tutors.

Secondly we established rules of 'netiquette' when posting to the peer group to maintain a professional environment for discussion and commentary. The level of self-disclosure is key, as blogs can help to develop a sense of professional /private spheres. We are also keen to avoid disclosure as a form of surveillance. Foucault (1995) argues:

This turning of real lives into writing is no longer a procedure of heroisation; it functions as a procedure of objectification and subjection. (p.17)

It is important to recognise that the blog can act as a space to explore the relationship between the professional and the personal, and to delineate those areas that can be discussed in the professional sphere and those that need to remain in the personal, so the blog can act as a 'sandbox[1]' to establish what is *professional not confessional.*

Assessing Blogs

A major question for us was whether and how to assess the blogs. Arguably some degree of assessment was required to make sure students actually maintained them, but not too formally because they are not the main product of the course, but rather a supporting feature to enhance the production and critical reflection of their photographic practice. Again, Moon (2006) provides guidance, advising that 'the assessment of secondary material is usually the preferable choice' (p.112).

We therefore treat the blogs with what we characterize as a 'light hand' and use them primarily for formative assessment during the research and production phase of the projects. The students then reformulate the material for their final critical report, which accompanies their major photographic project for the completion of their studies. The searchable and taggable nature of the blog format makes this process very efficient, as entries can easily be retrieved and reorganised to form primary source material for the later analysis. The blogs themselves are assessed on progress to a standard of completion with a required minimum number of weekly entries. As outlined earlier, we

ask the group to write personal statements at key points in the course to sum up their experiences, progress and their action plan for the future. These reflective letters form the basis of the one to one tutorials they then have via web-conferencing with their tutors, providing valuable insights into the student's work at crucial points in the course.

In this way we are seeking to assess *process* not *product* in the blogs. We regard this way of working with blogs as pedagogically sound as it encourages the return to the material and enhances secondary reflection. Additionally, it changes the blog from an assessment method to a tool for learning making it freer and more exploratory/ experimental. It avoids marking personal material, and the reformulated critical report is easier to assess against a set of criteria. Material from elsewhere can be included in the original blog and format and presentation issues are minimised, making the word count easier to handle.

However, several students who were very comfortable with the blog format have been allowed to present their critical report in the form of their blog. In several cases this has been very successful, particularly where the student used tags within his blog to identify key points where he critically interacted with his project in real time. The quote at the start of this chapter sums this up in the student's own words.

Volume of Postings

The volume of postings was an issue for both staff and students. Our student evaluations indicated that students felt that there were too many access points for information e.g. blogs, VLE, and emails; and that one centralised portal would be better. Running two blogs, one for project work and one personal was seen as counterproductive. Equally, the staff time needed to read and react to the blogs is significant, and in order to gain the greatest benefit this needs to be allowed for in determining allocation of staff resources. This process of reading the blogs can be greatly assisted by setting up a simple RSS feed to a blog reader, and by setting up a group blog to aggregate the entries from each individuals blog in one central point. It is then a simple matter of building the reading of blogs into the teaching schedule; typically just before a tutorial session the tutor can rapidly scan the relevant blog to see what progress the student has made. This significantly speeds up the process of getting to the heart of the issue that needs to be discussed in the tutorial, as the typical period at the start of a session when the student has to explain what they have been doing is negated, leading to a more fruitful interaction and greater student engagement. Also, due to their more informal nature, blogs can be 'scanned' and read relatively quickly, they do not demand the concentrated focus that a more academic style of writing would require. Thus the time spent – in our case typically five minutes in advance of a tutorial session – is well spent in terms of deepening the level of 'connected knowledge' with the student.

BENEFITS

Motivating Students

Feedback indicates that our students like blogs and find them useful. MA Photojournalism and Documentary Photography students are mostly digital immigrants with some digital natives (Prensky, 2001) however most are comfortable with technology, and use computers and the Internet in their existing professional practice. Some already had or read blogs before embarking on the course. Our evaluation from an MA cohort of 16 online students at end of first term is typical of both modes on the course. All the students responded that the process of creating the blog to aid studies had been very useful or useful and most students found the process of writing the blog useful or very useful in helping to deepen understanding of their own practice. All students

also responded that they found blogs useful or very useful in getting to know their fellow students and creating a sense of a group identity. In all these responses the majority were in the very useful rather than useful category. These figures are broadly in line with feedback we have from other years, and with other surveys of blogs in postgraduate education, e.g. the Brisbane Graduate School of Business (BGSB) MBA Blog (Williams and Jacobs, 2004).

Identity Construction and Personalisation

Arguably, the popularity and perceived usefulness of blogs among students comes from their role in enabling a personalised form of professional identity construction. This is likely to be valued by students where mass higher education has limited opportunities for personalised formal learning activities with academic staff. Blogs enable students to reproduce themselves in text and position themselves in relation to their knowledge through a process of self-narration (Chappell, Rhodes, Solomon, Tennant and Yates 2003). James and McInnes (2001) argue that writing is an act of self representation and Ivanic (1998) points out that the *process* of writing itself is a form of identity construction. Ewins (2005) reinforces this point particularly in the context of blogging where the process makes overt how identity construction is happening.

However professional identity construction is a social activity which happens through interaction with social processes and structures and so collaboration in a variety of ways is an important contributing factor.

Building a Collaborative Online Learning Community

There is a debate over the extent to which a Community of Practice can exist virtually. Kimble et al (2000) argue that the key issue is how to share soft knowledge. They argue that there are three methods of soft knowledge construction within a community: gathering specific knowledge, knowledge of working practices of the community; knowledge construction about the competencies of other members, often through story telling. They also argue for the importance of a shared artefact; a document in their case study and in ours, the blogs. They point out the role of document creation as a process which involves collaboration and sharing and embedding soft knowledge. Further, the document forms a mode of communication which both stimulates interaction and raises issues for discussion. This is similar to the role of the boundary object in Community of Practice theory (Wenger 1998) as an artefact or document that enables interconnections within and beyond the particular community. Kimble et al. (2000) argue that this works well in the kind of community where members share resources that are relatively easily translated to a distributed community but is more of an issue where there is an necessary face to face element in learning the job. Lueg (2000) sees this translation as more problematic since it raises questions about what the 'doing' is in a virtual community. He asks if there can be a community where members are distributed and there is little shared work practice. However he goes on to argue that there are other indicators of a community such as 'shared terms of good conduct as described in the so called netiquette, shared humour, and organised real-world meetings in selected newsgroups'. (p.4)

Overall we are convinced that blogs help the students understand more about what their fellow students are working on, strengthening the sense of community, especially valuable on group pieces of work. They quickly build a collaborative community, especially on the online course, as blogs give a rapid and deep insight into the personality and perspective of the blogger. Traditional models of student reflection can be critiqued as lacking in dialogue (Brockbank

and McGill 2007), particular in an era where there is limited tutor time to allocate to reading and feeding back on students' input. By building a collaborative learning community students are constantly in dialogue with each other and have to absorb and process the points made by other students as well as tutors.

The blog encourages students to support each other in the development of their professional identity, what it means to be a photojournalist, as this extract illustrates.
Comment:

I wouldn't be too worried about the fact that someone else has done on Thames Estuary work. Everything has been done-it's something I found time and time again over the years. At the NYT we would often gripe about reporters redoing stories (and us subsequently re-shooting it time and time again.). But as far as projects, subjects or ideas, realize that you have a unique eye and an original perspective on it, and most likely a strong personal vision that you will bring to your project that no one else will.

The following quote charts the development of a professional identity:

a friend/mentor told me years ago in New York that you should give yourself about ten years to develop as a photographer...the toughest part seemed not to give up...it's hard to pin down exactly where to mark the beginning of those ten years -- in china when I discovered light and shadow through the lens and experienced what something looks like when you make a photograph of it for the first time or when I was freelancing for the English language Indian newspapers in Madras, India in 1998 - that was the first time I was published... anyway...seems like things are rolling along now and I know I have so much more knowledge and understanding with how the business works and what exactly I want from it...

Brockbank and McGill (2007) point out the importance of dialogue for reflective learning since an individual's knowledge and understanding develops through response to critique. They argue that:

Dialogue that is reflective, and enables reflective learning, engages the person at the edge of their knowledge, their sense of self and the world as experienced by them. (p.65) The following post and comment show how this dialogue can take place at a deep level of empathy for the issues the students face:

(initial post)

I am taking stock this weekend about whether I have moved on at all since starting this MA. I feel I have, there are days when nothing works and I feel disillusioned but then if I really look back to say November or last year I realize that I am doing something everyday towards my work, whether its reading or actually taking pictures or making sure I see things I need to. Also I am beginning to think of myself as a photographer when people ask, rather than just saying nothing or mother.

(comment)

I read your comments about identity, motherhood, work...sounds like a good idea to start calling/ believing that you are a photographer !:) but I know what you mean...I declared myself a photographer in 1997 and moved to India for a year and a half to begin my career...I do remember at first though the hesitation and unsureness I felt in calling myself a 'photographer.' Also, I look younger than I am, so at 27, I probably looked like 21, 18...It's good you are recognizing these things...

With the project centred blog, tutors and other students are able to monitor and comment on each other's work in real time without having to wait for tutorials or other formal learning activities.

Students can post questions and ask for advice or comments on their work. The blogs then also form an instant communal archive of the creative process; this is especially valuable on group projects that have an extended life beyond the duration of the project. The ability to look back at previous years' blogs is an invaluable resource.

Students can also express their feelings about the course in a less self conscious way than in more formal contexts. By making the students more aware of the idea of blogs in general, it has made them search out relevant blogs in their area of practice, thereby increasing their understanding of the medium. Five of the previous group are still using their blogs one year after graduation as a platform for their work.

Widespread use of blogs could easily replace or supplement the traditional art and design student workbook, as it opens out the creative process to a wider audience, allowing much more interaction and feedback between the students and tutors, and documents in real time the trials and tribulations, and successes and failures of the e-flective practitioner.

Personalised Learning

Blogs help individual students organise their thoughts and document their workflow, essentially becoming an online workbook/sketchbook for their ideas, creating a space for reflective analysis of their projects in real time. In giving a 'warts and all' view of both their studies and of the course they develop an arena for healthy self-criticism of themselves and of the programme. As indicated earlier, the process of blogging helps build professional identity.

Most importantly they offer the tutorial staff an unparalleled insight into how the students think, work and relate to each other; thus they amplify 'connected knowledge' (Brockbank and McGill 2007) in a way that contact through tutorial sessions and classroom cannot match. Whilst the blog cannot replace more traditional tutorial sessions, it does get inside the student's work in a way that is not easily obtained by other methods. The best blogs offer an extraordinary insight into the students' practice, detailing the practical, conceptual and ethical issues they faced and documenting how successfully they overcame them. The blog format because of its informal nature allow students to express their ideas in a non threatening way, and get valuable peer group feedback as well as feedback from tutorial staff. It also permits students to present their other interests outside of course work, thereby enabling them to present themselves as more rounded individuals. They are 'authentic', in that grounded in experience, reflective diaries depict personal observations, making it difficult for others to fake. Tutors therefore have the insights about each student to make a real contribution to a more personalised form of learning.

We can see a number of possibilities for future research. We now have two years worth of blogs from both online groups and face to face groups. It would be profitable to carry out detailed analysis of the blogs including patterns of involvement and a more extensive analysis of how various forms of knowledge are negotiated and constructed.

Blogs can play a significant role in the development of communities of practice within a Schonian practicum that encompasses both the academic and the experiential zones. Both on an individual and on a group level they can serve to enhance the documentation of learning and reflection upon it, operating as collaborative vehicles to enhance not just the student's process of building a professional identity but also the whole group by sharing the differing viewpoints and activities of each participant with a controlled and appreciative audience. Their unique qualities of being in real time, and their expressive character that enables a more complete insight into the students practice greatly enhance the level of connected knowledge both with tutors and with their peer group. These attributes combine with their searchability and ease of re-contextualisation

to create the potential for technology to generate the e-flective practitioner.

REFERENCES

Alexander, R. (2008). *Essays on Pedagogy*. Abingdon, UK: Routledge.

Barger, J. (1997) Robot Wisdom WebLog for December 1997, *Robot Wisdom WebLog*. Retrieved September 6, 2008 from http://www.robotwisdom.com/log1997m12.html

Boud, D., Cohen, R., & Walker, D. (1985). *Reflection: turning experience into learning*. London: Kogan Page

Brockbank, A., & McGill, I. (2007). *Facilitating Reflective Learning in Higher Education*. Maidenhead, UK: OU Press.

Chappell, C., Rhodes, C., et al. (2003). *Reconstructing the Life Long learner: Pedagogy and identity in individual, organisational and social change*. London, RoutledgeFalmer.

Cowan, J. (2006), *On Becoming an Innovative University Teacher, 2nd Ed*. Maidenhead, UK: OU Press.

Delanty, G. (2001). *Challenging Knowledge: The University in the Knowledge Society*. Buckingham, UK: SRHE/OUP.

Eskow, S., & Trevitte, C. (2007). Reschooling Society and the Promise of e e-Learning: An Interview with Steve Eskow. *Innovate, 3*(6). Retrieved June 9, 2008 from http://www.innovateonline.info/index.php?view=article&id=502

Ewins, R. (2005). Who are you? Weblogs and Academic Identity. *Journal of E-Learning, 2*(4).

Ferdig, R., & Trammel, K. (2004). Content Delivery in the 'Blogosphere.' *T.H.E. Journal*, Feb 2004. Retrieved June 8, 2008 from http://www.thejournal.com/articles/16626/

Foucault, M. (1995). *Discipline and Punish*. New York: Vintage.

Giddens, A. (1990). *The Consequences of Modernity*. Cambridge, UK: Polity/Blackwell.

Goldin, S. (2008). Quoted in Technorati (2008) *State of the Blogosphere / 2008*. Retrieved Sept 18 2008 from http://technorati.com/blogging/state-of-the-blogosphere/

Graham, B. (1999). *Must See HTTP://, Sept 10, 1999*. Retrieved Feb 16 2009, http://www.bradlands.com/weblog/comments/september_10_1999/

Higher Education Academy UK Centre for Legal Education. (2008). *Introduction to Developing Reflective Practice*. Retrieved June 14, 2008 from http://www.ukcle.ac.uk/resources/reflection/introduction.html

Ivanic, R. (1998). *Writing and Identity*. Amsterdam: John Benjamins.

James, B., & McInnes, D. (2001). Interdependent Academic Identities: Language and Learning Practitioners and the Subject who writes. Retrieved February 15, 2009 from http://learning.uow.edu.au/LAS2001/index.htm

Kimble, C., Hildreth, P., & Wright, P. (2000). Communities of Practice: Going Virtual. In K.-P. Mehdi, (Ed.), *Knowledge Management and Business Model Innovation,* (pp. 220 - 234). London: Idea Group Publishing.

Klug, R. (2002) *How to Keep a Spiritual Journal. A guide to journal keeping for inner growth and personal discovery*. Minneapolis, MN: Augsburg.

Kolb, D. A. (1984). *Experiential Learning experience as a source of learning and development*. Upper Saddle River, NJ: Prentice Hall.

Lave, J., & Wenger, E. (1991). *Situated Learning: Legitimate peripheral participation*. Cambridge, UK: Cambridge University Press.

Lueg, C. (2000). *Where is the Action in Virtual Communities of Practice? Proceedings of the Workshop Communication and Cooperation in Knowledge Communities*. Paper presented at the D-CSCW 2000 German Computer-Supported Cooperative Work Conference "Verteiltes Arbeiten - Arbeit der Zukunft", Munich, Germany.

Merholz, P. (1999). "Peterme.com". The Internet Archive. Archived from the original on 1999-10-13. Retrieved February 16, 2009 from http://web.archive.org/web/19991013021124/http://peterme.com/index.html

Moon, J. (2004). *A Handbook of Reflective and Experiential Learning*. London: Routledge.

Moon, J. (2006). *Learning Journals: A handbook for reflective practice and professional development*. London: Routledge.

Nonnecke, B., & Preece, J. (2001). *Why lurkers lurk*. AMCIS Conference, Boston, June. Retrieved May 21, 2008 http://snowhite.cis.uoguelph.ca/~nonnecke/research/whylurk.pdf

Polanyi, M. (1967). *The Tacit Dimension*. New York: Anchor Books

Prensky, M. (2001). Digital Natives, Digital Immigrants. *Horizon, 9*(5).

Reich, R. (1992). *The Work of Nations*. New York: Vintage Books.

Schon, D. (1983). *The Reflective Practitioner*. New York: Basic Books.

Schon, D. (1987). *Educating the Reflective Practitioner*. San Francisco: Jossey-Bass.

Technorati (2008). *State of the Blogosphere / 2008*. Retrieved September 18, 2008 http://technorati.com/blogging/state-of-the-blogosphere/

Wenger, E. (1998). *Communities of Practice: Learning, Meaning and Identity*. Cambridge, UK: Cambridge University Press.

Wenger, E., McDermott, R., & Snyder, W. (2002). *Cultivating Communities of Practice: a guide to managing knowledge.* Boston: Harvard Business School

Williams, J. B., & Jacobs, J. (2004). Exploring the use of blogs as learning spaces in the higher education sector. *Australian Journal of Educational Technology, 20*(2), 232-245. Retrieved June 15h, 2009 from http://www.ascilite.org.au/ajet/ajet20/williams.html.

ENDNOTE

[1] The concept of a sandbox as a controlled area in which to experiment or practice is one common in software development, we use it here in the same way as the wikipedia sandbox see http://en.wikipedia.org/wiki/Wikipedia:Sandbox

Chapter 10
Building Practitioner Skills in Personalised eLearning:
Messages for Professional Development

Ruth Pilkington
University of Central Lancashire, UK

ABSTRACT

The chapter suggests the implementation of personalised learning within Higher Education raises fundamental issues and challenges when developing academic staff to support this form of learning and explores some of the challenges raised. It discusses the value of personalised learning for professional development in particular within the context of UK Professional Standards for HE staff. The chapter uses a case study to illustrate the issues and solutions offered by personalised eLearning and identifies particular issues of literacy, prior learning and comfort with respect to online delivery that need to be recognised for both developers and professional learners. The case study draws on a Joint Informations Systems Committee (JISC) funded project under the RePRODUCE banner and compares findings with existing traditional means of developing staff, as well as discussing the processes represented and the contributions that can be made when personalising learning more widely within HE.

BUILDING PRACTITIONER SKILLS IN PERSONALISED ELEARNING – MESSAGES FOR PROFESSIONAL DEVELOPMENT

Introduction

The emergence of personalised learning within the tertiary sector is an invitation for e-technology that must not be rejected. The web offers potential for students to access knowledge globally, and to individualise learning by using instant access to information as a learning resource. Social networking tools like Facebook, chat-rooms, discussion media and blogs can be used to share and build knowledge, reflecting a trend towards a socialised process of eLearning.

Professional development has become a significant activity within higher education (HE) as a result of initiatives to support and enhance learning

DOI: 10.4018/978-1-60566-884-0.ch010

and teaching activity in the UK higher education (HE) sector. These initiatives are embedded in HE as part of the Centres for Excellence in Teaching and Learning initiative, the work of The Higher Education Academy and its associated Subject Centres, and most recently through the introduction of a UK Framework of Professional Standards (UK PSF) for Teaching in HE (Higher Education Funding Council for England, HEFCE, 2006).

Academic and educational developers are employed within HE for the initial and continuing professional development (CPD) of HE staff. They often lead and support experienced staff in the enhancement of teaching and learning; provide initial teacher training to meet professional standards; and address a range of pedagogical themes and development needs in response to learning and teaching strategies and institutional priorities.

Personalised learning with its emphasis on learner centredness, diversity, empowerment of learners and flexibility (Beetham & Sharpe, 2007; MacDonald, 2006; Taylor, 2000; Phipps et al, 2008) could in principle provide an effective means of addressing the professional learning needs of academic staff within this context of initial and continuing professional development. This chapter explores whether this is in fact the case.

BACKGROUND

Professional Standards for the UK

In February 2006, the UK professional standards framework (UK PSF) for teaching in higher education was launched after extensive consultation. Backed by Universities UK, the Higher Education Funding Councils of Wales, England and Northern Ireland, the UK PSF presents three standard descriptors against which institutions of Higher Education are encouraged to accredit, reward and structure the initial and continuing professional development of staff employed in teaching and

learner support roles. The HE Academy provides a national accreditation process for universities that grants professional status to individual staff aligned to UK PSF. The PSF descriptors utilise five value statements to inform the professional ethos of HE staff. The PSF also specifies six expectations for professional knowledge and understanding and six areas of activity. By applying these descriptors to their own professional development frameworks for staff, universities can provide evidence of the quality and professionalism of their academic staff as well as contributing to the excellence of teaching and the student learning experience (www.heacademy.ac.uk).

Three of the value statements (a, c and d in table 1 below) focus attention on the importance of respecting the individual within the learning process and the social context of learning. These are characteristics of personalised learning. The areas of activity, knowledge and understanding identified within UK PSF highlight the informed development of practice when designing and supporting learning within the subject disciplines and the use of appropriate learning technologies to do so. This central requirement of UK PSF makes academic staff responsible for developing themselves and their practice when supporting an increasingly diverse, digitally-native student body.

The first standard descriptor can be used to accredit the professional development and status of a broad range of academic staff in teaching, learning support and research roles. The second focuses very specifically on the lecturer role, and the third descriptor emphasises leadership in academic practice (Pilkington, 2007).

The introduction of a UK Professional Standards Framework in 2006 for HE teaching staff has meant that, in addition to initial formal (taught) teacher education programmes linked to the core standards requirements, many higher education institutions are incorporating plans for continuing professional development using both formal and informal mechanisms to support the ongoing professional development of all staff. This

Table 1. Table showing values statements, areas of knowledge and activity for UK PSF

Six areas of activity	Knowledge and understanding of:
1. Design and planning of learning activities and/or programmes of study	1. The subject material
2. Teaching and/or supporting student learning	2. Appropriate methods for teaching and learning in the subject area and at the level of the academic programme
3. Assessment and giving feedback to learners	3. How students learn, both generally and in the subject
4. Developing effective environments and student support and guidance systems	4. The use of appropriate learning technologies
5. Integration of scholarship, research and professional activities with teaching and supporting learning	5. Methods for evaluating the effectiveness of teaching
6. Evaluation of practice and continuing professional development	6. The implications of quality assurance and enhancement for professional practice

The professional values are:
  a. Respect for individual learners
  b. Commitment to incorporating the process and outcomes of relevant research scholarship and/or professional practice
  c. Commitment to development of learning communities
  d. Commitment to encouraging participation in higher education, acknowledging diversity and promoting equality of opportunity
  e. Commitment to continuing professional development and evaluation of practice	

is resulting in the emergence of innovative and interesting approaches to professional development focusing on postgraduate CPD provision. These postgraduate courses tend to involve high levels of resource (Knight, 2006), and to focus on reflective, work-based learning delivered face-to-face through workshops (Kahn and Baume, 2003), mentoring and peer groups. At the same time the dynamic and increasingly complex environments of universities mean many lecturers have less time for formal face-to-face learning experiences, suggesting HE teachers may benefit from something more in line with the principles enshrined by the personalised learning agenda, that offers flexible learning opportunities aligned to problems and challenges in HE practice, socially constructed according to professional learning principles outlined in the next section.

Professional Learning

Professional learning encompasses the process of supporting the development requirements of the individual professional academic, at varied career points, in response to the different professional, personal and practice priorities faced. Within the literature professional learning is identified as being practice-focused and work-based. According to Eraut (1994, 1998), and Clegg (2006), professionals learn most effectively within the workplace, through informal, applied and experiential mechanisms. Wenger, (1998) suggests the creation of [professional] identity is integrated and defined in the course of engagement with practice (p76). The concept of 'Communities of Practice', the community around a domain or field of interest, has been linked by Lave and Wenger (1991) to notions of the professional developing within practice. Panda and Juwah (2006) suggest that professional learning, if meaningful, will be enacted within online communities of practice, but also – they emphasise – off-line within the real-life practice community of the practitioner (p207). This poses a challenge to the personalised eLearning agenda as to how these two aspects of professional learning can be effectively combined.

Negotiation of meaning is fundamental to professional learning which emphasises dialogue (Savin Baden, 2008), collaborative reflection with peers (Kahn et al, 2006; Brockbank & McGill,

2007), and reflective opportunities (Schon, 1987; Kuit and Reay, 2001). Eraut (1994) suggests that professional knowledge should be contextualised, individually applied and engaged with, which may be from a subject perspective as well as from an individual, locally relevant perspective. For professionals in HE who generally regard themselves as subject experts first (Becher & Trowler, 2001), this makes immense sense. This emphasis on the individual construction of relevant knowledge utilises a cognitive process called 'theorizing' (Eraut, 1994). Eraut continues that professional knowledge creation is primarily an experiential process resulting in potentially creative, unique and innovative practice. Panda and Juwah (2006) recognise this and place the 'self', the individual process of meaning making, centrally within professional learning online.

In conclusion then professional learning occurs best within an environment that can engender and facilitate communities of practice in which sharing and social collaboration and negotiation of meaning are fundamental components.

According to UK PSF professional development for HE academic staff should respect broader pedagogic knowledge alongside discipline specific agendas (Becher & Trowler, 2001; UK PSF Knowledge and Understanding criterion 1 – see Table 1). The postgraduate certificate awards for learning and teaching in the UK HE sector provide structured space for social and personal learning through dialogue that respects the influence of the practice environment, the role of peers, reflection, and scaffolded access to pedagogic knowledge and understandings (Vygotsky, 1978, Kreber, 2004). They also provide access to the language and concepts of education opening the route to development of conscious competence (Race, 2004: 13), and facilitating development through technical, pedagogic and curricular expertise (Kreber, 2004).

The author suggests that personalised eLearning can meet many of the conditions for professional learning because it involves professionals in theorizing (Eraut, 1994) by contextualising knowledge but also in discussing it with peers and/or with experienced 'others' (Vygotsky, 1978). This notion of an experienced 'other' is important in professional learning. It is related to ideas of support from an expert 'peer' as mentor or coach. Brockbank and McGill (2007) utilise the concept of 'cognitive apprenticeship' to characterise this 'expert peer' / 'learning peer' relationship and to also provide a notion of structured support. They suggest this is a viable and appropriate method of structuring professional learning in HE. The model focuses on dialogue over an indefinite period in which metacognitive apprenticeship skills are developed in partnership with an experienced 'other' who initially models behaviours, scaffolds professional learning using reflective processes, interrogation and engagement with self assessment and then gradually fades out as 'expert' (Boud & Falchikov, 2007: 130). Finally, Peel (2005) adds that professionals may often have to deal with dual status: being experienced in one area but acting as 'novice' in another. There will be elements in which the practitioner will be acting at the level of novice requiring considerable support, such as when developing eLearning for the first time. This reinforces an apprenticeship model of learning, especially in new fields of professional activity. This idea of novice/expert status is particularly relevant to the case study in this chapter which addresses the needs of academic developers who are experienced in pedagogy but inexperienced in eLearning, yet expected to provide leadership to academic staff that encompasses both elements.

Professional learning involves questioning, critique, and evaluation in the light of context and values, and judgement (Eraut, 1994, Boud and Walker, 1998). In this respect it reflects very much the three descriptor fields identified within UK PSF. It follows that the development of professional knowledge can be linked to the idea of a motivated, self-directed, autonomous and critical learner able to contribute pro-actively to the enhancement and re-creation of her own practice (Moon, 2004) and able to contribute to the development of the professional community and shaping of general professional knowledge.

The notion of a motivated self-directed autonomous learner has its roots in theories of adult learning (Knowles, 1989; Candy, 1991 in Tennant, 2006: 8-9). According to these theories adult learners are assumed to be self motivated, to prefer problem solving approaches, and to learn in response to social (or employment) roles and functions. The assumption is they are capable of self-direction and able to draw on accumulated experiences. Often issues needing clarification among professionals are allied to problems and solutions and hence professional learners may be motivated by needs linked to practice. This suits solution seeking adult learning approaches. Pratt (1993:17, cited in Tennant, 2006:17) adds two principles to adult learning requirements: that learning is actively constructed by the learner; and that it is an interactive process of 'interpretation, integration and transformation of one's experiential world'. It is worth considering these ideas within the context of personalised eLearning in which a fully empowered eLearner can flexibly act to take control of their own learning using e-tools, and engage in dialogue with others to construct and interpret that learning (Beetham & Sharpe, 2007:21).

Making collaborative learning through online dialogue available to staff for professional learning means the practitioner can apply existing subject and professional knowledge to problems or solution seeking as proposed within the learner centred, grounded instructional models outlined by Juwah (2006: 54; citing Nelson, 1992; Aamodt and Plaza, 1994; and Barrows, 1985).

Personalised Learning

Personalised learning is being strongly promoted within the primary and secondary sectors of the UK. Under the UK government policy initiative 'Every Child Matters' (www.everychildmatters.

gov.uk/ete/), personalised learning has been introduced as a means of engaging pupils more actively in their learning. This concept of personalised learning emphasises curriculum choice, learning beyond the classroom, frequent formative assessment, and the development of more responsive teaching and learning mechanisms as well as placing emphasis on partnership between teachers, learners and parents.

In HE personalised learning emerges from a response to increasing diversity of learners, retention and funding (Yorke & Longden, 2004). As with personalised learning in the secondary sector, in HE personalised eLearning incorporates expectations of flexibility, choice, and partnership. It recognises 'diversity, difference and individuality in the ways learning is developed, delivered and supported' (Kukulska-Hulme & Traxler 2007:184). It is coupled however with notions of the 'new learner' (Sharma and Juwah, 2006:229) for whom learning 'cannot be limited to formal settings alone. The whole world is a university that is at hand to offer limitless opportunities for learning'. This contains assumptions regarding experience of independent learning that may be valid for experienced learners, as with the professional HE practitioner, but may not be guaranteed for new HE students (Beetham and Sharpe, 2007:21). It also points clearly to the contribution of the world-wide web.

The web offers instant access to information as a learning resource. Suggestions are that in future students may access 'learning objects' at will which they will restructure for their own learning purposes, putting the learner in the place of the teacher (TESEP[1], cited as example by Beetham and Sharpe 2007:21). The idea of learning objects, free-standing learning packages that may be used for education and training (Oliver, 2001, Faidhi and Mohammed, 2004), is appealing to universities and potentially for learners within the context of personalised learning. They may also be attractive for overloaded academic staff seeking access to materials for lectures and seminars. This idea of open access resources, accessible at will to students and staff is important to notions of personalised learning. It also poses challenges to the individual learners in that they need to be a lot more effective as learners, and to have skills of judgement and selection, as well as clarity about their individual learning objectives. These are characteristics outlined by Tennant (2006) as associated with the adult learning. Ravenscroft and Cook (2007:216) recognise the challenge of self-directed learning and suggest that personalised learning may in fact involve provision of learning across a continuum from formally structured to free open-access and self-directed approaches. They suggest that within personalised learning it is important to recognise 'the degree of personalisation that the learner is comfortable with...this should be seen as part of the personalisation process itself'. This is important and relieves educators of the pressure to embrace personalised learning without question. It places learning and the needs of the learner-centred curriculum at the heart of personalised learning.

The advent of social e-tools (Facebook, Myspace, blogs, Wikipedia) to the eLearning experience is an important one. It provides access to tools for the social sharing and construction of learning. Goodfellow and Lea (2007) suggest that for young students who have grown up with these social networking tools as digital natives (so-called), information technology could lead to the development of a 'newly emerging generative order, linking students and academics into widening and increasingly eclectic knowledge-generating networks' (p7). They consider that eLearning used in this way can potentially change the way we learn, work and socialise and they describe a world in which learning may be supported less by formal e-delivered learning courses and more by learners accessing learning materials 'tagged' so that they can be deployed 'systematically from a database of materials to satisfy the needs of an audience of learners seeking just-in-time, individual learning' (p44). While recognising the value of technologies for personalising learning

approaches, Goodfellow and Lea raise significant and important concerns about the challenges of e-literacy and hence the ability of students, and indeed staff to engage with this new medium for learning purposes (p36).

Language is in fact not simply another kind of interface through which communication is conducted, but is in itself constitutive of communication in a very active way.... There has been so little attention paid to language in the context of eLearning...there is clearly a tradition of CBL [computer-based learning] failing to come to terms with it!

The issue of language is one also recognised by Russell in his activity theory approach (2002) which attributes a mediating role to language as both a cultural and learning tool (cited p139 in Goodfellow and Lea, 2007). When learning in a text-based medium, language is particularly important as other visual clues which normally aid communication are missing.

Having established that professional learning can be supported by personalised eLearning approaches, it is worth considering the professional development needs of academic staff as they are called upon to develop themselves to use personalised eLearning to support their students. What are the requirements for professional competence and knowledge and how can they be met?

A useful starting point is to identify professional competence and the skills needed for practitioners wishing to implement eLearning approaches in their teaching. Sharma and Juwah (2006) explore this in some depth, drawing on work by Dooley & Lindner (2000, cited Sharma and Juwah, 2006:234) which identifies the need for questioning skills, constructive criticism, an understanding of adult learning theory, technological knowledge, instructional design and communications skills. They also refer to Williams' (cited Sharma and Juwah, 2006:234) list of 30 e-teaching competencies which he groups into three areas: communication and interpersonal skills, administration and management and technology and instruction (pedagogic) skills. Finally Salmon (2000) outlines a range of competencies for e-moderators involving an understanding of online processes, technical skills, online communication skills, content expertise and personal characteristics. In particular she focuses on the skills necessary to support group work and learning for the social construction of knowledge. MacDonald (2006) talks about skills associated with managing asynchronous and synchronous discussion. These offer challenges because face-to-face teaching and classroom management skills do not transfer automatically to an eLearning environment.

Apart from the focused development of skills for facilitating, structuring and managing eLearning, there are critical questions of how to develop curricula in HE around the specific topic of eLearning. This generates additional professional learning needs for HE teaching staff with respect to curriculum design and is an important aspect of UK PSF. It stands out as a core professional skill in the values, areas of activity and knowledge and understanding. A consortium of Scottish universities working on eLearning delivery to support students concluded independently that five principles should underpin considerations on how to rethink learner centred e-design. Four of the five suggested principles reflect questions of learning design and relate directly to personalised learning.

1. Ensure every learner is as active as possible
2. Design frequent formative assessment
3. Put the emphasis on peers learning together
4. Consider whether learning tasks can be personalised
5. Consider how technology can help to achieve these principles. (www.jisc.ac.uk/media/documents/programmes/elearningsfc/sfc-booklettesep.pdf retrieved September 27th 2008 p5)

These clearly recall objectives in the areas of activity within UK PSF and create challenges for professional learning and development. They are also strongly reminiscent of personalised learning requirements.

In their consideration of how to support staff in the development of eLearning, Beetham and Sharpe (2007) make some very specific recommendations on how to develop academic skills and knowledge for eLearning. They recognise, for example, the need for technical updating and skills development. They recommend that academics should have opportunities to engage with technology in a staged, incremental way. The staged approach is one they feel can keep eLearning manageable for staff. To give this process a relevant learning purpose, Beetham and Sharpe (2007) emphasise that academics need to be encouraged to explore the use of eLearning as a means of making incremental improvements in the student learning experience. This means adopting a staged model of developing professional knowledge in eLearning design that specifically prioritises curriculum design and enhancement of student learning. They suggest examples of creating meaningful enhancement activity such as lecture slides to be used as a student e-resource; focused assessment tasks, using multiple choice questions; designing follow-on activity from lectures, introducing investigative projects. These types of eLearning activities mean that academic staff can develop their eLearning skills around specific interventions without requiring a complete redesign of learning. The development involved comes in manageable short bursts with specific skills sets built around generic workshops or short training courses.

This model of a staged engagement in eLearning cumulatively builds familiarity and understanding of the scope and value of eLearning. Beetham and Sharpe (2007) also suggest that for larger undertakings such as course redesign, staff need to work collaboratively, and to be given space to adopt an appropriate development cycle of piloting, evaluation and adjustment in the introduction of new courses so that improvements can be made and supported. Drawing on Beetham and Sharpe's work and the model proposed by the Scottish Enhancement Themes (TESEP) project cited above, it is possible to propose several points of good practice when engaging staff in eLearning.

1. Provide technical and skills training
2. Familiarise staff with e-technologies as users and learners
3. Explore with staff the (learning) purpose of e-technologies
4. Provide opportunities to apply different levels of eLearning application to support learning
5. Incorporate time and concrete activities to support implementation, e.g. using projects
6. Use a range of flexible, varied approaches across institutions
7. Incentivise professional development
8. Provide ongoing technical and educational support

These apply equally to the development of professional capability when introducing personalised learning with students as well as for those in academic development.

The Case Study

A project provides an excellent opportunity to build familiarity with eLearning and to develop staff in line with eLearning development models outlined above. This chapter uses examples from work undertaken for a project within a post 1992 university in the North West of England to show:

- How educational and academic developers can develop themselves to support others with personalised eLearning developments

- The experience of mature, non-digital native academic staff when trying to engage progressively with eLearning
- The perspectives of staff engaged in an online professional learning course and the issues that emerge relating to personalised professional learning
- How a formal professional learning programme can apply some of the personalised learning approaches in its design and delivery structure.

METHODOLOGY

The case study focuses on the work of a team of academic and educational developers linked to a postgraduate certificate award in learning and teaching. The education team are experienced developers of several years' standing and have worked together for a number of years on the Postgraduate Certificate in Learning and Teaching in HE. Several members of the team also contribute to a larger Masters in Education (MEd) continuing professional development award at the institution which incorporates numerous modules (20 credit units of study at masters level) and sub awards focusing on different areas of professional development. Before embarking on the project, the team had engaged sporadically with eLearning on the professional development programmes in line with staged development models of introducing eLearning (reflecting Beetham and Sharpe, above). This involved incorporating repositories of learning materials within a VLE (WebCT) and targeted use of discussions linked to individual assignments. They had become increasingly concerned about their expertise in the area of eLearning and technology and welcomed the opportunity to rewrite a core module worth 20 credits within the postgraduate certificate as a reduced, 10 credit, taught online course. It was intended as a support for part-time and hourly paid staff and for those based in university outposts without a professional teaching qualification, and was therefore linked to UK PSF. This was seen as an opportunity to gain experience in the e-facilitation of professional learning as first step to engaging with new social-networking and eLearning tools. Because the team lacked specific experience of designing curriculum for eLearning, they adopted an e-design model by Bird (2007), which emphasises three principles: creation of content, consolidation and construction of knowledge and favours structured engagement with asynchronous and synchronous communication tools for social mediation of learning.

The process of developing an e-programme provides an excellent opportunity to focus attention and acquire skills of eLearning (Laurillard, 2008; Donnelly and O'Rourke, 2007:35). Curriculum design activity is an appropriate mechanism for motivating professional learning: it provides a vehicle that has relevance to the individual's practice and therefore fits with professional learning principles. In this case the team worked with colleagues from a learning development unit. These colleagues provided mentoring, expertise and support with respect to the technology and tools required for the rewrite of the materials. This sort of collaborative development activity is useful because it promotes the academic and technical partnership necessary to design an effective learning environment, as well as mirroring the staged models and strategies for personalising eLearning proposed by Beetham and Sharpe (2007) and the Scottish Enhancement Themes (TESEP) Project. The outcomes were significant for the course development team in providing opportunities for their own targeted professional development.

The project was funded by JISC as part of the RePRODUCE[2] funding call in 2008. It involved redesigning existing and open access materials as a professional online learning course delivered over 12 weeks. The course was linked to the Staff and Educational Development Association's (SEDA) Professional Development Framework award in 'Supporting Learning' and UK PSF descriptor one. One outcome was the production of several reus-

able learning objects for professional development for JORUM[3], an open access resource bank. In this respect the team was responding directly to a personalised learning agenda. Research activity linked to the project involved qualitative action research (defined Kemmis, 1988 in Zuber-Skerritt, 1996: 147). It focused on the impact of designing the online course upon the team's development and subsequent changing perceptions to e-supported professional learning, as well as on the learning experience of the course students (also staff). This research involved interviewing the five member team midway and at the end of the course development and design process. Interviews were transcribed and analysed using an inductive approach, drawing out the themes and developmental aspects. Course participants (six) were also interviewed and transcriptions analysed for emergent themes. In addition, participants' work online within discussions and chat-rooms, and using a blog were analysed to expose the learning processes and evidence of learning construction through social mechanisms. A final collaborative event provided opportunity for the reflection and feedback process characteristic of action research to take place and for the course participants and team to discuss changes to the online course. In this way it was possible to draw preliminary conclusions about the online learning process for professional staff focusing on social construction of learning using reflective approaches. All participants gave their consent to the use of transcribed materials and documentation as part of the pilot and for research and dissemination purposes. The course comprised a taught package involving pre-defined and structured input, and also tried to replicate professional learning processes usual to facilitated, face-to-face workshops. Hence it drew heavily on a need to create social spaces (Savin-Baden, 2008) for collaborative learning that respects applied and active mechanisms, reflection on practice (Boud and Walker, 1998, Brockbank & McGill, 2007), application beyond the online context (Juwah, 2006: 207), and values-driven exploration of the participants' own development (SEDA; UK PSF; Eraut, 1994). Assessment tasks for the course and in the assessed online discussions were informed by Bird's scaffolding model for online learning (2007) and patchwork text methodologies (Winter, 2003). The patchwork text uses small incremental tasks to help learners develop their ability to write reflectively. The approach suited the small tasks linked to online discussion on the new course. Assessment is recognised as having a critical motivational role in learning (Brown et al, 1997), therefore the use of a patchwork text approach to the structuring of online discussions provided an effective way of incorporating reflective, peer-supported collaborative learning and social constructivist learning mechanisms.

From the outset of the project e-literacy and confidence with technology emerged as important barriers to how experienced staff, as non-digital natives, engaged with online learning. As the technical colleague commented, 'none of the course team is particularly technologically au fait...so it's been outside their comfort zone'. This attitude is recognized by Goodfellow and Lea (2007) as a barrier to eLearning. Although the development team had experience of social communication tools, for example three had experience with facebook and blogging, they expressed reservations about further involvement in what they regarded as time-consuming communications media. Technology is often secondary to the pedagogic and educational change issues for teaching staff and is addressed when it needs to be, often driven by the needs of learners (Beetham and Sharpe, 2007). The original face-to-face workshops for the 20 credit course emphasised a discursive, non-directed approach which the team regarded as appropriate to reflective, experiential learning. This attitude also influenced the team members to say that dialogue and the social and discursive structuring elements of face-to-face professional learning suffered when using text-based online tools.

- 'I still am not convinced that you get that dimension, that human interaction dimension with eLearning'. (Team member D)
- 'I think that my tendency is to be very interactive as a lecturer, almost a Socratic method, to pose questions and to sort of do exploration with students in that style, which is quite difficult to translate into an eLearning style. (Team Member B).
- 'In general, we have evolved to meet people face-to-face and we react to a wide variety of cues: physical posture; expressions on the face... Most of those are missing online, so you're really filtering everything, in most cases, through the textual expression and that means that it's not always that you're missing those other cues that you have come to rely on, that you're evolved to rely on, but also you're putting more of a burden on somebody to express themselves effectively using text'. (Team Member F)

This issue also stood out in participants' interviews. They found the lack of visual cues difficult to deal with in chat-rooms. They struggled with the synchronous chat-room process either because of typing speed or not being able to read, react and respond quickly enough, suggesting challenges of language, motor skills and literacy.

- 'I'm not very good reading a load of words on a screen and when words are coming at me in a random fashion and the topics are not sequential – it's all very random.' Participant A
- 'It's something to do with it being an alien environment and with it also being an immediate, sort of, synchronous event.' Participant B
- 'I'm not having difficulty following the threads, but sometimes being able to respond at the appropriate time – you know because we're talking about quite complex

concepts sometimes, aren't we?' Participant C

The text-based construction and reflection on learning in e-discussions was challenging but less difficult, although one person 'lurked' and gradually withdrew, having found the experience alienating 'I am totally a social learner which is why I do feel freaked out and alienated by the online environment'. In addition, participants were motivated to engage actively because discussions were linked to the patchwork text assessed element of the programme (Winter, 2003; Dalrymple and Smith, 2008). Participants' higher level of comfort with this medium comes across in comments:

* 'You can sit down and just type something that you think is a contribution to something and then just post it. That's not difficult.' Participant B
* 'Now, to my mind there's two issues there. I don't mind reflecting anywhere because I'm only going to reflect the bits that I want you to know anyway, so I might as well be on the discussion board and I might as well be being assessed' Participant A
* 'It's been good to see other people's ideas and to respond to that and then for them to respond to mine'. Participant C

These quotes imply that certain social eLearning tools were regarded as more accessible and familiar, as well as more supportive of collaborative learning. The difference in value and experience between discussions and chat rooms was quite marked; the chat rooms were viewed as having a generally negative impact. Salmon (2000) recognises specific advantages to discussions online in that they can be rewound to review comments, to pick out links and to rework the exchanged ideas in a way that is not possible in face-to-face dialogue. In this respect e-discussions offer genuine benefits to part-time professional learners as in this case study.

The students here were experienced professional learners and accustomed to reflection, but they nevertheless faced problems with e-literacy and communication using the electronic medium. This suggests challenges such as these will need specific attention when supporting online discussion for less experienced undergraduate learners operating in an unfamiliar academic context.

The course team's lack of familiarity with eLearning created problems with management of the eLearning process (Macdonald, 2006: 89), but overall it was apparent the discussion boards provided a more thoughtful social environment for reflecting and constructing professional learning, and the assessed aspects helped give this value. A team member commented that chat-rooms were particularly hard:

The experience I've had of chat-rooms in the past is that they can get a bit out of hand and the time delay is always a bit of an issue and..., for example you answer a question to one student and whilst you're typing that another question pops up into the chat-room, ...so the whole thing is supposed to be synchronous but it doesn't have coherence very often. (Team Member B)

The latter points are significant when considering personalised learning spaces using the written word. They indicate that there are distinct challenges associated with written e-mediated communication that may hinder collaborative social construction of learning online, namely: literacy, one-dimensional communication, comfort and aptitude.

It is possible to conclude that, because these participants were self-motivated and effective autonomous professional learners (Tennant, 2006), this would contribute to more effective learning. This expectation may not be as straightforward for undergraduate students. In fact Biggs (1999: 3) describes the majority of undergraduates as having difficulty with self-direction. Others (Biggs, 1999; Brown, 1997; Boud and Falchikov, 2007;

Bryan and Clegg, 2006) stress the importance of assessment to drive the learning process for this reason. Motivation is a criterion for success in personalised learning, but even though discussions were assessed, one participant withdrew.

The suggestion was that there might be a sense of insecurity and exposure in the text-based discussion because it can be disjointed and is visible in ways face-to-face exchange is not. In fact it appeared that the course team was more concerned about exposure than the participants from the following comment:

Whereas if you say something, it sort of goes in and out of people's minds and you sort of think well it's not going to be there forever, but there's a sense of permanence and visibility of you know… exposure. (Team Member A)

The course team was very concerned about the social aspects of the online module because for them the reflective, social and discursive aspects of professional learning and sharing that takes place in the face-to-face environment were lost. It ran counter to their concept of professional learning spaces and was influenced by their lack of familiarity. This perception would be challenging to overcome given the important role of the 'peer' in reflective professional learning (Kahn et al, 2006).

- 'Being actively involved in the process.. they learn best in a community, so it's really important that people have an opportunity to discuss things with their peers' (Team Member B)
- It's about layering, synthesizing and rebuilding it constantly in a social context'. (Team Member A)
- 'Learning is a social encounter' (Team Member D)

This suggests that the e-spaces of Savin-Baden (2008) or the social processes being promoted

within personalised learning may need effort, commitment and confidence from the facilitator if they are to form part of a structured learning experience (MacDonald, 2006: 48, 81; Savin-Baden 2008: 84). This is an area that may need considerable attention if lecturers are to be effective in supporting collaborative online personalised learning (Juwah, 2006). Feedback from participants on the original face-to-face course has always indicated in contrast that one of the substantial benefits for the workshop week was the fact that a diverse group of participants were being brought together to network and share perspectives. This came out strongly as an issue in course team concerns:

- 'I think that diversity is quite good because people can share experiences in the group and do have experiences to draw on'. And again, 'The sort of cross-university networking I think can be lost and just the human cut and thrust of being together in a classroom, the human element, and the coffee breaks, where after the class is over people can go off and talk about their experiences and so on.' (Team Member B)
- The [face-to-face course] is very interactive, well that week of sessions is very interactive and we say that some of the relationships that are developed between participants, ..it's really valuable for them to take those away and sustain those. (Team Member F)

Interestingly, the participants themselves did not perceive a difficulty about exposure or the group learning in the e-medium and dwelt positively on the value of the discussions:

- 'I don't mind reflecting anywhere because I'm only going to reflect the bits that I want you to know anyway' Participant A
- 'It's been good to see other people's ideas and to respond to that and then for them to respond to mine' Participant C

What didn't emerge in the interviews with either the participants or course team was the sense that a community of practice had been generated around the online module. This is unfortunate and is in contrast to the genuine networks and community of practice that have been observed as emerging around the face-to-face experience. Discussions with the e-course participants suggested their off-line community of practice was significantly more important in its contribution to their development as professionals than the online learning. This supports Panda and Juwah (2006) in their recognition that off-line learning in the real life community of practice of the practitioner can be a powerful component in professional learning. This suggests that further research may be required and that the emergence of a community of practice online is dependent upon factors not present in this case study.

Personalised learning implies the learner chooses and repurposes learning objects for her own use (Goodfellow and Lea, 2007: 44), whereas the experience of the project also emphasised the value of others providing structured learning materials reflecting the requirements of constructively aligned learning (Biggs, 1999) and addressing the novice/expert tension. The programme content itself was well received and regarded as important. Participants stressed the value of access and the usefulness of the learning materials because they were quite small chunks and therefore suitable to a self managed process:

- 'I really liked the links to online papers and stories relevant to the module' Participant D
- 'I think, looking through the units, they are actually broken down quite nicely into manageable chunks, aren't they? So, I found them quite good.' Participant B

The participants also welcomed the fact that they could access materials at a time of their own choosing and select what they felt they needed:

- 'This has had to fit in around other things and I haven't read every single bit of material that's been put up on WebCT or read all of the book you know.. I know where things are now, if I need to look at them in more depth'. Participant C
- 'I think the ones we've had on this course in terms of reading stuff online and being directed to different websites, I've found quite useful. That works for me in terms of doing it in my own time and sort of getting things organized'. Participant B

This aspect matched the objective behind the RePRODUCE project initiative: the creation of reusable learning objects for access at need by learners, a fundamental underpinning assumption associated with personalised learning. The online programme offered genuine value for professionals wishing to access learning and development at a time of their choosing. This advantage of the content was recognised by the team: it created a resource that was permanently available and accessible for the participants to revisit, complementing a personalised learning approach:

Students only seek information and retain it at a point where they want to use it and eLearning provides that opportunity for people to revisit stuff to access it when they need it. (Team Member B)

An additional conclusion in discussions with the team suggested the permanence of materials online and the more focused attention required to learn in this medium resulted in deeper learning than that in the fast-paced, fluid, face-to-face workshops.

- 'I think that they will get substance. I think that quite often what happens in the Toolkit classroom is transient, you know ideas are generated and thoughts are being created and they're not always captured by the materials that people take away and here you've got quite robust materials that can act as a good source of reference' Team Member B).

- 'So it may well suit people to reflect on the material and then at their leisure, in their study or whatever, think I'll just ask a question here or something. So, there are gains and there are losses I'm sure' (Team Member E)

Finally, the course team struggled with the idea of producing reusable learning objects, of creating something self-contained and meaningful, and questioned how a resource of materials (JORUM) even when organised with keywords around topics would be truly accessible to time-pressured staff seeking specific development. At the end, whilst the generation of the learning objects was relatively straight forward because they emerged naturally from the online course content, concerns about accessibility and usability remained. In personalised learning approaches, the onus is on the learner to contextualise and judge the value of the materials, and even to make them relevant for their own learning purpose. This may be difficult for even experienced professional learners who may be accessing resources and concepts from a 'novice' perspective. It suggests a need for mediation by a facilitator or educational developer to interpret or purpose learning objects (Brockbank & McGill, 2007; MacDonald, 2006). The application of materials as learning objects is something that needs further clarification and consideration to ensure accessibility for online personalised learning

FURTHER RESEARCH DIRECTIONS

From this brief discussion it is evident that further research into the impact of e-literacy and text-based communication is required, as well as for staff delivering personalised learning and in the context of designing learning objects and self-

directed learning. Whilst professional learning appears suitable to this form of delivery, there are areas where personalised eLearning appears less relevant; for example, for initial professional training and development of new lecturers, especially where it is linked to professional standards such as the UK PSF. Even for experienced staff seeking just-in-time solutions for continuing professional development (CPD) purposes, there are indications that facilitation of learning is important. It may be simply that 'novice' pedagogues need support to access concepts, pedagogic language and to determine what is valuable. This raises the question of personalised learning compared to facilitated eLearning (Ravenscroft and Cook 2007:216). Finally, the generation of communities of practice from online learning is not indicated by the findings of this case study. This needs further exploration. Communities of practice may be enhanced by eLearning but do not necessarily emerge if not already present.

CONCLUSION AND RECOMMENDATIONS

The case study provides insight into how eLearning can be experienced and developed as a professional learning tool. The impact on the development team of engaging with eLearning as e-designers and e-deliverers was very positive and the use of a project was invaluable. It helped the team members engage actively and meaningfully in professional development, building their own skills in eLearning. The case study indicates how, as students on such programmes, staff can also gain insights into the actual student experience of eLearning in HE. This is a significant benefit of such professional programmes and fulfils an important organisational objective of involving staff in eLearning delivery. Lessons and issues raised within this chapter provide a stimulus for reflection for readers in a wide range of roles - academic, development and training, technical and managerial - with respect to the experience and support of academic and educational development staff developing personalised learning spaces.

Some strong messages emerge from the reflections of both course designers and participants. These relate in part to the level of development of the team members themselves with respect to eLearning delivery, but also to some fundamental questions about professional learning and the capacity of eLearning to replicate an environment for effective professional learning. The restructuring of a face-to-face experience engaged the team with aspects of eLearning technology and although the structured learning on the new course was still distant from personalised eLearning ideals, it highlighted important questions of access, reflective dialogue, text-based communication, asynchronous and synchronous discussion and social learning. The case study confirmed the benefit of assessment and structure for all these aspects of the learning experience, and reinforced the value of co-ordinated staged professional development for those engaged in delivery.

According to the views outlined in team members' comments, many of them would not have engaged with the eLearning agenda without the driver of necessity. Having done so however, the process prompted thinking about how staff might utilise this learning to support colleagues' work around eLearning and how they can incorporate it further themselves, as well as drawing lessons from the process of restructuring the content.

The experience of delivering professional learning online indicates that when studying online, regardless of the personalised learning objectives, a structured experience for the students and staff is helpful in order to compensate for the loss of face-to-face cues and interaction, and from the perspective of constructing learning. There are questions as to whether personalised learning is appropriate for undergraduate learners given the early stage of development for most students regarding their autonomous and self managed learning capacity. For adult learners the issue may

be less significant. It can be assumed that professional learners should have greater capacity for self reflection, planning and identification of needs and of managing their learning. Early indications suggest this is not necessarily so, and this also fits what is understood about initial professional learning. Most postgraduate certificate courses for learning and teaching in HE provide crucial introductions to language and concepts of education for subjects specialists, for example. This is necessary for professionals within the context of UK PSF and the issue of being novice and expert simultaneously makes structure in learning important. The process of engaging with personalised eLearning design and delivery does, however, meet several of the statements on areas of knowledge, understanding and activity identified within the new UK professional standards framework.

In a CPD context, the example of the MEd award, especially one with a large number of modules, presents issues often shared by continuous professional learning across the sector. It is resource intensive, with demanding high level masters modules often offered to small groups. Personalised eLearning mechanisms can potentially support variety by providing the structured input for content and letting the deliverer focus on supporting the community, networking and reflective opportunities desirable for this type of learning. It is clear from the discussion in the chapter that such aspects within the eLearning process require substantial expertise however. In addition, staff development is necessary for the e-providers, plus considerable support, effort and skill-building for the participants. Even with this input, the desired creation of a community of practice to support personalised professional eLearning may not be guaranteed. Personalised learning is an important new approach within the HE sector. It offers benefits for the changing educational experience and emerging student needs. The emphasis on flexibility, choice and mechanisms to support inclusive learning around the classroom experience is critical. These elements are also desirable within a professional learning context.

The value of engaging in eLearning design and delivery in a way that ensures and facilitates a pedagogic exploration of its benefits and drawbacks is demonstrated as being significant for staff. Early adopters of new technologies and personalised learning will run ahead, but, for the majority of academic staff, support, structure, training and the opportunity to acquire confidence in the new medium are essential. It is valuable and helpful for those supporting such initiatives – the educational developers – to be familiar and empathetic to the issues, concerns and solutions offered by technology. Academics, developers and technologists should therefore work together to address the central learning questions identified in this chapter benefitting those associated with implementing personalised eLearning methodologies for themselves, as well as generating solutions that meet the particular learning demands of their students.

REFERENCES

Baldwin, C. (2004). X4L review: final report. *JISC*. Retrieved October 29th 2008 from http://www.jisc.ac.uk/media/documents/programmes/x4l/Baldwin, 2004.pdf

Becher, T., & Trowler, P. (2001). *Academic Tribes and Territories* (2nd Ed.). London: SRHE / OUP.

Beetham, H., & Sharpe, R. (Eds.). (2007). *Rethinking Pedagogy for a digital age*. Abingdon, UK: Routledge Falmer.

Biggs, J. (1999). *Teaching for quality learning at University*. London: OUP/SRHE.

Bird, L. (2007). The 3C model for networked collaborative eLearning: a tool for novice designers. *IETI, 44*(2), 153–177.

Boud, D., & Falchikov, N. (Eds.). (2007). *Rethinking Assessment in HE*. Abingdon, UK: RoutledgeFalmer.

Boud, D., & Walker, D. (1998). Promoting reflection in professional courses: the challenge of context. *Studies in HE, 23*(2), 91–206.

Brockbank, A., & McGill, I. (2007). *Facilitating Reflective Learning in HE* (2nd Ed). London: SRHE/OUP.

Brown, G., Bull, J., & Pendlebury, M. (1997). *Assessing student learning in HE*. Abingdon, UK: Routledge.

Bryan, C., & Clegg, K. (2006). *Innovative Assessment in HE*. Abingdon, UK: Routledge.

Dalrymple, R., & Smith, P. (2008). The Patchwork Text: enabling discursive writing and reflective practice on a foundation module in work-based learning. *IETI, 45*(1), 47–54.

Donnelly, R., & O'Rourke, K. C. (2007). What now? Evaluating eLearning CPD practice in Irish third-level education. *Journal of Further and Higher Education, 31*(1), 31–40. doi:10.1080/03098770601167864

Eraut, M. (1994). *Developing Professional Knowledge and Competence*. Abingdon, UK: The Falmer Press

Eraut, M., Alderton, J., Cole, C., & Senker, P. (1998). Learning from other people at work. In R. Harrison, F. Reeve, M. Cartwright, & R. Edwards. 2002 *Supporting Lifelong learning* (Vol. 1, pp. 127-145). Abingdon, UK: OUP / Routledge Falmer.

Fiaidhi, J., & Mohammed, S. (2004). Design issues involved in using Learning Objects for Teaching a Programming Language within a Collaborative eLearning Environment. *International Journal of Instructional Technology and Distance Learning, 1*(3), 39–54. http://www.itdl.org/Journal/Mar_04/March-04.pdf Retrieved October 29th, 2008.

Goodfellow, R., & Lea, M. R. (2007). *Challenging E-learning in the University: a literacies perspective.* London: SRHE / OUP.

Jaques, D., & Salmon, G. (2007). *Learning in Groups: a handbook for face-to-face and on-line environments,* (3rd Ed). London: Routledge.

Kahn, P., & Baume, D. (Eds.). (2003). *A Guide to Staff and Educational Development.* London: SEDA /Kogan Page.

Kahn, P., Young, R., Grace, S., Pilkington, R., Rush, L., Tomkinson, B., & Willis, I. (2006). *The role and effectiveness of reflective practices in programmes for new academic staff: a grounded practitioner review of the research literature.* Manchester, UK: University of Manchester, The HE Academy.

Knight, P. (Ed.). (2004). *Assessment for Learning.* Abingdon, UK: SEDA/RoutledgeFalmer.

Knight, P. (2006). *The Effects of Post-graduate Certificates.* EPGC Project in collaboration with Open University, Management passed to Tony Brand at Anglia Ruskin in 2006.

Knowles, M. (1989). *The Making of an Adult Educator.* San Francisco: Jossey Bass.

Kreber, C. (2004). An analysis of 2 models of reflection and their implications for educational development. *The International Journal for Academic Development, 9*(1), 29–49. doi:10.1080/1360144042000296044

Kuit, J. A., & Reay, G. (2001). Experiences of reflective teaching. *Active Learning in HE, 2*(2), 128–142. doi:10.1177/1469787401002002004

Kukulska-Hulme, A., & Traxler, J. (2007). Designing for mobile and wireless learning. In H. Beetham & R. Sharpe (eds.), *Rethinking Pedagogy for a digital age* (pp.180-192). Abingdon, UK: Routledge Falmer

Laurillard, D. (2008). The Teacher as Action Researcher: using technology to capture pedagogic form. *Studies in Higher Education, 33*(2), 139–154. doi:10.1080/03075070801915908

Lave, J., & Wenger, E. (2002). Legitimate peripheral participation in communities of practice. In R. Harrison, F. Reeve, A. Hanson, J. Clarke, (Eds.) *Supporting Lifelong Learning Vol. 1 Perspectives on Learning,* (pp. 111-126). London: OUP/Routledge

MacDonald, J. (2006). *Blended Learning and Online Tutoring: a Good Practice Guide.* Oxon, UK: Gower.

Moon, J. (2004). *Reflection in Learning and Professional Development: theory and practice.* Oxon, UK: Routledge.

Oliver, R. (2001). Learning Objects: supporting flexible delivery of online learning. *18th ASCILITE conference proceedings.* Retrieved October 29th, 2008 from http://www.ascilite.org.au/conferences/melbourne01/pdf/papers/Oliver,2001r.pdf

Panda, S., & Juwah, C. (2006). Professional Development of on-line facilitators in enhancing interactions and engagement: a framework. In C. Juwah (Ed.) *Interactions in online education: implications for theory and practice,* (pp. 207-227). Abingdon, UK: Routledge.

Peel, D. (2005). Dual professionalism: facing the challenges of continuing professional development in the workplace? *Reflective Practice, 6*(1), 123–140. doi:10.1080/1462394042000326851

Phipps, L., Stiles, M., Cormier, (2008). Reflecting on the VL system – extinction or evolution. *Educational Developments, 9*(2), May.

Pilkington, R. (2007). SEDA PDF – *A Tool for Supporting and Structuring Continuing Professional Development Frameworks.* London: SEDA Special 21 SEDA.

Race, P. (2004). *The Lecturer's Toolkit* (2nd Ed.). London: Routledge.

Ravenscroft, A., & Cook, J. (2007). New Horizons in Learning Design. In H. Beetham & R. Sharpe (eds.), *Rethinking Pedagogy for a digital age* (pp. 207-218). Abingdon, UK: Routledge Falmer.

Salmon, G. (2000). *E-moderating: The key to teaching and learning online*. London: Kogan Page.

Savin-Baden, M. (2008). *Learning Spaces: Creating opportunities for knowledge creation in academic life*. Maidenhead, UK:SRHE/OUP McGraw-Hill.

Schon, D. A. (1987). *Educating the reflective practitioner*. San Francisco: Jossey Bass.

Smith, H., & Higgins, S. (2006). Opening classroom interaction: the importance of feedback. *Cambridge Journal of Education, 36*(4), 485–502. doi:10.1080/03057640601048357

Taylor, P.G. (2000). Changing Expectation: Preparing students for flexible learning. *IETI 5*(2), November.

Tennant, M. (2006). *Psychology and Adult Learning* (3rd Ed). Abingdon, UK: Routledge.

Vygotsky, L. S. (1978). *Mind in Society*. Cambridge, MA: Harvard University Press.

Wenger, E. (1998). *Communities of Practice: Learning, Meaning and Identity*. Cambridge, UK: Cambridge University Press.

Winter, R. (2003). Contextualising the Patchwork text: addressing problems of coursework assessment in HE. *IETI, 40*(2), 112–122.

Yorke, M., & Longden, B. (2004). *Retention and Student Success in HE*. Maidenhead, UK: SRHE, OUP, McGraw-Hill.

Zuber-Skerritt, O. (1996). *New Directions in Action Research*. London: Falmer Press.

HE Academy, (2006, February). *The UK Professional Standards Framework*. HEFCE, UUK.

Staff and Educational Development Association website. www.seda.ac.uk

JISC Website. http://www.jisc.ac.uk, accessed September 2nd 2008

Higher Education Academy. website http://www.heacademy.ac.uk

Department for Children. Schools and Families. '*Every Child Matters*' on http://www.everychildmatters.gov.uk/ete/ retrieved November 21st 2008

ENDNOTES

[1] TESEP – Teacher Earth Science Education Programme, part of a technology initiative run from Napier University, Scotland, http://www2.napier.ac.uk/transform/

[2] Re-purposing & Re-use of Digital University-Level Content and Evaluation (RePRODUCE)

[3] JORUM is a **free** online service providing access to teaching and learning resources, for teaching and support staff in UK Further and Higher Education Institutions http://www.jorum.ac.uk/

Chapter 11
Using ePortfolios in Higher Education to Encourage Learner Reflection and Support Personalised Learning

Susi Peacock
Queen Margaret University, UK

Kate Morss
Queen Margaret University, UK

Alison Scott
Queen Margaret University, UK

Jane Hislop
Queen Margaret University, UK

Lindesay Irvine
Queen Margaret University, UK

Sue Murray
Queen Margaret University, UK

Simon T Girdler
Queen Margaret University, UK

ABSTRACT

Personalisation, with its emphasis on learner choice and lifelong learning, challenges educators to provide an innovative, student-centric educational experience. New technologies have great potential to support personalisation; however, institutions must review their approaches to assessment and feedback and their strategies to learning and teaching as well as increasing opportunities for collaborative learning and extending their external partnerships. This is a significant agenda for any institution. In this chapter, through the authors' four case studies drawn from different subject areas in a higher edu-

DOI: 10.4018/978-1-60566-884-0.ch011

cational institution, they illustrate how ePortfolios when integrated into the curriculum and combined with reflection can support personalised learning. The authors' also discuss the challenges of such an approach including lack of learner engagement with the reflective process, an increase in tutor time, restricted learner access to technology and the need for dynamic ePersonalisation. They offer suggestions for educators in addressing such issues in order to provide a truly personalised learning experience.

INTRODUCTION

The aim of this chapter is to contribute to current debate and inform practice on how, and in what ways, an ePortfolio can be used to encourage learner reflection and support a personalised learning experience in the higher education setting. In this chapter we:

- briefly outline personalisation and the theoretical and practical challenges that it presents for educators;
- discuss how reflective learning supported by an ePortfolio can help educators rise to these challenges and support learners to become independent, autonomous life-long learners;
- provide exemplars, drawn from a range of subject areas, to demonstrate 'ePortfolios in action';
- offer suggestions on how ePortfolios, when integrated within the curriculum, can encourage reflective learning and help educators to support a truly personalised learning experience.

PERSONALISATION OF LEARNING: AN OVERVIEW

Personalisation of learning has emerged as a key concept in the vision for the United Kingdom (UK) Government's reform of the public service sector including education. Although the discourse on 'personalization' originated in the United States, recent UK policy documents and political debates

imply that for school education, personalisation seeks to improve learner engagement, achievement and progression with the learner at the centre of a supported educational experience where there are opportunities for dialogue between learners and advisors (AoC, 2006; Pollard & James, 2004). Central to the personalisation agenda are:

- choice for pupils to decide what they learn and how they will learn it with the aim of removing barriers to learning and engaging all learners, especially vulnerable, disadvantaged and disengaged young people (DfES, 2006);
- developing learner autonomy and skills for lifelong learning which includes:
  ○ setting and having high expectations of learners;
  ○ developing the learning experience to reflect how learners learn, especially through interaction and collaboration;
  ○ focussing on the learning of skills as well as the transmission of knowledge;
  ○ fostering independent learning and decision-making so that learners can identify, plan and take responsibility for their own learning according to their specific needs. (DfES, 2006; Leadbeater, 2004; Miliband, 2004).

The Department for Education and Schools (DfES, 2004) has set out five key components of personalisation which schools need to address (see Figure 1).

Figure 1. Five components of personalisation. (Sources: DfES, 2004; Field, 2006; Pollard & James, 2004)

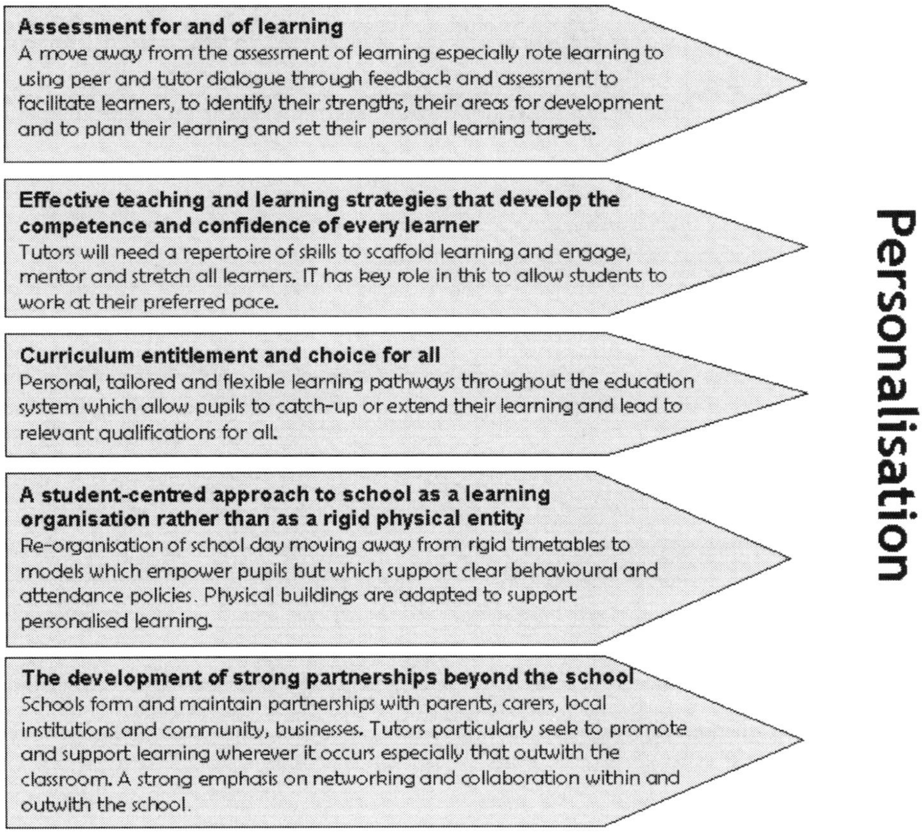

Assessment for and of learning
A move away from the assessment of learning especially rote learning to using peer and tutor dialogue through feedback and assessment to facilitate learners, to identify their strengths, their areas for development and to plan their learning and set their personal learning targets.

Effective teaching and learning strategies that develop the competence and confidence of every learner
Tutors will need a repertoire of skills to scaffold learning and engage, mentor and stretch all learners. IT has key role in this to allow students to work at their preferred pace.

Curriculum entitlement and choice for all
Personal, tailored and flexible learning pathways throughout the education system which allow pupils to catch-up or extend their learning and lead to relevant qualifications for all.

A student-centred approach to school as a learning organisation rather than as a rigid physical entity
Re-organisation of school day moving away from rigid timetables to models which empower pupils but which support clear behavioural and attendance policies. Physical buildings are adapted to support personalised learning.

The development of strong partnerships beyond the school
Schools form and maintain partnerships with parents, carers, local institutions and community, businesses. Tutors particularly seek to promote and support learning wherever it occurs especially that outwith the classroom. A strong emphasis on networking and collaboration within and outwith the school.

Personalisation

Despite general acceptance of the ideals of personalisation, concerns persist, including:

- raising expectations that cannot be met without significant increase in resources (Pollard & James, 2004);
- ensuring equity of experiences for all, including those who are less confident and less able to articulate their needs and wishes (Leadbeater, 2004).

THE ROLE OF TECHNOLOGY IN SUPPORTING PERSONALISED LEARNING: EPERSONALISATION

There seems little doubt that new technologies have great potential to support the implementation of personalised learning, 'ePersonalisation' (AoC, 2007; DfES, 2005; Knox & Wyper, 2008) and to meet the associated challenges:

… when we consider the systematic challenges posed by personalisation, it is clear without digital technologies, we are unlikely to be able to meet the needs of learners. (Green, Facer, Rudd, Dillon, & Humphreys, 2005)

Across all socio-economic classes, digital technologies are already used extensively by young learners for socialising, communication and learning (Prensky, 2001). Students extensively use social networking sites to discuss their learning, find resources and prepare assessments. In 2007 Facebook had 21 million registered users generating 1.6 billion page views each day (Ellison, Steinfield, & Lampe, 2007). Some schools are exploiting the popularity of social networking to facilitate collaborative learning and to encourage participation of all learners, especially the disadvantaged and disengaged (Green et al., 2005).

Technology has also pervaded the school environment through the use of Virtual Learning Environments (VLEs), interactive whiteboards, Personal Digital Assistants, laptops, wikis, and personal voting systems facilitated by high-speed educational networks. The implementation of such technology has transformed the traditional learning environment and enabled learners to develop new skills and access a wide array of resources (NCSL, 2006). Also, the technology has allowed teachers to explore new approaches to learning, teaching and assessment leading to improvements in access and equality as well as increasing student engagement and motivation; this has helped schools to meet the personalisation agenda (Green et al., 2005).

However, digital technologies may exacerbate some of the challenges of personalisation especially if there is limited access to computers and the Internet. Also, it cannot be assumed that all learners are comfortable with learning in a digital environment. In addition, concerns are now emerging that technologies only support a passive type of personalisation whereby learners have to adapt their learning preferences, styles and pathways to a specific system (typically a VLE). In such cases learners are required to identify themselves to this system by logging in and are then presented with one rigid pathway through pre-organised materials and activities. Although this provides some degree of freedom for the learner, for example by

working through the materials at a time and place that is convenient for them, the learning experience is often heavily controlled, structured, and tracked by the organisation (Fraser, 2006). This is the first stage of Fraser's three-stage model of ePersonalisation (illustrated in Figure 2). In the second and third phases, a more varied and flexible approach to system implementation can lead to a more dynamic form of ePersonalisation (Fraser, 2006).

Although this model reminds us that technology can, in some cases, limit the impact of the personalisation agenda, it is a model primarily about the choice of system or tools within that system. Whilst these choices are important, it is not the whole picture. A truly personalised learning experience should focus on embracing the five components of the DfES recommendations considering appropriate strategies for learning and teaching, assessment and feedback and learner choice within the curriculum. Personalisation also requires a learning institution to develop as a student-centred organisation with extended partnerships and opportunities for collaborative learning. This will be a significant agenda for any institution with constrained resources and increasing student diversity.

PERSONALISING THE LEARNING EXPERIENCE THROUGH REFLECTION AND EPORTFOLIOS

As educators we need to explore how technology can be used appropriately to meet the multiple goals of the personalisation agenda with the limited resources that are available to us. What is necessary is a technology which will support the centrality of the learners as individuals who are responsible for their own learning and skills development and are, therefore, critically reflective learners. Valued in many subject areas, reflection is associated with deep learning, encouraging learners to synthesise and integrate their learning from a

Figure 2. Levels of personalisation provided through technology. (Sources: Fraser, 2006; Knox & Wyper, 2008)

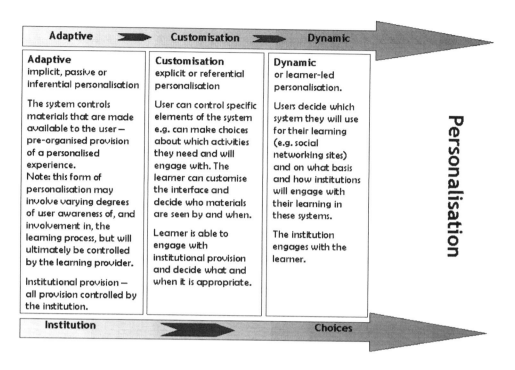

wide range of personal experiences and sources and to contextualise their learning (Donaghy & Morss, 2007; Schön, 1987). Reflection encourages learner 'ownership', allowing the student voice to shine through (Moon, 2005).

The reflective process requires the learner to reflect on what they know and to modify and change that knowledge in the light of their new learning experiences. Knowledge is personalised because reflection provides opportunity for 'working with meaning' (Moon, 1999, p. 139) by reasoning and making sense of new information. According to Moon (1999), the roles of reflection in learning are threefold. First, reflection on initial learning is about working with meaning to explore, organise and make better meaning. Second, reflection on the process of representing learning focuses on both the process and product of learning, that is, how one learns and how the learning can be demonstrated. Third, reflection can lead to an

'upgrading' of learning so that it becomes transformative. This transition to transformative learning is one which can involve a critical examination of beliefs, behaviours, perceptions and assumptions so that learning is enriched and becomes deeply personal (Mezirow, 1990).

WHY IS REFLECTION SO IMPORTANT TO LEARNING?

Fook and Gardner (2007) state that the personal perspective in reflection refers to the exploration of assumptions and personal experience through dialogue and questioning and they particularly stress the importance of social context and culture. The need for 'dialogue', both external and internal, as a means of achieving meaningful and deep self-understanding is a view held in common with other educationalists (Brockbank,

Figure 3. ePortfolios can support and improve the personalisation of learning. (© 2008, JISCinfoNet. Used with permission)

McGill, & Beech, 2002; Stefani, Mason, & Pegler, 2007).

External dialogue may occur through discussions, sharing materials and receiving feedback on their experiences and materials with friends, colleagues and/or tutors or even professional mentors. Internal dialogue, on the other hand, is an opportunity for quiet introspection which can provide another useful route to self-examination. It has been recognised that reflective writing can lead to a positive outcome, for example, to understand the process of learning, build theory, resolve uncertainties, defend decisions, empower or emancipate, explore emotions, understand, and plan self-development (Moon, 1999).

Whilst there are a number of technological solutions available to educators which may help to support learners to engage with and in reflective practice, the most flexible is the ePortfolio – frequently a web-based system – which can be used to record personal thoughts and ideas, for example, through a blog (web log). Learners can then explore these recorded experiences through internal and/or external dialogue with peers or tutors in order to make sense of them and to contextualise them. The tool can also facilitate the development, collection, selection and organisation of digital

resources or artefacts, such as photographs and multimedia, which when linked to blogs can both promote and provide evidence of transformative learning (Funk, 2004; Siemens, 2004).

A recent model of learning based on Kolb's (1984) experiential learning cycle developed by JISCinfoNet (2008) demonstrates how ePortfolios can support and improve the personalisation of learning, allowing individuals to develop skills, review and plan their learning, collaborate with many others in diverse settings, receive feedback and consider how their learning may be presented to others as an outward sign of achievement (see Figure 3).

EPORTFOLIOS AND QUEEN MARGARET UNIVERSITY (QMU)

At QMU we are exploring how ePortfolios can be used to support reflective learning and fulfil the five components of the personalisation agenda. QMU is a small institution in Edinburgh, Scotland which has recently gained university title and moved to a new campus. As throughout Scotland, most of our undergraduate programmes, especially in vocational areas, involve four years of study and

Figure 4. The PebblePad ePortfolio. (© 2008, Pebble Learning Ltd. Used with permission.)

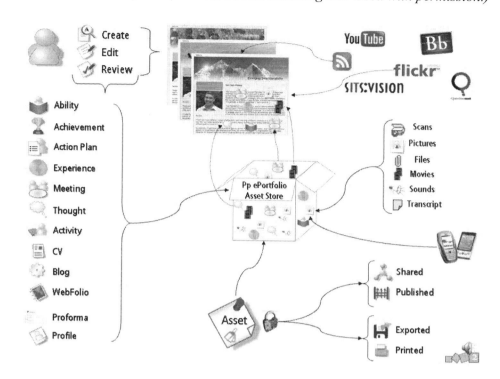

typically students start such courses from 17 years of age onwards. Generally, each year of study in a programme is referred to as a level.

Over the last five years technologies such as WebCT (our Virtual Learning Environment (VLE)), TurnitinUK (a plagiarism awareness tool), personal voting systems and Elgg (a social networking environment) have been implemented to meet the three primary goals of the Learning, Teaching and Assessment Strategy (QMUC, 2006) of:

- maximising potential through student-centred learning;
- developing QMU as a community of learners;
- ensuring quality assurance and enhancement.

In 2005, the institution introduced PebblePad as our institutional ePortfolio, which is similar to most ePortfolio systems, having tools such as web-based portfolios (webfolios), online diaries (blogs), competency checkers, online CVs and forms, activity logs as well as links to social software sites, such as Flickr. Learners can share and publish artefacts to the Internet or to a selected audience (see Figure 4). After leaving QMU, learners can either continue to use the ePortfolio system at this institution or transfer it to the site provided by PebblePad.

USING EPORTFOLIOS TO FACILITATE PERSONALISED LEARNING AT QMU: CASE STUDIES

In the following case studies, drawn from health, education and drama, we illustrate how an ePortfolio can be used as a tool to support reflection, address the multiple goals of personalisation and embrace the underlying philosophy of the personalisation agenda, in a higher education setting. Further information about each of the case studies is provided in Table 1.

The first two of our case studies are from the healthcare professions where reflective practice

is an integral part of the learning experience helping students to integrate theoretical and practical work-based learning. Students need to build skills and competencies and then demonstrate their learning and development (personal

Table 1. Case study details

Programme, Name of module, Mode of study	Level/s	Number of students	Tool/s used within the ePortfolio system	Role of the ePortfolio	Assessment
Programme BSc (Hons) in diagnostic radiography *Modules* Professional Practice (Level 1) Clinical Practice in Diagnostic Imaging 1, 2 and 3 (Levels 2 -4) Full-time	1-4 in an undergraduate programme	20- 30 students per level	Proforma Blog Thought CV Any other as desired by the learner which are collated into a webfolio	The ePortfolio system is primarily used to develop the skills required for students to reflect upon their learning in the clinical environment and to demonstrate the ability to link theory with practice. The learner can build a robust record of their learning by linking additional evidence of learning to their reflective accounts. Although a minimum requirement regarding structure is suggested, the learner may choose tools and presentation style. The ePortfolio is also used to record clinical activity to ensure appropriate clinical experience for the student throughout their final three years.	Being one element in a series of clinical assessments, the entire webfolio is assessed with the personal accounts of learning being appraised for structure and content. 0% weighting is applied since the webfolio is 'Pass/Fail.'
Programme MSc (pre-registration) Physiotherapy *Modules* Professional Studies Practice-based Learning Full and part-time	Level 1 in a postgraduate programme (Professional studies)	20 students per level	Webfolio Blog	Students use the blog to reflect on their experiences, critical events. These are used to form the basis of a webfolio which is submitted for the assessment.	Students write a 1,000 word reflective account of their learning demonstrating how they have linked their evolving subject knowledge with their experiences in the practice setting. The reflective account is weighted at 100% of the module credit.
	Levels 1 and 2 in a postgraduate programme (Practice-based learning)	20 students per level	Blog, proformas, SWOT analysis which are collated into a webfolio	Students use the ePortfolio system to develop and maintain a portfolio of evidence of learning during their studies. Students are encouraged to reflect on their academic and practice-based experiences using the blog and proformas tools. These experiences are then integrated into an online webfolio which is summated for assessment.	Summative assessment is a 3,000 word Personal Development Plan in which students are asked to reflect on their learning over the previous two years of the programme and to identify outstanding learning needs for their first year of employment.
Programme MSc in Professional Education *Module* Education in Action Part-time	1 in a postgraduate programme	30	Blog Achievement Thought which are collated into a webfolio	The ePortfolio system is used to assist learners in building a profile of their learning that has occurred throughout the module, providing evidence of their use of theory in practice. The system allows learners to link directly evidence with their commentary so that rationale, thinking, decision-making, design and actions are more transparent to them and their tutors. The reflective writing presented by the learners is personal, reflective and in some cases transformational. This offers the opportunity for greater personalisation of the work by allowing latitude in their presentation, choice of evidence and in the methods they use to teach in practice and support their own learners	The whole webfolio including the linked evidence, reflective critical commentary and released personal diary/blog elements are assessed.

Table 1. continued

Programme, Name of module, Mode of study	Level/s	Number of students	Tool/s used within the ePortfolio system	Role of the ePortfolio	Assessment
Programme BA/BA (Hons) Performing Arts Management *Modules* Practice 1 - 4 Full-time	Levels 1-4 in an undergraduate programme	Up to 16 students per level	Blog	Students are encouraged to find their own industry-based placements as soon as they are ready – usually in year 2. They need to reflect extensively on their learning experiences whether they are industry based or developed around the work of the School of Drama. An online learning journal (a blog) helps formalise the learners' reflections making their reflections more explicit and providing a focus for meetings with their tutors and peers.	The learning journal forms 40% of the mark in the first year, 50% in year 2 and 60% in year 3. Year four is a written journal and dissertation. The journal is 50% of the overall mark.

Note. Further information about these case studies is available at: http://www.qmu.ac.uk/eportfolio/

and professional) through the achievement of specified outcomes (Friedman Ben David et al., 2001; Jasper & Fulton, 2005). In each of these case studies learners spend a significant amount of time outwith the educational institution in the clinical setting where they are expected to develop skills of critical appraisal, evaluation and analysis in a multi-disciplinary work environment. Previously, assessment through paper-based portfolios, reflective logs and proformas have provided learners with opportunities to share their personal reflections upon their learning and development, to show their ability to link theory to practice and to demonstrate evidence of this development from a wide range of clinical settings. Our case studies show how paper-based portfolios have been moved online and we discuss the advantages and challenges of this change with regard to the personalisation agenda.

Case Study One: BSc (Hons) in Diagnostic Radiography, Levels 1 – 4

Our first case study illustrates how ePortfolios are used for summative clinical assessment of learning in a BSc (Hons) in diagnostic radiography. Approximately 20-30 students in each of the levels 2 – 4 create a reflective webfolio to demonstrate

their learning and personal and professional development in the placement setting. The tutor provides a model (see Figure 5) which guides the students in developing their personal webfolio and selecting and organising the evidence they have chosen for their assessment.

The elements of the assessment are:

- *A mandatory webfolio* (which is assessed 'Pass or Fail') containing
  - Online proformas which are records of clinical experience (see Figure 6). Minimum requirements are specified to achieve a pass, for example, level four students must demonstrate that they have performed a total of 40 mobile examinations of the chest and abdomen, 30 aided and 10 unaided by the end of semester two. The primary purpose of the proformas is to encourage the learners to record as many and as wide a range of procedures and techniques as possible to allow them to demonstrate the full extent of their clinical experience.
  - Reflective pieces about learners' experiences whilst in clinical practice. These accounts must include a full

Figure 5. A model for webfolio development in diagnostic radiography

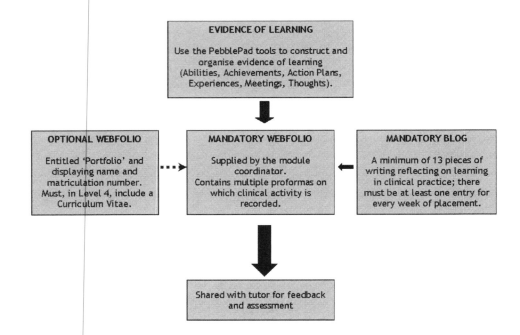

description of, at least one, interesting or challenging procedure, experience or encounter which calls upon blog entries for evidence.

A template of this mandatory webfolio is developed by the tutor and shared with the learners.

- *A mandatory blog* (which is assessed 'Pass or Fail') containing:
  ○ a minimum number of selected reflective pieces about the learner's experiences in clinical practice presented in a coherent order. Each account must include a full description of an interesting or challenging procedure, experience or encounter. These reflections will have originally been created in a personal blog where the learner is encouraged to reflect upon all their experiences in the clinical

setting. It is hoped that these private reflections will support the learner to engage in an internal dialogue about their learning from such experiences and to plan for future learning. The learner selects a specified number of entries from the personal blog as evidence in the mandatory blog.
  ○ further evidence of learning, such as a list and content appraisal of all clinical tutorials.

Multimedia evidence such as images, video and web links are encouraged. However, learners are advised to make explicit the relevance and purpose of all the evidence that they provide. The mandatory webfolio and the blog are shared with the tutor for assessment. Some students elect to create an additional optional webfolio to act as a title page or index with links to the two mandatory elements. In level four of their diagnostic radiog-

Figure 6. A clinical activity record (Proforma) within a webfolio

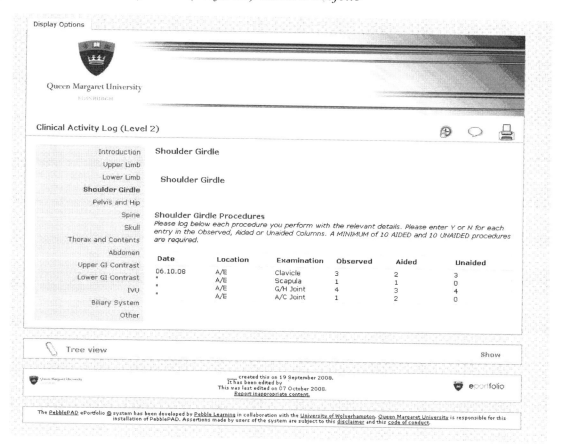

raphy studies, students start to apply for positions and write covering letters and CVs which they send to managers. Students may create an online CV in the ePortfolio; this is a document that could be shared with a future employer.

All of the learners are provided with a demonstration of the tools within the ePortfolio system (see Figure 4). Although not all of the tools are required for assessment, many may assist learner reflection. An example is the achievement tool which requires the learner not only to identify areas of success and development but also to provide evidence of learning gained by reflecting on the achievement. Learners are encouraged to explore these tools during the introductory session and to choose those appropriate for them and their learning style. Learners are also shown how to share their webfolios with peers and are encouraged to work collaboratively. However, not all learners opt to use this facility preferring to engage in an internal reflective dialogue. Others like to share with peers and the comments and feedback provided are recorded on the webfolio and can be viewed during the assessment process. Some students have difficulty with both the technical aspects of the software and/or the key concepts of evidencing clinical activity and the reflective process. The tutor facilitates additional group and one-to-one sessions to prepare students adequately for the requirements of the assessed webfolio; however, for a busy academic, there are clear tensions between the desire to provide support for personalised learning for between 20-30 students and the constraints of an overcrowded timetable.

To help resolve this tension, central services provide a weekly drop-in session for students to discuss issues when using the ePortfolio system; this seeks to reduce the amount of technical support required of the tutor.

Additional support for students is also provided through WebCT which holds a range of reference materials for students whilst in the university and on clinical practice. Diagnostic and professional practice PowerPoint presentations from all levels of the programme are made available, as well as an illustrated glossary for reference, clinical handbooks, assessment forms and examples of previous examinations. The tutor uses the announcement and noticeboard tool on a regular basis to inform students about forthcoming events, assessment deadlines and new resources.

Extensive, written formative feedback through the comment tool in the ePortfolio system is provided at least once, and often twice, on draft webfolios. Typically, the focus will be on the quality of the writing, descriptive content, identification of key learning experiences, level of reflection and degree of evaluation of practice. Additional evidence of learning presented by the student is also scrutinised and comments on its value given. Students are asked to acknowledge the feedback, also using the comment tool, and to retain these comments as part of the summative assessment. This way, the tutor can decide whether or not the original feedback has been useful to the student and whether or not changes and improvements have been made. For example, learners at level 2 submit a draft webfolio following the first and second blocks of clinical placement with the tutor offering feedback on strengths and areas for improvement. Students are asked to engage in reflection on this feedback and to outline their plans for future development in the light of the tutor's comments.

The webfolio is assessed at the end of semester 2 and approximately six to eight webfolios of the overall 20-30 can be marked in a day. An external assessor typically takes two hours for each level.

All are graded either pass or fail. Some learners will produce the minimum requirements and are awarded a 'pass' which is the same grade as those who have submitted an excellent piece of work. This may appear unfair, but mirrors the accreditation provided by the Health Professions Council (HPC, 2007) which will either re-accredit or not - they will not award distinctions for effort. It also reinforces that learners are responsible for their own learning and will need to continue with this in their professional life through continuing professional development (CPD). It is clear that those learners who perform well in the webfolio are also likely to do well in other summative assessments; this may, therefore, predict academic and future professional success.

The quality of reflection within the webfolios and blogs increases with the level of the learner. Level 2 learners tend towards the descriptive with incremental development of reflection, critical appraisal and evaluation of practice over time. Some students never fully 'get it' whilst there are the natural reflectors that produce deep, insightful reflections from day one. The mandatory reflective writing contained within the blogs or webfolios are the elements that encourage students to develop this skill. Good feedback, particularly in the early stages, is vital to this development; hence the need for students to respond to feedback in level 2 to ensure they are engaging with feedback especially if it focuses on reflection.

For the future it is anticipated that more formal links to external partners will be provided through the ePortfolio. Proformas, currently paper-based, are completed by placement supervisors for staged and continuous assessment purposes. Learners, at present, usually scan such documents after completion to include in the webfolio as examples of evidence. Such forms could be completed online within the ePortfolio system by the supervisors. However, such initiatives may be limited by restricted access to computers within the National Health Service.

Case Study Two: MSc (Pre-Registration) Physiotherapy Programme, Levels 1 – 2

The MSc is a two-year programme for science graduates who wish to pursue a career as a physiotherapist. Many of the graduates have high-level subject knowledge in related areas such as anatomy and human physiology but have little, if any, experience of how to work as a reflective health practitioner in a multifunctional team. The core module, Professional Studies, runs in semester 1 and 2 of level 1, which is the first year of the two-year MSc programme, with each semester being 14 weeks. The five core Practice-based Learning modules run as six-week placements in the clinical environment in semester 3 of both level 1 and 2 of the programme. Both the Professional Studies and Practice-based Learning modules aim to support students in developing a reflective approach to their learning, both in and out of the practice setting. The ePortfolios in these modules are used as a space where the 20 learners can link all aspects of their learning together in one place. WebCT is used by the tutors to provide additional supportive materials, such as handbooks, narrated PowerPoints and details of placements. Online asynchronous discussions are also a vital part of the programme encouraging students to share experiences especially about the placement setting.

At the start of the programme, in the Professional Studies module, learners are introduced to reflection, the advantages of reflective writing and the importance of becoming a reflective health practitioner. They are asked to identify their learning styles and shown how models such as Kolb's experiential learning cycle can help support their development in writing and reflecting. Learners are encouraged to explore their assumptions and personal experience through dialogue and questioning and to use reflective writing as a vehicle for this. In semester 1 of level 1, students shadow an undergraduate student for half a day in a clinical site. This allows them to discuss and share their thoughts on the ethical and professional issues encountered by physiotherapists in clinical practice with a fellow student. Later they will record this experience and then through quiet introspection start to explore in greater depth their learning, their emotions related to the experience and plans for future self-development.

In the first semester, students are introduced to the ePortfolio system and encouraged to use the different tools as a medium for generating, selecting and collating their evidence which they can then integrate into their reflective accounts in the webfolio. Some learners, not all, keep a reflective private blog on a regular basis outlining their reflections on their learning experiences. For example, their reflections on their clinical visit as well as their generic learning from self study, tutorials and experiences outwith the institution. Such use of the blog supports learners with their internal dialogue about how these experiences relate to their theoretical learning within the institution and their expectations of life as a physiotherapist. Extracts from their blog are then included to support their personal reflective accounts of learning in the webfolio. Learners may also use customised proformas, such as those available on their professional body's website, the Chartered Society of Physiotherapy (CSP). The CSP has developed a series of proformas, such as templates for a critical incident report and SWOT analysis (strengths, weaknesses, opportunities and threats) which are available to all members of the CSP, including student members. Such forms can be housed in the ePortfolio system and used as appropriate as evidence of learning and for the identification of future learning needs. Finally, learners are shown how to customise the webfolio, how to select materials and are provided with guidelines about the type of evidence that is required. They are also shown an exemplar webfolio developed by the tutor that helps them to visualise their own webfolio and start to plan its structure.

In the summative assessment for the Professional Studies module at the end of semester 2, students are asked to write a 1,000 word reflective account of their learning, describing critical events and outlining learning outcomes which should demonstrate how they have linked their evolving subject knowledge with their experiences in the practice setting. The reflective account is weighted at 100% of the module credit. This assessment allows tutors to provide students with feedback on their reflective writing and generates material which students can draw upon within their summative assessment of the practice-based learning placements.

The summative assessment for the final practice-based learning module, submitted at the end of the programme, is a 3,000 word Personal Development Plan (PDP). This assessment is weighted at 50% of the final Practice-based learning module credit. The assessment is staged through the Practice-based learning placements with students undertaking a formative portfolio task in each placement. Students obtain formative feedback from their peers, for example through sharing a SWOT analysis in their third placement and feedback from academic staff through undertaking a critical incident report at the end of their second practice-based learning module which is submitted at the end of level 1. Evidence of learning from a range of experiences must be provided. Students also identify their learning needs and develop an action plan describing future personal development. To further contextualise the second-year assessment, and provide the students with experience which could be beneficial in terms of their employability, the students are asked to focus on their skills and learning and development needs in relation to a post-qualification job outline (see Figure 7). These assessments are created in the webfolio tool and shared with the tutor.

The advantage of using the webfolio tool is that it allows students to access and organise an ongoing portfolio of evidence, including

evidence of reflection, whilst in the academic and clinical setting. The blog function and the profession specific proformas are particularly useful to students on placement as a resource for recording informal reflections on clinical experiences. Given that the placements are undertaken over a two-year period this means that students can quickly access archived material which can form the basis for further reflection. In addition the webfolio tool allows students to share work with their peers and academic staff when they are remote from the academic institution. The feedback from peers and academic staff and the students' reflections on this, encourages a deep, personalised learning approach.

Case Study Three: MSc in Professional Education, Module Education in Action

Our third case study is taken from a master's programme in Professional Education designed to develop theory and practice of teaching at higher education level. The programme is accredited by the Higher Education Academy and the Nursing and Midwifery Council; it is primarily designed for professionals with a high level of subject expertise and experience but who wish to enhance their professional development in teaching or training. Students are from diverse professional backgrounds and cultures and have a varied level of technological experience. The core introductory module on this programme, Education in Action, encourages learners to spend time studying an extensive range of theories, approaches, models and strategies for learning, teaching and assessment and evaluating practice. Participants are required to be engaged in some teaching, to allow application and integration of learning to the workplace. Thus the module is grounded in the dynamic process of supporting individuals to build on their expertise and experience to enhance skills necessary to teach effectively in a complex changing educational environment and

Figure 7. Example of webfolio where the student has identified personal learning needs, learning outcomes and an action plan for their first year in employment

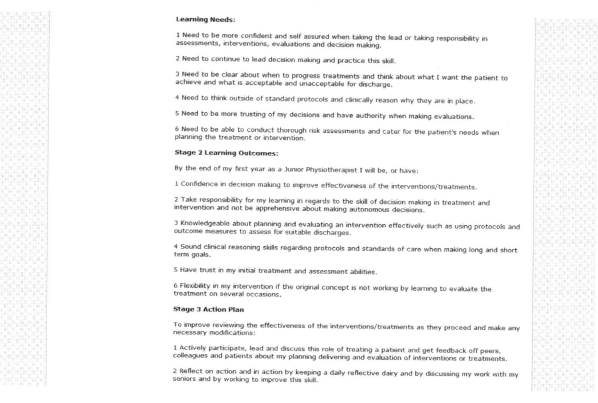

Learning Needs:

1 Need to be more confident and self assured when taking the lead or taking responsibility in assessments, interventions, evaluations and decision making.

2 Need to continue to lead decision making and practice this skill.

3 Need to be clear about when to progress treatments and think about what I want the patient to achieve and what is acceptable and unacceptable for discharge.

4 Need to think outside of standard protocols and clinically reason why they are in place.

5 Need to be more trusting of my decisions and have authority when making evaluations.

6 Need to be able to conduct thorough risk assessments and cater for the patient's needs when planning the treatment or intervention.

Stage 2 Learning Outcomes:

By the end of my first year as a Junior Physiotherapist I will be, or have:

1 Confidence in decision making to improve effectiveness of the interventions/treatments.

2 Take responsibility for my learning in regards to the skill of decision making in treatment and intervention and not be apprehensive about making autonomous decisions.

3 Knowledgeable about planning and evaluating an intervention effectively such as using protocols and outcome measures to assess for suitable discharges.

4 Sound clinical reasoning skills regarding protocols and standards of care when making long and short term goals.

5 Have trust in my initial treatment and assessment abilities.

6 Flexibility in my intervention if the original concept is not working by learning to evaluate the treatment on several occasions.

Stage 3 Action Plan

To improve reviewing the effectiveness of the interventions/treatments as they proceed and make any necessary modifications:

1 Actively participate, lead and discuss this role of treating a patient and get feedback off peers, colleagues and patients about my planning delivering and evaluation of interventions or treatments.

2 Reflect on action and in action by keeping a daily reflective dairy and by discussing my work with my seniors and by working to improve this skill.

to use theory and research findings to develop their own practice.

This transparent focus on continuous personal and professional development through critically reflective self-appraisal of practice within a complex and changing environment requires an assessment vehicle which allows individuals to 'tell their own story' – a personalised, customised reflective portfolio of practice. The portfolio is based on the concept of assessment *for* learning (QAA, 2007), integrated with all learning activities (Biggs & Tang, 2007) and gives students complete responsibility for it. The criteria specify there should be evidence of: critical reflection and personal insight based on systematic evaluation of practice; deep knowledge and application of educational theory and principles of good practice; ability to critically evaluate and debate relevant research and scholarship. Evidence is required for specific justification of appropriate choices and decisions in relation to teacher/learner context such as subject area. The nature of the students and the cultural context is required to be substantiated along with examples of good practice in teaching, assessment, support and feedback to their own learners. Therefore, students are expected to provide sound rationales for strategies, applications, tools and materials which they choose or develop in the course of their teaching. They may select whatever evidence is most relevant, of highest quality and in the most appropriate format – text, diagrams, pictures and video. They are expected to evaluate and track their progress by frequently reflecting on self, peer and tutor feedback thus planning for their further development. Opportunities for external and internal dialogue to underpin this reflection are continuous and varied since they are 'built into' the design of the module.

At the beginning of the module, in depth group discussion of the concepts of reflection, reflective practice, evidence-based practice and portfolio-building occurs so learners can begin their portfolio journey. Technical training is part of the introductory sessions to ensure learners feel competent to undertake the portfolio development, as many have limited experience of working in a technological environment. In these sessions, learners are provided with guidance on how to customise the webfolio and how to upload evidence that is appropriate to their individual learning.

The module is based on a blended learning model in which learners engage in highly interactive classes once a month and in online activities during the intervening periods. The guiding principles which underpin the module is that tutors always have a guiding and facilitative role, attempting to give as much leadership and ownership of discussion as possible to students. All electronic communication, group work, discussion and posting of work during the interim periods are facilitated through WebCT so that students have control over when and where they engage with each other online. Although online activities are broadly outlined by tutors, students have choice over topics, modus operandi and presentation format. The products of this work can also be transferred from WebCT into each individual's webfolio as evidence of learning. For example, a group critique of assessment strategies presented in poster format may lead to the adoption by an individual of a different assessment tool which may be implemented and evaluated as evidence in the webfolio. The story of that journey may become part of the reflective commentary.

Throughout the module learners are encouraged to engage with the tools within the ePortfolio, integrate it with their interim activities and use it for on-going external and internal dialogue and reflective writing. At the end of the year, learners bring together these reflections and select appropriate evidence to complete their webfolio, which demonstrates their learning and development, to include skills, knowledge and plans for their on-going future continuous professional development.

All the webfolios are highly individual, often very creative in their presentation of evidence, and contain materials that are completely personalised in that they refer only to the learners' perspective, values, strategies and critical evaluation of themselves. The electronic system allows learners to link directly evidence with their commentary so that rationale, thinking, decision-making, design and actions are more transparent to them and their tutors. There is no question that the reflective writing presented by the learners is personal, reflective and in some cases transformational, with the ePortfolio approach freeing the learner from the traditional writing required of academic study. This offers the opportunity for greater personalisation of the work by allowing greater latitude in their presentation, choice of evidence and in the methods they use to teach in practice and support their own learners. For example, learners tell the story of their learning underpinning it with theory, and illustrating their learning with personal selection of episodes of significance to them. These may be positive or negative episodes but the ePortfolio allows the freedom of selection. The electronic nature of the ePortfolio seems to allow students to feel more able to disclose exciting or uncomfortable personal experience than if they were writing traditionally.

Case Study Four: BA (Hons) in Performing Arts Management

Our final case study is taken from performing arts management. In this programme students combine practical activity (working in the placement setting) with their academic studies: each contributes 50% to the overall mark for the programme. The students are encouraged to find and undertake industry-based placements in order to develop an in-depth understanding of the processes of performance management in the theatre setting.

Reflection and reflective writing is core to this development. At the beginning of the programme, learners (approximately 16 per year) are introduced to the blog tool within the ePortfolio system which they use to develop and maintain an online journal. Extracts from this journal are shared with peers and tutors for feedback to support internal and external dialogue and to encourage learners to reflect on their personal learning journey.

Initially, the tutor provides an extensive introduction to the purpose of the online journal, which is to document and record learner experiences, outline future learning needs and to applaud achievement and growing self-awareness. The tutor explains that the students need to develop a 'management head' for their professional roles and that the online journal is a 'mental gym' where they can record critical events, reflect on them through thoughtful internal dialogue and then, if required, shared with the tutor for feedback which is usually written and occasionally face-to-face. They are encouraged to write about new knowledge and skills that they have developed, especially when on placement, and to relate these

to their developing theoretical knowledge of the subject area.

The online journals are then marked; in the first year they form 40% of the mark, in year 2, 50% and in year 3, 60%. In year four students submit a written journal which contributes to 50% of the mark. Each learning journal is marked against a set of criteria (see Table 2) and points are allocated to each of the criteria.

Through the continued use of the blog, constant self analysis and writing, the tutor has observed significant learner development especially in the ability to think strategically and to plan for future activity which leads to purposeful outcomes. Students have started to assess their own abilities and to link their studies with their future career development. Not all students have found the experience fruitful or engaging. Some dislike using computers and others have a lack of understanding of the purpose of self analysis. There is often a resistance to what may be seen as a chore – writing a reflective online diary – especially in the early stages of the programme. Learners also talk about the 'fear of the blank sheet' and are reluctant to

Table 2. Criteria for assessment and allocation of points for the learning journals in BA (Hons) performing arts management

Criteria for assessment of online learning journals
Does the student demonstrate an understanding of learning outcomes commensurate to their experience and time on the course? (20 points)
Does the student demonstrate an understanding of good management practice commensurate to their experience and time on the course? (20 points)
Is there evidence of self analysis demonstrated throughout? (20 points)
Does the journal demonstrate the student's attention to detail, taking into account any problems a student may have with the written word and presentation? (20 points)
Does the journal draw from experiences and examples of activity demonstrating that it has been written using entries compiled across the academic year? (20 points)

Allocation of points for the learning journal	
0 to 5 points	little evidence
5 to 10 points	good evidence
10 to 15 points	excellent evidence
15 to 20 points	outstanding evidence

share reflections about an experience that was not successful which results in learner overcompensation by writing too much. The tutor provides extensive feedback, especially at the beginning of the programme, challenging learners to explore what happened in uncomfortable experiences, like working in dysfunctional groups, their emotional responses and to consider how they will handle similar incidents in the future, especially in the intensive working environment of the theatre. The most effective way to avoid the negative response has been for the tutor to work consistently with students individually. By supporting students' understanding of personal development, the learning journals become more pertinent and the resistance to using ePortfolios lessens.

DISCUSSIONS

Our case studies demonstrate that through the judicious use of ePortfolios as a tool to support learner reflection we are responding to the multiple goals of personalisation and embracing the underlying philosophy of the personalisation agenda, as appropriate for our institution. In all of our case studies, learners have significant choice in what they learn, and how and when they learn and, as well, how they demonstrate their learning. By the latter stages of their programmes, our learners are beginning to take responsibility for how they learn and also for what they need to learn – key skills for lifelong learning.

We now return to the five components of personalisation and discuss how we have engaged with these in our case studies.

Assessment for and of Learning

In all of the case studies, innovative approaches to formative and summative assessment have tried to combine assessment 'for' and 'of' learning whilst meeting, in three of the four case studies, the assessment guidelines provided by the professional bodies. Learners use the ePortfolio to present their personal learning journey and provide tangible evidence of learning. Blogs or other digital artefacts, such as videos or images, can be used as evidence to show growing self-awareness and critical self-evaluation and identify areas for development and plans for future learning, for example as demonstrated earlier in Figure 7. Such types of assessment add validity, truthfulness, meaningfulness, and authenticity to the assessment procedure.

Feedback, formative and summative, individual and group, is an essential element of the assessment process. The ePortfolio offers educators extensive opportunities to provide both formative and summative feedback and for students to reflect and act on this feedback. In all the case studies, formative feedback is used to question and probe learner's assumptions and encourage deep learning. Early conversations with students in radiography, physiotherapy and education suggest that they value opportunities to submit their draft webfolios for feedback, with motivation increasing through the provision of reassurance and encouragement about performance. Performing arts management learners find that the extensive feedback on their blogs whilst away from the institution keeps them focussed and develops their 'management' head.

However, learner engagement with the ePortfolio does not always need to be assessed. Not all blog entries are submitted for assessment such as in physiotherapy and diagnostic radiography; students are encouraged to use the ePortfolio tool to support their individual learning and personal development.

Effective Teaching and Learning Strategies that Develop the Competence and Confidence of Every Learner

All our case studies show how ePortfolios can be used in conjunction with innovative learning and teaching strategies to engage learners, improve confidence and lead to increased competence, especially our education case study, in the higher education setting. However, critical to the success of these case studies is learner engagement with the reflective process. All of our learners at the early stages of their studies are introduced to reflection and the purpose of reflective writing. In the education case study, learners are given examples of writing and asked to work in teams to discuss if they consider the exemplar to be reflective, academic or descriptive. In the radiography and physiotherapy case studies, webfolio templates are developed by tutors and shared with students; these are accompanied with guidance about how to select evidence and how to link this evidence to their reflective accounts.

The flexibility provided by the ePortfolio affords learners many opportunities to engage in the reflective process. With its wide range of tools, learners can select the appropriate one for them, their preferred learning style and level to develop their confidence in using the system to support reflection. In radiography learners are offered guidance about the different ways to use the blog tool for reflection. Each posting to the blog is called a 'thought' and can be constructed in two ways:

- a student who is skilled in the reflective process may utilise the simple 'journal' option and write a reflective piece (a thought) with no automated prompts from the system;
- the learner requiring more guidance might select the 'reflective cycle' option which provides a step-by-step process to writing a reflective thought. At each stage the learner is provided with hints and tips about what they may wish to include in their reflective account.

Curriculum Entitlement and Choice

The underpinning curriculum design in each case study has sought to provide as much choice as possible for learners through the approaches to learning and teaching and assessment. However, in many professional programmes in higher education, such as health and education, learning outcomes, core content and structure and allocated time spent in the clinical setting may be subject to regulation by the professional body. Fortunately, the use of the webfolio provides some scope in how outcomes can be met, particularly through choice in the development, selection, organisation and presentation of the student's work. The blog allows learners to reflect on personal experiences and make sense of their learning in the different settings.

A Student-Centred Approach to School as a Learning Organisation Rather Than as a Rigid Physical Entity

In the higher education setting, timetabling and scheduling of lectures, seminars, tutorials and workshops provides many challenges for any institution. Our case studies have not sought to tackle this issue which is often outwith the control of a programme. In our new campus we provide a wide variety of innovative spaces for learners, as individual and as groups, to discuss and reflect on their learning, for example, students can book rooms within our learning resource centre to come together, explore their learning in the placement setting and then record these dialogues within their blogs (QMU, 2008).

Our learners spend a considerable amount of time in the placement setting and we have sought to maximise the flexibility afforded by this learning. We have focussed our limited resources on the implementation of a student-centric web-based ePortfolio system that can support a personalised learning experience and give some sense of control and ownership to our learners, wherever they may be learning. This contrasts with our institutional VLE, which in most of our case studies has been developed and maintained by tutors to provide extensive support to learners in a very structured and controlled environment. The VLE is used to provide an interactive learning environment through the thoughtful implementation of online discussions, quizzes, videos and narrated PowerPoints but these are controlled, selected and managed by the tutor. The ePortfolio differs to the VLE by affording more choice for our learners in how they engage with the system. There are more opportunities for customisation of fonts, images and animations, as seen in our radiography example (see Figure 8). In this case

the learner has developed an individual webfolio through the innovative use of photographs, which reflects personal interests.

The Development of Strong Partnerships beyond the Institution

Like any institution, QMU has developed extensive partnerships with the institutions that provide placement opportunities for our learners, such as hospitals and organisations running events and festivals. However, the ePortfolio is proving to be a vehicle for strengthening these links and in some cases developing new ones. Blog entries are shared with tutors and sometimes with clinical supervisors for feedback and dialogue. In a

Figure 8. Personalised but unstructured radiography webfolio

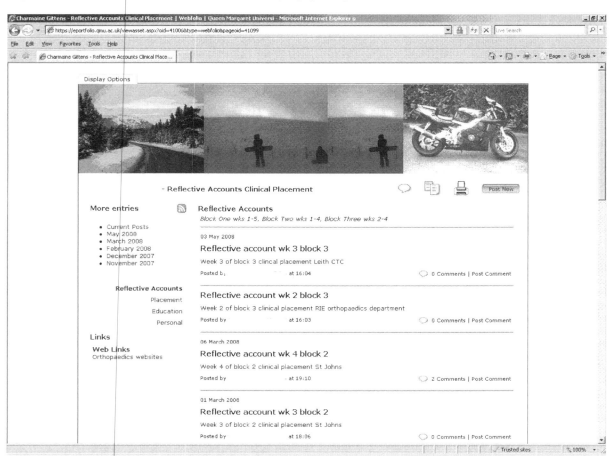

community and public health nursing programme, supervisors provide feedback directly into a shared webfolio. For the future it is hoped that unnecessary paper-based form-filling can be transferred to the ePortfolio and completed in situ by supervisors. Not only is this bringing these institutions in contact with the ePortfolio system but also with our approach to learning and teaching and the institution itself.

Learners have shown a keen interest in using webfolios to demonstrate evidence of learning to potential employers and to share online CVs. Learners particularly like the fact that when they share a webfolio it states that it is housed on the institution's ePortfolio system and provides a type of formal link to where they have been studying.

Our case studies illustrate the different ways that we have engaged with the five components of the personalisation agenda through the use of reflection supported by an ePortfolio. For each institution, their engagement with these areas will vary according to their subject area and their strategies for learning and teaching, as well as their engagement with the ePortfolio system. Institutions may wish to use these components as a guide to planning the implementation of ePortfolios to support personalisation.

THE CHALLENGES OF PERSONALISATION

Although our case studies demonstrate that many of our learners have used the ePortfolio to engage in reflection and meet some of the goals of the personalisation agenda, issues have emerged including:

- lack of learner engagement with the reflective process;
- increased tutor time to support personalisation;

- limited learner access to, and use of, technology;
- a lack of dynamic ePersonalisation.

In this section we discuss these issues and offer some suggestions for those implementing ePortfolios to support the personalisation agenda.

We cannot assume that because our learners are using the technology to record and reflect on critical events that reflection leading to deep learning is always taking place. Many of our learners, especially in the early stages, did not possess the skills and ability to be reflective (DiBiase, 2002) and did not always enjoy the reflective process. Others did not immediately understand the benefits and relevance of reflection in higher education and wanted, and expected, a more didactic approach to learning and teaching. In physiotherapy, students often found it difficult to engage with the reflective process when they were experiencing a steep learning curve in the skills and knowledge required to complete their programme of studies. To cope with this, they often took a strategic approach to learning and disliked having to make additional time to reflect, write reflectively and to use these reflections to prepare for future learning needs. Assessment plays a central role, focussing the learner on the task and helping to engage them in the reflective process. In some of our case studies, such as radiography, this had led to debate about whether to allocate a percentage of the total module mark to the webfolio after developing robust assessment criteria based upon content, structure and presentation such as that in drama. However, it is often only after our learners have completed their studies that they start to understand the purpose of reflection and its role in their continuing professional development; in some cases, this has led them to opt to use our ePortfolio system after graduation.

Learners at the early stages of their studies often will lack confidence and experience and need structured personal development support

(Beetham & Strivens, 2005). To overcome such issues, having a framework for structuring and supporting reflective accounts seems most productive, if not essential. Such frameworks suggest using a reflective model (Boud, Keogh & Walker, 1985; Johns, 1994) or providing 'prompter' questions to guide thinking and establish a kind of dialogue between the learner and the question. Rees, Forbes & Kubler (2007) have developed an excellent set of questions to enable learners to reflect on a wide range of attributes such as communication, leadership, judgement, creativity and learning and development; these could be used in conjunction with the more structured elements of the ePortfolios such as the action planner. The ePortfolio system can also assist the tutor in scaffolding the learner experience through the sharing of templates and exemplars, which guide the learner in the development of their reflective accounts. Sharing blog entries or webfolios in the early stages of a programme also provides an opportunity for feedback and helps guide the learner, as in the physiotherapy and radiography case studies above. Given the apparent importance of dialogue to facilitate and deepen reflective thinking, it is advisable for tutors to design in as many opportunities for feedback as possible.

Providing such personalised feedback has had significant resource implications for tutors. In radiography level 1, students in their induction session were asked to create a blog and reflect upon a key learning experience in their first weeks at the institution. This was then shared with the tutor. The tutor required approximately six hours to provide appropriate individual feedback, for a cohort of 35 students. Although this engaged new and especially vulnerable students, and substantially improved their motivation, it significantly increased tutor workload. In the first iteration of using the ePortfolio, tutors in our education case study found marking online a challenge and initially required more time to navigate systems and familiarise themselves with the structure and organisation of the webfolios compared with a

paper-based portfolio. Protected time is essential for tutors to familiarise themselves with the system and to explore how it may be used to fulfil the personalisation agenda without a significant increase in their commitments to the programme. For example, peer feedback is now being explored, accompanied by more limited and focussed tutor feedback in drama. In radiography, in early trials, a learner submitted an individualised webfolio (see Figure 8) and although the quality of presentation was high and the content appropriate, the structure was so difficult for the assessor to navigate that the evaluation required in excess of two hours. Learners in this subject area are now provided with a model (see Figure 5) to guide them and to provide a more consistent structure for tutors to follow.

It is expected that technology will address the challenges of personalisation but in some cases it seems that by embracing technology in learning, the very inequities that personalisation is trying to address are being reinforced. Some of our education students felt disadvantaged simply because access to technology was a challenge in busy households with only one family computer. They would struggle to have access to a computer which was required for homework, family communication and leisure activities. Others lost work through their lack of knowledge about backing-up materials prior to uploading into the ePortfolio system. Physiotherapy, radiography and education students struggled to access the ePortfolio on clinical placement as institutional firewalls inhibited and sometimes prohibited access to the system. Performing arts management students requested access to the ePortfolio system through mobile phones, wanting to record experiences as they happened, and then to reflect on these whilst on placement in theatres away from the institution.

For each of our case studies, a practical hands-on session was required to help familiarise students with the ePortfolio system. Afterwards, top-up sessions were offered and in some cases, one-to-one sessions, as well as weekly drop-in sessions. This was time-consuming for support and academic staff, but allowed tutors to prepare learners for the challenges of using technology intensively for their studies. In the education and physiotherapy case studies, students were warned about the issues of firewalls and as part of their action planning for the modules were asked to explore different options for access which included working from libraries and internet cafes. Early trials of our ePortfolio system in other institutions have shown that mobile devices can be used to add blog entries (PebbleLearning, 2008) and for the future may improve access. Despite such technological challenges, by the end of their studies, many of our learners were thrilled at the development of their IT-skills through engaging with the tool and this led them to feel more confident when using technology in their professional and personal lives, and has led to them opting for alumni access to the system.

Our case studies demonstrate technology supporting learner reflection, but we acknowledge that it is not true dynamic ePersonalisation as envisaged by Fraser (2006). Our learners currently do not have a choice of the system they wish to use and they may prefer to interact with a familiar social networking site such as Facebook for their learning, reflecting and presentation of materials. In such cases, it would be anticipated that the institution – the tutor and the administration – would engage with the learner's preferred system. Such an approach has many advantages but raises issues such as the reliability of the chosen web 2.0 service – will the social networking site be available throughout the programme of studies and on a regular basis? These and other issues related to web 2.0 services in the learner environment are discussed elsewhere (Edinburgh University, 2007), but it is possible that they may compromise the integrity of a programme and the learner experience. Using Web 2.0 would also have significant resource implications. Tutors

and external examiners would be required to log into all the different preferred systems and then familiarise themselves with the various formats and styles before assessing the work.

In the future, a learner will have access to numerous ePortfolio systems - educational, professional, regional and even national, such as the EELs project (JISC, 2008). Higher education will need an approach that accommodates learner choice but one that is also sustainable without significant resourcing implications. It is possible that institutions will elect to have an ePortfolio system where students will have access to templates, exemplars, support and guidance, such as the model developed for radiography students (see Figure 5) outlining the structure of an assessed webfolio. The ePortfolio will also serve as a gateway from which learners will be able to link to a system of their choice. Physiotherapy learners may select to use the CSP ePortfolio whilst our drama learners may wish to link to private entries posted to Facebook. Alternatively some learners may prefer to use the institutional ePortfolio which is structured and supported. For assessments, work held on Web 2.0 services will then need to be 'copied' to the institutional ePortfolio system from the learner's system. Technical solutions to this are currently being explored by CETIS including Portfolio interoperability prototyping (CETIS, 2008).

IMPLEMENTING AN EPORTFOLIO TO ENCOURAGE LEARNER REFLECTION AND SUPPORT PERSONALISED LEARNING

Through our case studies, specific areas have emerged that educators should address when implementing an ePortfolio system to support personalised learning and the personalisation agenda including the following.

Learner Introduction to Reflection

A thorough introduction to reflection should be provided to all learners, explaining the purpose of reflection in learning and its role in future personal development. Examples of reflective writing, both good and bad, as well as frameworks for structuring and supporting reflective accounts help students to start writing reflectively. Learners must know the difference between descriptive and reflective writing; sharing early attempts at reflective writing with 'blogging buddies' who, at a later stage of their studies, could provide valuable, timely feedback.

Assessment Design

Diverse assessment mechanisms, such as learning journals and the creation and maintenance of personal development plans, should be used to engage learners with reflection and the ePortfolio system on a regular basis. Formative and/or summative assessment will provide the best results, encouraging learners to reflect and use the ePortfolio as a support mechanism for the reflective process.

Feedback

Formative and summative feedback is essential especially in the early stages of ePortfolio use. Learners should be encouraged to engage actively with such feedback by commenting within the ePortfolio system on the feedback that they have received and by providing outlines of future activities in response to this feedback. Face-to-face sessions with learners should specifically refer to the feedback within the ePortfolio system and reinforce key messages.

Familiarity with the ePortfolio System

The system can become a barrier for learners, causing them to focus on the tool rather than the learning activity. Learners require at least one hands-on demonstration of the ePortfolio system and then regular 'top-up' opportunities. Easy-to-use documentation and video guides to using the tools within the system are essential, as well as drop-in sessions.

Exemplars and Models of Learner Use of the ePortfolio System

It takes time to visualise an online portfolio and how the different elements may, or may not, be integrated to support learning. Students need to be able to make informed decisions about which tools to use within the system, and when, for example, recognising when a blog would be a useful addition to a webfolio. Exemplars from previous student work help learners develop an understanding of what the system can do for them and why. A model, outlining how the different tools could be integrated, is also helpful in this process.

CONCLUSION

In this chapter we have demonstrated how reflection, when integrated with an ePortfolio, can meet the multiple goals of the personalisation agenda as appropriate for our particular case studies in higher education. We have also shown how technology can be used to help meet that agenda but it is important to recognise that technology, and especially the choice of system used by the learner, is not the complete picture regarding personalisation; it is all too easy to fall into the trap of focussing on system selection rather than addressing the bigger, more complex issues of personalisation, such as strategies to learning and teaching and approaches to assessment and feedback (Pollard & James, 2004). Crucially, through our examples, we have shown that significant planning and careful integration within the curriculum are required to ensure that the ePortfolio supports the personalisation process. ePortfolios must become *part* of the learning process where a student's learning is documented and tracked, re-visited, revised, expanded and where collaborative activities and discussion are linked directly into the personal portfolio building experience. At the moment, as educators in higher education, we are still in the formative stages of personalisation (Pollard & James, 2004) and further research is required to explore how personalisation develops in higher education. Nevertheless it is clear that:

There is evidence that students [in HE] value personalisation of their learning experience and that the benefits manifest in engagement with their studies, motivation and self-confidence. Empowering students to be autonomous and independent learners also has beneficial consequences in terms of giving them control over important aspects of their own learning. (Knox & Wyper, 2008, p5)

ACKNOWLEDGMENT

The authors would like to thank the tutors and students who kindly participated in the case studies and the reviewers for their invaluable feedback and comments.

REFERENCES

Association of Colleges. (2006). *Personalisation in electronic environments: A definition and check list*. (Briefing: AoC NILTA 15/06). London: Association of Colleges.

Association of Colleges. (2007). *Personalising further education: Developing a vision*. London: Association of Colleges.

Beetham, H., & Strivens, J. (2005). *Current e-Portfolio developments in the 14-19, adult and continuing learning sectors*. Commissioned by the National Learning Network Transformation Board.

Biggs, J., & Tang, C. (2007). *Teaching for quality learning at university* (3rd ed.). Maidenhead, UK: Open University Press.

Boud, D., Keogh, R., & Walker, D. (1985). *Reflection: Turning experience into learning*. London: Kogan Page.

Brockbank, A., McGill, I., & Beech, N. (2002). *Reflective learning in practice*. Aldershot, UK: Gower.

CETIS. (2008). *Portfolio interoperability prototyping*. Retrieved November 13, 2008, from http://wiki.cetis.ac.uk/Portfolio_interoperability_prototyping

Department for Education and Skills. (2004). *A national conversation about personalised learning*. Retrieved June 10, 2008, from http://www.innovation-unit.co.uk/images/stories/files/pdf/PersonalisedLearningBooklet.pdf

Department for Education and Skills. (2005). *Harnessing technology: Transforming learning and children's services*. Retrieved June 25, 2008, from http://www.dfes.gov.uk/publications/e-strategy/docs/e-strategy.pdf

Department for Education and Skills. (2006). *2020 Vision: Report of the teaching and learning in 2020 review group*. Retrieved September 19, 2008, from http://www.teachernet.gov.uk/_doc/10783/6856_DfES_Teaching_and_Learning.pdf

DiBiase, D. (with Zembal-Saul, C., Melander, G., Sabre, J., Schall, J., Howard, D., Spielvogel, E., Rademacher, H., Mathews, J., Burlingame, P., & Orndorff, R.). (2002). *Using ePortfolios at Penn State to enhance student learning. Status, prospects, and strategies*. College Park, PA: Education Institute, The Pennsylvania State University. Retrieved June 24, 2006, from: https://www.e-education.psu.portfolios/e-port_report.shtml

Donaghy, M., & Morss, K. (2007). An evaluation of a framework for facilitating and assessing physiotherapy students' reflection on practice. *Physiotherapy Theory and Practice*, *23*(2), 83–94. doi:10.1080/09593980701211952

Edinburgh University. (2007). *Guidelines for Using External Web 2.0 Services*. Retrieved November 13, 2008, from http://www.vp.is.ed.ac.uk/content/1/c4/12/45/GuidelinesForUsingExternalWeb2.0Services-20070823.pdf

Ellison, N. B., Steinfield, C., & Lampe, C. (2007). The benefits of Facebook "friends:" Social capital and college students' use of online social network sites. *Journal of Computer-Mediated Communication*, *12*, 1143–1168. doi:10.1111/j.1083-6101.2007.00367.x

Field, S. (2006). *Personalised learning*. The Teacher Training Resource Bank. Retrieved October 6, 2008, from http://www.ttrb.ac.uk/viewarticle2.aspx?contentId=12406

Fook, J., & Gardner, F. (2007). *Practising critical reflection: A resource handbook*. Maidenhead, UK: Open University Press.

Fraser, J. (2006). *Personalisation: customisation – is it enough?* Entry posted to EdTechUK, archived at http://fraser.typepad.com/edtechuk/2006/10/personalisation.html

Friedman Ben David, M., Davis, M. H., Harden, R. M., Howie, P. W., Ker, J., & Pippard, M. J. (2001). AMEE medical education guide no.24: Portfolios as a method of student assessment. *Medical Teacher, 23*(6), 535-551. Retrieved October 18, 2007, from http://dx.doi.org/10.1080/01421590120090952

Funk, K. (2004). Brief or new: student learning portfolios: Balancing tradition with innovation. *Occupational Therapy in Health Care*, *18*(1), 99–105. doi:10.1300/J003v18n01_10

Green, H., Facer, K., Rudd, T., Dillon, P., & Humphreys, P. (2005). *Personalisation and digital technologies*. Retrieved June 10, 2008, from http://www.futurelab.org.uk/resources/documents/opening_education/Personalisation_report.pdf

Health Professions Council. (2007). *Standards of proficiency: Radiographers*. Retrieved October 30, 2008, from http://www.hpc-uk.org/assets/documents/10000DBDStandards_of_Proficiency_Radiographers.pdf

Jasper, M. A., & Fulton, J. (2005). Marking criteria for assessing practice-based portfolios at master's level. *Nurse Education Today*, *25*, 377–389. doi:10.1016/j.nedt.2005.03.006

JISC. (2008). *At the cutting edge of educational technology*. Retrieved November 13, 2008, from http://www.jisc.ac.uk/news/stories/2008/02/labgroup.aspx

JISCInfoNet. (2008). *e-portfolios*. Retrieved June 24, 2008, from http://www.jiscinfonet.ac.uk/infokits/e-portfolios

Johns, C. (1994). Guided reflection. In A. Palmer, S. Burns, & C. Bulman (Eds.), *Reflective practice in nursing: The growth of the professional practitioner* (pp. 110-129). Oxford, UK: Blackwell Scientific.

Knox, H., & Wyper, J. (2008). *Quality enhancement themes: The first year experience: Personalisation of the first year*. Retrieved June 20, 2008, from http://www.enhancementthemes.ac.uk/documents/firstyear/Personalisation%20-%20Final.pdf

Kolb, D. A. (1984). *Experiential learning: Experience as the source of learning and development*. Englewood Cliffs, NJ: Prentice-Hall.

Leadbeater, C. (2004). *Learning about personalisation: How can we put the learner at the heart of the education system?* Retrieved June 17, 2008, from http://www.demos.co.uk/files/learningaboutpersonalisation.pdf

Mezirow, J. (1990). *Fostering critical reflection in adulthood: A guide to transformative and emancipatory learning.* San Francisco, CA: Jossey-Bass.

Miliband, D. (2004). *Personalised learning: Building a new relationship with schools.* Retrieved June 17, 2008, from http://publications. teachernet.gov.uk/eOrderingDownload/personalised-learning.pdf

Moon, J. (1999). *Reflection in learning and professional development: Theory and practice.* London: Kogan Page.

Moon, J. (2005). *Learning through reflection: Higher Education Academy guide for busy academics Number 4.* Retrieved June 23, 2008, from http://www.heacademy.ac.uk/resources/detail/ id69_guide_for_busy_academics_no4_moon

National College for School Leadership. (2006). *An overview of the summary report findings.* Retrieved September 19, 2008, from http://www. ncsl.org.uk/media-579-61-personalised-learning-overview.pdf

PebbleLearning. (2008). *News.* Retrieved November 12, 2008, from http://www.pebblelearning. co.uk/news.asp

Pollard, A., & James, M. (Eds.). (2004). *Personalised learning: a commentary by the teaching and learning research programme.* Economic and Social Research Council.

Prensky, M. (2001). Digital natives, digital immigrants. *On the Horizon 9*(5). Retrieved February 26, 2009, from http://www.marcprensky.com/writing/Prensky%20-%20Digital%20 Natives,%20Digital%20Immigrants%20-%20 Part1.pdf

QAA. (2007). *Integrative assessment: Balancing assessment of and assessment for learning, guide number 2.* Gloucester, UK: QAA. Retrieved October 6, 2008, from http://www.enhancementthemes.ac.uk/documents/IntegrativeAssessment/ IABalancing.pdf

Queen Margaret University. (2008). *New campus.* Retrieved November 13, 2008, from http://www. qmu.ac.uk/the_university/new_campus.htm

Queen Margaret University College. (2006). *QUELTA goals and aims: 2003-8: Quality enhancement of learning, teaching and assessment (revised spring 2006).* Retrieved December 12, 2007, from http://www.qmu.ac.uk/quality/ documents/QELTA%20Strategy%20revised%20 June%202006.doc

Rees, C., Forbes, P., & Kubler, B. (2007). *Student employability profiles: A guide for higher education practitioners* (2nd ed.). Higher Education Academy. Retrieved October 24, 2008, from http://www.heacademy.ac.uk/assets/York/documents/ourwork/tla/employability_enterprise/ student_employability_profiles_apr07.pdf

Schön, D. (1987). *Educating the reflective practitioner.* San Francisco, CA: Jossey-Bass.

Siemens, G. (2004). *ePortfolios.* Retrieved November 9, 2007, from http://www.elearnspace. org/Articles/eportfolios.htm

Stefani, L., Mason, R., & Pegler, C. (2007). *The educational potential of e-portfolios: Supporting personal development and reflective learning.* Abingdon, UK: Routledge.

Chapter 12
Personalised Learning:
A Case Study in Teaching Clinical Educators Instructional Design Skills

Iain Doherty
University of Auckland, New Zealand

Adam Blake
University of Auckland, New Zealand

ABSTRACT

The authors consider personalised learning in the context of delivering a specialist postgraduate course – ClinEd 711, ELearning and Clinical Education – at the Faculty of Medical and Health Sciences, University of Auckland. They describe the pedagogical theory underlying the course design and their experience of delivering ClinEd 711 with particular reference to the personalised learning process that the course design facilitated. They present their research results for the student experience of ClinEd 711 and discuss changes made to the course as a result of student feedback. They make reference to the introduction of student-led modules to further personalise the students' learning experience. ClinEd 711 is a specialist postgraduate course with low student numbers; with this in mind the authors discuss the implications of their pedagogical approach for those educators involved in teaching larger classes. They conclude their paper with a discussion of the role of the educator in personalised learning.

INTRODUCTION

The Learning Technology Unit (http://www.fmhs.auckland.ac.nz/faculty/ltu/) and the Centre for Medical & Health Sciences Education (http://www.fmhs.auckland.ac.nz/faculty/cmhse/default.aspx) at the Faculty of Medical and Health Sciences, University of Auckland jointly offer a fifteen week course – ELearning and Clinical Education (ClinEd 711) – as part of a clinical education postgraduate degree program. The overall objective of ClinEd 711 is to bring the learners – who are typically educators in the field of medical and health sciences – to the point of understanding themselves as instructional designers capable of converting one of

DOI: 10.4018/978-1-60566-884-0.ch012

their traditional face-to-face courses for flexible/distance delivery. ClinEd 711 was offered for the first time in Semester 1, 2007 as a fully online distance education course. The course was offered for a second time in Semester 1, 2008 and at the time of writing (March 2009) the course is being offered for a third time. From the outset, ClinEd 711 was designed to locate the student at the centre of the learning process in order to provide students with a personalised learning experience. However, as a result of feedback from students and after critical analysis of the first iteration of the course, ClinEd 711 was re-designed to create an even more personalised learning environment. This was achieved through the introduction of student-led modules in which the students had to take responsibility for the creation and delivery of a particular course module to be "studied" by their peers.

In this chapter we: outline our understanding of personalised learning; detail the research approach that we took in designing and evaluating ClinEd 711; explain how the course was designed to situate the learner at the centre of the learning process; describe the personalised learning processes that the approach facilitated; outline the differences between the first and second iteration of the course; and provide the reasoning behind the changes that were made for the second iteration of the course. Our chapter will make particular reference to the student-led modules that were introduced in the second iteration of the course, as the rationale for this innovation was to provide students with greater learning autonomy and with greater responsibility for their learning outcomes. As we shall see, these are two of the central features of personalised learning. We are aware that ClinED 711 is a specialist postgraduate course with a relatively low number of student enrolments and with this fact in mind we will discuss the potential challenges of offering this particular form of personalised learning to larger class sizes. We conclude our chapter by discussing the relationship between the role of the educator and the independence of the student in a personalised learning environment before briefly considering future research directions.

PERSONALISED LEARNING

A key characteristic of personalised learning is that the student is located at the centre of the learning process. Personalised learning meets the individual learning needs of a diverse range of students whilst encouraging independent learning (Johnson, 2004) through learners taking greater responsibility for their own learning and through learners being more actively engaged in the learning process (Hannafin & Land, 1997; Ong & Hawryszkiewycz, 2003). It is the design of a particular type of learning environment "shaped by its foundations and assumptions about learning, pedagogy and the learner" that provides the conditions for personalised learning (Hannafin & Land, 1997, p. 197). For example, teachers can facilitate personalised learning by adopting teaching strategies that meet the needs, abilities and aptitudes of each student thereby providing for an individual learning pathway (Sun & Williams, 2004). This can be achieved through shifting responsibility from the teacher to the student for discovering, organising, analysing and synthesising content (Brush & Saye, 2000; Downes, 2005). Such strategies can maximise student motivation and attainment so that students realise their full potential (Johnson, 2004). However, the role of the educator remains crucial if students are to succeed (Hannafin & Land, 1997) with the educator fulfilling the necessary roles of facilitator and mentor (Johnson, 2004; McLoughlin & Lee, 2007; Ong & Hawryszkiewycz, 2003).

In cases where class sizes are large with lecturers often being "time-poor" (Goodyear, 2005, p. 2), it has been said that personalised learning must necessarily be about offering students learning choices within the framework of a particular curriculum or course (Johnson, 2004). In practice this means providing a teaching framework that offers a solution to the problem of teaching to a large group of students whilst also meeting the diverse learning needs of each particular student so that learners, "are actively engaged in the learning experience with their preferred content" (Sun & Williams, 2004, p. 2). The Harvard University virtual world project "River City" – a project to teach school aged children science – provides an excellent example of a development that seeks to achieve a balance between providing a standard framework for learning whilst also offering learners individual choice in order to cater to diverse student abilities (Clarke, Dede, Ketelhut, & Nelson, 2006). In "River City" this balance is achieved through providing standardised features in the virtual world whilst also offering customisable features within the environment. For example, "River City" has an individualised guidance system in which student activities are logged in a database. The database maintains a personalised history of the activities undertaken by each student with levels of guidance in the form of "hints" being offered for each individual student in terms of the student history of interaction in "River City". This – along with other design features – has enabled the creators of "River City" to offer an educational innovation that meets the diverse needs of learners and educators.

ClinEd 711 is a specialist postgraduate course and the number of students enrolling has been relatively low. We did not, therefore, have to deal with the challenge of providing personalised learning opportunities to a large numbers of students. Even so, we found that it was challenging to create and manage a learning environment that allowed learners to engage in the learning experience in terms of a project of their own choosing and with their preferred content. Whilst creation of ClinEd 711 was time consuming, the essential difficulty that we faced had to do with the demands placed on the tutor in terms of supporting students in their learning and in terms of marking assessed work. We will discuss both of these challenges

in this chapter. We will also discuss the extent to which the learning design implemented for ClinEd 711 might be "scaled up" and implemented on a course with much larger student numbers. This will involve us in critically considering how to provide a standard teaching framework that provides a solution to the problem of offering a personalised learning environment when student numbers are large.

It should not be thought that our conception of personalised learning is synonymous with "individual" learning. Rather, interactional theories of cognitive development (Bruner, 2006; Vygotsky, 1978) posit that the social dimension of learning is crucial in pedagogical terms so that students are exposed to a variety of opinions and perspectives that will challenge and inform their own perspectives (Hannafin & Land, 1997; McLoughlin & Lee, 2007). Thus, students might work cooperatively so that their learning is "participatory and social" (McLoughlin & Lee, 2007, p. 664) whilst retaining choice concerning their learning content, their preferred learning style and their use of particular types of social software for communication and collaboration (McLoughlin & Lee, 2007). Students can also be offered flexibility concerning where and when they learn. ClinEd 711 is very firmly rooted in a social constructivist pedagogical framework. Again, despite relatively low student numbers, managing the 'social' component of the learning process led to distinct challenges that will be discussed in this chapter.

BACKGROUND

We deemed design research to be an appropriate research methodology for our ClinEd 711 research project – particularly when compared with research approaches grounded in an objectivist and scientific methodology (Collins, Joseph, & Bielaczyc, 2004; Reeves, Herrington, & Oliver, 2005). Whilst design research has had difficulties gaining traction in the broader research community

(Collins et al., 2004), it is a method that is being applied successfully and is championed by a number of prominent researchers (Bannan-Ritland, 2003; Clarke et al., 2006; Herrington, Oliver, & Reeves, 2002; Kelly, 2003; McKenney, Nieveen, & van den Akker, 2006; Reeves, 2000, 2006; Reeves et al., 2005). Our research approach utilised six design research tenets as explicated by Reeves, Herrington, & Oliver (Reeves et al., 2005):

1. A focus on broad-based, complex problems critical to higher education;
2. The integration of known and hypothetical design principles with technological affordances to render plausible solutions to these complex problems;
3. Rigorous and reflective inquiry to test and refine innovative learning environments as well as to reveal new design principles;
4. Long-term engagement involving continual refinement of protocols and questions;
5. Intensive collaboration among researchers and practitioners, and learning communities;
6. A commitment to theory construction and explanation while solving real-world problems.

We considered the question of how to engage lecturers in a "pedagogically principled way" (Burden & Atkinson, 2008, p. 4041) with technologies for teaching and learning to be a challenge that was sufficiently broad based and complex to warrant adopting the design research approach. We also conceived of the creation of ClinED 711 as a real world problem. The reasons for coming to these conclusions included the fact that the Medical Faculty is the largest Faculty within the university with five Schools and, potentially, a pool of very diverse students. Teaching with technologies is an issue that affects all five Schools because of a demand for delivery of flexible/ distance postgraduate courses and because of a perceived need to produce technology-enhanced teaching materials for undergraduate students.

In addition, factors at a Faculty and University level – such as lecturer time to learn new skills and prepare new content, cultural ethos, pressure to engage in discipline research and the question of incentives for teaching with technologies – all potentially impact on whether or not students on ClinEd 711 actually implement what they have learned. At the outset, we had a long-term commitment to the ClinED 711 research project with the University of Auckland ethics committee approving the research project for a period of three years. A long terms commitment to educational research is important in order to avoid the mistake of conducting an isolated one off study that is of questionable value in terms of meaningful research results. The way in which the remaining tenets of the design research approach have been put into practice will be made evident in the following sections as we describe the creation of ClinEd 711 and the revisions that were made in light of our teaching experience on the course.

COURSE DESIGN

Both iterations of ClinEd 711 have been based upon social constructivist theory (Gillani, 2003; Mergel, 1998). This pedagogical philosophy (Goodyear, 2005, p. 85) "guides learners to conduct and manage their personalised learning activities and encourage [sic] collaborative and co-operative learning for critical thinking and problem solving" (Sun & Williams, 2004, p. 2479). At the level of the individual, constructivist theory suggests that learning is a search for meaning or significance. Students learn in terms of a pre-existing conceptual schema or framework within which they ideally fit new knowledge. Constructivism should therefore be understood as a description of the way in which individuals might go about their learning rather than as a description of the way in which they do in fact go about learning. It is the job of the educator to provide the conditions in which constructivist learning might take place.

This is achieved through providing an educational framework in which course content and activities might be personally meaningful for the students. At the social level, interaction with others can serve to change an individual's conceptual structure or personal interpretation of particular phenomena whilst simultaneously influencing the collective interpretation of those phenomena. In the context of designing a learning environment, educators can create experiences that are personalised – that is individually meaningful, relevant and tailored as far as possible to a learner's particular needs – whilst also ensuring that the learning experience is social thereby exposing individual learners to the perspectives of other learners.

Regarding the second tenet of design research – the integration of known and hypothetical design principles with technological affordances to render plausible solutions to complex problems – ClinEd 711 was designed around six pedagogical principles with the first principle bearing directly on the constructivist learning philosophy:

- Learning should be meaningful for the learner (Ausubel, 1963; Bransford, Brown, & Cocking, 2000);
- Learning should be organised around core concepts and cognitive flexibility to develop expert rather than novice knowledge (Ausubel, 1963; Bransford et al., 2000; Driscoll, 2005);
- Learning tasks should replicate real world problems in an authentic context (Bransford et al., 2000; Lave & Wenger, 1991; Lemke, 1997);
- Learning should involve the collaborative construction of knowledge thereby providing learners with multiple perspectives on particular issues and concepts (Bruner, 2006; O'Donnell, 2006; Vygotsky, 1978);
- Learning should employ strategies that appeal to multiple sensory modes and cognitive capabilities (Driscoll, 2005; Gardner, 1983; Mayer, 2003; Paivio,

1986; Spiro, Feltovich, Jacobson, & Coulson, 1995);
- Learning tasks should encourage meta-cognitive capabilities and reflective practice (Bransford et al., 2000; Schön, 1987).

In line with recommendations for publishing design research as it unfolds, the research basis for implementing these design principles has been reported elsewhere (Blake & Doherty, 2008; Doherty & Blake, 2007). In this chapter we will be focussing on those aspects of the learning environment that pertain directly to personalised learning and on the challenges of providing personalised learning to students.

COURSE CONTENT AND LEARNING PROCESS

The postgraduate degree programme in clinical education within which ClinEd 711 is offered is aimed at health professionals and academics (doctors, nurses, pharmacists and others) involved in clinical teaching. Students might be full time academics or they might primarily be clinicians with some teaching responsibilities within the Faculty. This is an interesting point with respect to meeting the needs of all learners. Whilst academics with some clinical responsibilities will have a professional identity defined to a significant degree by their teaching, clinicians who teach only part time are much more likely to have a professional identity that is defined by their clinical responsibilities. This point obviously bears upon offering personalised learning to students since the course tutors have to be sensitive to the fact that some students will not come to ClinED 711 with an understanding of themselves as teachers. Students participating in the first 2 iterations of the course have had the characteristics described in Table 1.

Whilst student enrolments have been relatively low, we can see that students on ClinEd 711 have

Table 1. Characteristics of ClinEd 711 students, 2007 and 2008

	Field of clinical education practice	University of Auckland staff member?	Resident in Auckland?
First course iteration, 2007 (4 students)	Psychiatry	Yes	**Yes**
	Palliative care nursing	No	**Yes**
	General medicine	No	**Yes**
	Pharmacy	Yes	**Yes**
Second course iteration, 2008 (6 students)	Anaesthesia	No	**Yes**
	Surgery	No	**No**
	Psychiatry	Yes	**Yes**
	Mental health nursing	No	**Yes**
	Physiology	Yes	**Yes**
	Psychology	Yes	**No**
n (total) = 10		**UoA staff = 5**	**Auck. resident = 8**

been diverse in terms of their field of clinical practice. We can also see that the majority of students have been resident in Auckland with half of the students being Auckland University staff. Since this was a wholly distance course, the physical location of the students was not a factor in the student learning experience since all content and interaction was carried out online. Both iterations of ClinEd 711 required students to progress through the course in terms of an eLearning project of their own choosing. In this way, students engaged in authentic, personalised and meaningful learning through selecting one of their own courses for their project and through developing that course for flexible or distance delivery.

The emphasis in ClinEd 711 was on the personal relevance of the learning for the learner's teaching and learning philosophy and for their clinical education practice. The reference to clinical practice is important as it bears upon the sixth tenet of design research, "A commitment to theory construction and explanation while solving real-world problems". ClinED 711 emphasised that students needed to consider how their teaching practice would impact on real world health care problems. There was, therefore, an emphasis in

ClinED 711 on students creating flexible/distance courses that would lead to, for example, improved health care in the workplace. Students were directed to take ownership of their learning from the very beginning of the ClinED 711. This situated them at the heart of the learning process and as a result the course became personally relevant and meaningful to the students. Students typically chose to focus on a course that they were already teaching, although in some cases they chose to create a new course. This provided each student with an individual pathway through ClinEd 711. Progression through the modules of ClinEd 711 was centred on two core instructional design documents that are used within the Learning Technology Unit at the Faculty of Medical and Health Sciences for eLearning project developments. The use of these two core documents provided an authentic, real-world learning scenario in which learners could learn to think like instructional designers.

The first document – Needs Analysis Document – clarifies the potential social and pedagogical usefulness of the project and captures key information necessary for converting a traditional face-to-face course for flexible/distance delivery.

The Needs Analysis Document asks for the following information: project goal; project rationale; staff who will contribute to course development; whether the course is university approved; completion date for development work; current course format and mode(s) of delivery; new provisions required; available budget; frequency of updates for the completed development; staff available to carry out the updates and head of school approval. The document therefore functions to ensure that there is a clear reason for converting the course for flexible or distance delivery and completion of the document also indicates broadly that the project is viable in terms of the development work required during the allotted timeframe of fifteen weeks. In project management terminology, the Needs Analysis Document is the functional equivalent of a project mandate document, which serves to determine in broad terms whether, or a not a project is worthwhile. Students on ClinEd 711 were expected to complete the Needs Analysis Document during the early weeks of the course. The course tutor then marked the Needs Analysis Document. In the real world of project management the Needs Analysis Document is crucial as it provides the information required to gauge whether or not the project is viable. The same is true in the context of ClinED 711 and, therefore, students were made aware of the importance of completing the document to a high standard. The course tutor marked the Needs Analysis Document and if the document did not meet the required standard – that is, if the document did not define the project as both worthwhile and viable – students were given the opportunity to revise the document.

The Second Document – Course Development Document – requires students to detail the pedagogical thinking and development work required to successfully convert their course for flexible/distance delivery. This is the project management equivalent of a project initiation document which functions to ensure that the project has a sound basis. Since the Course Development Document is so central to ClinED 711, we have provided an example of the document in Appendix One. Completion of this document ensures that the student's chosen course is appropriately developed in terms of meaningful course content, meaningful student activities, and meaningful student-teacher and student-student interaction (Hutchins, 2003; Rourke, Anderson, Archer, & Garrison, 1999). This is achieved through requiring the student to detail for their chosen course development project: module topics and associated learning tasks; student roles and activities on the course; delivery mode or modes; teaching and learning resources; tutor support roles; and methods of assessment and feedback. Students on ClinED 711 completed the Course Development Document as they progressed through the course modules so that by the end of the semester the students had a "blueprint" for developing and implementing their own flexible or distance learning course. We can see, therefore, that the student learning was both authentic and personalised as the module content related directly to the students' own projects in terms of completing the Course Development Document.

Subject content for ClinEd 711 was selected in terms of key concepts and knowledge required for the practice of instructional design and the course was structured to foster reflective practice (Bruce, Edwards, & Lupton, 2006, p. 5). The ClinEd 711 modules included:

- The major learning theories of behaviourism, cognitivism and constructivism.
- Instructional design principles and practice;
- Methods for quality assurance in developing flexible and distance courses; and
- Sourcing particular learning objects whilst justifying their pedagogical value, and demonstrating an understanding of copyright issues with respect to their chosen learning object.

The primary theme running through course tasks and assessment was for students to relate course concepts to their personal pedagogical beliefs and their own teaching context. Thus, in addition to the personal relevance of choosing their own eLearning projects, students were encouraged to engage in learning processes that enabled them to see the meaning of what they were learning as it applied to their own teaching practice. With respect to social participatory learning, learners engaged in collaborative exercises through participating in online discussions and through engaging in peer critique exercises. Reflective practice and meta-cognition were encouraged through peer critique activities, self-reflection activities and through comprehensive feedback provided by the course tutor in accordance with detailed marking rubrics. Finally, the course utilised a variety of media including text, images, multimedia resources and podcasts in order to accommodate different learning preferences.

FIRST ITERATION TEACHING, LEARNING AND ASSESSMENT

The first iteration of ClinEd 711 encouraged personalised learning in terms of students choosing their own eLearning project and in terms of requiring each student to reflect on their own teaching and learning perspectives. For example, having chosen their own course to develop for flexible/distance delivery in ClinED 711, online discussion of topics prompted students to relate course concepts from each module to their own teaching beliefs and teaching practices. The purpose of this self reflection was to encourage students to think about how their beliefs about teaching and learning impacted on their teaching approaches. For example, having learned about constructivist learning theories students might reflect on the educational value of constructivist learning and on whether or not their own approach to teaching included constructivist elements. This

sort of reflection was particularly challenging for students who came to fundamentally question their approach to teaching and the tutor providing feedback on the reflective exercises had to exercise a degree of sensitivity and understanding as students questioned beliefs about teaching that had not previously been considered.

Although learning was personalised for students in these ways, the tutor extensively managed the first iteration of ClinED 711. This was particularly evident in the assessment activities. Each of modules 2-10 required submission of an assessed piece of work. One of the authors acted as primary course tutor and assessor, with the second tutor providing assessment moderation for all student submissions. There was, therefore, a tension between the desire to offer personalised learning – particularly in terms of students taking responsibility for their own learning – and the requirement for students to conform to a rigid assessment schedule throughout the course. The disjoint between the assessed activities and the aim of encouraging students to take responsibility for their own learning only became apparent to the tutors as the course progressed. The tension caused by the assessed modules is evidenced by the following overview of course tasks and assessment activities provided in Table 2.

ClinEd 711 course web pages providing detailed course information and the overview of tasks, interaction, and resources for each module were created using MindManager mind mapping software (http://www.mindjet.com). MindManager was chosen because one of the course tutors preferred a visual approach to development work and had used the software extensively. MindManager further recommended itself because it has an export feature that quickly and easily allows the user to export the Mind Map as a set of HTML pages to be uploaded to a server. The exported web pages were hosted within the university's Learning Management System (LMS). Online discussion was facilitated primarily via threaded discussion in the LMS. Students were supported in

Table 2. Overview of ClinEd 711 course tasks and assessment (first iteration, 2007)

Coursework item	Module(s)
Online group discussion around course-related material demonstrating critical reflections on your learning and linking of learning to your own context (15%)	Modules 1-10
Completion of Needs Analysis Document (15%) (formative feedback provided prior to final completion)	Module 2
Literature-based development of principles around learning technology and media (5%) (small group/pair assignment)	Module 3
Literature-based development of principles around the role of the teacher (5%) (small group/pair assignment)	Module 5
Sourcing and applying learning objects (10%)	Module 7
Course Development Document (50%), comprising:	
Reflective commentaries on completion of key aspects of the Course Development Document (20%)	Modules 4, 5, 6 & 10
Critique of a peer's draft Course Development Document (10%)	Module 8
Completion of final document (20%)	Modules 9-10

setting up individual blogs using Blogger (http://www.blogger.com) in order that they might post their reflective commentaries. For the two small group/pair assignments (detailed in the table above), students were supported in using PBWiki (http://pbwiki.com/) to collaborate, but were also encouraged to experiment with any other collaboration environment of choice. For example, in the second small group/pair assignment, one pair used the collaborative concept mapping application, Bubbl (http://bubbl.us).

Despite the low student numbers (n=4) on the first iteration of the course, students were relatively active in the threaded discussion forums (135 student messages contributed during the course). Students appeared to have little difficulty with the practical aspects of posting discussion forum messages. Students also found setting up their blogs and wikis relatively easy. We would attribute the lack of difficulty with the various technologies to the fact that students were provided with detailed step-by-step instructions for these tasks. This is one of the ways that we ensured that we designed ClinED 711 in terms of the total student learning experience (Alexander, 2001), taking into account not only course content but

also supports required to ensure the quality of the student learning experience. Although the initial intention had been for students to post their Course Development Documents to their blogs for peer critique, the inability to post file attachments to blogs meant that the LMS discussion forum tool was used for this activity.

As detailed in Table 2 above, students were required to create a reflective commentary on their completion of key aspects of the Course Development Document. Students were provided with a blog to facilitate their reflective practice and a 'blogs' tab was provided within the LMS, with links to each of the student's blog. Because students showed little inclination to post comments in response to their peers' reflective commentaries, the course tutor used a blog conglomeration tool, Blogdigger (http://blogdigger.com) to collate all of the blog entries in chronological order on one webpage. The tutor also provided a link to the collated blogs within the LMS. The aim was to make it easier for the students (and the tutor) to review the postings, and to provide more of a sense of connection within the group in relation to their reflective postings. However, students still did not engage in interaction by way of commenting on their peers' blogs. One of the reasons for this may be that no marks were associated with posting comments on other students' blogs. As we shall see below, we attempted to address this issue in the second iteration of the course.

Students were provided with rubrics detailing the key areas of performance required for each assessed task. The rubrics described 5 levels of performance for each area ranging from exemplary through to inadequate. The course tutor used these rubrics, with an additional column added for comments, to provide feedback to each student on each of the assessed tasks. Students used the Course Development Document rubric to provide critique on their assigned peer's work. Using rubrics in this way worked well to provide clarity on task requirements and to communicate high expectations of performance. However, those high expectations create a matching expectation for quality feedback; if a student was graded as not having achieved exemplary performance within a particular area of a task, then the tutor was responsible for clearly showing how that student had failed to meet expectations. The tutor also had a clear responsibility to show students how they might improve their performance.

In our introduction we made reference to the fact that providing a personalised learning experience for students was challenging on ClinED 711 despite the fact that student numbers for each iteration of the course were relatively low. The challenge concerned the creation of the course in the first instance as we sought to create a course with both standardised elements and individualised elements (Clarke et al., 2006). Whilst the creation of a new course is always time consuming, the commitment to designing a course that would deliver a personalised learning experience for students entailed a substantial number of hours spent in course design. In particular, we spent a lot of hours creating a learning environment that would be personally relevant for the students. We also spent a considerable number of hours in creating authentic or "real world" learning activi-

ties. Finally, the creation of the assessed activities together with detailed marking rubrics for each activity also took a considerable amount of time. Whilst it is not possible to be specific in terms of the time taken to create ClinED 711 compared with the time taken to develop other ClinED courses, we are very aware that we committed considerably more hours to course creation than tutors who followed a more traditional route.

As we shall see below, the time that we spent on creating the course was worthwhile with the external assessor remarking on the quality of the course particularly in terms of the learning activities and tutor teaching practice. With these points in mind we would certainly deem the time and effort spent on ClinEd 711 to have been worthwhile. However, the number of assessed tasks throughout the course combined with the detailed feedback entailed by the marking rubric meant that assessment and feedback activities were extremely time-consuming despite low student numbers. For example, in the first iteration of the course the tutor spent approximately twelve hours assessing the Needs Analysis Document and the Course Development document for the four students. We can see quite clearly that higher enrolments would lead to the need for additional tutors to deal with marking and to monitor the message board. There would certainly come a point at which the format for this course would become unfeasible because we would not be able to commit the requisite tutor time to the course. This would be true even if we employed additional tutors. It is difficult to specify the point at which the ClinEd 711 format would no longer be feasible. However, we can safely say that this level of tutor support would not be possible with a class of two hundred students. Whilst this scenario is unlikely to occur for a specialised Masters course, the question of appropriate learning designs for personalised learning in large classes is a real one.

The difficulty with dealing with large class sizes comes down to offering students an individualised and authentic learning pathway in which they take greater responsibility for their learning in the context of a structured and somewhat standardised framework provided by the educator. We believe that there is an issue here to do with course creation – discussed above – as the creation of a course that offers personalised learning opportunities is time consuming when compared to offering a course that consists solely of standard components. The second issue is the amount of time that the tutor has to spend supporting each student throughout the course and, in particular, providing appropriate feedback on assessed tasks. Whilst, as already suggested, this problem might be overcome initially by employing additional tutors, this will not always be feasible and even when it is feasible there will come a point when student numbers are too great even with the use of additional tutors. The question then becomes how to continue to offer an individual learning pathway with authentic learning activities in a way that does not place impossible demands on teaching staff.

A peer review process – in which students take responsibility for marking the work of other students – suggests itself as a possibility to overcome demands on tutor time. However this option still requires that tutors oversee the peer review process with a minimum requirement being that they moderate peer reviews across a range of allocated grades. The peer review option also requires an appeal process so that students who feel that they have not been marked fairly by their peers have recourse to the tutor. A second possibility is to reduce the number of assessed tasks. In the case of ClinEd 711, for example, we might reduce the number of assessed activities to two; the first assessed activity would be completion of the Needs Analysis Document and the second assessed activity would be completion of the Course Development Document. Other activities – for example, peer critique of the two core course documents – might be built in to the course structure but not assessed. Students would then be responsible for engaging with others in order to learn from others and to contribute to the learning of others. Unfortunately, our experience on ClinED 711 together with research in the area would suggest that students engage in online group activities only when marks are allocated for those activities. In the final analysis, motivation is extrinsic; students want to see tangible rewards for their efforts. Reducing the tutor workload through putting more of an emphasis on students' self-learning may not, therefore, be feasible.

The previous paragraph highlights issues that will be encountered when attempting to create a personalised learning environment for a large class. Whilst we have not offered a solution to the problem, we have identified a core issue to do with tutor time spent on providing formative feedback and marking assessed activities. It is our opinion that the learning design for a large class size would of necessity look very different from the learning design for a small class such as ClinED 711. The specialist nature of our course means that we are extremely unlikely to find ourselves in a situation in which we have to fundamentally change our learning design.. However, we know that the learning design is a good one – measured in terms of feedback from the external moderator and in terms of student feedback – and it is therefore a design that we would look to implement for other courses including courses with larger student numbers. We will, therefore, have to continue to think about how to transpose the teaching principles to courses with larger numbers.

FIRST ITERATION RESEARCH RESULTS

In line with the sixth tenet of design research – a commitment to theory construction and explanation while solving real-world problems – the research project associated with ClinEd 711 was originally designed to allow us to answer a number of key questions with respect to teaching clinical educators about developing their courses for flexible or distance delivery. In particular we were concerned with:

- The preparedness of lecturers to teach with technologies;
- The success or otherwise of ClinEd 711 in terms of teaching clinical educators instructional design skills;
- The factors that impacted positively and negatively on lecturers' intentions with respect to flexible or distance learning development once they had completed the course.

For the first iteration of the course, students were given a pre-course survey to determine their extant levels of knowledge concerning teaching with technologies. The same survey was administered at the end of the course. Students also completed a university evaluation questionnaire concerning the course, and following standard procedures for first-time delivery, the course underwent review by an external assessor. Finally, a one-year follow up telephone interview was conducted with students. However, this did not take place before the development of the second iteration of the course and is not reported here.

The outcomes of our research into the first iteration of ClinEd 711 have been reported in detail elsewhere (Blake & Doherty, 2008). In summary, indications were that the course was very effective overall. The external assessor praised the course design and teaching practices writing that, "The creative and practically-oriented assessment tasks are to be lauded. It seems that the course teachers are modelling excellent tutoring techniques." Students reported that: the course motivated them to learn; was intellectually stimulating; and enabled them to enhance their teaching practice. Each student successfully developed a design blueprint for their chosen course, demonstrating learning outcomes that focussed on improved patient care. Areas of concern on the part of the students related to volume of work and the pace

of the course. The external assessor also queried the assignment load and recommended greater assessment weighting for collaborative tasks together with a reduction in the number of assessed components on the course. This bears on the point that the number of assessed activities was at odds with the desire to provide a personalised learning environment and this feedback from the external moderator was considered to be particularly useful. Our experience of teaching the course was one of finding the teaching experience rewarding whilst being aware of several challenges. It should be noted that whilst the number of assessed tasks was deemed problematic, the rationale for including a large number of assessed activities was sound; we wanted to provide students with frequent feedback.

From a teaching perspective, it was very rewarding to be involved with the students as they engaged with learning theory and design issues as part of online discussion, collaboration and reflection tasks, and to see their insights deepen as they developed sound eLearning design blueprints for very worthwhile health education projects. The large number of assessable tasks, each with a detailed rubric, meant that students received frequent and detailed personal feedback. The volume of course tasks however led to expressions of fatigue by students late in the course and meant a fairly high instructor workload despite low student numbers. Although students were generally active in collaboration and communication, the low student numbers also meant that for the most part there was a lack of the 'critical mass' that enables really productive discussion forum exchanges to develop (Blake & Doherty, 2008, p. 100).

In terms of the third tenet of design research – rigorous and reflective inquiry to test and refine innovative learning environments as well as to reveal new design principles – the outcomes of these initial evaluations together the comments from the external moderator and considered re-

Table 3. Overview of ClinEd 711 course tasks and assessment (second iteration, 2008)

Coursework item	Module(s)
Online discussion/research/reflection throughout course demonstrating critical reflections on content and others' contributions, locating and sharing relevant resources, and linking learning to your own context (25%)	Modules 1-8
Completion of Needs Analysis Document (20%)	Modules 2-3
Student-led module: Creation/moderation of content/learning activities/discussion for one module (20%) (small group/pair assignment)	Module 3, 5, or 6
Course Development Document (35%), comprising:	
* Critique of a peer's draft Course Development Document (10%)	Module 7
* Completion of final document (25%)	Module 8

flection on the part of educators, led to a desire to revise the course so that students would:

- Experience a greater sense of independence and control over their learning.
- Maintain and deepen their engagement with course concepts while dealing with less assessment.
- Engage in authentic communication and collaboration with their peers beyond the 'standard' online threaded discussion.
- Gain more experience of 'hands-on' teaching with technologies.
- Be inspired to tap into their creativity to further personalise their learning.

SECOND ITERATION TEACHING LEARNING AND ASSESSMENT

For the second iteration of the course we responded to the assessor and student feedback by:

- Removing the two small-scale collaborative tasks implemented in the first iteration;
- Combining individual reflective tasks within a broader courselong "discussion/ research/reflection" assessment category;
- Providing a new academic social networking environment (ClinEd711 Network) for course communication;

- Restructuring the content to reduce the number of modules;
- Introducing student led modules.

An overview of the revised course tasks and assessment is provided in Table 3.

The ClinEd711 Network for course communication and file sharing was facilitated using the open source software, Elgg (http://elgg.org). The software was installed and configured on one of the university's servers by a web administrator, and the course tutor was then able to administer student access. Since there were only six students this was not a particularly onerous task. One can see, however, that administering student access for two hundred students would be a somewhat more time consuming affair. For ease of access, a tab was added within the course in the LMS, providing a link to the Network. Elgg features include a personal profile page for each student, a blog, file storage space, and RSS feeds. All blog entries were collated and presented in date order on a scrolling page to enable students to view peer contributions and to respond by way of comments. The six students who took part in the second iteration participated comfortably in the ClinEd711 Network from the beginning of the course. We did not, therefore, have to spend time supporting students in the use of the social software. Over the duration of the course a total of 124 original blog entries were posted along with

204 comments [note however that this includes the course tutor's postings, which the threaded discussion forum total of 135 for the first iteration did not]. One of the drawbacks with Elgg was that it did not offer a feature to easily view the most recently posted comments. At our request, the web administrator reconfigured the software to provide this feature.

Combining all discussion and reflection tasks within a single discussion/research/reflection task (with amended rubric) relieved the pressure on students to post reflections at fixed times and in response to set questions. Pressure on the course tutor to provide rubric-based feedback on these reflections was also relieved, with feedback being provided more informally by comments in the Network from both peers and the tutor. For two of the students, participation levels and depth of reflection were perhaps lower than might have been the case if they had been required to post reflections. To help focus students on the depth of engagement that was expected, the course tutor provided each student with formative feedback half way through the course using the discussion/research/reflection rubric. Unfortunately this did not solve the problem of lack of engagement on the part of the students in question. It is the view of the tutors that the original reflective tasks structure would have obliged the students in question to contribute. The revised structure meant the students were penalised less for their lower level of contribution. This points to a tension between the control exercised through assessed tasks and the responsibility students have for their own learning in a personalised learning environment. Overall, however, the new assessment structure and networking environment appeared to provide a greater level of personalised learning by promoting greater intrinsic motivation to engage with peers and course concepts. Additionally, the course tutor experienced the workload as manageable although it has not be noted that marking the Needs Analysis Docu-ment, the Course Development Document and the student led modules (detailed below) still took a considerable amount of time.

STUDENT-LED MODULES

The second iteration of ClinEd 711 provided for students to lead one of three modules (out of a total of eight modules) that had previously been tutor-led in the first iteration of ClinEd 711: Technologies and Media, Role of the Teacher, or Quality in ELearning Design and Teaching. The student-led modules were created as collaborative tasks in which a pair or small groups of students (up to 4) would be assigned to one of the three designated modules. Students were provided with only a brief introduction to the module together with a set of learning objectives that they were to assist their peers to achieve. Each module lasted 2 weeks, with students expected to collaborate ahead of the scheduled start date to ensure their module was ready to 'go live' on the due date. As we have seen, one of the key aspects in personalised learning concerns students taking responsibility for their own learning. Providing student-led modules, therefore, made a significant contribution to ClinED 711 as a personalised learning environment. The social component of ClinED 711 was further enhanced through the fact that students were also taking responsibility for the learning of their fellow students. If the students allocated to a particular module failed to complete the learning activity, then their fellow students would not have the requisite content for that particular module. The overview of the task provided to students is set out in Figure 1.

Of the 20% of the total course mark allocated to the student-led module task, 12% was for the creation of a web-based module resource. The description provided in the rubric for the ideal performance for this task was:

Figure 1. Overview of the student-led modules for students in the ClinEd 711 course

Student-led modules

The student-led modules provide you with a hands-on opportunity to work with one or more assigned colleagues to take the learning objectives for an assigned module (Module 3, 5, or 6) and create an engaging online module that will help your colleagues to achieve the module's objectives.

During Module 1 your instructor will notify you of your assigned colleague/s, and the module you will be preparing and moderating.

The student-led modules provide you with an opportunity to:

- become more familiar with the literature as you conduct your own research to locate suitable readings for your assigned module
- use software tools for collaboration, planning & production of web-based resources
- apply learning theory to the design of an online module
- build a 'teaching presence' into online materials
- set up and moderate online discussion
- reflect on the process of creating and moderating the online learning for your module.

You may wish to use the module layout used in this course (and the questions included there) to help inform your work.

You and your assigned colleague/s are able to choose which software platform you will use to create and moderate your module. Options include:

- A wiki or blog (both of which enable content to be presented and discussion to take place via a 'Comments' function)
- The eXe elearning editor (which is able to produce webpages that can be uploaded to the ClinEd 711 course in Cecil), in conjunction with discussion conducted via a wiki or blog, or in the ClinEd 711 Network
- Setting up a Community in the ClinEd 711 Network, which enables files to be uploaded and discussion to occur in the community's blog
- Some other web-based option that will enable you to present your content and links to readings, as well as to facilitate online discussion (if you're unsure, ask your instructor).

We appreciate that this is a challenge! Your instructor will be available to assist.

Assessment

Your collaborative efforts on your student-led module are worth 20% of your total mark for the course. Detailed information and assessment rubrics are set out here. **Make sure you use the detailed rubric for the Collaborative Module to guide your work. Note the weightings for each category, and use the description of ideal performance for each category as your target.** If you do not carry a fair share of the workload you may incur a penalty.

Group members provide an engaging website, wiki, blog or other resource for the allocated module with original content and links to relevant scholarly materials together with case studies or other interactive tasks that can serve to stimulate discussion and reflection. Taken as a whole the resource provides a sound platform for peers to successfully fulfil the module's learning objectives.

A further 5% was allocated to moderating module tasks and online discussions engaged in by peers as they undertook the module, and the remaining 3% to accurately evaluating the success of the module design, resource, and moderation.

STUDENT RESPONSE TO THE STUDENT-LED MODULES

As noted earlier, we had initiated our redesign for the second iteration of the course (including introduction of the student-led modules) in the hope that students' engagement with the course concepts, with their peers, and with educational technology tools would be enhanced. The student-led modules embodied all of our 6 core learning design principles, but there was a particular focus on the first principle: that learning should be personally meaningful for the learner. Our hope – indeed our design conjecture (Sandoval, 2004) – was that the challenge of collaboratively creating and moderating a module for peers would lead to positive intermediate outcomes or "observable patterns of behaviour predicted by a model of how an embodied conjecture functions to support learning" (Sandoval, 2004, p. 215). We predicted that these intermediate outcomes would include student research activity in order to offer a variety of resources and perspectives, creative module learning designs, use of a range of technologies, and engaged moderation of tasks and discussion during the modules.

Our predictions were largely fulfilled in the manner in which students engaged with the student-led module task. All three pairs collaborated successfully to produce online modules that were ready on time. The first pair used the open source eXe eLearning editor (http://exelearning.org) to produce their module resource, and moderated peer discussions in the ClinEd711 Network social networking environment. The second pair used a wiki (http://www.wikispaces.com) to both present their resource and to facilitate discussion. The final pair used an eLearning development tool (CourseBuilder) created by a web developer at the University of Auckland, and facilitated peer discussions in the ClinEd711 Network. Each pair took a different design approach to achieve their module's learning objectives, and provided a range of readings and resources for their peers to draw on in undertaking module tasks and discussions. One of the modules was exemplary when measured objectively in terms of the marking rubric. Moderation of discussions was inconsistent for one module, but the student pairs were otherwise active in moderating their modules. Students reflected well on their learning designs for the modules that they created, on the moderation that had been effective, and on what they would do differently next time.

At the end of the course, students were asked to complete the revised post-course questionnaire. This included questions regarding the student-led modules. Five out of six students who undertook the course completed the questionnaire. Students were asked:

Was it helpful for your learning to collaborate with a peer to develop and moderate your student-led module? Why or why not?

All respondents answered in the affirmative with three of the respondents referring directly to the benefit of gaining a different perspective on their topic, two students referring to the benefit of sharing the workload and one respondent expressing the view that the task provided an insight into expectations that are placed upon their students. Students were also asked:

Did you learn more from the student-led modules (led by your peers) than from those led by the course coordinator? Why or why not?

Some students answered from the perspective of developing and moderating their own student-led module whilst others responded in terms of their participation in the modules that were led by the other students. Three of the five respondents indicated that they had learned more from the student-led modules with one respondent referring to the need to actively learn about a module in order to present it effectively and two respondents reporting on the value for their own learning of leading a module.

Finally, in engaging with this research over two years we have shown fidelity to the fifth tenet of design research: intensive collaboration among researchers and practitioners, and learning communities. We have achieved this through working as academic partners in reflecting on and refining teaching approaches and course and research design, working with ClinEd 711 students as academic colleagues who can offer valuable insights into the effectiveness of the course design, and through our informal discussions with other researchers about the project. At the time of writing we are in the final year of our research project and we are committed to carrying out evaluations of the their iteration of the course in order to improve ClinED 711 further.

THE MORE THINGS CHANGE, THE MORE THEY STAY THE SAME

The technologies available today may open up a wider world for information gathering and provide for multiple means of social interaction through, for example, the use of Web 2.0 applications and services such as blogs, wikis and social networking spaces such as FaceBook. However the fundamental model of personalised learning with a social dimension, in which students make use of multiple media sources to work collaboratively on a particular problem, is not new. The issues and challenges faced in previous implementations of what can be considered to be personalised learning – albeit under the different name of student centred learning (Brush & Saye, 2000; Hannafin & Land, 1997) – need to be borne in mind in the current educational climate.

We are all I suspect familiar with the now somewhat tired notion of the shift from the sage on the stage to the guide on the side and possibly even the meddler in the middle (McWilliam, 2008). However, the question of the changing role of the educator in a personalised learning environment – and by implication the role(s) of the students – is significant. Whilst personalised learning may shift responsibility for learning to the student, it is the educator who is designing the learning environment thereby providing the parameters within which the learning takes place. Thus, whilst learning may be personal, that learning has to be focused on something and that something has to do with course objectives, learning outcomes, provision of content and appropriate forms of assessment. In other words, there must still be careful course and lesson planning. If not, then students may experience a sense of "frustration" and "disorientation" (Brush & Saye, 2000, p. 79 & 88) with some students failing to understand the nature of the task or problem that has been set for them (Brush & Saye, 2000, p. p.90). Whilst it may not be in vogue for educators to transmit knowledge, they are still subject matter experts

in their particular field and they need to fulfil the essential roles of advising, guiding, supporting, discussing and critiquing the student's learning (Salmon, 2001).

Educators need to accept that students who are engaged in personalised learning are going to find resources, develop perspectives and create work that will fundamentally challenge the educator as subject matter expert. In the opinion of one writer, the educator will become "a usefully ignorant co-worker in the thick of the action" (McWilliam, 2008, p. 263). Whilst the notion of the educator as an ignorant co-worker is certainly ill considered hyperbole – a heart surgeon with twenty years experience and a wealth of theoretical knowledge to impart is anything but ignorant – it is true that personalised learning is a very different scenario from the lecturing scenario in which the lecturer as "guru" (McWilliam, 2008, p. 266) is distanced from the students and transmitting knowledge. In contrast, personalised learning brings proximity – the educator in the midst of the learning – and the concomitant challenges that come with proximity; for example, the educator has much less control over the actual learning process and may find him/herself in unfamiliar territory both in terms of subject matter and technologies. This suggests that educators require support (Brush & Saye, 2000; Hannafin & Land, 1997) in transitioning from a traditional role to a new role in a personal learning environment. This is particularly apparent if we conceive of a student's personal learning environment (Downes, 2005). In this case, the learner is situated at the heart of the learning environment whilst being connected to communities of interest, learning communities, communities of practice, social spaces, Web 2.0 tools, multiple sources of information and, finally, to multiple forms of media. Amine provides an excellent graphical representation of such a personal learning environment (Amine, 2007).

Teacher management strategies remain important in a student-centred learning environment (Brush & Saye, 2000, p. 92). It cannot be assumed that students will simply work effectively either as individuals (Hannafin & Land, 1997, p. 191) or in groups (Brush & Saye, 2000, p. 88). Educators need to structure activities in terms of, for example, "individual accountability, group goals and rewards, and, most importantly in the case of student-centred learning, methods for providing students with opportunities to learn and practice group management and decision making skills" (Brush & Saye, 2000, p. 81). The educator must also retain the role of ensuring that student interactions are both socially and academically appropriate. For example, maintaining appropriate decorum on message board discussions or, if the learning space is physical, within the classroom (Brush & Saye, 2000, p. 88). However, if the educator is successful in the task of establishing an environment conducive to personalised learning then s/he can gradually fade into the background as students develop the requisite skills to become self-directed learners (Hannafin & Land, 1997, p. 194). It is at that point that we might describe the learning environment as truly personal. We would note, however, that the tutor still has a role at this stage. That role covers both the affective activities conducive to good teaching – encouragement, support and understanding for example – and the 'intellectual' activities that are a part of teaching well. Examples of such activities would include providing students with sources of information, assessing their work at both a formative and Summative level and providing constructive feedback to help students improve.

FUTURE RESEARCH DIRECTIONS

It is time perhaps for a slight confession. We have two issues with our future research direction. The first issue concerns the use of design research as an appropriate research methodology. We are fundamentally questioning the value of this approach to research. Our concerns in this area lie with whether or not the research results warrant

the time and effort that has to be spent analysing the quantitative and qualitative data. Despite the fact that student numbers have been low on ClinED 711, we have put considerable time into analysing student coursework, student blog postings and student discussion board postings in order to determine whether the changes that we made to ClinED 711 resulted in an "improved" learning experience for students. Whilst we would say that our changes have led to improvements in the course – particularly in terms of personalising the learning for students – we are of the opinion that reflective teaching practice might have achieved the same results with considerably less work. Reflection can be understood as "learning through questioning to lead to a development of understanding" (Loughran, 2002, p. 134). This questioning is prompted by something that is common to all reflection; the centrality of a problem in a practice setting (Centre for Support of Teaching and Learning, 2008; Loughran, 2002). Reflection would differ from a more formal research approach in terms of the fact that changes to particular courses would be made in terms of the judgment and experience of the practitioner. Furthermore, reflective practice does not necessarily result in peer reviewed publications of any sort. Whilst we have not focused on research methodology in this paper, the point is an important one in terms of the feasibility of carrying out this sort of research on a larger scale. Just as there would be problems scaling up the pedagogical approach of ClinED 711 in order to offer the course to much larger class sizes, so there would be problems scaling up the research.

Our second issue with our research concerns where to go next. The fact is that ClinEd 711 has been rated very highly by both the external examiner and by students. We have made a number of changes to the course with the result that we have provided a more personalised learning experience for students and our current judgement is that whilst we might make minor revisions to the course, ClinED 711 provides a quality learning experience for students. Furthermore, ethics approval for our research comes to an end this year (2009) and we are not envisaging asking for an extension. It is time to look for a new research direction. We have made mention throughout this chapter of the fact that student numbers on ClinEd 711 are relatively low. However, the Learning Technology Unit produces distance postgraduate courses where student numbers are considerably higher. Nursing, for example, regularly offers postgraduate courses with student numbers approaching two hundred. One logical direction for our research would be to consider how we might take the learning principles applied in ClinED 711 and apply them to courses with much larger class sizes. In essence this would entail considering how we might offer meaningful and authentic learning tasks with students taking responsibility for their own learning whilst also learning according to their preferred learning style. Taking over the pedagogical tactics (Goodyear, 2005) or the specific learning activities from ClinEd 711 is unlikely to work for reasons already cited; the demand on the teacher's time would simply be too great. The challenge will be, therefore, how to apply our pedagogical philosophy (social constructivism) and high level pedagogy (meaningful and authentic learning tasks) whilst changing our teaching tactics (Goodyear, 2005).

If we are to scale up the pedagogical approach that we have taken in ClinED 711 then there are number of key areas that we need to consider. At the level of the learning activities in which students engage we will have to address the issue of monitoring blog entries and discussion board postings. In a course of two hundred students or more the potential workload for the teachers responsible for monitoring discussions and postings is enormous. We would also have to look at the nature of our assessed activities. With large student numbers it would just not be feasible to be marking – for example – two hundred discussion board postings against a detailed marking rubric that required extensive feedback for students.

It is interesting that the idea of students taking responsibility for their own learning is one of the key elements of a personalised learning environment. If students really did take responsibility for their own learning – and by extension the learning of others in a social constructivist framework – then the tutor role might be reduced to one of providing guidance throughout the course whilst also providing extensive feedback on two major assessed activities. Taking this direction would make the teacher workload much more manageable. The core research question would then be one of how to increase the intrinsic motivation of students. There is a certain logic in considering this question since the heart of constructivist learning theory is the notion that student learning is a search for significance or meaning. If this is the case, then one of the key roles of the educator would be to understand the student, particularly in terms of what motivates each student to learn. This would be – in part at least – a question of eliciting already held beliefs from the student. It would also be a question of understanding student attitudes. For example, which students are taking the course simply to progress their careers? Which students are taking the course because they are passionate about learning? Which students prefer to learn individually rather than in a group situation? These seem to be important questions if one adheres to a constructivist teaching philosophy and yet these questions are seldom asked (Holt, Smissen, & Segrave, 2006).

CONCLUSION

In this chapter we have described the process of designing and delivering a personalised learning environment for students. We have acknowledged that the course in question – ClinED 711, ELearning for Clinical Educators – is a specialised postgraduate course with relatively low enrolments and we have discussed the difficulties of "scaling up" the course design in order to deliver a course based on similar principles to much larger student numbers. Finally, we have recognised that there are two areas that require further research; the first is the implementation of constructivist learning theory and the second is how to offer personalised learning to larger classes. Overall, student feedback together our own experience of teaching ClinED 711 suggests that personalised learning is a valuable approach to teaching that results in a rewarding learning experience for students.

REFERENCES

Alexander, S. (2001). E-learning developments and experiences. *Education and Training, 43*(4/5), 240–248. doi:10.1108/00400910110399247

Amine, M. (2007). *My PLE/PKM.* Retrieved 11th September, 2008, from http://mohamedamine-chatti.blogspot.com/2007/06/my-plepkm.html

Ausubel, D. P. (1963). *The psychology of meaningful verbal learning.* New York: Grune and Stratton.

Bannan-Ritland, B. (2003). The role of design in research: The integrative learning design framework. *Educational Researcher, 32*(1), 21–24. doi:10.3102/0013189X032001021

Blake, A., & Doherty, I. (2008). An instructional design course for clinical educators: First iteration design research reflections. *Journal of Learning Design, 2*(2), 104–115.

Bransford, J., Brown, A. L., & Cocking, R. R. (2000). *How people learn: Brain, mind, experience, and school.* Washington, DC: National Academy Press.

Bruce, C. S., Edwards, S., & Lupton, M. (2006). Six frames for information literacy education [Electronic Version]. *Italics, 5.* Retrieved August 8th 2008, from http://www.ics.heacademy.ac.uk/italics/vol5-1/pdf/sixframes_final%20_1_.pdf

Bruner, J. S. (2006). The course of cognitive growth. In J. S. Bruner (Ed.), *In search of pedagogy, volume 1: The selected works of Jerome S. Bruner.* (pp. 67-89). Oxford, UK: Routledge.

Brush, T., & Saye, J. (2000). Implementation and evaluation of a student-centered learning unit: A case study. *Educational Technology Research and Development, 48*(3), 79–100. doi:10.1007/BF02319859

Burden, K., & Atkinson, S. (2008). Beyond content: Developing transferable learning designs with digital video archives. In J. Luca & E. R. Weippl (Eds.), *Ed-Media 2008 World Conference on Educational Multimedia, Hypermedia & Telecommunications* (pp. 4041-4050). Chesapeake, VA: AACE.

Center for Support of Teaching and Learning. (2008). *Reflective practice.* Retrieved 13th September, 2008, from http://cstl.syr.edu/cstl2/home/Teaching%20Support/Teaching%20Practice/141000.htm

Clarke, J., Dede, C., Ketelhut, D. J., & Nelson, B. (2006). A design based research strategy to promote scalability for educational innovations. *Educational Technology, 46*(3), 27–36.

Collins, A., Joseph, D., & Bielaczyc, K. (2004). Design research: Theoretical and methodological issues. *Journal of the Learning Sciences, 13*(1), 15–42. doi:10.1207/s15327809jls1301_2

Doherty, I., & Blake, A. (2007). Teaching instructional design principles to clinical educators: A design research approach. In C. Montgomerie & J. Seale (Eds.), *Ed-Media 2007 World Conference on Educational Multimedia, Hypermedia and Telecommunications* (pp. 2799-2804). Chesapeake, VA: AACE.

Downes, S. (2005). E-learning 2.0 [Electronic Version]. *eLearn Magazine.* Retrieved September 18th, 2008, from http://www.elearnmag.org/subpage.cfm?section=articles&article=29-1

Driscoll, M. P. (2005). *Psychology of learning for instruction*. Boston: Pearson Education, Inc.

Gardner, H. (1983). *Frames of mind: The theory of multiple intelligences*. New York: Basic Books.

Gillani, B. (2003). *Learning theories and the design of e-learning environments*. Lanham, MA: University Press of America Inc.

Goodyear, P. (2005). Educational design and networked learning: Patterns, pattern languages and design practice. *Australasian Journal of Educational Technology*, *21*(1), 82–101.

Hannafin, M. J., & Land, S. M. (1997). The foundations and assumptions of technology-enhanced student-centered learning environments. *Instructional Science*, *25*, 167–202. doi:10.1023/A:1002997414652

Herrington, J., Oliver, R., & Reeves, T. C. (2002). *Patterns of engagement in authentic online learning environments*. In A. Williamson, C. Gunn, A. Young & T. Clear (Eds.), *Ascilite 2002, Winds of Change in the Sea of Learning: Charting the Course of Digital Education* (pp. 279-286). Auckland, New Zealand: UNITEC Institute of Technology.

Holt, D., Smissen, I., & Segrave, S. (2006). *New students, new learning, new environments in higher education: Literacies in the digital age*. Paper presented at the 23rd Annual Ascilite Conference: Who's learning? Whose technology? Sydney, Australia.

Hutchins, H. (2003). Instructional immediacy and the seven principles: Strategies for facilitating online courses. *Online Journal of Distance Learning Administration*, *6*(3).

Johnson, M. (2004). *Personalised learning - an emperor's outfit?* Southampton, UK: Institute for Public Policy Research.

Kelly, A. E. (2003). Research as design. *Educational Researcher*, *32*(1), 3–4. doi:10.3102/0013189X032001003

Lave, J., & Wenger, E. (1991). *Situated learning: Legitimate peripheral participation*. New York: Cambridge University Press.

Lemke, J. (1997). Cognition, context, and learning: A social semiotic perspective. In D. Kirshner & J. A. Whitson (Eds.), *Situated cognition: Social, semiotic, and psychological perspectives* (pp. 37-56). Mahwah, NJ: Erlbaum.

Loughran, J. J. (2002). Effective reflective practice: In search of meaning in learning about teaching. *Journal of Teacher Education*, *53*(1), 33–43. doi:10.1177/0022487102053001004

Mayer, R. (2003). The promise of multimedia learning: Using the same instructional design methods across different media. *Learning and Instruction*, *13*(2), 125–139. doi:10.1016/S0959-4752(02)00016-6

McKenney, S., Nieveen, N., & van den Akker, J. (2006). Design research from a curriculum perspective. In J. v. d. Akker, K. Gravemeijer, S. McKenney & N. Nieveen (Eds.), *Educational design research* (pp. 67-90). London: Routledge.

McLoughlin, C., & Lee, M. J. W. (2007). Social software and participatory learning: Pedagogical choices with technology affordances in the web. In Atkinson, R.J., McBeath, C., Soong, S. K. A., Cheers, C. (Eds.), *24th Annual Conference of the Australasian Society for Computers in Learning in Tertiary Education, ICT: Providing Choices for Learners and Learning* (pp. 664-675). Singapore: Centre for Educational Development, Nanyang Technological University.

McWilliam, E. (2008). Unlearning how to teach. *Innovations in Education and Teaching International*, *45*(3), 263–269. doi:10.1080/14703290802176147

Mergel, B. (1998). *Instructional design and learning theory*. Retrieved 14th June, 2007, from http://www.usask.ca/education/coursework/802papers/mergel/brenda.htm

O'Donnell, A. M. (2006). The role of peers and group learning. In P. A. Alexander & P. H. Winne (Eds.), *Handbook of educational psychology* (pp. 781-802). Mahwah, NJ: Lawrence Erlbaum Associates.

Ong, S. S., & Hawryszkiewycz, P. I. (2003). Towards personalised and collaborative learning management systems. In V. Devedzic, J. Spector, D. Sampson, Kinshuk (Eds.), *3rd IEEE International Conference on Advanced Learning Technologies* (ICALT'03). CA: IEEE Computer Society.

Paivio, A. (1986). *Mental representation: A dual coding approach.* New York: Oxford University Press.

Reeves, T. C. (2000). *Enhancing the worth of instructional technology research through "design experiments" and other development research strategies.* Paper presented at session 41:29, of the Annual Meeting of the American Educational Research Association (pp.1-15).

Reeves, T. C. (2006). Design research from a technology perspective. In J. V. D. Akker, S. Gravemeijer, S. McKenny & N. Nieveen (Eds.), *Educational design research* (pp. 52-66). London: Routledge.

Reeves, T. C., Herrington, J., & Oliver, R. (2005). Design research: A socially responsible approach to instructional technology research in higher education. *Journal of Computing in Higher Education, 16*, 96–115. doi:10.1007/BF02961476

Rourke, L., Anderson, T., Archer, W., & Garrison, D. R. (1999). Assessing social presence in asynchronous, text-based computer conferences. *Journal of Distance Education, 14*(3), 51–70.

Salmon, G. (2001). *E-moderating. The key to teaching and learning online.* London: Kogan Page Ltd.

Sandoval, W. A. (2004). Developing learning theory by refining conjectures embodied in educational designs. *Educational Psychologist, 39*(4), 213–223. doi:10.1207/s15326985ep3904_3

Schön, D. A. (1987). *Educating the reflective practitioner.* San Francisco: Jossey-Bass.

Spiro, R. J., Feltovich, P. J., Jacobson, M. J., & Coulson, R. L. (1995). Cognitive flexibility, constructivism, and hypertext: Random access instruction for advanced knowledge acquisition in ill-structured domains. In L. P. Steffe & J. Gale (Eds.), *Constructivism in education* (pp. 85-107). Hillsdale, NJ: Erlbaum.

Sun, L., & Williams, S. (2004). *An instructional design model for constructivist learning.* In L. Cantoni & C. McLoughlin (Eds.), Ed-Media 2007 World Conference on Educational Multimedia, Hypermedia and Telecommunications (pp. 2476-2486). Chesapeake, VA: AACE.

Vygotsky, L. S. (1978). *Mind in society.* Cambridge, MA: Harvard University Press.

APPENDIX ONE

Table 4. Course Development Document

Outline the learning tasks students will complete for which you seek LTU development support:						
Module/Topic, Learning Objective and Learning task	**Student Role / Activities** (what will students do?)	**Delivery Mode(s)**	**Resources** (what materials or information will students draw on to complete the task?)	**Tutor Role** (how will you support the students as they undertake the task?)		**Assessment/Feedback** (how will you assess or provide feedback on the students' work?)
				Text-Based Supports	**Personal Supports**	
e.g. Microbiology module - Small group collaboration (1 week) to produce individual summary of particular disease organism and process	e.g. Students will work in groups of 3; each group will be allocated one of 3 disease organisms; will individually develop summary of organism and disease process and submit to group members for critique; will refine and submit to lecturer for marking	e.g. Online, via LMS small group discussion forums	e.g. Lecturer's PowerPoint summaries of disease organisms Journal articles Weblinks	e.g. Instructions outlining task and student roles Rubric for disease summary Rubric for participation Disease processes template (Word doc) Announcements at start/midpoint/ completion to keep students focused	e.g. Facilitate small group discussions online by moderating as required	e.g. Assessment of disease summary based on rubric (12%) Assessment of participation based on rubric (3%)

Chapter 13
Research–Led Curriculum Redesign for Personalised Learning Environments:
A Case Study in the Faculty of Information Technology

Len Webster
Monash University, Australia

Patricie Mertova
Monash University, Australia

Kim Styles
Monash University, Australia

Lindsay Smith
Monash University, Australia

ABSTRACT

This chapter provides a case study outlining strategies which represent a starting point in the development of a personalised learning environment (PLE). The initial strategies focus on student engagement in two units run by the Faculty of Information Technology at Monash University, Australia. The case study looks at changing the approach to a more personalised learning environment in the respective IT units, and it also outlines how the changes were made based on a meta-analysis research of the Australian Course Experience Questionnaire (CEQ).

INTRODUCTION

Personalised Learning Environments (PLEs) offer many advantages to learning and teaching in higher

education. To become implemented broadly, they will need to be able to address challenges within the higher education sector including large class sizes, multiple national and international campuses, diverse student cohorts and collaboration within

DOI: 10.4018/978-1-60566-884-0.ch013

diverse and isolated teaching teams. This chapter explores commencement of implementation strategies adopted for a PLE-based approach within one such landscape of challenges in a large Australian university with multiple campuses (including overseas). The PLE approach was implemented in a Faculty of Information Technology, and was a response to a number of problems identified by the Faculty over recent years with its core undergraduate subjects. Overall, the chapter argues that PLEs may become a potentially powerful strategy to improve the student experience and engagement.

BACKGROUND

In the last decade or more, with significant changes in the student population (more diverse student cohorts, including mature-age students), a large intake of international students and also a general massification of Australian higher education, students have become one of the most important stakeholders in higher education. The student cohorts are more diversified than was the case in the past. They now display more varied levels of academic, cultural and linguistic preparation for tertiary study. As a consequence, they also exhibit a more diverse range of expectations and needs. Despite this realisation, universities in general have been slow to recognize the role of student views in monitoring and changing the learning and teaching environments (OECD, 1998; Meek, 2000; Fiocco, 2005).

Research over the past decade has recognised that student perceptions are important parameters of the social and psychological aspects of the learning environments (Fraser, 1998; Ramsden, 2005). Research studies have consistently confirmed a strong correlation between learning and teaching environments and levels of satisfaction (Fraser, 1998; Nair and Fisher, 2001). Recently, many providers in the higher education sector have realised the need to re-evaluate their approaches

to provision by placing a greater emphasis on meeting the expectations and requirements of their stakeholders, and particularly their students (Cheng and Tam, 1997; Lee et al, 2000; Wright and O'Neil, 2002; Griffin et al, 2003; McInnis, 2003).

As the student body has become increasingly more diversified in recent years, one way in which universities have approached the process of determining the needs of their diversifying body of students was through the collection of student perceptions via surveys. The significance of student surveys in determining student needs and the value of the student voice in curriculum restructure was highlighted, for instance, in the recent extensive study (undertaken by Scott between 2001 – 2004) involving approximately 95,000 graduates from 14 Australian universities (Scott, 2006).

The aspect of taking account of the changing student body, their needs and also the range of factors which need to be considered as part of student experience (including a regular review of the relevance of particular surveys) was emphasised in a study by Griffin et al (2003). The study involved nearly 4000 students from 15 Australian universities and focused on the extent to which the current Australian Course Experience Questionnaire (which is posted to all recently graduated students across Australian universities) covered different aspects of student experience.

Implicit in the gradual diversification of student cohorts and also in the realisation of the necessity to cater for student needs is the focus on developing personalised learning environments. In order to manage the changing student demographics and contemporary views on educational approaches, and thus in search of more personalised learning systems, many universities turned to web-based and technology-enhanced approaches to course delivery to improve student learning (Becker et al, 2007).

The idea of personalised learning environments (PLEs) has become topical in the last approximately 5 years and, as Attwell (2007) pointed out, it has become a "trendy" concept. However, despite all the "buzz" around PLEs, there has been a relative lack of consensus on what personalised learning environment actually means. Nevertheless, there was some agreement that personalised learning environments are an approach to using new technologies for learning. At the heart of this approach is the changing face of learning in a changing world. Although it might be debated whether technology has brought about change, there is substantial educational literature that shows that the change to learning approaches has been a constant factor across many decades, from behaviourism, through cognitivism to constructivism and beyond. Common themes in recent literature identify the importance of context and engagement for learning to be successful. Indeed, engagement and context might be classified as "resilient pedagogies", and are as relevant now as a decade or more ago.

Attwell (2007) pointed out several key aspects of personalised learning environment. Firstly, he highlighted that personalised learning relates to the concept of lifelong learning. It recognizes the continuity of the learning process throughout individuals' lives and also seeks tools to support that learning. This aspect also underlines the role of an individual in organizing their own learning.

Secondly, personalised learning is associated with the notion of informal learning. Attwell referred to the findings of the US Institute for Research on Learning (IRL), which indicated that formal learning and training only accounts for at most 20 per cent of how individuals learn for their jobs (Attwell, 2007).

Thirdly, personalised learning brings together all modes and means of learning, including informal learning, workplace learning, learning in the home, learning driven by problem solving, learning driven by personal interest and other forms. Personalised learning environment can thus provide a more holistic learning environment which is capable of bringing together disparate sources

and contexts of learning. It can also enable students to take responsibility for their own learning and it may bridge the "walled gardens" of educational institutions and the "worlds outside" (Attwell, 2007). It is this third perspective that underpinned the case study described in this chapter.

Regarding new technologies supporting personalised learning, Oravec (2002) observed that, for instance, the blog has many dimensions that are suited to representing the student voice. It can empower students, and also encourage analytical thinking in them. However, Williams and Jacobs (2004) found that there was very little existing academic research and very few publications on the use of blogs in education.

Further, Coates (2005) pointed out that despite recent wide and rapid adoption of learning management systems (LMSs) by many tertiary institutions and also despite recognition of the potential that these systems hold for personalised learning, their understanding is in relative infancy. Coates pointed out that these systems have a potential to significantly enrich student learning experience by offering them access to a greater range of interactive resources, and making course content more cognitively accessible to students.

Hambleton et al (1998) highlighted the fact that students display particular approaches to learning in response to the perceived context, content and demands of their learning tasks. In that context they emphasised the value of personalised or at least context-specific instruction. Hambleton et al carried out a study using personalised instruction system with a group of students, and this study indicated enhanced levels of understanding of the subject matter among the participating students.

Laurillard (2006) has also supported the value of developing personalised learning systems, utilising new technologies effectively in ways that would serve enhancement of student educational experience. Laurillard outlined four aspects in which student learning experience may be impacted by new personalised learning technologies. These aspects are of:

- *cultural* nature – students are familiar with such systems of communication and information searching from other parts of their lives;
- *intellectual* nature – new mode of engagement offering social and material interaction;
- *social* nature – offer reduction in social difference and thus enable students to take greater responsibility for their own learning;
- *practical* nature – enable managing quality at scale, sharing resources across networks, and also greater flexibility in provision in terms of place and time and thus support widening participation.

This section has summarized overlapping understandings of personalised learning. The authors of this chapter are of the view that personalised learning is a complex and multi-factorial concept incorporating a wide range of aspects. The authors agree with the view expressed by Attwell (2007) that personalised learning incorporates all modes of learning (including lifelong, informal, distance and online learning). The authors believe that personalised learning ought to be as holistic in nature as possible in order to accommodate individual needs of learners, therefore it ought to account for cultural, intellectual, social and practical aspects of individual's learning (Laurillard, 2006). In that the authors are of the view that new technologies may be beneficial in accommodating this range of aspects incorporated in personalised learning.

The case study presented in this chapter is attempting to highlight the fact that any change towards a more personalized learning environment requires a starting point. This case study achieves some elements of a PLE, but, more importantly, sets a stage for further development. In that respect, the authors argue that to achieve a PLE in such a complex setting (as is a multi-campus large University) requires an iterative and change-managed process. The authors further maintain that the risks in attempting to create a PLE in a single iteration (with multiple campuses, different staff and large student numbers) are too high. Therefore, this case study describes a limited attempt to develop a starting point in achieving a PLE environment. The strategies outlined in the case study draw from a PLE model – especially relating student learning to work contexts and the access to learning resources from a variety of locations (including home).

CONTEXT

Monash University is a large internationalised, research-intensive institution with approximately 56,000 students from around 130 countries. It consists of eight campuses: six are located in Australia and two offshore (in Malaysia and South Africa). It further offers a number of courses in partnerships set up in other countries, such as, Singapore, Hong Kong and Indonesia. Monash University is also a member of the Group of Eight (Go8) leading Australian universities.

This case study concerns the Faculty of Information Technology (FIT), which is one of the University's ten faculties. The Faculty has recently redeveloped a suite of its undergraduate first-year subjects comprising a number of core subjects for all students. The overall aim of this redevelopment was to make undergraduate programmes in the Faculty more personalised in accordance with the findings of a major strategic review undertaken in 2004. The new programmes were developed throughout 2005 according to the recommendations of the 2004 FIT Strategic Review. Integral to the structure of the new degrees was a suite of seven common core units. In light of this, the Associate Dean for Education in the Faculty consulted the director of the Centre for the Advancement of Learning and Teaching (CALT) at Monash University, to assist the Faculty in planning, implementation and evaluation of the core units in the undergraduate programmes.

The evaluation aimed to be outcome-focussed. Its intention was to inform future curriculum development in line with best practice in tertiary teaching and learning, thus contributing to the Faculty's existing quality assurance initiatives for teaching and learning. The evaluation strategy was mindful of the recent and extensive restructuring in the educational governance of the Faculty.

The broad purposes of the evaluation were to:

1. Evaluate each unit's pedagogy, in particular:
    a. the relationship between intended learning outcomes and teaching and learning approaches;
    b. the assessment strategy employed and in particular the alignment of unit objectives, pedagogical strategies and unit assessment tasks;
    c. the educational efficacy of current approaches to lectures/workshops/ practicals or laboratories;
2. Review the existing course materials including unit outlines, distance education materials and a sample of teaching and learning support materials from each core unit for pedagogical relevance and publication quality;
3. Evaluate each unit's curriculum from a "workload" perspective for students and teaching staff;
4. Determine the students' experiences of teaching and learning in the core units;
5. Ascertain the effectiveness of the special interest groups as an organising framework for curriculum development across the core units;
6. Make recommendations for change and improvement based on the evaluation findings.

Evaluation of the seven core undergraduate units in the FIT Faculty was undertaken by the CALT over 2006-2007. One of the key findings was the urgent need for teaching improvement that would move curriculum thinking in the Faculty beyond "content-for-delivery" and a deficit model of student learning. The evaluators highlighted the fact that the starting point for quality improvement has to be a shared view of student-centredness. The evaluation did not suggest that innovative pedagogical practices were absent in the core curriculum, however it pointed to a "silence" surrounding student-centred learning and an in-grained transmission model of teaching.

Other findings in the evaluation provided valuable insights into students' conceptions of "good teaching" and their perceptions of what counts for successful learning. Student perceptions of "good teaching" were understood as significant reference points guiding the development of a more personalised learning curriculum model. Overall, the evaluation revealed that students described "good teaching" as teaching which included:

1. Provision of clear objectives;
2. Access to "helpful" teaching staff;
3. Fair assessment that has clear criteria and is timely to allow for useful feedback;
4. Lecture, tutorials and laboratory sessions that complement each other and assist students' learning development;
5. Teaching staff are animated, committed and interested in their subject matter;
6. Teaching and learning approaches that students perceive as relevant and interesting, included:
    a. structured opportunities to practise what they were learning when appropriate to the unit content;
    b. access to strategies to support remediation;
    c. small group work and problem solving activities; and
    d. opportunities to be taught by industry experts where appropriate.

Many of these findings build on concepts of a personalised learning environment. This case study details the evaluation and restructuring of two core first-year units, FIT A and FIT B which have introduced steps in moving towards a PLE for the students. As a starting point on the pathway to a more fully-developed PLE approach, the success of the initial changes are critical. Based on some of the recommendations arising from the CALT evaluation in 2006, the Unit Evaluations in 2007 indicated increased satisfaction for unit FIT A. The FIT A and FIT B teaching and developer team have redeveloped resources, teaching and assessment strategies throughout semester 1 of 2008. Following the redevelopment process and implementation of most recommendations from the 2006 – 2007 CALT Evaluation, the latest Unit Evaluation results in semester 1 of 2008 have indicated further improvements in student satisfaction with units FIT A and FIT B on most Monash University campuses except for the South African campus. This has confirmed the validity of the recommendations and the utility of the restructuring process to incorporate a PLE approach. There is no doubt that over the next few years, the PLE approach will be continually developed and move rapidly towards a PLE for students.

EVALUATION METHOD: MIXED METHOD DESIGN

The move to a PLE approach was supported by qualitative and quantitative data that assisted the design of the preliminary steps for getting a PLE approach established within the core subjects of the degree. The 2006 CALT Evaluation team chose a mixed method evaluation design in keeping with contemporary approaches in the field of programme evaluation (Greene, 2002; Johnson, Onwuegbuzie, 2004; Patton, 1996, 2002; Powers, 2004; Tashakkori, Teddlie, 2003). Such an approach suited the purpose of the study and enabled the evaluation team to gather the most

comprehensive data, given resourcing and time constraints. Therefore, both quantitative and qualitative methods were used in the evaluation.

CALT provided the FIT Faculty Associate Dean for Education with a draft evaluation plan which was discussed and approved. The two key CALT evaluators and a senior FIT academic representing the Associate Dean for Education then finalised the operational plan for the evaluation and the FIT Faculty provided administrative support for the project.

QUANTITATIVE DATA

The quantitative part of the evaluation consisted of gathering and analysing data through Monash University's standard Unit Evaluation Surveys undertaken at the end of Semester 1 2006. The Centre for Higher Education Quality (CHEQ; a central quality evaluation unit at Monash University) oversees the administration and descriptive analysis of this data. More detailed statistical analysis has been undertaken as part of the evaluation for the FIT Faculty. These unit evaluations by the CHEQ were also repeated in 2007 and 2008.

QUALITATIVE DATA

To add a qualitative dimension to the study, students, unit coordinators and academic teaching staff and tutors were invited to participate in the Evaluation (through face-to-face interviews). The qualitative data provided an opportunity for participants to discuss their various experiences in the "core units" and for the evaluation team to seek more "in-depth" data than might be provided by a purely quantitative approach. The qualitative data was aggregated in reporting and "direct quotes" from the data sources used where appropriate throughout the final report.

Further, a survey and subsequent interviews

were carried out with academic staff teaching in FIT A and FIT B at all Monash University campuses. The survey and interviews concerned the issue of communication among FIT academic staff across all Australian and overseas campuses and whether this impacted on the quality of the delivery of the two units. The most frequent communication concerning the unit contents and their delivery occurred among staff on Australian campuses. There was less contact with staff on the Malaysian campus and South African campus.

DESIGNING PERSONALISED LEARNING ENVIRONMENT

The development of units FIT A and FIT B has been undertaken with input from students and teaching staff at all Monash University campuses and utilising Scott's 2006 research into the student voice undertaken at the University of Western Sydney (UWS). The overall strategy was aided by the aim of developing personalised learning environments for the students, especially the principles of bringing together all modes and means of learning (including informal learning, workplace learning, learning in the home, learning driven by problem solving, learning driven by personal interest). Uses of technology were considered to make a linkage to work-related contexts (see FIT A) and provide flexibility in access to materials (see FIT B).

CHALLENGES

There were a number of barriers to overcome in getting this change commenced.

Rapid turnover of teaching personnel in FIT B has presented a challenge in the development process. For the redevelopment to be fully successful, it would have explicitly demanded for the unit restructure to have closely followed Scott's identified model and would have required

a dedicated project manager. However, due to insufficient resources, a research assistant has been appointed and the project was overseen by a coordinator. The lack of a dedicated project manager has limited the capacity of the group particularly in the time and depth that could have been applied to tasks.

The project was further benchmarked against a similar development project at the UWS. The IT Faculty senior research staff attended a benchmarking workshop at the UWS and discussed relevant strategies. CALT reviewed the concept of benchmarking with respect to learning and teaching, raising key issues including validity of benchmarking between universities with different historical background, missions, status and course outcomes. Ultimately, the benchmarking exercise provided little additional assistance in designing the PLE strategies.

Further, to enhance the teaching practices, technology was utilized to enhance contact and sharing of feedback (on teaching approaches) between students as well as among academic staff. The purpose of this was to bring the IT academics together more as a team and to help them reflect on and improve their teaching practices. This proved more difficult than originally considered. For example, the review of the project brought a realisation that the development of a PLE approach for the core units delivered across campuses nationally and internationally would have required a more team-based planning approach.

IMPLEMENTATION

There were a number of interventions applied in the running of the two units in the Faculty of Information Technology aimed at improving student engagement along the lines of a more personalised learning environment. This involved aspects, such as flexibility, communication and relationship to workplace.

Firstly, to contextualize the IT teaching material, a number of IT professionals were interviewed in a workplace context and the interview data was then incorporated into the teaching material (see detailed description of units FIT A and FIT B below).

Secondly, web-based teaching materials related to individual lectures were posted on the university website prior to the lectures, to enable students to contextualise material, become familiar with basic concepts and allowing more complex issues and personal interests to be addressed in class time. One of the unanticipated outcomes of this intervention was that teachers, particularly tutors, benefited from access to online materials to improve their own teaching. This opened the opportunity for the resources to become a new means or approach to academic staff development where the teaching teams are dispersed across national and international boundaries and cultures.

In the second semester of 2008, streamed video in place of lectures was trialed for a three-week module in one of the IT units (FIT B) to further personalise the teaching and learning for students (see below for a detailed description).

The overall aim of these interventions was to provide a high quality student experience and flexibility of access in course delivery, regardless of the geographical location. The case might, therefore, provide some guidance to other tertiary institutions similar to Monash University attempting to enhance student experience with particular focus on international delivery, or to tertiary institutions contemplating setting up teaching programmes in overseas locations.

UNIT FIT A

Restructuring unit FIT A, the FIT team with assistance of a CALT evaluator have attempted to link theory and practice in the tutorials, to demonstrate to students that there was a direct link between the subject contents and their poten-

tial future careers. The unit contents were made more structured and direct. The team have also incorporated more learner-centred and engaging approaches in the delivery of the unit suited to students making the transition to tertiary education. Team and collaborative assessment and tutorial activities were set in actual context using role plays supported by scripts for teachers, and construction artefacts.

Lectures were repositioned as reinforcement of the conceptual content rather than as primary content delivery which was provided in weekly Study Guides. The lectures provided actual examples of the concepts in action, presented small cases and problems, and were rich with visual images and video. Initially the learning design required students to come to lectures prepared with questions from the study guides to be explored in depth in the lectures. In week five of classes, a student survey was conducted and it indicated low student engagement due to the large class size. Subsequent lectures were designed in such a way that they provided a brief outline of main points around which examples and cases were structured. Lecture resources for teachers incorporated detailed teaching notes and indicated points at which local examples were required. In subsequent evaluations, the "Best aspects" feedback from students consistently identified lectures as positive contributors to their learning experience.

The IT Faculty established that first-year students generally did not have a good understanding of what to expect in their future IT careers. To provide credible, current advice on skills, jobs and applications of IT education in the workplace, the lecturers were assisted by the Monash University Employment and Career Development, who made a series of short videos for use in the lectures and tutorials. Major employers in the IT industry including IBM, Google, Accenture and others were interviewed using a series of questions based on the Unit learning objectives and interpretations of Scott's (2006) definitions of engagement. Four career orientated resources were produced, aimed to provide IT students with:

1. Advice on securing their first IT job – how to prepare themselves for their first job while studying; by Google, IBM, Accenture, Ernst & Young.
2. Knowledge needed for IT careers – what students need to take away from their degree studies to achieve their career ambitions; by IBM, Kodak, Accenture, ACS.
3. Roles available in the IT industry – the jobs that are available (reinforced by the content of the unit); by Google, IBM, Accenture, Sage Technology, Ernst and Young.
4. Skills and Attributes of the IT professional – with explicit links to the activities and content in the unit; by Kodak, Google, Managesoft, IBM.

The resources were part of the holistic PLE approach to the subject and were used to motivate students in their studies, to enhance their understanding of the reality of the IT workforce, and to give them opportunities to synthesise the content of the Unit with their own career ambitions. Formal evaluation of the impact of these resources is currently being undertaken by Careers and Development section of the University.

Throughout the implementation process, the teaching team have worked closely across the multiple campuses to ensure coordination of the PLE approach across the various campuses teaching the subject.

In using a PLE approach, other issues were also identified. These were, for example, the timetable and teaching space. One campus has, for instance, identified the issue of tutorials being scheduled for the same day as lectures, thus they needed to be rescheduled. There were also some issues of a lack of teaching space identified.

UNIT FIT B

When restructuring unit FIT B, new PLE-aligned approaches were trialled. For instance, team activities were incorporated in tutorials. First, a range of theoretical questions were presented and then they were addressed through team involvement. When introducing group assessment in tutorials, problems with the actual forming of groups were identified.

A new approach to delivering lectures was also trialled. This involved pre-recording the lectures using a video and posting them electronically on the Unit website for individual student use and review. Subsequently, a survey was conducted among students, which showed that this approach was received positively by them.

VIDEO LECTURE TRIAL

An initial step in exploring PLE approaches is to trial some possible implementations in a trial module within the Unit (subject). Such a trial was conducted in weeks 7 - 9 of the FIT B unit, when streamed video lectures were offered to students. The Unit consists of a one two-hour lecture for all students and a series of two-hour laboratory sessions. In second semester of 2008, the Unit was offered on six campuses, four in Australia and two overseas. The weeks 7 – 9 material was chosen for the video trial as it allowed lecturing staff to develop the resources during the first six weeks of the semester, and also academic staff could get to know their students during that time.

Due to hosting difficulties, lectures were offered as downloadable iPod format videos for the use on student mobile devices. Each week's material was divided into two or three sections depending on suitable transition points in the study material to produce files of around 50Mb with a 30-minute playing time. The content was produced using ScreenFlow (http://www.flip4mac.com/screenflow.htm) on Apple Macintosh computers. ScreenFlow enables the author to record the current screen contents, audio and the feed from the desktop video camera simultaneously. The software also has in-built editing facilities and a range of export formats. Using ScreenFlow, it was possible to record an MS PowerPoint screenshow and a "talking head" of the presenter to make the presentation more personalised.

On two campuses where the Unit was offered, the recorded lectures were used to replace standard lectures (2 hours per week) during weeks 7 – 9. On two other campuses, the recorded lectures were viewed during the standard lectures and discussed with the lecturer, and on the remaining two campuses the standard lectures were held as normally. Only students who were enrolled by Off-Campus Learning on the last two campuses used the recordings as supplementary material. On the campuses where standard lectures were suspended during these three weeks, the lecturer was available for student consultation during the regular lecture time.

The total number of enrolments in unit FIT B was around 480 students, with approximately 130 based in South Africa and Malaysia where bandwidth issues tend to limit students' ability to access some resources directly from Australian-based servers. This was one of the reasons why these two campuses were selected to use the recording under the lecturers' guidance in weekly seminar-like sessions.

OUTCOMES

The above described curriculum restructuring approaches aimed at greater personalisation in the delivery of the two core first-year units in the FIT Faculty were received positively by students. This was confirmed in the results of the latest Monash University Unit Evaluations undertaken by the Centre for Higher Education Quality (CHEQ). There was an increased satisfaction expressed by the FIT students with the two units across all Monash University campuses compared to the 2006 evaluations of these units. The Unit Evaluations administered by the CHEQ consist of ten standard questions common to all Monash University faculties and individual faculties also have the opportunity to use up to ten questions specific to the particular faculty. Table 1 below outlines improvements in student satisfaction with unit FIT A (across three Monash University campuses) in relation to the faculty-specific questions between years 2006 and 2008. The latest CHEQ evaluation data for unit FIT B was not available at the time of writing of this chapter, the authors, therefore, do not include it here.

Frequency of "Best aspects" comments in 2008 was improved from previous offerings of the Unit in 2006 and 2007, with the majority of comments specifically identifying the quality of the lectures, tutorials and the relevance of the Unit for their future careers in IT. Student responses generally verified the improved engagement of the restructured teaching and learning approaches utilised in the Unit.

CONCLUSION

The success of the PLE restructuring strategies developed for the units FIT A and FIT B may serve as examples for the wider restructuring process of other core units within the Faculty of Information Technology at Monash University. The experience gained by the development team assists in the formulation of strategies to commence the movement to a more fully implemented PLE. Evaluation following the restructure of the FIT A and FIT B units has indicated that more personalised and innovative approaches to delivery were positively received by students. One of the challenges in developing personalised learning environments for subjects with large student enrolments (such as the two IT units) is to effectively combine and utilise information technologies and expertise of academic staff regardless of their location (campus or country). The capacity of this approach to address the unique issues associated with motivation and engagement of students in core subjects with large enrolments delivered across multiple campuses

may serve as a model for other universities dealing with similar issues.

The ultimate objective of the FIT A and FIT B development teams was to create more personalised learning environments and to motivate and

Table 1. Unit Evaluation Scores for FIT A at three Monash University Australian Campuses (Source: CHEQ)[1]

Unit Evaluation Survey Question	S1 2006	S1 2007	S1 2008	Change 07→08
Campus A				
Q 3. I found the unit intellectually stimulating	3.5	3.71	4.43	+0.73
Q 5. I received constructive feedback on my work	4.29	4.07	4.57	+0.50
Q 8. I was satisfied with the quality of the unit	3.75	3.79	4.43	+0.64
Q10. Topics in this unit complemented my degree	4.38	4.15	4.71	+0.56
Q12. The face-to-face classes I attended helped me learn	4.25	3.67	4.75	+1.08
Q15. The teaching and learning approaches used in the unit worked for me	3.88	3.57	4.29	+0.72
Q16. The ungraded learning activities, such as tutorial and other exercises, case studies, etc., provided me with feedback to support my learning	4	3.85	4.67	+0.82
Campus B				
Q 3. I found the unit intellectually stimulating	3.37	3.47	3.5	+0.03
Q 5. I received constructive feedback on my work	3.56	3.76	3.92	+0.16
Q 8. I was satisfied with the quality of the unit	3.58	3.9	3.89	-0.01
Q10. Topics in this unit complemented my degree	4.12	3.72	3.73	-0.01
Q12. The face-to-face classes I attended helped me learn	3.81	4.08	3.99	-0.09
Q15. The teaching and learning approaches used in the unit worked for me	3.56	3.76	3.96	+0.20
Q16. The ungraded learning activities, such as tutorial and other exercises, case studies, etc., provided me with feedback to support my learning	3.59	3.87	3.83	-0.04
Campus C				
Q 3. I found the unit intellectually stimulating	3.29	3.60	3.74	+0.14
Q 5. I received constructive feedback on my work	4.57	3.50	4	+0.50
Q 8. I was satisfied with the quality of the unit	4.43	3.53	3.96	+0.43
Q10. Topics in this unit complemented my degree	3.67	3.57	3.61	+0.04
Q12. The face-to-face classes I attended helped me learn	4.29	3.73	3.74	+0.01
Q15. The teaching and learning approaches used in the unit worked for me	4.5	3.73	4.09	+0.36
Q16. The ungraded larning activities, such as tutorial and other exercises, case studies, etc., provided me with feedback to support my learning	4.14	3.80	3.61	-0.19

[1] The Chapter presents the evaluation results for three Australian Monash University campuses because Unit FIT A was run in all the three years only at the these campuses.

engage first-year students in making their learning experience more relevant and purposeful. Students have rated positively this novel approach to delivering these two units, thus indicating appreciation of more personalised approaches to delivery and also greater contextualization or connectedness to real-world experiences. Therefore, this case study may serve as an example of an approach to delivery of similar large enrolment first-year units in the Faculty of Information Technology, in other faculties at Monash University and also other Australian and international universities.

REFERENCES

Attwell, G. (2007). The Personal Learning Environments - the future of eLearning? *eLearning Papers, 2*(1,). Retrieved November 21, 2008 from http://www.elearningpapers.eu/index.php?page=doc&doc_id=8553&doclng=6

Becker, K., Kehoe, J., & Tennent, B. (2007). Impact of personalised learning styles on online delivery and assessment. *Campus-Wide Information Systems, 24*(2), 105–119. doi:10.1108/10650740710742718

Cheng, Y. C., & Tam, M. M. (1997). Multimodels of quality in education. *Quality Assurance in Education, 5*, 22–31. doi:10.1108/09684889710156558

Coates, H. (2005). Leveraging LMSs to enhance campus-based student engagement. *EDUCAUSE Quarterly, 1*, 66–68.

Fiocco, M. (2005). *'Glonacal' Contexts: Internationalisation Policy in the Australian Higher Education Sector and the Development of Pathway Programs*. Digital PhD, Murdoch University, Australia. Retrieved October 10, 2008 from https://wwwlib.murdoch.edu.au/adt/browse/view/adt-MU20060502.154739?PrintFriendly=1

Fraser, B. J. (1998). Science learning environments: Assessment, effects and determinants. In B.J. Fraser & K.G. Tobin (Eds.) *The international handbook of science education* (pp. 527-564). Dordrecht, The Netherlands: Kluwer.

Greene, J. (2002). Mixed-method evaluation: a way of democratically engaging with difference. *Evaluation Journal of Australasia, 2*(2), 23–29.

Griffin, G., Coates, H., McInnis, C., & James, J. (2003). The development of an extended course experience questionnaire. *Quality in Higher Education, 9*(3), 259–266. doi:10.1080/135383203200015111

Hambleton, I. R., Foster, W. H., & Richardson, J. T. (1998). Improving student learning using the personalised system of instruction. *Higher Education, 35*, 187–203. doi:10.1023/A:1003031601307

Institute for Research on Learning. (2008). Retrieved October 10, 2008, http://portal.acm.org/citation.cfm?id=142750.142991

Johnson, R. B., & Onwuegbuzie, A. J. (2004). Mixed Methods Research: A Research Paradigm Whose Time Has Come. *Educational Researcher, 33*(7), 14–26. doi:10.3102/0013189X033007014

Laurillard, D. (2006). E-learning in Higher Education. In P. Ashwin, (ed.), *Changing Higher Education: The Development of Learning and Teaching*. London: Routledge. Retrieved October 10, 2008, from http://www.bacs.uq.edu.au/CurriculumReview/DianaLaurillard.pdf

Lee, G., Jolly, N., Kench, P., & Gelonesi, B. (2000). *Factors related to student satisfaction with university.* Paper presented at the First year in Higher Education Conference: Creating futures for a new millennium, Brisbane, Australia.

McInnis, C. (2003). *New Realities of the Student Experience: How should Universities respond?* The 25th Annual conference of the European Association for Institutional Research.

Meek, V. L. (2000). Diversity and marketisation of higher education: incompatible concepts? *Higher Education Policy*, *13*(1), 23–39. doi:10.1016/S0952-8733(99)00030-6

Nair, C. S., & Fisher, D. L. (2001). Learning Environments and Student Attitudes to Science at the Senior Secondary and Tertiary levels. *Issues in Educational Research*, *11*(2), 12–31.

OECD. (1998). *Redefining tertiary education*. Paris: OECD.

Patton, M. Q., (2002). *Qualitative Research and Evaluation Methods*. Thousand Oaks, CA: Sage.

Patton, M. Q. (1986). *Utilisation-Focussed Evaluation*. Newbury Park, CA: Sage.

Powers, A. (2004). An Evaluation of Four Place-Based Education Programs. *The Journal of Environmental Education*, *35*(4), 17–32. doi:10.3200/JOEE.35.4.17-32

Ramsden, P. (2005). *Using Research on student learning to enhance educational quality, Deliberations*. Retrieved October 10, 2008 http://www.londonmet.ac.uk/deliberations/ocsld-publications/isltp-ramsden.cfm

Scott, G. (2006). *Accessing the Student Voice: Using CEQuery to Identify What Retains Students and Promotes Engagement in Productive Learning in Australian Higher Education*. Canberra, Australia: Higher Education Innovation Program and the Collaboration and Structural Reform Fund, Department of Education, Science and Training.

Tashakkori, A., & Teddlie, C. (2003). *Handbook of Mixed Methods in Social and Behavioural Research*. Thousand Oaks, CA: Sage.

Williams, J. B., & Jacobs, J. (2004). Exploring the use of blogs as learning spaces in the higher education sector. *Australasian Journal of Communication Technology*, *20*(2), 232–247.

Wright, C., & O'Neil, M. (2002). Service Quality in the Higher Education Sector: An Empirical Investigation of Students' Perceptions. *Higher Education Research & Development*, *21*(1), 23–39. doi:10.1080/07294360220124639

Chapter 14
Video–Enriched Learning Experiences for Performing Arts Students:
Two Exploratory Case Studies

Alberto Ramírez Martinell
Lancaster University, UK

Julie-Ann Sime
Lancaster University, UK

ABSTRACT

To close the gap between formal education and professional practice, Higher Education (HE) practitioners need to be aware of the importance of offering realistic learning scenarios where students can profit from personalised learning opportunities and meaningful learning. In this chapter, the authors study the extent to which viewing video recordings of the individual performances of dance and music students benefited the learning process. Evidence was gathered from two groups of undergraduate performing arts students at a HE institution in the United Kingdom, and from their corresponding teachers, who independently offered their students a personalised way of accessing visually relevant feedback on their performances via a virtual learning environment. Results suggest that this access to personalised learning facilitated critical reflection and learning from experience. It enabled the students to reposition themselves in relation to their actual performance, fostered their will to learn, and reaffirmed them as potential professional performers.

INTRODUCTION

In the field of personalised learning, video can be used to nurture the student experience, it *"can transport the viewer to places and times that he or she would not otherwise be able to see"* (Pinnington,

1992, p. 11), it can offer just-in-time meaningful visual representations and it can be used to enhance the student's motivation and will to learn (Barnett 2008). For performing arts students this represents a major breakthrough. By viewing video recordings of their own performances, students are able to step out of their bodies and see themselves from the audi-

DOI: 10.4018/978-1-60566-884-0.ch014

ence point of view, as well as develop a realistic view of their own performance. This enables them to reflect and critically analyse their performance with a view to iterative improvement.

Researchers on video as a learning aid for performing arts students claim that "*students are most likely to benefit from video recordings; these can help them to develop a more realistic and rich description of their practice*" Leijen, Lam, Wildschut, Simons & Admiraal (2009, p. 170). Leijen et al (2009) conducted a study on how streaming video could be used to support dance students in carrying out reflection and concluded that video leads to a more personalised instruction. In their study, they used online peer feedback to help performers reflect on how the audience may perceive their act; build up a professional identity; and ground their experiences in the relevant professional context. Their motivation was to explore reflection of dance students, which despite its relevance and inclusion in educational practices, has been identified as a challenging activity that needs further facilitation (Leijen et al, 2009). Among the lessons they learned from the inquiry, were that students saw video as an effective medium for carrying out self-evaluations and to facilitate students to overcome worries about the judgments of others. They concluded that video in this academic context enhances three processes of reflection: "*describing an experience, evaluating an experience, and relating to multiple perspectives*" (Leijen et al, 2009, p. 175).

Technology supported learning environments are commonly used in Higher Education (HE) to support students' reflection – by means of forum posts, guided readings, online debating, etc – however students, including those of performing arts disciplines, may lack objectivity and criteria to be able to cope with the task without appropriate guidance (Leijen, et al, 2009). A technology supported learning environment should be a safe atmosphere for the students to get such guidance, trust and opportunities for proactive interaction. It should provide the necessary information and

support for students to deal with challenging and even emotional situations (Parizotto-Ribeiro & Hammond, 2003). Students should trust the validity of their experiences without spending a lot of time worrying about the judgements of others (Leijen, et al, 2009) which can result in negative consequences that may even extend beyond the training period (Ende, 1983). A technology-supported environment should provide prompt and objective feedback that students can trust, and embedding feedback in the videoed performance of the students seems to meet these demands.

In this chapter we will examine two cases and explore the extent to which a video enriched virtual learning environment can provide opportunities for personalised learning and be capable of providing sufficient opportunities to: foster performing arts threshold competencies (Meyer & Land, 2003), nurture the students' will to learn (Barnett, 2008), support critical reflection (Leijen et al, 2009), and offer access to realistic, ill-defined and meaningful content for analysis in accessible and flexible ways. This study examines the complex relationship between production of educational video, its use within an academic setting by performing arts teachers and the students' use, and experiences of using, the video resources. The focus is on the academic practice of two performing arts teachers and the experiences of their students as they use video to support reflection and promote critical analysis of their own performance and that of peers. In the first case, video is used as a visual record, of the iterative development of group choreography by dance students, and in the second, video provides visual feedback on conducting to music students.

BACKGROUND

The smooth integration of technology into the every day life of the HE student and the popularisation of web-based applications for learning purposes, social networking and other technological paradigms, have emphasised the inflexible and rather outdated character of some traditionally academic norms and trends that still stand out in HE institutions and leave the importance of nurturing the student's learning experience aside. In 2000, Gilly Salmon stated that traditional teaching methods in HE structures were still prevalent in the average academic setting. Yet, in some academic scenarios such a dependence on old practices may hinder the incorporation of technology-supported instruction (Salmon, 2000). Almost a decade after those claims, in an era where most undergraduates have grown up surrounded by technology and are what Prensky (2001) calls digital natives, predominantly education can still be seen as a pedagogical approach where a teacher projects the knowledge and students are expected to grasp it. Students are still explicitly asked to be part of a traditional teacher-learning dialogue (Salmon, 2000) and regardless of the young people's sophisticated technical skills and learning preferences (Bennett, Maton, & Kervin, 2008), HE programmes tend to be aimed at a kind of student who studies full-time at a given pace, and that requires to attend to an academic institution at stipulated times. Residential education does help students foster the development of their interpersonal and communication competencies, to build up teamwork and leadership skills; and to enable them to engage in self-verification processes (Swann, 1983) aiming to reaffirm themselves (Barnett, 2008), but on its own residential learning *"might be too restrictive, too expensive and often even inappropriate"* (Parchoma, 2008, p. 3). In residential learning, both learners and teachers have the opportunity *"to take advantage of relative cues to make points and to verify that a point or a question has been understood"* (Yang and Liu, 2007, p. 172), but today's knowledge economy *"requires that the citizenry and workforce be able to harness information and communication technologies in order to remain competitive in a global scale"* (Knox, 2006, p. 31). Nadolski and colleagues identify rapid changes in today's labour

market that may *"require suitable approaches to lifelong education"* (2008, p. 338), and rethinking the definition of academic life and providing the student with realistic, flexible and personalised instruction seems to be the ways to attend such demands. *"Today's students need to know how to apply their knowledge in a real-world environment by thinking critically, analyzing information, comprehending new ideas, communicating, collaborating in teams, and solving problems"* (Bruett 2006, p. 27). These are all skills that employers have identified as essential competencies for a twenty-first century world (Bruett, 2006; Knox 2006; Levy & Murnane 2006).

Modern-world graduates need to be flexible enough to adapt to a professional environment in which self-awareness of personal and professional development, and a continuous process of updating and learning, are basic skills that most employers expect (Stefani, Clarke & Littlejohn, 2000). Such self-awareness has started to emerge among HE students (Conole, de Laat, Dillon & Darby, 2006), and their institutions are conscious of these new demands (Laurillard, 2002). However, HE institutions are in a transitional stage in which the goals are: to accommodate non-traditional students in more flexible ways for learning; to offer a life-long learning approach for traditional and non-traditional students (Parchoma, 2008); to provide opportunities to foster threshold competencies (Meyer & Land, 2003); to promote the development of twenty-first century skills (Bruett 2006); and to nurture the students' will to learn (Barnett, 2008).

Studies in the field of Personalised Learning (ePortfolios, personal development plans, the student experience, attitude treatment interaction, learning styles, enquiry-based learning, practice-based learning, reflective practice, changing practices, competence-based knowledge structures, and graduates' employability) suggest that the experience in HE should not solely be determined by the spatiotemporal prerequisites dictated by the course and the style of delivery of instruction, but by the transferability of knowledge and experience to real or near-authentic contexts. In other words the experience in HE should be oriented to foster the student's employability (Hills, Robertson, Walker, Adey & Nixon, 2003) and capability to successfully integrate to the workplace. HE students should be empowered to develop the competencies that may enable them to cope with the demands of real-world, ill-defined situations. Additionally there is evidence (Hills et al 2003, Cade 2008) that points to a mismatch between what the students are learning in HE institutions and what they – according to employers – will need to know after graduation. Jochems, Merriënboer & Koper (2004) stress that there is a need to close the gap between formal education and professional practice, and to strengthen the transfer of acquired competencies from the classrooms to the workplace. As Goodyear (2001) would say HE institutions need to support students in their acquisition of discursive competences by offering a deep understanding of some discursive realm and an insight into what it is like to handle, with confidence, the concepts, theories and ideas of a field of thought within an informed, critical and active attitude. In terms of Meyer and Land (2003), HE institutions should enable students to constantly re-elaborate on their existing body of knowledge – even if troublesome – in order to open up previously inaccessible ways of thinking about given aspects of the subject in question (Meyer & Land, 2005), and by means of a transformative, irreversible, integrative, troublesome and bounded process of getting to know, these threshold concepts may potentially transform the student's learning experience and reposition him or her in relation to the subject.

HE institutions need to adopt a student-centric view and provide flexible opportunities for students to get involved in academic – or non-academic – activities designed to develop threshold competencies and bridge links between theory, practice and the workplace. The promises of student-centric learning are to *"open the door*

for students to learn in ways that match their intelligence types in the places and at the paces they prefer by combining content in customized sequences" (Horn & Johnson, 2008, p. 39); to enable personalised training schemes tailored to the learner's current and future needs; to facilitate flexible access to lifelong learning and just-in-time training as continual processes rather than a distinct event; and to provide new learning models for efficient integration of training into workplaces (Sampson, Karagiannidis & Kinshuk, 2002).

A student centric approach to learning is about giving what seems to be relevant to the learner and about providing confirmation bias in self-verification processes (Swann, 1983). In a technology supported environment personalised confirmation opportunities can be offered in many forms (e.g. by means of peer reviews and online collaboration, lurking in peer generated content, analysing data and data representation and by means of multimedia rich content) but a one-size-fits-all approach may not fulfil the needs of students of all disciplines.

In performing arts disciplines – such as dance, theatre and music – students' performances are usually assessed by means of the tutor's appraisal and feedback; on-site vicarious reinforcement (Bandura, 1971); and the students' subjective appreciation of what they see in mirrors during a performance, or in a video recording of themselves after the performance. Video as a process – rather than as an end – can be used as a powerful means of expression (Pinnington, 1992) towards a pedagogy of affirmation (Barnett, 2008). Video is able to provide students with specific and global self-views of themselves (Swann, Chang-Schneider, & McClarty, 2007) and enhance the student's self-reaffirmation. In its own right, video enables students to disembody themselves from what they have done allowing them to make enough distance to adopt a more critical view of their own performance.

In a nutshell *"video in performing arts provides an opportunity for students that neither mirrors nor verbal feedback can, which is reviewing one's performance asynchronously either right away after having reflected on the feedback received or even after the students have mastered the skills"* (Ramírez Martinell, 2009, p. 180).

RESEARCH FRAMEWORK

Participatory action research and a pragmatic lens have been employed as the research framework of this inquiry for three main reasons: 1) participatory action research enables the researchers to internally validate findings by means of an iterative process in which what emerges from the inquiry becomes an assumption to be observed for the following iterations; 2) voicing the main stakeholders helps researchers build up a reliable process in which the *"research is conducted with people rather than on people"* (Heron & Reason, 2001, p. 179); and 3) because the pragmatic character of action research enables researchers to identify the ways forward for the application of findings in real or near-authentic scenarios facilitating the generalisation of findings.

In this participatory action research, the students, teachers and researchers were placed as co-creators of a whole. For Reason and Bradbury (2001, p. 9) *"a participatory worldview is a political statement, as well as a theory of knowledge that implies democratic, peer relationships as the form of inquiry"*, being the political imperative not just a matter of ethical inclusiveness and considerations about a representative sample of subjects, but the democratic foundations of inquiry. Subjects and objects are bounded, and due to being part of a whole, they are unquestionably actors within it, and therefore the results of inquiry and reflection imply a pragmatic character (Reason & Bradbury, 2001). As such it is the right of students and teachers to participate with each other in the establishment of agreements, in the creation of resources, the discovery of the impacts of one's actions on the others and in the creation of usable knowledge.

Participatory action research is a legitimate form of educational inquiry (Zeichner, 2001) that is only possible with, for, and by people and communities, ideally involving all stakeholders, both in the questioning and sense-making that informs the research, and in the action which is its focus. Thus, knowledge is an evolving process of coming to know rooted in everyday experience (Reason & Bradbury, 2001).

Action research respects the voices of the participants and values their experience. Students and teachers bring knowledge to the inquiry, and the researcher can get integrated in the rituals and routines established by the participants. Practice, theory and reflection are brought together with the aim of redefining roles and changing practices and social structures.

PERFORMING ARTS

Two different groups of performing arts students, and their teachers, from the same HE institution participated in the research: one group studying dance and the other music. During the academic year, the groups convene once a week and the students were video recorded while on-stage. After the face-to-face sessions the videos were hosted in the institutional virtual learning environment (VLE), that students were already familiar with, where students had the chance to view the streaming video of their performance.

The feedback of the teachers was a recursive element in both groups although it was presented in different ways. In the dance group the teacher gave feedback immediately after the students' performances and thus the feedback was also video recorded. In the music group the teacher took notes during the rehearsals or concerts and, before dismissing the class, handed them to the performing student.

The dance students were eighteen 18-19 year old females and the music students were five 19-20 year old males and females. Both courses were taught to undergraduates, and no one expressed difficulties in using the online environment. For the production of the videos, neither of the teachers called upon institutional help either from the television unit or the audiovisual department. In both cases, the teachers used departmental resources and equipment and, according to the teachers, the activity did not represent any major preparation or a significant change to their academic load. In this respect the music teacher said:

transferring video (from tape) to the computer, and encoding it to RealPlayer could have been easier, I have to say. It is indeed time consuming, but I neither watch it nor wait for my computer to finish, I have other things to do and I just let it do the work.

Both teachers worked full time in the university and their duties include teaching, research and performing. Although, both teachers conducted similar video-enriched learning activities, they were not aware that another performance arts teacher within their institution was conducting a similar activity, and therefore they were not able to share experiences. None the less, the sessions were composed of similar elements: the expository participation of the tutor and the performance of the students accompanied by the corresponding feedback, either oral or written. During the observed sessions, both courses relied to a large extent on the students' physical performances.

Generating the Video-Enriched Learning Activities

Generation of the video-enriched learning activities was similar, to some extent, in both scenarios. Students and teachers convened in the classrooms as they usually did for any other session and proceeded to follow the normal class routines, for the dance group this consisted of: warming up, teacher-controlled drills, less controlled drills and students' presentations divided into teams. For the music

group, it mainly consisted of the presentations of the students' rehearsals, followed by the teacher's feedback and an "improved" performance of the student conductor. Each session focused on the work of one of the five students who was asked to conduct the orchestra. During the individual conducting sessions all classmates were to give oral feedback to the conductor in turn.

A single camera array was used in both courses. In the dance group the camera operator – one of the researchers – was located in a corner of the room with a tripod and a consumer tape-based video camera from where performances and the teacher's oral feedback were recorded. The camera operator did not know the dance routines and the final videos had undesired camera panning, which could have been avoided with a multi-camera setting and additional editing time. In the music group, it was the teacher who recorded the students' performances. He sat in the back of the room, positioned the tripod and the consumer tape-based video camera right next to him and started to record the students' performances. These videos were steady and no camera techniques were used nor required (e.g. camera panning, zooming, etc), however other kinds of problems emerged. During the encoding process there were some output time delays, and the audio and video tracks in the final recording ended up being out-of-phase, nonetheless students found no problems with the audio delay. They coped with the quality limitations of the media and got the most out of its benefits. To this respect two students said:

I think the videos were fine, I had no complaints. (dance student)

Well, yes the audio was delayed and it could have been better, but I was paying attention to other things (...) I wanted to see what the teacher meant (in the feedback). (music student)

Both teachers attempted to avoid creating a feeling of disruption as a result of the presence of the camera – and the camera operator in the case of the dance group, and although it was evident, the students saw it as non-intrusive. One dance student said:

I barely paid attention to the camera and the camera operator.

and another one added:

it was like if the camera had always been part of the classroom arrangement.

On the whole, the production experience in both groups was smooth – the presence of the camera did not modify the behaviour of the students, the technical difficulties did not hinder the primary objective of the media and in both cases, the video did not represent a major change in the approach to teaching. Both teachers commented that the face-to-face interaction without the video would have been the same, however video was used as a pedagogy of affirmation and new learning opportunities were clearly enabled by its use: the feedback the teacher gave the students was validated by means of on-demand and personal viewing sessions and a critical attitude towards the students' performances was fostered. The practitioners were aware that the video-enriched activities would be more demanding for students outside the classroom than they would have been during the academic gathering, but at the same time, they thought students were going to recognise the value of the tasks and the direct benefit to their personal development if done on their own. Students claimed that having access to the videos either from their rooms or from the library allowed them to study the performances without the social pressure normally faced while being in the hall.

It is generally very intimidating to receive feedback in front of your classmates, especially because you gave your best and you do not want to ac-

cept your weak points (she laughs) or at least you don't want to accept them in front of everyone. (music student)

I tend to view the videos with my boyfriend because he doesn't see them in the same way we do in class, he cheers me up and I explain him what the exercise was about. (dance student)

Both teachers agreed that the experience was worth it. For the dance teacher this was the first time he had used this type of video-enriched learning activity as a way to provide visual and verbal feedback to his students. The music teacher however had been using this activity since 2002 and over the years he had found that the experience of watching yourself while performing/conducting helps students to develop a sense of awareness of the feedback they receive. This was, however, the first time he had worked with online video.

Teacher Implementation and Student Use

The video production process in both scenarios was very simple. They both used a consumer camera with a tripod, and then the video was transferred to the computer and encoded in an appropriate format for streaming. The dance teacher opted for windows media video and the music teacher preferred to go for the real player format. This decision did not make any difference to the students' perceptions. To make the videos available to the students, both teachers uploaded them to the University VLE and asked their students to watch the material after class hours.

The dance students were highly motivated by the activity. In the session when they were video recorded for the first time, they were eagerly asking when the videos would be available online, and once the footage was hosted in the VLE, 6 unique visits were registered on each thread, suggesting that the 6 students of each group promptly accessed the videos. They were aware that being filmed during class would require them to watch the videos out of class time.

The dance teacher attributed this positive attitude towards the medium to a latent appeal of theatre and dance students to being on camera, he however questioned that an activity of this type would be useful for other disciplines. In this respect the music teacher said that it was not only the appeal to being on camera that determined the success of the activity and he thought that other performing disciplines where the students' physical effort was relevant for their academic achievement could benefit from this type of video-enriched approach for learning in a personalised manner.

Although the level of excitement varied, the attitude of the music students was not different – this was the second course they had taken with this teacher and the second time they had used video for revising their performances (in the first time videos were delivered via DVDs).

I think the videos have become an essential part of this subject. I cannot imagine the class without them. (music student)

When the dance teacher was asked whether the engagement of the students was driven by the novelty of the video-enriched activity, he discarded a Hawthorne effect. He said that:

video is a conventional teaching aid, and the students are accustomed to watching videos of dance work forms along the sessions anyway, so working with video did not distract them from their academic commitments.

The teacher's perception was supported by data gathered in a set of questionnaires. 86% of the dance students have, indeed, made use of video for learning purposes before this activity took place: for making their own video productions (69%); for analysing the technique of professional performers (15%); for watching interviews (7%); or even for recording TV segments on request (7%). None of them, however, admitted having used video in such a personalised manner, before.

Both teachers were aware of the learning impact of the activity and they decided to use this approach because they were expecting to achieve certain learning objectives. Their aim was to foster awareness in the students and promote reflection on performance, but different learning strategies were intended. The teachers' job was to point to the areas of opportunity, but it was the student who decided whether to follow the suggestions or not. On the one hand, the dance students were asked to watch the video of their own and of their peers and think of the feedback and improvements suggested by the teacher during their performances and to construct a written argument based on their factual experience. After watching the videos, a clear course of action was required from the students. They needed to construct a better version of the presented performance, in which the teacher identified the iterative improvements in individuals and in the group and provided the pertinent feedback. On the other hand, the videos for the music students were to support the feedback the teacher gave them on their rehearsals and their concerts. The extent to which they followed the suggestions of the teacher, and tried to improve their performance, was up to them.

Data Collection

The design of the instruments for data collection is based on the premise that teachers and HE students are active participants in their teaching/learning processes, who are able to adapt their previous knowledge to engage in learning activities that will potentially develop their critical thinking skills, either alone or in collaboration with others. The instruments for data collection used in this research include participant observations, questionnaires, formal and informal interviews, and semi-structured focus groups. Participant observations occurred in 60% (N=10) of the dance sessions and 30% (N=17) in the music group. Each participant observation was accompanied by a corresponding research journal. The objectives of the participant observations were to gather qualitative data from the groups; to recognise the intrinsic characteristics of the learning environments where the video enriched learning activities were used and to enhance the understanding of the use of video as a reaffirmation means. The questionnaires were applied to gather qualitative data on the students' opinions, and preferences about the experience, to define the profile of the students, to find out how many active users were using the video resources and to gather the impressions of the students towards the experience as a whole. The questionnaires were completed at the beginning and at the end of the inquiry, and in the case of dance students an additional questionnaire was completed five weeks after the course finished. The interviews were used to get to know the perspectives and opinions of both teachers and to get spontaneous responses from the students. The interviews were conducted in the teachers' offices and at the end of two of the sessions. Due to the interest and participation of the students in what originally was planned to be an interview the third interview session had to be treated as a semi-structured focus group, where the dance students talked about their learning experiences. The reach and limitations of each of the instruments of data collection is grounded in the idea that the participants involved in the research were free to provide as much or as little information as they would feel confident with and that it is their subjective perceptions towards the medium that has been used as evidence in the research.

DANCE STUDENTS

This case study was conducted from October 2007 to February 2008. Eighteen female 2nd year students were involved in the case study. The objective of the inquiry was to observe, document and understand the purpose of an activity in which students were video recorded during the iterative development of a group choreography with the specific aims of: 1) enhancing personal development situations; 2) providing collaborative work opportunities for the implementation of group choreographies; and 3) for referencing purposes in a final academic essay.

At the beginning of the term, the students were asked to prepare a choreographic piece which was going to be presented to other peers and staff at the end of the term. For didactic purposes, students were assigned to work in three teams of six. The course convenor redistributed the three-hour weekly workshop into one-hour slots to provide a more personalised instruction to each team. In the fifth week of the course, the teacher asked the students to individually prepare a series of fixed movements which they would be able to present several times in the week after. In that week, after having devoted time for conducting a series of total-class activities, the class was dismissed and each team reconvened with the teacher as scheduled. The performances of the three teams and the feedback given by the tutor were video recorded. After the session the footage was encoded in Windows Media Video format and made available for streaming to the students via the VLE in three different threads, one per team.

By means of the activity tracking features of the VLE it was possible to get an idea of the activity in each thread. The online presence of the students was high; however, the written activity in the threads was not what made this activity valuable. Before the weekend, each thread had a total of 6 unique visits which suggested that the team members had accessed the team thread. In a rather unexpected behaviour, a day before the following session it was found that each post had accumulated 18 unique visits. Students were clearly prioritising the revision of their team footage, but once they had more time, they lurked into the other teams' video threads either to compare whether their team's weak points were something to worry about or to validate the positive feedback they received.

I couldn't resist the urge to lurk on the other teams' videos (...) and I have to say that our raw material was as good as theirs, I do not understand why the teacher was so harsh with us.

It is very useful because you can analyse your own work, see where the choreography is weak and work on it, and you can always peep on your peers' work (she laughs).

In week 7, during class time, the students presented the revised versions of the original presentations, again in separate teams. At the end of that session the course convenor assigned the students a fellow classmate to work with and asked them to combine their performances and present them the following week. In week 8 each pair presented their choreography to their teammates and received feedback and orientation from the course convenor. The assignment for this week was to put together a team choreography, where each of the 6 members had to provide certain input in the choreography. In week 9 the students performed for the course convenor in the allocated session slot. They received final feedback and prepared for the stage performance in week 10.

The online behaviour remained constant across the weeks; students were going online to lurk on the video threads rather than to comment on them. Team threads accumulated 6 unique views before the weekend and a much higher number after the weekend. 77% of the students (N=18) said it was useful to watch their peers' videos because they could: 1) criticise their performances (36%); 2) analyse them (23%); 3) reflect on what they did and the feedback they got (23%); 4) compare their own performances with their classmates' (5%); and 5) even enjoy them (13%).

During the focus group in week 9, the students agreed that listening to the teacher's feedback while watching the video recordings of their performances was useful because they could analyse what they were told and improve their technique, they also said that embedding the videos in a familiar learning environment such as in the VLE they are used to working with helped them deal with the medium without the hassle of learning – or getting used to – new learning environments.

you don't have to download the video, I am familiar with the VLE and my group members can comment on my work. I also feel comfortable because only me and the dance students can watch it.

In this group, the course convenor focused on his teaching duties and left the work of video recording, encoding and uploading the videos to someone else – one of the researchers. The commitment of the students and the motivation were remarkable. The development of each individual student was kept as a video *memoir* of their iterative development and once the term finished, a DVD was authored and handed to the course participants for their personal portfolios. The course convenor asked the students to reference the videos of their performance for their analytical final essay. Five weeks after the stage performance, and with the aim of getting a retrospective view of the activity, the students were questioned about how useful it was to have such a feature in the course. All of the students, referred to the activity as the most personalised learning experience they have ever taken part in. One student claimed:

This is what I call an up-close-and-personal coaching experience.

MUSIC STUDENTS

This study took place with a group of orchestra-conducting students, comprising five 2nd year music students. The enquiry was carried out from January to April 2008. The aim of the study was twofold: 1) to investigate the experience of students using video as a learning artefact in the processes of developing their skills in front of an orchestra; and 2) to gather understanding of the use of video for learning purposes. In an interview with the course convenor, an enthusiastic practitioner, who since 2002 has used this medium as a means of providing feedback, he claimed that

... video is especially useful for performing arts students because they need to get prompt and accurate feedback to realise whether they are doing accordingly.

Since his first experience with the medium, the course convenor had always intended to foster a more objective view of the students' performances by creating a certain distance between themselves as observers and themselves as performers. By having this created distance the students were able to reflect, on the feedback the teacher had given them, in a more objective way. In this respect, the course convenor said that

when a conducting student receives feedback on the way he or she performs, there is always a possibility of students not believing – or not wanting to believe – the feedback because according to the way they perceive their actions, they might think they are doing it the right way. When the teacher tells them that their movements are not powerful enough and they see what the teacher means by actually viewing themselves in a video, a whole new way of accepting feedback and reaffirming what they think and validating themselves as students arise.

Students become more critical and objective by reflecting upon past performances while viewing the videos; they are able to reflect in the midst of action without the need to interrupt it (Schön, 1983), a threshold concept that performing arts teachers need to nurture without competing for space in the curriculum (Levy & Murnane, 2006, p. 58).

Performing arts students are required "*to learn how to shape their perceptions and understanding of the world and to create a physical manifestation of that perception*" (Corner, 2002, p. 148) and video can help them step back from their performance, allowing them to assume the place of the observer. This separation of their performing selves and the appreciation point of view during their performance, may enable them to become more aware of what they are doing while being engaged in their own performance. Four students said:

It is weird to see yourself in a video, but you don't see the videos to find you there as a person, but as a performer. I watch them because I want to see what the teacher meant not because I want to see how handsome I am (he laughs).

I watch them because I want to see me through the eyes of the teacher so to say it.

I watch the videos because I want to improve my technique (...) we have very few opportunities to see ourselves performing and we have to take advantage of them.

Thanks to the videos I have compared the way I conducted last year and the way I am conducting this year, and I can really tell the difference (...) it feels good (she smiles).

The performing arts undergraduate student needs to learn how to understand and manipulate the teacher's feedback and their appreciation of their own performances. They need to be taught to analyse, develop technical and practical skills and combine these elements into a physical realisation. Schön (1987, p. 26) would consider this a stage of development in their professional practice towards being a reflective practitioner.

Based on the Myers-Briggs indicators, Alisa Roost (2003) states that performing art students are extroverted and perceiving, and that reflective activities such as writing or analysing readings or, in this case, videos, may enable them to think critically and make connections across fields. In a categorisation of the performing art student, Roost defines them as outgoing and quick thinkers who, despite procrastinating, achieve the academic tasks generally energised by the last-minute deadline. In an interview with the music teacher, he revealed that although his students tend to be considered as outgoing and extroverted individuals, based on the feedback he has received from 225 students since the year 2002, an extrovert attitude is developed, to a certain extent, by exposure to videos of themselves while performing. Analysis of course feedback revealed that nearly 90% of his students showed a recursive feeling of shame and social pressure when first exposed to video of themselves, and a growing confidence, self awareness and openness to criticism with further use of the medium. To this matter a student commented:

The feeling of embarrassment indeed decreased along the course, but I wouldn't talk about feeling confident with seeing me onscreen and being criticised by my classmates.

With respect to the students' fondness for the last-minute rush, the music teacher considered that it might affect their being critical of their own work hindering valuable reflective time. He is convinced that providing feedback backed up with video has helped his students to improve in the course. During interview it emerged that his enthusiasm and affinity with the medium have been critical factors in this particular, successful use of video as an academic resource. The tutor has refined his method of using video to provide visual feedback to the students, for over 6 years. During his professional practice, he has used many different ways of delivering video – tape, DVD and, this year, online video. Since he began to use video in his academic practice, he has dealt with all aspects of video production and despite the fact

that he does not have a technology background; he has managed to test the technology at hand and decide what suits his academic purpose. Technology has neither driven the production decisions nor the educational use of video; it has always been the teacher's intention to offer a personalised learning experience - the learning purpose and the students' needs have been the driving force.

LESSONS LEARNED

Many lessons have been learned from these case studies within the performing arts. For a more detailed consideration of the production, encoding and delivery of the videos, see Ramírez Martinell, Sime & O'Donoghue (2006) and Ramírez Martinell & Sime (2008). For more detail on the integration of the video-enriched activities into academic practice, see Ramírez Martinell (2009) where an additional 6 case studies are discussed. Here, we discuss the lessons learned about: technology acceptance; video as a support for personalised learning; student engagement; and teaching practice.

Technology Acceptance

The advent of consumer produced video, desktop postproduction, video sharing platforms, and web 2.0 services has helped video to cross the chasm in technology adoption (Moore, 1999). User Generated Video (UGV) is one of the most used resources in the web. For instance, Youtube.com, a video-sharing platform, currently receives up to 19% of global Internet users' visits (according to Alexa.com), making it the third most visited site in the world. Millions of people produce and watch online video everyday. The viewers' tolerance to non-broadcasting quality – and even to low quality – video has increased, viewing habits have changed, and attitude towards UGV has also adapted to the medium. Despite minor problems with the quality of the videos, there were no complaints from students in these two cases; there was no problem with acceptance of video that did not meet broadcast standards.

As with any other technology, the extent to which learning opportunities are fostered by video enriched learning activities depends on the integration within a learning environment and their use for enabling and transforming the learner (Luckin, Shurville & Browne, 2007). The success of a technology supported learning strategy not only depends on its potential to enhance learning, but also on its latent degree of acceptance. According to some researchers (Rogers, 1962; Moore, 1999; Dagdilelis, 2005; Luckin et al, 2007; Sime & Kemp, 2008; Parchoma, 2008) innovation and technology supported learning strategies can consolidate themselves as effective means for fostering learning if the diffusion of the innovation is effective and the adoption is strengthened. "*Diffusion is the process by which an innovation spreads (…) from its source of invention or creation to its ultimate users or adopters*" (Rogers, 1962, p. 13). To consolidate the adoption of a medium like video three criteria for its successful utilization should be met: "*it must address an unmet need; it must provide better utilization of existing resources and it must be cost-effective*" (Sprey, 1997, p. 44). Based on the accomplishment of these criteria, it can be claimed that in these practices video was effectively used: it allowed performing arts students to be affirmed as potential professional performers, by means of visual meaningful feedback at minimal additional cost.

One of the most controversial issues in the students' acceptance of educational video is the length and the consequences that derive from it – such as concern over the students' attention span and the ever-increasing potential to procrastinate and get distracted during an online viewing sessions (Elvers, Polzella & Graetz, 2003, p. 159) (e.g. reading and writing e-mails, checking profiles and activity in social-networking sites, reading RSS feeds, or browsing the web). But contrary to reported drawbacks over long form video and

a prescriptive top limit length, that can oscillate from twenty to thirty seconds (Alessi & Trollip, 2001, p. 74) to even 15 minutes (Noam, Groebel & Gerbarg, 2004, p. 225), the students in these case studies did not show any negative concern towards the duration of the videos, which, in comparison to reported ideal lengths, were not particularly short. The dance students watched an average of 4 videos a week for 5 weeks and the music students 1.8 videos a week for 17 weeks. The average length of the videos is 9 minutes and 8 seconds for the dance students and 21 minutes and 38 seconds for the music students. The longest video in the dance course, a 20 minute 03 second video, was watched by 94.4% students while the longest video in the music course, a 29 minute 28 second video, was watched by 100% the students. When asked whether the duration of the videos put the students off watching them, they overwhelmingly said length did not matter, they thought the contents of the videos were "*about right*" and length was only a consequence. In this respect, two dance students claimed:

some videos were about a minute long some others about ten minutes, it didn't matter I watch them all, especially when I was the one on the video. (…) in some cases I even thought they were too short, I wanted more of me, I just can get enough (she laughs).

Personalised Learning

Repurposing the use of video from a presentational medium to a means of providing visual feedback to performing arts students generated various learning opportunities for the students. Students were able to view their performances and to make sense out of the teacher's feedback in a flexible manner; video kept students motivated and willing to take part in the technology supported dynamics. On the whole video bridged a link between the face-to-face sessions and the students' work outside the classroom. Students were required to commit quality time to the revisions of their performances, and in some cases to the revision of their classmates' performances. Students reported that the VLE appeared to have evolved from an online repository and course forum to an online personal development portfolio in which they could have on-demand access to personalised videos and their feedback.

The whole VLE makes perfect sense, when I log in, what I see is my work, my areas of further development and my teacher telling me what to do to achieve it. (dance student)

The flexibility of access to the online videos enhanced opportunities to learn in a place-dependent discipline like performing arts, regardless of place, learning pace and time. Students became more aware of their personal development, and thanks to the visualisation of their performances, their areas for improvement became more evident and achievable. Videos enabled students to take distance from their work and to exercise a well informed self-critique of their own practices. By means of video, the students could step out of their own perspective and see what they have done from the point of view of a different person, from the point of view of the audience or from the point of view of the teacher. According to the music teacher, this seems to be particularly helpful because

(...) by means of self-confrontation students are able to interpret the tutor's feedback in a more objective way.

For the dance students, this practice helped them to reflect on their performance and to analyse in a more conscious way the rationale of the movements they chose for their choreographies. The students of both courses claimed that watching the video clips made them become aware of areas of opportunity that, without the media, would have been difficult to accept and therefore to improve.

They agreed that distancing oneself during the artistic performance, and having the opportunity to watch it from the point of view of a third person was a useful experience in the sense that they could evaluate their performance in a more critical fashion and were more prepared to accept – and understand – well-founded criticism.

Student Engagement

According to the data gathered, students felt satisfied with the activity. They felt the teacher was going for the extra mile and in return they did not want to let him down.

it is like if he were working extra hours for this class, so why shouldn't I? (music student)

The moral authority of both teachers was remarkable. Both groups were doing whatever the teachers were asking them to do with no questioning at all. Students from both groups were aware of the prestige of their teachers and they seemed to devote their time and effort to what the class required.

we are in good hands (...) if he says I should do it his way, it is because I should do his way. (dance student)

The data gathered suggests that this level of commitment also took place out of the classroom. From the tracking features of the VLE a quantitative analysis of the videos viewed was conducted. A total of 20 videos with a running time of 3 hours 2 minutes and 44 seconds were produced during 5 weeks for the dance course; and 34 videos were produced during 17 weeks for the music course with a running time of 12 hours 15 minutes and 20 seconds. Each dance student was videoed 5 times (an average of 45 minutes) and the music student was filmed an average of 7.4 times (2 hours 27 minutes. A decrease in viewing interest was expected as the term progressed however;

the students' viewing awareness in both groups remained high throughout the whole course. At the end of the term, 77% of the videos were viewed by the dance students during the term and the music students did similarly with 72% of the videos. That is, that each student in the dance group watched an average of 2 hours 20 minutes of video in 5 weeks; and 8 hours 49 minutes in the music group for 17 weeks. The time committed to viewing the material suggests that the student engagement was high and that the video-enriched learning activities added 28 minutes a week (for 5 weeks) for the dance students and 31 minutes a week (for 17 weeks) of devotion to the course.

From the students' perceptions, gathered through questionnaires, it was found that 77% of the dance students and 80% of the music students were extremely satisfied with the activity and with the results. Students thought that this activity was valuable because it created opportunities for self-confrontation and verification and for reflection. To these points three dance students claimed:

it was very useful to see the raw movements of the other teams. It made me feel confident about my academic performance.

watching the videos allowed me to analyse my performance neutrally and to see the whole piece as an audience member rather than a performer.

the videos were useful because you can analyse your own work to see where your performance is weak and work on it.

Teaching Practice

During the inquiry it was obvious that the performing arts teachers were fully aware of the pedagogical implications of using video in HE. Compared to the role of teachers observed in a further 6 case studies (Ramírez Martinell, 2009), the performing arts teachers seemed to have a clearer justification of why to use video and a better understanding of appropriate learning goals. Both teachers used video in very confident ways, and made transparent to the students the technical side of the production, implementation, encoding and delivery of the video elements. Video, for both teachers, was "*an extension of their capabilities*" (Bransford, Brown, & Cocking, 2000, p. 230) and as such it never interfered with their main academic task. Both teachers were very enthusiastic and committed to their teaching and showed a particular interest in the use of video within teaching practice. In terms of Moore's technology adoption lifecycle, both teachers played the role of early adopters, that is, someone who integrates new technology into their teaching practice before most other people do (Moore 1999). The early adopter is a pragmatist who eagerly explores and adopts new technologies to suit his or her own purposes. While not being the most innovative or daring, these enthusiasts are on the same side of the barrier to technology adoption, as the innovators who champion new technologies. The enthusiasm, commitment and increased sense of awareness towards the use of video and its integration into their teaching practice was probably a significant factor in their success, as such, it is uncertain as to whether these practice would easily transfer to other practitioners in the field of performing arts.

WAYS FORWARD

Grounded in actual class experience these case studies may contribute to the development of a general understanding of the relevance of video technology for personalised, active and flexible learning in the field of performing arts. Further research is still required to validate the claims and to investigate whether what has been said also applies to other teaching and learning settings.

Video in performing arts courses tends to be used as a source of information, by means of documentaries or teacher produced videos; for illustration purposes by means of pre-recorded performances, theatrical events, concerts, or documentaries; as a creative element when students are asked to produced their own videos, or to create video installations; for retrieving visual feedback by means of videoing the students performances and making them available for the students to review; and as it was presented in these two cases: as visual elements that facilitate a personalised learning instruction aiming to encourage self-confrontation, personal development and critical reflection.

During interview, the dance teacher asserted that video for performing arts students is like books for literature students, in the sense that they are (or at least, they should be) familiar learning resources. He claimed that familiarity with the medium as a learning artefact enables students to benefit from the video resources without the problem of overcoming fears of use or becoming confident and comfortable with the medium. According to the music teacher, the use of video in performing arts courses is more pragmatic and justified than in other subject areas, claiming that almost every single video clip used during a course is a necessary element of the students' integral preparation.

This framework of reference suggests that the performing arts students may tend to be more tolerant with length and video quality, and that they might be more likely to lean-in towards an educational video – that is "*that the viewer may adopt a reflective and an attentive posture towards the medium*" (Ramírez Martinell & Sime, 2008, p. 1325) – engage with its contents, and reflect upon it more than the average undergraduate student. In interviews with the students, they recognised that activities of this kind could also be successful if implemented in any practical subject that may require rehearsals and the physical engagement of fellow students. All the students agreed that using video to provide visual feedback to trigger critical thinking and an out-of-the-body experience to enhance reflection was useful.

CONCLUSION

The main purpose of these case studies was to help develop a better understanding of the way video can be used to enhance students' self perception of their performances and as a confirmation bias in self verification. It was found that video as an extension of the teacher's capabilities enabled students to access a personalised way of reflecting and learning from their previous performances and on the feedback they received from the teacher thus enabling them to become competent with the threshold concepts the teachers wanted students to develop: relating themselves to multiple perspectives and creating a physical manifestation of the world based on their perception and understanding.

During the inquiry, it was observed that videoing students while performing and promptly making the videos available in a safe online learning environment provided a flexible and personalised means for learning. In the tailor-made videos students were able to see the specific areas of opportunities and improvement of each and every individual on the course and the collective experience of the group. Although there was a general course pace, the videos, the feedback and thus the mental and physical engagement were shaped by the academic performance of each individual. It was observed that by implementing this type of video-enriched learning activity in performing arts disciplines, HE institutions are beginning to close the gap between the expectations of employers and the skills of graduates, through improved personal development programmes that not only provide relevant material for the creation of personalised students' portfolios, but also enhance the students commitment and willingness to learn.

Additionally, the inclusion of technology-supported activities within performing arts courses fosters the development of ICT skills among the students; enhances the possibilities for the student to develop self direction, personal and social responsibilities, people skills, teamwork skills and adaptability in work related environments (e.g. dance company, concert hall); and opened a valuable space for students to become the administrators of their own learning processes.

REFERENCES

Alessi, S. M., & Trollip, S. R. (2001). *Multimedia for learning: Methods and development,* (3rd ed.). Boston: Allyn & Bacon.

Bandura, A. (1971). Vicarious and self-reinforcement processes. In R. Glaser (Ed.) *The nature of reinforcement* (pp. 228-278). New York: Academic.

Barnett, R. (2008). *A will to learn*. London: Open University Press.

Bennett, S., Maton, K., & Kervin, L. (2008). The 'digital natives' debate: A critical review of the evidence. *British Journal of Educational Technology, 39*(5), 775–786. doi:10.1111/j.1467-8535.2007.00793.x

Bransford, J., Brown, A., & Cocking, R. (2000). *How people learn: Brain, mind, experience and school: Expanded edition.* Washington, DC: National Academy Press.

Bruett, K. (2006). Why American business demands twenty-first century learning: An industry perspective. *New Directions for Youth Development, (2006)*110, 25–30. doi:10.1002/yd.163

Cade, A. (2008) *Employable graduates for responsible employers*. Report to the Higher Education Academy Education for Sustainable Development. Retrieved February 2009, from http://www.heacademy.ac.uk/projects/detail/esd_employable_graduates

Conole, G., de Laat, M., Dillon, T., & Darby, J. (2006). *JISC LXP: Student experiences of technology.* Draft final report. Retrieved February 25, 2009 from http://jisc.ac.uk/media/documents/programmes/elearningpedagogy/lxp_project_final_report_nov_06.pdf

Corner, F. (2002). What to teach? Qualitative research into fine art undergraduate programmes. In *Enhancing curricula: Exploring effective curricula practices in art, design and communication.* (pp. 144-160). Retrieved October 18, 2008, from http://www.arts.ac.uk/docs/cltad_2002corner.pdf

Dagdilelis, V. (2005). Integrating ICT in universities: Some actual problems and solutions. In S. Mishra & C. Ramesh (Eds.) *Interactive multimedia in education and training* (pp. 113-134). Hershey, PA: IGI Global.

Elvers, G., Polzella, D., & Graetz, K. (2003). Procrastination in online courses: Performance and attitudinal differences. *Teaching of Psychology, 30*(2), 159–162. doi:10.1207/S15328023TOP3002_13

Ende, J. (1983). Feedback in clinical medical education. *Journal of the American Medical Association, 250*(6), 777–781. doi:10.1001/jama.250.6.777

Goodyear, P. M. (2001). Psychological foundations for networked learning. In C. Steeples & C. Jones (Eds.). *Networked learning: Perspectives and issues,* (pp 49-75). Berlin: Springer Verlag.

Heron, J., & Reason, P. (2001). The Practice of Co-operative inquiry: Research "with" rather than "on" People. In P. Reason & H. Bradbury (Eds.), *Handbook of action Research: Participative inquiry and practice.* London: SAGE.

Hills, J. M., Robertson, R., Walker, M. A., Adey, A., & Nixon, I. (2003). Bridging the gap between degree programme curricula and employability through implementation of work-related learning. *Teaching in Higher Education, 8*(2), 211–231. doi:10.1080/1356251032000052456

Horn, M. B., & Johnson, C. W. (2008). *How disruptive innovation will change the way the world learns.* New York: McGraw-Hill Professional.

Jochems, W., van Merriënboer, J., & Koper, R. (Eds.). (2004). *Integrated e-learning: Implications for pedagogy, technology and organization.* London: RoutledgeFalmer.

Knox, A. (2006). Why American business demands twenty-first century learning: A company perspective. *New Directions for Youth Development, (2006)*110, 31–37. doi:10.1002/yd.164

Laurillard, D. (2002). Rethinking teaching for the knowledge society. *EDUCAUSE Review, 17*(37), 16–25.

Leijen, A., Lam, I., Wildschut, L., Simons, R.-J., & Admiraal, W. (2009). Streaming video to enhance students' reflection in dance education. *Computers & Education, 52*(1), 169–176. doi:10.1016/j.compedu.2008.07.010

Levy, F., & Murnane, R. J. (2006). Why the changing American economy calls for twenty-first century learning: Answers to educators' questions. *New Directions for Youth Development, (2006)*110, 53–62. doi:10.1002/yd.167

Luckin, R., Shurville, S., & Browne, T. (2007). Initiating e-learning by stealth, participation and consultation in a late majority institution. *Journal of Organisational Transformation and Social Change, 3*(3), 317–332. doi:10.1386/jots.3.3.317_1

Meyer, J. H. F., & Land, R. (2003). Threshold concepts and troublesome knowledge (1): Linkages to ways of thinking and practising within the disciplines. In C. Rust (ed.) *Improving Student Learning - Ten Years On,* (pp 412-424). Oxford: OCSLD.

Meyer, J. H. F., & Land, R. (2005). Threshold concepts and troublesome knowledge (2): Epistemological considerations and a conceptual framework for teaching and learning. *Higher Education, 49,* 373–388. doi:10.1007/s10734-004-6779-5

Moore, G. (1999). *Crossing the chasm: Marketing and selling technology products to Mainstream customers,* (2nd Ed.). Oxford: Harper Business.

Nadolski, R., Hummel, H., Van den Brink, H., Hoefakker, R., Slootmaker, A., Kurvers, H., et al. (2008). EMERGO: A methodology and toolkit for developing serious games in higher education. *Simulation & Gaming, 39*(3), 338-352. Retrieved August 22, 2008, from http://sag.sagepub.com/cgi/content/abstract/39/3/338.

Noam, E., Groebel, J., & Gerbarg, D. (2004). *Internet television.* London: Lawrence Erlbaum Associates.

Parchoma, G. (2008). *Adoption of technology enhanced learning in higher education: Influences of institutional policies and practices.* Saarbrücken, Germany: VDM Verlag Dr. Müller.

Parizotto-Ribeiro, R., & Hammond, N. (2005). *Does Aesthetics affect the users' perceptions of VLEs?* Paper presented at the meeting of the International Conference on Artificial Intelligence in Education. Workshop on motivation and affect in educational software, Amsterdam.

Pinnington, A. (1992). *Using video in training and education.* London: McGrawHill Training Series.

Prensky, M. (2001). Digital natives, digital immigrants part 1. *Horizon, 9*(5), 1–6. doi:10.1108/10748120110424816

Ramírez Martinell, A. (2009). *Educational online video: Exploring the complex relationship between production, educational use and audience.* Unpublished PhD Thesis, Lancaster University, UK.

Ramírez Martinell, A., & Sime, J.-A. (2008, July). *Who is watching our Educational Videos anyway? An analysis of target audiences and their responses to different kinds of educational video.* Paper presented at the 8th International DIVERSE Conference, The Netherlands. Retrieved February 25, 2009 from http://www.inholland.nl/INHOLLAND-COM/Studying+at+INHOLLAND/Events/Diverse2008/Papers+abstracts+and+posters/Papers+abstracts+and+posters.htm

Ramírez Martinell, A., Sime, J.-A., & O'Donoghue, M. (2006). Design of a Constructivist Virtual Learning Environment composed by video summaries. In *Proceedings of the International EDUTEC 2006 conference: Education in Virtual Environments: Quality and Effectiveness in E-learning.* Tarragona, Spain: Rovira i Virgili University.

Reason, P., & Bradbury, H. (2001). Inquiry and Participation in Search of a World Worthy of Human Aspiration. In P. Reason & H. Bradbury (Eds.), *Handbook of action Research: Participative inquiry and practice* (pp. 1-14). London: SAGE.

Rogers, E. M. (1962). *Diffusion of Innovations.* New York: The Free Press.

Roost, A. (2003). Writing intensive courses in theatre. *Theatre Topics, 13*(2), 225-233. Retrieved April 2008, from http://muse.jhu.edu/login?uri=/journals/theatre_topics/v013/13.2roost.html

Sampson, D., Karagiannidis, C., & Kinshuk, . (2002). Personalised Learning: Educational, Technological and Standardisation Perspectives. *Interactive Educational Multimedia. Special Issue on Adaptive Educational Multimedia, 4*, 24–39.

Schön, D. A. (1983). *The Reflective Practitioner: How professionals think in action.* London: Temple Smith.

Schön, D. A. (1987). *Educating the reflective practitioner.* San Francisco: Jossey-Bass.

Sime, J.-A., & Kemp, B. (2008). A 3D Multi-User Virtual Laboratory: Is Successful Implementation Enough? In J. Luca, & E. R. Weippl, (Eds.). *Proceedings of ED-MEDIA 2008: World Conference on Educational Multimedia, Hypermedia and Telecommunications* (pp. 3539-3547). Chesapeake, VA: AACE.

Sprey, J. A. (1997). Videoconferencing as a Communication Tool. *IEEE Transactions on Professional Communication, 40*(1), 41–47. doi:10.1109/47.557518

Stefani, L., Clarke, J., & Littlejohn, A. (2000). Developing a Student Centred Approach to Reflective Learning. [United Kingdom: Routledge.]. *Innovations in Education and Teaching International, 37*(2), 163–171. doi:10.1080/13558000050034529

Swann, W. B., Jr. (1983). Self-verification: Bringing social reality into harmony with the self. In J. Suls & A. G. Greenwald (Eds.), *Psychological perspectives on the self* (pp. 33-66), Hillsdale, NJ: Erlbaum.

Swann, W. B., Jr., Chang-Schneider, C., & McClarty, K. (2007). *Do people's self-views matter? Self-concept and self-esteem in everyday life.* American Psychologist.

Yang, Z., & Liu, Q. (2007). Research and development of web-based virtual online classroom. *Computers & Education, 48*(2), 171–118. doi:10.1016/j.compedu.2004.12.007

Zeichner, K. (2001). Educational Action Research. In P. Reason & H. Bradbury (Eds.), *Handbook of action Research: Participative inquiry and practice* (pp. 273-282). London: SAGE.

Chapter 15
Enabling Personalised Learning through Formative and Summative Assessment

Neil Andrew Gordon
University of Hull, UK

ABSTRACT

This chapter considers some ways in which personalised learning can potentially be delivered by means of appropriate assessment and the use of associated technologies. Recognising that for many students, learning is driven by summative assessment, the chapter considers how by blending summative and formative assessment, students can be encouraged to develop and take responsibility for their own learning along with ways in which technology can make this assessment be tailored to the individual student. The approaches described can support and encourage self-regulated learning – itself an effective way of providing the more general concept of student-centred learning. The framework of learning that is engendered – with the use of technology – has the potential to allow an educational pathway which reflects individual students' needs and aptitudes, and which can thus provide a form of personalised learning. This chapter describes some of the relevant theory – which forms the context within which this work is based and has developed - before then describing two case studies where this blend of formative and summative assessment is described and analysed. This is followed by a discussion of some of the more general issues.

INTRODUCTION

This chapter considers the experiences of the author in introducing technology based interventions intended to deal with issues such as increasing class sizes and an increasing breadth of diversity within

a given cohort, issues that are now present in many areas of U.K. Higher Education (tertiary education), and further afield. The interventions considered are focussed on using technology to provide individual support for students within a typical Higher Education (H.E.) learning environment, where large class sizes and restrained contact hours typically mean that the opportunity to personalise the learning experi-

DOI: 10.4018/978-1-60566-884-0.ch015

ence can seem limited. However, the flexibility and support offered through technological solutions can provide a way to provide this personalised learning. Assessment is well acknowledged as a driver for student engagement – whether the assessment is formative or summative in nature and the chapter describes how to utilise this to encourage elements of student centred and personalised learning. Furthermore, technology offers a way to offer more flexible and individual assessment approaches, as well as more generally offering more flexible learning pathways, which offers further opportunities for a personalised learning experience.

In terms of assessment, the main focus of this chapter is on the use of diagnostic based approaches to assist students in developing their own learning and to consider the way in which technology can offer some opportunity to personalise that learning. We make use of case studies to demonstrate some specific examples, where the assessment can help students in:

1. Developing approaches to self regulated learning;
2. Developing self-analytical skills, and through these learn to identify areas of knowledge or skills that require training and enhancement;
3. Developing time management skills;
4. Developing an understanding of assessment criteria;
5. Developing an appreciation of the benefits of learning itself – not just remaining with the "marks are all" mantra.

BACKGROUND: ISSUES IN HIGHER EDUCATION

In considering personalised learning, it can be helpful to first explore some of the wider context around learning issues, in particular the relevant areas of assessment which influence the case studies that we discuss below. A more general discussion on some of the wider contextual issues is explored after the case studies.

The use of assessment within the learning context is well-known, and the use of formative and summative assessment is well recognised and documented (Biggs, 1998). Whilst it is common to distinguish between these in terms of the feedback and expected outcomes, in practice the distinction between formative and summative can be less clear (Brown, 1997), and in many respects and instances it can be more productive to combine these into single forms of assessment.

Formative assessment itself is characterised as assessment which can be used to modify learning and teaching (Sadler, 1989). In this respect, the results can apply equally to teacher and to learner. Formative assessment is typically done during a learning process and provides information which can help the learner in developing their understanding, and can help the teacher in modifying their teaching to ensure that the learning objectives are met.

In contrast to formative assessment, summative assessment may be typified as having no learning value itself, but is purely a way to measure performance. In this respect, summative assessment is usually considered as taking place at the conclusion of the learning process. Summative assessment within tertiary education has been typified as the *finals* – the exams at the end of a period of learning. Whilst commonly these would be the end of academic year exams, the focus on modular teaching, with immediate assessment has placed more focus on end of semester assessments.

In a traditional approach to teaching – as typified by a common view of traditional university teaching – material would be taught, with comments from a teacher to the students on formative assignments to assist the student in their learning, and to assist the teacher in focussing their teaching, and this would be followed by the summative assessment, usually exams.

The above dichotomy of assessment appears clean, but is not reflective of the more complex interplay between formative and summative assessment which is now the reality of much of H.E. In practice, formative and summative assessments can combine – even with exams; students are encouraged to use the exam results to help them prepare for future learning by reflecting on their learning strategies and techniques in the light of their previous performance. Similarly, summative assessment results can assist teachers in adapting their teaching for the same and future cohorts.

Within the context considered above, one role of H.E. can be seen to be that of developing self-learning approaches for students – i.e. methods and skills to allow the student to take more responsibility for their own learning. Depending on how far the emphasis is placed, this can fall within the gambit of self-regulated learning (Pintrich & De Groot, 1990), an approach where the focus of control of learning is with the learner rather than the teacher and can be an effective way of developing student-centred learning. This has long been a feature of H.E. but is something which can potentially be more efficiently and effectively developed by utilising technology – something considered later in the case studies.

Student centred learning has become a key feature of many educational policies in recent years – considered by many as a way to improve the effectiveness of education, and to improve student engagement. In the context of the work described below, the key points for student centred learning are that the student is responsible for their own learning and takes an active part in the learning process. One aim for student centred learning is for an increased level of engagement by the student, the intention being that this lead to deep learning. In student centred learning, there is often a change in the role of the lecturer, from that of a provider of knowledge and a director of the learning process, to that of a provider of material and acting as a facilitator in the learning process (O'Neill, 2005; Gibbs, 1995). One way

to potentially develop student centred learning is to use self regulated learning – where the learner takes on the role and responsibility of the manager of the individual learning process. This still requires the teacher as a manager of the overall learning process – but potentially with a reduced interaction with the individual student. In this way, the teacher becomes a manager of the process, rather than necessarily directly managing the student. The approach of student centred learning seems to fit well with some key characteristics of personalised learning, which has been promoted within the U.K. education system as a way to give the learner choices in what, when and how to learn (DCSF, 2008).

A particular aspect of assisting students in identifying the focus for their learning is the approach of utilising goals - the so called goal orientation approach (Booth, 2004; Bouffard, 1995). This approach can focus on the goals of the teacher and/or the goals of the learner. By taking account of the orientation of these goals, and by considering in particular the way in which the goals of the student can be actively orientated the learning process can be improved. Self-regulated learning requires that the learner has a clear notion of what they wish to achieve, how they may achieve it, and mechanisms by which to regulate or assess their learning. Goal orientation is relevant to the first of these three concepts – providing a way to ensure that the learner is focussing on learning which is conducive to the learning outcomes that are appropriate.

Within the context of self-regulated learning, the second issue mentioned in the previous paragraph – namely that of the learning considering how they can achieve their learning goals – can be expanded to include the issues of how to learn, and how to manage that learning process. One feature that students can struggle with on the transition to tertiary education is the amount of autonomy and self-management. In particular, time management can become an issue in an environment where teacher instructions and timetabled lessons are radically reduced when compared to the previous levels of education. This places the onus on the learner to take more responsibility for their own learning processes. By allowing for this in the design of learning materials and assessment, students can be assisted in developing the appropriate skills.

The third point mentioned above under self-regulated learning is that of having mechanisms by which to regulate and assess their own learning. This encompasses a number of related issues. The first is that of knowing what to learn. Learning outcomes are commonly used to describe learning – from the learning outcomes expected within an individual learning activity such as a lecture or workshop, to module level outcomes, and ultimately to programme level outcomes. Whilst these have become the norm for teaching staff - partly reflecting the growth of auditing processes within H.E. such as the Quality Audit Agency in the U.K. – students' understanding of these terms and descriptions cannot be assumed. By linking assessment explicitly with learning outcomes, and moreover linking both of these with the type of indicative content which students can more readily appreciate, students can begin to take more responsibility for the content of their own learning.

A related aspect to those covered in the previous paragraph, is that of developing an understanding for assessment criteria. This topic can be quite contentious, since views on assessment criteria vary from those who see them as definitive descriptors of what needs to be achieved and assessed, to those who perceive it as something more ethereal, that reflects the professional interpretation and context of the marker. However, within the pre-tertiary arena the demands for standards which allow for comparisons of performance on at least a national scale, along with the volume and need for systematic approaches means that assessment criteria and descriptions of levels is accepted as common practice. Within the context of learning general, an understanding of what is wanted – i.e.

what are the assessment criteria – can assist the learner in focussing their activity on that which is identified by the assessor as important (Rust, 2003). One aspect that we consider below is the use of assessment to drive the student learning activity, and in this context the value of clear assessment criteria which the students appreciate is critical.

The role of summative assessment - more specifically the role of marks - as a driver for student activity is something which teachers frequently make use of. However, as teachers the aim – particularly in the context of encouraging lifelong learning – is often to develop an appreciation of the benefits of learning and to get away from the "marks are all" mantra. Paradoxically, allowing students more flexibility in the way that they take assessments, and in placing the onus on learning more on them, we can potentially encourage this. Whilst a bare pass may be sufficient for many students and others would wish to achieve the highest mark, allowing flexible environments where the student can determine the amount of effort they wish to put in to a particular subject in order to achieve a target mark means that there is the potential for the accumulation of marks to be tied more closely to what is learnt. This becomes clearer when we consider some of the flexible learning and computer supported learning aspects below.

Flexible learning is often used to refer to distance learning – but more generally reflects learning where the learner is given more control and in particular choices in their learning process. The essence of flexible learning is that the learner can choose the where, when and how of the learning process (Becker, 2007). The degree of choice and freedom within these three degrees of freedom characterises different levels of flexibility on offer. Within traditional tertiary education, there is usually limited choice within a traditional course. However, the introduction of Virtual Learning Environments and other innovations mean that flexible learning is available to a wide number of students, and across the full educational spectrum. The emphasis within flexible learning is to put as much of the choice and flexibility into the hands of the learner. This contrasts a little with the traditional views on personalised learning, where the focus is often on providing a personalised approach to learning, catering for the individual needs of the learner. In the context of pre-tertiary education – particularly in the U.K. – this has led to funding to assist in the implementation and development of personalised learning plans for individual students. The intention is to provide structured approaches to learning and to involve students as partners in their own learning (DFES, 2008). In tertiary education, the same model can apply – but the greater maturity of the learners means that more of the responsibility can be placed on to the learners.

Computer Based Learning and Teaching is well established in all levels of education. For professional training and development, computer based materials and assessments provide efficient ways to support learning in a flexible way that suits employers and employees. Within Higher Education, the use of technology to support teaching – through I.C.T., Internet and Intranet resources, and through the more specialised and application specific Virtual Learning Environments is common practice. However, making appropriate and effective use of these technologies is a non-trivial task and one that still raises many questions. Shifting lecture notes and teaching materials to electronic distribution adds some flexibility, but does not of itself offer any truly new learning opportunities. Effective use of electronic communications such as email, forums and Web 2.0 technologies such as Wikis and Blogs can provide some new flexibility in communication and delivery and for distance learning offers some real benefits. But for a campus based institution, the main benefits may be more to do with resource, and making up for increasing levels of student to staff ratios which have reduced the face-to-face learning opportunities that tertiary education was respected for.

Computer Based Assessment can be seen as another facet of dealing with large classes and reduced resources. The assessment mechanisms that computer based assessment encourages is perceived as some as encouraging a more surface level of assessment and reflects an inability to assess the deeper understanding of students. This type of criticism is frequently directed at Multiple Choice Questions and short answers, where computer marking does offer real resource benefits, but does mean that the teacher needs to question the appropriateness of the assessment. However, the use of advanced multiple choice questions – such as blind multiple choice – and through the design of suitable questions some of this criticism can be alleviated. Furthermore, more open approaches of assessment are possible with technology, and as these advance the opportunity to use these to allow flexible assessment become more viable.

One way in which multiple choice questions can take particular advantage of computerised testing is through branched or tailored testing, also known as Flexilevel testing (Lord, 1980). Multiple choice question sets based on branched testing can be developed by identifying the key skills in a topic, and how these skills interrelate. Then a student who gets a question wrong, may be asked more refined questions around that topic, whereas one who gets it right would immediately go on to more complex topics. These types of question banks are based on the analysis of how different topics and skills can be placed in a hierarchy. This approach means that students get individualised and different question sets, and leads to questions about the equivalence of the assessment and issues of fairness. However, with careful and appropriate use these types of approaches can provide more flexible and individualised assessment schemes. Flexilevel testing seems to offer some promise with regards to providing a form of personalised learning. The ability of the system to automatically tailor the questions to the individual needs of the learner offers one way to personalise the learning experience and the learning material.

In the case of mathematics, and some related sciences, the opportunities for computer assessments are increased as the standard formal approaches to interpreting and manipulating expressions mean that students can be given questions which are generated by the computer, with certain elements randomised. A simple example to test a students numerical skills would be a question such as "what is x+y?" Here, rather than setting a specific set of data (answer the question "5+9" say) the computer can be given a range of values to choose between. So setting a question of the type "X+Y" where X and Y are in the range 1 to 10 would lead to 10*10=100 different questions. One good example of this – widely used in H.E. in the U.K. - is Diagnosys (Appleby et al, 1997), an expert system providing an effective way to assess the mathematical skills of students at the interface of secondary to tertiary education. Further details of Diagnosys are considered later in this chapter where the principle of supporting personalised learning through technology are illustrated with two case studies and the potential benefits of using Computer Based Assessment in dealing with large classes and in providing immediate feedback to students.

CASE STUDIES

This section provides details of the use of diagnostic learning technologies in teaching, where the intention is that the feedback from the diagnostic tests would assist the students in identifying for themselves what areas of knowledge and skills to develop, and considers how these offer one way of providing some personalised learning. The author has used this approach in a number of modules over several years, teaching different topics and subjects. By comparing these case studies colleagues can become aware of the positive

and negative points to this type of student centred and personalised learning.

The case studies are based on experience teaching within the discipline of Computer Science. These case studies consider the use of Computer Based Assessment in teaching mathematics and in teaching IT, in a way that is intended to provide a flexible learning approach for the students. The two subjects that form the focus of these case studies are themselves core (also known as key) skills and thus are relevant to students of other disciplines than Computer Science. Having said that, it is worth noting the curious situation that Computing as a discipline is in – within the UK it seems that few institutions require that students have formal advanced qualifications in either Mathematics or computing, yet many students do have these qualifications. This means that the early stages of computing courses typically include material which is considered as core to the discipline, yet which for some students may essentially be revision of prior learning, whilst for others will be brand new material. This situation provided a catalyst for considering ways in which to deal with students with very different learning needs – i.e. how to personalise the learning experience. The case studies describe an approach to flexible personalised learning utilising various technologies which are appropriate to this context, as well as considering some of the problems that arise with this particular approach - including the delicate balance between formative and summative assessment. This also encompasses the apparent need to encourage students to engage with work by allocating credit to what would ideally be formative development.

Context to the Case Studies

The two case studies which we consider below share a number of common features and are located within a common context. Both modules are taught within a portfolio of Computer Science degrees at a traditional U.K. university (a pre-92 sector university). The case studies document the experiences of the author in teaching modules within a medium sized department, to student cohorts of a medium size (60 to 140 students per module). As a lecturer of computer science, who has also taught within the mathematics subject and with a range of experiences of teaching across level 3 to level 7 (A-level equivalent up to taught Masters provision), the two case studies will describe the implementation of flexible approaches to learning utilising assorted technologies.

Case Study I: A Flexible Approach to Teaching Mathematics with Technology

Background

This case study considers a first year (level 4), optional module which has expanded from a cohort size of approximately 40 four of five years ago, to the current cohort size of around 98 students. Essentially a mathematical methods module, it is called "quantitative methods for computing" to reduce the negative impact that having mathematics in the title can produce. This reflects changes in the intake requirements for computer science degrees at my institution and generally – where the traditional requirement for advanced (A-level) mathematics has gradually decreased across the sector, in recognition of the changes in the secondary provision of mathematics, and the changes in the need for prior mathematical skills in computer science students. The module content is designed to develop the theory and skills that supports the fundamental mathematics and formal methods that are considered as key to computing, and which support later study within the degrees offered. This requires reviewing some mathematics which is familiar to school and college level, as well as developing this out to specialist applications that are necessary to understand the theory of computer science and which are essential tools in applying the theory.

One feature of the widening participation agenda – key to this module – is the large variety in educational history and the corresponding variation in mathematical skills and experience across the cohort. In practical terms for this particular module it means that some students taking the module may not have taken mathematics beyond GCSE (secondary school) level, and that may have been at the lowest tier (grade C or below). Conversely, other students taking the module may have top grades in advanced (A-level) mathematics, and sometimes in Further Mathematics or equivalent. Furthermore, the module is offered as an option within the free-elective scheme operated at our institution, meaning that students taking the module may be from other departments and may even be in their second year (level 5) of study.

Aims and Definitions

Given the context described in the previous section, one issue that become an increasingly pressing one was that of coping with the allied pressures of increasing class size and a widening range of knowledge and skills within the cohort. A traditional approach to teaching mathematics – lectures supported by small group tutorials – was successful with small cohorts, but was under pressure as the cohort increased and the familiar concerns about resources encouraged consideration of alternative approaches.

Thus, the aims of the approach adopted were to

i) provide support for a subset of the content that needed to be taught;

ii) support the students in identifying what areas of mathematics they needed to revise and develop;

iii) allow for differentiation within the class so that students with different backgrounds could find a suitable level of challenge;

iv) encourage students to engage with the work in a timely way, and develop their self management skills.

These aims align closely with many of the characteristics of personalised learning, and the approach described below in achieving these aims demonstrates the way in which technology can provide some support for personalised learning when resource constraints may otherwise preclude it.

Development and Implementation of this Approach

In the 1990s, a number of U.K. projects under the government funded Computer in Teaching Initiative were producing a range of materials that offered support and materials to encourage the use of computers in teaching. Through evaluations at this time, under a variety of educational technology projects, I had come across a complete – albeit somewhat limited in its range of topics – computer assessment tool called Diagnosys (Appleby, 1997). This system implemented a knowledge net based on assumptions on the hierarchy of mathematics skills that engineering, mathematics and similar students would be expected to typically have on entry to higher education. The approach used in Diagnosys is a good example of the flexilevel type of test described earlier. I introduced the use of this particular tool in its intended diagnostic role within our mathematics degrees at the time (Gordon, 2005A). This was later used in engineering and other science subjects at my institution. In this role, the software was used to test the students in the first few weeks of starting their course, and was used to provide them with advice on what areas they may need help with. This particular system also had the capacity to provide an overall profile of the class for teaching staff, so that they could tailor their teaching to cover material that was identified as a potential difficulty for a large proportion of the class.

Whilst the diagnostic approach just described is valuable, the engagement by students was somewhat limited – empirical evidence from the students showed that many were apparently unwilling to follow up the guidance on areas where they should concentrate their revision etc. In 2000, when my own focus shifted from supporting educational technology for others, to teaching as a lecturer, I decided to incorporate the diagnostic approach within the summative assessment for a module. Specifically, to provide flexibility to students and to encourage the students to engage with the material, I made use of this system to provide summative assessment. Students still undertook the diagnostic test early on in their university level studies, but they were then required to continue to use the software as a way of tracking their own learning and to provide an element of the summative assessment for the module. By giving the students a wide period to take the assessment in, and allowing them to decide for themselves when to be content with their results, the responsibility for their learning was placed in their own hands. The testing was supported with some lectures, formal workshops and optional drop in sessions. Some elements of this specific material were also subsequently tested in a formal exam. The students were allowed to take the assessment when they wanted, as many times as they wished. The mark for this element of the module was to be the maximum mark achieved in the allowed timeframe.

Evaluation: The Benefits and Pitfalls

The approach just described has a number of benefits which include

i) given resource constraints, to support the (repeated) assessment of large student cohorts with immediate feedback and guidance to students;

ii) the flexilevel approach offered by Diagnosys, with some randomisation of variables in questions, meant that individual students got unique question sets and thus they could be given flexibility in when and where they took their tests;

iii) The intention was to encourage students to begin to manage their own learning. By looking at the empirical evidence, a number of students undertook the assessment many times, slowly improving their mark as they apparently learnt and applied new skills;

iv) the individuality of the assessment means that students cannot simply copy other students work, but would need to coerce another student into taking that assessment for them;

v) Some students seem to treat this material as a game. The fact that it is marked by a computer, and allows users to retake the assessment means that it seems similar to a game – indeed some students would keep working on the material and the test until they could achieve 100%, and compared "high scores" within the class;

vi) The students could tailor their learning to their own personal skills and objectives. The assessment could be ended when they had achieved their desired aims (e.g. a bare pass, or in some cases getting to 100% and mastery of the subject).

Pitfalls with this approach:

i) A primary concern – something especially pertinent given the wider considerations of the role of coursework in assessment within the U.K. – is that of ensuring that students do not use unfair means in these assessments. The flexibility offered to the students in the way that this was used for assessment means that this cannot be guaranteed – but in the context of this module, and by reducing the weighting of this assessment to 10% (i.e. one class boundary) this was felt to be acceptable;

ii) Whilst the use of computer based assessment meant that allowing numerous reattempts was viable, the amount of time involved in system administration, and in collating results can become considerable;

iii) The lack of integration with other learning environments and learning databases on campus meant that collating the results cannot be fully automated;

iv) Whilst the system adopted has been robust in itself, changes in other campus infrastructure has led to numerous problems over the years, which undermined confidence in the system amongst both staff and students.

Case Study II: Using IT to Provide a Flexible Approach to Teaching IT

Background

This case study considers another first year (level 4) module – but one which is core and has had grown from 100 students to approximately 140 students over the last few years. This module covers the type of IT skills and core concepts which are essential for students on computing courses, yet which some students may have already studied to some extent in earlier IT or computing qualifications. Whilst there are clearly some similar issues between the two cases, there are also some distinct differences. One primary difference is that whilst some students claim to be surprised at the requirements to study mathematics topics within a computing degree, most accept and expect the type of IT coverage that they meet in their first year.

As with the first case study, the range of experience within the cohort causes potential difficulties for teaching. As a key skill most students who have gone through the education system in recent years will have had some education in ICT or IT, although this experience – as with mathematics – can itself be somewhat negative with respect to the subject itself. However, for students who have determined to continue on to a computing course, this was not an overwhelming barrier. Furthermore, many computing students will actually have studied some form of advanced computing course – which may be a academic style qualification (such as A-level computing in the U.K.), or a more vocational approach such as the National Diploma – although this distinction is likely to become less clear within the U.K. as the new Advanced Diploma in I.T. develops (Qualifications and Curriculum Authority, 2008).

Aims and Definitions

The range of module options within advanced computing courses, in combination with the range of qualifications themselves, means that some form of differentiation within the teaching of this has potential advantages. But within H.E. the ability to differentiate within a class is limited by the resources available given the cohort sizes. Because of these reasons, there is a clear advantage to considering the use of technology to provide some form of personalised learning support where we can support differentiated, tailored learning and assessment.

Thus, the aims of the approach adopted were to

i)   provide support for a section of the IT curriculum required for the module;

ii)   assess the students in a way which would encourage them to identify their own learning needs and areas to develop;

iii) allow for differentiation within the class so that students with different backgrounds could find a suitable level of challenge;

iv)   encourage students to engage with the work in a timely way, and develop their self management skills and to encourage student engagement with PDP and the early stages of career planning.

It should be noted that some of the above aims are common to those in the first case study and again these aims align closely with many of the characteristics of personalised learning.

Development and Implementation of this Approach

As mentioned in the previous section, there were a number of similarities in the aims of this and the other case study. However, there were also some differences. Alongside the specific IT skills that were the focus of students learning, the focus on PDP and on career development meant that an alternative approach to implementing a personalised learning environment would be beneficial. Another feature of the context at this time was being considered, changes in departmental policy meant that lab demonstrators – typically research students – were no longer allowed to play a direct part in assessing student work, regardless of the weighting of that element of assessment. Having come across some materials for teaching and diagnostically assessing the ECDL (European Computer Driving License), it seemed opportune to consider how to use this material in a similar way to the previous case study.

Whilst the use of this diagnostic system offers some superficial similarities to the Diagnosys approach, differences included the fact that this was a task orientated assessment with specific solutions (e.g. click on a particular part of the screen to simulate a menu selection) and so was not suitable for an entirely flexible approach (anytime, anywhere). So for this particular system, the approach adopted was to require that the assessments were done in allocated labs. However, students would be allowed to retake some of the assessments. For the purposes of the module being taught, 4 of the ECDL learning units were utilised, and students could choose to retake one or possibly two of these.

Due to licensing restrictions, this approach was subsequently amended, to use an online Multiple Choice Questions (MCQ)/short answer computer based assessment implemented in the university's Virtual Learning Environment (VLE). However, the principles were the same.

Evaluation: The Benefits and Pitfalls

The approach just described has a number of benefits which include

i)   the fact that this work was linked with a separate qualification, which the students could do, encouraged them to think about the value added issues around their studies – something directly related to their PDP;

ii) The opportunity to retake tests encouraged students to work on improving their knowledge of specific areas identified in the assessment;

iii) Students did take the opportunity to retake assessment, with improved results;

Pitfalls with this approach:

i)   The lack of alternative routes through the assessment (except potentially for the order of questions) meant that the assessment needed organising in labs, placing restrictions on the flexibility of delivery;

ii) The use of fixed MCQ or tasks meant that there is little flexibility in the level of the material;

iii) Using yet another separate system (ECDL originally, and an alternative VLE more recently) has further complicated the collating of results.

iv) Students who had already taken the full ECDL assessment resented the requirement to demonstrate the same skills that were already certified. This is an issue, but in the context of a small part of a module, demonstrating that these skills are known was felt to be worth the potential negative feelings;

v)   As an off-site resource, organised by another section of the institution, last minute changes in the license and provision caused serious problems for delivery and use with students.

Further details and analysis of the above case studies can be found in Gordon (2007) and (2005B).

DISCUSSION

Widening the earlier context considerations, it is opportune to consider how policy within the U.K. to widen participation in H.E. has been successful in so far as increasing student numbers. However, one corollary to this expansion has been a wider variation in the knowledge, skills and readiness for H.E. in the overall student body and experienced by many teaching in H.E. Combined with changes in the teaching methods used in secondary and further education, this has led to growing concerns about the general preparedness of students entering H.E. This issue is not unique to the U.K. but some of the features of the H.E. system within the U.K. make this more of an issue – where institutions are still expected to maintain high rates of retention and where students are still expected to complete an honours course within a three year period. The increase in class sizes – in my own experience doubling in some cases, can make it harder to provide individual support for students, something which technology can address. In practical terms, the unit of teaching resource is limited and there is ongoing pressure to improve efficiency, which has tended to be interpreted as increasing the student to staff ratio. This naturally puts pressure on the ability of staff to provide feedback to students.

One of the key features that has altered within pre-H.E. in the U.K. over recent years has been a growing use of coursework, and a change in the use and practice in exams. For example, students entering H.E. may have had little experience of examinations, or have taken exams but been allowed multiple reattempts. This can alter the approach to assessment – to one where students are used to an environment where the feedback and assessment cycle is an ongoing one that only ends when a satisfactory level of achievement is achieved. This is quite different to that which is still the most common one in H.E., where reassessment opportunities can be limited, and where class sizes and the philosophy of learning still focus on the final assessment. This expectation of being able to get formative feedback on assessment on a regular and rapid basis is an example of students' expectations to be able to choose the how and what is assessed, and is a good example of students' increasing expectations of some form of personalisation in their learning.

The Widening Access agenda appears to lead to a more diverse student cohort, which creates many challenges for the teacher – challenges that are common in the pre-H.E. environment, but which have been less common in H.E. and where the expectations of staff can cause tensions within the new education environment. Furthermore, the increasing variety of student qualifications, attainment and experiences pre-H.E. means that there is a growing need to provide more support for differentiation in the H.E. class – something familiar to the secondary and F.E. world, but often quite unnatural for H.E. Educators.

One further consequence of the changes in the wider educational agenda is that student engagement with their learning is quite different. As it has become more of an expectation that students will enter H.E. and as they do so for career and social reasons, their engagement with their learning on entering H.E. can be more limited and challenging to develop.

I.C.T. technology has long been recognised as offering potential benefits in teaching and learning generally. Within the U.K. H.E. context, a number of government and other initiatives through the 1990s onwards encouraged projects to develop approaches to utilise computing solutions for H.E. – the Computers in Teaching Initiative (CTI) and associated centres being particularly instrumental in this respect. However, whilst policy makers and practitioners recognised potential benefits, the nature of these benefits was – and

still is – less agreed. Some – typically policy makers and management – may take the view that technology can offer resource benefits; potentially reducing contact hours and allowing an increase in student to staff ratios. However, those who have used technology often find that the use of technology here does not reduce the support that learners require – but changes the nature of it. The benefits then are typically not in the overall resource requirements, but rather in the change in the learning process that I.C.T. can afford and in particular the engagement with those students who may not respond to the typical approaches to learning engendered in H.E.

The role of Universities in providing education and the type of education they provide has also become a concern. A number of countries (the U.S.A., Australia, the U.K.) have begun to consider the role of research in informing education (Boyer, 1998; Clark, 2003), and this has led to a growing interest in the role of inquiry based learning (Brayshaw & Gordon, 2008) and other learning models in ensuring that students benefit from their University education and that this has a wider benefit on society. This emphasis on students as inquirers into knowledge increases the focus on students' problem solving and critical analysis skills. Similarly, the wider concerns about preparing students for work has led to a growing emphasis on embedding appropriate generic (key / core / transferrable) skills into curricula. This includes aspects such as team work, and more recently many countries have begun to reflect on the role of H.E. in raising awareness of wider social aspects – within the U.K. there is growing pressure for H.E. to embed sustainable development education within their provision. A further aspect of H.E. is the recognition of the need to encourage students to take more ownership of their learning, and to begin to see learning as a lifelong concept. In the U.K. this was promulgated by the Dearing report (Dearing, 1997) which recommended that U.K. H.E. institutions develop means to embed this into their provision, and which has latterly been incorporated into the quality review process of H.E.

Personal Development Planning can offer a structure in which to encourage the self-analysis that students require in order to be effective in regulating their own learning. Within the U.K. this was another consequence of the Dearing Report (Dearing, 1997). This includes the identification of areas of knowledge that require development – and this in turn is ideally done by utilising diagnostic approaches. Computer based assessment (CBA) can provide an efficient way of carrying out diagnostic assessment for students, and combined with appropriate advice – whether automatically provided by the computer system or provided by the teacher – can be an effective way of assisting the student in self-diagnosis and corrective study

Self-regulated learning can be seen to have a close relationship with Personal Development Planning (PDP) and other approaches which aim to improve the engagement of students with learning, and with the aim of developing students as lifelong learners. Requiring students to monitor and track their own progress fits in naturally with the role of PDP as a means to encourage learners to reflect upon and plan their own learning in a more general context, and in particular to become aware of the need for lifelong learning. This can fit in well with approaches where students can decide what assessments to retake, and what areas they need to work on to improve their skills and knowledge. This is another contentious area itself, and one where the role of summative assessment becomes key. The use of coursework, and the opportunity to retake assessments, has a poor reputation in many areas. For example, in the U.K. coursework is being phased out of many A-level qualifications (Qualifications and Curriculum Authority, 2005; 2006) as the general perception was that it opens up too many opportunities for work that does not reflect the students' own abilities and leads to an inflation of final marks which means that grades themselves become poor

indicators of future performance. Having said that, in opening up the opportunity for self-regulated learning, a truly flexible approach should allow for the learner to choose for themselves where a reattempt would be valid. This requires trust in the learner – and is an area where technology can offer some potential solutions, or at least alleviate some of the particular areas of concern.

I was made starkly aware of the importance of assisting students in the transition to tertiary education when a student knocked on my door, and enquired if I would look at and tell them whether the coursework answers they had prepared were correct or not. This was sometime before the coursework deadline, yet the student was surprised to be told that whilst I would indicate if their work looked reasonable, I would not state if it was absolutely correct or not. The reason for their surprise was that at college their teachers had habitually given this advice before work was formally submitted. Whilst I was conscious of this issue in a general way, I was personally surprised at the level of this, and more generally the impact this has had on how students learn and perceive learning should not be underestimated. Whilst changes in pre-university education may alleviate this situation, the appropriate use of personalised learning environments at university offers an immediate way for universities to tackle this type of problem, by encouraging students to take more responsibility for their own learning, supported by technology that allows a truly flexible and personal approach.

The above discussion points have identified some of the wider contextual issues that demonstrate the growing need for personalised learning, whilst also considering some of the constraints on educators that limit the opportunity to offer it. The case studies demonstrated some approaches using formative and summative assessment and the potential for the use of flexilevel approaches which can allow some form of personalisation in the learning experience (for example, see Wen, 2008). Technology can offer even more flexible approaches – for example through allowing learners to identify and use web based learning resources. One area where there is particular scope for future research and development is in providing tools to assist educators in identifying and structuring learning pathways, along with the functionality to allow learners to access these and to potentially aggregate their own choice of learning and assessment materials which reflect their own favoured learning styles and approaches to the assessment process.

CONCLUSION

We have considered some of the context and background which makes personalised learning with technology an important and pertinent issue for higher education to consider at this time. The opportunities that technology offers for changes in how we teach, and how learners learn, are great and increasing. The above case studies, evaluated here from a practitioner point of view, demonstrate some of the benefits and pitfalls of introducing flexibility within teaching in higher education. The use of technology offers the potential for new approaches – especially in terms of tailoring learning material using Flexilevel and diagnostic type approaches. Technology also offers flexibility in terms of the location of learning and assessment, and can be aligned with other issues of teaching in tertiary education, such as improving student engagement, coping with widening participation and encouraging students to take responsibility for their own learning.

Contrasting the two case studies, the first one utilised flexibility of time and place of assessment, with teaching supported by more traditional lectures and workshops, along with numerous web based support resources. The second one allowed some flexibility in assessment, but restricted the place and time of assessment. However, the main learning materials were all web based, but supported with supervised labs which also provide the

venue for the supervised assessments. However, they both shared the common feature of putting the onus on the students in terms of determining what areas of knowledge and skills to work on, and in requiring the students to begin to make the decision – supported by teaching staff – of where to place their focus of work and when to cease study of a particular area.

Future developments that offer more opportunities for tailoring the learning to the student include further personalisation of the learning spaces, particularly the virtual learning spaces that many students now use. Another area that offers numerous development opportunities is in providing more flexible approaches to the ordering of material and assessments. The case studies considered in this chapter have focussed on individual assignments. Encouraging and developing team work and collaboration is another key skill that universities are commonly expected to develop. Tools such as WebPA offer opportunities to encourage group work and peer and self-assessment (Gordon, 2008) along with more flexible marking schemes which reflect these elements of assessment. Furthermore, Web 2.0 technologies such as Blogs, Wikis and other collaborative tools offer further flexibility in delivery and approaches to teaching and learning.

Placing the onus of learning onto the student, and managing the changing role of the teacher from imparter of knowledge to an assistant manager of the learning process seems to require a change in view and approach by teaching staff. Allowing students the greater freedoms offered by flexible learning environments, and encouraging an environment where personalised learning can flourish requires a level of trust between teacher and students – something highlighted by the issues in the case studies of the concerns over unfair means within assessments. In my experience the workload for staff is not reduced – indeed, given the consideration into the design of assessment and teaching, the discovery, evaluation and implementation of suitable technologies to implement it, and the management of both the systems and the students and their data it can begin to make end of teaching summative written exams an attractive proposition. However, in my view the benefits to students and staff when personalised learning is offered far outweigh any difficulties.

REFERENCES

Appleby, J., Samuels, P., & Treasure-Jones, T. (1997). Diagnosys - a knowledge-based diagnostic test of basic mathematical skills. *Computers & Education*, *28*(2), 113–131. doi:10.1016/S0360-1315(97)00001-8

Becker, K., Kehoe, J., & Tennent, B. (2007). Impact of personalised learning styles on online delivery and assessment. *Campus-Wide Information Systems*, *24*(2), 105–119. doi:10.1108/10650740710742718

Biggs, J. (1998). Assessment and Classroom Learning: a role for summative assessment? *Assessment in Education: Principles . Policy & Practice*, *5*(1), 103–110.

Booth, D., Edwards, P., Gordon, N. A., Khait, A., & Taylor, I. (2004). Goal orientation in mathematics education for computer scientists and engineers. In L. Price (Ed.), *Undergraduate Mathematics Teaching Conference* (pp. 73 – 82). Birmingham, UK: Birmingham University Press.

Bouffard, T., Boisvert, J., Vezeau, C., & Larouche, C. (1995). The impact of goal orientation on self-regulation and performance among college students. *The British Journal of Educational Psychology*, *65*(3), 317–329.

Boyer, E. (1998). Reinventing Undergraduate Education: a Blueprint for America's Research Universities. *Boyer Commission on Educating Undergraduates in the Research University*. Retrieved October 10, 2008, from http://naples.cc.sunysb.edu/Pres/boyer.nsf/

Brayshaw, M., & Gordon, N. A. (2008). Inquiry based learning in computer science teaching in Higher Education. *Innovations in Teaching and Learning in Information and Computer Sciences*, *7*(1), 22–33.

Brown, G., Bull, J., & Pendlebury, M. (1997). *Assessing Student Learning in Higher Education.* London: Routledge.

Clarke, C. (2003). *The future of higher education.* White Paper, HMSO.

DCSF. (2008). *Personalised Learning: a practical guide.* HMSO.

Dearing, R. (1997). *Higher Education in the learning society.* London: Stationery Office.

DFES. (Department for Children, Schools and Families), (2008). *About Personalised Learning.* Retrieved October 1, 2008, from http://www.standards.dfes.gov.uk/personalisedlearning/about/

Gibbs, G. (1995). *Assessing Student Centred Courses.* Oxford, UK: Oxford Centre for Staff Learning and Development.

Gordon, N. A. (2005A). Experiences of embedding information technology into discipline based teaching. *Innovations in Teaching and Learning in Information and Computer Sciences*, *4*, 1–9.

Gordon, N. A. (2005B). The use of diagnostic software in teaching a mathematics module for computer science students. In H. Steed & U. O'Reilly (Eds), *Annual Conference of the Subject Centre for Information and Computer Sciences* (pp. 34 – 38). Ulster, UK: Higher Education Academy Subject Centre for Information and Computer Sciences.

Gordon, N. A. (2007). Issues in teaching IT within H.E. computing courses. In H. White (Ed.), *Annual Conference of the Subject Centre for Information and Computer Sciences* (pp. 131-134). Ulster, UK: Higher Education Academy Subject Centre for Information and Computer Sciences.

Gordon, N. A. (2008). Group work in Higher Education computing courses. In H. White (Ed.), *Annual Conference of the Subject Centre for Information and Computer Sciences* (pp. 35-39). Ulster, UK: Higher Education Academy Subject Centre for Information and Computer Sciences.

Lord, F. (1980). *Applications of Item Response Theory to Practical Testing Problems.* Hillsdale, NJ: Erlbaum.

O'Neill, G., & McMahon, T. (2005). Student–Centred Learning: What Does It Mean For Students And Lecturers? In O'Neill, G., & Moore, S., & McMullin, B. (Eds), *Emerging Issues in the Practice of University Learning and Teaching, Dublin: AISHE.* Dublin: University College Dublin.

Pintrich, P., & Dr Groot, E. (1990). Motivational and self-regulated learning components of classroom academic performance. *Journal of Educational Psychology*, *82*(1), 33–40. doi:10.1037/0022-0663.82.1.33

Qualifications and Curriculum Authority. (2005). *A review of GCE and GCSE coursework arrangements.* Retrieved October 5, 2008, from http://www.qca.org.uk/qca_10407.aspx

Qualifications and Curriculum Authority. (2006). *QCA announces changes to coursework.* Retrieved October 5, 2008, from http://www.qca.org.uk/qca_9678.aspx

Qualifications and Curriculum Authority. (2008). *The Diploma.* Retrieved October 20, 2008, from http://www.qca.org.uk/qca_5396.aspx

Rust, C., Price, M., & O'Donovan, B. (2003). Improving students' learning by developing their understanding of assessment criteria and processes. *Assessment & Evaluation in Higher Education*, *28*(2), 147–164. doi:10.1080/02602930301671

Sadler, D. (1989). Formative assessment and the design of instructional systems. *Instructional Science*, *18*(2), 119–144. doi:10.1007/BF00117714

Wen, L. (2008). *Flexible Virtual Learning Environments: a Schema-Driven Approach using Semantic Web Concepts.* Unpublished doctoral dissertation, University of Hull, UK.

Section 3
Technological Issues

Chapter 16
"You Can Take Out of it What You Want":
How Learning Objects within Blended Learning Designs Encourage Personalised Learning

Debbie Holley
London Metropolitan University Business School, UK

Lyn Greaves
Thames Valley University, UK

Claire Bradley
London Metropolitan University, UK

John Cook
London Metropolitan University, UK

ABSTRACT

This chapter shows how a suite of learning objects were developed by the Centre for Excellence in Teaching and Learning for Reusable Learning Objects (www.RLO-CETL.ac.uk), one of 74 CETLs being funded by the UK's Higher Education Funding Council for England. The learning objects were used to support students within a blended learning context. It shows student personalised learning: learning that can be any time (in the 24 hour digital world), any place (the university experienced in the home or workplace), any where (limited only by the students choice and internet access – trains, boats, planes, global learning). It focuses on two case studies at UK Higher Education institutions that demonstrate any time, any place learning. London Metropolitan University (London Met) and Thames Valley University (TVU), have both used and reused learning objects in different contexts. In each case study the background and the resulting blended learning design is outlined, followed by evaluation data illustrating the student experience and how the learning design and the learning objects have encouraged personalised learning. The chapter concludes with the start of the third iteration of use – to facilitate informal learning 'any where', through the incorporation of learning objects that can be used on mobile phones.

DOI: 10.4018/978-1-60566-884-0.ch016

INTRODUCTION

This chapter explores the metaphor of any time and any place personalised learning. In its simplest form, personalised learning focuses on the customisation of education to an individual's needs, interests and aptitude, giving the learner a degree of ownership of the learning process. Such a view has the potential to refocus learning from the student perspective, in addition to the institutional viewpoint of providing appropriate learning environments. Indeed, given the current interest in the student learning experience, for example see the JISC report 'In their Own words' (JISC 2007), institutions are increasingly examining PLEs (Personal Learning Environments) as a way to enable any time and any place learning:

The idea of a PLE (Personal Learning Environment) is that learners can configure different services and tools to develop their own learning environment, bringing together informal learning from the home, the workplace as well as more formal provision by education institutions. The PLE is controlled by the learner and as well as offering an environment for accessing different information and knowledge allows access to web based publishing and other opportunities for creating content and expressing and exchanging ideas. The idea behind the PLE is to harness the power and potential of social software and web 2.0 applications for learning. (Atwell, 2008).

However, we contend that from a Higher Education perspective, the whole personal learning agenda needs exploring with formal learning in mind, i.e. where a more deliberative approach to scaffold learning takes place to complement the more informal social activities that may go on using social software. Cook (2009) has argued that we need Personalised Learning Environments, which he defines as a loosely coupled set of tools and resources that are learner defined, i.e. where the learner creates their own context for learning

(hence the use of the word Personalised as opposed to Personal). The European Commission funded MATURE project (http://mature-ip.eu/en/start) and the work of Van Harmelen (2007) provides a good example of the development of Personal Learning Environments and tools to support work-based learners on a learning journey. Cook (2009) describes the learner's perspective within a Personalised Learning Environment, based on his involvement in the MATURE project, as follows. The learner is supported on a learning journey as they: (i) set their own learning goals; manage their learning (by managing both content and process); communicate with others across multiple contexts in the process of learning (i.e. support student experience of eLearning as they move between work/life/learning contexts); appropriate digital tools and media into the learning practice; and thereby achieve learning goals.

But Personalised Learning Environments (or PLEs from now on) are also about imposing the personal on the technical and providing 24/7 access to educational support. Because there is a real need to support more formal education, this paper looks at the work of the Centre for Excellence in Teaching and Learning (CETL) in Reusable Learning Objects (RLOs) and how this work on formal learning has been used to promote personalised learning at two UK Higher Education Institutes (HEIs). These reusable learning objects provide bite-sized scaffolding for learning and can be seen as one of the building blocks for the PLE, which we conceived as a loosely coupled set of tools and resources.

The CETL in Reusable Learning Objects is one of 74 CETLs being funded by the UK's Higher Education Funding Council for England (http://www.rlo-cetl.ac.uk/). It is developing a range of multimedia learning objects that are stored in repositories, accessed over the Web or from mobile phones, and integrated into course delivery. London Metropolitan University (London Met) is the lead site, in partnership with the Universities of Cambridge and Nottingham. The RLOs are designed with pedagogy as a central concern, along with the requirement that they should be able to be reused by other tutors and institutions, and in different contexts (Boyle & Cook, 2001) and accommodate different types of users (students and tutors). In this sense RLOs have the potential to be added into the mix of a PLE at a time when a learner decides they need specific support.

CASE STUDIES OF ANY TIME, ANY PLACE LEARNING

The London Met case study was the first pilot. Its primary purpose was to evaluate student experiences of using RLOs. To support their learning, students were able to engage with module materials any time of day, and self-select their place of learning and the materials that best suited their development needs. In terms of the accepted PLE approach (Cook 2009), these students are moving along a continuum from a starting point of selecting their own learning goals and beginning to manage their learning in terms of both content and process. The second case study at Thames Valley University (TVU) used and evaluated RLOs in a different context. Rather than the serendipitous self-discovery approach presented in the first case study, the aim of this project was to offer the students a carefully constructed learning experience. The experience guided them through the content of the module to an individual threshold concept point (Land 2008) where the students would appropriate digital tools and media for themselves. TVU redesigned their module to offer a scaffolded environment not only for classroom contact but for out of class independent learning activities as well. The blended learning designs are outlined for each study, and can be seen as the basis for an evolving PLE for HE; they form a bedrock in that they can scaffold learning in a range of PLE contexts, to support student experience of eLearning as they move between work/life/learning contexts (Cook 2009 op.cit).

Case Study 1: Introduction of the Study Skills RLOs at London Met

London Met is an inner-city University, committed to widening participation. This agenda can lead to challenges in meeting the needs of a diverse student body. Two-thirds of our students are mature learners, many with English as a second language. Students experience financial hardship, and many are trying to combine full-time study with nearly full-time work, well above the national average of 15 working hours per week.

On more traditional campus-based Universities one factor for student success is that students are physically present. In the Business School where this case study is located, gate entry data (i.e. from swipe cards as students enter the University) indicates that many students attend University only for their scheduled teaching. Research on previous student cohorts (Holley et al 2004) report of students being unreflective, lacking motivation, being surface learners and unengaged with the learning process. Fear and a lack of self-confidence are also known to have a real impact on the student learning experience, and inhibit that learning. The unequal power relations of educational discourse can very easily reinforce negative self-perceptions (Sinfield, Burns & Holley 2004).

In an attempt to encourage students to engage more meaningfully with their course, a large, first-year cross campus core module was redesigned. The 'Studying Series' is a set of modules that all first year Business School students take. It underpins the transferable skills needed by students to their academic writing and writing within their discipline.

The Revised Learning Design

The teaching team considered how students could personalise their engagement with university life virtually. Collis & Moonen (2001) explore the meaning of the term 'virtual' as applied to University life, and within this paper, virtual applies in terms of mobility, where a student can stay at home (or another location of choice) to access materials. The new design aimed to erode the time and place barriers to formal study inside the classroom with more personalised access to materials outside the classroom, thus moving to an 'anytime anyplace anywhere' model of access (Goodyear 2006). The notion of a 'virtual' learning experience as part of the blend, was seen as critical to the success of the redesign.

The redesigned modules comprised a series of weekly lectures, attended by the whole student cohort and delivered in a traditional lecture theatre, linking the core disciplinary area with learning about the discipline. Weekly seminar activities were completely redesigned to be interactive, to scaffold the assessment tasks and to encourage students to form friendship groups. The most innovative intervention was the development of multimedia learning objects (RLOs), to support areas of the curriculum students found difficult. Four were developed initially, on Referencing Books, Referencing Journals, Referencing Websites and Reflective Writing. The RLOs were designed by the module tutor, working closely with students as part of a development team that included a multimedia developer, other tutors, and the RLO-CETL manager. The virtual presence of each module was realised through a supporting website, which had links to resources to accompany each teaching week (http://learning.londonmet.ac.uk/LMBS/study/lectnotes_marketing.htm) - please see week 4 as an example (the RLOs are listed as 'multimedia resources' for students).

The RLOs are developed in Adobe Flash, and incorporate rich multimedia and interactive techniques to both engage students and put them in control of their learning. They include interactive simulations, 3D graphics, animations, and in the case of Reflective Writing, audio clips and video interviews with past students to bring the subject matter to life. From initial introductions to the subject matter, animations are used to step through processes that need breaking down for

easier understanding, such as how to create a reference for text quoted in a report. Scaffolding is thus provided to help the students understand the topics that are being covered. The RLOs conclude with a set of self-test activities, in which students test their understanding of what they have covered. Reflective Writing includes a self-diagnostic questionnaire that enables students to identify their preferred learning style. They are all web-based, so that students can work through the objects in their own time and at their own pace, and they are designed so that they can revisit any part of the object at any time, such as to help understanding, or for revision at a later date. Figure 1 provides screen shots of examples of two of these RLOs. All RLOs produced by the RLO-CETL are freely available for educational use (http://www.rlo-cetl.ac.uk). Reflective writing is accessible at http://www.rlo-cetl.ac.uk:8080/rlo/reflective_writing/reflective_writing.html and Referencing Books at http://www.rlo-cetl.ac.uk:8080/rlo/referencing_books/v2/index.html.

The aim of the new learning design was to move along the PLE continuum to provide a more personalised learning experience, enabling students to engage flexibly with module materials at a time and place of their own choosing. Thus the students managed their individual learning development and blended their home and university learning activities in a way that was useful for them.

The Student Experience

In this section student evaluation data provides evidence of why and how students welcome the additional support of RLOs to aid their learning.

The first cohort of students taking the module incorporating the RLOs was asked to complete a questionnaire (15 were completed, representing 21% of the group). The profile of the students was typical of those taking the module: 80% were female and 20% male; 40% were aged between 18-20, 53% 21-25 and 7% 26-35. 13 students had access to the web at home, with the other 2 ac-

Figure 1. Screens from the Referencing Books and Reflective Writing RLOs

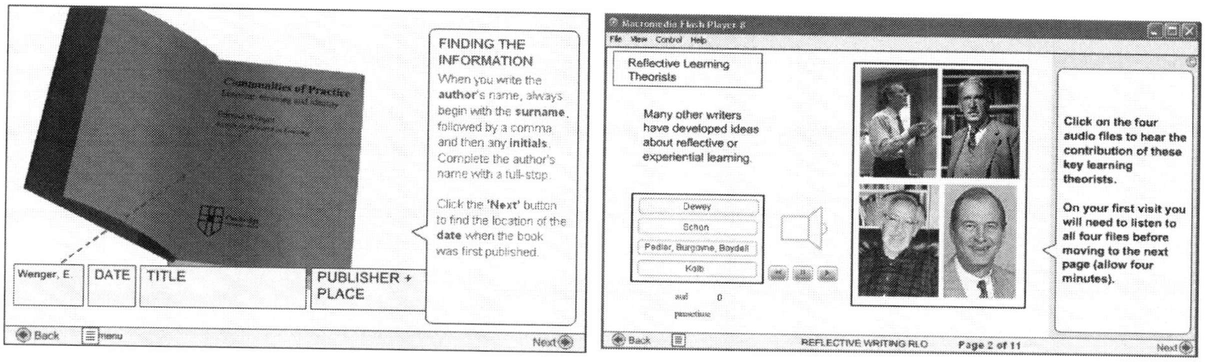

cessing from within the university or elsewhere. 87% (13) rated their confidence in using computers as high. No students reported technical problems accessing the learning objects.

The learning objects were well received by the students (see Table 1). The majority of students (87%) agreed that they enjoyed being able to learn on their own. A similar number (86%) agreed that they would like more of these learning objects in other modules, and 94% agreed that they would recommend the learning objects to other students with similar learning needs.

To ascertain more precisely what they like, they are asked to rate the importance of a number of attributes of the learning objects (see Table 2). 60% thought the visual components were important, 100% interactivity, 80% assessment/ self-test exercises, 100% access anytime, 93% access anywhere and 93% working at my own speed. The responses to the last 3 questions, that they could access the learning objects at any time,

from any where and work at their own speed were particularly important to the students. The majority rated 'very important' for each one, indicating the benefits that online learning objects can provide to allow flexible and personalised use.

We can tell by looking at when the RLOs are accessed (from the server log files) that students do adopt flexible learning patterns and access them at any time. For example, when the second cohort of students used the RLOs, 16% of accesses were made at weekends. Looking at the hours of the day they were accessed, 49% were made during the day between the hours of 9.00am and 6.00pm, showing that 51% of accesses were outside of these hours. Accesses were actually made in every hour of the day, including the early hours of the morning. Such figures give us evidence of when students are learning outside of their face-to-face teaching sessions.

Table 1. Student views on using the learning objects

Question	Rating (%)			
	Strongly agree	Agree	Disagree	Strongly dis-agree
I enjoyed being able to learn on my own	26.7	60	6.7	6.7
I would like more of these Learning Objects in other modules	29	57	14	0
I would recommend these Learning Objects to another person with similar learning needs	40	54	7	0

Table 2. Student views on the attributes of the learning objects

Please rate how the following attributes of the Learning Objects have contributed to your learning:	Rating (%)			
	Very important	Important	Not very important	Not at all important
Visual components (e.g. video, animations)	33	27	40	0
Interactivity	60	40	0	0
Assessment/self-test exercises	33	47	20	0
Access any time	67	33	0	0
Access any where	46.7	46.7	6.7	0
Working at my own speed	53	40	7	0

Student Personal Stories about Their Approach to Learning

A focus group was held with a later cohort of students to explore in more depth their use of and attitudes towards the learning objects. Because there were only 3 students (several dropped out at the last minute), each contributed in-depth views and opinions, and these have been extracted to produce a personal story for each student, which provides a valuable insight into their individual practice. It became apparent from their comments, that each student had a different approach to the learning objects and the way they study, and that this was affected by several factors, such as their character, their personal situation and their preferred way of learning. Note that student's names have been changed to preserve anonymity.

Hanna's Story

Hanna is female, a full-time mature student, and has children. She describes herself as not being very computer literate, and seems to lack confidence in her abilities as a student "for me it's very helpful at home. My husband says 'the only way you can learn is if you sit behind it and try and play with it', so that is what I do". She described the learning objects as 'very helpful' and liked the fact that they give guidance "I would say it's very helpful - because it's better when you know

how to do something than when you don't have any guidance at all – so it seems like a sort of guidance". She likes the fact that you can access the learning objects at any time and that at the University there are lots of computing facilities. But she accesses them more from home "for me I find that I can practice more at home whereas over here I feel a bit intimidated". She feels more comfortable at home, and can spend more time learning and understanding things.

She particularly liked the use of animations in the learning objects, saying "mm the animation, it breaks it up, you know and catches your eye, just in case you are about to fall asleep, I think it wakes you up! I think it's such a good idea." She would like LOs for other modules "it would be very useful and very helpful", as she finds some of the other teachers very challenging because of their teaching style, e.g. because she can't hear what they're saying, she feels she can't ask a lot of questions if she doesn't understand things or they don't make sure that you have understood. She says "Whereas if we have this online, that would guide you and that would go to explain further what they meant by whatever they were saying."

Joanne's Story

Joanne is a young female student, and rated herself as only having 'adequate' computer skills, although she talks later on about being confident with navigating through information. She has come straight to University after taking her 'A' levels. She described the learning objects as being "user friendly" and that "it backs up everything you say in the seminars and gives you more in-depth knowledge of what you need to know". She mainly used the objects for about 3-4 weeks in the middle of the Semester, for the duration of the coursework. She prefers to be able to access the learning objects from home "mainly because the IT studios are really hot and really slow". She says she has a short attention span, and often when she looks at learning objects she's more interested in the first half, and wants to get the basic information from them, saying "once I got the basic information and found out what I wanted, that was all I wanted to get from them really".

She didn't like the student interviews on video in Reflecting Writing, because "you know when you just want to get something done and I just don't think seeing other people's opinions of it, didn't really help me". She went on to say "sometimes they were a bit long", and "the point is that you want to get a basic knowledge so you can go on to do your own work or use the systems". She made several comments about the use of multimedia and interactivity in the learning objects. "I think that's one of the best, the strongest points about them is they're not just a block of text … "the pictures and the interactivity as well, is really, really good". She was probed about what it was about interactivity she liked, and she said "you can take out of it what you want", so it suits her learning style perfectly. "You can interact and click on this click on that and find out more information." She went on to say that she preferred the audio to the video. She likes online material that she can access when she needs to.

On having learning objects in other modules she says, "I think it would be really helpful say like it complements the course and if you didn't maybe perhaps understand quite what they were saying. Whereas, at school or college you can go

back to the teacher and say sorry I didn't quite get that. It's not really quite the same in university. You just have a lecture and you go."

Joanne doesn't like to learn by reading: "Personally, I find it very hard to read through textbooks, but I am trying! But I do find it very, very monotonous, especially when you have to read a whole chapter at a time … if I am set questions I maybe go to the questions at the end of the chapter because it helps me sort of focus and remember what I have learnt rather than just read it, and not take any of it in." When studying she starts with the computer "I'm very much with computers, yeah. And then I'll try and read as much as I can from the book … But, yeah, I always start with the computer and that's why I found the learning objectives [objects] so helpful last semester."

Mai's Story

Mai is a young female student from China. Her English isn't very fluent, and she is keen to practice regularly to develop her language skills. She rates her IT experience as 'good'. She found the Reflective Writing LO 'useful', because it helped her to improve her English, and the questionnaire helped her to know what she is good and bad at. She accesses the LOs more from home, and finds the University Internet connection really slow. "And also I don't need always to go to the teacher's office because they're busy; so I can learn it at home." She finds them an easily accessible form of help, which is there when she needs it. She thinks this module is good, because it's different from the others in its design and less "traditional", because of the module booklet, the QuickStart website card, the website and integration of the learning objects. She thinks that if things are different or use new ideas, that people are more likely to pay attention to them. She goes home after the lecture and seminar (which follow each other) and accesses the module website and online resources and reviews what was covered that day, saying "I can review it all".

She remarks that the way she likes to learn is a little different from the other two in the group "because I'm learning the subject but also I need to learn English". She had some advice from a school teacher who said don't study too much information, but practice everyday. She went on to say that "I am not interested in reading at all, I fall asleep. But I do like to practice something or like maybe answer a question. … and also I like creating something." She summarised by saying "what I'd like is to use a new idea of study". She agreed that she liked to use different kinds of learning "because it's interesting. If you always use the same way I think you're boring." She felt that the learning objects helped with that "yeah, yeah it's interesting. As I said it's different from another so it's made me interested." She liked the use of video in the learning objects "I think the video is good and helpful". She likes the fact that the learning objects are online and accessible any time "it's good because, maybe if someone's busy with their work or suddenly something happens and they can't go to the lecture. And after they go home the student can still check the information. It's good." Also, if you have a question or a problem that you can't ask about in a lecture, you can resolve it when you get home. She concluded, referring to the RLOs "And this one is good and exciting, it's not too traditional and it's new, it makes me pay attention, it's interesting."

Case Study 2: Reuse of the RLOs at TVU

The Thames Valley University (TVU) case study takes the notion of the personal learning agenda with formal learning in mind. The module in this case study follows a carefully constructed curriculum where the focus is on the student accessing subject content through a skills development process approach. This differs from the focus of the previous case study, which develops skills through the discipline. The RLOs and a supporting virtual learning environment (VLE) were introduced into an existing curriculum for a core foundation module 'Critical approaches to research and study in HE' which was designed to support progression and develop academic competence. The work reported here builds on the work of a previous investigation (Greaves 2007) that evaluated the effectiveness of a strategy designed to underpin academic competence in a Business Studies degree. This learning experience offered the students the opportunity to reach their individual personal 'threshold concept point' (Land op.cit). The purpose of embedding the RLOs within the scaffolded curriculum for non-contact activities was to explore possible further gains in learning and progression rates.

Adapting the Teaching Approach

In the original learning design a decision was made that students should be taught the required 'learning how to learn' skills through a structured approach (Harvey and Knight 1996). Previous studies (Greaves 2006, Greaves & Hadzic 2007) had shown that our inclusive entry policy was best supported by teaching our learners to engage effectively with subject content. We recognised our academic world as a complex and connected activity system (Cole 2005) which we should make visible for our students at point of entry. Using the notion of Vygotsky's 'zone of proximal development' (described in Cole 2005) to inform our curriculum design, critical academic competence activity is made explicit and practised by the learner. We suggest to the learner that entering a University is similar to entering a new country that they seek to belong to. An understanding of language, customs and local behaviours will facilitate a more successful experience and integration into community membership and belonging. We suggest that tutors are key members of this community and will be their personal guides to help them make a successful transition. This strategy is delivered through a transparent, shared and jointly tutor/student owned Learning Development Pathway (LDP).

In their first semester students enter the LDP, designed to ensure effective engagement and deep learning of skills required to underpin critical enquiry and effective academic writing. During the contact session students are introduced to a critical skill. They then deploy this skill independently within a subject based activity during their personal learning time. The activities are linked and developmental. Outputs from their independent activities are brought to contact sessions on a weekly basis. Students are supported to a level of deep understanding through timely and appropriate educational interventions given as formative feedback. Students are challenged on superficial and weak learning habits (e.g. cutting and pasting when asked to undertake a précis activity) and required to re-deploy the critical skills in a new activity. Previous findings indicated that while students understood these critical skills at the time of explanation, they faced challenges in subsequent independent applications. For example, they would understand how to undertake Harvard referencing during the session but then become confused when trying to apply it in an essay context. RLOs were introduced as a mechanism for addressing this problem.

The LDP assumes that linked technical skills underpin an ability to identify the relationship between procedural and declarative knowledge and to undertake the cognitive shift to conditional and functioning knowledge (Biggs 2003). The acquisition of academic competence does not necessarily guarantee an ability to critically enquire, however, the lack of certain technical and process skills and an understanding of the links between them will seriously impede progress and ability. The repeated developmental activities build links between key academic competencies, and thus encourage deep learning.

The Blended Learning Design

Having measured student learning gains as a result of engagement in the LDP in the previous year, findings indicated that while students understood these critical skills at the time of explanation, they faced challenges in subsequent independent applications. A need was identified for interactive support outside of contact sessions. RLOs were seen as a mechanism for addressing this problem. Blackboard was being used in the University for its eLearning platform 'TVU Online', it was supported by a central department, and was considered to be an ideal platform to integrate the online components within the module framework. Four multimedia learning objects developed by the RLO-CETL at London Met were selected to be incorporated within the module: Referencing Books, Referencing Journals, Referencing Websites and Reflective Writing (the same RLOs used in Case Study 1).

The RLOs were supplied to TVU and were embedded locally within Blackboard. The Blackboard VLE was designed to act as a repository of information and materials to support the module. It includes the basic module information with the aims and the learning outcomes, staff information, assessment details and marking criteria. The RLOs were integrated into the linked activities at the point in which they could help the students complete their weekly tasks and written assignments outside of the contact sessions. They thus directly supported the linked activities that the students were required to do. Homework questions provided in the contact sessions were posted into the VLE each week. In effect, everything that the students needed outside of their contact sessions to support the development of their academic competence and independent learning in their personalised learning activities was provided within the VLE.

The Student Experience

In this section we present some of the evaluation data gathered from the first student cohort (30+ students) that used this new blended learning design. For this first cohort of students it was important to find out if the students were using the VLE and RLOs and what they thought about them, to give us an indication of their effectiveness. If they did not use the VLE, they would not get the links through to the assignment details and accompanying RLOs. To explore these issues, a student evaluation session was held at the end of the module, attended by 17 students, who completed a questionnaire and took part in a focus group. Feedback also came from RLO feedback forms, and collectively provides evidence of why and how students welcome this additional support to aid their learning, and how it is making them become more independent as learners. Statistics from the VLE provide an insight into when students are choosing to do their learning, which is not confined to university hours, and indicates an extremely flexible approach to when they study. There is also a comparison of the student cohort from the previous year, which shows that the intervention of the RLOs and Blackboard VLE had an impact in improving students' learning (Greaves et al., 2008).

Student Use and Perceptions of the Effectiveness of the VLE and RLOs

The statistics from Blackboard provide evidence of the level of use of the VLE and when it was used. From the 30 students who were active in the module beyond Week 5, a total of 4,342 hits were made over the module duration (125 days). This indicates a substantial use of the Blackboard VLE by these students, with a mean average of hits per student of 145, but with the number of hits ranging amongst students from 0 for one student to 390 for another. Mondays saw the largest level of activity (943 hits, 22%) followed interestingly by Sundays (873 hits, 20%). Sunday would be the last chance that students had to complete their assignments for submission on Monday, which could explain this high level of activity. Face-to-face teaching took place on Monday, so students were evidently logging in before they handed in their work, or afterwards to prepare for the next assignment. Each hour of the day saw some Blackboard activity, even though between 03.00 a.m. and 04.00 a.m. only registered 2 hits. The highest activity was between 12.00 p.m. and 13.00 p.m. (9%), with most activity occurring between 11.00 a.m. and 20.00 p.m. However there was a reasonable amount of activity in the evenings up until midnight, and surprisingly between 01.00 a.m. and 02.00 a.m.

In the questionnaire all the students agreed that the Blackboard site was really useful (44% strongly agreed). Table 3 shows some of the comments made about Blackboard in the focus group, which illuminate their views. Students described it as being "good", "useful" and "helpful". It was helpful because "all the assignments are posted on Blackboard", "or if you need to see the question again without finding somebody or looking for papers, it's there". Several students mentioned the discussion board, which was good because it "allows you to get feedback from your classmates and teachers", you can ask others for help, and you can share ideas and resources. Several thought that "it helps you keep on track with your work", with some feeling that it is was helpful if you couldn't go to some of the classes, but a couple of students suggested that if attendance wasn't so important, they wouldn't go to classes and just use Blackboard.

Focusing in on the use of the RLOs, in the questionnaire, students indicated that online, any time access to the RLOs was valued; 87.5% of students agreed that they liked being able to access the RLOs at any time, any where. We probed into student's study patterns in the focus group. The majority accessed the RLOs from home, providing they had access to a PC and the Internet (not all

Table 3. Comments about Blackboard and how it helped with the module

Yeah, it's helpful
It's good.
All the assignments are posted on Blackboard so ...
And it allows you to get feedback from your classmates and teachers, the discussion board.
And, the discussion board, yeah, that's good.
Some questions are quite hard and then we'll just share ideas, like give links to good sites and stuff, so it's really useful.
It helps you keep on track with your work
Or if you need to see the question again without finding somebody or looking for papers, it's there.
I think Blackboard's so good that if attendance wasn't that important for the students, you can just deal with blackboard.
It's more like why go to a website, why not just use blackboard or the learning objects, and you can get all the information from there.

did). One student commented that those students that didn't, would use them at the University or in the library. They were asked which days of the week they tended to use them, and comments were expressed that they would use the RLOs after the classes when they started to do their assignment work, i.e. on Tuesdays and Thursdays, and then on Saturdays and Sundays before their assignment was handed in at the class on Monday morning.

Students said that all of the RLOs were useful in the questionnaire, with each having their individual preference about which they found most useful. 94% of the students agreed that the RLOs were really useful. All the students except one said that they used each RLO more than once, indicating that most students were referring back to the RLOs as the module progressed. When students were asked what they thought about the RLOs, the responses were that they were "easy to use", "easy to understand", "easy to navigate" and were "useful". Evidence that the students found the RLOs beneficial is illustrated by the fact that 94% of the students agreed that they would like RLOs in other modules. Table 4 below shows some of the comments made in the RLO feedback forms and the evaluation questionnaire about what they liked about the RLOs.

Some of the comments relate to the helpfulness and usefulness of the content, that they gave relevant and useful information and were not complicated. Many comments relate to the presentation of the content, that it was clearly explained, easy to understand, broken down into small steps and colourful. This led to "better understanding". Ease of use was also mentioned. One liked the audio in Reflective Writing, and another liked the interaction, indicating personal preferences about what helps them to learn. A dialogue that ensued between two students in the focus group illustrates how they particularly appreciated the RLOs. The first student thought that they were colourful and would help people with short attention spans, and because you're interacting with the object and creating a reference and getting feedback on the results, this will be easier for some people to understand. The second student said "they give you examples of it, if you looked at it in a book you wouldn't follow it at all", and that the objects show you what to do and how to do it. The first student when probed about what it was about interactivity that helped said "because you're actually like reading it then putting into practice what you're doing" and went on to say that the object shows you how to do the reference, and where to get the information from. This is important as the RLO is acting as the tutor in the student's PLE. Only three negative comments were given when they were asked about what they didn't like. These were that it needs to be explained a bit more and be more detailed, sometimes it was a

Table 4. What TVU students like about the learning objects

Referencing Books
The way it was presented, which was easy to use and understand.
Helpful to someone who is relatively new to the referencing world
Referencing Journals
The steps that it went through so you can get a better understanding.
Very helpful covers all aspects of referencing.
Referencing Websites
Very helpful thank you.
Easy to follow and understand.
Reflective Writing
The diagram at the end which showed areas on which I could improve on.
They had information available to what I needed for my work.
They were there to help.
They were easy to access and easy to use and easy to understand.
It explains everything clearly.

bit slow, and it could be slightly confusing to use, although we don't know precisely which RLOs they were referring to.

Student Learning and Progression

Student learning and progression has been compared with the previous cohort using baseline data, see Figures 2 and 3.

The original investigation in 2006-7 collected four written artefacts at three-week intervals. Us-

Figure 2. Cohort A (2006/07)

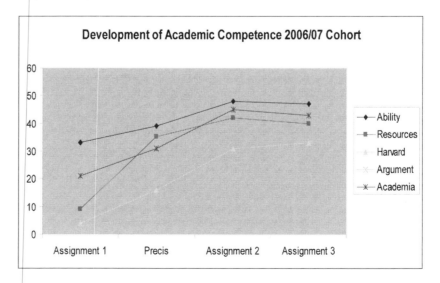

Figure 3. Cohort B (2007/08)

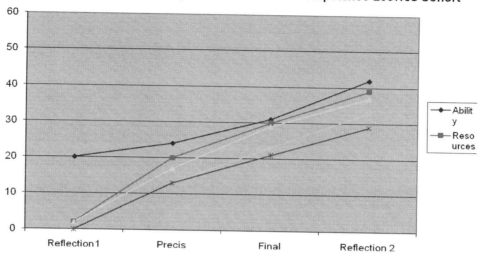

Development of Academic Competence 2007/08 Cohort

ing the learning outcomes denoted as key words – Ability (to identify and retrieve resources), Resources (select appropriate resources for a given purpose), Harvard (make effective use of resources in terms of referencing and citation), Argument (use subject material effectively to present and develop an argument), and Academia (conform to a recognized academic written level and standard) - each written assignment was graded using a Likert Scale of 1-5, with 1 as the lowest grade and 5 as the highest. Each student's progress was recorded as an individual chart. The collective findings of the members of the cohort who submitted work at the four formative assessment points and attended at least 80% of the taught sessions were then put into a table showing the cohort average. This approach was replicated for Cohort B in 2007/8. The sample for 2006/07 was composed of 10 students and the cohort for 2007/8 of 11. The age (19-25), ethnicity (Asian and Black African), and entry qualifications (no GCSE's, A' level or equivalent qualifications) profile of both cohorts was very similar. There was however a difference in the gender differential with a ratio of approximately 2:1 male/female in

2006 and 3:1 male/ female in 2007. The same tutor taught both groups and facilitated the LDP, the only change was the strategically introduced VLE and RLOs for Cohort B.

The above figures show that there are significant differences between the two cohorts. There is clear evidence of gradual and sustained development for Cohort B, who had the additional support of RLOs in their PLEs. Initially it appears that Cohort A have made more rapid progress, however, this is not the complete picture. What is not visible from the graphs in the progress made, is that Cohort A students during their experiential independent activities made use of 'cut and paste' as a mechanism for completing the work. A key part of the learning design is that flawed or superficial learning strategies should emerge so that they might be challenged. Cohort A's focus was on the artefact and not the process. Learning through doing is the key to the LDP and the first submission is the point at which the tutor deals with best academic practice in using resources, and the précis submission is the point where the tutor has the opportunity to raise issues of plagiarism.

When placed in the same learning design and undertaking the same learning activities, Cohort B was additionally asked to engage with specific RLOs to support their PLE learning activities. Interestingly they did not select 'cut and paste' as an assignment completion strategy. Their focus was on being able to articulate the process with less emphasis on the artefact. As a group, Cohort B worked co-operatively from the outset, selecting to undertake the online activities together. They were able to articulate and share with each other and the tutor their conceptual struggle in understanding the application of their new knowledge. Unlike Cohort A, who had to be challenged on superficial learning strategies and led to an understanding of the role of each of the competencies and the links between them, Cohort B demonstrated through their questioning and observations during the taught sessions that they were engaged in deep learning. For example, unlike cohort A who would use the contact sessions to ask predominantly 'how' questions (such as 'how do we do referencing?'), Cohort B would come in with the technical skill acquired through the RLO and ask the 'why' questions. Questions such as 'Why do we need to do referencing in the body of the text as well as the end?' led us to issues around citation, argument development, evaluation of appropriate sources and so forth.

This gradual 'coming to know' is reflected in the lower, yet more evenly distributed, scores of the précis assignment. Unlike Cohort A, who had staggered development in each of the areas, with development following only after a tutor intervention, Cohort B demonstrated all four areas of academic ability as developing simultaneously. As may be seen from Figure 3 this even development continued over the duration of the module. In stark comparison to Cohort A whose argument development was quite weak until the third assignment, Cohort B, although from a lower starting ability than Cohort A, were able to sustain a steadier and more rounded growth in their academic competence skills, particularly in argument development.

All 11 students in Cohort B indicated they had made use of the RLOs to inform preparations for assignment work. The original intention of using only RLOs was not possible, as by the third submission Cohort B students had searched for and made use of other online resources to support their learning that they had not been directed to. Additionally, although not directed to or tutor supported, by Week 6 Cohort B were also making use of the BlackBoard discussion area as an informal learning space to share findings. We can see here that from the 'safe' position of a scaffolded environment the learners were confident to harness web tools and materials and construct a wider PLE which was not tutor scaffolded or directed.

Both cohorts made good academic competence progression as a result of the LDP, however, the second cohort appeared to have a deeper and more coherent learning experience as a result of the introduction of the RLOs. Whilst we cannot claim this for certain, we do know from the extensive student evaluation of the project that both the VLE and the RLOs have been useful and helpful to the students, and that they have in fact made use of them. The VLE helped them to keep on track with their work as it acted as a central store of information and resources, and enabled them to collaborate and share ideas and resources with others (an unexpected outcome). Student comments about the RLOs indicate that they did use and value them. The intention was that the online learning environment and interactive RLOs would provide additional support for students, providing them with access when it was most useful and convenient. The evaluation has shown that this was in fact the case, and we are confident that our learning design has helped the students to succeed. Learning gain experiences like this can provide a learning design template for blended eLearning, regardless of the technology used to mediate learning.

Conclusions from the Two Case Studies

Coming powerfully through both Institutional case studies are very strong messages from the students that they like using the RLOs in their PLEs. Why? Top of the list is the ease of access and instant feedback. These were positive themes highlighted by both case study groups. Being able to repeat the exercises and check their own understanding through the interactive activities was a recurring topic in their feedback. Both groups indicated that they liked the RLOs as they were easy to navigate and allowed immediate practice of a skill. Having the power to select and decide when and where learning was to take place was clearly empowering and enabling for both London Met and TVU students.

This flexible approach to supporting learning fits well within the work/life needs of our students. Learners accessed the RLOs in multiple location contexts outside of the university between the taught sessions. The statistics indicated many students often repeated an exercise to gain deep understanding. This learning need is easily supported by the RLOs, effectively ensuring 'tutor' access whenever and how often a learner feels the need to check their understanding. It is the equivalent of having a 'tutor in their pocket' that will have the patience to explain the concept as many times as requested.

Students also like the multimedia components within the RLOs, with several commenting that they are attracted to and learn more effectively from certain media types (graphics, animations, video, audio), according to their individual preferences. Thus the RLOs contribute to increased personalised learning, as students can choose to learn from what suits them.

A key message for busy tutors is that the students liked being guided further in their learning 'out of hours'. Once designed into the curriculum the RLOs do the work for the tutor in developing the understanding and application of the concept.

The tutor is then able to concentrate on checking the quality of learning that is occurring. The ease with which the RLOs can be utilised by tutors means that this high quality curriculum enhancement is readily available for embedding into existing curriculums. The generic skill RLOs are particularly well designed for easy transferability across disciplines. This is particularly important within the emerging employer/work-focused/work-based learning agenda for two key reasons. Firstly the student can combine their learning with their work and personal needs, enabling them to determine when and where they undertake their learning; secondly curriculum designers can move rapidly to respond to the changing needs of employers in the design of negotiated courses. Key to this is that although the students are able to personalise their individual learning it is within a carefully scaffolded experience, which is designed, supported and monitored by the tutor.

FUTURE OF PLEs AND RLOs: MOBILE TECHNOLOGY

Many educators and parents have been sceptical, until now, about the value of mobile devices in learning. However, the educational potential enabled by these devices – especially when used in combination with social networking applications – are significant (Knell, 2009). Mobile devices that belong to the learner are in some ways an obvious choice for acting as a platform for a PLE. Furthermore, in the introduction we pointed out that we view reusable learning objects as being able to provide bite-sized scaffolding for learning and that they can be seen as one of the building blocks for the PLE, which we conceived as a loosely coupled set of tools and resources. This is particularly important in the light of emerging evidence that the kind of critical and reflective thinking we wish to encourage in HE may not be happening when users access the Internet. For example, a report commissioned by JISC and the

Figure 4. Different types of mobile learning support

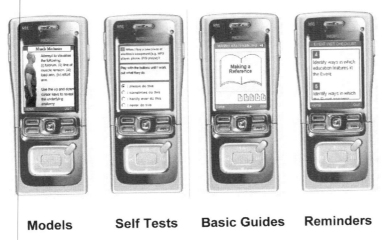

Models   **Self Tests**   **Basic Guides**   **Reminders**

British Library (UCL, 2009) counters the common assumption that the 'Google Generation', i.e. young people born or brought up in the Internet age, as being the most adept at using the web. The report claims that although "young people demonstrate an ease and familiarity with computers. They rely on the most basic search tools and do not possess the critical and analytical skills to assess the information that they find on the web." Indeed, a recent report for Becta (2008) on Web 2.0 and social software usage found that there are "only a few embryonic signs of criticality, self-management and meta-cognitive reflection".

In anticipation of this trend over the past 3 years the CETL for Reusable Learning Objects has explored the utility of making mobile learning objects that can be used by the learner as elements of their PLE that can be accessed via a mobile device. We have started to repurpose the study skills RLOs described in the case studies above for use on mobile phones, and this really offers the students the ultimate experience in personalisation. Briefly, in our exploratory work, a selection of the 200+ internet based RLOs that the CETL has produced have been developed for mobile phones and have been evaluated with consistently positive results (see Bradley et al. 2007; Smith et al, 2007). For example, in a pilot

evaluation of the 'self-tests' and 'basic guides' shown in Figure 4 below, Bradley et al. (2007) found that there were indications from students that they would use mobile learning objects: 83% would find it useful to be able to access learning materials on their mobile. Frequently raised comments were that they welcomed the idea of having learning resources that were convenient to use, in the sense that because they always have their phone with them, they could do some learning in what was referred to as 'dead time', such as whilst travelling, having lunch or where there is no access to computers.

Whilst we acknowledge that the number of students involved in this preliminary initial evaluation (Cook et al., 2007) is small (n=7), there were however, indications from students that they would use mobile learning objects. One said about the learning objects on the phone "I love them ... I can see so many different uses". One thought it was "a good idea" as you could look at something you needed to on the way home from University. Another said "I think it's got a lot of potential. I would definitely use it if it was applicable to my course."

Possible criticisms of the RLO approach when applied to the mobile phone include that it simply replicates the desktop experience; it is simply extending traditional pedagogic practice, and not taking advantage of the ability of mobile devices to enhance context-to-context learning or indeed conversations across contexts (Sharples, Taylor and Vavoula, 2006). However, one advantage of the RLO approach is that it provides rich, bite-sized learning that can be used outside and inside the classroom to reinforce learning. The design of these mobile learning objects is not simple (see Bradley et al.) and sound is used more in the mobile versions in order to avoid having lots of text on a small sized screen. Indeed, this approach allows learners to take a 'proxy' of the teacher off-site with them as they engage in a field-study learning task. For example, in Figure 4 the 'Reminders' resource was used in a recent study (Cook, Pachler and Bradley, 2007) where learners went into the field to gather content with smartphones for an assignment with the 'Reminders' RLO on their phones which provided scaffolding for the learning task.

Mobile devices have a number of unique educational affordances such as increasing portability, functional convergence of technological devices, social interactivity, context sensitivity, connectivity and individuality. Consequently they provide an ideal platform for a PLE for HE; put quite simple nearly all of our students already own their own mobile phones which are increasingly becoming more sophisticated (more like handheld computers). Our initial evaluations show that students carry their phones with them and use them any time, any place and that the students value resources that enable them to study without time and space limits, when they want to be able to learn. This work is starting to explore the affordances of social interactivity, connectivity, or individuality. Issues surrounding interoperability of different phones types and service providers are proving a barrier for scalability. However, this work is still at the early stages but we feel it holds great potential.

Emerging issues from the work described above are significant from the perspective of personalised learning. A key question is: what indicators should be used when flagging personalisation in terms of learner preferences? These could include media options, ease of use and quickness, self-tests, feedback; however, all these may not be provided in lectures/seminar environment (e.g. feedback). Consequently it is important to enable a range of delivery methods if the goal is to deliver greater personalisation where students can choose what suits them. This has implications for practitioners and institutions alike, who need to plan and design the services and tools available in the PLE; they also need to provide interoperability with tools, resources and services, for example phones, iPods, PDA's, that are 'already out there' and that may emerge over the coming years. This is a none-trivial task! Another key issue is the interactivity, design and structure of RLOs; they need to enable ease of 'taking what you want' at the point in time in which you want it. A third key issue surrounds the combination of different media used in the RLOs to suit individual's preferences according to how they like to learn and learn more effectively. Our evidence base on this is growing, and this paper contributes to this, but more work is needed. However, what is clear is that if the rhetoric surrounding personalised learning and PLEs is to move on then systematic work like that described above should become the rule and not the exception.

CONCLUSION

This chapter explores the metaphor of any time, any place, any where, personalised learning. We compared the findings from two institutions, looked at the lessons learned and examined the contribution that blended learning and learning objects can make to increased personalised learning opportunities for HE students.

The first study found that students have a different approach to the learning objects and the way they study, and that this was affected by several factors, such as their character, their personal situation and their preferred way of learning. For example, for Hanna, the learning objects are very helpful as they give guidance and provide extra help if she doesn't understand something. She likes online, anytime access, as she can access them when she wants, and in the comfort and privacy of her own home. She likes reading from textbooks, but likes the animations in the learning objects, as they break up the learning material and keep you interested. Furthermore, the evaluation data from the first case study provided the unexpected result regarding the degree to which RLOs facilitate more flexible study patterns and provide options for students to take control of their learning and implement a greater degree of personalised learning than they would have had from the previous and more traditional model of on-campus lectures and seminars. The second case study at TVU conducted a comparison of the student cohort from the previous year who had studied within a carefully scaffolded contact curriculum, and showed that the intervention of additional scaffolded non-contact learning with the RLOs and VLE also had an impact in improving students' learning. Both cohorts in this second case study made good academic competence progression, however, the second cohort appeared to have a deeper and more coherent learning experience as a result of the introduction of the RLOs. They also demonstrated that when scaffolded in their learning they were confident to step outside of the scaffold, and appropriate digital tools and media for themselves to meet their own emerging PLE needs.

Coming powerfully through both Institutional case studies are very strong messages from the students that they liked using the RLOs as they were easy to navigate and allowed immediate practice of a skill. A key message for busy tutors is that the students liked being guided further in their learning 'out of hours'. The students in the first case study draw down RLOs and other online materials to meet their individual needs. By way of contrast, case study two students had very little flexibility and autonomy in terms of materials to be accessed. However, these students reached their threshold concept point, evidenced by their exploration of online materials outside the module and bringing these inside the module – thus personalising the blend of the formal and informal learning spaces in a way that was unique for the individual. The learning design is the significant factor in both cases studies. The students enjoy the freedom and flexibility of any time, any where, any place learning; however, it is the scaffolded approach that achieves a richer and more effective and deeper learning experience. Supporting the individual to their threshold concept point enables the individual to embark confidently on a personal journey of effective selection and appropriation of digital tools and media for the design (Cook op cit) of their personalised learning environments for the transferability of learning to their future studies.

We concluded with a section on plans to extend this work more informally to facilitate learning 'any where', through the incorporation of learning objects that can be used on mobile phones in the context of our notion of a PLE for HE. We contend that our vision of personalised learning, where RLOs are available from the Internet or from a learner's own mobile phone, is a productive working example of personalisation that is transferable across multiple institutions' platforms, subject areas and curriculum delivery models.

ACKNOWLEDGMENT

The learning objects described in this chapter were produced by a team of people that also included Richard Haynes, Carl Smith and Martin Agombar.

REFERENCES

Attwell, G. (2008). *Social Software, Personal Learning Environments and the future of Education.* Keynote presentation at the Conference on Web 2.0, University of Minho, Braga, Portugal, October 10th. Retrieved October 23, 2008, from http://www.pontydysgu.org/wp-content/uploads/2008/09/portplesfin.doc

Biggs, J. (2003). *Teaching for Quality Learning at University,* (2nd Ed.). Berkshire, UK: Open University Press.

Boyle, T., & Cook, J. (2001). Towards a pedagogically sound basis for learning object portability and re-use. In G. Kennedy, M. Keppell, C. McNaught & T. Petrovic (Eds.) *Meeting at the Crossroads. Proceedings of the 18th Annual Conference of the Australian Society for Computers in Learning in Tertiary Education,* (pp. 101-109). Melbourne: Biomedical Multimedia Unit, The University of Melbourne. Retrieved August 18, 2008, from http://www.ascilite.org.au/conferences/melbourne01/pdf/papers/boylet.pdf

Bradley, C., Haynes, R., Cook, J., Boyle, T., & Smith, C. (2009). *Chapter 8 Design and Development of Multimedia Learning Objects for Mobile Phones.* In M. Ally (ed). *Mobile Learning: Transforming the Delivery of Education and Training,* Athabasca University Press.

Bradley, C., Haynes, R., Smith, C., Cook, J., & Boyle, T. (2007). *Multimedia Learning Objects for Mobiles.* Mobile Learning, 5-7 July 2007, Lisbon, Portugal.

Cole, M. (2005). Putting Culture in the middle. In H. Daniels, (ed). *An Introduction to Vygotsky,* (2nd Ed.). Routledge: London.

Collis, B., & Moonen, J. (2001). *Flexible learning in a digital world: Experiences and expectations.* Kogan Page: London.

Cook, J. (2009). *The Digitally Literate Learner and the Appropriation of New Technologies and Media for Education.* Inaugural Lecture, Learning Technology Research Institute, London Metropolitan University, 3 February 2009. Retrieved February 4, 2009, from http://www.slideshare.net/johnnigelcook

Cook, J., Pachler, N., & Bradley, C. (2008). Bridging the Gap? Mobile Phones at the Interface between Informal and Formal Learning. *Journal of the Research Center for Educational Technology,* Spring. Retrieved September 23, 2008, from: http://www.rcetj.org/?type=ci&id

Goodyear, P. (2006). Technology and the articulation of vocational and academic interests: reflections on time space and e-learning. *Studies in Continuing Education, 28*(2), 83–89. doi:10.1080/01580370600750973

Greaves, L. (2006). *Developing Student Academic Competence: an investigation of curriculum designed to support progression and achievement.* TQEF Funded Project, Thames Valley University.

Greaves, L. (2007). Developing Student Academic Competence: the successes. *Faculty of Professional Studies Learning and Teaching Journal,* 4.

Greaves, L., Bradley, C., & Cook, J. (2008). A Blended Learning Design to Support Student Learning. In *Proceedings of World Conference on Educational Multimedia, Hypermedia and Telecommunications* 2008 (pp. 4643-4651). Chesapeake, VA: AACE.

Greaves, L., & Hadzic, V. (2007). *Developing Student Academic Competence: a longitudinal investigation progression and achievement.* TQEF Funded Project, Thames Valley University.

Harvey, L., & Knight, P. (1996). *Transforming Higher Education.* Buckingham, UK: SRHE/Open University Press.

Holley, D., Andrew, D., & Pheiffer, G. (2004). Exploring the usefulness of new technology with new students: a case study. *Investigations in university teaching and learning, 2*(1), Summer. JISC, (2007). *In their own words: Exploring the learner's perspective on e-learning.* Retrieved October 12, 2008 from http://www.jisc.ac.uk/intheirownwords

Knell, G. E. (2009). *Pockets of Potential: Using Mobile Technologies to Promote Children's Learning*, Joan Ganz Cooney Center. Retrieved January 10, 2009 from http://joanganzcooneycenter.org/publications/index.html

Land, R., Meyer, J. H. F., & Smith, J. (Eds.). (2008). *Threshold Concepts within the Disciplines.* Rotterdam: Sense Publishers. Meyer, J. H.F. & Land, R. (2005). Threshold concepts and troublesome knowledge (2):Epistemological considerations and a conceptual framework for teaching and learning. *Higher Education, 49*(3), April, 373–388. *RLO-CETL website* (n.d.). Retrieved August 18, 2008, from http://www.rlo-cetl.ac.uk

Sharples, M., Taylor, J., & Vavoula, G. (2006). A Theory of Learning for the Mobile Age. In *The Sage Handbook of EL-earning Research* (pp. 221-247). Retrieved October 7, 2008, from http://telearn.noe-kaleidoscope.org/openarchive/browse?resource=215_v1&back=%2Fstats%2Flast_week_popular_publications.php

Sinfield, S., Burns, T., & Holley, D. (2004). Outsiders looking in or insiders looking out? Widening participation in a post 1992 University. In J. Satterwaite, E. Atkinson, & W. Martin, (Eds.), *The Disciplining of Education: new languages of power and resistance,* (pp. 137-152). Trentham, Stoke on Trent UK.

Smith, C., Bradley, C., Holley, D., Cook, J., & Haynes, R. (2007). Learning objects and blended learning designs for the net generation. In *Second International Blended Learning Conference, University of Hertfordshire*, June 14, 2007.

UCL. (2009). *Information Behaviour of the Researcher of the Future. Executive Summary.* Ciber Briefing Paper for JISC and the British Library. Retrieved January 10, 2009 http://www.jisc.ac.uk/media/documents/programmes/reppres/gg_final_keynote_11012008.pdf

Van Harmelen, M. (2007). *Personal Learning Environments*. Retrieved December 23, 2008 http://octette.cs.man.ac.uk/jitt/index.php/Personal_Learning_Environments

Chapter 17

Into the Great Wide Open:
Responsive Learning Environments for Personalised Learning

Dirk Thißen
IMC (UK) Learning, UK

Volker Zimmermann
IMC AG, Germany

Tilman Küchler
IMC AG, Germany

ABSTRACT

Personalisation is a key requirement to motivate learners to use learning technology and self-paced content. Whereas most research and technologies focus on personalisation of content, this paper focuses on the personalisation of the tools and platform technologies for learning. When designing a learning environment, most organisations worked in the past on their internal business processes and content but did not focus on what the learner really does with the learning tools the organisation provided to them. Changing the perspective to the user shows, that they create today "around the organisational solutions" their own technology-enhanced learning world using a whole set of technologies: Learning management system (LMS) of the company, learning management system of a further education institution or of a university, different social network platforms, search engines, open web services in the internet like blogs or wikis, and a lot more other applications. Therefore the challenge for organisations today is how they can manage this variety of technologies by also enforcing the creativity and motivation of the users to personalise and individualise their learning environment. This paper proposes a solution by describing an architecture for a responsive and open learning environment. It delivers examples and a procedure how such a solution can be built step-by-step. The approach can be used in schools, higher education institutions, corporations or further education institutions.

DOI: 10.4018/978-1-60566-884-0.ch017

INTRODUCTION

Since Sidney Pressey, who was first to use "intelligent" machines for educational purposes in 1926 (Pressey, 1926), and Benjamin Bloom (Bloom, 1984), who argued that the most effective way of teaching is one-on-one tutoring, the idea of personalized tutoring has been in the focus of psychological, pedagogical, and didactic theory and practise, particularly with respect to technology-enhanced learning. Intelligent and adaptive educational systems have attempted to support the learner and the teacher by providing meaningful, relevant, and appropriate educational content. Over the past years, research and development in the area of intelligent and adaptive educational systems has made significant progress and the evolution of such technology – including their psycho-pedagogical foundations – proceeds continuously. In the focus of existing approaches to intelligent and adaptive learning is the content: Adaptivity particularly refers to personalised presentation of contents and adaptive navigation through the contents.

One crucial aspect of personalisation and adaptation to the learners, their preferences and needs is largely untouched by current educational technology: the personalisation of the entire learning environment, its components, tools, and functionalities. The broad range of different demands – digital natives versus technological novices, learners preferring strong guidance versus learners preferring a large degree of freedom, mass-individualisation (in a company) vs. the needs of very specific individuals (e.g., apoplexy patients) – and the dynamics of demands over time, ultimately requires such higher-level approaches to adaptivity and adaptability. Additionally, an appropriate balance between system controlled, self-controlled, and peer/teacher-controlled environments contributes to that requirement.

Moreover, there is a significant change – a "perfect storm" (Vice-Chancellor of the UK Open University) happening in educational technology.

This change is essentially driven by the strong use of learning management systems in corporate as well as higher education environments, but nowadays also driven by Web 2.0-developments, where learners increasingly create their own content (e.g., in WIKIs).

The pattern is of a shift from "push for learning" (the dominance of organisation-driven models of learning) to "pull for learning" (a learner-driven demand for informal and lifelong learning, in which learners control what they learn, how they learn it, and with whom).

Simple peer-to-peer networks between virtual learning environments (VLE) have not solved these questions in the past. There is a need to enable the learner to mashup the services in his/her personal learning environment (either on social network technologies or within collaboration and portal platforms in an enterprise setting). There is a need to integrate the technology into the whole application scenario of corporations or higher education institutions, where the LMS controls the processes in a form, that the learner can adapt and personalize his own scenario in combination with Web 2.0 technologies and other learning resources as well as open content.

This is of particular relevance in the critical lifelong learning transition phases when inhomogeneous groups of learners are treated in a one-size-fits-all way since there is no way to respond to their individual strengths and weaknesses. Even worse, in such transition phases learners are typically required to become accustomed to working with an entirely new VLE.

At this point, promising starting points for innovation in learning technology occur. One of the main question is how to enable the individual learner as well as groups of learners to adapt the learning environment to their very specific needs and, more importantly, how to enable the system to adapt its functionalities and components to the very concrete and individual demands concerning learning environment and learning strategies.

And yet, there is a need to go even a step further beyond such novel perspectives on personalisation and adaptation in educational technology. In the future, it is necessary to enable the individual learner or groups of learners to generate (to mashup) new components and functionalities on the basis of existing web-based software tools, so-called web services.

This vision is quite ambitious. On the one hand, the technological realization must allow 'non-technicians' to generate new tools and functionalities. This necessarily includes the need for research regarding adaptive learner support for service composition and orchestration of adaptive tools (what may be called meta-responsiveness), including support and motivation regarding 'learning how to learn'. While the so-called "digital natives" are utilizing many aspects of technology to support their learning, inexperienced learners need suitable support. On the other hand, technological research and development must ground on psycho-pedagogical theories of intelligent and adaptive education, learning psychology, and sound didactic principles and strategies. Moreover, aspects of self-regulated learning must be considered particularly in this context.

Therefore, we will discuss a framework for personalization in this document, which will provide learners with adaptivity and personalisation of their own learning environment, the used tools and functionalities. The framework is being researched within the context of the European Project ROLE – Responsive Open Learning Environments (EU IST Program FP 7 – Technology enhanced Learning).

From a technical point of view, such a framework does not have to bring all learning tools and technologies into one infrastructure – as it is the approach of service-oriented architectures or peer-to-peer-integration of technologies. There is strong need for a flexible composition of technologies by the end user in the sense of mashing-up learning tools and technologies at the 'clients' side (Zimmermann, Faltin 2006). The vision is

to combine the best features of virtual learning environments in one 'bundle', further called a "responsive open learning Environment". The responsive open learning environment will federate the best open tools, most practical functionalities from an learning management system and best open content by using webservices and loosely coupled systems that integrate into a very flexible solution. "Best" means "best" for an individual learner or a specified group of learners.

BASELINE CONCEPTS

When discussing to build an open virtual learning environment, the state-of-the-art of key baseline concepts must be analysed. In this chapter, we give a short overview on the core baseline concepts on which a personal learning environment will be built upon.

Learning Technologies

Taking a look at today's technologies used to build a virtual learning environment, a large variety of different software systems and components are being used depending on the learning processes that organisations aim to support. Figure 1 contains the most important software tools and platform components.

Learning Management Systems (LMSs) are in a modern virtual learning environment the core (Grohmann et al., 2007). They take over the role of integrating the different technologies into a common learning infrastructure. They are the mainstream technology and prevalently used in the educational context, as examined for a large number of European institutions by (Paulsen, 2003). Arising from so-called course management systems and emerged to web-based and didactic-aware eLearning systems, LMSs primarily focus on the management of learning and training processes, distributing the learning content, supporting the learning process, and serv-

Figure 1. Technologies within a personal learning environment

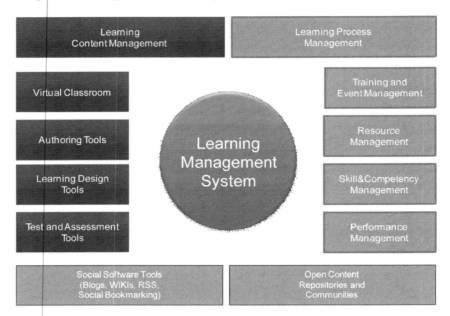

ing as general communication point and interface between learner and teacher (Helic, 2006). Using an LMS, the organisation collects data to enable decisions in order to create better learning, to fulfil compliance needs and to manage an efficient education and training business. No other technology allows a teacher to support learners in such a structured, systematic way, driven by learning objects (Kraemer et al., 2007).

Integral parts of an LMS are content management components and learning process management components. The content management enables an organisation to manage a large scale of different learning objects, to reuse and repurpose them in different courses or learning settings. The process management allows the organisation to manage the workflows and business processes such as booking of courses, notifications to inform learners and teachers about events or learning activities, setting up a learning process / syllabus and run training programs.

On the instructional designer side and to share or create content, a lot of tools are available. Virtual classroom tools support activities of synchronous learning like sharing of workspaces and resources as well as live discussions between different participants. Authoring tools allow to create and to publish content using standard technology to integrate the result of the creation process into the platforms (e.g. SCORM). A differentiation between recording tools where a learning object is created through recording a live lecture or class, and constructive authoring tools, where the content is created by special media designers and programmers including the development of simulation or animations in order to build an interactive learning object. Test and Assessment systems allow to create exercises, to integrate them into tests and to run tests in order to proof the knowledge and certify people for a specific knowledge level.

On the organisational side, many additional components extend a learning environment. Training and event management systems support the management of onsite training events, such as administrating participants, waiting lists, confirmation lists and cancellation of class participations. Resource management systems help to optimize the resources needed to execute training and education, such as rooms administration, reservation and booking of trainer resources, ensuring, that all training resources such as projectors and overhead are available etc. Skill and competency management systems allow to describe as-is- and planned-skills of persons as well as skill and competency profiles for job roles. They support a skill-gap-analysis in order to create a competency and training plan for people according to the course offering in the LMS. Performance management systems help to track the learning outcome of people through courses, link the training with evaluations and 360 degree feedback in order to create content that leads to higher performance of an employee.

Collaborative, social and informal learning plays more and more an important role within a virtual learning environment. WIKIs, Blogs, Search Functionality, RSS-Feeds etc. help to support learners by sharing and creating knowledge, either within a course or in a self-organised form. Social Network systems and open content platforms support the exchange of information, knowledge and learning objects, interlink people around content and create networks of common interest. Either these objects are standing-alone technologies in the web 2.0, integrated through mash-ups or they are integral part of an LMS.

A modern Personal Learning Environment (PLE) nowadays can be built on the technology of an LMS using an integration technology to interlink the technologies. Also integration to HR management systems (in corporations) or campus management systems (in higher education) is being done. Modern LMS systems allow a natural and learner-centric approach and is characterised by the freeform use of a set of lightweight services and tools that belong to and are controlled by individual learners. On the one hand, such a system integrates different services with application logic, the idea is to provide the learner with a plethora of different services and hand over control to her to select and use the services the way she deems

fit. Such a VLE (virtual learning environment) or PLE (personal learning environment) driven approach does not only provide personal spaces, which belong to and are controlled by the user, but also offers a social context by offering means to connect with other people for effective knowledge sharing and collaborative knowledge creation (Chatti et al., 2007). A PLE build on LMS will be a composition of subsystems, e.g. collaboration technology, test and assessment technology (Van Harmelen, 2006; Wilson et al., 2006) – as described above.

An example for an LMS that can be used to build a PLE and integrated into an organisational infrastructure is the software CLIX shown in figure 2. A course design consists of a combination of formal learning processes with community and social learning tools as well as virtual classroom.

LMSs are getting more and more open and extensible, allowing developers to integrate new learning functionality and allowing to integrate the functions into employee portal or collaboration systems. Despite their popularity, LMSs are criticised for their focus on supporting learning management, which often results in behavioural approaches to learning (Schulmeister, 2002). But – as explained above – the integration of social learning technology has proven, that this is not anymore true. Moreover, in an LMS-driven approach, a strong emphasis is being placed on how to centralise and standardise the learning experience. All learning activities and materials in an LMS-based course are organised and managed by and within a managed system which is driven by the needs of the institution and consequently often not adopted by the learners. This is a future challenge.

Open Content

The term of Open Content (OC) is not yet clearly defined and can be misunderstood. Open Content in a narrow sense denotes sharable and re-usable content for the purpose of learning, education

Figure 2. Course design within an LMS system (sample: CLIX)

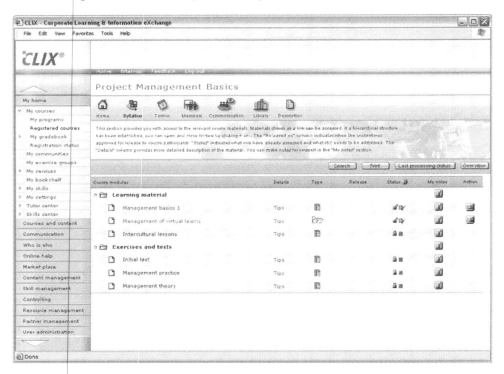

and training. However, a variety of content can be used for educational purposes: Besides ELearning modules a huge amount of content for knowledge management purposes is available on the internet. In Communities of Practice (CoP), users share their knowledge on specific fields (Lave & Wenger, 1991, Reimann, 2007). They do not solely provide documents or information but work in a common field towards a common goal (e.g., problem solving).

Therefore, Open Content can be seen as shared, distributed, and re-used content by stakeholders for educational and knowledge management purposes (Küchler et al., 2008). Open content in the field of ELearning can significantly improve the access to content by learners, content providers and other stakeholders (Attwell, 2005, Vuorikari, 2004). Open content must be re-usable, accessible, interoperable to allow stakeholders to re-use open content – if this condition is met, open content can initiate a community-based, cooperative produc-

tion process leading to an exponential increase of content – similar success stories can be found in the field of open source software (Baldi et. al, 2002) or open access publishing (Björk, 2004).

However, currently only very few stakeholders use this opportunity. Therefore it is necessary to adopt and evaluate Open Content Models regarding their potentials for knowledge sharing, knowledge distribution and business models.

Several communities provide open content for different purposes. The MIT OCW Open Courseware project in the USA and several US universities provide their content freely available via the web. It can be argued that this content provision is done for marketing purposes as a degree from those high-profile universities is the main attraction to students, not the content itself. However, many European universities have formed communities sharing and distributing content using Creative Commons licenses (Creative Commons, 2002). One major initiative is the Open Content initiative OpenLearn (McAndrew, 2006) by the Open University UK. Other initiatives which mainly provide repositories to share OER are EducaNext, SLIDESTAR, Ariadne, Gateway to Educational Material, Merlot or the JISC Collections (cf. OECD, 2007, Geser, 2007).

A business-oriented activity for user-generated Open Content has been started recently as web 2.0 community service under the name SLID-ESTAR. The objective is to allow professors and students to publish and share eLectures and lecture resources free-of-charge. Figure 3 shows a screenshot of SLIDESTAR. The users sees a preview of the content that fits to a specific topic and can access and view this content directly from the portal. If the content is a recorded eLecture, the user is able to listen to the eLecture immediately without download. Another focus is to create a social network between these stakeholders by linking related content and support the evaluation of lectures by the students themselves.

It is expected that open content activities will impact the quality and excellence of teaching by creating more transparency and benchmarking possibilities as well enabling a stronger person-alisation and individualisation of the learning process through solving the bottleneck of content availability.

Instructional Design

The general aim of educational systems is to help and assist learners in acquiring and improving certain skills. Instructional design is the concep-tional definition of the process how to teach the learner containing a description of which activities have to be performed by learners and instructors. The result of the instructional design is a syllabus containing learning activities (self-paced, onsite, collaborative, etc.) in a specific sequence under specific conditions such as learning outcome.

To take into account various characteristics of learners and to overcome the traditional one-size-fits all approach, research in technology-enhanced

learning over the last years focused on realising the concept of personalisation in technology-enhanced learning as key instructional design paradigm. The idea is to be able to personalize a standard syllabus to the specific needs of a single learner.

In educational systems personalisation is strongly related to the adaptation of the system's behaviour to a learner's characteristics, for ex-ample a learner's goals/tasks, knowledge, back-ground, hyperspace experience, and preferences (Brusilovsky, 2001).

Generally, there are three main types of adapta-tion within instructional design:

- adaptation on content level - adaptive presentation support (De Bra et al., 1999; Hohl et al., 1996),
- adaptation on link level - adaptive naviga-tion support, (Brusilovsky, 1999; Conlan et al., 2002; DeBra, 1997, 1998), and
- adaptation on problem solving level - adap-tive problem solving support (Brusilovsky, Schwartz & Weber, 1996).

Self-Regulated Learning

Self-regulated learning has become increasingly important in educational and psychological re-search as well as instructional design. The tenor is to give the learner a greater responsibility and control over all aspects of technology-enhanced learning, e.g. (Kay, 2001), which is beneficial for their actual learning outcomes (Steffens, 2006). Another reason is seen in the advance of life-long learning, and thus, of non-academic learning environments, where instead of instructor- and teacher-orientation more learner-orientation is requested (Steffens, 2006).

However, although there has been a lot of re-search on self-regulation in areas of metacognition, motivation and evaluation/feedback, there are still only a few models trying to integrate results into a complete model of self-regulated learning. Among

Figure 3. Open content repositories like SLIDESTAR - an important technology for social learning

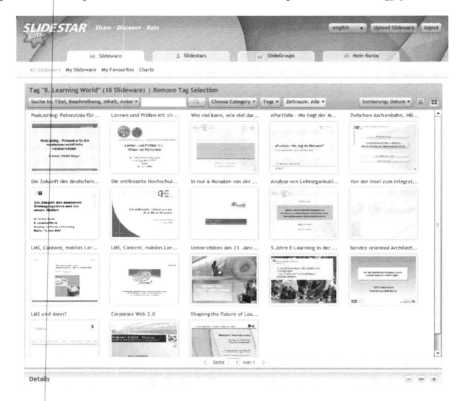

the proposed models are the Model of Adaptable Learning (e.g. Boekarts, 1997, 1999), the Process-oriented Model of Metacognition (e.g. Borkowski, 1996), the General Framework for Self-Regulated Learning (Pintrich, 2000, 2004), the Four-Stage Model of Self-Regulated Learning (Winne, 2001) as well as the Social Cognitive Model of Self-Regulation (Zimmerman, 1998, 2000). Most of these models deal with self-regulation as a process that involves goal setting and planning, monitoring and control processes, as well as reflection and evaluation processes.

The need to reflect and promote self-regulated learning in technology environments requires the development of highly sophisticated technology. To date some efforts have been made to build learning systems that integrate tools for fostering processes of self-regulation. Four broad categories of pedagogical tools have been identified (Dabbagh & Kitsantas, 2004): web-based hypermedia

tools (e.g. search engines, use of browsers), web-based multimedia tools (e.g. applications that enable the viewing of non-html files in a browser), collaborative and communication tools (e.g. email, chat, discussion forums, audio and videoconferencing tools), and content creation and delivery tools (e.g. html editors, authoring tools). Among key self-regulatory processes that are targeted by these tools are goal-setting, self-monitoring, self-evaluation, help-seeking, time-planning and management, and use of task strategies, whereas different types of tools might be used to support the same or different processes of self-regulation.

Collaboration in Networked Learning Communities

Success stories in the use of learning technologies are often based on large-scale approaches, most in large companies or in the public sector, when targets groups are addressed, where it is worth the effort to provide learning technologies in a large scale. New trends in the Internet, subsumed with the term Web 2.0 (O'Reilly, 2005) and commonly known due to large user communities or strong media attention, have already started to influence technology-enhanced learning (Rollett et al., 2007; Ullrich et al., 2008) to achieve more active participation of learners (Vassileva, 2002; Kamel Boulos & Wheeler, 2007), particularly in the field of higher education (Kieslinger et al., 2006). Educational experts such as (Downes, 2005) see significant potential for Web 2.0 in education. Recently, researchers have been focusing on how to incorporate the new Web trends into the learning process and how to harness and apply Web 2.0 concepts to create new learning experiences and learn across communities. Aiming at a more active involvement of learners in the learning process, current Web 2.0-driven learning technology focuses on the perspective of learners, allowing them to design their learning environments individually on the basis of given tools and services, giving them full control over the learning environment, supporting communication and collaboration with other learners (Mödritscher & Wild, 2008), and, in sum, leading to a learning network of actors, artefacts (resources), and activities (Koper et al., 2005).

Collaborative learning can be a powerful instrument for achieving an active learner involvement (Dillenbourg et al., 1995), e.g. by promoting reflective interactions (Baker & Lund, 1997). However, existing pedagogical frameworks are expert-driven, which conflicts with the learner-driven paradigm of Web 2.0 (Ullrich et al., 2008). Thus, collaboration in learning environments also deals with offering adequate publishing functionality, providing high-quality content responsive to the learner's context, and sharing learning experiences with other learners (Rollett et al., 2007).

Learning systems more and more need to respond to the learners' needs and preferences in an all-embracing way. Especially the learning customs and preferences associated with each of the tools that a learner chooses for their initial learning environment must be adapted by getting community-based recommendations and offers of supplementary learning tools according to the learners' profiles, particularly in terms of skills and competences, not only regarding domain specific issues, but also concerning self-regulation and skills required for using tools. The consequence is, that an instructional design made by experts also must be in the future get enhanced by end user feedback and experiences of learners.

TOWARDS AN RESPONSIVE OPEN LEARNING ARCHITECTURE

The Problem and the Solution Idea

In the previous chapter we described the state-of-the-art-technologies and relevant aspects from an organisational view as well as from instructional design view. A school, higher education or corporate organisation has the perspective, how to design the technology, the content and the design methods for personalised learning.

But this is only one perspective. When changing the perspective from the organisation to the user, the whole picture changes. A user - a student or an employee – creates "his/her own world of learning" based on what he/she gets offered from his institution, where he/she works, what is available in the web and what he/she gets from other organisations – such as a further education institution where he/she participates in a course. This perspective is difficult to plan for an organisation, there is not one solution to be used, there are many solutions that might be used from the learner.

Figure 4 describes this situation by presenting a possible scenario from a user perspective. In this corporate scenario, the user learns within the company using an LMS that is provided by the

Figure 4. Scenario of a user's learning world - a wide range of technologies might be used

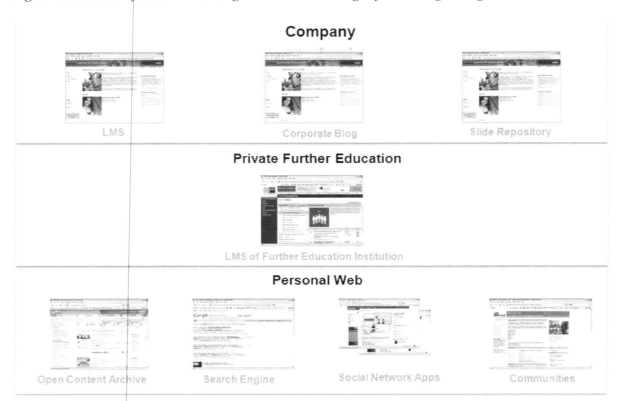

company. This LMS might contain various tools and technologies as described above. It might be full of courseware and content. In addition, the company provides in this scenario a corporate blogsphere for learning and a repository with documents that contains relevant knowledge such as slides, PDF documents etc. Besides the corporate world for learning, in this scenario, the user also attends a training class in an external further education institution, which runs their own LMS. So the user has a second account in another LMS. This LMS might be a different one than that used in the company. So the user has to follow other learning logics, tools and didactics in this LMS. In the scenario, besides the LMS based activities within the company and within the further education institution, the user has decided on his own to use open and common available web tools – collected by him-/herself: Search engines

to retrieve relevant content, social networking platform to share experiences or books or just to chat with other learners. The user also uses in this scenario open content repositories to share slides and other learning material.

In sum, this scenario makes clear how diverse the "real" learning world of an end user might look like. It is just an example, but it reflects the situation that most learners face. An employee has a corporate offering, a private one through further education institutions and also a large offering of web 2.0 tools. It is on his/her own decision how and to what extend he/she uses the different technologies.

It is not realistic today to think, that all learning will take place in one single system – this is an overcome organisational view. In a responsive open learning architecture, the challenge is to support this "real" world from the user perspec-

Figure 5. Architecture of a responsive open learning environment

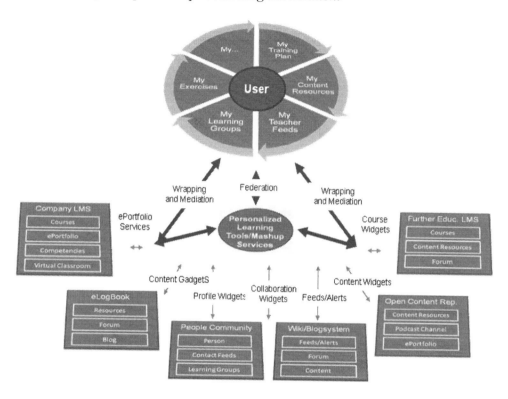

tive. Learning technologies must be mashed-up upon user's needs by enabling organisations to manage and control the learning process as well as offering the rooms for creative and flexible social learning – but not by creating a monolithic learning infrastructure.

Providing solutions to the end users is primarily a question on how to design a flexible, web-based, open environment by federation, composition and mash-up of learning services on a personal, individual level. This is named a "responsive open learning environment". The design principle is the creation of individual worlds for learning with personalisation intelligence on the user's side (learner and teacher). Personalisation intelligence concerns

- the adaptation of learning processes,
- the intelligent content selection and sequencing,
- the personalized skills management,
- individual learning as well as,
- focussed teaching.

Technical Solution Description

Figure 5 shows an architecture of a responsive open learning environment. Aim is to provide solutions that fulfil the need of end users by combining services from different technical solutions as well as organisations. This should be flexible customizable from the user him-/herself . The user can use for this an open web environment such as open social from Google or a portal technology within the corporation. The composition and mash-up of learning services happens then on a personal, individual level, the system delivers to the end user recommendations how to mash-up these services.

To realize such an environment from a technical point of view, each system like an LMS, library system, community platform, WIKI, blogsystem or open content repository must offer webservices or widgets, that can be composed on an open platform such as facebook, iGoogle or a corporate Portal like SAP Netweaver, MS Sharepoint or other using the interfacing technology of the relevant portal (iViews, Webparts etc.). Key element in this architecture is a personalisation mash-up service or engine that combines these independent services logically by using meta data of services, of content and of the user profile (competency data, learner preferences). The user data mainly come from the LMS / competency management systems.

A technological issue in this environment is the interfacing technology. The most direct way is the integration of services through Application Programming Interfaces (APIs). This is today state-of-the art, but it usually requires that the services to be integrated have been developed in the same programming language. Over the past years more loose ways to connect services gained

increasing importance. Web services with SOAP (Simple Object Access Protocol) and REST (Representational State Transfer) technologies found particular attention. In SOAP technology web services exhibit interfaces with formally defined methods to be called with arguments of types which are also formally defined. REST is a more simple way to call web services. It uses a restricted number of methods. WSDL (Web Service Description Language) is used as a language to describe these interfaces. It enables other services to detect ways in which a given service can be contacted. There are software tools available which create WSDL files and code fragments from models of software systems and business processes.

Unfortunately both SOAP and REST services lack in semantics, but semantic data are needed to federate services in an intelligent form. Recently SA-REST (semantically enhanced REST) has been developed. It is a very promising standard as its clean design makes it suitable to integrate REST

Figure 6. CLIX Architecture - supports the integration of services into other platforms such as portals or communities through webservices, webparts/iViews or widgets

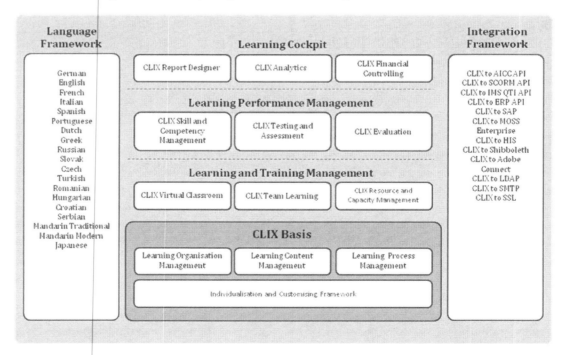

based services with little or no programming in semantic mashups, so called smashups (Lathem et al., 2007). Smashups enable the transfer of additional data between widgets and open applications and by this enable the better realization of above described solutions.

A LMS that already supports such an open environment is the software CLIX. The architecture of CLIX is being described in Figure 6.

It offers many different components as personalised widgets that are open to be harvested into a portal. Users need to be authentified by a common user management most of the time driven by the portal system.

Having explained the technical architecture, the question leaves open how organisations can build such a system. It is recommended, to do this step-by-step from "inside to outside". Figure 7 provides a step-by-step-procedure.

In the first step, a organisation should build an integrated learning platform on the basis of an LMS. This leads to efficient educational or training business processes. This technical basis is needed as the benefit will be to have a base-

line infrastructure with functionalities to track learners, to offer eLearning and blended learning. The next step should be to implement various content technologies and content repositories. This helps to create a channel to access learning resources. Once this step has been reached, the learners should be using tools to create content on their own, collaborate and share learning experiences. Wikis, Blogs, Feeds etc. should be part of such a solution. Up to step 3, the world of learning is very much in the management hand of the organisation. Therefore, the 4th step is to open the solution towards social network communities and platforms through widgets and mash-up technologies. The result is an increasing degree of building an adaptive and responsive learning environment and openness of the whole environment.

Use Case: Combined Learning Methods in Higher Education

Figure 8 describes three different learning methods that are the most important ones in higher

Figure 7. Procedure to a responsive system

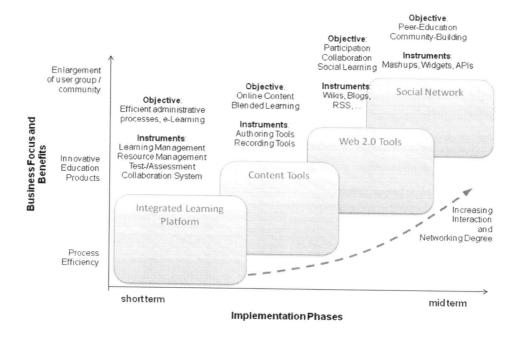

Figure 8. Learning methods from a user's perspective

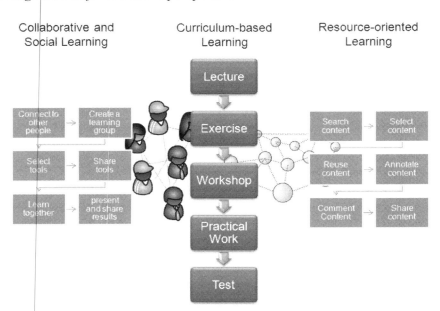

education. The typical instructional model in a higher education institution is the curriculum-based learning that contains a number of lectures and exercise sessions, combined with student workshops, practical work phases and ending with a final test. Along to this curriculum based learning process, the students connect themselves within a social network and work collaboratively on presentations or seminar papers. Besides this, students use search engines and content repositories to search for literature, relevant learning objects or other learning material that they might use for learning or reading.

The above described open learning environment enables the student to support all these processes with technology. In the centre stands the learning management system, that manages the curriculum based learning process. Social network components support the collaborative learning and content repositories support the resource-based learning by searching and finding content. In an open learning environment the student can compose all these technologies on his/he web-based workdesk by mashing-up

the different technologies in one open platform such as Facebook.

Figure 9 shows an example, how a learning widget of SLIDESTAR (Open Content Repository) and CLIX (LMS) as open content repository can be integrated in Facebook using widget technology. Many services in that direction are currently under development in many learning systems, and we can expect that open learning environments like describe will be the standard in the future.

CONCLUSION AND FUTURE RESEARCH DIRECTIONS

The objective of this paper was to show, how a flexible, web-based, open environment for the federation and mash-up of learning services on a personal, individual level should look like today on the basis of open standards for tools and interoperability. Aim is to create an individual world for learning with personalisation intelligence on the user's side (learner and teacher).

Figure 9. Sample open learning environment using Facebook as starting point, integrating an open content repository and an LMS

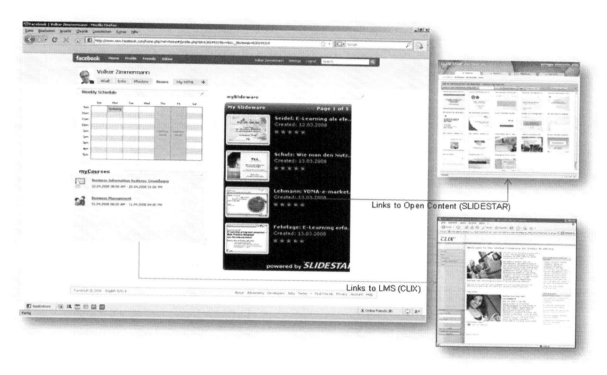

Personalisation intelligence concerns the adaptation of learning processes, the intelligent content selection and sequencing, the personalized skills management and individual learning as well as focussed teaching. This will create a more effective adaptivity and mass-personalisation approach than a central, instructional driven approach can reach, as it uses the intelligence and user profiles of the learners and teachers as well as learner oriented syndication/federation and competency bartering systems. In addition, the conception is open and enable the use of the newest technologies to federate and mashup services and tools in an intelligent way, e.g. LMSs, eLogBook, wikis, blogs, repositories, etc. and by this differ from any other recent approach. This can be reached by enabling the learner to easily construct and maintain his/her own personal learning environment (PLE) consisting of a mix of preferred learning tools, learning services, resources and other related technologies that combine the best features of push and pull. In this way the level of self-control and responsibility of learners will be strengthened, which is seen as a key motivation aspect and success factor of self-paced, formally instructed as well as informal/social learning.

Numerous research issues arise here, since in general it is not straightforward to effectively compose an individual learning environment that is in line with current preferences and goals of the learner and dynamically takes account of changes in their domain knowledge, skills, competencies and learning.

Therefore, the future research questions are:

- How will learners work with a large **choice of interoperable, institution-independent learning tools**.

- **How will the learning outcomes improve** by transferring responsibility for the choice and configuration of the learning environment from the teacher to the learner.
- How can the **learning tools itself be made responsive to events in the context of the learner** including responsiveness to events in the learner's social context (i.e. ensure that the tool designs are compatible with insights from providers and the offers from those providers).

These questions will be investigated in a new EU research project ROLE that starts in 2009 co-funded under the 7th European Research Framework.

REFERENCES

Attwell, G. (2005). What is the significance of Open Source Software for the education and training community? In M. Scotto, & G. Succi, (Eds.), *Proc. Of the First International Conference on Open Source Systems*, Genova, 11th-15th July 2005.

Baker, M., & Lund, K. (1997). Promoting reflective interactions in a CSCL environment. *Journal of Computer Assisted Learning, 13*(3), 175–193. doi:10.1046/j.1365-2729.1997.00019.x

Baldi, S., Heier, H., & Stanzick, F. (2002). *Open Courseware vs. Open Source Software – A Critical Comparison*. ECIS 2002, Gdansk.

Bloom, B. S. (1984). The 2 Sigma Problem: The Search for Methods of Group Instruction as Effective as One-to-One Tutoring. *Educational Researcher, 13*(6), 4–16.

Boekarts, M. (1997). Self-regulated learning: a new concept embraced by researchers, policy makers, educators, teachers and students. *Learning and Instruction, 7,* 161–186. doi:10.1016/S0959-4752(96)00015-1

Boekarts, M. (1999). Self-regulated learning: where we are today. *International Journal of Educational Research, 31,* 445–475. doi:10.1016/S0883-0355(99)00014-2

Borkowski, J. G. (1996). Metacognition: theory or chapter heading? *Learning and Individual Differences, 8,* 391–402. doi:10.1016/S1041-6080(96)90025-4

Brusilovsky, P. (1999). Adaptive and Intelligent Technologies for Web-based Education. *Künstliche Intelligenz, 4,* 19–25.

Brusilovsky, P. (2001). Adaptive Hypermedia. *User Modelling and User-Adapted Interaction,* 11(1-2), 87-110. Hingham, MA: Kluwer Academic Publishers.

Brusilovsky, P., Schwarz, E., & Weber, G. (1996). A Tool for Developing Hypermedia-Based ITS on WWW. In *Proceedings of Workshop "Architectures and Methods for Designing Cost-Effective and Reusable ITSs" at Third International Conference on Intelligent Tutoring Systems (ITS 1996),* Montreal, Canada.

Chatti, M. A., Jarke, M., & Frosch-Wilke, D. (2007). The future of e-learning: a shift to knowledge networking and social software. *International Journal of Knowledge and Learning, 3*(4/5), 404–420. doi:10.1504/IJKL.2007.016702

Conlan, O., Hockemeyer, C., Wade, V., & Albert, D. (2002). Metadata Driven Approaches to Facilitate Adaptivity in Personalized eLearning systems. *Journal of Information Systems Education, 1,* 38–44.

Creative Commons. (2002). Licenses Explained. Retrieved from http://creativecommons.org/learn/licenses/

Dabbagh, N., & Kitsantas, A. (2004). Supporting Self-Regulation in Student-Centered Web-Based Learning Environments. *International Journal on E-Learning, 3*(1), 40–47.

De Bra, P. (1997). Teaching through adaptive hypertext on the WWW. *International Journal of Educational Telecommunications, 3*, 163–180.

De Bra, P., Brusilovsky, P., & Houben, G.-J. (1999). Adaptive hypermedia: From systems to framework. *ACM Computing Surveys, 31*(4). doi:10.1145/345966.345996

Dillenbourg, P., Baker, M., Blaye, A., & O'Malley, C. (1995). The evolution of research on collaborative learning. In E. Spada & P. Reimann (eds.), *Learning in Humans and Machine: Towards an interdisciplinary learning science* (pp. 189-211). Oxford: Elsevier.

Downes, S. (2005). E-learning 2.0. *eLearn Magazine, 10*(2005). New York: ACM.

Grohmann, G., Kraemer, W., Milius, F., & Zimmermann, V. (2007). Modellbasiertes Curriculum-Design für Learning Management Systeme: Ein Integrationsansatz auf Basis von ARIS und IMS Learning Design. In A. Oberweis, et al. (Eds.), *Tagungsband 8. Internationale Konferenz Wirtschaftsinformatik "eOrganisation: Service-, Process-, Market Engineering"* (pp. 795-812). Karlsruhe, Germany.

Helic, D. (2006). *A Didactics-Aware Approach to Management of Learning Scenarios in E-Learning Systems*. Graz, Austria: Graz University of Technology.

Hohl, H., Böcker, H.-D., & Gunzenhäuser, R. (1996). HYPADAPTER: An adaptive hypertext system for exploratory learning and programming. *User Modeling and User-Adapted Interaction, 6*(2-3), 131–155. doi:10.1007/BF00143965

Kamel Boulos, M. N., & Wheeler, S. (2007). The emerging Web 2.0 social software: an enabling suite of sociable technologies in health and health care education. *Health Information and Libraries Journal, 24*(1), 2–23. doi:10.1111/j.1471-1842.2007.00701.x

Kay, J. (2001). Learner control. *User Modeling and User-Adapted Interaction, 11*, 111–127. doi:10.1023/A:1011194803800

Kieslinger, B., Fiedler, S., Wild, F., & Sobernig, S. (2006). iCamp: The Educational Web for Higher Education in an Enlarged Europe. In P. Cunningham & M. Cunningham (eds.), *Exploiting the Knowledge Economy: Issues, Applications, Case Studies* (pp. 1440-1448). Amsterdam: IOS Press.

Koper, R., Rusman, E., & Sloep, P. (2005). Effective Learning Networks. *Lifelong Learning in Europe, 1*, 18–27.

Kraemer, W., Milius, F., & Zimmermann, V. (2007). Von WINFO-Line zum Corporate Learning Management – Nachhaltiger Transfer wissenschaftlicher Konzepte in wettbewerbsfähige Produkte. *IM Information Management 20*(Special Edition), 50-67.

Küchler, T., Pawlowski, J., & Zimmermann, V. (2008). Social Tagging and Open Content: A Concept for the Future of E-Learning and Knowledge Management? In Gaiser, B., Hampel, T., Panke, S. (Eds.), *Good Tags – Bad Tags: Social Tagging in der Wissensorganisation, Münster et al.* (pp. 131-140).

Lathem, J., Gomadam, K., & Sheth, A. (2007). SA-REST and (S)mashups: Adding Semantics to RESTful Services. In *International Conference on Semantic Computing (ICSC 2007),* (pp. 469-476).

Lave, J., & Wenger, E. (1991): *Situated learning: Legitimate peripheral participation*. Cambridge, UK: Cambridge University Press

McAndrew, P. (2006, October 26-27). *Motivations for OpenLearn: the Open University's Open Content Initiative*. OECD experts meeting on Open Educational Resources 2006, Barcelona, Spain. Available at http://kn.open.ac.uk/public/document.cfm?docid=8816

Mödritscher, F., Neumann, G., García-Barrios, V. M., & Wild, F. (2008). A Web Application Mashup Approach for eLearning. In *Proceedings of the OpenACS and. LRN Conference*, (pp. 105-110).

O'Reilly, T. (2005). *What is Web 2.0?* Sebastol, CA: O'Reilly Media Inc., Retrieved March 07, 2008 from http://www.oreilly.com/pub/a/oreilly/tim/news/2005/09/30/what-is-web-20.html

OECD. (2007). *Giving Knowledge For Free: The Emergence Of Open Educational Resources*. Paris: OECD.

Paulsen, M. F. (2003). Experiences with Learning Management Systems in 113 European Institutions. *Educational Technology & Society*, *6*(4), 134–148.

Pintrich, P. R. (2000). The role of goal orientation in self-regulated learning. In M. Boekaerts, P.R. Pintrich & M. Zeidner (Eds.), *Handbook of Self-regulation*. San Diego, CA: Academic Press.

Pintrich, P. R. (2004). A conceptual framework for assessing motivation and self-regulated learning in college students. *Educational Psychology Review*, *16*, 385–407.

Pressey, S. L. (1926). A simple apparatus which gives tests and scores - and teaches. *School and Society*, *23*(586), 373–376.

Reimann, P. (2007). Communities of Practice. In Kinshuk, Pawlowski, J.M., Sampson, D. (Eds.), *Handbook on Information Technologies for Education and Training, 2nd Edition, International Handbook on Information Systems Series*. Berlin: Springer.

Reload (2006). *PLEX: Personal Learning Environment Download Page*. Reload. Retrieved March 31, 2008 from http://www.reload.ac.uk/plex/index.html

Rollett, H., Lux, M., Strohmaier, M., Dösinger, G., & Tochtermann, K. (2007). The Web 2.0 way of learning with technologies. *International Journal of Learning Technology*, *3*(1), 87–107. doi:10.1504/IJLT.2007.012368

Schulmeister, R. (2002). *Grundlagen hypermedialer Lernsysteme*. München, Germany: Oldenbourg.

Steffens, K. (2006). Self-Regulated Learning in Technology-Enhanced Learning Environments: lessons of a European peer review. *European Journal of Education*, *41*(3/4), 353–379. doi:10.1111/j.1465-3435.2006.00271.x

Ullrich, C., Borau, K., & Shen, R. (2008). Collaboration and Learning in the Social Web of the Future. In *Proceedings of the Conference on Integrated Design and Process Technology (IDPT 2008)*.

Van Harmelen, M. (2006). Personal Learning Environments. In *Proceedings of the IEEE International Conference on Advanced Learning Technologies (ICALT 2006)*, (pp. 815-816).

Vassileva, J. (2002). Motivating Participation in Peer to Peer Communities. In *Proceedings of the Workshop on Emergent Societies in the Agent World (ESAW 2002)*, (pp. 141-155).

Vuorikari, R. (2004). *Insight Special Report: Why Europe Needs Free and Open Source Software and Content in Schools*. Retrieved from http://ww.eun.org/insight-pdf/special_reports/Why_Europe_needs_foss_Insight_2004.pdf

Wilson, S., Liber, O., Beauvoir, P., Milligan, C., Johnson, M., & Sharples, P. (2006). Personal Learning Environments: Challenging the dominant design of educational systems. In *Proceedings of the first Joint International Workshop on Professional Learning, Competence Development and Knowledge Management (LOKMOL 2006 and L3NCD 2006)*, (pp. 67-76).

Winne, P. H. (2001). Self-regulated learning viewed from models of information processing. In B. J. Zimmerman & D. H. Schunk (Eds.), *Self-regulated learning and academic achievement: Theoretical perspectives*, (pp. 153-189). Mahwah, NJ: Lawrence Erlbaum Associates.

Zimmerman, B. J. (1998). Academic studying and the development of personal skill: a self-regulatory perspective. *Educational Psychologist, 33*, 73–86. doi:10.1207/s15326985ep3302&3_3

Zimmerman, B. J. (2000). Attaining self-regulation: a social cognitive perspective. In M. Boekarts, P.R. intrich & M. Zeidner (eds), *Handbook of Self-regulation*. San Diego, CA: Academic Press.

Zimmermann, V., & Faltin, N. (2006). Integration of Business Process Management Platforms and Learning Technologies: The PROLIX Process-oriented Learning Life Cycle. In *Proceedings eLearning 2006 Conference, Helsinki.*

Chapter 18

Personalisation and the Online Video Narrative Learning Tools V–ResORT and the ViP

Gordon Joyes
University of Nottingham, UK

ABSTRACT

This chapter describes two tools for personalised learning that were outcomes of projects led by the author for use in educational settings. These are the Virtual Resources for Online Research Training (V-ResORT) and the Virtual Interactive Platform (ViP) learning tools. The former was designed to support post graduate research students to develop an understanding of educational research through an exploration of researcher video narratives. The latter was designed to support online communities in sharing and critiquing videos of practice. These tools support the development of a learner identity characterized by proactive participation in construction and reconstruction of knowledge rather than pure consumption. This involves an engagement with communities of practice which it is argued is central to personalised learning.

INTRODUCTION

The Virtual Resources for Online Research Training (V-ResORT) and the Virtual Interactive Platform (ViP) learning tools are described in the following. These use online video in quite different ways though their intentions are the same; to engage learners with communities of practice. Their origins arise from a reconceptualisation of personalisation and some re-thinking about what might be termed a personalised

tool for learning. These considerations present the rationale for the design of the tools and as such are an important starting point for the chapter.

Dede (2007) states that "Our ways of thinking and knowing, teaching and learning are undergoing a sea change, and what is emerging seems both rich and strange" (p.25). New technologies offer the potential to change the nature of learner identity and are already doing so, particularly in lifelong learning contexts. For educationalists (policy makers, curriculum developers, teachers, lecturers, mentors and researchers) new technologies bring

DOI: 10.4018/978-1-60566-884-0.ch018

with them a wake up call to focus on the skills and competences required by learners in a globalised knowledge rich environment (Laurillard, 2007). The curriculum needs to support learners in adopting new modes of learning which may seem strange in formal educational settings, but which may seem natural and common place in informal social networking ones. Online learning brings with it the potential for not only student-centred leaning but an engagement with networks or communities as part of the curriculum. In this context of supporting the forming of new identities for learners, notions of what is meant by personalisation need to be rethought. Recent research into UK school student expectations of university and use of new technologies in order to inform Higher Education indicate that traditional approaches to teaching and learning such as face-to-face lecture and seminars predominate their thinking. This JISC (2007) report states that "they are excited by technological options which they imagine will assist and complement their studies, but not by ones which they imagine will complicate or inhibit them, or take them out of their comfort zones with regard to teaching and learning" (p.29). There are issues to be addressed in relation to learner support and induction when engaging any learner in new and strange pedagogic approaches and new technologies can add a further potentially troublesome dimension. Simply making technologies available themselves will not result in changes in learner identity. However this chapter argues that technologies carefully designed with clear pedagogic purposes in mind can engage learners in developing new understandings of their roles as learners and prepare them for their roles as lifelong learners. These tools for learning can act as enablers of new approaches to learning.

The term tool for learning is used within the chapter and a distinction is made between a resource and a tool. Beetham (2007) states that "resources are content based artefacts that use various representational media such as text, images, moving images and sound" (p. 33). The

Vygotskian perspective is that tools play a mediational role in the construction of knowledge; a change in tool has the potential to change the structure of a learning activity (Vygotsky, 1981). In this chapter it is argued that online resources when combined with pedagogic features such as powerful navigation, suggested learning pathways, opportunities to upload resources and make meaning of them etc. constitute tools for learning. Tools for personalised learning have a conscious pedagogic intent in their design.

The chapter provides the rationale for the design of the V-ResORT and the ViP tools that use video narratives as a pedagogic device. V-ResORT is described together with the action research development and evaluation process. Some strengths and limitations of V-ResORT are then discussed. The ViP is introduced and contrasted with V-ResORT. The ViP evaluation projects that are underway are then described and these provide an insight into the ways this is being used to mediate or shape learner identity within communities of practice. The chapter concludes with a discussion of future research and an invitation for partners to be involved in ViP research projects.

PERSONALISED TOOLS FOR LEARNING

Issues, Controversies, Problems: Defining Personalised Learning

Definitions of personalised learning emphasise the need to move from the world of the teacher to the world of the learner in designing learning. Ravenscroft & Cook (2007) state that "personalisation and learner-centredness mean starting from the learner's own devices, preferences and behaviours" (p. 213). In addition:

The logic of education systems should be reversed so that it is the system that conforms to the learner, rather than the learner to the system. This is the

essence of personalisation. It demands a system capable of offering bespoke support for each individual that recognizes and builds upon their diverse strengths, interests, abilities and needs in order to foster engaged and independent learners able to reach their full potential. (Green et al. 2005, p.1)

However this 'sympathetic' approach as expressed by Green *et al.* can lead onto notions of intelligent and automated learning with the learners' every online move being tracked and their pathways mapped out in sympathy with these moves with assumptions being made that the learners preferred learning style or mode of learning is somehow fixed and/or desirable and has to be supported. The business of education and in particular Higher Education is to challenge learners, to introduce 'troublesome knowledge' (Perkins, 1999) and uncomfortable spaces in which the learner's very notions of what it is to be a learner move on. Kakulska-Hulme & Traxler (2007) equally emphasise the need to recognise the learners starting points. "By personalised learning we mean learning that recognises diversity, difference and individuality in the ways the learning is developed, delivered and supported " (p. 184). However Kakulska-Hulme & Traxler additionally emphasise context and authenticity as central to a personalised learning experience. This notion is further developed by Mayes & de Freitas (2007) who articulate a Web2.0 notion of personalisation in which Web2.0 tools for learning can provide increased flexibility in control of learning "through processes allowing rich dialogue with others with whom the learner can identify " (p. 21).

It is not simply the intellectual engagement that seems important with Web 2.0 tools such as blogs. wikis, social bookmarking and media sharing applications etc. it is the finding of others with shared 'interests' and it is the socio-emotional engagement (Hall *et al.* 2007) with these others. This self disclosure through the sharing of profiles, preferences, interests, views, thoughts, ideas, photos, videos provides a level of social behaviour and interaction that promotes a sense of community. Choices are made to belong to online groups/communities/networks which serve to operate at both intellectual and social levels. These notions of personalisation include both the cognitive and affective domains, i.e. elements of personal intellectual challenge and of emotional and empathetic engagement within a community. The former is more usually associated with formal or course based learning and the latter with social networking. Effective tools for online learning could usefully combine these to support the development of a Web 2.0 learner identity in formal course based educational settings that involves engagement with communities of practice.

There is evidence of construction of knowledge occurring in educational settings through Discourse within communities with shared agendas (McConnell, 2000). Narratives or storytelling seem particularly well suited to Web 2.0 ways of knowing and sharing. Bruner (1996) argues that deductive-logical approaches to education tend to be valued by formal courses but there are narrative and storytelling approaches that need to be equally valued.

A system of education must help those growing up in a culture find an identity within that culture. Without it, they stumble in their effort after meaning. It is only in the narrative mode that one can construct an identity and find a place in one's culture. Schools must cultivate it, nurture it, cease taking it for granted. (Bruner, 1996, p. 42)

University studies initiate learners into subject cultures which are recognisably distinct (Becher & Trowler, 2001). Each subject area/ discipline develops its own declarative, procedural knowledge and cultural practices with its own Discourse. These Discourses are socially recognized ways of using language, gestures and other semiotics (images, sounds, graphics, signs, codes), as well as ways of thinking, believing, feeling, valuing, acting/doing and interacting with people and things. Discourse establishes the culture and it establishes our identity within this community enabling others to recognise us as a member (Gee, 1996). We might be seen as a novice or expert, an academic and/or practitioner, a student or lecturer, an enthusiast, a sceptic etc. Wenger (1998) points out that this Discourse involves a 'reification' (stratification and codification) of knowledge that provides a barrier to those new to a discipline. The legitimate forms in which this knowledge exists and is therefore shared tends to be written, i.e. text books, journal articles and conference papers and the Internet has not significantly changed this practice other than to make these forms more accessible. A form that is missing is the narrative or story telling about practice - though YouTube videos and Blogs do provide narratives these are not (as yet) considered legitimate forms of knowledge to be formally shared within academic communities and do not in themselves represent these communities. However as part of an academic or research community these narratives and reflections on them are part of the lived experience of collaborative working and may even form part of the research data.

Lave and Wenger (1991) describe learning as a process of social participation in communities of practice. Learners move from being newcomers to established members through a process of legitimate peripheral participation in which they engage in initially small but useful tasks within the community. Legitimate peripheral participation suggests that access to the community, opportunities to observe practice and listen to members discussing practice all mediate membership and hence learning. However legitimate peripheral participation is problematic when narrative about practice is not an established form of sharing this and when the opportunity to engage with narrative involves being part of collaboration, i.e. already being a community member. The tools for learning discussed in this chapter are two quite different solutions to this dilemma, V-ResORT

shares the 'hidden' narratives that provide authentic insights into practice, the ViP establishes an online community of practice around the sharing of narratives.

SOLUTIONS AND RECOMMENDATIONS: EXAMPLES OF PERSONALISED TOOLS FOR LEARNING

The need to develop tools for personalised learning that engage learners with their communities of practice and develop their identity as learners has been discussed as has the intended pedagogic device, the narrative. The following discusses two quite different tools that were outcomes of projects led by the author that utilise video narratives. The first tool, V-ResORT supports beginning researchers to develop their understanding of the research process through an exploration of video streams of researcher narratives. The second tool, originally perceived as complementing V-ResORT is the ViP which allows learners to upload their own media and construct their own narrative around this in online learner communities. Each tool was consciously designed with a learning context in mind and the ways these narrative tools mediate learning (Laurillard, 2002) will be discussed.

A Tool for Personalised Learning: Virtual Resources for Online Research Training (V-ResORT)

Lave & Wenger (1991) state that "for newcomers the purpose is not to learn from talk as a substitute for legitimate peripheral participation; it is to learn to talk as a key to legitimate peripheral participation" (pp.108-9). For research students the key issues are as presented earlier: How can learning technologies support their engagement with their community of researchers, when the 'legitimate' and formal forms of presenting research can be difficult to engage with? How can the design of a tool for personalised learning lead to legitimate peripheral participation in the communities of practice with which beginning researchers need to engage? V-ResORT was consciously designed to respond to these questions and the project constructed a flexible online learning experience that incorporated the use of videos of researchers providing narratives about their research.

V-ResORT was developed with funding from the Higher Education Funding Council for England (2004-8) and is a freely available online tool for learning designed to support the training of educational studies research students at masters and doctoral level. It involved four UK partners, the Universities of Sheffield, Bath and Canterbury Christ Church and the University of Nottingham who led the work. The need for the resource that led to the successful bid for funding was developed at two national conferences attended by 22 UK Higher Education Institutions and supported by the UK Education Subject Centre ESCalate www. escalate.ac.uk. The outcome of these workshops was a recognition that new online approaches to educational research were needed and examples of video narratives of research that were shown were enthusiastically received - further developments in this area were encouraged.

The project adopted an action research approach in recognition of the need to engage the community of potential users and contributors with the development of the materials if they were to be widely adopted. These users were to be beginning researchers in education studies, their lectures and supervisors and the original focus was to be doctoral students. However as part of the ongoing action research a particular need was expressed for researcher narratives of master's students exploring the development of their dissertation studies and so these were included. A steering group of national experts in educational research informed the plan, act, review cycles throughout the five action research cycles and began with a development of a conceptual framework. This framework was used successfully to build the storyboard for the different video narratives and consists of six main questions about the research journey that could be asked of any researcher or about any research. This framework has been found to be successful in revealing authentic research 'stories' that the research students can find connections with.

These questions are:

1. Where did the ideas for the research come from? - **Where?**
2. What is the aim/purpose of the research? - **What?**
3. Why were the theoretical and methodological approaches chosen? - **Why?**
4. How was your research project designed and conducted? - **How? When? Who with? Where?**
5. How was the research reported and communicated to a range of audiences? - **Communication?**
6. What happened to the research after it was completed? -**And then?**

These questions represent a researcher journey and the ways these are represented within an inquiry pathway on the website is shown in figure 1.

Initially one video narrative of research was captured and presented as a prototype on the V-ResORT website and the profile of this researcher is also shown in figure 1. Microsoft Producer was used to create the videostreams and a bespoke Adobe Flash interface using open source PHP linking to a MySQL database was developed for the website. The interface navigation enables a user to select a question, a researcher by name, and then one of the short video clips shown. A short profile of the researcher including their picture and the research is included so that users can select the narratives that are of relevance to their own context. Selection of one researcher and then the questions in turn reveals a complete research journey. Selection of a question and

Figure 1. The research journey and a researcher profile

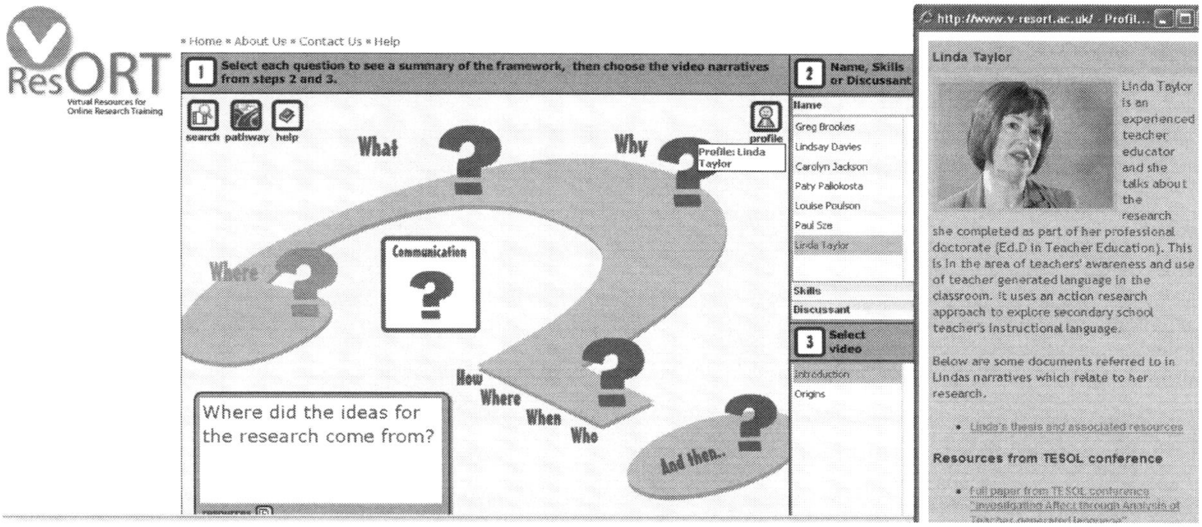

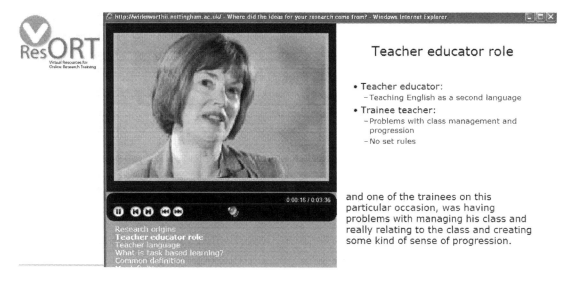

then the researchers in turn enables comparisons between all of the research around that question to be made. Figure 2 shows an example of a video narrative clip.

This prototype was user tested with both students and academics and refined. Initially cartoon images of bassett hounds were included on the website researcher journey page alongside each question. The notion was that this would

represent the research process as the search for or the 'sniffing out' of evidence. Feedback during the first action research cycle strongly suggested that many international students would find this image offensive and so it was removed from the default view of the page. The website was then used to engage the four partner universities in further developing the website design and re-sulted in their each contributing one researcher

Figure 2. A research narrative

narrative, chosen because this was perceived as something that could be usefully used on courses at the donor institution. This approach assured the project materials would initially be used and evaluated in at least four universities in the UK. Subsequent action research cycles involved workshops with new partners and their contributions of new video narratives. By the end of the fourth action research cycle nine UK universities had contributed materials and were utilising the courses with their students. A key feature of the approach to 'localise' the website has been the identification and use of local 'mentors', i.e., respected academics who have worked in realistic ways to not only support other staff in the use of the resource, but to inform the project about the local context. Part of their role and as part of the evaluation strategy was to gather information from academics and students about the ways they were using the website and to gather suggestions for improvements. Where these represented learning activities using the website these are represented as learning pathways accessible on the research

journey page. In this way pedagogy in use has been embedded into the materials.

A key feature of the V-ResORT website is the way the materials are integrated into a meaningful learning tool. The complete research narratives are linked to reports, articles, data, thesis chapters and other useful online and text based resources. Skills training is provided that relates directly to skills referred to within the narratives, i.e., the use of interviews, focus groups. Figure 3 shows a skills based training video clip covering approaches to writing at research degree level which is also used for analysis of the conduct of focus groups.

Discussant narratives are also included that explore general methodological issues that arise directly from the research narratives. This internal referencing was a deliberate pedagogic choice, the researcher narrative providing context and meaning for the learner - something research methodology texts often fail to do.

Figure 1, the research journey, represents one approach to navigation around the video narratives. A second approach uses a key word search

Figure 3. Skills training, discussing writing and analysing the focus group

facility as shown in Figure 4. If a lecturer or a student enters a key word such as 'ethics' all the video narrative clips that engage with this issue are presented. This was thought to be of particular use in research training within taught components of research courses.

Evaluation data was gathered in a range of ways during the project not least through the ongoing action research cycles with the user academics. Users have to register on the website, leave an email address and agree to email contact for evaluation purposes. Emails were sent to the over 20,000 registered global users in October 2007 who were requested to complete an online survey. Many of the email addresses were no longer valid but 627 users responded to this survey. The survey asked users to describe the ways they had used the web site and to describe how it had impacted on their learning. It also requested volunteers

for telephone interviews and in all 52 volunteers were interviewed; each interview was recorded and transcribed. As was expected a large number of users (97%) identified themselves as students, 1% identified themselves as both lectures and students, the rest being lecturers. 89% were studying education at doctoral level in the UK and of these 43% were from the nine universities involved in the project. Some 26% were doctoral students or researchers studying or working at non-UK universities, e.g. in China, Taiwan, Malaysia, Germany, Sweden, Holland etc. This survey and interview data revealed the ways the website represented a community of practice for these users and this is discussed in the following.

As discussed earlier V-ResORT was designed to provide opportunities for personalised learning not simply because of its inbuilt pedagogic flexibility, but importantly because of the ways

Figure 4. Key word search facility

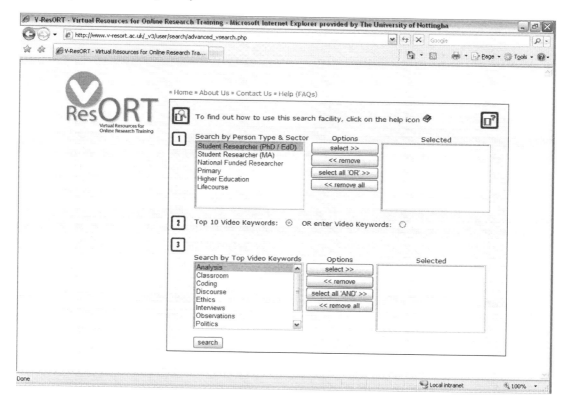

it represents the community of practice the users are joining. The narratives provide authentic accounts of research in ways the learner can identify with and in which their notions of being a learner/ researcher are challenged. The evaluation survey data provides evidence of student as well as lecturer learning with 61% of respondents indicating that they browsed the video narratives to find a researcher who they could identify with, e.g., they were international, they were a doctoral or master's student. For 83% of student respondents the precise nature of the topic or method was not at first the major factor in deciding to watch a narrative.

The following example is one in which the user identified themselves as a lecturer and was using the website for their personal development needs.

*I looked through the materials (I think it was the first three) which stimulated thinking on research design. I liked the videos and the **link to a paper written by the person whose research I was most interested in.** (Senior Lecturer at a post 1992 university)*

Lecturers who had been introduced to the materials as part of their research training were also recommending the materials for their students who were also undergoing research training. There is also evidence of the ways the students identified with the researcher narratives from within a Masters in Research Methods course. This was another rich source of data as the project had access to the discussion forum and blog activities, where the students were actively using the V-ResORT materials and it was possible to triangulate this data with the survey data:

*I met this resource as part of my masters course in research methods and found the video narratives compulsive viewing. I particularly liked the Patya video as**I related to the ways she seemed to be still exploring the methodological issues.**I*

watched this from start to finish one evening at home, it was so useful in developing an understanding of the real research process. The course readers are of course helpful but the video brought the research process alive for me. The realities of doing research are there. (Masters student at a pre 1992 UK university)

There was evidence that the resources were useful at all stages of the research process not just in initial research training. This student was using the resource at the end of her doctorate and gives a sense of ways the resource can help a student overcome the sense of isolation that can be felt at this stage.

*At my stage (final months of PhD write-up) the resources are valuable for those of us (probably most of us) working at a distance from our institutions ... it is nice to **feel part of a wider network of people** going through the same agony!* (Professional Doctoral student at a pre 1992 UK university)

The words highlighted in the quotes above provide evidence of the ways the resource provides opportunities for learners to identify themselves as part of a network of researchers - developing their sense of being part of a community. This is a particular strength of the video narrative approach, but it is also strengthened by the underlying conceptual framework that was developed at the start of the project, i.e. it represents an authentic account of the research journey. Wenger's notion that the 'reification' of knowledge provides a barrier to those new to a discipline gives an insight into the reasons why beginning research can often be problematic, not only for research students but for new lecturers in education. "There is a pedagogical cost to reifying that requires additional work - even possibly, a new practice - to make sense of the reification" (Wenger 1998, p. 264). The reified account of the research process provides a rather tidy separation of choice of methodology, methods, field work, analysis and writing. The project found that researchers talk quite openly of the messiness of the whole process adhering to a complexity model rather than a more simplistic one. The conceptual framework allows for the description of this complex process. For example, question 4 (How was you research project designed and conducted?) allows for literature review, fieldwork, analysis, further fieldwork, refining of research questions and so on to be reported in the ways the process happened. This tends not to be the ways research is reported in the literature which can be a confusing misrepresentation for those new to the area and an approach students cannot easily identify with - representing a barrier to their identity as members of a researcher community. There is evidence of learners beginning to identify with these authentic versions of research as ones that rang true to their personal experiences of the realities of professional practice - most doctoral students in educational studies have several years of professional experience.

Well I had made my research plan as it seemed that was something I should do.. but at what level of detail? **In fact it did not feel an appropriate thing to do at all and the videos reinforced this - it became clear that my 'experience' of pursuing my research would help me refine things and that the process could not be tightly defined.** *I knew my research area was complex and refining questions, methodology would need to evolve as I understood my research context and the literature more and it was good to have it confirmed from the videos that this was OK - I sort of knew this from my experience in the area.. but somehow it seemed I had to have the research plan now. (Professional Doctoral student at a pre 1992 UK university)*

The above has provided the rationale for and some evidence for the V-ResORT design, its effectiveness and the ways this has mediated learning. The conceptual framework provides the pedagogy,

i.e., activities that compare the same parts of the research process are 'highlighted' by means of the questions that support easy navigation across different researchers. This allows learners to identify their own issues and explore these across the research narratives as well as follow any research narrative from start to finish. The design was a conscious attempt to provide this facility through an in-depth understanding of the issues faced by those new to educational research.

The visual as well as the authentic nature of the resource was central to its value to learners. It was as much to do with *what* was being said as *who* was saying it and *how* they where saying it that allowed the resource to resonate with the users. The visual aspect added value helping rapid identification with researchers with the same gender, ethnicity, background, age, occupation, confidence etc. These cues can be initially important to users as much as research topic, methodology covered and the course being studied when those new to research are beginning to discover and understand the nature of their research community and the nature of its Discourse. This is of particular importance to courses that attract international students and for courses that are promoting themselves as exploring research globally.

It was hoped that V-ResORT would shape pedagogic practice in the teaching of research. The evaluation found little evidence of any change in the ways lecturers taught research methods as a result of the project, most lecturers would recommend V-ResORT to students rather than integrating it within their courses as a means of introducing students to the research process. In fact 63% of the surveyed students responded that they had been recommended the site by another student, 26% found it on a search engine and only 7% had been directed to the site by their lecturer or supervisor. What is needed is a discussion of the value of researcher narratives that provide an authentic account of the research process for sharing practice and this chapter represents one way the project is raising this.

The evaluation identified key strengths of V-ResORT to be the quality of the video and the ways all the resources are integrated and are easily searchable. The academics involved dictated the need to have high quality video for the narratives and for it to have a search facility as well as the research journey navigation. This does enable flexibility of use and enable the website to be presented in seminars and lectures. However the production process was relatively costly as professionals were employed to capture the video and prepare this for online delivery. In addition the process was time consuming as a storyboard for the clips for each video narrative needed to be created so that each narrative could be presented in a uniform way, according to the questions in the conceptual framework. The audio also needed to be transcribed and the text accompanying each clip cut into small chunks in Dreamweaver, PowerPoints had to be constructed and then organised in an MS Producer file. The requirement for transcripts and PowerPoints highlighting key points was a requirement of the users, something discovered at an early stage of the project. The language used within research can be quite specialised and concepts, names and key texts are mentioned. The spellings for these are important for the user who after all has chosen a narrative because they are interested in the research. Additionally UK regional and international English accents can be difficult to understand and so the text is needed to support the user. Once the MS Producer file was created it was then uploaded to the video streaming server. Key search words and resources were then added and then the video would be viewed in its draft form by a review group of students and lecturers as well as the researcher whose narrative it was. After revisions it could then go live. A typical video narrative would involve the creation and the weaving together of over 30 video clips, over 100 PowerPoint slides and over 200 text clips and this could take between six and eight weeks, but initially it took longer.

The following describes a tool for learning that also uses visual learning and authentic accounts of practice but which involves these to support the co-construction of knowledge. The quality of the video and the narrative is dictated by the user and so overcomes the complex and time consuming production process involved in V-ResORT. In this instance videos and their associated narratives are owned by each member of the community - so rather than observing a research community constructed by 'others' as a prelude to engaging in practice the users *are* the community of practice.

A Tool for Personalised Learning: The Virtual Interactive Platform (ViP)

The Virtual Interactive Platform (ViP) was originally conceived as a complementary tool to support V-ResORT. The original idea for the context for use was to enable the uploading and sharing of practice research interviews and focus groups. Users would be introduced to the practice of conducting interviews and focus groups in V-ResORT through analysing the skills video. Then they would work within a beginning researcher community of practice within the safety of an online and private group. The context for trialling this was to be the online professional doctorate in Teacher Education at the University of Nottingham, UK and this will still occur in the future, however the ViP was not available in time to be used when the module was taught in 2008. In this context the ViP would be used within an already established online international community of research students. What was of interest was the ways it could be designed and could be used to establish and sustain a community of practice. Lave & Wenger (1991) state that "a community of practice involves much more than the technical knowledge or skill associated with undertaking some task. Members are involved in a set of relationships over time" (p.98). A sense of joint enterprise and identity is achieved because communities develop around the things that matter to the members (Wenger 1998).

As in V-ResORT the ViP was designed as a platform in which narratives or stories of practice could be told. The ViP differs from V-ResORT in that there is no guiding conceptual framework in which the video narratives have to fit. It is a more flexible tool for learning in that it allows anyone to upload video to the ViP server and construct a narrative around this - see figure 5.

It couples media-sharing features supported by personal commentaries, resources and an interactive discussion forum with the creation of social groups around the media content. It builds upon Web 2.0 video-sharing and social networking concepts scaffolded by a flash animation and alternative pdf format user guide.

The ViP provides an integrated online environment for:

- the uploading and transcoding of media content (in this case video, audio and animation);
- the addition of supporting commentaries and associated resources;
- the formation of groups of friends and peers to share public or private materials;
- the engagement in an interactive discussion forum where users can pinpoint snippets within video files and embed them into the discussion area text.

The ViP is pedagogically driven, allowing distributed learners to share multimedia content with whom they choose, to critique their own meaning and develop understanding of their practice. It moves a traditionally teacher-centred approach to a learner-centred one that encourages reflection and criticality. A key design feature is

Figure 5. ViP video narrative commentary and discussion

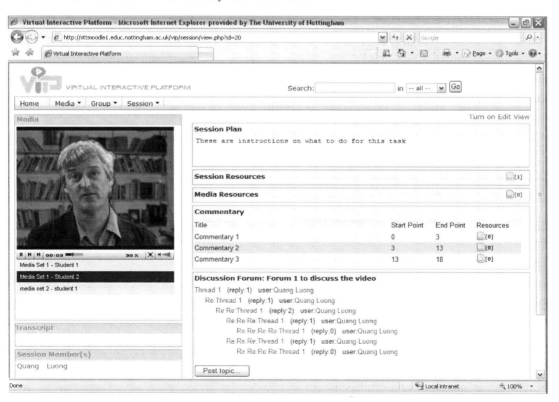

the way the author can add text commentaries to their uploaded video which are then highlighted when the video plays. This transforms the video into a narrative which is a reflection upon the video content. Importantly the author can select to keep their video private or share this within a small group or make this openly available. The author can invite others to add their own ideas around the video in the discussion forum and so multiple perspectives can be shared around the same video. This is achieved through a text based discussion around the video in which learners in a post can select and link to one or more video snippets from a variety of video sources within the ViP. Discussion around video can be difficult particularly when the video is long or there is a large number of clips to refer to. This selection and linking facility within a discussion post has been designed to support the exploration and analysis of the video. So for example, if a video of a focus group were being analysed, the discussion posting might want to point out the strategies the facilitator was using to engage all of the group members in the discussion. They could refer to strategies in the post within any part of the text and place a video link icon that would take the viewer to the precise place in a video clip where the strategy was being used. Further video links could be added to illustrate that one strategy and further strategies could be added with further video links.

The ViP is server based and the user creates their narrative around the video once it is uploaded to the server. Compression and conversion to Flash happens automatically. The ViP uses mostly free and open source client-side and server-side web technologies. At the client side, the ViP uses XHTML and CSS and utilises the Yahoo User Interface (YUI) Javascript library. Multimedia content is displayed using Flash. At the server side, PHP middleware scripting interfaces with a MySQL database. Videos are converted to Flash format via ffmpeg and Red5, a Java-based Flash server is used to stream the content. The website

is currently hosted on Apache web server and Linux operating system.

The ViP is currently operating as a Beta version. The evaluation strategy has involved ongoing user testing of the functionality, but the current focus is on the ways the tool may support communities of practice. There are various contexts for use where the ViP would be a useful personalised learning tool. Research has shown that making reflective videos can benefit both teachers (Barton & Haydn, 2006; Gebhard, 2005) and students (Triggs & John 2004). Demonstration of the tool within the University of Nottingham and at International conferences such as ALT-C and Ascilite has been used as an opportunity to explore with the higher education community contexts for use. As a result of this dissemination the development team at the educational development innovations technology lab (ed:it) within the School of Education, University of Nottingham have established and are continuing to form research partnerships with academics, researchers, teachers etc. Examples of these ViP projects are presented below.

A ViP Evaluation Project to Support the Continuing Professional Development of Teachers across Technology Rich Schools in Malaysia (2008-9)

The ViP is being used in this context to value teacher knowledge and support the sharing of classroom practice within three subject based online communities of teachers across Malaysian Smart schools which are designated as technology rich. This research involves twenty volunteer teachers from five Smart schools working within English, Maths and Science teacher communities of practice and supported by mentors from the Universiti Kebangsaan Malaysia (UKM), who are funding the project. Technology support and consultancy advice is provided by ed:it and a team from the School of Education, University of Nottingham, UK. Teachers capture on video one lesson in which they integrate new technologies, upload this to the ViP, add commentaries and resources (lesson plans, worksheets, examples of children's work) and then within their subject community discuss aspects of practice. The commentaries allow a reflection on practice and represent the teacher perspective and the ensuing discussion allows for other perspectives to be shared. The research is comparing the use of a text based blog, which was used initially by the teachers to discuss practice in their communities, to the use of the ViP. The focus is on the teacher's personal narratives, their changing foci and pedagogic language within their communities, the nature of the different subject communities and changes in teacher identity as a result of engagement in the community. This learning context is a radical departure from the 'top down' training these teachers are used to - one which has failed to move their practice forwards (Siti Suria Salim & Mohd. Nor, 2005; Hajar Mohd. Nor, 2005; Azizah Yaacob et al, 2005; Lee, 2007). The research is exploring this personalised approach to continuing professional development - one in which self theories and new identities are forged and the intention is to continue to work with these communities and also develop them in different regions in Malaysia.

A ViP Project within an Already Established Online Community of Teachers in the Carribean (2009-10)

This is a doctoral studies project that is working with the Caribbean Education Network (CEN) which is a NING based social network of over 300 teachers from the English Speaking Caribbean. A small group of ten volunteer teachers will explore the use of the ViP in this context. This is an informal network and the ways the ViP might mediate professional development is to be studied.

A ViP Project with Masters TESOL Students at the University of Nottingham (2009-10)

The users of the ViP are the module tutor and the eight students studying the Teacher development: from theory to practice' (elective) module on the MA TESOL course 2008-9

The ViP has been adopted after attempts at using podcasting because initial trails showed that it had two main benefits:

- enabling video snippet selection within a discussion so that there is focused discussion around particular video episodes - a difficulty with podcasts;
- ease of use, so that participants who may not be particularly tech-savvy will find it easy to communicate (and form a community).

This project has two phases. Phase 1 (Spring 2009) in which participants on the module will use ViP to:

- Upload reflections on their teaching beliefs/practice (in audio and/or text and/or video form, using audio-recordings of in-class discussions, previously composed written reflections and talking-to-camera videoblog recordings);
- Upload two 15-minute recordings of their microteaching in video form (these may be in 15-minute clips, or shorter clips to comprise 15 minutes of teaching from each of two microteaching sessions in the module);
- Create transcripts/commentaries for key sections of their microteaching;
- Engage in ongoing discussion around the issues raised by the clips and using the video snippet link facility in ViP;
- Store all the semester's thoughts and practice in a convenient space so that it is easy to describe, exemplify and reflect on the

learning process for the end-of-module assignment.

Phase 2 (August 2009 onwards) in which participants will use the ViP on their return to their various home countries to:

- Continue to share their beliefs, experiences and practice, uploading and commenting on brief audio/video excerpts from lessons or post-lesson reflections (text/audio/video);
- Help form a learning / practising community.

A ViP Project with Teachers in 16-19 Colleges across Europe (2009-2011)

This is a project currently seeking funding from the EC Transversal programme that will follow a similar approach to the Malaysian continuing professional development programme. It involves 16-19 colleges in the UK, Sweden and Poland and the University of Nottingham working initially with teachers of modern foreign languages to explore practice who will later become mentors to support the development of communities of practice across the colleges in other subject areas, where the use of English as a medium may be problematic. A key element of this project is the use of the ViP to support collaborative action research into effective practice within classrooms across Europe.

FUTURE RESEARCH DIRECTIONS

There a several directions research in this area can take some of which is already beginning to be explored. The V-ResORT tool for learning has inspired and informed the development of a Virtual Graduate School (VGS) at the University of Sheffield, UK in which different subject communities are developing both generic and subject specific resources to support their research students. The use of video is a key feature of the VGS and what is of interest is the different video genre that each subject community uses to represent its area, for example video of different cultural contexts is as important for cultural studies as is the narrative of the researcher exploring these contexts.

The ViP has wide application in situations where visualisation of practice and focussed reflective commentary is a key part of the learning process - particularly where sharing of videos needs to be in private spaces. Research into its use within teacher education could involve the training of mentors to support student teachers in schools and the sharing and discussion of advanced skills by 'expert' teachers. These would involve the development of communities of practice in these contexts. Its use across other subject areas within Higher Education would also be of interest as would student use in these settings. However the ViP was designed to be able to be used by anyone and would be suitable for school based, work based and lifelong learning contexts. The ViP already allows for upload via the internet from mobile devices and high quality low priced digital camcorders are already available and these facilities will soon become standard in mobile phones. As technologies improve the creation of the commentaries, discussion posts and viewing of video will all become possible using mobile technologies rather than laptops. This opens up possibilities for just-in-time sharing of practice and rapid feedback from the community of practice but potentially provides a facility for reflection in practice as well as on practice (Schön, 1983). My particular research interest is in the nature of these communities and the ways the technologies shape their identities, but there are other equally important research areas to be explored not least the design of effective tools for personalised learning.

CONCLUSION

This chapter has discussed the nature of personalised learning in a connected world; discussed the importance of narrative in learning and the ways this may not be valued within formal course based learning and the associated subject cultures; explored the design of tools for personalised learning that involve video narratives to engage learners with their communities of practice. The evaluation of the use of V-ResORT has provided evidence of the ways video narratives of researchers can support identification with a community as a means of legitimate peripheral participation for newcomers. The ViP provides exciting new ways for learners to share practice and establish their identities as members of a community. The role of higher education institutions beyond research and development of these tools needs careful consideration. There is real potential within teacher education for a community of practice model to form part of masters and doctoral degree studies for the teacher's involved and this could also extend to undergraduate level. There is also potential for teachers to identify their training needs within their communities with the possibility for universities to provide the requested support. This fits well with a model of Higher Education responding to the needs of lifelong learners and local communities that is necessary in a world where individuals and businesses are faced with reinventing themselves to survive in the global economy.

V-ResORT is a freely available tool and can be found at www.v-resort.ac.uk. ViP will become available for wider application when it has been further evaluated - information about the ViP is available at http://editlab.nottingham.ac.uk and contact information for those wishing to explore its use is available there.

REFERENCES

Barton, R., & Haydn, T. (2006). Trainee Teachers' Views on What Helps Them to Use Information and Communication Technology Effectively in Their Subject Teaching. *Journal of Computer Assisted Learning, 22*(4), 257–272. doi:10.1111/j.1365-2729.2006.00175.x

Becher, T., & Trowler, P. (2001). *Academic tribes and territories. Intellectual. enquiry and the cultures of disciplines.* Buckingham, UK: Open University Press.

Beetham, H. (2007). An approach to learning activity design. In H. Beetham & R. Sharpe(Eds.), *Rethinking Pedagogy for a digital age: Designing and delivering for e-learning* (pp. 26-40). London: Routledge.

Bruner, J. (1996). *The Culture of Education.* Cambridge, MA: Harvard University Press.

Dede, C. (2007). Introduction: A Sea Change in Thinking, Knowing, Learning and Teaching. In G. Salaway., & J. Borreson Caruso (Eds.), *The ECAR Study of Undergraduate Students and Information Technology. ECAR: USA.* (pp. 19-26). Retrieved June 28, 2008, from http://net.educause.edu/ir/library/pdf/ers0706/rs/ers0706w.pdf

Gebhard, J. (2005). Teacher Development through Exploration: Principles, Ways, and Examples. *TESL-EJ, 9*(2), 1-15. Retrieved June 28, 2008, from http://web.icu.ac.jp/lrb/vol_22/Kota%20LRB%20V22.pdf

Gee, J. (1996). *Social Linguistics and Literacies: Ideology in Discourses*, (2nd Ed.). London: Taylor & Francis.

Green, H., Facer, K., Rudd, T., Dillon, P., & Humphreys, P. (2005). *The personalisation and digital technologies report.* Retrieved November 3, 2008, from http://www.nestafuturelab.org/research/personalisation.htm

Hall, C., Hall, E., & Cooper, L. (2007). A socio-emotional approach to building communities of learners online. In H. Spencer-Oatey (Ed.), *e-Learning initiatives in China: pedagogy, policy and culture* (pp. 79-93). Hong Kong: Hong Kong University Press.

JISC. (2007). *Student expectations study*. Retrieved November 3, 2008, from http://www.jisc.ac.uk/media/documents/publications/studentexpectations.pdf

Kakulska-Hulme, A., & Traxler, J. (2007).Designing for mobile and wireless learning. In H. Beetham & R. Sharpe (Eds.), *Rethinking Pedagogy for a digital age: Designing and delivering for e-learning* (pp.180-192). London: Routledge.

Laurillard, D. (2002). *Rethinking University Teaching: A Conversational Framework for the Effective Use of Learning Technologies,* (2nd Edition). London: Routledge.

Laurillard, D. (2007). *The Kaleidoscope scientific vision for research in technology enhanced learning*. Retrieved January 12, 2008, from http://telearn.noe-kaleidoscope.org/warehouse/Kaleidoscope-Scientific-Vision-v1.pdf

Lave, J., & Wenger, E. (1991). *Situated Learning, Legitimate peripheral participation*. Cambridge, UK: University of Cambridge Press.

Lee, K. (2007). *ESL Teacher Professional Development & Curriculum Innovation: The Case of the Malaysian Smart School Project*. Unpublished doctoral dissertation, Lancaster University, UK.

Mayes, T., & de Freitas, S. (2007). Learning and e-learning: the role of theory. In H. Beetham & R. Sharpe (Eds.), *Rethinking Pedagogy for a digital age: Designing and delivering for e-learning* (pp. 13-25). London: Routledge.

McConnell, D. (2000). *Implementing Computer Supported Cooperative Learning,* (2nd Ed.). London: Kogan Page.

Nor, H. M. (2005). *Conditions facilitating the implementation of Information and Communication Technology (ICT) Integration in the Malaysia Smart School*. Unpublished doctoral dissertation, Universiti Putra Malaysia, Serdang, Selangor.

Perkins, D. (1999). The many faces of constructivism. *Educational Leadership*, *57*(3), 6–11.

Ravenscroft, A., & Cook, J. (2007) New horizons in learning design. In H. Beetham & R. Sharpe (Eds.), *Rethinking Pedagogy for a digital age: Designing and delivering for e-learning* (pp. 207-218). London: Routledge.

Schön, D. (1983). *The reflective practitioner*. New York: Basic Books.

Siti Suria Salim & Sharifah Mohd. Nor. (2005). Teachers as Implementers of Change: The Smart School Experience. *International Journal of Learning*, *12*(10), 197–204.

Triggs, P., & John, P. (2004). From Transaction to Transformation: Information and Communication Technology, Professional Development and the Formation of Communities of Practice. *Journal of Computer Assisted Learning*, *20*(6), 426–439. doi:10.1111/j.1365-2729.2004.00101.x

Vygotsky, L. (1981). The instrumental method in psychology. In J. Wertsch. (Ed.), *The Concept of Activity in Soviet Psychology* (pp. 134-143). New York: Armond.

Wenger, E. (1998). *Communities of practice: Learning, meaning and identity*. Cambridge, UK: Cambridge University Press.

Ya'acob, A., Mohd Nor, N. F., & Azman, H. (2005). Implementation of the Malaysian Smart School: An Investigation of Teaching-learning Practices and Teacher-Student Readiness. *Internet Journal of e-Language Learning and Teaching, 2*(2) 16-25. Retrieved from http://www.eltrec.ukm.my/ijellt

Chapter 19

Shared Spaces and 'Secret Gardens':
The Troublesome Journey from Undergraduate Students to Undergraduate Scholars Via PebblePad

Marina Orsini-Jones
Coventry University, UK

ABSTRACT

This chapter illustrates a curricular intervention carried out at Coventry University (UK) with undergraduate students reading English. It explores how the students maximised their use of the tools available within the ePortfolio software PebblePad. It discusses how the software tools were used to enhance and personalise the students' learning experience and engage in the discourse of 'becoming researchers' in the second year module Dissertation Methods and Approaches. It proposes that the use of some ePortfolio tools helped many students to become critical and to actively engage in their ontological journey of transition to becoming independent thinkers. However it also reports that some problematic issues surfaced following the implementation of the curricular action: some students find active learning and active engagement in the scholarship of research 'troublesome'. Finally this chapter gives consideration to how to integrate the lessons learned from this experience into the curriculum for the next cohort of students.

INTRODUCTION

In this chapter I initially provide an overview of the inquiry-based nature of the curriculum design of the undergraduate BA English Degree course that started in academic year 2006-2007 at Coventry University (UK). I then focus on a second-year mandatory module (*Dissertation Methods and Approaches*) that

is aimed at equipping students with the 'armoury' of research skills necessary to complete their final year dissertation independently. I discuss in particular how the ePortfolio software PebblePad supported the students' learning journey on this module with particular reference to the creation of an assessed task: their dissertation plan.

In my roles of principal investigator for this study and module leader, I evaluated the learning experience of the 2007-2008 cohort of students on

DOI: 10.4018/978-1-60566-884-0.ch019

the above-mentioned second year module, 42 in total (32 female and 10 male, between 19 and 45 years of age). I had carried out previous cycles of curricular action-research interventions that had demonstrated that sharing knowledge construction with the dedicated ePortfolio PebblePad tools such as the *webfolio* and the *action plans* had helped students with understanding difficult grammar concepts (Orsini-Jones & Jones, 2007; Orsini-Jones & Sinclair, 2008). For this curricular intervention I hypothesised that the ePortfolio tools could be utilised to support second year students in their individual 'research journey' that is required for the design of their assessed dissertation plan for module *Dissertation Methods and Approaches*. I believed that the e-tools would provide students with the opportunity to personalise their research journey while also giving them a platform for sharing their 'research artefacts' with the tutors and peers if they wanted to. So the ePortfolio could be compared both to a 'secret learning garden' for the students' personal use only (hence the reference to the famous novel by Burnett, 1909), while also offering them the opportunity to be their public research 'arena' (i.e. the shared *gateway* where they could display the *webfolio* of their dissertation plan).

I made the assumption, based upon evidence collected for other modules in previous academic years, that embedding ePortfolio tools aimed at developing reflective skills in the syllabus of the research module would impact positively on the students' research learning journey. I hypothesised that by using such e-tools for the creation of their dissertation plan, students could be encouraged to become critical. I was hoping that via a carefully structured e-supported task I would help students to actively engage in their ontological journey of transition from being at the 'receiving end' of their learning experience, to becoming independent thinkers. This would also include the active participation in a scholarly critique of each other's work, both face-to-face and online.

Engaging students in active learning and preparing them for, in Barnett's words, a disturbed and disturbing 'age of supercomplexity' (Barnett, 2000, p.155), proved to be challenging in some cases. The data I collected highlighted that some students find active learning and active engagement in the scholarship of research overwhelming. It emerged that some students were finding the assessed individual *webfolio* task 'troublesome' for both epistemological reasons (e.g. alien subject-related terminology and concepts) and ontological ones (e.g. fear of the solitary aspects of the research journey paired with unease about the assessed task format that took them out of their 'comfort zone' and undermined their confidence).

What had started as an evaluation of the use of PebblePad on the module became therefore a wider investigation into 'troublesome knowledge' repositioning my study in the relatively new field of transactional curriculum inquiry (Cousin, 2009, pp. 201-212) known as 'threshold concepts' and developed by Erik Meyer and Ray Land (Meyer & Land, 2003; 2005; Meyer, Land & Smith, 2008). A threshold concept is:

- troublesome: the learners will find it problematic;
- transformative: once understood, its potential effect on student learning and behaviour is to occasion a significant shift in the perception of a subject;
- integrative: it exposes the previously hidden interrelatedness of concepts that were not previously seen as linked;
- irreversible: the change of perspective occasioned by acquisition of a threshold concept is unlikely to be forgotten; and
- bounded: any conceptual space will have frontiers, bordering with thresholds into new conceptual areas (Meyer and Land, 2003, p. 412).

Thus the analysis of the data brought about an unexpected outcome: the attempt to identify which 'threshold concept' undergraduate students need to cross to see the link between the 'epistemic tools' necessary to carry out research in English Studies and the 'cognitive and identity shift' (Cousin, 2009, p.201) needed at the ontological and personal level to start 'thinking like a researcher of English Studies'.

The chapter's objectives are therefore: firstly, to illustrate a curricular intervention aimed at 'developing students as researchers'; secondly, to investigate the students' reactions to the learning experience of actively engaging in research and sharing scholarship with the support of PebblePad; thirdly, to discuss the troublesome knowledge identified and, finally, to propose a way forward for the next cohort of students in view of the findings.

BACKGROUND 1: CURRICULUM DESIGN TO FACILITATE THE TRANSITION 'FROM STUDENTS TO SCHOLARS'

The creation of the new degree course in English that was launched in academic year 2006-2007 offered staff in the English Language Unit at Coventry University the opportunity to design an inquiry-based course that had the following generic aims (Programme Specification Document 2005):

- to enable students to develop a range of skills which will help them to develop their future careers;
- to provide students with a range of related skills which they can transfer to other contexts;
- to equip students with the scholarly skills needed to undertake undergraduate study and to progress to postgraduate study on completion of the course;
- to encourage students to develop confidence and an independent mind which questions and develops a critical awareness;

- to enable students to conduct their own independent research.

The curriculum design was therefore underpinned by modules that aimed to encourage students to engage with scholarship and experience research at first hand. The integration of a research ethos within the English provision mirrored the right-hand side of the 'Curriculum design and research-teaching nexus' model proposed by Healey (2005, p.70, Healey & Jenkins, in press: Figure 1).

Following recommendations in relevant literature (e.g. Brew, 2001, 2006 & 2007; Jenkins, Healey and Zetter, 2007; Trowler 2007; Healey 2005a & 2005b; Healey and Jenkins, 2008) the curriculum was designed to introduce students to an ethos of inquiry-based learning where lecturers make the epistemological links between teaching and research explicit at each stage of a student's ontological journey towards 'being a scholar'. Although the research-teaching nexus ethos permeates the whole of the curriculum, three modules in particular were designed to focus on its active development: *Academic and Professional Methods and Approaches* at level 1, *Dissertation Methods and Approaches* at level 2 and *Dissertation* at level 3. I am the module leader for all three modules.

It must be stressed that in this study 'undergraduate research' is not intended as the production of original knowledge. In the words of Jenkins and Healey, the focus:

is on student learning and on being assessed in ways that mimic how research is conducted in the discipline...what is produced and learned is not to be new knowledge per se; but it is new to the student and, perhaps more significantly, transforms their understanding of knowledge and research. (2008)

At level 1 the students' transition to scholarship is for example encouraged in module *Academic*

Figure 1. Curriculum design and the research-teaching nexus (© Healey, 2005 and Jenkins and Healey, 2008). Used with permission.

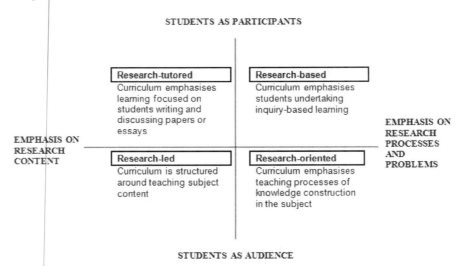

and *Professional Methods and Approaches,* the aims of which are:

...to prepare students for academic study at degree level, to illustrate the nature and processes of research in humanities and to introduce students to research methodology. The module will also aim at providing practical experience of applying these skills in actual case studies relevant to their study programme. Extensive use of information and communication technology will be made in the learning, teaching and assessment of this module. The module will include elements of on-line assessment, both summative and formative, such as a test on information retrieval skills and weekly contributions to online discussion forums. Students will be given the opportunity to reflect upon and record their Personal Development with the ePortfolio PebblePad. (Module Information Directory, 2008)

In the above modules students have to develop academic essay-writing skills. Instead of providing students with 'ready-made' essay titles, one of the assessed tasks requires them to identify the sources of a set of quotations provided by the tutor, to reference them, to find scholarly sources on the same topic and to build an argumentative essay around the sources found. They have two weeks to prepare for the assessed in-class assessed essay writing task based upon their research. As recommended in relevant literature on assessment task design (Boud, 1995; Elton, 1996; McDowell & Sambell, 1999; Race, 1999; Biggs, 1999), the assessed essay-writing task aims to actively engage the students and to foster an intrinsic approach to learning, rather than an extrinsic one, by encouraging them to take ownership of their learning experience and to become more involved in the decision-making process related to the assessment task. In this way students start searching for information and approaching controversial topics in a similar way to their lecturers', and mirroring research practice in the discipline studied - English - as recommended by Jenkins, Healey and Zetter (2007) and Barnett (2000). Also, students take a 'personal' route into the topic set in the question and identify their preferred sources to support their argumentative essays. It is an open-book 'seen' task that students can prepare beforehand;

they also are allowed to bring unmarked sources to the in-class test and access e-resources.

Students are also encouraged to make use of all the eLearning tools available within the tailor-made Coventry University Portal (CUOnline) that includes the VLE (*Blackboard Vista*, formerly *WebCT*), the ePortfolio software PebblePad and links to the e-Library to support their 'active learning journey'. As part of the development of an inquiry-based culture, students are asked to reflect, both individually and in groups, on the way they have carried out their tasks with the support of PebblePad and of the discussion forums in the VLE, so that their inquiry-based task also becomes a socio-collaborative one. As previously argued (Orsini-Jones & Sinclair, 2008; Orsini-Jones, *et. al.,* 2008), encouraging students to engage in 'metareflection' can be conducive to effective learning.

The level 2 module *Dissertation Methods and Approaches* builds on the students' experience of scholarly practice at level 1 and takes it further. It aims to develop independent research management skills in undergraduates and encourages students – all students - to engage in inquiry-based learning. The module also provides practical experience of applying research methods and approaches in actual case studies, relevant to each student's programme, with particular emphasis on developing a viable research design plan in preparation for the third-year dissertation. This practical experience includes more specific attention to information gathering and advanced literature searches in paper and electronic forms. It counts for 10 credits out of 120 on the students' second year programme and ran for the first time in the second term of year 2 in academic year 2007-2008. Students are asked from the very beginning to identify a provisional topic for their dissertation in year 3. The module learning outcomes are that on its completion students should be able to:

- Construct a viable research design plan for a dissertation;

- Apply their understanding of qualitative and quantitative methods in the research design;
- Retrieve, analyse and evaluate materials from a number of different sources for both academic and professional purposes; and
- Present their research plan to tutor/peers both orally and as a PebblePad *webfolio*, reflect upon the feedback received and comment on their peers' plans. (Module Information Directory 2008)

The module is assessed via an individual presentation of a dissertation research plan - 40% of the module mark- and a draft research proposal for the dissertation – 60% of the module mark.

I decided to base its structure on a module on research methodology that I had taken myself for my MA in Learning and Teaching in Higher Education in 2006-2007. Part of the assessment for the MA module was to present an individual research plan to my tutor and peers and to discuss it with them after the presentation. I had found the process of sharing my work with my 'community of practice' (as used by Wenger 1998) very beneficial and inspiring. I therefore decided to try out the process with the undergraduate students on the module *Dissertation Methods and Approaches*, but with the added support of the use of PebblePad. The students were asked to use the PebblePad *webfolio* tool to produce the outline for their presentation. This was done to enable both presenter and participants to have a 'sharable' research plan, a learning object that would be available both for the duration of the module in 2007-2008 and also subsequently, in 2008-2009, so that the 'ripples' of the students' work (and the staff and students' comments on their work) could reach into the next academic year and inform the students' subsequent research choices as illustrated in the FREE model discussed below.

BACKGROUND 2: KNOWLEDGE CONSTRUCTION WITH THE *VLE* AND WITH PEBBLEPAD

At Coventry University staff have many e-tools at their disposal within the institutional portal to support learning and teaching. These range from 'old(er)' – e.g. the VLE - to 'new(er)' technology - e.g. *Wordpress,* for the easy creation of blogs and wikis. As previously discussed (Orsini-Jones & De, 2007), VLEs and other proprietary systems like PebblePad are subject to criticism these days (e.g. Beetham & Sharpe, 2007; Phipps, Cormier & Stiles, 2008), possibly because they are being used by many Higher Education institutions as static repositories for (mainly) administrative content, or because their interface no longer reflects the dynamic interaction available within other social-software platforms available on the world wide web (such as *Facebook*). It has also been reported in the relevant literature that many students find the navigation of proprietary systems puzzling in comparison to the e-platforms they use for private and social purposes - there are various JISC reports on this point, see for example Conole, 2008.

Web 2.0 freeware advocates however overlook the fact that serious pedagogical and management issues could arise from the adoption of non-proprietary systems in a formal educational setting. This is particularly true if the purpose of the lecturer is that of designing and managing assessed tasks for taught courses. Proprietary systems are still the most valid solution for the setting of tasks that offer students a mixture of personalised and social-collaborative learning opportunities within an ethically sound environment. Also, this does not prevent students from accessing and using Web 2.0 technologies from within the proprietary system adopted by the institution that they happen to be studying at (e.g. students producing a video for *YouTube* for their assessed presentation and putting a link to it in their PebblePad *webfolio*). Further analyses of the way in which a VLE can enhance the learning

environment in higher education can be found in O'Donoghue (2006) and in Brett's chapter in particular (2006, pp. 160-175), with examples provided from other institutions.

With reference to PebblePad in particular, in the words of one of its creators, Shane Sutherland (Email communication, 2009):

Part of the misunderstanding around using Web 2.0 rather than a system like PebblePad concerns a lack of differentiation between 'learning' and 'assessment'. So, there are many Web 2.0 tools I can use to support my learning (individual, constructivist, social-constructivist) but the process of assessment becomes unmanageable where e.g. 30 students submit work for formative or summative feedback in a range of different tools/styles. This is especially problematic if the work is intended to be 'private' in some way as a multitude of passwords are required by both the students and the assessor to be able to access and comment upon each others' work. (Also) we can argue that PebblePad is more like a personal learning system because it provides tools (wizards) that are obviously beneficial to users recording things like action plans, thoughts, meetings etc. Web 2.0 tools don't normally do this - that's not their purpose. (Sutherland, 2009)

The above view was shared by the Personal Development Planning University Group at Coventry University, that took the decision of adopting PebblePad campus-wide in academic year 2005-2006 (following a pilot in 2004-2005) and to provide all students with PebblePad training and handbooks in both induction week and throughout the year from 2006-2007. PebblePad became the platform of choice for the production of the personal development planning portfolios that all students have to create as part of their mandatory 10 credit employability modules – one per year - since 2006-2007. The setting up of a 'flying squad' of PebblePad helpers based in both the careers office and the eLearning Unit

Figure 2. The FREE – Fluid Role Evolving Environment – through WebCT Model (© Orsini-Jones and Davidson 1999)

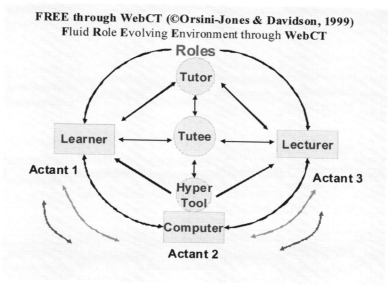

supported students with overcoming most of the initial navigational problems that they had experienced and reported in the pilot year of campus adoption (Orsini-Jones, *et. al.,* 2007). The higher profile of PebblePad following its campus-wide adoption and the provision of dedicated manuals made its integration into the curriculum easier. It also allowed staff and students to experiment with recording reflections and creating materials in a novel way (e.g. Courtney & Deane 2006; Webb, 2006; Bull & Webb, 2007; Orsini-Jones, *et al.* 2007b; Awang, 2008, Orsini-Jones & De, 2008). PebblePad appeared to offer more than a VLE in terms of the opportunities for the personalisation of the student's learning experience.

I decided to try and implement an eLearning model I had designed with a colleague from health studies with PebblePad. The model is called the Fluid Role Evolving Environment (FREE) through WebCT (Figure 2). It is based on constructionist foundations (Ackermann, 1996; 2001; 2004), as I ascribe to the principle that knowledge is "not something that a person has or doesn't have" (Burr, 2003, p. 9), but rather "something that people do

together" (*ibid*). The model illustrates how students' scholarship could be integrated into the curriculum and be made visible on a permanent basis. Examples included case-studies from languages and health studies, where learning objects created by students were studied by other students even in subsequent academic years and evolved thanks to the fact that they could be shared, discussed and modified by staff and students within the VLE (Orsini-Jones & Davidson, 1999).

As previously mentioned, PebblePad encourages students to engage in reflective practice when writing an entry – or 'asset' - as it is called in PebblePad. It also provides a blog facility, and makes it easy to create active hypertextual nodes. Moreover, assets can be shared via a *gateway* that operates like a 'content-rich' forum, where students can peer-review each other's work. The building of web pages can be collaborative and the *webfolio* tool provides opportunities for group reflective practice and socio-collaborative creation of hypermedia environments (Orsini-Jones *et. al.,* 2007; Orsini-Jones, 2008). For this reason it appeared that it would be possible to operationalise

Figure 3. The 'Secret Garden' - The hidden world of a student's private PebblePad environment

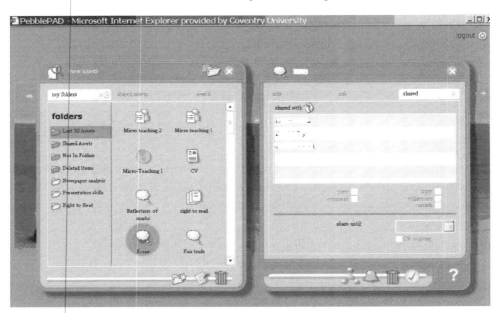

and adapt the model via the integration of the new available software into the curriculum. The main difference with the previous implementation of the FREE model was that this time students would engage in an individual task, rather than a group one.

Also, there are aspects of PebblePad that differ considerably from the VLE. The ePortfolio area is managed individually by the student and is private to him or her – like a walled secret garden - but s(he) can choose to share some of her/his entries with peers/tutors (see Figure 3: The "Secret Garden" - The hidden world of a student's private PebblePad environment). This aspect of student-centred control differentiates PebblePad from a VLE. The tracking of students' work is not possible in PebblePad unless students are instructed to post work to the shared gateway. This can be frustrating in terms of research needs of the staff involved, but it is quite empowering for the enhancement of a truly personalised approach to learning for students. Also, as highlighted by most of the literature available on ePortfolios (see for example: Beetham, 2005 and Jafari &

Kaufman, 2006) ePortfolios are ideal tools for process-based approaches to learning and teaching and for personalised learning. In fact, in the words of the provost of the famous innovative Alverno College in the USA, where ePortfolios were pioneered, they are ideal as personalised "Learning Construction Zones" (O'Brien, 2006).

There are various definitions of what constitutes 'personalised learning' (see for example Powell, Tindal & Millwood, 2008). I am in agreement with Ackermann that learning occurs when there is a dialectic tension, a 'dance' between personal and shared learning spaces: "Without connection people cannot grow, yet without separation they cannot relate." (Ackermann, 1996, p. 32). Because of the way the software is built, PebblePad can be 'navigated' by students either at a private or at a public level on their cognitive journeys. Its adoption at Coventry University allowed me to structure the inquiry-based tasks for module *Dissertation Methods and Approaches* around the affordances of the software bearing in mind the overall principles below (Orsini-Jones & Sinclair, 2008, p. 76):

- An eLearning activity must be very carefully designed and is defined as 'a specific interaction of learner(s) with other(s) using specific tools and resources, orientated towards specific outcomes'. (Beetham, 2007, p. 28, italics in original)
- As implied by McLuhan (1967) the medium (or media) chosen for the task affects the students' learning experience and cognitive journey.
- Learning, as argued by Vygotsky, 'is a socially mediated activity in the first instance, with concepts and skills being internalized only after they have been mastered in a collaborative context'. (Vygotsky 1986, cited in Beetham, 2007, p. 36)
- For learning to be effective, tasks set need to challenge the learner's approach to learning and 'worldview': learning can be troublesome (Meyer and Land, 2006).

Developing as Scholars via Shared Spaces and Secret Gardens in Module Dissertation Methods and Approaches: Students' Perspectives and Troublesome Knowledge

This work started as a reflective evaluation of the students' experience on the new module *Dissertation Methods and Approaches* in its first year of delivery (2007-2008). It was initially triggered by the desire to evaluate the use of the ePortfolio PebblePad to support the students' research journeys within the framework of the FREE model, but then developed into a bigger scale investigation – that is still in progress – to identify curricular actions that can help students with overcoming the fear to engage with research at undergraduate level.

The change in direction of the investigation was triggered mainly by the evaluation of the students' feedback on the module and the marks that the students obtained. I was concerned by the relatively low average mark obtained by the

students for their individual *webfolio* presentation task for this second year module (50%, see Appendix 1 with the instructions for the task). I felt that I needed to engage in a systematic analysis of what had gone wrong as these results did not tie in with my initial expectations derived from the previous case studies of integration of PebblePad in other modules. In the other case-studies there had been evidence that the targeted use of certain PebblePad tools had enhanced the students' learning experience (Orsini-Jones *et. al.*, 2008; Orsini-Jones & Sinclair, 2008). Although it was somewhat reassuring that students obtained a higher average mark in their second assessed task for module Dissertation Methods and Approaches – the dissertation project plan (58%) –, it was necessary to investigate further the issues that had arisen from the presentation task.

One of the major issues was that some students found the subject matter – engaging in research – obscure. This was also reflected in the pass rate for the module: 20% of the students failed at their first attempt. Although the students who failed this module also failed many of their other modules, it was still of concern to me that the pass rate for a second year module was so low, which is why I decided to identify the main areas of difficulties in discussions with students in order to action-research changes for future academic years.

There have already been some studies aimed at identifying troublesome concepts related to 'becoming a researcher' at postgraduate level (e.g. Kiley & Wisker 2006; Wisker, Kiley & Aiston 2006; Trafford, 2008) and attempts to design taxonomies of undergraduate research skills following the identification of troublesome research knowledge (e.g. Willison & Remenda, 2008; Willison & O'Regan, 2006). The distinctive features of this work are that it tries to identify threshold concepts at undergraduate level that relate to 'being an undergraduate researcher in English Studies' and investigates the role that dedicated e-tools can have in supporting such experience.

The evaluation of this curricular intervention is based upon both qualitative and quantitative data:

- the questions that students asked in class;
- the queries that they posted in the VLE (both in module mail and in discussions);
- the observation of the assessed individual presentations and the marks obtained for the presentation *webfolios* and project plans;
- the reflective action plans that students wrote and posted in PebblePad before and after their presentations;
- the written comments posted by students on their peers' *webfolios;*
- the informal conversations carried out with students throughout the year;
- the formal supervisions carried out with each student in preparation for the submission of the final version of their research plan;
- the semi-structured interviews carried out with a self-selected group of final-year students in November 2008 – after the module had finished and at the beginning of their 'dissertation journey';
- the feedback provided by students in the anonymous online module evaluation questionnaires created using the assessment/survey tool in the VLE and standard for all modules at Coventry University (14 returns out of 42 students);
- the feedback provided to me by the colleagues who moderated the task; and
- the feedback provided at Course Consultative Committees, a forum for students to comment on their course to their lecturers.

The analysis of the feedback in the module evaluation questionnaires showed that the students who had responded had found the module interesting and stimulating and particularly valued the opportunity to learn how to plan for their dissertation before the final year, e.g.: "I believe this module gave us the chance to think and prepare notes and express our thoughts for next year's final project. It was also helpful to do the action plan, the oral presentation and also the tutors' feedback". As for the negative comments, in the survey some students stated that the nature and assessment of the module had been too demanding: e.g. "The module is too intense and puts students under pressure".

During the semi-structured interviews (that I carried out in adherence with British Educational Research Association guidelines in academic year 2008-2009 after the students had completed the module), the four self-selected female students who agreed to discuss their learning experience stated that they had found the action-plan tool in PebblePad particularly useful for the purpose of outlining their research proposal. The tutor's choice to opt for a model mirroring her experience on the MA programme also proved to be successful as students maintained that receiving feedback from their peers and tutors after the presentation had been the most valuable aspect of the module:

Student 1: What I really liked was that when you do a presentation, any presentation or a piece of coursework, you only ever get something in from your lecturers because they mark it, but for the presentation you were faced by everybody you are studying with and you know they gave you both positive and negative points. And even if some people find that daunting it did help because it was useful; it was coming from the peers (stress in the voice marked with underlining).

Student 2: That really taught me that it was a big project and it needs to be.

Student 3: The presentation is a huge support... and it's all very well if you are having the lecturer saying do this, this and this, but when your peers point out things to you it means more.

Student 2: And you do take it on board. The presentation must be kept.

Encouraging remarks were also made by students on the written comments received on their research plans in the shared *gateway* in PebblePad:

Interviewer: And then, after you received the oral feedback, did you have a look at the written comments? Was there anything useful?

Students 1, 2 and 3 (together): Very useful.

Student 1: Mine especially, people said it was too vast and it was going to take up my whole life. So I reduced my data collection to 6 months.

Student 2: Me too. Comments said that I was not being very realistic and that made me re-think my plan. Some also commented that my plan did not make clear sense in places, so I revisited it and made changes.

During the semi-structured interviews students were furthermore asked if they felt that using PebblePad had helped them to 'become researchers' and to structure their work. They stated that they had valued the way in which the tools in PebblePad had indeed helped them to structure their research project:

Interviewer: Did it help at all to use the Pebble-Pad webfolio to structure your draft dissertation presentation?

Chorus of 'yes'

Q. Why and How?

Student 1: Because the structure is already there, isn't it really, it's easy to follow. It's just so user-friendly, I think. That helps with structuring the sections.

Student 2 (interjecting): It was useful to be forced into specific headings.

Interviewer: So you found that it forced you into structuring what you were doing?

Students 1 and 2: Yes.

Interviewer (addressing the third student): You found that as well?

Student 3: Yes. In my own head I found it extremely difficult to decide what should go first and second and after. You were forced to produce an introduction. And for me that's very, very helpful because I need to have help with structuring and I struggle with this. It was not that easy to begin with, but then I found it user-friendly too and I like the fact that I can personalise the interface.

It can be seen from the words of student number 3 that being able to customise the PebblePad environment is important to her. The students who participated in the interviews also stated that they all used the ePortfolio for their own private use too, and one of them was even keeping a personal driving test diary, documenting her difficulties in trying to pass the test and action-planning her mistakes. It was apparent that they were maximising the use of the tool for both personal and academic use and valued what had been referred to previously as the 'dance' between their private and their public learning spaces. These students also valued the 'private learning space' provided by PebblePad and felt 'safer' within in that in other environments:

Interviewer: Have you ever communicated amongst yourselves in PebblePad for personal reasons?

Student 1: Yes, with some friends around campus.

Interviewer: And why do you think you used PebblePad as opposed to Facebook?

Student 1: I didn't really use Facebook when I started using PebblePad. And you can keep it private in PebblePad.

Interviewer: So you like the fact that PebblePad is 'closed'?

Student 2: Yes, we like it because it is private.

Student 1: It is difficult to be private in Facebook

However, although the feedback on the use of PebblePad was very positive from the students who volunteered to be interviewed, others made negative remarks about it both in the evaluation questionnaires ("cumbersome") and face-to-face (some students had had problems in accessing it from home and/or with creating the *webfolio* and/or posting to the *gateway*). I therefore asked the interviewees to comment on why some of their peers, unlike them, had found the tool challenging and/or were against its use. The interviewees claimed that in their opinion it was not so much a matter of computer-phobia (even if they admitted that this could be the case for a minority of their peers), but that it had to do more with PebblePad being associated with doing what was perceived to be difficult work for the university:

Student 1: I think it's because they were introduced to it at University and so many people think 'oh PebblePad means University, it's academic, it's work'. And so they think it's boring and it's difficult because we had to use it for the dissertation.

The above words would appear to confirm the outcome of research carried out for JISC, Conole

(2008), indicates that students can 'resent' what they perceive to be institutional tools. The fact that many students thought that PebblePad was a Coventry University in-house-created piece of software is telling in this respect. The tensions that emerged in the way students positioned themselves towards the use of PebblePad reflect the content of a talk given by Hartley (2007) and well summarised by Samuel (2008). Hartley suggests that the students' learning experience has become a "collision of learning spaces", as students these days have to journey amongst three main eLearning zones:

- The formal, public, controlled. The institutional world of control and individual assessment, the VLE (*the museum*);
- The collaborative, informal, exploratory. The world of facilitation and enquiry, Google, wikis, Facebook and MySpace (*the playground*); and
- The personal, private and exclusive. Talking to invited friends only: iPODs (*the refuge*).

Hartley sees education as the "new fight in the playground" (2007). It could be argued that PebblePad has characteristics that would fit in each of the above three learning zones, particularly in the light of the feedback obtained in the semi-structured interviews. However, the complexity inherent in handling all the above spaces can prove to be confusing for some students, particularly those who resist transition into the higher education ethos of independent learning, are challenged by inquiry-based learning and would rather be told what to do. The higher than normal failure rate for the webfolio presentation task in the 2007-2008 cohort could be partially justified by the fact that the cohort was weak (which will have to be verified against the marks obtained by students in 2008-2009), but it could also be partially ascribed to the inability of some students to negotiate amongst different learning spaces.

Some students associate personalisation only with leisure, rather than with personal development planning and struggle to grasp the differences in the 'discourse' of each eLearning space used. So, for example, many research plans were written like colloquial blogs and presented characteristics that in 'threshold concepts' terminology are associated with 'mimicry'. 'Mimicry' means faking understanding (Cousin, 2009, p.204), so, for example, some students wrote in their research plans for English literature, where they had chosen to analyse the themes of a particular literary texts, that they would use 'both qualitative and quantitative data' – which was irrelevant for their chosen topic and betrayed their puzzlement about relevant research methodologies.

It has been previously argued (Orsini-Jones, 2008), that a constructivist approach to knowledge development like the one represented by the FREE model does not suit all learners, as it requires a high level of cognitive engagement and, to put it with Perkins, "not all learners respond well to the challenge". (2006, p.36)

The testing nature of the tasks set in module *Dissertation Methods and Approaches* was also explored with the students interviewed in November 2008. Both from the data collected and from the interview transcripts it emerged that the troublesome knowledge appeared to be mainly linked to difficulties to do with:

- the 'epistemic game', the linguistic tools (Perkins, 2006) required to engage with the 'discourse' of research in English Studies; and
- the ontological shift of identity required to 'being/becoming' a researcher.

Both of the above troublesome areas impact upon the students' attitudes towards the e-tools available to them – whether they use them for personal or public use. In fact I would like to propose that this inability to cope with a shift in focus from receiving knowledge from an authority to collaborating with lecturers and peers to create knowledge is also clearly reflected in some students' resistance to the adoption of the e-tools used to support them in 'becoming researchers'. Some students will therefore blame the e-tool for their inability to engage, while it is in fact their deep-seated suspicion and/or resistance to inquiry-based learning that prevents them from crossing conceptual thresholds.

The resistance to engaging in the discourse of research encountered amongst some students always appeared to encompass the two above-mentioned areas. Despite having encountered resistance to independent learning before, I was still taken aback by the levels of anxiety encountered when asking students to decide on a provisional research topic for their dissertation at the beginning of the module. As the students were English specialists, I also wrongly assumed some epistemic knowledge on their part that they did not have. For example, it became obvious that some students did not understand the difference between 'literature' as a subject that they were studying and 'literature review', despite the fact that it had been covered during the face-to-face sessions in class. This is illustrated in the following extract from one of the research plans by one of the students posted in their PebblePad *webfolio* under the heading "Literature review": "At this point in time I have no set pieces of literature to work from as this will be a language-based investigation."

Another incorrect assumption I made was to think that students had become acquainted with the concepts and 'epistemic arsenal' relating to critical and analytical thinking extensively covered in all the modules in the first year and in particular in module *Academic and Professional Methods and Approaches*. Again this was not the case for many students who did not seem to be able to distinguish between the daily use of certain terms and their use in an academic context, e.g. "criticise" and "argue". They associated their semantic field with the negative connotations that the two terms have in a daily, conversational use, rather than within academic conventions. One student stated for example: "I don't want to argue" to her supervisor, who was trying to explain to her how to build an academic argument in her literature review. This difficulty in engaging with the 'discourse' of research mirrors the results found when analysing the troublesome concepts that languages students encounter when engaging in formal meta-grammatical analysis (Orsini-Jones & Jones 2007; Orsini-Jones, 2008).

At the level of the 'ontological shift', the students interviewed ascribed their difficulties to the following factors (Semi-structured interviews November 2008):

- lack of confidence in carrying out independent research;
- fear of criticism because it is a personal project ("it's personal, it's very close to you") and difficulties in handling criticism (possibly also to do with the 'literal' understanding of the term, as illustrated above); and
- a feeling of loneliness, inability to compare their own work with that of their peers ("carrying out your own research project is not like having to write the same essay that we all have to do").

The last point could partially explain why the use of PebblePad to support the crossing of conceptual thresholds in grammar understanding had been successful (Orsini-Jones and Sinclair 2008). In that study, students had engaged in group *webfolio* creation. However, the purpose of module *Dissertation and Approaches* is to prepare students for their individual dissertation journey in the final year, so they need to practise working on their research project on their own, even if they can share and discuss the outcomes of their project.

As for the epistemic tools, apart for the above-mentioned issue of the literature review,

students struggled to understand the difference between data collection and analysis on the one hand and research methodology on the other. There was, furthermore, a certain resistance to engage with electronic journal articles and e-books amongst some students. It is somewhat ironic that the children of the digital revolution often complain that "there are not enough books in the library" (module evaluation questionnaire). Intensive library training in the use of e-journals and databases organised in collaboration with the subject librarian for English did not seem to solve the problem. Many students found it too time-consuming to scan and skim so many database articles and often resorted to the 'quick Google fix' that only produced irrelevant and/or inappropriate material. One minor positive outcome was that, possibly because of their familiarity with Google, it was at least possible to engage them in the use of Google Scholar.

On a positive note, the students who successfully completed the tasks despite having encountered initial problems ascribed their achievement to having shared their draft research plans in PebblePad and to having presented them to their peers: "…it was important to do the presentation and talk to your peers. There is light at the end of the tunnel, it helps to talk to peers". (Semi-structured interviews November 2008).

It is difficult to state with certainty if a specific 'research threshold concept' has been identified in this study. It is undeniable however that the successful students, those who managed to produce outstanding research proposals following their initial bewilderment at the idea of having to do so, appeared to have crossed a conceptual threshold. Meyer and Land (2003) define a threshold concept as something:

…akin to a portal, opening up a new and previously inaccessible way of thinking about something. … It represents a transformed way of understanding, or interpreting, or viewing something without which the learner cannot progress… As a con-

sequence of comprehending a threshold concept there may thus be a transformed internal view of subject matter, subject landscape, or even world view...This transformation may be sudden or it may be protracted over a considerable period of time, with the transition to understanding proving troublesome. (Meyer & Land, 2003, p. 412)

It could be argued that the weaker students on module *Dissertation Methods and Approaches* were finding it difficult to conceptualise themselves as researchers. With reference to doctoral students engaging in PhDs, Trafford maintains that the threshold concept has to do with the ability to conceptualise with reference to the subject matter chosen (Trafford, 2008, pp. 280-284). But Trafford is illustrating case studies of postgraduate students who have already gained the confidence to engage in serious research by enrolling on a PhD. In view of the results of this study, it is proposed that the curriculum intervention to help undergraduate students with coming to terms with 'being researchers' has to be targeted at the threshold concept of 'seeing themselves as researchers'. The issue of "lack of confidence in being a researcher" recurs in the interviews and the feedback collected for this work. It would appear that while the epistemological aspects of the methodology must also be taught, students will not 'buy in' the research discourse unless more stress is put on helping them with conceptualising themselves as researchers.

It is also necessary to point out to them that they need to come to terms with the fact that learning can be troublesome (Meyer & Land, 2006). With reference to the lessons learnt for 2008-2009, I tried to put less stress in my teaching on 'what is research?', and more on encouraging students to ask themselves 'how can I think like a researcher?'/'how can I become a researcher'. I also realised that it is important to set clearer ground rules referring to what research means at undergraduate level, so that students do not feel that they must produce an original piece of research;

however, it should also be stressed to them that original research might be a possible outcome of their project proposal. Providing examples from the best dissertation plans produced in PebblePad by the students who managed to cross the threshold concept (see for example Figure 4: *Sample Plan Screen Shot (extract): The shared world of research to be peer reviewed – the Dissertation Plan Proposal (Language Acquisition)* should also help. This was of course not possible in academic year 2007-2008, as the module was running for the first time.

FUTURE RESEARCH DIRECTIONS

The second occurrence of the module, January-April of academic year 2008-2009, offered the module leader an opportunity to implement action-research-led curricular change (McNiff 1988; McKernan 1992). The outcomes of this study have already fed into the planning of the syllabus and delivery of the module. An evaluation of the actions taken will then be carried out at the end of academic year 2008-2009 and will feed into the re-planning of the module for academic year 2009-2010 in an action-research cycle as the one illustrated in Figure 5 (Stages in and Action-Research Project). I will base the methodology for this curricular intervention around the one I used to action research threshold concepts for an investigation in the understanding of formal grammar learning with the support of eLearning tools. (Orsini-Jones, 2008; Cousin, 2009, p.209)

The troublesome research knowledge identified in this study will therefore be investigated further as well as its links with the utilisation of different eLearning spaces by students. More research must be carried out on how technology works or does not work to support personalised learning, bearing in mind what Hartley claims when eLearning spaces do not work: "… technology is a symptom – it is not the problem" (2007).

Figure 4. Sample plan screen shot (extract) - the shared world of research to be peer reviewed - the dissertation plan proposal (Language Acquisition)

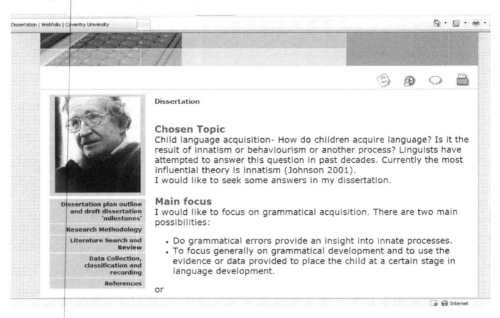

Figure 5. Stages in an action-research project

1. A problematic issue is identified (**reconnaissance** stage);
2. Change is **planned** collaboratively (staff and students) to address the issue;
3. The change process is **implemented – 'acted out'**;
4. All agents involved in the change process **reflect** upon its outcomes, both while it is happening and at the end of the first phase of implementation;
5. Actions are taken to **re-plan** the changes and the second phase of the action-research cycle starts (McNiff, 1988; McKernan, 1992; Kemmis & McTaggart, 1990 and 2005; Kember, 2000).

With reference to the evaluation of the validity of the FREE model in the current eLearning landscape, it could be argued that its principles of constructionist and inquiry-based knowledge building still apply. However, its graphic representation (Figure 1) does not do justice to the complexity of the ICT affordances (Conole 2005) of the new and emerging e-tools and e-zones. A new FREE has therefore been designed (Figure 6). An 'E' for 'ELearning' has been added to the acronym that now reads: Fluid Role Evolving ELearning Environment (FREEE). It tries and represent how the three spaces identified by

Hartley affect learning at the local institutional level (students use all three 'zones' on a regular basis): "museum", "playground" and "secret garden" (I prefer this to "refuge", as from the title of this chapter) and the way the same three 'zones' are linked to and interact with the wider, global e-village we now live in. The role of the lecturer has also changed, as he/she cannot ignore how students are using technology, but needs to provide support (hence the 'supporting' link arrow) to enable students to use technology in an academically and professionally enabling way. Moreover, the new e-tools (both local and

Figure 6. The new FREEE (Fluid Role Evolving ELearning Environment). © Orsini-Jones 2009[1]

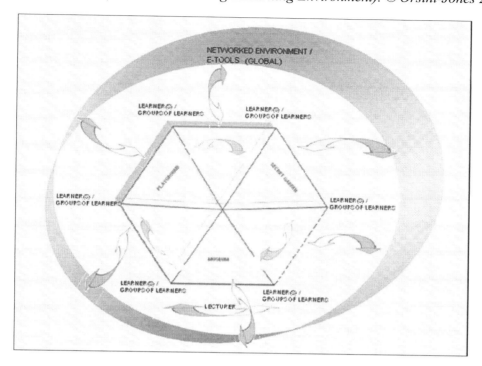

global) allow learners to interact individually or in groups with other learners in ways not even imagined ten years ago. As stressed before, there still is a considerable amount of work needed in terms of information literacy though (or multiliteracies: New London Group 1996; Warschauer & Ware 2008): Mason and Rennie report that students may have the technical skills "to find, cut and paste information, but not the pedagogical literacy skills to make it their own" (Mason & Rennie, 2008:135).

Also, the analysis of the data collected for this study appears to somewhat contradict what Hartley claims. It might be true that higher education institutions are fighting for the "playground" eLearning space, but it could be argued that learning at university level might take place more in an "interactive museum" and in a "secret garden" than in a "playground". Perhaps the will of undergraduate students to keep their academic learning spaces separate from their playgrounds (which is amply documented in the literature, including in

Hartley, 2007) should be respected. It would be interesting to know how Hartley would classify PebblePad. Having observed students using it for the last 5 years, I would like to propose that it is part *museum*, part *refuge* (or, better still, *secret garden*) and part *playground*. It is a proprietary system, but it allows students to own, control and personalise their learning space while at the same time providing them the opportunity to engage with highly structured reflective formal tools like the 'action planning' one.

CONCLUSION

The initial evaluation of the first occurrence of the running of module *Dissertation Methods and Approaches* has provided an opportunity to explore how students relate to a task which is aimed at developing their research skills and is supported by a variety of reflective e-tools, available both in shared and in private spaces.

This study has underlined that for some students the use of such tools can help them to develop their independent research skills and to build up their confidence as researchers and personalise their learning experience. These students are able to move easily between their public and private eLearning spaces and are able to maximise the benefit of the e-tools available to them in both academic and personal ways (and/or both).

However it has also emerged that other students find the complexity of engaging in research and in inquiry-based learning very challenging, and instead of maximising the benefits deriving from the use of the reflective eLearning tools available, they see them as another difficult hurdle to jump. They also appear to be confused by the eLearning spaces available to them and do not appear to grasp their relevance to either their academic or personal development.

It was observed how sharing the research proposal plan learning objects (the *Webfolios*) via the gateway in PebblePad caused a positive ontological shift in some of the students in the second group, who started to come to terms with the fact that engaging in research is troublesome, but can be a rewarding and confidence-building challenge.

It was also ascertained that there might be links between students' attitudes towards learning and the way they perceive the institutional tools that have been put in place to support their cognitive journey. Students can find challenging the e-tools that they associate with what they perceive to be 'difficult' assessed tasks.

The use of the ePortfolio PebblePad would appear to suit the learning preferences of the students who thrive on personalising their learning experience: they appear to see clearly that the tool can be used for both their personal learning needs and their social-collaborative ones and can maximise its use to their benefit. On the other hand, students who struggle to engage with inquiry-based learning and constructionist tasks also find it difficult to 'conceptualise themselves as researchers'. It

is proposed that the latter is a threshold concept that needs further investigation.

With reference to the stimulating model of eLearning spaces proposed by Hartley, it must be pointed out that it does not appear to cover personalised collaborative learning in formal settings and more research is needed in this field.

Finally, it has emerged that the less independent students might need further support with becoming better acquainted with the different 'discourses' inherent to each of the eLearning spaces that they use.

REFERENCES

Ackermann, E. (1996). Perspective-Taking and Object Construction. In Y. Kasai, & M. Resnick (Eds.), *Constructionism in Practice: Designing, Thinking and Learning in a Digital World* (pp. 25-35). Mahwah, NJ: Lawrence Erlbaum.

Ackermann, E. (2001) *Piaget's Constructivism, Papert's Constructionism: What's the difference?* Retrieved July 20, 2008, from http://learning.media.mit.edu/content/publications/EA.Piaget%20_%20Papert.pdf

Ackermann, E. (2004). Constructing knowledge and transforming the world. In M. Tokoro & L. Steels (Eds.) *A learning zone of one's own: Sharing representations and flow in collaborative learning environment* (pp. 15-37). Washington, DC: IOS Press.

Awang, D. (2008, November). *PebblePad: Big Splashes or mini Ripples? Reflections on Electronic Portfolio Usage on a Blended Learning Course.* Paper presented at ECEL 2008, 7th European Conference on E-learning. Grecian Bay Hotel, Agia Napa, Cyprus.

Beetham, H. (2005). *JISC report on e-portfolios in post-16 learning in the UK: Developments, issues and opportunities*. Retrieved October 20, 2008, from http://www.jisc.ac.uk/uploaded_documents/eportfolio_ped.doc

Beetham, H. (2007). An approach to learning activity design. In H. Beetham, & R. Sharpe (Eds.) *Rethinking Pedagogy for a Digital Age – Designing and delivering e-learning* (pp. 26-40). London: Routledge.

Biggs, J. B. (2003, 2nd Edition). *Teaching for Quality Learning at University*. Buckingham, UK: SRHE and Open University Press.

Boud, D. (1995). Assessment and Learning: Contradictory or Complementary? In P. Knight (ed.) *Assessment for Learning in Higher Education* (35-48). London: Kogan Page.

Brett, P. (2006). Staff using an institution-wide VLE for blended e-learning. In J. O'Donoghue (Ed.) *Technology supported learning and teaching: a staff perspective* (pp 160-175). Heshey, PA: Idea Group Publishing.

Brew, A. (2001). *The nature of research: inquiry in academic contexts*. London: Routledge Falmer.

Brew, A. (2006). *Research and teaching: beyond the divide*. London: PalgraveMacmillan.

Brew, A. (2007). Research and teaching from the students' perspective. *International policies and practices for academic enquiry: An international colloquium*, Winchester, UK, April 19–21. Retrieved November 1, 2008, from http://portal-live.solent.ac.uk/university/rtconference/2007/resources/angela_brew.pdf

British Educational Research Association (BERA). (2009). Retrieved February 21, 2009, from http://www.bera.ac.uk

Bull, K., & Webb, L. (2007). E-portfolio as a tool for online collaborative group research and experiences of running a whole school module on PDP. In F. Deepwell, (Ed.), *ELATE (Enhancing Learning And Teaching Environments) Conference 07 – Internationalisation Conference Proceedings* (pp 95-96). Coventry, UK: Coventry University Press.

Burnett, F. H. (1909). *The Secret Garden*. New York: HarperCollins.

Burr, V. (2003). *Social Constructionism* (2nd Ed.). London: Routledge.

Conole, G. (2005, December). *Designing for effective e-learning - feeding pedagogical research into practice*. Paper presented at the Higher Education Academy E-Learning symposium: pedagogy and practice, University of Southampton, Southampton, UK.

Conole, G. (2008). Listening to the learner voice: The ever changing landscape of technology use for language students. *ReCALL, 20*(2), 121–140. doi:10.1017/S0958344008000220

Courtney, K., & Deane, M. (2006). Collaborating to Strengthen Students' Writing Skills. *Impressions: Newsletter of the Centre for the Study of Higher Education (CSHE), 1*(15). Coventry, UK: Coventry University. Retrieved November 5, 2008 from http://www.corporate.coventry.ac.uk/content/1/c6/01/49/14/CSHE%20Newsletter.pdf

Cousin, G. (2009). *Researching Learning in Higher Education: An Introduction to Contemporary Methods and Approaches*. London: Routledge.

Elton, L. (1996). Strategies to enhance Student motivation: A conceptual analysis. *Studies in Higher Education, 21*, 57–68. doi:10.1080/03075079612331381457

Facebook (n.d.). Retrieved from http://en-gb.facebook.com/

Hartley, P. (2007). New technology and the modern university. In *Next Generation Environments, JISC*. Retrieved November 9, from http://www.jisc.ac.uk/media/documents/events/2007/04/next_gen_keynote.ppt

Healey, M. (2005a). Linking Research and Teaching to Benefit Student Learning. *Journal of Geography in Higher Education, 29*(2), 183–201. doi:10.1080/03098260500130387

Healey, M. (2005b). Linking research and teaching exploring disciplinary spaces and the role of inquiry-based learning. In R. Barnett (Ed.), *Reshaping the university: new relationships between research, scholarship and teaching* (pp. 30-42). Maidenhead, UK: McGraw-Hill/Open University Press.

Healey, M. & Jenkins, A. (2008, October). Developing students as researchers. *UC (University and College) Magazine,* 17-19.

Jafari, A., & Kaufman, C. (2006). *Handbook of Research on e-Portfolios*. Hershey, PA: Idea Group.

Jenkins, A., & Healey, M. (in press) Developing the student as a researcher through the curriculum. In C. Rust (ed.) *Improving Student Learning through the Curriculum*. Oxford: OCSLD.

Jenkins, A., Healey, M., & Zetter, R. (2007). *Linking Teaching and Research in Disciplines and Departments*. Retrieved 30 June 2008 from http://www.heacademy.ac.uk/ourwork/research/teaching

Kiley, M., & Wisker, G. (2006, December). *Learning leaps and strides: when and in what ways do doctoral research students cross conceptual thresholds and achieve threshold concepts?* Paper presented at the Beyond boundaries: New Horizons for Research into Higher Education Conference, Brighton, England.

Land, R., Meyer, J. H. F., & Smith, J. (Eds.). (2008). *Threshold Concepts Within the Disciplines*, (pp. 59-74). Rotterdam: Sense.

Mason, R., & Rennie, F. (2008). *E-Learning and Social Networking Handbook*. London: Routledge.

McDowell, L., & Sambell, K. (1999). The experience of Innovative Assessment: Student Perspectives. In S. Brown, & A. Glasner, (Eds.) *Assessment Matters in Higher Education* (pp. 71-82). Buckingham, UK: SRHE/Open University Press.

McKernan, J. (1992). *Curriculum Action Research*. London: Kogan Page.

McNiff, J. (1988). *Action Research: Principles and Practices*. London: Routledge.

Meyer, J. H. F., & Land, R. (2003). Threshold Concepts and Troublesome Knowledge (1). Linkages to Ways of Thinking and Practising within the disciplines. In C. Rust (Ed.), *Improving Student Learning – Ten Years On. 10th International Symposium, The Oxford Centre for Staff and Learning Development* (pp. 412-424). Oxford: OCSLD.

Meyer, J. H. F., & Land, R. (2005). Threshold Concepts and Troublesome Knowledge (2): epistemological considerations and a conceptual framework for teaching and learning. *Higher Education, 49*, 373–388. doi:10.1007/s10734-004-6779-5

Meyer, J. H. F., & Land, R. (2006). *Overcoming barriers to student understanding: Threshold concepts and troublesome knowledge*. London: Routledge/Falmer. *Module Information Directory* (n.d.). Coventry, UK: Coventry University. Retrieved November 5, 2008, from http://mid.coventry.ac.uk

New London Group. (1996). A pedagogy of multiliteracies: Designing social futures. *Harvard Educational Review, 66*(1), 60–92.

O'Brien, K. (2006). ePortfolios as Learning Construction Zones: Provost's Perspective. In A. Jafari & C. Kaufman (Eds.) *Handbook of Research on e-Portfolio,* (pp.75-82). Hershey, PA: Idea Group.

O'Donoghue, J. (Ed.). (2006). *Technology supported learning and teaching: a staff perspective.* Heshey, PA: Idea Group Publishing.

Orsini-Jones, M. (2008). Troublesome language knowledge: identifying threshold concepts in grammar learning. In R. Land, J. F. H. Meyer & J. Smith (Eds.), *Threshold Concepts within the Disciplines* (pp. 213-226). Rotterdam, The Netherlands: Sense.

Orsini-Jones, M., Adley, D., Lamari, C., Maund, N., & Paruk, K. (2008). Integrating PDP (Personal Development Planning) and PebblePad into the curriculum – Students' perspectives. In F. Deepwell, (Ed.), *Proceedings of the ELATE (Enhancing Learning and Teaching Environments) Conference 2007: Internationalisation.* Coventry, UK: Coventry University. Retrieved November 9, 2008, from http://www.english.heacademy. ac.uk/explore/publications/casestudies/technology/eportfolio.php

Orsini-Jones, M., & Davidson, A. (1999). From reflective learners to reflective lecturers via WebCT. *Active Learning, 10*(1), 32–38.

Orsini-Jones, M., & De, M. (2007). Research-Led Curricular Innovation: Revisiting constructionism via e-portfolio shared assets and webfolios. *Coventry iPED Conference 2007: Researching Academic Futures,* September 10-12, (pp. 65-76). Retrieved November 10, 2008, from http://www. corporate.coventry.ac.uk/content/1/c6/02/15/41/ iPED_2007_Proceedings.pdf

Orsini-Jones, M. & Jones, D.E. (2007). Supporting Collaborative Grammar Learning via a VLE: a case study from Coventry University. *Arts and Humanities in Higher Education: an international journal of theory, research and practice, 6*(1), 90-106.

Orsini-Jones, M., Kurowska, M., McTavish, A. M., & Mills, S. (2007). Personal Development Planning Perspectives from the Faculty of BES (Business, Environment and Society). *Proceedings of the Internationalisation – ELATE (Enhancing Learning and Teaching Environments) Conference,* 26-27 June, (pp. 65-72).

Orsini-Jones, M., & Sinclair, C. (2008). Helping students to GRASP the rules of grammar. In C. Rust (Ed.), *Improving Student Learning – For What?* (pp. 72-86). Proceeding of the 2007 15th International Symposium – The Oxford Centre for Staff and Learning Development. Oxford: OCSLD.

PebblePad – Pebble Learning (n.d.). Retrieved November 10, 2008, from www.pebblelearning. co.uk

Perkins, D. (2006). Constructivism and troublesome knowledge. In J.H.F. Meyer & R. Land (Eds.), *Overcoming barriers to student understanding: Threshold concepts and troublesome knowledge* (pp. 33-47). London: RoutledgeFalmer.

Phipps, L., Cormier, D., & Stiles, M. (2008). Reflecting on the virtual learning systems – extinction or evolution? *Educational Developments, 9*(2), 1–4.

Powell, S., Tindal, I., & Millwood, R. (2008). *Personalised Learning and the Ultraversity Experience.* Inter-Disciplinary Inquiry-Based Learning Project, University of Bolton, Institute of Educational Cybernetics, Retrieved February 18, 2009, from http://idibl.bolton.ac.uk/resources/ publications/Personalised%20Learning%20 and%20the%20Ultraversity%20Experience.pdf/ view

Samuels, P. (2008). Report on JISC Next Generation Environments Conference. *MSOR Connection, 7*(4), 26-29.

Sumner, N. (2006). *PebblePad ALT-N, (5)*. Retrieved November 8, 2008, from http://newsletter.alt.ac.uk/e_article000611550.cfm?x=b11,0,w (Trafford, V. (2008). Conceptual Frameworks as a Threshold Concept in Doctorateness. In R. Land, J. F. H. Meyer & J. Smith (Eds.), *Threshold Concepts within the Disciplines* (pp. 273-288). Rotterdam: Sense.

Trowler, P. (2007, September). *Disciplinary Differences and the Teaching-Research Nexus.* Keynote paper presented at the Researching Academic Futures: Emergent Pedagogies, Global Perspectives Leading Academic Learning, iPED (Inquiring Pedagogies) Conference. Coventry, UK: Coventry University Technocentre. Summary retrieved November 10, 2008, from http://www.corporate.coventry.ac.uk/content/1/c6/02/15/41/iPED_2007_Proceedings.pdf

Warschauer, M., & Ware, M. (2008). Learning, change, and power: Competing discourses of technology and literacy. In J. Coiro, M., Knobel, C. Lankshear, & D. J. Leu (Eds.), *Handbook of research on new literacies* (pp. 215-240). New York: Lawrence Erlbaum Associates.

Webb, L. (2006). Personal Development, Planning - Case Study from Graphic Design. *Impressions: Newsletter of the Centre for the Study of Higher Education (CSHE)1*, 8-9. Coventry, UK: Coventry University. Retrieved November 5, 2008 from http://www.corporate.coventry.ac.uk/content/1/c6/01/49/14/CSHE%20Newsletter.pdf

Wenger, E. (1998). *Communities of practice: Learning, meaning and identity.* Cambridge, UK: Cambridge University Press.

Willison, J., & O'Regan, K. (2008). *The Research Skill Development Framework.* Retrieved November 1, 2008, from: http://www.adelaide.edu.au/clpd/rsd/

Willison, J., & Remenda, V. (2008, June). *Embedding Research Skills Development in Undergraduate Courses or Stuck in Blue-Sky Research in the Disciplines.* Paper presented at the second conference on Threshold Concepts: From Theory to Practice, Queen's University, Kingston, Ontario.

Wisker, G., Kiley, M., & Aiston, S. (2006). Making the learning leap: Research students crossing conceptual thresholds. In M. Kiley & G. Mullins (Eds.), *Quality in Postgraduate Research: Knowledge creation in testing times* (pp. 195-201). Canberra, Australia: CEDAM, The Australian National University.

Wordpress (n.d.). Retrieved February 21, 2009, from http://wordpress.com/

APPENDIX A

Module *Dissertation Methods and Approaches*: Assessed Coursework 1

Individual Presentation of the Dissertation Research Plan.

You will have to deliver a 5-minute individual presentation to illustrate to the rest of the class and your tutor(s) your proposed dissertation plan. You will use the PebblePad *webfolio* tool to do this and include in it the headings indicated in the marking scheme. You can use all the other tools available in PebblePad (the action planning one will be particular useful).

At the end of the session there will be a 5-minute feedback/discussion session and you will receive feedback on your plan from your tutor and your peers. After the session is finished and no later than one week from the date of the delivery of your presentation, you will have to write up an action plan in which you address the issues raised and compare these with issues raised in the research action plan you wrote before the presentation.

This piece of assessment counts for 40% of the module mark and reflects the MID learning outcomes 1, 2, 3 and 4.

Table 1. Marking scheme

1. Dissertation plan outline and draft dissertation 'milestones' **(10 marks)** *Presentation of the topic chosen - illustration of overall aims and objectives and of the draft planned timeline for dissertation writing* What have you chosen? Why? What focus? Have you thought of a hypothesis to test? (If applicable)
2. Research methodology (10 marks) *Illustration and discussion of the research method to be adopted.* *Tools to be used. Ethical considerations.* Rationale for the research method. Reflection on your choice and on how/why it was reached. Ethical forms.
3. Draft literature search and review (10 marks). *Critical review of chosen literature and illustration of how/why/where from it was retrieved. Plans for future searches in view of current findings.* How was the relevant literature found? What tools were used? Why were these texts/article selected? Were others 'discarded'? Why? How? Who did you ask for help?
4. Data collection, classification and recording (5 marks). *Outline of how the relevant data/literature is going to be identified/collected/classified/recorded. Tools to be used.* Methods/tools used for recording data. Where? How? When?
5. Personal reflection and action planning for the dissertation (5 marks). Written reflection in PebblePad in view of the feedback received after the presentation. You must use the action plan tool. What actions will your take now? Are you giving some consideration to the comments received? Are you considering changing anything?

Chapter 20
Physical Metaphorical Modelling with LEGO as a Technology for Collaborative Personalised Learning

Stuart Nolan
Hex Induction, UK

ABSTRACT

LEGO Serious Play is a business development process where users build metaphorical models from LEGO bricks in order to explore and share their perceptions of various aspects of their working lives. They model important symbolic elements of their personality, emotions, working practices, organization, and the relationships between these elements in order to share stories that aid the construction of organizational knowledge. This chapter reports on trials using LEGO Serious Play with HE students from a range of subject areas who used metaphorical modelling to articulate their learning autobiographies, current situations, orientations to learning, and aspirations. The models helped students make informed choices and helped staff to understand their needs and personalise the learning provision appropriately.

INTRODUCTION

It is in playing and only in playing that the individual child or adult is able to be creative and to use the whole personality, and it is only in being creative that the individual discovers the self. (Winnicott, 1971, pp 54)

In its simplest form, personalised learning is about tailoring education to the individual's needs, interests and aptitude, giving the learner a degree of ownership of the learning process. This deceptively simple statement sets out two very clear but complex challenges, how do we discover what the needs, interests and aptitudes of an individual are and how do we facilitate the learner's attempts to own the learning process? To rephrase this from a speculative learner's perspective, "How do I know what my *relevant* needs, interests and aptitudes are

DOI: 10.4018/978-1-60566-884-0.ch020

and what exactly is this learning process that I'm supposed to own?"

This chapter describes the evaluation of a process that attempts to deal with both of these challenges by having students physically model their needs, interests, aptitudes and learning processes in order to model the learner journey itself. Students then use these models in metaphorical storymaking and storytelling in order to articulate their learning autobiographies, current educational context, orientation to learning, and aspirations to other students and to staff. Models are revisited and reconfigured throughout the learners engagement with Higher Education (HE) and are used to help them make choices related to course and module options, placements, projects, training, and other personal and professional development planning. We refer to this process where groups of students help each other to understand their learning processes and make decisions based on this understanding as *collaborative personalised learning*. The strengths and weaknesses of this process will be the primary focus of this chapter.

BACKGROUND

Initiated in 2004 by Hex Induction (an independent consultancy with experience in training, change management, and research) The Playful was a research project that looked at the use of pedagogical games in HE. Funding for the project came from areas with an interest in: play and learning (the University of Huddersfield Teaching and Learning Research Fund); digital game design (the Centre of Excellence in Digital Design at the University of Huddersfield and The Centre for Excellence in Media Practice at Bournemouth Media School); and performativity and learning (the University of Huddersfield Drama Department).

The initial aim of The Playful was to find workable, playful, teaching and learning methods, with a broad potential application across HE, that would appeal to learners for whom visual thinking

and aesthetics are important and which would not put shy learners in difficult situations.

Before describing the trials with students the next section will look at the LEGO Serious Play process: why it was developed, how it works, its basis in learning theory, and how it is used in business contexts.

THE LEGO SERIOUS PLAY PROCESS

Kjeld Kirk Kristiensen, the owner of LEGO, and Bart Victor and Johan Roos, professors at the Swiss business school IMD, developed LEGO Serious Play in 1996 in order to find a way to generate more engagement, imagination, and playfulness in staff meetings (Roos & Victor, 1998). It is now is an established business development tool used by companies such as Google, eBay, Roche, NASA, AstraZeneca, the International Red Cross and DaimlerChrysler as an alternative to traditional planning meetings. Participants use LEGO bricks to *build* models of themselves, their teams, the organization, and business strategies (Roos & Victor, 1999). The process discourages the making of literal models, which would be no more useful than traditional tools such as flipcharts and diagrams, by focusing on *metaphorical* and *symbolic* representations.

This is best explained with an example. Figure 1 shows a model made by a final year student representative to describe a negative attitude exhibited by senior managers at their University. The model shows two managers looking away as the University "cash cow" feeds on the bones of students who haven't been supported properly.

Simple metaphors are combined in a model to represent pretty much anything that is important to the individual, team or organization. Often, it is the individual, team or organization that is built but specific issues or problems can also be modelled.

Figure 1. This model uses a common metaphor, "cash cow", and extends it by adding original metaphors to create a powerful, complex of metaphors that generated much discussion and storytelling (© 2007, Stuart Nolan. Used with permission.)

The process draws on the constructivist learning research of Jean Piaget (1984) who suggested that intelligence grows from the interaction of the mind with the world. Seymour Papert, a student of Piaget, used this idea in his notion of constructionism which he refers to as "learning-by-making' but warns that this description doesn't do justice to a process that is "much richer and more multifaceted" than one might think (Papert, 1991).

Although the *hands-on* act of making metaphorical models is, in itself, helpful for knowledge construction it is perhaps the telling and sharing of stories about the models that can truly facilitate emotionally engaged, reflective learning experiences (Roos, 2006). Sharing perspectives through narrative helps participants learn about each other and about themselves. This can be related to the Johari window, a metaphorical tool used to help people understand their interpersonal communication (Luft & Ingham, 1955).

The LEGO Serious Play facilitator's training is a week of intense and well-structured workshops where every aspect of the process is both experienced and practiced. The facilitator's role is to take the participants through a series of exercises that ensure that they are able to make LEGO models easily and are able to create and use physical metaphors. The facilitator guides the participants through the storytelling process and makes decisions on what the next round of building should focus on but it is not necessary for the facilitator to have knowledge of the subject the students are studying.

The next section describes how the methodology was chosen.

METHODOLOGY

In order to devise the research questions and methodology a session was organized with a group of experts, each with an interest in play, creativity, and teaching & learning. The session aimed to explore and experience the techniques in order to gain as great an understanding of the process as possible before beginning live trials with students.

Participants began by constructing models of their organizations. They then added physical metaphors that explored how, why, when and where play and learning occurred in these models. They modelled how play and learning are managed and their aspirations for both for themselves and their organizations. Finally they combined their models to represent the key issues for play, education, management and creativity in the future (see Figure 2). This image shows one way that collaborative learning can be modelled once individual models have been made and stories about them shared. The shared model in the centre of the table includes everything that has been previously modelled in the individual models about the issues being discussed. During the building of this shared model the metaphors are refined, elaborated and clarified as metaphors are combined and choices are made between different metaphors. In later trials, students would also build such shared models in order to collaborate on the personalisation of their learning e.g. they would build a shared model of the forthcoming academic year and use it to discuss their choices as learners.

The day provided a framework for developing The Playful, suggesting a number of ways that LEGO Serious Play could be used by each of the participants beyond its original intended use as a management process. Here are some indicative examples:

- As a research tool for understanding rhetorics of play within HE and in the creative industries.
- As a tool for participatory and collaborative design. Architecture and town planning are just two examples where the perspectives and feelings of stakeholders need to be captured and considered. It was also seen a tool for developing a design brief with a client.
- As a way of organizing research networks.

- As a way of designing collaborative, interactive narratives.
- As a research tool for understanding a student's orientation to learning.

The group then considered the use of LEGO Serious Play as a technology for the collaborative personalisation of learning and a framework for research was devised. This is outlined in the next section.

RESEARCH QUESTIONS AND METHODOLOGY

The key research questions were as follows:

1. Can metaphorical modelling help the students to reflect on their learning?
2. Can the sharing of stories about the models facilitate a collaborative personalization of their learning?
3. Can this reflection and collaboration help them to learn more effectively?
4. What organizational issues are there in integrating metaphorical modelling into an Undergraduate course?

The favoured research methodologies were unstructured, open interviews with staff and students and unstructured group discussions with students. These methods chosen for the following reasons:

1. We consider personalised learning to be, almost by definition, quite personal and we wished to examine the affective nature of the experience of collaborative personalised learning. Unstructured interviews allowed space for both students and staff to relate the emotional aspects of the experience.
2. We wished to use research methods that would capture the metaphorical content of

Figure 2. The expert group considers their emerging shared model, which represents the use of play in creativity and learning (© 2007, Stuart Nolan. Used with permission.)

the experience. Metaphors are fundamental to discourse in education (Cameron, 2003; Taylor, 1984) and the personal metaphors created by students are of more practical use in teaching than statistics and evaluation forms.

3. We wished to use research methods that respected the views of the participants by allowing them to relate their experiences in their own way and at their own time. Open interviews allowed participants to refer to the models if they wished but did not put pressure on them to do so. We also wished to respect the professional experience of the tutors involved by trusting their opinions.

Although we used attendance, grades, retention and student evaluation forms to get a general sense of how the students were responding to the experience such qualitative methods are not considered to be as important as the views of the staff and students involved. This is not just for the statistical reasons that a sample of 327 students is too small to produce information of statistical significance and that students were drawn from such a wide range of courses that audit-based comparisons would be fallacious. It is also because such pseudo-scientific methods are driven by an urge to view learning as more tractable and mechanical than it really is and, encouraged by audit systems with little relation to teaching and learning, are increasingly undermining the role of the professional teacher (Evans, 2005) and we are reluctant to add to this problem.

The consensus of the expert group was that the timing of use during a students learning journey would be important. Metaphorical modelling works best at times of choice, change, crisis, and challenge when the learners existing internal metaphorical model needs to adapt (Roos, 2006).

Externalizing the conceptual modelling process at these times supports an emotional need and the process is more valuable. Modelling during times of steady, unchanging work is a far less effective use.

The following section describes the trials with students in a number of Higher Education contexts.

TRIALS IN HIGHER EDUCATION

The main trial was with 76 Multimedia final year undergraduate students. A further 251 students from a range of courses have also used the process.

Use of metaphorical modelling for collaborative personalised learning focused on two key moments of the student's learning journeys,

1. The beginning of the academic year, when they are making choices and orientating themselves to a new set of challenges.
2. The period of preparation for final crits, during which they have to demonstrate their progress and describe their learning process.

University of Huddersfield, Multimedia BA(Hons) Undergraduate Final Year 2005

The pilot trial was with a group of 28 final year Undergraduate students from *Multimedia Design* and *VR with Animation* courses. LEGO Serious Play was first used in the week before their final presentations, a tense and difficult time for them when they are asked to present their work and to explain and defend the learning choices throughout the final year. Many of the students find presentations daunting and these particular presentations count a lot towards their final marks. Many say they have difficulty planning presentations and 6 of them had been diagnosed as dyslexic and found

this an additional barrier to planning. 18 of them stated that they suffered from nerves when presenting and four of them reported extreme difficulty presenting in the past. These reported difficulties are common and the group was not unlike previous final year groups in this subject area.

After a series of warm up games designed to help them familiarize themselves with the LEGO materials, to think and model metaphorically, and to feel comfortable telling stories about the models, each student was asked to metaphorically model the presentation they were to give the next week. Figure 3 shows an example of a presentation model. The ghost in a tree to the left of the model represents the learning choices that weren't taken in the past but which are remembered by the student and still influence their decisions.

University of Huddersfield, Multimedia BA(Hons) Undergraduate Final Year 2006

In 2006 we introduced LEGO Serious Play as a core process for the Multimedia subject area final year. This final year comprises students from *Multimedia Design* and *VR with Animation* courses and some transfer students. In addition around 75% will have taken a placement year in industry while the rest have come straight from the second year.

The final year places great emphasis on a self-directed studio project where time management and planning are essential. We wanted to help students cope with this by having them model their understanding of their final year and to revisit the process at key points throughout the year. From a longitudinal research point of view it was hoped that we could investigate how repeated use over time would change the way the process worked. Over the year, LEGO Serious Play was used three times with all of the final year students:

1) Modelling The Final Year: This session aimed to introduce students to the process, to each other, to the staff, to the final year, and to

Figure 3. An example of a metaphorical presentation model (© 2007, Stuart Nolan. Used with permission.)

the options for personalisation available to them. In the first week all 48 students modelled their skills and competencies in regard to their final year and then modelled what they felt the final year entailed. They later focused on how their choices of dissertation topic, studio project, and skills workshops could be personalised to suit their orientation to learning, vocational objectives, skills, and competencies. 41 of the models used metaphors of journeys with steps towards a final goal. This representation of a journey can be clearly seen in Figure 4. The steps and the goal often lacked detail in the first round of model making but the metaphors led into a sharing of feelings, ideas, and strategies to cope with the journey. Every student modelled a degree of uncertainty and nervousness about the year. The value of this sharing of concern should not be underestimated as many admitted to feeling that they were alone in their worries and were much relieved to find that others shared their trepidation.

In one round of building each student was given the name of another student present and asked to keep the name a secret. They were then asked to model something that they thought was true about that student but which had been left out of the model the named student had made for themselves. They then talked about the model only revealing the name at the end when they would give the model to the person they had made it for. This activity works well both for established groups and for those who have just met. It was always a positive activity - nobody used the model to insult someone - but perceptive and challenging insights can be revealed. After the session it was noticeable how the students socialized more easily and more quickly than in previous years. This is a clear example where collaborative per-

Figure 4. Richard models his perception of the forthcoming final year. The journey can be read from left to right. (© 2007, Stuart Nolan. Used with permission.)

sonalized learning can improve both individual and group learning.

At the end of the sessions photographs of the models were taken and put online for the students to refer to. Most of the students also chose to take photographs of their models to show their friends, to put on their blogs and to refer to later. This capturing of the models through photography is important as the models are broken up at the end of a session. This moment has to be carefully handled as the participants have invested a lot of emotion in their models.

2) Aspirational Modelling: In the Spring term students undertake a week of intensive concept development where they are introduced to a number of media industry concept development techniques that they apply to their studio projects. This takes place at The Media Centre in Huddersfield rather than at the University and they receive talks and tutorials from visiting industry practitioners and

focus on career options and how their work can best be developed, displayed and promoted to achieve a good grade and portfolio. They have to make key decisions about the support they need from the School and which workshops to attend.

In contrast to the previous session where they modelled their perception of the final year and focused on their journey as a learner they are now asked to model their work, their work processes and their aspirations as a practitioner. They begin by modelling their working practice as it is in the present time. This initial model must be a *warts and all* representation, incorporating both strengths and weaknesses. After sharing the story of this model they are asked to change the model to show how they would like their working practice to be in an ideal world. By discussing how the model has changed they developed strategies for making choices and planning their future as a learner and practitioner. The session

Figure 5. An example of an aspirational model (© 2007, Stuart Nolan. Used with permission.)

was followed up with tutorials focused on post-graduation plans, portfolio and CV writing. This session worked particularly well for students who were feeling bogged down with the workload of the final year helping them to take a step back and see the bigger picture.

Although the models vary greatly certain images, metaphors and themes arise during aspirational modelling. Figure 5 shows a number of these themes. Towards the left of the model a number of goals are represented with a flag, gold coins, and balls in a basketball net. Separated from these goals are a number of figures with different hats, tools and costumes each representing an aspect of themselves that the student feels they need to develop in order to reach the goals. Notice that, even in an aspirational model, the figures are still facing away from the goals and are separated from them. This student was having difficulty connecting their learning options with their aspirations. A second aspirational model made two weeks later

simplified the range of characters represented and connected them to the goals.

3) Presentation Modelling: This was essentially a repeat of the previous years session of presentation modelling held a week before their final assessments. Again, this session helped students to plan their presentations. The only addition was that time was given at the end for the students to take detailed notes of the models if they felt they required them.

The following examples of use come from contexts that are quite different from the main study just described.

MPhil/PhD Students at the Digital Research Unit (DRU), University of Huddersfield

A 1-day LEGO Serious Play session was run with 12 post-graduate students who were all beginning their research at the same time and were being asked to work as a research team. They were all artists working with media technologies but their practice varied widely. Some of them knew each other's work, two pairs had worked together on projects, but in general they knew little about each other. They spent the morning modelling their individual practice and research and the afternoon combining their individual models to create a model of the research team. Their needs as both individual students and as a research team were modelled and this model was used to plan provision for them.

It is interesting to note that when using LEGO Serious Play with practicing artists and designers their personal aesthetic tastes can initially slow them down as they try to make aesthetically pleasing models rather than meaningful ones. As metaphorical meaning and visual aesthetics cannot be easily disentangled the facilitator must carefully manage this issue.

Performing Arts Students at the Central School of Speech and Drama (CSSD)

Working over 3 days with 36 second-year Performance Studies students we modelled their individual practice and approach to performance. Some focused on their performance skills others on staging, scenography, the process of devising a production, or their responses to theatre. A few students initially regarded the process as a form of improvisation and care was taken to keep them working with their perceptions of reality rather than creatively inventing scenarios. They were less inhibited about using the workspace than other students, often building their models on the floor and building larger models than usual.

PhD Students at the Helsinki University of Technology

In August 2006 we ran a week of Magic and Technology workshops at The Telecommunications Software and Multimedia Laboratory (TML) in Helsinki that included a number of LEGO Serious Play sessions. 15 delegates from the Helsinki University of Technology, Helsinki University of Art and Design, The Finnish State Broadcaster YLE, and three Finnish games companies explored how the philosophies and practice of conjuring can play a part in the creative technology design process and examined the relationships between media, magic, game design and technology (Nolan, 2006). On the last two days we used LEGO Serious Play to ask where *designing the magical* plays a role in the practice of the participants.

Using LEGO Serious Play as part of a series of workshops is a novel and innovative form of reflective learning. It provides a playful, emotionally connected way of reflecting, as a group, on the learning that has taken place. It focuses on the experiential learning rather than the information presented and on the understanding that learners are seeking ways to relate the learning to their own practice.

Seven of the participants were working on their PhD studies and we ran a collaborative personalised learning session in which they modelled their research and practice. This required five rounds of modelling asking participants to "focus in" on specific aspects of their models with each new build. Complex topics can be dealt with in this way and phrases like "zooming in", "double clicking", or "opening up" help guide the participants to add detail and meaning to their models. Figure 6 shows a first attempt at modelling the student's PhD research. Further builds added complexity, emotional issues, and more external factors. A round of aspirational modelling was particularly useful in identifying, prioritizing, and personal-

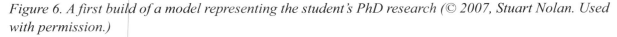

Figure 6. A first build of a model representing the student's PhD research (© 2007, Stuart Nolan. Used with permission.)

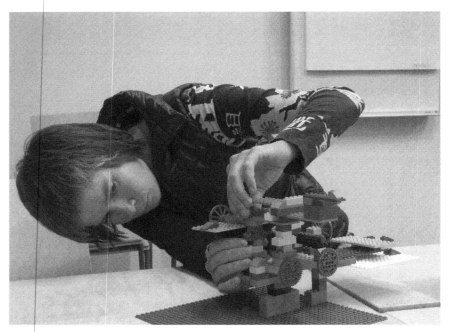

ising further work that needed to be undertaken both by the student and the University.

Post-Compulsory Education and Training (PCET) at the University of Huddersfield

A half-day session was organized for 5 lecturers in the Post-Compulsory Education and Training (PCET) at the University of Huddersfield. They were introduced to the process and spent time modelling how learning occurred in their students and how they dealt with personalising the provision for learning. Students are often on placement and a key part of PDP is the reporting and reflecting on their experience in the classroom and workplace. Support for the students is personalised depending on the context of their placement.

Having experienced the process the PCET lecturers adapted some of the methods for their own use occasionally using the LEGO bricks in both group and individual PDP. They also created

methods derived from the focus on physical objects and metaphor. One of these they refer to as *Teaching in a Bag* - student teachers are asked to bring a carrier bag full of found objects that they think metaphorically represent their experience of teaching practice. They talk about the objects and the resulting discussion of their teaching practice is more reflective, emotional, and detailed that is usually experienced.

The PCET group has since included the use of metaphorical modelling in a training DVD and are in the process of writing a paper on the experience.

MENTORING INDUSTRY PLACEMENTS WITH NORTH-WEST VISION AND MEDIA

We have used LEGO Serious Play with four mentees on placements with media companies in the North West. They modelled their placement experience, their aspirations prior to completing the placement, and their skills and competencies to date. The models were used to help improve their CVs and to determine further training needs. This successful use suggests that the process could lend itself well to formal Training Needs Analysis for organizations.

Student Reflections

Of the 327 students involved all have stated that they found the process either useful or very useful in planning their learning. Fourteen stated that it was the best workshop they had ever attended.

We found that the statements the students made about the process tended to describe a number of specific issues: clarity, control, revealing options, open visibility, play, and personal and shared metaphors.

Clarity: Students spoke of the process of modelling their learning as a way of gaining *clarity*. This increased clarity could be both inward looking - concerning skills, competencies, emotions, and orientations to learning – and outward looking – concerning educational programs, choices, placements, planning, and professional relationships with staff and other students.

Sometimes the clarity was concerned with gaining an overview of their situation,

I have a problem seeing the big picture because I can get bogged down in working on one thing and ignore everything else. I modelled a bird up high in the sky as part of my model of the final year because it's the only time I've been able to see the whole picture. (Pritesh, Final Year Multimedia Student)

At other times the clarity was focused on a particular issue,

There's this thing I do when I'm given choices because I'm always worried about making the wrong choice so I try to do everything and it's

a mess and exhausts me. But I'd never realized that was what I did and by zooming in on that bit of my model I realized what the man with 8 arms and 12 different tool was a problem rather than something good. (Robbie, Final Year Multimedia Student)

Notice how the making of the metaphor becomes before the moment of clarity. Models are often made and then interpreted showing that the process is not a simple mapping of existing knowledge but a creation of new knowledge.

Control: Students spoke a lot about getting a sense of control over their learning. They spoke of gaining a better grasp of why they made the decisions they did and of feeling more comfortable about their decision-making.

When I compared my second model to the one I'd made months before I could see how I was in control of how it was growing. It was like a garden and I was planting what I wanted and then seeing how it would grow up. (Javier, Final Year Multimedia Student)

The metaphors of *tending gardens, taking journeys,* or *building houses* occurred in many of the models.

Revealing options: Students often spoke or *discovering* or *revealing* options that were previously *hidden* to them.

I hadn't realized that I could structure my options this way until I moved the palm trees from the technical swamp and put them in the river with the job fish. It was like finding something buried on Time Team. (Sam, Final Year Performing Arts Student)

The options were mainly revealed through aspirational modelling of possible futures.

When I made my model of how I wanted things to be in the future all these different versions started happening and I could change them easily just by adding or removing the metaphors. I could change the number of hats on the ladders and see how that changed my options for studying and it was fun. I couldn't do that on paper. Boring. (Nav, Final Year Multimedia Student)

This perception of a difference between boring, inflexible pen and paper planning and playful, flexible metaphorical modelling was very common. Although this may be partly explained by the novelty of the process we believe that there is a valuable difference that is worth exploring further.

The *open visibility* of a physical model was often commented upon.

For me I reckon the big difference between making models and using pen and paper is that you could always see everything you'd said. And everything everyone else said. Its all there in front of you and its like you can go on a walk through it and notice things. Differences. And its all easy to remember. (John, Final Year Performing Arts Student)

The models were often seen as more easy to remember than written equivalents. The design courses involved have a high percentage of students with dyslexia spectrum issues. Having a non-text based process for PDP has helped a number of them with concept development, project planning, presentation planning, and personalisation and ownership of the learning process. Many found that, rather than having to rely on written notes, they could easily hold an image of their model in their minds and mentally refer to it while presenting.

I have dyslexia and find writing too dry and dull. With LEGO I can say anything I want in my own words. Except they aren't words, they're better than words. I can feel them not just think them. (James, Final Year Multimedia Student)

Personal metaphors: Many of the students commented on how useful they found the basic idea of using metaphors to describe their learning. Students modelled learning styles and modes that could be related to learning style theory but which were metaphorically their own. For instance, one student modelled a busy, physical, making mode of learning as a bunch of flailing chains with monkeys at the centre. Her description of this model could be related to theoretical concepts of body-kinaesthetic learning (Gardner, 1993) and d-mode thinking (Claxton, 1998) but her reflective relationship to it was emotionally engaged rather than coldly theoretical.

Sometimes I love my chain flailing monkeys. Other times they get all knotted up and I need to untangle their chains and calm them down. I look after them but they get on my nerves a bit. (Sarah, Final Year Multimedia Student)

Notice that she expresses a number of emotions about her "monkeys". The students expressed complex and wide-ranging emotions about their metaphors.

Collaborative metaphors: What begins as a personalisation of learning through personally meaningful becomes, through the sharing of these personal metaphors a collaborative personalisation of learning through what are now collaborative metaphors.

We all really liked Sarah's crazy monkeys with chains cos we all have them a bit so we all decided that the monkeys should go into the shared model. Its become something we have a laugh about. I'm having a chain-monkey day. Its good we all have them. (Ben, Final Year Multimedia Student)

Collaboration occurs through asking questions about each other's models, building models of each other, and building shared models. Notice that the shared metaphors continue to be used by the participants of a specific session and enter into the shared language of the group. This also helps the group to get to know each other.

As well as helping me to get an overview of what the final year had in store it also helped to get to know the other students and the tutor. (Joe, Final-year Student, Multimedia Design.)

Staff Reflections

Once students and staff have learned the techniques they can continue to build effective models without a facilitator and core elements of the process can be easily taught to staff in less than a day. In total 30 members of staff from the participating institutions were interviewed about their experience of the process.

The overall response was very positive with 100% of them hoping that the process can be used more with their students. Unprompted, 19 of them expressed a wish to be trained in the process so they could use it themselves. 12 of them reported that they had adapted the methods for use in their teaching.

We found that the statements the staff made about the process tended to describe a number of specific issues: windows into learning, spotting problems, working relationships, and enriching communication.

Windows into learning: 25 of the staff claimed that the process gave them a way of seeing the actual learning of the student.

Despite assessment, tutorials, and group discussions its really hard to ever feel like you are seeing how the learning of an individual is actually happening. You get glimpses. But this modelling is like getting a clear window into their heads. You can see exactly how they think and learn. And you can spot the problems. (Gary, Multimedia Tutor)

Spotting problems: Every member of staff mentioned the fact that potential problems can be seen in advance and steps taken to avert them.

Through their models, students revealed many things about their orientation to learning that are very useful for a tutor to know, discussing issues such as time management, lack of focus, narrow vision, too broad a vision, and difficulties with technology, reading, motivation and ambition. The process helps tutors to quickly gain a deep and complex understanding of a student's practical and emotional learning needs and, where possible, they can tailor learning support to fit these needs.

I knew one student was having serious trouble with the technical modules by the way they talked about them in the model. They would never have told me directly because they were the kind who puts on a brave face. I gave them some extra help. (Stuart, Multimedia Tutor)

These insights also proved invaluable to the staff as they personalised the educational provision to the student's group needs.

All the students modelled problems their understanding of theory in the second year. Individually, they all thought it was just their own problem but we realized that the way we were teaching it was problematic for all of them and we could improve it. (Karen, Senior Lecturer in Multimedia Theory)

Where specific learning options are being offered a LEGO Serious Play session can give the staff a focused understanding of the students needs.

Working relationships: 27 of the staff discussed the fact that the modelling sessions helped the group to bond, to understand each other, and to achieve a good working relationship.

It is hard to be specific about how much this helps the group to bond but it usually takes around a month to develop a close working relationship with the final year group and the use of metaphorical modelling probably shortened the time to a week. (Jen, Final Year Tutor)

It was noted that once the students have built a few models they could rapidly model projects, issues, or brief concepts during tutorials. Just having the bricks around to play with was seen as beneficial. Even when not actively modelling the bricks have a relaxing effect that helps conversation flow and encourages a creative playfulness.

It is useful to have LEGO bricks around for tutorials just so that students can fiddle with the pieces while chatting. (Catherine, Tutor)

Enriching communication: The value of the shared metaphorical language developed by participants was mentioned by 18 of the staff.

Being able to say 'How are the elephants, Dave?' to a student is much better than 'How is your problem with scoping projects'. (Alan, Tutor)

The shared metaphorical language made collaborative personalised learning more playful, detailed, precise, and memorable. This applied to discussions with student and discussions about students.

To say, 'the pig has left the wheelbarrow and is nearer the trees,' tells us much more about an individual student's learning than the fact that their last assessment was 1 grade higher than the previous assessment. (Catherine, Tutor)

17 staff suggested that metaphorical modelling could be used to replace or support existing forms of assessment, tutorial, and interview. A question that arises from work with the University of Huddersfield School of Education and Professional Development is whether LEGO Serious Play can be used as an alternative to the current individual PDP tutorials that attempt to help trainee teachers reflect on their professional practice and their identities as teachers? Rather than have a series of 30 minute, individual PDP tutorials a group of trainee teachers would have a 2-hour modelling session together. Annotated photographs of the models would replace the current documentation. Individual tutorials would be reserved for student teachers wishing to raise private issues.

14 staff were impressed that facilitators using the techniques have no need for subject specific knowledge and each subject area relates to the process by referring to its own, familiar, metaphors. There is also an unexplored strength in a technique that can be applied in research, teaching and learning, and management contexts by the same individuals and teams.

The next session deals with problematic issues raised by both staff and students.

ISSUES WITH LEGO SERIOUS PLAY

There are some intrinsic aspects of the LEGO Serious Play process that limit its use in HE. The core method of sharing stories through metaphorical modelling is only effective for groups of between 5 and 12. With more than 12 participants the process becomes cumbersome and too time-consuming for participants to maintain their focus and to effectively communicate as a group. With less than 5 participants there are not enough stories being told to stimulate valuable discussion. A group of 8 is optimum. The exception to this is when the technique is used in mentoring where one person can effectively share issues of their professional and personal development with an experienced mentor. With this limitation it is difficult to run a session with a whole group, as most HE courses will have at least 15 students. Obviously, the course students can be split into smaller groups, and I have worked with groups of 45 students by running 5 separate sessions, but there is then no communication between the groups and the process takes a long time. When splitting groups in this way it is valuable to have a show and tell session with the whole group where images of models are shown and key findings are shared.

LEGO Serious Play demands an initial skills

building session with all participants which takes between and 60 and 90 minutes for a group of up to 5-12 participants and this initial time investment is likely to be a barrier to its use in most HE institutions. As much of the value of the process comes from repeated use, with students taking more ownership of the process, this extra time commitment may also be problematic. The physical use of the materials requires an amount of manual dexterity and is therefore unsuitable for those with certain disabilities. One member of staff with impaired sight found the process quite difficult but could manage when given extra time.

The initial materials expenditure is high compared to traditional pen and paper methods, though not compared to software solutions. However, the materials are robust and easy to maintain, replace, and expand. One question often raised by staff is whether materials other than LEGO could be used more or less effectively. Materials that are more flexible, such as clay and Plasticine, might offer more scope for creativity but they introduce an aspect of artistic creativity that causes a problem. Some people are very good at sculpting with clay-like materials and their enjoyment of making aesthetically pleasing models distract them from telling useful stories. Conversely, those that find sculpting with clay very difficult can get frustrated with the materials. The LEGO Serious Play materials have been selected to offer a lot of *ready-made* metaphors such as animals, people, tools, windows, plants, and parts of buildings. These enable anyone, regardless of their modelling skills, to make meaningful metaphors. In addition there are plenty of non-specific bricks that allow for the creation of new, original metaphors. Any materials used in place of LEGO should also provide this mix of the ready-made and the flexible.

LEGO is regarded as a design classic being voted Best Toy of the 20th Century and is well liked by students in creative fields. The visual nature of the models also provides good materials for marketing, promotion, and recruitment and these design and taste issues are very important when encouraging engagement with learning. However, there can be an occasional negative reaction from conservative staff to the idea of using a toy for serious educational matters and perceptions of this sort do need to be carefully addressed by facilitators. First hand experience of the process quickly demonstrates that it is not trivial but occasionally a manager will be more concerned about the perception than the actuality. Highlighting the number and range of large companies who have successfully used it can help to counter initial cynicism.

LEGO Serious Play is marketed and sold via trained partners and, at present, only certified partners are permitted to use the methodology. This provides a network of practitioners with which to communicate and partner but there are some downsides. A week of training in Denmark or the US and a yearly fee is required to become a certified LEGO Serious Play facilitator. This cost is a serious barrier to extensive HE use but LEGO are in the process of developing a 1-day training session for organizations that only wish to use the process internally. This training carries no additional yearly fee and would be suitable for HE institutions but there is resistance from existing partners who are worried that the quality of delivery of the process may suffer. This concern is justified as the process can appear simple to those with little experience of facilitation and there is a danger of staff attempting to apply the methods without adequate preparation. There is, of course, no reason why the core methods cannot be adapted and used by anyone as long as no attempt is made to sell such use as LEGO Serious Play.

Until the 1-day training becomes available one approach is for the HE institution to have members of staff trained in the full process and to offer it to businesses as external consultancy. Revenues raised could then be used to fund educational use. However, few HE institutions are able to set up such a system as education and consultancy tend to be kept separate. Ideally, a single centrally funded LEGO Serious Play facilitator would work with all Schools and Departments but that would require a coordination that few institutions are capable of.

LEGO Serious Play is philosophically opposed to organizational structures that block the flow of communication, ideas, and creativity. In practice, the process challenges organizational hierarchy, individual power, chains of command, and excessive bureaucracy. The organizational nature of most HE institutions means that they are unlikely to use the process for the organizational development it was originally designed for. This may not matter when considering its use in the personalisation of learning but it does limit its usefulness when working with HE staff. Having said that, the process provides a playful and provocative way of managing strategy in an organization and could be particularly useful for tackling the issues that arise when schools and departments collaborate.

FUTURE RESEARCH DIRECTIONS

Play is a form of experimentation and as such, is the R&D of mammalian life. (Cheyne, 1989)

These following future research directions may appear quite disparate and unrelated but they all have at their core a concern with the importance of narrative, storytelling, emotion, and play in the creation of knowledge and the personalisation of learning.

Visual and participatory research methods are high on the agenda in social and educational research and Gauntlett (2007) has begun the work of using LEGO Serious Play to research the construction of social identities and the way we view ourselves as learners in particular. My research has been primarily concerned with developing a pragmatic tool for the personalisation of learning but the use of this tool generates models that are well suited for the study of learner identities. With the addition of audio and video documentation

many questions about the construction of learner identities, the experience of learner journeys, and the affective elements of personalisation and learning could be asked.

Using LEGO Serious Play as a replacement for formal research interviews in certain contexts has been suggested. An example here is the need for more research into issues of retention. Asking students why they choose to stay in formal education or choose to leave it is notoriously difficult. Having new students model their expectations and concerns at the very beginning of their engagement with a HE institution could provide a way of examining these issues.

A close look at the common metaphors used by students may identify patterns that could provide early signs of problems that would help target those in need of extra support. It has been proposed that metaphorical modelling may be useful in student counselling and that experts in this field should evaluate it.

LEGO Serious Play is a tool developed for business development and educational institutions could learn more from this field by looking at change management and organization theory. For instance, a student's time at a HE institution is perhaps the time of greatest change in their lives and although change management techniques may appear to deal fundamentally with organizational change they often do so through addressing the effect of change on the mental models of individuals (Karp, 2005).

In the early 80's organization theorists first documented the ubiquity of narratives in organizational settings and in organization theory itself (Martin, 1982). Attention has focused in different areas of narrative since then: in organizational stories (Gabriel, 2000; Boje, 2001), in the role of narrative in organizational communication (Fisher, 1987; Taylor, 1993), and in narratology as a source of methodological inspiration (Czarniawska, 1997; Cooren, 2000). Narrative is also important in learning. In particular, autobiographical memory has been shown to have a key influence on reflective, intentional, and habitual facets of learning (Boekaerts, 2000) and on self-efficacy in both learning (Schunk & Pajares, 2002) and work (Stajkovic & Luthans, 1998). The use of expressive autobiographical writing can be a way of understanding this influence and improving the students' experience of learning (Hauk, 2003). These issues are highlighted when supporting students with varied cultural orientations to learning (Boekaerts, 2003). It is proposed that the use of physical metaphors in the construction of learner autobiographies would further research into the role of personal narratives in learning.

As the process is as much about modelling affect as cognition it may be useful for examining both intuitive and reflective practice. Intuition in teaching practice is regarded as an important area but one that is notoriously difficult to research (Atkinson, 2000). It has been noted that education is founded on metaphors (Taylor, 1984) and it is proposed that further research examines the metaphors that our educators use to construct their identities.

We have used metaphorical modelling with HE teaching and management teams for strategic planning and decision-making and feel that this use is relevant to personalisation issues as staff and students can develop a shared metaphorical language that affects their communication and should be researched further. LEGO Serious Play can be considered a *material-semiotic* method in that it allows one to map relations that are simultaneously material (between things) and semiotic (between concepts) and could be a useful tool for an actor-network theory (Latour, 2005) approach to the study of educational networks.

CONCLUSION

Claxton (1999, pp 305), discussing Higher Education in the context of lifelong learning, suggests that,

In general, in the learning society, it is more and more up to individuals to assess for themselves what they know, and what they need to know. To be able to monitor and check your own progress; to know when you have done good work; to diagnose your own learning strengths and needs; to take stock of achievement: for all these reasons, the cultivation of the disposition and the ability to self-assess is invaluable.

This ability to self-assess is at the core of personalised learning and our aim was to explore whether metaphorical modelling could facilitate a *collaborative* self-assessment. We now return to the original questions.

1. Can Metaphorical Modelling Help the Students to Reflect on Their Learning?

These trials with LEGO Serious Play indicate that students benefit from techniques that help them to construct conceptual models of their learning. By using physical metaphors students can construct knowledge of their work patterns, skills and competencies, relationships, cognitive processes and emotions. The use the models to reflect on their learning and to self-assess by noting strengths and weaknesses and modelling changes over time. They can then personalise their learning experience by making decisions informed by their improved understanding of their own ways of learning.

Metaphorical modelling may support multiple learning styles by engaging visual-spatial intelligence through the active creation of new images and constructions, linguistic intelligence through the explanations participants provide for their constructions, and bodily-kinaesthetic intelligence through the physical act of building with LEGO bricks. Learning is as much an emotional journey as a cognitive process and personal metaphors help a learner reflect on their journey in a way that suits them best.

2. Can the Sharing of Stories about the Models Facilitate a Collaborative Personalization of Their Learning?

Students generally reflect on their personal learning needs by themselves, through discussion with support staff and tutors, or informally with friends and family. Through *collaborative personalisation* using metaphorical modelling with a group they can articulate their learning needs through storytelling, learn strategies from each other's models, contribute to each other's models, and compare their models with those of their peers. It is the combination of building metaphorical models and the subsequent sharing of stories about them that gives LEGO Serious Play its educational potential.

The performative nature of knowledge construction is important in the process as students construct metaphorical models and tell stories about these models. The performance occurs through the models with pieces of the model *acting as* aspects of the student's personality. This is an aspect of play with physical objects that engages the emotions while also giving a certain amount of emotional distance to the storytelling. It makes the process very approachable and non-threatening in comparison to techniques involving role-play. Each participant constructs their own models and all stories are given equal time and respect providing a safe environment for even very shy participants to contribute.

3. Can this Reflection and Collaboration help Them to Learn More Effectively?

Student feedback indicates that they felt the process helped them to learn more effectively. This observation is backed up by the reflections of the staff and by various assessments of work, attendance, retention and satisfaction.

4. What Organizational Barriers are there in Using Metaphorical Modelling in HE?

Despite some limitations imposed by cost and materials metaphorical modelling with LEGO Serious Play has been very successful as a technology for the collaborative personalisation of learning. We have already discussed the various organizational barriers in some depth in the Issues With LEGO Serious Play section.

What can we learn from the use of metaphorical modelling as a tool for collaborative personalised learning that could be transferable to other technologies for personalisation of learning? Lets consider some of the most important aspects of metaphorical modelling in this regard.

Play: The concept of *play* is important in the LEGO Serious Play process and a playful framework for learning has been show to facilitate emotional expression on a number of levels (Winnecott, 1971). Our feedback shows that participants enjoy the socially engaged experience of this playful *emotion work* (Hochschild & Russel, 1979). Huizinga (1996) argues that cultures can be understood through their play and recent commentators suggest that we live in an increasingly ludic society with notions of play becoming crucial in both business (Schrage, 2000; Beck & Wade, 2004; Kane, 2005; Dodgson *et al*, 2005) and education (Stephenson, 1998; Terr, 2000; Prensky, 2000; Gee, 2003). Innovation in both education and business is often considered as a kind of play (Dodgson *et al*, 2005). We would argue that technologies for the personalisation of learning should consider playfulness as a critical part of their interaction design.

Metaphor: In play, one thing can easily be used to represent another and these metaphorical representations can be informative and revealing. In contrast, modelling in education tends to be both literal and while literal modelling certainly has its uses, much of the strength of metaphorical modelling from the use of conceptual metaphors that are fundamental to all conceptual understanding (Lakoff & Johnson, 1999). We would learn very little if we asked a group of students to build their learning context and they then constructed a literal model of their University and hall of residence. If technologies for personalisation do not allow for rich metaphorical construction then they may risk limiting the conversations that can take place.

There are implications here for the design of virtual learning environments (VLEs) that tend to be more literal than metaphorical. It is worth noting that the popular virtual worlds allow their users a more flexible and expansive use of metaphor than VLEs. Can VLEs be designed to allow students to easily create their own metaphorical spaces, places, and objects? Even if we can build such worlds what is the difference between virtual and physical modelling from a constructionist learning point of view? Is the construction of knowledge different if it isn't physical and if so what is lost and what is gained?

Hands-on: Most technologies for the personalisation of learning are software based and, even if using hand-held devices, are not physically hands on in the same way as LEGO. The differences between the physical and the virtual need to carefully considered when designing technologies for the personalisation of learning. Perhaps the main consideration is how the physical and the virtual may engage the emotions in different ways?

Emotion: Hands-on metaphorical modelling engages the emotional and personal aspects of learning. Emotions are very important when attempting to personalise learning and must be carefully managed. When students take ownership of learning the various emotions that come with a sense of ownership can be engaged. The *experience design* of the technology becomes as important as its core functionality. Both LEGO and the LEGO Serious Play process were designed with the emotional experience in mind. Technologies for learning are often designed by technical and academic staff with little understanding of the field

of experience design. This can lead to a functional but unemotional experience for the user.

It is easy to forget that the processes of assessment, measurement and audit that have become so ubiquitous in recent years are themselves technologies with intrinsic affordances and concepts of learning. When we compare these processes to the process of metaphorical modelling considered in this chapter we find that they are dramatically different. LEGO Serious Play considers learning as play rather than work. It values the specific stories of learners and teachers with their rich metaphors rather than the literal formulations of generalized guidelines and criteria. It is inherently democratic rather than bureaucratic. It promotes emotion work rather than paperwork. Unfortunately, the final conclusion of this chapter is that while metaphorical modelling has much to offer learners as a technology for the personalisation of learning the current organization of HE institutions in the UK will severely hamper any attempt to use it.

REFERENCES

Atkinson, T. (2000). *The Intuitive Practitioner: On the Value of Not Always Knowing What One Is Doing.* Buckingham, UK: Open University Press.

Beck, J. C., & Wade, M. (2004). *Got game: How the gamer generation is reshaping business forever.* Cambridge, MA: Harvard Business School Press.

Boekaerts, M. (2003). How do students from different cultures motivate themselves for academic learning? In F. Salili & R. Hoosain (Eds.) *Research on Multicultural Education and International Perspectives: Vol. 3. Teaching, learning and motivation in a multi-cultural context.* (pp. 13-31). Greenwich, CT: Information Age Publishing.

Boekaerts, M., Pintrich, P. R., & Zeidner, M. (Eds.). (2000). *Handbook of self-regulation.* San Diego: Academic Press.

Boje, D. M. (2001). *Narrative methods for organizational and communication research.* Thousand Oaks, CA: SAGE.

Cameron, L. (2003). *Metaphor in educational discourse.* London: Continuum.

Cheyne, J. A. (1989). *Serious Play from Peregrination to Cultural Change: A Bateson-Gadamer-Harris Hypothesis.* [online]. Retrieved January 23rd, 2007 from http://watarts.uwaterloo.ca/~acheyne/Misc/SeriousPlay.html

Claxton, G. (1998). *Hare Brain, Tortoise Mind.* London: Fourth Estate.

Claxton, G. (1999). *Wise-Up.* London: Bloomsbury.

Cooren, F. (2000). *The organizing property of communication.* Amsterdam: John Benjamins.

Czarniawska, B. (1997). *Narrating the organization: Dramas of institutional identity.* Chicago: University of Chicago Press.

Dodgson, M., Gann, D., & Salter, A. (2005). *Think, Play, Do: Technology, Innovation, and Organization.* Oxford, UK: Oxford University Press.

Evans, M. (2005). *Killing Thinking: The Death of the Universities.* London: Continuum International Publishing Group Ltd.

Fisher, W. R. (1987). *Human communication as narration: Toward a philosophy of reason, value, and action.* Columbia, SC: University of South Carolina Press.

Gabriel, Y. (2000). *Storytelling in organizations.* Oxford, UK: Oxford University Press.

Gardner, H. (1993). *Multiple Intelligences.* New York: Basic Books.

Gauntlett, D. (2007). *Creative Explorations. New Approaches to Identities and Audiences.* London: Routledge.

Gauntlett, D., & Holzwarth, P. (2006). Creative and visual methods for exploring identities. *Visual Studies, 21*(01), 82–91. doi:10.1080/14725860600613261

Gee, J. P. (2003). *What Video Games Have to Teach Us About Learning and Literacy.* New York: Palgrave Macmillan.

Hauk, S. (2003). Understanding entering students via mathematical autobiography. Committee on the Undergraduate Program in Mathematics (Eds.), *Undergraduate Programs and Courses in the Mathematical Sciences* (pp. 79). Washington, DC: Mathematical Association of America.

Hochschild, A. R. (1979). Emotion Work, Feeling Rules and Social Structure. *American Journal of Sociology, 85*(3), 551–575. doi:10.1086/227049

Huizinga, J. (1950). *Homo Ludens: A Study of the Play Element in Culture.* Boston: The Beacon Press.

Kane, P. (2005). *The play ethic: A manifesto for a different way of living.* London: Macmillan.

Karp, T. (2005). Unpacking the mysteries of change: mental modelling. *Journal of Change Management, 5*(1), 87–96. doi:10.1080/14697010500057573

Lakoff, G., & Johnson, M. (1999). *Philosophy in the Flesh.* New York: Basic Books.

Latour, B. (2005). *Reassembling the Social: An Introduction to Actor-Network-Theory.* Oxford, UK: Oxford University Press.

Luft, J., & Ingham, H. (1955). The Johari window, a graphic model of interpersonal awareness. In *Proceedings of the western training laboratory in group development.* Los Angeles: UCLA

Martin, J. (1982). Stories and scripts in organizational settings. In A. H. Hastrof & A. M. Isen (Eds.) *Cognitive social psychology*. New York: North Holland/ Elsevier.

Nolan, S. (2006). Building Magical Realms: Responses to Pervasive and Locative Technology. *Digital Creativity*, *17*(3), 185–192. doi:10.1080/14626260600882489

Papert, S., & Harel, I. (1991). Situating Constructionism. In *Constructionism*. Norwood, NJ: Ablex Publishing Corporation.

Piaget, J. (Trans. P.A. Wells). (1982). *Psychology and Epistemology: Towards a Theory of Knowledge*. London: Penguin Books Ltd.

Prensky, M. (2000). *Digital Game-Based Learning*. New York: McGraw Hill.

Roos, J. (2006). *Thinking from Within: A Hands-on Strategy Practice*. New York: Palgrave Macmillan.

Roos, J., & Victor, B. (1998). In search of original strategies? How about some serious play? *Perspectives for Managers*. International Institute for Management Development, Lausanne.

Roos, J., & Victor, B. (1999). Towards a model of strategy making as serious play. *European Management Journal*, *17*, 348–355. doi:10.1016/S0263-2373(99)00015-8

Schrage, M. (2000). *Serious Play: How the world's best companies simulate to innovate*. Cambridge, UK: Harvard Business School Press.

Schunk, D. H., & Pajares, F. (2002). The development of academic self-efficacy. In A. Wigfield & J. Eccles (Eds.), *Development of achievement motivation* (pp. 16-31). San Diego: Academic Press.

Stajkovic, A. D., & Luthans, F. (1998). Self-efficacy and work-related performances: A meta-analysis. *Psychological Bulletin*, *124*, 240–261. doi:10.1037/0033-2909.124.2.240

Stevenson, W. (1988). *The Play Theory of Mass Communication*. New Brunswick, NJ: Transaction Books.

Taylor, J. R. (1993). *Rethinking the theory of organizational communication: How to read an organization*. Norwood, NJ: Ablex.

Taylor, W. (Ed.). (1984). Metaphors of Education. *Studies in education, new ser., 14*. London: Heinemann Educational Books for the Institute of Education University of London.

Winnecott, D. (1971). *Playing and Reality*. London: Tavistock.

Chapter 21
Using ePortfolios to Evidence Practice Learning for Social Work Students

Samantha Osborne
University of Kent, UK

Ruben Martin
University of Kent, UK

Louise Frith
University of Kent, UK

ABSTRACT

The University of Kent is piloting the use of ePortfolios in a number of departments; the School of Social Policy, Sociology and Social Research took the opportunity to pilot ePortfolios to investigate whether ePortfolios could improve communication and collaboration between student, placement supervisor and academic tutors whilst Social Work students are out on work-based placement. Social Work students are required to complete two reflective practice documents during each of their two placements during Years 2 and 3 of their degree to assess their competence against a set of National Standards. The chapter will discuss the adoption of a Personalised Learning Environment for recording assessed practice and how the tools provided can enhance the different categories of users' experiences both in terms of reflective practice and personal development. The chapter gives a background to the pilot and describes the different profiles of each user group which are students, academic staff, practitioners, and other stakeholders. It will also examine to what extent the pilot is in line with government initiatives such as the Leitch Review and Burgess Report and research into the use of ePortfolios for reflection; the issues surrounding the introduction of new technology to non-traditional students and outside organizations; how technology has changed student and practitioner's perceptions and expectations in the production of a collaborative body of evidence; and the future pedagogical implications of using technology with Social Work students and practitioners.

DOI: 10.4018/978-1-60566-884-0.ch021

INTRODUCTION

Over the past 12 years, initiatives by government have increasingly emphasised the development of Higher Education students' skills and employability. The National Committee of Inquiry into Higher Education (Dearing 1997) recommended that students be encouraged to record, reflect upon and plan their progress in Higher Education. The Quality Assurance Agency (QAA) accepted these recommendations and set a lead time of five years for institutions commencing in 2005 which was designed to give universities time to devise their own plans for developing Personal Development Planning. The Leitch report (2006) reviewed the nation's long term skills needs and recommended partnership between employers, government and individuals. In 2007, The Burgess Report recommended that the Higher Education Achievement Report (HEAR) should become the main vehicle for measuring and recording a student's achievement. The report proposed that the HEAR, a supporting document which gives a wider indication of the student's performance against certain criteria, be developed and tested over a four year period alongside the existing degree classification which currently encapsulates student achievement in a single number. ePortfolios are being developed to support students' Personal Development Planning which the Burgess Report encourages the use of to further strengthen the evidence found in the HEAR.

The University of Kent's Unit for the Enhancement of Learning and Teaching has been carrying out a number of pilot projects to encourage students to reflect on their personal development and record their progress using an ePortfolio. The University's Social Work degree programme seemed to be a perfect match for the use of ePortfolios because it encourages reflection as part of learning and students are expected to record evidence of practice in order to demonstrate that they have met Social Work standards. Since students are all required to produce reflective writing as part of their assess-

ment for work-based placements, it seemed an ideal opportunity to introduce ePortfolios to assist them with completing the required documentary evidence of competence.

The process of introducing ePortfolios has not been without its difficulties; many of the assumptions about students being 'digital natives' because of their easy acceptance of mobile phones, MP3 players, online chat and social networking sites have been dispelled. The profile of the students enrolled on the Social Work course is mainly mature with many originating from overseas and a considerable number being from low socio-economic groups.

Using ePortfolios can add educational value to the learning experience of students, Practice Assessors (Social Work practitioners who assess practice placements) and teaching staff; however, some of the issues that have been encountered have raised questions as to whether ePortfolios are being used simply to adapt to government life-long learning initiatives such as progress files and the widening participation agenda proposed by Dearing (1997) and those developed since.

The piloting of the ePortfolio by the Social Work degree programme at Kent was a leap of faith as the question whether the use of ePortfolios would truly benefit students needed to be tested in practice. This chapter will trace the roots of what has proved to be a difficult journey of translating a paper portfolio to a collaborative ePortfolio and will share the valuable lessons, both pedagogical and technological, which have been learnt and continue to be evaluated and incorporated into the teaching of the degree programme.

BACKGROUND

The National Student Survey in 2005 showed that the student experience of Personal Development Planning (PDP) at the University of Kent was not equitable across different departments. As a result, the University undertook a campus-wide review of PDP practice in 2006. The review exposed a considerable lack of awareness of PDP amongst students. However, it also confirmed that Kent's approach to PDP being discipline-based was deemed, pedagogically, to be a strength but laid the University open to accusations of inequality. Lecturers commented that PDP should be a largely student-owned process supported by academic staff. Consequently, curriculum developers embarked on finding a way of strengthening PDP, making it student–owned and more visible to students yet retaining a variety of discipline-based approaches.

Research into PDP support systems indicated that an ePortfolio might prove to be a useful tool for Kent. ePortfolios have a number of advantages including:

- They have the ability to make PDP a tangible process. Yancey states that 'ePortfolios make learning visible and thus faculty members and students focus on learning in new ways' (Yancey 2001).
- They facilitate a student-owned approach to PDP because they are based on constructivist philosophy, students are expected to take responsibility for selecting artefacts, making connections to standards and interpreting their own learning. (Strudler & Wetzel 2005)
- Being in an electronic form, ePortfolios are compatible with the method which most students use to produce their work now. (Batson 2002)

The University of Kent introduced the Pebble-Pad ePortfolio in December 2006 with the initial investment of 100 licenses. A small-scale pilot project began on a Clinical Psychology module with 20 students who volunteered to use the portfolio for the reflective journal element of their work. The students and lecturers on this module were interviewed about their experience and feedback was mainly positive. Based on this pilot, access to ePortfolio software was opened up to other departments. However, the project remained a pilot with consultation and evaluation built-in following Ayala's (2006) recommendations which advise a slow, democratic, constructivist approach to the introduction of ePortfolios.

One of the first programmes to take advantage of the ePortfolio was the Social Work degree. The question of using ePortfolios for the assessment of competence was a subject which has been of interest; particularly in the past 5 years with the growing interest in using them for reflective practice in areas such as medicine, social care and nursing (McMullan et al, 2003). Reardon, Hartley & Lucas (2007) state that a starting point for the introduction of ePortfolios is to identify a problem that needs to be solved. For Social Work, the problem arose on the assessment of practice element of the programme. Students undertake two 100 day placements for which they provide evidence validated by a Practice Assessor (PA). This was done via emailed Word documents which gave rise to problems of version control and lost feedback. The ePortfolio was introduced into the Social Work programme to address these two problems. At the start of the academic year 2006/7 Social Work students and their Practice Assessors were shown the ePortfolio software and given a choice to use it or to continue with the emailed Word documents. Just under a third of the 33 students in the cohort volunteered to take part which gave us a pilot of study of 9 students.

Evaluation of the ePortfolio in the Social Work programme was built into the pilot and based on the Sampson, Reardon, Peterson and Lenz (2004) Diagnosis, Prescription, Process, Outputs, Outcomes (DPPOO) Model which is:

- Diagnosis of what the problems identified by staff and students were; version control and lost feedback
- Prescription, that the ePortfolio was introduced to replace emailed Word documents

- Process, plans of the PebblePad pilot projects were discussed and agreed at Department and University level.
- Outputs, the primary effects so far have been to enhance the collaborative aspect of the assessment of practice
- Outcomes, the outcome of the primary effects so far have been that the student on placement is better supported and has gained confidence using transferable IT skills.

This project is now in its second year which represents a very early stage for reporting as Hall and Hord (2001) view change in education as a complex process that takes a minimum of 3-5 years. The information contained in this chapter is very much the initial findings of a work in progress.

The professional Social Work qualification in the UK changed in 2003 from a 2 year diploma to a 3 year degree programme. The diploma required students to complete 130 days of practice which was assessed through a detailed report from a Practice Teacher from the organisation in which the student was placed. The process was time-consuming and could lack objectivity as final judgments were left to the Practice Teacher. With the introduction of the Social Work degree, the amount of assessed practice increased to 200 days with the students being required to produce a portfolio of evidence based on National Occupational Standards for Social Work (TOPPS England, 2004 and Department of Health, 2002) which is validated by a Practice Assessor (previously Practice Teacher role), who makes a Pass/Fail recommendation. For organisations that do not have a qualified practitioner (Practice Assessor) to assess the student, the validation for assessment is undertaken by an off-site assessor traditionally referred to as a Long-Arm Practice Teacher (LAPT) who works with an on-site supervisor who provides day-to-day support and allocation of work. The University of Kent meets the practice

requirement through the provision of two 100-day placements which occur during the second and final years of the degree. Once the portfolios of evidence are submitted, a Practice Assessment Panel of Social Work practitioners from local authorities and voluntary organisations that work in partnership with the Social Work programme read them to establish that the evidence given supports the Practice Assessor's recommendation of meeting National Occupational Standards.

The portfolio of evidence includes a document called the Assessment of Practice Tool which the student completes with guidance from their Practice Assessor who is required to have a formal weekly supervision session with the student to discuss progress. In order to provide material for this process, students complete a Weekly Practice Learning Record throughout the duration of the placement from which sample evidence can then be transferred to the Assessment of Practice Tool at interim and final assessment stages. Students were originally given these documents as Microsoft Word files on a floppy disk and files were emailed back and forth between student and Practice Assessor. Occasionally, Practice Assessors and students encountered problems with emailing files and it could be difficult to keep track of the latest version of the document. In addition, the University had decided to introduce Office 2007 on campus which saves files in a radically different file format which was not always compatible with older versions of Office unless a converter was downloaded. This increased the risk of files becoming corrupted in transit. It was decided to investigate the use of the webfolio tool in PebblePad in order to facilitate and enrich the exchange of information between the student and their Practice Assessor.

HOW THE PERSONAL LEARNING ENVIRONMENT WAS SELECTED

In 2006, Kent's Unit for the Enhancement of Learning and Teaching (UELT) started investigating Personal Learning Environments (PLE) and two main options were considered: WebCT/ Blackboard Web Portfolios and PebblePad. The decision about which PLE to use was made by the University's Learning and Teaching Unit after seeing presentations from WebCT and PebblePad and in consultation with interested tutors including Social Work tutors. The following discussion outlines the concerns that Social Work tutors expressed and it was found that many of these concerns were echoed by tutors from other departments such as Clinical Psychology, Architecture and Sports Science.

The final choice of PLE depended on five factors: confidentiality, interoperability, extraction, look and simplicity.

Confidentiality is a key concern for Social Work students, practitioners and teaching staff. As Social Work students and others are in a situation where they need to be able to express their thoughts and feelings in a safe environment, confidentiality is a factor of utmost importance. Students who had already been using WebCT may have perceived that their tutors were able to track their movements and read their ePortfolios as they may have understood that teaching staff have ultimate control over what is available in WebCT. However, as PebblePad offers a confidential space in which only the students have control over the material which they can add to and share from their ePortfolios; it was felt that the sense of ownership and privacy offered by PebblePad would encourage students to use the tool for their reflections and enable them to feel comfortable with recording those reflections due to the more confidential nature of the PLE.

The issue of interoperability was another important factor as the tool that students, teaching staff and practice placement assessors would use needed to be available on as many platforms as possible. As Social Work students and their Practice Assessors complete their work whilst out on placement, the tool needed to be compatible with as many different systems and web browsers

as possible. Although WebCT was an embedded technology within the University, it still required that a number of prerequisites be met before it worked properly and did not support many other web browsers apart from Internet Explorer and required users to have installed a particular version of Java. As PebblePad required the use of Flash which is easily obtainable via a free download and also has a browser checker on their website so users can check the compatibility of their browsers and software, it seemed like a better fit for the intended user groups.

Although both systems offered the option to share data with others, the PebblePad option was the more attractive as the possibilities for extraction included an option to collaborate on work which proved to be a good fit for the delivering the Weekly Practice Learning Record and Assessment of Practice Tool as students and Practice Assessors need to be in constant dialogue. The ability to work on one document together is a significant asset which was not a feature of WebCT's ePortfolio tool when we assessed the systems. In addition, WebCT placed strict access protocols and usage restrictions on the licence of their system so we may potentially have had problems with using it for the purpose intended because of the number of different user groups we had to deliver the material to.

PebblePad also offered students the option to keep their PebblePad account active after graduation so it was felt that it would be useful in the future as a vehicle for recording the student's lifelong learning activities. With the introduction of the requirement for social workers to record their Continuing Professional Development activities as part of their re-registration process, it was felt that the ability for students to be able to carry on using the tool after graduation would be a good motivator. (Department of Health, 2002)

The appearance of the interface was another key factor in choosing which system we chose. Even though the WebCT interface (Figure 1) was already familiar to the students it seemed that it

Figure 1. Sample of ePortfolio offered by Blackboard/WebCT © Peter Chalk, London Metropolitan University, 2007

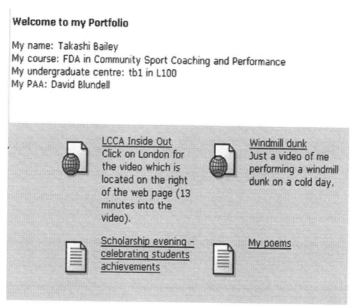

might provide an element of confusion as the style of the ePortfolio was very similar to what students would see when they logged into their WebCT modules. In the separate ePortfolio section, students would have had to use different tools from the ones which they had been used to.

Despite seeming like a good integrated solution, since Social Work students have been encouraged to make use of WebCT from the start of their course in order to pick up course material and access online resources; the integrated WebCT solution was not viable for the Social Work students and the Practice Assessors as the interface meant that students had to acquire a different set of skills from those which they normally needed to navigate through their WebCT modules. It was felt that this could be confusing for them.

The PebblePad interface (Figure 2) seemed to be simpler and easier to navigate due to its uncluttered layout and simple numbered steps which users are required to follow in order to create and manipulate files. Additionally, it was not certain whether Practice Assessors would be

allowed to access students' WebCT ePortfolios due to licencing restrictions about different users imposed by WebCT's owners.

We commenced our PebblePad pilot in September 2007 and the first cohorts of students have been through their 100 day placements with the option of using either the established method of using Microsoft Word and email or using the PebblePad webfolio to record evidence for their Assessment of Practice Tool and Weekly Practice Learning Record. It was decided that all students in that year and their Practice Assessors would have the choice of deciding between the two methods during the pilot so participation was voluntary and by mutual agreement. The benefit giving students and practitioners a choice meant that those who were interested could try it if they wished and this did not disadvantage those who did not feel confident enough could opt not to use PebblePad. We have now started to embed this technology into the curriculum and our second cohort of students have just begun the first of their 100 day placements and demand from students and practitioners

Figure 2. Sample of ePortfolio offered by PebblePad © Samantha Osborne, University of Kent, 2008

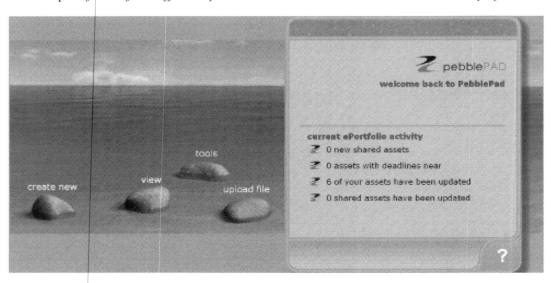

to be part of the pilot has led to the need to run further sessions for interested practitioners who may have heard about PebblePad from their peers or enthusiastic students.

USER PROFILES

The Kent Social Work programme's ePortfolio pilot involved three main categories of users: students, users from outside university (Practice Assessors and Long-Arm Practice Teachers) at the student's placement and, to a lesser extent, University tutors.

Students

There are approximately 45 Social Work students per year at the University, based at our Medway campus, and these students come from a variety of different backgrounds. Many students had already been in employment before they started their university degree course with students ages ranging from 21 to 53 years with a high number mature of students. Kent's focus at the Medway campus has been to encourage and develop the

Widening Participation agenda and many of the students on the course were found to be from a less affluent socio-economic background than students at the Canterbury campus.

It was clear that many of our students were not the 'digital natives' we anticipated and on further investigation into of the kinds of students that had been recruited we discovered some potential explanations for the difficulties that some students were experiencing. Figure 3 demonstrates that the majority of Social Work students engaged in the ePortfolio trial were over the age of 30 (over 65%) which may be a factor in some of the pedagogical issues encountered. When questioned further, students admitted they had to seek help from their peers and, in some cases, their children to understand some of the concepts that were discussed.

All students at Kent are required to hand in word-processed assignments and there have been moves to digitize hand-in to allow use of online plagiarism detection tools. Consequently, there is a steep learning curve for many students who have not had a lot of exposure to using computers prior to coming to university. IT is one of the key skills which has been identified by the General Social

Figure 3. Analysis of student ages of social work cohort piloting ePortfolio use (© 2008, Samantha Osborne, University of Kent)

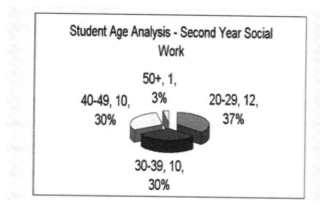
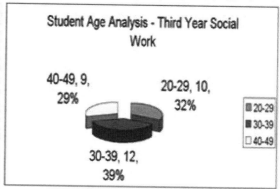

Care Council and TOPPS England (now Skills for Care) as essential for the social care workforce and students are assessed for CLAIT or ECDL, or an equivalent, during the Social Work degree programme (TOPPS England, 2000). Despite the training that is offered to students, some still struggle with IT and cannot immediately make the link between skills learnt during the course of the ECDL or CLAIT and how they can be used in other computing applications.

Committed students proved to be crucial to the success of the pilot. We gave our students and practitioners the choice of whether they would use PebblePad or the Word document which meant that ownership and commitment to the pilot came from the end-users. As it can take time for new initiatives such as using ePortfolios to become embedded in a programme, attaining a high level of commitment from students can result in student-led development. In turn, this ensured that the innovation was able to gather momentum and, consequently, carry the more reluctant students and practitioners along with it. By persevering with the pilot, we have been able to win over the students who have questioned why they needed to use new technology and have also created an expectation that the new initiatives are accepted as standard practice on the Social Work degree course at Kent.

University Tutors

University tutors generally possess a high-level of IT literacy as they are used to dealing with the different interfaces for the University systems however there remain some tutors who still struggle with new systems and avoid them if possible. Although the student's personal tutor is not directly involved in assessing the student's practice, it became clear during the pilot any future plans for a full implementation of the use of PebblePad on the programme would rely on the full participation of committed tutors to provide encouragement to those students and practitioners who might not feel as confident about embracing new technology. In addition, there was supportive leadership from the Head of Social Work at the University of Kent. As tutors did not attend training in the pilot year, we have since learnt that it is important that all tutors receive training in order to enable them to support and guide their students. We will be addressing the issue of tutor training by inviting them to the introductory, support and refresher sessions offered so that they may learn alongside Practice Assessors and Long-Arm Practice Teachers.

Practice Assessors and Long-Arm Practice Teachers

As Practice Assessors and Long Arm Practice Teachers are from different social work and social care organisations and have different levels of IT literacy; this particular group can prove to the be the most challenging in terms of setting up and maintaining the interaction through the ePortfolio. Practice Assessors and Long Arm Practice Teachers are invited to training days before and during the placement however they are not always able to attend. Initially, those Practice Assessors and Long Arm Practice Teachers who attended placement training were given a simple demonstration of how the software would work and asked to volunteer for the pilot. It was felt that the process they had to complete was simpler than what the students needed to do to share their ePortfolio; however, it became clear that some Assessors and Long Arm Practice Teachers found that they had difficulty with the concept of and using webfolios. Subsequent, hands-on sessions and drop-ins were arranged in order to enable them to get better acquainted with ePortfolios and be able to provide further support to their students.

Academic Culture

The academic culture of the Social Work degree seeks to encourage students to engage in reflective thinking. As a student's reflections are part of the assessment criteria, the nature of these types of assessments can prove difficult for weak students. The course provides a unique interaction between Practice Assessors (and Long Arm Practice Teachers when necessary), tutors and students. By working together to produce a document that is collaborative, students are given guidance and feedback throughout their placements in order to help them to prepare their reflections. Students are assessed on their reflective practice and, consequently, become more engaged in the process.

Right from the beginning of the first term of their degree programme, Social Work students are expected to use reflective writing in all their academic assignments and, in particular, whilst completing participative modules such as 'Communications Skills' which is assessed through students keeping a reflective diary during the entirety of the module and a video role play with a 1,000 word analytical commentary. Additionally, students complete the 'Values, Ethics and Equality' module where they are required to keep a reflective log during a 10-day practice observation placement. During the two 100-day practice placements both the Weekly Practice Learning Record and Assessment of Practice Tool require students to give evidence of practice which is then linked to underpinning theory and values as well as adding their own analysis and reflection.

The academic culture of reflective practice in the Social Work programme is quite different from many other departments where reflection on learning and reflective writing is not generally an accepted part of the academic culture. The prevailing culture of the Social Work degree programme increases the likelihood of projects involving Personal Development Planning and life-long learning initiatives succeeding.

COLLABORATION WITHIN THE UNIVERSITY

The success of this pilot hinged on effective collaboration between the main project implementers. Figure 4 details the partners and their roles:

The pilot benefited from initial promotion and encouragement by the University's Personal Development Planning coordinator, who contributed a wider knowledge and experience of use of personalised learning and ePortfolios to departments and programmes. The department agreed that the Departmental IT Manager could be released to devote sufficient time to this pilot on the Social Work degree programme, being one

Figure 4. Collaboration between main project implementers (© 2008, Louise Frith, University of Kent)

Partner	Social Work academic tutor	Practice learning Coordinator	Departmental IT Manager	UELT PDP coordinator
Role	Academic support for the student throughout the programme of study	Arranging and coordinating practice placements. Ensuring Practice Assessors are available, trained and supported	Devising ePortfolio format for required documentation. Training students and staff to use the new software	Promote and evaluate innovative ways to enhance the curriculum and address new initiatives such as PDP

of many programmes in a large academic department. The Social Work degree programme has a full-time Practice Learning Coordinator who coordinates the organisation and development of training events as well as acting as a personal tutor for a group of students. The programme's Director of Studies was also personal tutor to some of the students and supported the pilot at programme and individual level.

It is usually very difficult to achieve effective collaboration between partners. Part of the reason that this collaboration was successful was the definition of clear roles and responsibilities during the project pilot and the establishing of good communication between partners.

EXTERNAL COLLABORATION WITH OUTSIDE ORGANISATIONS

The Social Work degree programme already had good relationships with external social work and social care organisations such as local authorities and other service providers and has worked in partnership with them to provide the students' practice learning opportunities in assessed placements. However, arranging practice placements for all students is a difficult task as it depends on organisations being willing to host a student for 100 days and the availability of qualified Practice Assessors. In allocating placements a number of factors have to be balanced such as student's interests and learning needs, geographical location, and the student's previous experience and characteristics. It may disadvantage a Black student, for instance, to be placed in a predominantly White

Figure 5. Screen shot of students' My Assets area (© 2008, Samantha Osborne, University of Kent)

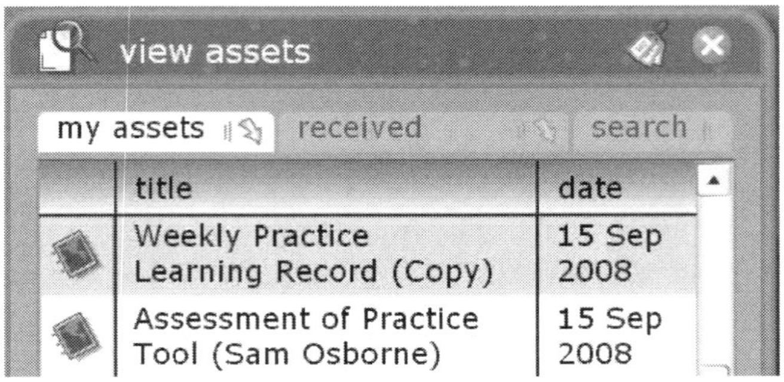

area where all practitioners in the work team are White. The number of placements is limited so this also reduces the choice for each student. Practice Assessors are invited to preparation and support meetings, however Practice Assessors take on the commitment as part of their busy workloads and it often not convenient to attend. Employers should provide a workload reduction to allow a practitioner to take a student but, in practice, this rarely happens.

Placements commence with a learning agreement meeting attended by the student, Practice Assessor, on-site supervisor (if different from the Practice Assessor), and the student's personal tutor. The ePortfolio facilitates ongoing communication between this group due to the ability to share materials electronically via the internet. When students begin to evidence their practice in the Weekly Practice Learning Record and Assessment of Practice Tool, they are able to seek comments from both their Practice Assessor and personal tutor. However, tutors must accept that during practice placements Practice Assessors are primarily responsible for assessing the students and must be satisfied with the evidence provided by the student. There is a danger that tutors could give contradictory advice or mixed messages to students and such issues are best resolved in close collaboration between all parties.

Students are provided with a webfolio template which is sent to their received folder by the depart-

mental IT Manager. The individual students are then required to take ownership of the portfolio by copying it into their My Assets area (Figure 5) where they will edit and adapt the ePortfolio until they are ready to share it with their Practice Assessor/Long Arm Practice Teacher or whoever else they wish to share it with (Figure 6).

As students write their documents collaboratively with active input from their Practice Assessor/Long Arm Practice Teachers, the issue of ownership of the ePortfolio can prove problematic. When students are given their PebblePad accounts, they are told quite explicitly that they are in control of who can see the items that they create and are given training on how to share and unshare items with others. Due to the nature of the Social Work course, it is vital that students are able to trust that the mechanism for recording their personal thoughts and feelings is secure.

Students out on placement are encouraged to visualize themselves as a professional practitioner working largely through establishing relationships with service users. The Assessment of Practice Tool, therefore, has an element of personal development planning. It is also a tool for assessment of competence and it is ultimately the Practice Assessor who recommends whether the student has passed or failed the practice element of their degree. Students may question their ownership of the ePortfolio when a Practice Assessor is commenting on their failure to meet standards and

Figure 6. Screen shot of webfolio for assessment of practice tool (© 2008, Samantha Osborne, University of Kent)

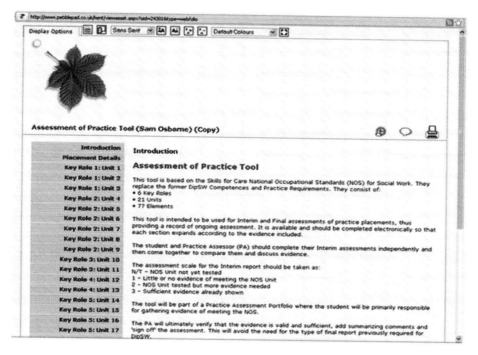

their risk of failing the placement. It is difficult to give the student the responsibility for providing evidence of their own weakness or failure.

TECHNICAL ISSUES

The concept of using ePortfolios for the Assessment of Practice Tool and Weekly Learning Record to students was first introduced in 2006/07 academic year just before the second and third years students were due to go out on their 100 day placements. Two document templates based on the existing Microsoft Word files were created in the form of webfolios and these were shared via PebblePad with the students so that they could copy the items into their own personal spaces. Students are then responsible for sharing their own personalised webfolios with the Practice Assessors so that both parties can work on them collaboratively. Students could have uploaded

their webfolios to an assessment gateway however this would have added an extra layer of complexity to a new process and they would not have been able to make use of the immediate feedback of the collaborative feature of the webfolio (Figure 7).

Students were all given a brief introduction to the PebblePad and the concept of an ePortfolio during a lecture and then they had an hour-long hands-on training session where it was explained how they would work with their Practice Assessors on producing their documentary evidence together. There were two main areas where students struggled with using ePortfolios:

1. The inability to transfer their knowledge of using Microsoft Word to edit documents to the webfolio interface.
2. Having a limited understanding of the difference between a standalone software application and a tool delivered over the internet.

Figure 7. Screen shot of webfolio for weekly learning record (© 2008, Samantha Osborne, University of Kent)

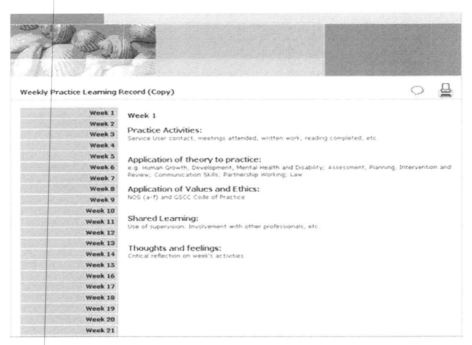

It became clear in these initial training sessions that not all students were not comfortable with the technology and despite the clear interface; the concepts of collaboration and sharing need further emphasis. Despite all students being assessed for computer literacy, it is clear that some students continue to struggle with using keyboard shortcuts for cutting and pasting and other simple functions. As students and practitioners had the choice of using PebblePad or not during the pilot, support offered was needs-based.

As Social Work students are required to return to university for recall days, this gives them the opportunity to discuss any problems they may have in working with ePortfolios during an informal 'clinic' session. Many students benefited from the individual attention and often went on to help their peers. It was often the case that students found it difficult to disassociate what they could do in Microsoft Word from the basic functions that were available in the simple online text editor. The text

editor also had an inherent issue where the cursor returned to the first letter of the entire document whenever the student pressed the return key which caused frustration particularly when they were working on a long section of their document. The issue of the cursor was fixed in a subsequent release of PebblePad but there was still a sense that it was a source of residual frustration and contributed to the students' feelings of distrust of the software.

A further issue was the speed of internet connection as students did not fully understand that as they were working on a document via internet the speed of the connection and other connectivity issues affected how quickly the application responds. Many students commented that loading and typing into the text editor could be slow. One student did not have access to broadband at home so refused to use PebblePad at all despite a high-speed internet connection and fairly recently upgraded PCs being available at University. Reasons that students gave for not using facilities at University would often include childcare issues and lack of time.

There were also questions of whether the ePortfolio tool will be compatible with assistive software such as those for dyslexia or vision impairment. One student reported that she was unable to get her PebblePad webfolio to 'cooperate' with the software which she uses for dyslexia and the only solution for her was to use the Word document otherwise she would have had to cut and paste out of her webfolio every time a change was made.

Although it was assumed that most Practice Assessors would be able to understand the simple interface of the PebblePad webfolio, many were not keen to learn something different right at the start of a placement, despite the offer of hands-on training, very few took up the offer and continued to use Microsoft Word with their students. As Practice Assessors are not compelled to attend the preparation for placement training days that are offered by the University, not all the students' Practice Assessors were available to receive the information on how their students could use webfolios to share their Assessment of Practice Tool and Weekly Learning Record. Some of the Practice Assessors who agreed to participate on the pilot had to rely on their students being able to help them navigate the PebblePad interface and this contributed to some of the issues that students had with using ePortfolios for their assessments. Coupled with a licencing requirement which meant that Practice Assessors had to apply for a Kent IT account in order to be able to have a PebblePad account; some Practice Assessors found the process laborious and decided not to participate, although others welcomed the link with the University which also enabled them to use the University library. Another issue that came up was that many organisations have rigorous firewall restrictions which sometimes do not allow applications using Flash or block connections to the PebblePad server. Some IT departments were

willing to cooperate and gave their staff and our students the ability to access PebblePad at their workplace. Other organisations, although willing to cooperate, found that their firewall and access issues proved to be insurmountable. Despite these issues, the Practice Assessors involved were interested enough to log into PebblePad from home and continue working on the ePortfolios with their students. Some Practice Assessors were so impressed by the perceived benefits of working collaboratively that they took up the offer of extra training sessions and encouraged some of the more reluctant students to take part in the pilot.

ASSESSMENT

The University of Kent has not yet fully embraced the whole concept of the ePortfolio as the assessment panel still requires students to submit their Assessment of Practice Tool in paper form. The assessment panel comprises of twenty practitioners from a variety of local authority and voluntary sector organizations who are not all involved in the supervision of students on placement.

Social Work students are required to submit a number of documents to evidence their practice which are:

*   The Assessment of Practice Tool
*   Direct Observations of the student's practice – written by Practice Assessors
*   Process Recordings – written by students to describe interactions with service users
*   Service user feedback – feedback from service users that the students have dealt with
*   Feedback from other professionals that the students have dealt with (e.g. health care and educational professionals)

Many of these documents are not in a standard format and are often hand-written. Consequently, as students did not have easy access to scanning facilities, it was felt that in order to keep the documentation together, it was better to print out the APT so that the evidence could all be sent in one format to the panel. We are still in the early stages of determining the benefit of using ePortfolios during the placement and need to establish the benefits of invest time and expenditure in training and supporting the assessment panel in using the software as well as providing scanning equipment for student use in order to make the assessment fully electronic.

As the APT webfolio was intended to be viewed on screen, the format of the printed copy can look inferior as the printed text appears very small and some pages print out just the menu options which can be an issue for students who have to pay for printing by the page. Some students used the option to convert their webfolio into a Microsoft Word file and have spent quite a considerable time changing the formatting in order to make their documents more presentable for print despite being given reassurances that the panel would not penalise them for the formatting of the printed ePortfolio as it appeared.

FEEDBACK FROM THE PRIMARY PILOT PHASE

Although the opportunity to trial ePortfolios was given to both the second and third year cohorts; it was second years who took the opportunity to try out the ePortfolio option. As the third year students were already used to and comfortable with using the Microsoft Word system, there was great reluctance to try out something new but students were given the opportunity to use PebblePad if they wished to. Eighteen students out of the second year cohort which numbered 33 responded to a short 8 question survey about their use of the ePortfolio at the end of their first 100 day placement. Half of the students had stated that they used the ePortfolio template to complete their Assessment of Practice Tool and Weekly Learning Record. Only one of the 9 students had given up

using the ePortfolio giving the reason that it was too slow. Three of those students gave in-depth individual interviews about their experiences.

Case Study 1

O is a 43 year old third year Social Work student. In O's second year, a PebblePad trial was carried out with second and third year students. Like many of his cohort, O came to university with limited knowledge of using computers and technology and was reluctant to begin using PebblePad as he considered it as an extra activity that would have been more time-consuming even after he had attended a hands-on training session. As all students had been given the option of using either the Microsoft Word template or using a webfolio template in PebblePad; O, like many students, felt that it was easier to stick with the Word option. In particular, students like O felt that they did not want to participate in the PebblePad trial since they had also been the first Social Work cohort to use the VLE WebCT the previous year. However, with some encouragement from his Practice Assessor, who had attended some hands-on training; O reluctantly started using the webfolio and soon found that it was beneficial.

He found that it was useful for his Practice Assessor to work on the same document as he was; however, it was frustrating for both of them if she forgot to save the document and the web connection went down sometimes meaning that they had lost a lot of work but he had a good relationship with his Practice Assessor so they persevered with it together. Although he was reluctant to use an ePortfolio at first, he really started to see the benefits of using it. He liked that he was able to access his webfolio from wherever he was in the world and that his changes would be seen instantaneously by his Practice Assessor in the UK. O was in Nigeria at one point during his second year winter break and his comment was that it would not have been so easy if he'd used a flash drive (memory stick).

Even though O did find some of the aspects of editing the webfolio difficult; he was so keen to increase his use PebblePad that he has asked to have his required Process Recordings included and has even added a page in his webfolio in order to do this. O did end up using the 'Convert to Word' option in PebblePad when he finished work on his ePortfolio as he felt that he would be penalized for the layout of his printed evidence and spent quite some time reformatting the document for print.

O has proven to be a keen convert to using ePortfolios and is planning keen to carry on using PebblePad even after he graduates to keep a record of his Continuing Professional Development.

The feedback questionnaire consisted of mostly free text answers as we wanted to encourage students to have the freedom to write the comments and any explanations they felt they wanted to give. It was felt that this kind of commentary would be more helpful to the pilot coordinators than just using a rating scale at that stage of the pilot.

Questions covered the following areas:

- Why students did not use the ePortfolio
- What was the most useful aspect of using PebblePad
- Sharing work with Practice Assessors/ Long-Arm Practice Teacher
- Training
- Improving the take-up of the ePortfolio in future years
- Use of other tools in PebblePad
- Further suggestions (see Figure 8)

Out of the 14 reasons that the 9 students had given for not using the ePortfolio, the responses fell into three main categories: speed of the connection, Practice Assessor/Long-Arm Practice Teacher involvement and technical issues. In particular, the comments that a student had "Lost confidence early on" and one student's "PA did not know how to use it", has helped shaped some of our future

planning for future stages of the pilot as it helped us to be more aware about the anxieties that our students feel about technology and consequently plan for better integration of awareness-raising and support of ePortfolios for subsequent cohorts of students. We have been able to report back to the vendor the comment from one user regarding the incompatibility with dyslexia software. Only one student reported their economic situation as a barrier to using the ePortfolio: "I cannot afford internet at home, so could not access it then."

The nine students who responded that they were using the ePortfolio provided twelve statements with which the majority of the group agreed that the collaborative aspect of the ePortfolio was the most useful (Figure 9). A third of the respondents said that being able to access their ePortfolio via the internet was the most useful aspect for them, one commented that: "Placement wouldn't allow me to use the USB data stick." The evidence provided by the student and Practice Assessor who took part in the interviews for the Case Studies at the end of this chapter agreed with these reasons.

When students were asked about whether using the ePortfolio was helping them share their work with their Practice Assessor, the responses for and against approximated to the take-up of the pilot; namely an almost fifty-fifty split. The main reason that the students gave for the ePortfolio not helping them share their work was that the Practice Assessor "did not know how to use it". One of the 9 students who had Practice Assessors who worked with them on their ePortfolio were very positive about their experience: "This feature was great!". The availability of Practice Assessors and Long-Arm Practice Teachers for training has previously been discussed, however, the availability of this feedback has demonstrated the importance of practical demonstration of the ePortfolio and hands-on training for this group of stakeholders. In response to the feedback, we have improved and extended our training and support for Practice Assessors which seems to have trebled the number of requests for PebblePad logins in

Figure 8. Reasons students gave for not using PebblePad (© 2008, Samantha Osborne, University of Kent)

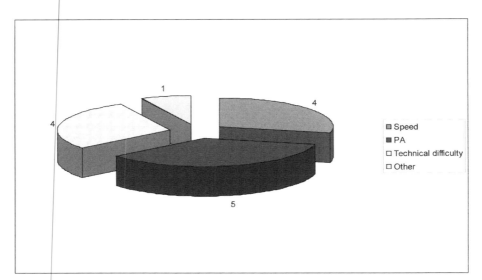

comparison to previous years. We have also given Practice Assessors/Long-Arm Practice Teachers the incentive of being able to access University library eResources through the provision of a Kent IT Account. Students, however, indicated that they had sufficient training and support opportunities with 15 out of 16 responding positively to the question on whether or not they had sufficient training opportunities in how to use PebblePad (Figure 10).

When students were asked what would encourage other students to use ePortfolios in the future, the responses were fairly mixed with 25 responses from the 18 students. The majority of responses were concerned with improving the functionality and speed of PebblePad itself. It was realised that many students did not understand that the speed of editing and accessing the ePortfolio was dependent on the speed and reliability of the internet connection. In order to address this, the next cohort of students who were to pilot PebblePad on their placement were told explicitly to remember that they were editing a document on the internet and sometimes it might be slow if their connection was slow. Just under a fifth of responses said that it

would be better if it was more like Microsoft Word so and in order to address this point, this year's training emphasised the restrictions of publishing to the web and the trainer briefly explained about the underlying code of a website which meant that not all of the underlying sophistications available in Microsoft Word were not available. A useful comparison was with social networking sites or webmail and students have started to understand the technicalities of editing and sharing files using an ePortfolio.

Case Study 2

J is a Long-Arm Practice Teacher who supervised three students in the 2007/08 academic year. Two of her students used PebblePad webfolios to record their evidence of practice. J was not confident about using webfolios at first but after attending a hands-on session, she saw the benefits of a collaborative provision.

J particularly enjoyed the immediateness of using a collaborative ePortfolio as it was easy to add something straight away particularly after she met with her students. It could be difficult

Figure 9. What students found most useful about using the ePortfolio (© 2008, Samantha Osborne, University of Kent)

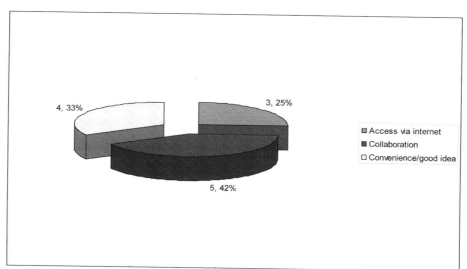

because it was not like Word but she worked out a system using different fonts and colours so that she and the student could keep track of when they made changes. J keeps a log in each student file and asks students to let her know which units of competence they were working on in order to make sure that she covered all the required areas as it was difficult to see straight away when a section was changed. J found that her older students were not very confident but with encouragement, they did eventually start using the webfolio.

As Practice Teachers do not receive extra time or reward for taking on students, J felt that it was important to emphasise the benefits which come with adopting the use of PebblePad as the recording instrument for the required evidence: being library access, the opportunity for them to have their own account with space to record their own professional activity and the opportunity to improve their own IT skills. J commented that by agreeing to supervise and assess students through the use ePortfolios, it was something that Social Workers could demonstrate as a CPD activity.

Informal interview feedback from 2 volunteers amongst the Practice Assessors/LAPTs. Case

Study 2 details one of the respondents' feelings about using PebblePad. The other participant said that "It looks like a really useful way of working but we really couldn't get it to work at our establishment but I wanted to see if we could do it and tried it out at home instead. It is a good way of keeping track of where we are as I don't have to depend on the student sending me their APT, I can just go in there and have a look for myself and encourage the student to work on areas they haven't completed or need to do extra work on."

From the evidence that we have received so far, it seems that the ePortfolio adds value to the practitioner-student relationship despite the issues that the students have indicated. Informal feedback from Year 2 students seems to be much more positive and requests from Practice Assessors to have access to a PebblePad account and training have increased three-fold this academic year. We have really been encouraged that this second group of students who are piloting the ePortfolio appear to be quite engaged and enthused about using the software as a number of them requested that a proforma for the process recordings they have to carry out be put on PebblePad.

Figure 10. How would students be encouraged to take up the use of PebblePad (© 2008, Samantha Osborne, University of Kent)

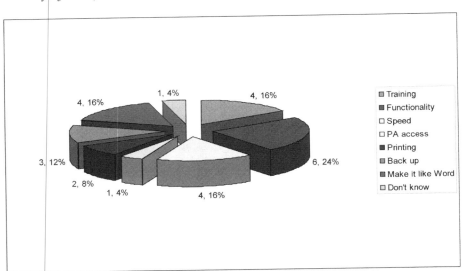

SOLUTIONS AND RECOMMENDATIONS

Valuable lessons were learned during the initial stages of the pilot during the first term of practice placements. Most importantly, it is clear that not all students are comfortable with new technology despite support being available during all of the recall days, the chorus of disapproval from the more vocal students could be quite discouraging for those students who had volunteered to try ePortfolios. As part of the evaluation of the pilot, feedback was gathered from the students and practice assessors via questionnaires and interviews of a selected sample of students discussed in the previous section, it seemed that the problems and issues mentioned were not insuperable and proved to be mainly pedagogical i.e. not enough training and technical support. As students were introduced to PebblePad and the concept of webfolios just before their placements, many of them expressed the opinion that they would have preferred to have had some time to learn about how to use it before they went out to their placements.

In order to address the pedagogical issues which the students' had expressed, it was decided to further embed the use of PebblePad into the programme. First year Social Work students are required to go on a ten day placement during their second term at university and produce reflective written assignments based on the placement; this seemed like an ideal opportunity to introduce them to the concept of an ePortfolio for recording their thoughts during that period. A detailed information sheet was written and distributed to all students giving much fuller detail on each of the items in the webfolio in order to address some of the technological difficulties. As students were not required to produce a webfolio for their ten day placement, many did not participate at all despite being told that it was integral to their 100 day placement in the following years of their degree. Some students did express the need for extra support so a hands-on session and some one-to-one support was arranged for those who expressed interest. A final session a week before students went out on placement was arranged in order to teach students how to collect the webfolio templates and collaborate with their Practice Assessors was given. It did seem that some of the pedagogical issues which had been experienced by the previous cohort had been addressed as students were more familiar with the interface and the concept of editing a webfolio.

Initial feedback from student placements this academic year has been more positive than the previous year. It can be concluded that it has proved useful to further embed the technology into the degree programme that students will view it as a core technology rather than a nuisance add-on. As the students who received training on PebblePad during the first year of their degree programme despite not being compelled to use it seem to be more receptive to the use of ePortfolios than the previous cohort, we felt that this was something worth repeating. As the students had more time to learn how to use the tools and were given more support, it was felt that these elements are a key to the success of the project.

Future opportunities may involve making the ePortfolio for the first year 10 day placement compulsory so that students are compelled to learn to use the editing and collaborative tools and also increases the inclusion of the Social Work tutors.

Practice Assessors were also given extra opportunities before the start of the placement for the second pilot year to come in for hands-on training which a quarter of the total number of Practice Assessors/Long Arm Practice Teachers attended. Together with the Practice Assessors who used PebblePad the previous year before and those who were not able to attend training but requested access nonetheless; there appears to be a significantly larger number of students who are keen to use ePortfolios during the placement than before. Exact numbers of how many students are using the ePortfolio will not be available until the end of the academic year but the current numbers engaged on this second phase of the pilot are encouraging. Students have been told that using the ePortfolio is the main way that they should fill in their As-

sessment of Practice Tool and Weekly Learning Record and that the Word template is only to be used in exceptional circumstances. It may be the case that the only way that we will convince all Practice Assessors to use the ePortfolio method of working on the documents is to compel them to attend training and not give the students an alternative method of completing the documents. Julie Hughes at the University of Wolverhampton compels student teachers and their placement co-ordinators to only use PebblePad to communicate their practice reflection (Hughes, 2008) This is not something which we have considered at Kent as we are still in the early stages of adopting ePortfolios for practice. We have had some interesting feedback from Practice Assessors who feel that their role is likely to be more proactive because of the use of collaborative ePortfolios as working on one document together means that they are able to encourage students to work on the different key roles rather than the old system where they relied on the student to sending them bits of work piece meal by email and only finding out when the email has been received what the student has or has not done.

One consideration is whether we could increase the support which can be provided by university tutors through use of the ePortfolio so that when students are on placement tutors could be able to view their student's Assessment of Practice Tool and provide clarification and comments on the evidence provided. As explained earlier, tutors are not formally involved in assessing practice so their role is supportive and advisory. It is the Practice Assessor's responsibility to verify evidence in the ePortfolio, make comment and make a Pass or Fail recommendation.

We are currently in our second year of using ePortfolio to deliver the Assessment of Practice Tool and Weekly Practice Learning Record therefore as an institution, we are still considering the usefulness of this technique of gathering collaborative evidence. A fully electronic process for producing, submitting and assessing the Assessment of Practice Tool is something that we would envisage happening in the near future possibly with the assessment panel being sent the ePortfolio via an assessment gateway and the assessment panel meeting being conducted with an on-screen version of the Assessment of Practice Tool. As more students and Practice Assessors/Long Arm Practice Teachers become more conversant with and are able to access the ePortfolio at their work places, this option will become more viable as we will have a case for further funding for extra training, support and equipment. The ePortfolio tool which we are using is constantly changing so we need to ensure that we are fully confident with what we are asking our users to do and that our own systems can provide up to date support.

Consequently, we are looking at ways we can support the Practice Assessors and Long Arm Practice Teachers who give up their time to come for ePortfolio training. We give Practice Assessors and Long Arm Practice Teachers the use of a PebblePad account free of charge, we encourage them to use their accounts to record their own personal development if they wish to. As all Social Workers are now required to renew their Social Work registration every three years which includes a requirement to provide evidence of completion of 90 hours or 15 days worth of post-registration training and learning (PRTL). In 2009, we will be embarking on the first phase of a pilot programme of using ePortfolios to enable social care staff to reflect upon and record their continuing professional development activities. We hope to build a set of ePortfolio templates in order to help staff with the reflective and recording process and will be seeking support from the General Social Care Council.

We are keen to look at more creative ways of supporting and encouraging our user groups in their use of ePortfolios and will be looking at ways of fostering students' interest. One such means is the use of 3G on mobile phones since it is now possible to create a quick blog entry via the simple text interface that PebblePad introduced

last year. Another question is raised by this instant use of blogging: will we want to look at more creative ways of gathering evidence to meet national standards such as the use of blogs espoused by Julie Hughes with her teacher trainees at the University of Wolverhampton. (Hughes, 2008) We could ask our students to maintain a blog during their placement then attach relevant blog entries to the national standards but this could mean that although the webfolio might have many links to different blog entries the student does not fully address the required competencies for each unit of National Occupational Standards. Although less suitable for the type of assessment for which students are currently required to use ePortfolios; opportunities for encouraging students to use blogs to reflect upon their own feelings in their personal portfolio space are to be promoted and supported and could potentially replace the Weekly Practice Learning Record webfolio as a form of recording thoughts to put into the Assessment of Practice Tool. This kind of use for ePortfolios will only be successful if students can be convinced of the personal benefit of carrying out what is often perceived as an 'extra' activity.

CONCLUSION

The adoption of ePortfolios to gather evidence of practice for the Social Work degree programme at the University of Kent has not been an easy process and continues to be a challenge. However, many of the benefits evidenced by students, tutors and Practice Assessors encourage us to persevere with our efforts. We have learnt a number of lessons from our experiences namely not making assumptions about our student cohort's transferrable IT skills and also embedding the use of ePortfolios into the degree programme from the first year.

We still have a long way to go before the ePortfolio is considered a core technology and the assessment can be fully electronic as there are still a number of issues to be dealt but it cannot be denied that when the technology works the synergy between user groups works very well. The adoption of ePortfolios has meant that some lasting partnerships have been created and it is certainly true that once all parties have embraced the technology relationships between the different user groups have been encouraged and advanced.

REFERENCES

Ayala, J. I. (2006). Electronic Portfolios for Whom? *EDUCAUSE Quarterly, 1*, 12–13.

Batson, T. (2002). The Electronic Portfolio Boom: What's It All About? *Syllabus, 16*(5), 14–17.

Burgess, R. (2007). *Beyond the honours degree classification: Burgess Group Final Report.* Retrieved August 15, 2008 from http://www. universitiesuk.ac.uk/Publications/Bookshop/ Documents/Burgess_final.pdf

CareStandards (2000). Retrieved October 1, 2008 from Office of Public Sector Information http://www.opsi.gov.uk/acts/acts2000/uk-pga_20000014_en_1

Dearing (1997). *Higher Education in the Learning Society.* Retrieved August 15, 2008 from The National Committee of Inquiry into Higher Education http://www.leeds.ac.uk/educol/ncihe/

Department of Health. (2002). *Requirements for Social Work Training.* Retrieved October 1, 2008 from Department of Health http://www.dh.gov.uk/ en/Publicationsandstatistics/Publications/Publi- cationsPolicyAndGuidance/DH_4007803

Hall, G. E., & Hord, S. M. (2001). *Implement- ing Change: Patterns, principles and potholes.* Needham Heights, MA: Allyn & Bacon.

Hughes, J. (2008). Exploring ePortfolios and weblogs as learning narratives in a community of new teachers. [JISTE]. *Journal of International Society for Teacher Education, 12*(1).

Leitch, S. (2006). *Prosperity for all in the global economy - world class skills: Final Report.* Re- trieved September 30, 2008 from HM Treasury http://www.hm-treasury.gov.uk/d/leitch_finalre- port051206.pdf

McMullen, M. (2003). Portfolios and assess- ment of competence: a review of the literature. *Journal of Advanced Nursing, 41*(3), 283–294. doi:10.1046/j.1365-2648.2003.02528.x

Reardon, R., Hartley, C., & Lucas, S. (2007). Pro- gram Evaluation of E-Portfolios. *New Directions for Student Services, 119*, 83–97. doi:10.1002/ ss.251

Sampson, J. P., & Reardon, R. C, Peterson, G.W., & Lenz, J.L. (2004). *Career Counselling and Services: A cognitive Information Processing ap- proach.* Pacific Grove, CA: Wadsworth-Brooks/ Cole.

Strudler, N., & Wetzel, K. (2005). The diffusion of Electronic Portfolios in Teacher Education: Issues of Initiation and Implementation. *Journal of Research on Technology in Education, 37*(4), 411–433.

TOPPS England. (2000). *Modernising the Social Care Workforce.* Retrieved September 3, 2008 from www.topssengland.net/files/1%20MSCW%20 training%20strategy%20FINAL.pdf

TOPPS England (2004). *The National Occu- pational Standards for Social Work.* Retrieved October 1, 2008 from http://www.skillsforcare. net/view.asp?id=140

Yancey, K. (2001). Introduction: Digitized student portfolios. In B. Cambridge (Ed.) *Electronic portfolios: Emerging practices in student, faculty and institutional learning*, (pp.15-30). Washington, DC: American Association for Higher Education.

Chapter 22
Effective Assignment Feedback through Timely and Personal Digital Audio Engagement

Anne Nortcliffe
Sheffield Hallam University, UK

Andrew Middleton
Sheffield Hallam University, UK

ABSTRACT

Audio feedback is a method that can provide rich, personal and detailed feedback that can convey more than the written word. This is particularly achieved through the capturing of the expressive quality of the speaker's voice. Audio feedback has the potential to promote student engagement in the feedback process, as it is not associated with the negative connotations of written feedback. This chapter will draw upon the growing literature base and recent research. It will indicate how different approaches to using audio technology can enhance the learning experience and the feedback process through its personal and timely qualities. The chapter will conclude with guidelines for best practice for implementation of audio feedback.

INTRODUCTION

This chapter explains why well-designed audio feedback offers an effective tool for promoting student reflection in supporting their ongoing development. It describes and considers various methods of implementation and the factors that determine the approaches that can be taken. Drawing upon a growing literature base and evidence from recent research, the main focus is on how audio can be designed to enhance a meaningful feedback

process through its ability to support personal and timely intervention. The chapter also provides further analysis of the students' perceptions of audio feedback, how they value it, and its impact on their learning. It pulls together findings from several pieces of work by the authors including previously unpublished research.

We begin by introducing some important themes that underpin understandings of effective audio feedback implementation. We then introduce and examine five approaches to providing audio feedback: broadcast feedback; personal tutor monologue; peer review; peer conversation; and personal feedback

DOI: 10.4018/978-1-60566-884-0.ch022

conversations. We draw upon a range of data, using various research methods, to analyse each approach in more detail.

The Purpose of Feedback and Important Themes in the Design of Effective Feedback

Effective feedback creates a learning opportunity enabling and motivating students to identify what they need to do (Sadler, 1989). Students at Sheffield Hallam University appear to share this view,

If you do a task and you don't get feedback after, it's like you've just written something and you have submitted it, but it's not really important. But if you get that feedback, you know that you were lacking this and that.

This comment indicates how students who receive useful feedback are able to use the assessment as a formative opportunity. A similar comment by a Sheffield Hallam University student emphasises how feedback can encourage ongoing engagement with the work,

You can actually go back to the assignment, read it and just see exactly what the feedback was talking about. If you don't get the feedback obviously there's no point in going back and looking at the assignment you've done.

In this digital age it is useful to consider, therefore, how technology can be used to encourage greater engagement with feedback, especially where it can support the feed forward of advice, enabling a quick focus on aspects of work in need of improvement (Chickering & Ehrmann 1996). Previous educational research demonstrates how audio technology can enhance learning through the provision of feedback. Moore's (1977) studies of analogue audio feedback indicated that the students preferred audio feedback to written

feedback and this has been echoed over the years by Sipple (2007) and others. Johanson (1999) noted that analogue audio feedback promoted self-reflection and the students' ability to improve subsequent assignments through encouragement to feed forward.

Rotheram (2007) emphasises that audio can be used to introduce a personal, pastoral dimension to tutor feedback, a quality that can enhance the student learning experience, whilst at the same time satisfying administrative demands, including those of the external examiner.

Timeliness of Feedback

The students benefit from receiving feedback when it is given in a timely fashion, although Orrell (2006) found that students studying teaching and nursing education courses believe that the majority of feedback is inadequate and not timely. Hartley & Chesworth (2000) noted that 59% of their respondents felt feedback was too late to be of any use, i.e. they were not able to apply the specifics of the feedback into their ongoing learning. Gibbs & Simpson (2004) stress that the timeliness of feedback is a key component of good assessment feedback, reinforcing the earlier recommendations from Brown & Knight (1994) that feedback should be returned when it is still relevant in order to impact student learning. Where timely and informative feedback has been given, students become better problem solvers and are more able to assess their own work (Grant, 2006).

However, 'timeliness' needs to be clarified in the context of the digital age: it is not simply about feedback that is turned around quickly; it is about feedback that is highly accessible and available for whenever it is needed. Rather than seeing the student as recipient, it may be useful to understand the student as the person in control, deciding for himself or herself when it is best to listen back to the feedback and affect their own learning. This may be hours, days, weeks or months later (Middleton & Nortcliffe, 2008). This need for accessibility also suggests that timeliness may also be dependent upon being available in the most appropriate *format*. Persistence, format and access become important considerations, therefore. At the same time feedback design needs to recognise that the life of feedback may now extend well beyond the initial turn around of assessed work: it may be accessed and used at any time, depending upon when the student needs to draw upon it and make connections from previous learning to future work, i.e. their next assignment, module or task (Nicol & MacFarlane, 2006).

Personal Nature of Feedback

Students also prefer more personal feedback (Huxman, 2007). However, student performance is particularly likely to be enhanced if students receive a combination of personal and generic feedback. Personal feedback has been shown to promote student learning and improve the quality of future submissions (Davis & Fulton, 1997). This is further supported by our own research in which student focus groups reflected upon lab-based audio feedback conversations (Middleton & Nortcliffe, 2008), for example this Sheffield Hallam University student's reflection,

I find it useful as long as it's personalised. Not just a sheet circled like a marking scheme: 'You've done this at this percentage and this is why.' It's just generic - I don't find it particularly useful like that, but when it's personalised and written for you I think it's good.... I think I take more notice of it if it's personalised..... If it's written in the lecturer's own hand writing and talking about what you wrote then it's more useful.

Audio is a particularly personal channel, as the following student's (2008/2009) comment makes clear. Here they respond to a question about the first time they had received personal audio feedback from the tutor,

It was useful. A lot better than handwritten... as you don't tend to read the written comments in great detail... written comments you tend to think, "How many did they write exactly the same comment?" ...You want to know it is unique.

This reveals how some students approach feedback with a degree of cynical mistrust, and that a 'unique' and personal engagement with their tutor is valued.

Iteration of Feedback

When feedback is properly integrated with the curriculum design, opportunities emerge for an iterative feedback process where connections are made within and across tasks, assignments and modules. An iterative feedback cycle in the assessment process can be used to encourage students to act upon the feedback whilst allowing them the chance of demonstrating their development and their assimilation of feedback into feed forward action. This cyclical view of feedback encapsulates an expectation of continuous improvement in both the students' work and their learning (Taras, 2006). However, a timely iterative feedback cycle is largely missing from current assessment practice in undergraduate education, with the exception of tutoring around final year projects or dissertations. In reality the feedback given by academics is usually a summative justification of marks, and this fails to achieve the objective of facilitating student learning and, in turn, it can discourage students from acting upon the written comments (Orrell, 2006).

Negative Associations of Abundant Feedback

Many students respond negatively to returned work that includes a lot of handwritten annotations from the tutor, particularly when they are made using a red pen associating it with school experiences where assignments and coursework may have been 'defaced' by the teacher's pen to highlight errors. So this can cause students to be less inclined to read feedback consequently missing constructive comments. This is highlighted by the following 2008/2009 students,

Your work has got marks on and it is in red pen. So it is negative, you can't get really get the context of what people are saying, whereas you can with the audio feedback.

Most people have a mental association with a red pen as a negative thing, so if everything is marked in red, as people tend to do, even if the positive marks/comments are in red, they still have negative mental association.

Feedback at university needs to be differentiated from school work to highlight the change in emphasis from correction to personal development. The use of audio feedback can emphasise the personal, caring and constructive nature of the feedback process at university; criticism is absent from the constructive voice. Recent work shows that audio feedback has been received more positively because it is novel and is free of prior associations of previous student experience (Rust, 2001; Rotheram, 2007; Middleton & Nortcliffe, 2008). This is supported by a student from the 2007/2008 cohort reflecting on the benefits of audio feedback against his experience of written feedback,

Generally the text written feedback on assignments would tend to be brief and just what you've done wrong or where the mistakes are: you could go into a lot more in detail with the audio feedback. If that much was written no one would bother to read it.

This is also confirmed by a 2008/2009 student,

[It is] nice [when] you got the detail on each question. Each question got about 30 seconds of feedback, which was nice. You don't always get that… detail [with written feedback].

Richness of Feedback

Audio feedback is often much richer than written feedback and has the capacity to convey much more than the written word. Rust (2001) highlighted audio's capacity to communicate understanding through the expressive qualities of the voice: tone, nuance, informal language, humour, sincerity, honesty, pace, pitch, the personal, and so forth. These attributes add layers of meaning for the listener that cannot be conveyed easily using other media, and they can be manipulated to emphasise significance. A 2008/2009 student explained how audio conveys more for them than written feedback,

You can hear the emotion as people are saying it, so if something is not meant negatively you can tell it was not meant negatively, whereas written you can't tell straight away.

Audio's extended capacity is also noted by King *et al.* (2008), who describe how audio is less constrained than written feedback, which is often limited by the space available for writing; tutor guidance is affected by pre-determined constraints including unused areas of the page (e.g. margins, line spacing), feedback summary quotas, or the feedback templates used in some institutions. Audio, in terms of both duration and style, offers more room to the tutor in engaging their students in meaningful ways. As shown by 2008/2009 student explaining how audio conveys more feedback information than written feedback,

You can hear the emotion as people are saying it, so if something is not meant negatively you can tell it was not meant negatively, whereas written you can't tell straight away.

Good feedback should "foster positive self-esteem" and encourage the receiver to act upon the feedback, using it to feed forward, directly or indirectly, into their future learning (Young, 2000). The previous student comment highlights how 'intention' becomes implicit in oral communication, though is often absent in written feedback. When the well-meaning intention is not present, tutor or peer criticism can be read as derisory, becoming unintentionally destructive, sometimes to a devastating degree. Audio feedback, through vocal intonation, reiteration and other techniques, reduces the possibility of miscommunication, even if the grammatical structures are somewhat freer than in well-written language. Rotheram (2007) picks up on this, finding that the digital audio revolution had made it possible to fulfil Rust's (2001) pastoral aspirations for audio feedback.

A REVIEW OF AUDIO FEEDBACK APPLICATIONS

In this section we introduce some of the approaches that are being taken in using digital audio to provide feedback.

Broadcast Feedback

This approach aims to provide feedback quickly to a large group, i.e. a whole cohort of students. The average size of the cohort at Sheffield Hallam University, where this method has been applied, is 56 students ranging from 25 to 80 students per cohort.

Broadcast feedback is sometimes known as 'generic feedback', and referred to by some students as 'general feedback'. However, these terms can be misleading, conjuring up images of feedback that is general in nature, instead of feedback that is concerned to make specific, points, which are relevant and useful to the cohort. Done properly, broadcast feedback accommodates

each listener as an individual, each making use of the message, as they believe it applies to them. The method involves the marking of a sample of the assessment submissions in a very short time and the noting of common recurring themes in the assessment sample. The academic focuses on providing constructive, timely feedback to all students so that each student can affect their ongoing and future work.

The feedback is recorded by the academic on a PC or MP3 recorder and then distributed to the students by broadcasting the feedback through, for example, the virtual learning environment (VLE), the module podcast channel, or as an email attachment.

This method does not replace individual feedback, being typically combined with a more individual feedback method such as personal tutor monologue audio feedback, written comments on an assessment grid, or written comments on an assessment submission (e.g. marginalia; summary statement; marks in the text) that are returned to the students at a later date.

Review of the Broadcast Approach

In developing an understanding of the effectiveness of the broadcast model, Computer Network Engineers in two consecutive years (2007/2008, 2008/2009) participated in semi-structured focus group discussions and the 2008/2009 cohort was also surveyed by questionnaire. The academic view of this approach was ascertained through a small survey of those using audio feedback from across the university. The findings from these activities are presented and discussed in the following paragraphs.

It should be emphasised that broadcast audio feedback needs to evoke personal engagement. For example, one way of achieving this is through the reiteration of key learning points targeted at an ambiguous "you." This was discussed by the following 2007/2008 student who received broadcast feedback that was not phrased personally (i.e. "you all could do better," "you all need to take on board"),

If it was personal and you knew it was, then I think I would be more inclined to listen to it because it's there, rather than read a sheet of paper.

These 2007/2008 students responded to the more personalised approach where "you have," as opposed to "you all have," was used. Although it was subtle, they thought,

It was good to give us at least some indications ...before we got the official mark and [written] feedback.

It was quite personal.

However, they still have a preference for feedback that is more specifically targeted at individuals or groups,

It still can be quite generic 'you' still by itself ...if you used our names [it would be more personal]. That would be better I think.

[The broadcast feedback] still addresses the points we need to know ...then why not do it in groups and pick up on the same points?

The results indicate that broadcast feedback is a useful method of providing feedback to the entire cohort, but that it should not be used as a substitute for more targeted personal feedback and that it should preferably be used in conjunction with personal feedback, of one form or another. If it is true that the speed of turn-around is critical to feedback's effectiveness, how soon should broadcast feedback be delivered, and how does this relate to the delivery of accompanying personal feedback? Computer Network Engineering students said it was good that the broadcast feedback was turned around within 24 hours and that,

ideally, the personal feedback would be useful if returned within "about a week,"

Just before the next lecture... so you can discuss it in that if there is anything you don't agree with or unsure of.

Students' expectations for turn-around timescales are high. Broadcast feedback helps to address this, but the expectation for an abundance of rapid personal feedback needs to be carefully managed, especially where large cohorts are involved.

The focus group results also highlighted the need to keep the broadcast feedback concise, between two and five minutes,

If [the audio feedback was to last] more than 5 minutes no-one would bother [with it]. If it's generic then people would just get bored, so it probably needs to be short and sharp.

The 2008/2009 cohort agreed and suggested that feedback lasting more than two or three minutes would need a reiteration of key points "to bring it back together."

Three academics using the broadcast approach in various university faculties were presented with a set of factors that may have influenced their decision to use audio feedback. These were based upon Nicol's (2008) eleven principles of assessment design. Two of the three academics selected the same top three factors in deciding to take this approach:

- Timely access to feedback for when the student needs it
- Delivers high quality feedback information
- Helps students to close the gap between current and desired performance.

The 2008/2009 cohort of students were surveyed in a similar way to the academics, this time

Table 1. 2008/2009 cohort responses using Gibbs & Simpson, 2003 feedback conditions

Question	Strongly Agree	Agree	Disagree	Strongly Disagree	Don't Know/ MAYBE/ CAN BE/ NEUTRAL
Is the feedback adequate in detail?	6	21			4
Was the feedback provided quickly enough to be useful?	12	19			
Was the feedback understandable and meaningful?	9	14			6
Have you acted upon the feedback to improve your work?	5	14		2	6

using a framework based upon Gibbs & Simpson's (2003) conditions under which assessment supports student learning. Their response to the broadcast approach (see Table 1) indicated that 45% of the cohort of 68 students had listened to the broadcast feedback a week after receiving it via an email attachment. This had been broadcasted 24 hours after the submission of their formative assessment. It should be noted that two students added written comments to their survey stating that personally they prefer written feedback, and this is in keeping with Sipple's (2007) findings.

A further survey was conducted a week later, this time based on Nicol's (2008) Principles of Assessment Design, as used with the academics (see Table 2). 47% of the 2008/2009 68 strong cohort had listened to the broadcast feedback that had been distributed by email. This indicates that the research itself, which used a survey tool in the VLE, may have encouraged greater engagement with the feedback.

Both survey results indicate that, in general, the students found the broadcast approach offered feedback that was timely, of good quality and of sufficient detail, and that it encouraged further engagement with the module. This result is consistent with the academic perspective. Where

academics had been asked to highlight the three *most important* factors, students were asked to indicate *any* factors that contributed to a positive experience, and they indicated that broadcast feedback addressed all assessment principles.

France & Ribchester (2008) have an interesting approach, related to the broadcast method, described here: a generic stub is appended with a personal message - the best of both worlds perhaps, though incurring extra work to produce. However, the broadcast approach, more than anything else, should allow for a quick response and one that allows each individual to measure their progress against the cohort as a whole. It is not a substitute for individual feedback, written or otherwise, but it is a useful method of distributing feedback efficiently to a number of students so that they can check their progress and apply the feedback to ongoing work.

PERSONAL TUTOR MONOLOGUE

The personal tutor monologue approach to audio feedback involves the tutor assessing submitted student work, such as essays or project reports, whilst recording their response in the form of a

Table 2.Student's perceptions of broadcast feedback measured against Nicol's (2008) Principles of Assessment Design

Question	Strongly Agree	Agree	Disagree	Strongly Disagree	Don't Know/ MAYBE/ CAN BE/ NEUTRAL
Has the feedback helped you engage more with the learning activities in this module?	5	18	2		7
Has the feedback had positive motivation upon your learning and self-esteem?	5	16	2		9
Is the feedback of good quality?	8	17	1		6
Has the feedback encouraged more peer and tutor dialogue of the your learning?	2	17	3		10
Has the feedback promoted personal connection with your peers and tutor?	4	11	4	1	12
Has the feedback promoted engagement in module topics?	2	14	2	2	12
Does the feedback capture the level of your time and commitment to this module, in and outside the classroom?	4	12	3	1	12
Has the feedback helped you improve your performance?	5	16	2		9
Has the feedback provided information for the tutor to improve their teaching?	4	14	2		12

personal tutorial. The tutor uses either audio recording software on their PC or a portable audio recording device. The latter allows the academic flexibility to record in places and at times that are more convenient to them. Whatever technique is used, this approach involves the tutor recording the feedback in isolation from the students and is similar, therefore, to most written feedback procedures.

Johnason (1999) used the personal tutor monologue approach to provide detailed personal feedback in a way that related the audio response to annotations on the student's work. Croke (2008) used a similar method with a cohort of 40 students, also referencing written markers in the submitted work. This simple technique addresses the issue of disjuncture between the feedback and the submitted work. One author (Nortcliffe) has adopted a mixed approach that connects audio feedback with written comments and annotations on an assessment criteria grid. The audio component offers personal audio feedback appended by an overall commentary of the class performance, a similar approach to that used by Ribchester *et al.* (2008), thus providing the opportunity for individuals to benchmark their relative performance to the module cohort. Others, such as Micklewright (2008), have provided each student with a personal MP3 feedback file without any complementary forms of feedback, written or otherwise. Micklewright's cohort was 68 in number. The literature describes this method of audio feedback as being more constructive, less terse and more engaging for the learner than written feedback, and is no more time-consuming than other methods of feedback for either the academic or the student. A small survey of academics using audio feedback at Sheffield Hallam University identified this was by far the most common method. One academic commented on how her students had engaged with this method,

[The] majority of students really liked it and liked the amount of feedback. The odd one chooses not

to engage with it before they have even heard it. I have an academic on my current module from Canada who thinks it's simply gimmicky!

This is consistent with the perceptions of other tutors in the literature; however this method is not for everyone. Research at Sheffield Hallam University has indicated that novelty may be a factor in engaging students. This Computer Network Engineering (2007/2008) student raised this,

It's curiosity I think. Media files and that when you see them on the Internet, or even if it's on Blackboard, it's rare isn't? Nobody else has got it. If it just says something like 'Audio Feedback' you'll think, "Oh, audio." And you'll click on that and listen won't you?

Claims for student engagement need to be treated with caution therefore. However, on reflection students and staff value the virtual proximity effect of audio feedback, as demonstrated by a Computer Network Engineering (2008/2009) student. The method may be novel, but on reflection it also offers much more than written feedback,

[It was] weird at first. It was the first time we ever had audio feedback. It was quite interesting. Quite a nice way of marking I think, instead of red pen on paper, which can be quite harsh. You can hear the emotion as people are saying [the feedback], so if something is not meant negatively you can tell it was not meant negatively, whereas with written you can't tell straight away.

A 2007/2008 student's perception of this method shows an appreciation for the personal approach and the clarity of the feedback,

I think audio is more personal. I think, by audio it comes across differently to if it had been written down on paper. Like, someone could say something and mean it bluntly, but you might take it in the wrong manner. Whereas with audio you can tell by

the tone of the voice, pitching, etc, whether they're being nasty, being polite, helpful. Whereas on a piece of paper it's just one [dimensional]. Some people take a lot of things wrongly.

A 2006/2007 cohort student who received audio feedback using this technique, in response to group work, valued the personal dimension,

The audio feedback that we used to get last year ...to me it felt like, although it was a group thing, it felt like she was talking to me personally and I thought that was quite useful because sometimes her tone of voice, you know, suppose she had emphasised that bit, I would see the importance of that.

The suggestion here is that audio feedback is perceived as being more useful to them as it conveys more than is possible through the written word and, irrespective of whether the feedback was targeted at groups or individuals, students interpret the feedback personally.

Students' perception of the feedback is that it can provide timely, personal feedback in a similar way to personal face-to-face feedback from the tutor; recorded audio obviously has the advantage that it can be revisited at times that suit them, both now and in the future. For some, this will mean they find value in the feedback beyond the assessment process. Five academics at Sheffield Hallam University reported that they had used this audio feedback method and all agreed that the key driver for them was that it was a way of delivering high quality feedback information, when selecting the three most important factors derived from Nicol's (2008) eleven principles of assessment design. Three also selected, 'supports timely access to feedback for when the student needs it', and two chose 'helps students to close the gap between current and desired performance.'

There appear to be drawbacks to this method too. Takemoto (1987) noted that it provides no opportunity for student-tutor interaction. A

Table 3. 2008/2009 student response to personal audio feedback

Question	Strongly Agree	Agree	Disagree	Strongly Disagree	Don't Know/ MAYBE/ CAN BE/ NEUTRAL
Is the feedback adequate in detail?	9	20			3
Was the feedback provided quickly enough to be useful?	13	17	1		1
Was the feedback understandable and meaningful?	10	20		1	1
Have you acted upon the feedback to improve your work?	8	16	1		8

2008/2009 student said this was not an issue, however, if the feedback was issued before their next lecture, tutorial, or seminar. The main point here is that the technology does not have to support the whole conversation, and in fact we would argue that audio feedback should always be understood holistically as one of many components in a teaching strategy in which conversations amongst tutors and peers take various forms. Kelly and Ryan (1983) reported on this too, noting that Open University students still appreciated audio feedback, despite the lack of interaction, as it provides a degree of personal contact, and a better critique and review of their assessment submission in comparison to the tutor's written comments. This is supported by a previous 2008/2009 student comment that the audio feedback is less harsh than written feedback.

Again, the duration of the audio is important, as with broadcast feedback. 2008/2009 students indicated that they preferred audio feedback lasting between two to three minutes. They said they would like feedback that is "short and sweet" and that if it is "any longer you would start to fade out, [and that] any shorter it wouldn't be relevant." A survey of Computing Networking Engineering students (2008/2009) on the use of the personal tutor monologue model indicates that 58% of 55 students had listened to their personal audio feedback 3 days after receiving notification of its availability and this method of audio

feedback can satisfy the conditions under which assessment supports student learning (Gibbs & Simpson, 2003).

The same students completed the additional survey based upon Nicol's (2008) Principles of Assessment nine days after their audio feedback was made available to them. 60% of 55 students had listened to it.

The survey indicates that this method of feedback can be used to provide timely, high quality, detailed, useful and meaningful feedback that enables students to engage more with the module learning activities, and that it can have a positive effect on the student learning, self-esteem and performance. The results from this study showed that this method strongly supported: effective communication; timely access to feedback for when the student needs it; the delivery of high quality feedback information; the engagement of students in deep, not just shallow, learning activities; the encouragement of positive, motivational beliefs and the development of self-esteem; and the support of students to close the gap between current and desired performance. The students and academics concur, therefore, that this method can address all of Nicol's principles. This method of audio feedback also has potential to promote self-assessment if students are encouraged to periodically listen back to the feedback. This 2008/2009 student focus group highlight their awareness of this,

Table 4. 2008/2009 cohort responses using Nicol's (2008) Principles of Assessment Design not previously covered in the survey based upon Gibbs & Simpson, 2003 feedback conditions of Personal Tutor Monologue Audio Feedback

Question	Strongly Agree	Agree	Disagree	Strongly Disagree	Don't Know/ MAYBE/ CAN BE/ NEUTRAL
Has the feedback helped you engage more with the learning activities in this module?	8	18	3		5
Has the feedback had positive motivation upon your learning and self-esteem?	5	20	3		6
Is the feedback of good quality?	9	18	3		4
Has the feedback encouraged more peer and tutor dialogue of the your learning?	3	15	5	1	10
Has the feedback promoted personal connection with your peers and tutor?	1	18	4		11
Has the feedback promoted engagement in module topics?	1	18	4	1	10
Does the feedback capture the level of your time and commitment to this module, in and outside the classroom?	4	15	5	1	9
Has the feedback helped you improve your performance?	9	14	1	1	9
Has the feedback provided information for the tutor to improve their teaching?	3	16	6		9

If we wanted to we could download it and archive it onto our hard-drive so we could look at and see how we have changed since we started and compare how we are now, and how our responses have changed.

See how we have improved.

Or [on] ...the next assessment, they could then go then through it and critically analyse their actual assessment ...and performance in the same way as the previous assessment and see if the same points are been highlighted again or if people have actually learnt over the year.

A multi-layered approach emerges (figure 1) therefore. It is composed of a cycle that includes reflection on the first engagement with the audio feedback; a second listening with reflection leading to a feed forward of their learning into the second assessment; and then a comparative reflective listening, enabling students to reflect and gauge the depth of their learning progress. This metacognitive process may be particularly useful to students undertaking quite practical work where it can be difficult to separate learning from the task in hand.

It should be noted that distribution of this method of feedback needs careful consideration and planning. The cassette tape method used by Johanson (1999) easily resolved this problem as it required each student to submit an audio tape with their work, which was returned later with their marked work. However, the digital solution, which requires each student to download their personal file from the tutor's PC in class (Croke, 2008) is time-consuming and reduces the actual class teaching contact time. A more efficient method

Figure 1. Potential layers of learning using personal tutor monologue audio in a feedback cycle

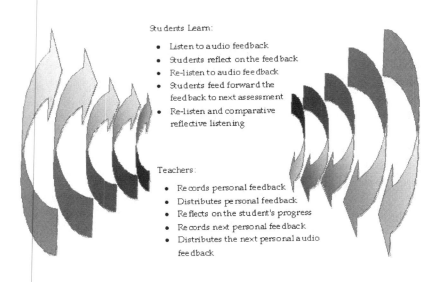

Students Learn:

- Listen to audio feedback
- Students reflect on the feedback
- Re-listen to audio feedback
- Students feed forward the feedback to next assessment
- Re-listen and comparative reflective listening

Teachers:

- Records personal feedback
- Distributes personal feedback
- Reflects on the student's progress
- Records next personal feedback
- Distributes the next personal audio feedback

is to distribute the audio files via the VLE or an online content system, as used by Mickwright (2008) and the authors.

Much of the discussion in this section on the personal tutor monologue model has described approaches where detailed feedback is given. However, the authors have previously (Middleton, 2008) drawn attention to methods where the audio feedback is highly selective and used in combination with other objective techniques (e.g. grids and marginalia) that cover the detail. In this way audio does what it can do best: that is highlight key areas for student attention, motivate them and show tutor interest in and care for the students.

PEER REVIEW OF PERSONAL TUTOR MONOLOGUE

The Peer Review of Personal Tutor Monologue model has been developed by the Computer Network Engineering students themselves as a way of developing a broader and deeper understanding of their work through a joint review of, and reflection upon, the personal tutor monologue

feedback that they had experienced individually. Students decide who they would like to share their personal feedback with and then listen together to each other's personal feedback. This provides an opportunity to discuss similarities and differences. It allows them to benchmark their own progress with that of others. By discussing their feedback they deepen their knowledge and understanding, reinforce the common points made in the feedback, and broaden their understanding where different issues were covered.

2008/2009 students explained why they had developed the approach,

It doesn't really bother me listening with my friends. They would probably look at it anyway, whether it was written down or whether spoken, so it made no difference to me. We like to share things anyway. Everyone knows everything about everyone. Yes it was nice to share it and hear other people's and compare [our feedback] to other people's.

I thought it was good because we all listened, because all of us got different answers. We all

Figure 2. Layers of learning through the Peer Review of Personal Tutor Monologue feedback cycle

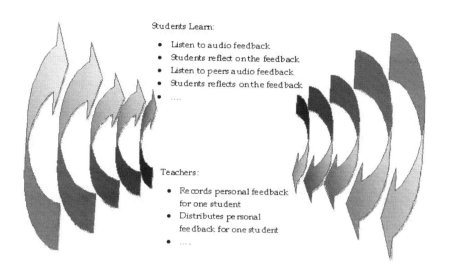

have different plusses and minuses ...as everyone answered different ones [questions]. So we managed to get the right answers for each of them ...[and] we got a much larger quantity of feedback than if we had answered all five questions and kept [the feedback] to ourselves.

My arguments, I didn't think, were very good, X's were very good ...It was useful getting his feedback, that was quite useful.

The sharing of the personal tutor monologue, therefore, has the potential to add more layers of learning to the audio feedback cycle, figure 2.

The sharing of the files amongst peers reassured the students and reinforced the assertion that the personal tutor monologue feedback was intended to be of use, primarily, to individual students. Recognition of this is highlighted by the following 2008/2009 student,

The benefit of hearing everyone else's [was that] we knew that [the academic] was not doing a standard version for each person. It did vary.

PEER CONVERSATIONAL AUDIO FEEDBACK

This method involves the recording of supportive peer conversations, with or without the tutor, in which participants discuss either a student's contribution to group work, or individual and group progress in general. The recording is distributed back to the group via the VLE. The students appreciate this approach in helping them to reflect more objectively on more intensive peer exchanges. A Computer Network Engineering (2007/2008) student commented that,

If you have got an argument going off, one is on one side and one on the other side ...A lot of people just have that one view and they find it hard to take the other person's view into account. Whereas, if you sit back and listen ...90% of the time you think they were right [and] if you could go back change things you would. Listening to someone else's view again is good.

This is substantiated by other Computer Network Engineering (2007/2008) students who appreciated the way it enabled the groups to come to consensus after listening to the audio recording of a group meeting,

I can see that working, because you have no, like, feelings behind it when you listen to it or not as much.

[It's] much more objective. You have calmed down and [you're] ready to listen.

The recordings also enabled group members to engage in parts of the conversation they missed during the live discussion, especially when it is not always possible to hear everything that is said, as described by these Computer Network Engineering (2007/2008) students,

When you are talking with three people ...it is sometimes easier to tune out one person for a second and then miss out on certain sentences or parts of the conversation.

I think it is a lot better because you actually engage with what you said before ... you listen back to it [and] you pick up on the comments you actually said and the other person's said. You know what you personally said, but did you take into account what the others said?

Four academics at Sheffield Hallam University are applying this method of audio feedback, three of whom agreed that its capacity to deliver 'high quality feedback information' is a key principle in their decision to use it. Selecting from Nicol's 2008 principles of assessment design, two of the four agreed that audio feedback also helps them to support 'timely access to feedback for when the student needs it', and 'helps students to close the gap between current and desired performance.'

PERSONAL FEEDBACK CONVERSATION

One solution to Takemoto's (1987) concern that audio feedback is a one way conversation can be resolved using a personal feedback conversation model, as described by Nortcliffe & Middleton (2007), whereby a student-tutor formative conversation is recorded in the lab, studio, or workshop. It is then distributed to the students for later reflection. This method lends itself to any scenario where a tutor and student have a discussion on the student's learning, i.e. studio 'crits', coursework or project progress discussions, or discussions around dissertation writing. It can be used with either a small group or with individuals. The model is described in figure 3.

Again, this acknowledges that live discussion can be a very noisy, active and even anxious experience, resulting in little substance once the moment has passed. Recording the conversation ensures that the learner's construction of knowledge is supported not only through the live discussion, but through revisiting the feedback, where new trains of thought and understanding may emerge (Nortcliffe & Middleton, 2007). In this way the feedback avoids being obscured by time and provides a valued resource that continues to assist students in successfully feeding forward their learning. A sample of the 2007/2008 student focus group's results indicate that the method of formative audio feedback conversation on the progress of software engineering projects was helpful in encouraging student learning,

I listened to a couple. I just did the basic minimum when I used to go into class and she'd tell me where I could improve stuff ...Because it's such a long project, again I left it 'til quite late on to get on with it - seven or eight weeks. It was handy to go back and listen to what she'd said earlier on. How I could improve myself. It upped my grade.

Figure 3. An iterative feedback cycle involving layers of learning through the use of audio feedback

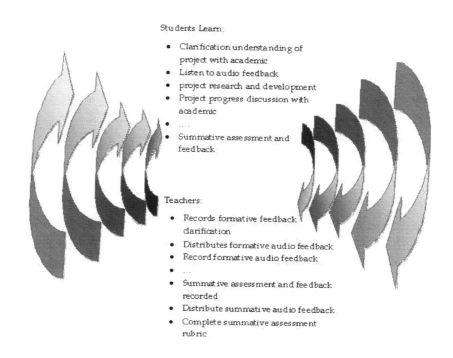

Upped my grade from a 60% to over a 70% for that project. I was looking at 60% without audio feedback. With audio feedback it pushed me back into a 1st.

A 2006-2007 student explained how audio feedback had helped them,

I have got a pretty bad memory as it goes, so it was nice to go back and listen to our conversation again, have another listen to what was suggested.

Another 2007-2008 student explained its value to them,

When you listen to it you remember you'd forgotten half of the stuff you [the academic and yourself] said on the recording.

A fellow student from the 2007-2008 cohort concurs that the audio was a valuable memory aid,

It is really useful, because within the short interviews, or in that time, you forget what you said. Going back to it a week later, I can't recall what needs to be changed to the documentation. So having the audio files is a really good way of remembering what was said and getting done what needs to be done.

Both these students describe how the audio recording is timely and how, without it, the potential impact of the live feedback would have been lost with the passing of time. A student from the 2006-2007 cohort further corroborates this,

If there was something I'd forgotten about I'd go back in and review what she had said to me.

Students interpret the feedback personally and note how they can improve themselves personally. Audio feedback provides a personal feedback artefact with which students engage,

It helps me to jot down what exactly I need to be working on, what I need to show in the next labs. Also it kind of helped me to listen to myself and the way I think and the way I put myself forward, and express my ideas. So I can see a few weaknesses I can improve upon ...put your ideas forward more accurately and just makes you kind of think, "I didn't want to say that, I want to say this instead." Reflecting on your own thinking.

Audio feedback provides an opportunity to support learning and practice on both professional and key skills. It enabled this student to reflect upon their communication skills and their thought processes. Two academics at Sheffield Hallam University, who are applying the Personal Feedback Conversation method, agreed that their rationale for using it in respect to Nicol's Principles of Assessment Design, is that it 'supports timely intervention by tutor' and that it 'delivers high quality feedback information.'

CONCLUSION

Audio is a versatile medium ready to be applied in many ways within education given that our technological infrastructures are increasingly capable of supporting its use. In this chapter, by taking a broad view of what academic feedback can mean, we have considered several approaches being taken by both academic staff and students. These approaches have been shown to promote deeper and broader learning through assignment feedback.

Audio also shows its potential as a tool with which to engage learners in their feedback, both during the assignment process and beyond. The advantages of audio feedback is that; it can be revisited by the learner as their needs change, the quality of such approaches is enhanced, compared to transient methods (i.e. live conversation) or methods that are less accessible due to their format (i.e. written feedback associated with marks on paper).

Audio feedback, like any feedback, is of course only as good as the message that is being carried and the action that follows. Its versatility allows it to fit in with the many contexts in which it is being used in virtual and physical environments, and across the curriculum. This flexibility increases the chance of student engagement and the potential, therefore, for them to learn.

Used well, audio feedback supports the provision of feedback that is personal, meaningful, timely, profound, and that can positively affect student motivation and self-esteem. Live feedback conversations between the academic and students can, of course, satisfy the principles for effective feedback discussed here, but academics are a limited resource and cannot readily respond with the same versatility as recorded conversations or comments. Audio feedback can effectively complement and develop the tutor-student relationship, and the presence of recorded feedback clearly signals the importance of conversation in learning. Selecting the best form of audio feedback is dependent upon a lot of contextual factors including the practicalities of work and study loads, the size of cohorts, and the subject and type of assignment. Other forms of feedback should also account for such factors, yet this is an area where many academics conform to what they have experienced themselves or to existing practice. Audio appears to be so different to many academics that its consideration prompts pedagogic creativity as demonstrated by the diversity of models referenced in this chapter.

This novel opportunity needs to be taken seriously for many reasons, not least because, for many students, written annotations on a student's work can carry negative associations derived from prior experiences at school where, in extreme cases, students have perceived feedback as being a destructive, defacing process. The constructive, pastoral approach of the personal tutor monologue feedback, for example, contrasts sharply with this.

Providing timely personal audio feedback, especially in the case of large cohorts, is time consuming, but less so than good written feedback (Rotheram, 2007). Following the example of France & Ribchester (2008), there are techniques that can combine the individual feedback method with the broadcast audio feedback to provide personalised, high quality and timely feedback. Such methods can encourage peer benchmarking whilst directly supporting individuals.

The methods discussed here are really only useful if they promote learner reflection, and this will not happen just because the feedback is given. Students need to understand what they are meant to do with the feedback and need to be encouraged to engage with it, and re-engage with it.

All of the methods discussed here are best used if they are understood in the context of iterative feedback cycles, where they evoke multiple layers of deeper learning (Nortcliffe & Middleton, 2008). This does not necessitate any extra work on the part of the academic and incurs only a little extra effort on the part of the student. If the audio is stored in an appropriate way, and the feedback has been designed so that it fits with future usage scenarios, the experience of revisiting the feedback should be highly rewarding to the students. The advice from one of the 2007-2008 students to students in subsequent years was,

Make use of it, don't forget it is there or come back to it at the end of the year ...keep it fresh.

As a result of continuous investigation into audio feedback over recent years the authors have produced some good practice recommendations. This is an evolving area so it is expected that this understanding will grow. However, the following

may prove useful to anyone devising their own audio feedback method:

1. The authors cannot recommend one audio recording device over another as models are soon superseded; however, the authors have used a variety of devices and suggest the best devices for academic use offer a limited set of options, a simple interface for recording and playback, a pause button for managing the recording process and USB connectivity.

2. Introduce the value of audio feedback to students beforehand and develop personal engagement with students in class. This makes it easier to develop the relationship and trust in the feedback.

3. Be clear about scalability; consider a pilot study; manage your commitment and consider local factors, i.e. staff training requirements, distribution options, etc.

4. Practice makes perfect, so get to know how to use your recorder, e.g. confidence in talking into a recorder and the possible benefits of the 'pause' button over the 'stop' button.

5. For personal audio feedback methods remember to include the student's name, assignment title or stage, and the date of each recording; for broadcast models include the assignment title or stage and the date of the recording. Name the audio files systematically so you can visually browse and organise them.

6. Keep audio feedback brief and engaging, and be selective in what you choose to address. If the feedback has to be lengthy, summarise the key points the student or students must note. This ensures that the feedback carries both emphasis and detail, with your voice conveying meaning. In addition you may want to annotate submitted assignments, to provide feedback correlation.

7. Don't edit your recordings - it will take too long. Make use of the pause button.

Restart the recording if you make a major slip up. If recording in your office, invest in a 'Recording - do not disturb' sign.

8. Blend approaches, using each method according to its strength, e.g. audio and assessment grids for quick detail with breadth; broadcast feedback with follow-on personal audio or written feedback for quick feedback followed by detailed feedback.

9. Use a clear, structured approach with signposting in the feedback, especially if is long. This will help students to be clear about the relationship between the points that are made; reiterate key points where necessary.

10. Either omit the grade or leave it towards the end as a way of emphasising the formative nature of the feedback.

11. The feedback should clearly explain how the students can improve and what they are expected to do when they have finished listening, especially where the tutor has devised or contributed feedback. Encourage the students to make notes when listening and to archive the feedback so they can revisit it later. Explain how they should connect what they have learnt to future work and if possible suggest when to listen again, i.e. in preparation for next assessment or following receipt of the next assessment feedback.

REFERENCES

Brown, S., & Knight, P. (1994). *Assessing learners in higher education*. London: Kogan Page.

Chickering, A., & Ehrmann, S. C. (1996). Implementing the seven principles: technology as lever. *AAHE Bulletin*, October, 3-6. Retrieved January 7, 2008, from http://www.tltgroup.org/programs/seven.html

Croker, K. (2008). Giving Feedback via audio files. *HEA Assessment SIG 5th June 2008 Meeting*, York, UK

Davis, W., & Fulton, J. (1997). The Effects of professors' feedback on the growth of students' overall writing quality in two college freshman English courses. *EDRS Research Report*. Retrieved June 24, 2008, from http://www.eric.ed.gov/ERICDocs/data/ericdocs2sql/content_storage_01/0000019b/80/15/17/cb.pdf

France, D., & Ribchester, C. (2008). Podcasts and feedback. In Salmon, G., & Edirisingha, P. (Eds.), *Podcasting for learning in universities*. Maidenhead, UK: Society for Research into Higher Education/Open University Press

Gibbs, G., & Simpson, C. (2003). Measuring the response of students to assessment: the Assessment Experience Questionnaire. In [*th International Symposium Improving Students Learning: Theory, Research and Scholarship*, Hinckley, UK. Oxford, UK: Alden Press.]. *Proceedings of the, 2003*, 11.

Gibbs, G., & Simpson, C. (2004). Conditions under which assessment supports students' learning. *Learning and teaching in higher education, 1*, 3–31. Retrieved June 5, 2005, from http://www.glos.ac.uk/departments/clt/lathe/issue1/index.cfm

Grant, P. (2006). Examining your practice: feedback as part of assessment. *National Middle School Association . Middle Ground, 9*(3), 18–20.

Hartley, J., & Chesworth, K. (2000). Qualitative and quantitative methods in research on essay writing: no one way. *Journal of Further and Higher Education, 24*, 15–24. doi:10.1080/030987700112282

Huxham, M. (2007). Fast and effective feedback: are model answers the answer? *Assessment & Evaluation in Higher Education, 32*(6), 601–611.

Johanson, R. (1999). Rethinking the red ink: audio-feedback in the ESL writing classroom. *Texas Papers in Foreign Language Education, 4*(1), 31–38.

Kelly, P., & Ryan, S. (1983). Using tutor tapes to support the distance learner. *International Council for Distance Education Bulletin, 3*, 1–18.

King, D., McGugan, S., & Bunyan, N. (2008). Does it make a difference? replacing text with audio feedback. *Practice and Evidence of Scholarship of Teaching and Learning in Higher Education, 3*(2), 145–163.

Micklewright, D. (2008). Podcasting as an alternative mode of assessment feedback. *Higher Education Academy Hospitality Leisure, Sport and Tourism Network Assessment Case Studies*. Retrieved October 26, 2008, from http://www.heacademy.ac.uk/assets/hlst/documents/case_studies/case129_-podcast_feedback.pdf

Middleton, A. (2008). Audio feedback: timely media interventions. In *Proceedings of The Third International Blended Learning Conference, "Enhancing the Student Experience,"* University of Hertfordshire, UK

Middleton, A., & Nortcliffe, A. L. (2008, in press). Understanding effective models of audio feedback. In Roy, R. (ed.), *Engineering Education*.

Moore, G. E. (1977). *Individualizing instructional feedback: a comparison of feedback modes in university classes*. Paper presented at the Annual International Conference for Individualized Instruction, West Lafayette, Indiana

Nicol, D. (2008). Assessment as a driver for transformational change in HE. *HEA Education Subject Centre advanced learning and teaching in education (ESCalate) Newsletter* 10. Retrieved October 14, 2008, http://escalate.ac.uk/4451

Nicol, D. J., & Macfarlane-Dick, D. (2006). Formative assessment and self-regulated learning: a model and seven principles of good feedback practice. *Studies in Higher Education, 31*(2), 199–218. doi:10.1080/03075070600572090

Nortcliffe, A. L., & Middleton, A. (2007). Audio feedback for the iPod generation. In *The Proceedings of the International Conference on Engineering Education 2007*, Coimbra, Portugal

Nortcliffe, A. L., & Middleton, A. (2008). Blending the engineer's learning environment through the use of audio. In *Proceeding of the Engineering Education 2008 Conference*, Loughborough, UK.

Orrell, J. (2006). Feedback on learning achievement: rhetoric and reality. *Teaching in Higher Education, 11*(4), 441–456. doi:10.1080/13562510600874235

Ribchester, C., France, D., & Wakefield, K. (2008). *'It was just like a personal tutorial': Using podcasts to provide assessment feedback*. Paper presented at 'Transforming the student experience' Higher Education Academy Annual Conference, Harrogate, UK. Retrieved October 28, 2008, http://www.heacademy.ac.uk/assets/York/documents/events/conference/ 2008/Chris_Ribchester.doc

Rotheram, B. (2007). Using an MP3 recorder to give feedback on student assignments. *Educational Developments, Staff and Educational Development Association, 8.2*, 7-10

Rust, C. (2001). A Briefing on the assessment of large groups. *LTSN Generic Centre*. Retrieved January 10, 2008, http://www.heacademy.ac.uk/resources/detail/ourwork/tla/assessment_series

Sadler, D. R. (1989). Formative assessment and the design of instructional systems. *Instructional Science, 18*, 119–144. doi:10.1007/BF00117714

Sipple, S. (2007). Ideas in practice: developmental writers' attitudes toward audio and written feedback. *Journal of Developmental Education, 30*(3).

Takemoto, P. A. (1987). Exploring the educational potential of audio. *New Directions for Adult and Continuing Education*, (3): 19–28. doi:10.1002/ace.36719873405

Taras, M. (2006). Do unto others or not: equity in feedback for undergraduates. *Assessment & Evaluation in Higher Education, 31*(3), 365–377. doi:10.1080/02602930500353038

Young, P. (2000). 'I Might as well give up': self-esteem and mature students' feelings about feedback on assignments. *Journal of Further and Higher Education, 24*(3), 409–418. doi:10.1080/030987700750022325

Chapter 23
Contemporary Music Students and Mobile Technology

Thomas Cochrane
Unitec, New Zealand

ABSTRACT

Five billion songs, and counting, have been downloaded (completely legally) through Apple Computer's online iTunes Store. The iTunes University links free educational content from over seventy tertiary institutions worldwide, and is now available to New Zealand tertiary institutions. The Internet has revolutionised the delivery and access of media and education – making access to a worldwide audience or market merely a Google (or iTunes Store) search away! But, what are the real-world practicalities of this for contemporary music students and teachers today? How can these tools be utilised to facilitate personalised learning environments. Within this context, this chapter presents and evaluates a mobile learning case study at Unitec in the Diploma of Contemporary Music on the Waitakere campus.

INTRODUCTION

This section introduces the underpinning concepts related to mobile Web 2.0 and personalized learning environments upon which the example research project is based. This introductory section is then followed by a section describing the case study, an evaluation of the results and findings, and finally a discussion on the future of the project for 2009.

Mobile Learning

While there have been many attempts to define the unique essence of mobile learning (mLearning), most have either focused on the mobility of the device, the learner, or on the facilitation of informal learning beyond the confines of the classroom (Kukulsa-Hulme & Traxler, 2005; Laurillard, 2007; M Sharples et al., 2007; Wali et al., 2008). Mobile learning, as defined by the author of this chapter, involves the use of wireless enabled mobile digital devices (Wireless Mobile Devices or WMD's) within and between pedagogically designed learning

DOI: 10.4018/978-1-60566-884-0.ch023

environments or contexts. From an activity theory perspective, WMD's are the tools that mediate a wide range of learning activities and facilitate collaborative learning environments (Uden, 2007). Laurillard's definition of mLearning emphasises the critical role of the educator: "M-Learning, being the digital support of adaptive, investigative, communicative, collaborative, and productive learning activities in remote locations, proposes a wide variety of environments in which the teacher can operate" (Laurillard, 2007). MLearning can support and enhance both the face to face and off campus teaching and learning contexts by using the mobile wireless devices as a means to leverage the potential of Web 2.0 tools. The WMD's wireless connectivity and data gathering abilities (e.g. photoblogging, video recording, voice recording, and text input) allow for bridging the on and off campus learning contexts – facilitating "real world learning". It is the potential for mobile learning to bridge pedagogically designed learning contexts, facilitate learner generated contexts, and content (both personal and collaborative), while providing personalisation and ubiquitous social connectedness, that sets it apart from more traditional learning environments.

Mobile Web 2.0

The term Web 2.0 was coined in 2005 (O'Reilly, 2005) within a context of how businesses were changing the way they interacted with clients via new interactive Web-based tools. The term has been popularised as a way of characterizing the emerging interactive, user-centred Web based tools that have been revolutionizing the way the Internet is conceptualized and used. These tools include: blogs, wiki's, image-sharing (e.g. Flickr), video-sharing (e.g. YouTube), podcasting etc… Many educators have harnessed Web 2.0 tools for creating engaging student-centred learning environments. This appropriation of Web 2.0 tools within a social constructivist pedagogy facilitates what has been termed "pedagogy 2.0".

Pedagogy 2.0 integrates Web 2.0 tools that support knowledge sharing, peer-to-peer networking, and access to a global audience with socioconstructivist learning approaches to facilitate greater learner autonomy, agency, and personalization (McLoughlin & Lee, 2008).

Herrington (A. Herrington & Herrington, 2007) argues that "the advances in philosophical and practical developments in education have created justifiable conditions for the pedagogical use of mobile technologies" based on newer learning theories that find their roots in social constructivism such as: authentic learning, communities of practice, distributed intelligence, distributed cognition, connectivism, and activity theory. Social constructivism focuses upon students being involved in learning environments as an explorative and social process. This is in contrast to the instructivist pedagogies that have dominated tertiary education in the past that focus upon the teacher/lecturer as the expert holder of knowledge from whom students learn directly. In general, education based on social constructivist pedagogies is interested in enabling students to develop creative, critical thinking, and collaborative skills, rather than focusing upon course content. The underpinning pedagogy of a course will determine how particular tools and technologies are used and integrated within the course.

The main focus of this research project is on the support and enhancement of both the face to face teaching and learning context and the off-campus informal learning contexts by using wireless mobile devices (iPod Touch and iPhone in this case) as a means to leverage the potential of current and emerging collaborative and reflective eLearning tools (e.g. blogs, wikis, RSS, instant messaging, podcasting, social book marking, etc…). These are often called Web 2.0 or "social software" tools. Many of these tools are formatted specifically for access via mobile devices, compensating for smaller screens and slower text input methods, and facilitating the use of built-in cameras and GPS (Global Positioning Systems) etc... The iPod's wireless connectivity and data gathering abilities (e.g. Web browsing, photoblogging via email, video playback, voice playback, and text input) allow for bridging the on and off campus learning contexts – facilitating "real world learning".

The research is focusing on social constructivist approaches to education (Bijker et al., 1987; Lave & Wenger, 1991; Vygotsky, 1978; Wenger et al., 2002) and a conversational model (Laurillard, 2001, 2007) of teaching and learning. The disruptive nature of Web 2.0 and mobile technologies (Mike Sharples, 2000, 2001, 2005; Stead, 2006) facilitates a move from instructivist pedagogies to social constructivist pedagogies. The personal, social networking, and context awareness of mobile devices democratise power relationships and are best suited to open learning environments. Disruptive technologies are those technologies that challenge established systems and thinking, requiring change and are thus viewed by many as a threat to the status quo. Disruptive technologies democratise education environments challenging the established power relations between teachers and students. Integrating such technologies into a curriculum requires significant pedagogical change. Mishra et al (2007) argue that "appropriate use of technology in teaching requires the thoughtful integration of content, pedagogy, and technology".

Personalised Learning Environments

Within the context of tertiary education, personalized learning environments (PLE) are those that facilitate student ownership, customization, and sharing of content and social networking. However most institutional learning management systems (LMS's), such as Blackboard or Moodle, are hosted by the institution and require secure login access, limiting customization and sharing beyond the enrolled class and lecturers. In contrast, a combination of the Web 2.0 and mobile devices described above can be used to create flexible personalised learning environments (PLE). Many educators see this second approach as the future of online learning environments. Attwell (2006) aptly describes this concept:

Social software is used here in the meaning of software that lets people rendezvous, connect or collaborate by use of a computer network. It supports networks of people, content and services that are more adaptable and responsive to changing needs and goals. Social Software adapts to its environment, instead of requiring its environment to adapt to software. In this way social software is seen as overcoming... Social software underpins what is loosely referred to as Web 2. Whereas Web 1 was largely implemented as a push technology - to allow access to information on a dispersed basis, Web 2 is a two way process, allowing the internet to be used for creating and sharing information and knowledge, rather than merely accessing external artefacts... The idea of the Personal Learning environment is in effect a Web 2, social software concept (Attwell, 2006).

Jafari (Jafari et al., 2006) presents a theoretical next-generation eLearning environment based on these concepts:

Stakeholders across the spectrum want an anytime, all-the-time, personalized experience of teaching and learning - one that utilizes all the currently available social tools, intuitive tools, smart agents, and interactive environments of Web 2.0 and social computing. In short, faculty, students, and administrators are waiting for an eLearning environment that is smart, environmental, archival, multi-modal, collaborative, and mobile (Jafari et al., 2006).

The establishment of such personal learning environments is aimed at producing the following learning outcomes for students:

- Developing critical reflective skills
- Experiencing and developing group communication skills
- Developing a life-long online ePortfolio that showcases their potential
- Developing a potentially world-wide peer support and critique and support network
- Learning how to maximise technology to enhance their learning experience across multiple contexts

The Wider Research Project

The case study summarized herein is part of a wider research project (Cochrane, 2008a) investigating the potential of mobile Web 2.0 for enhancing tertiary education through a series of action research projects in a variety of disciplines, including: Bachelor of Product Design (using Nokia N95 smartphones and Apple iPhones), Diploma of Contemporary Music (using Apple iPod Touches and iPhones), and the Diploma of Landscape Design (using Sonyericsson P1i smartphones). Compilations of 2008 student and staff VODCasts (Online video recordings) are available on YouTube:

- BProduct Design Year 1 http://www.youtube.com/watch?v=8QUfw9_sFmo
- BProduct Design Year 2 http://www.youtube.com/watch?v=6jwAFXBZAz0
- BProduct Design Year 3 (and Lecturers) http://www.youtube.com/watch?v=8Eh5ktXMji8
- DipContemporary Music http://nz.youtube.com/watch?v=0It5XUfvOjQ
- DipLandscape Architecture http://nz.youtube.com/watch?v=c8IZSVtaMmM

This chapter focuses upon the impact of mobile Web 2.0 upon one of these projects (Diploma of Contemporary Music), analyzing feedback gathered from the students and the academic staff involved.

Methodology

The research uses a participatory action research methodology. Yoland (Wadsworth, 1998) identifies the key characteristics of 'participatory action research': the researcher is a participant, the researcher is the main research instrument, it is cyclical in nature, involves action followed by reflection followed by informed action, and is concerned with producing change. This change is ongoing throughout the process, and the research is interested in input from participants/stakeholders. This allows for the continual development and improvement of the projects based on the feedback from participants at regular points in the projects.

The Research Questions

What are the key factors in integrating Wireless Mobile Devices (WMDs) within tertiary education courses?

What challenges/advantages to established pedagogies do these disruptive technologies present?

To what extent can these WMDs be utilized to support learner interactivity, collaboration, communication, reflection and interest, and thus provide pedagogically rich learning environments that engage and motivate the learner?

To what extent can WMDs be used to harness the potential of current and emerging social constructivist eLearning tools?

Data Gathering

Pre-trial surveys of lecturers and students, to establish current practice and expertise.

Post-trial surveys and focus groups, to measure the impact of the wireless mobile computing environment, and the implementation of the guidelines.

Lecturer and student reflections via their own blogs during the trial. The blog is also an online ePortfolio facilitating the collection of rich media resources capturing critical incidents and providing a dynamic journal of student projects and lecturer input (both formative and summative).

The survey tool and focus group questions can be viewed in the appendix. An action research methodology is used, creating a reflective research environment that continually seeks to improve the student learning outcomes based on regular student and lecturer feedback.

Course lecturers were asked to reflect on the impact of mobile Web 2.0 at several points throughout the trial, and used a variety of media to capture their reflections, including: posts to their blogs, VODCasts (video recordings uploaded to their blogs and YouTube), paper surveys, discussions and brainstorms with the researcher.

MLEARNING CASE STUDY: DIPLOMA OF CONTEMPORARY MUSIC

This section describes and analyses a mobile learning project that illustrates several issues surrounding the potential of mobile Web 2.0 to facilitate personalized learning environments.

Background

The Diploma of Contemporary Music is a newly established two-year level five (equivalent to first year University) Diploma programme. Its unique elements include a focus on the local community, a broad overview of music performance, theory, composition, and technology within a relatively broad scope of musical styles (from classical to contemporary). Traditionally music education focuses upon a pedagogical model that is similar to apprenticeship, with an expert teacher/performer providing mainly one-on-one training and guidance to the student. However the course curriculum was written to allow for the embedding of new technologies with a focus on

student-centred, social constructivist pedagogies, and group performance. 2008 was the second year of the programme, and it is in the process of building up a profile and student numbers within the local region. Compared to national statistics, the region is under-represented in tertiary education achievement, therefore most students enrolled in the course are classed as under-achievers or second-chance tertiary students. The use of mobile Web 2.0 technologies within the course has been investigated for pedagogical reasons (to facilitate the move from traditional instructivist pedagogies to social constructivism), as well as a way to establish the programme as innovative and engaging to students. Contestable funding for innovation in programme delivery was made available for 2008, and a proposal from the researcher for funding to implement mobile Web 2.0 within the programme was accepted. This allowed for the purchase (in February 2008) of a class set of iPod touch's, and funding to purchase a class set of 3G iPhones when they became available in New Zealand in July 2008.

The programme director was a member of a Community of Practice established in late 2007 to explore the educational potential of Web 2.0 tools alongside of the addition of the Campuspack (adding Blog, wiki, and podcast tools to Blackboard) to the institutional Leaning Management System. Including other lecturers on the Music programme in a Community of Practice was logistically problematic, as most of the lecturers for the course are part-time. Hence the other two lecturers involved in the iPod/iPhone project did not have the previous experience of the Community of Practice or the educational use of Web 2.0 tools before the start of the project.

Setting up the Trial: Choices and Design

The iPod Touch was chosen as the wireless mobile device (WMD) for the Contemporary Music trial after discussions with the lecturers at the end of

Table 1. Diploma of Contemporary Music mobile trial milestones

Date	Project Milestones
October to December 2007	Community of Practice with lecturers focusing on the integration of Web 2.0 technologies and Blackboard.
December 2007 to February 2008	Brainstorm mobile web 2.0 project goals and course integration with course Lecturers
20 February 2008	Purchased iPod Touch's (16GB) Investigated Synching via iTunes over the network to the xserve. Setup Blackboard support course (iPASA)
26 February	Provided course lecturers with iPod Touch and tutorials on setup.
7 March	Provided students with iPod Touch and began weekly technology support sessions (Community of Practice with staff, students, and the 'technology steward').
March – June	Supported students and staff during trial via weekly 'technology workshops' Monitored student progress via their Vox Blogs/ePortfolios
June	Student and staff surveys Focus group Data analysis and report write up. Re-evaluation of Trial for second semester 2008
July	Re-launch of trial with iPhones replacing the iPod Touch's
November	Final Data gathering, analysis, and report write up.

2007 as it aligned closely with the curriculum and delivery choices of the programme. The course is based around Apple Macintosh computers and software, providing close integration with Apple software such as iTunes and Garageband. Students and lecturers were provided with an iPod Touch (16GB) for the duration of the 2008 trial. Participants signed an acceptable use policy, agreeing to look after and return the device at the end of the trial, and were encouraged to treat the device as if it were their own for the period of the trial, including customisation, downloading of media, and installation of third party applications. Internet connectivity is available via Unitec's WiFi network while on campus. This provides free Web access while on campus. An intentional Community of Practice model is used to create a collaborative learning community between the lecturers, the students, and a 'technology steward' (Cochrane, 2007; Cochrane & Kligyte, 2007). Wenger (Wenger et al., 2005) defines a 'technology steward' as a member of the community of practice with the experience and expertise to guide and advise the group on appropriate technolo-

gies to choose for supporting and facilitating the groups communication and goals. Thus the project was guided and supported by weekly "technology sessions" facilitated by the researcher as the 'technology steward' (Table 1).

Students volunteered to participate in the iPod trial from across the Diploma of Contemporary Music programme. As a pre-requisite, students were required to have already passed two of the introductory core papers of the course.

Participants:

- 11 students – students volunteer to participate in the trial using the provided iPod Touch. The average age of the students is 22, and the gender mix is 6 female student and 5 male students.
- Course Lecturers
- Technology Steward (Thom Cochrane – CTLI)

iPod Touch details: Apple iPod Touch. (New Zealand iPhone details TBA circa June/July 2008)

- WiFi
- 16GB flash memory
- Built-in virtual keyboard
- Multi-Touch screen
- iTunes synchronization via USB

Learning Management System: Blackboard 7 with added Campuspack for Podcasting, RSS, Wiki's, and Blogs.

Mobile Web 2.0 Pedagogies

The core activity of the project was the creation and maintenance of a reflective Blog as part of a course group project, creating a collaborative context independent learning environment. The blog host chosen (http://www.vox.com) provides free creation of a blog, an ePortfolio (collections of student media), and social networking (via VOX's 'neighbourhood' feature), and provides access to a potentially worldwide peer learning community. The iPod can be used to enhance almost any aspect of the course. The project was centred on preparing students for the music technology paper that is part of the Diploma of Contemporary Music which is due to run for the first time in semester one of 2009. In this course students will experiment with and evaluate current music creation and delivery technologies, including podcasting and sharing via blogs, ePortfolios, and social networking. The goal of the trial was to illustrate the potential of a PLE, facilitated by mobile Web 2.0 technologies, that was unconstrained by the limitations of the institutional LMS. For semester one of the trial lecturers and students were provided with an iPod Touch (16GB) each, which was to be replaced by a 3G iPhone in semester two when they become officially released in New Zealand. While the iPod Touch is not a smartphone, it has WiFi and is essentially an iPhone without the phone or camera capability, thus it provides a limited connectivity version of the iPhone until they were made available. Although the iPod Touch has limited content creation capabilities (no camera

for still image or video capture, no microphone input for audio recording, and no built-in GPS for geotagging or geolocation) it is a powerful mobile internet device suited to text-based input and one of the best mobile media viewing devices currently available. The iPod/iPhone includes a virtual keyboard for text entry as part of its touch-screen interface. Another limitation of the iPod Touch (and the iPhone) is the reliance upon media synchronization via iTunes software on a computer. The iPod Touch and iPhone thus require users to have access to a computer and an iTunes Store online account. User content creation was thus facilitated by using the Apple iMac computers in the Music Lab, using their built-in Webcams, microphone, and the use of external audio and midi equipment attached to the iMacs.

The project initially focused on investigating the use of the iPod Touch synchronized with iTunes software on desktop computers (Apple iMacs) for the following activities:

- A reflective Blog (http://www.vox.com)
- An ePortfolio (http://www.vox.com)
- Email (GMail)
- RSS (Google Reader)
- Shared Calendars (Google Calenders)
- Image Blogging (Flickr)
- Video Blogging (YouTube)
- Podcasting
- Instant Messaging (http://www.mundu.com)
- Accessing the Course Management System (Blackboard http://bb.unitec.ac.nz)
- Document reading (Word, Excel, PowerPoint, PDF using email attachments and Google Docs)

Lecturers were encouraged to model the use and integration of mobile Web 2.0 in their own daily work-flows and to provide regular formative feedback to students via posts on their blogs and other media. The following diagram (Fig.1) is a concept map outlining the integration of the key

Figure 1. Mobile Web 2.0 concept map

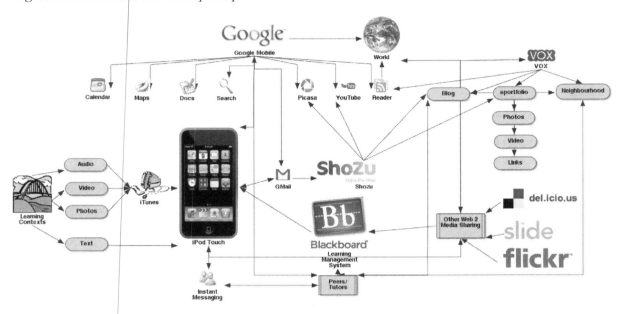

mobile Web 2.0 tools used in the project. It was partially inspired by Jafari's (2006) conceptual diagram of future personal learning environments. The iPod Touch (or iPhone) is used to provide a bridge between learning contexts as a media synchronization and collaborative communications device. A variety of mobile friendly Web-based tools are used to host, record and share the participants learning experiences. The iPod/iPhone provides a link between learning contexts, course content, user-generated content, peers and teachers, aligning with the interactive elements of Laurillard's conversational model of learning (2001). There is an interactive online concept map (Figure 1) illustrating the generic model used for all the mobile Web 2.0 projects available at http://ltxserver.unitec.ac.nz/~thom/mobileWeb2concept2.htm.

Supporting Mobile Web 2.0

The project was guided and supported by weekly "technology sessions" facilitated by a 'technology steward' (Wenger et al., 2005) who is the researcher and an Academic Advisor in eLearning and learning technologies in the Centre for Teaching and Learning Innovation (CTLI) at Unitec. The project was a collaborative project between the 'technology steward', the course lecturers, and the students on the course. The institution's Learning Management System (LMS) was used to provide scaffolding and support for both lecturers and students, while externally hosted Web 2.0 tools were used to create a more customisable and flexible personal learning environment for the students work. Table 2 below summaries the main topics and sequence of the weekly 'technology support sessions' throughout the project.

The main limitation of the iPod Touch is it's wireless connectivity being limited to wifi hotspots only. With the update of the iPod Touch to the 1.1.4 software the iPod Touch became a capable wireless internet PDA (Personal Digital Assistant). The software update removed the reliance upon Web-based tools by including an email application, a calendar, Google maps, notes, a YouTube player, and stocks. The version 2 software update opened the iPod Touch to the vast array of third party ap-

Table 2. Outline of mobile web 2.0 support session topics

Topic	Outline of Content
Trial Documentation	Acceptable Use Policy, Research consent, initial participant survey
Setting up your iPod	Info to get you started, including How to setup WiFi access Basic Navigation Email Setup Creating Web Bookmarks
Blackboard Homepage	Edit your Blackboard Homepage (In the 'Tools' menu). Include the following info: A headshot photo A brief introduction of yourself Your GMail address Links to your Blog and Web2 accounts (To follow...)
GMail Setup	Creating a GMail account, accessing web-mail on the iPod Touch, and setting up the email client application on the iPod Touch.
Blog setup	Creating and customising your Vox Blog.
Subscribing to VOX Blogs	Using Google Reader to subscribe to each other's VOX blogs
Email uploading to your blog	Using Vox's email to post facility on the iPod touch.
Web 2.0, Web Apps	Setting up your Web2 services: EPortfolio YouTube Flickr Google Mobile RSS Feeds Etc...
Creating a VODCast Show	How to create a Video Cast using QuickTime Pro and YouTube
Using VOX to create a PODCast Show	Using Vox collections and RSS feeds to upload an audio file and create an online podcast show.
iTunes U	An overview of music related resources available via iTunes U
Lecturerial PODCasts	Video Demos of the iPod Touch - these are collated in the Podcast Show for the course - see the 'iPod tutorials' link on the left.
iPod Touch Updates	How to update the iPod Touch software and the benefits of updating
iPod/iPhone Applications	With the V2 software update (included on the iPhone 3G or a $12 update for he iPod Touch) the iPod/iPhone becomes a powerful multimedia device that can play games & work with web2 sites in a much more integrated way. A variety of free (and some paid) applications are explored.
iPod/iPhone Accessories	Enhancing the iPod/iPhone with external hardware
iPhone Vodafone NZ setup	Network settings for 'unlocking' the iPhone

plications available through the iTunes application store. Table 3 summarizes a few of the third party applications that were experimented with.

The iPhone significantly improved over the iPod Touch's limited content creation capabilities, including a built-in camera for still image capture, a built-in microphone for recording audio, a built-in speaker for audio and video playback, and a GPS (for geotagging and various geolocation ap-

plications). Participants who were upgraded to an iPhone were also reimbursed the cost of a 200MB per month 3G data plan, but paid for their own accompanying voice and txt plans. The iPhone's 3G cellphone connectivity reduced the reliance of connectivity and communication via wifi hotspots. The iPhone reduced the dependence on a computer for media creation, and added the dimension of context independence for capturing, reflecting

Table 3. Overview of free iPod and iPhone applications

Free iPod/iPhone Apps	Description
Blogit	A web app for text blogging using Safari on the iPod or iPhone
AIM	An instant messaging application for the AIM protocol
MySpace	An iPod/iPhone application for managing a MySpace account
NetNewsWire	An RSS reader application for iPod/iPhone
Facebook	An iPod/iPhone application for managing a Facebook account
Remote	A remote control application for wirelessly controlling iTunes
Scratch	A DJ sound effect application
Shozu	A multiclient web 2.0 media and blogging client for iPod/iPhone
PangeaVR	A QuickTime Virtual reality scene player and search application
Google	A shortcut for logging into the Google suite of iPhone optimized web apps
Wordpress	A wordpress blogging application for iPod/iPhone
Palringo	A multi-client instant messaging application for iPod/iPhone
2D Sense	A 2D mobile code decoder for the iPhone
Cellspin	A multi-client web 2.0 media and blogging client for the iPod/iPhone
MoPhoto	An application to manage a Flickr online image sharing account
Speedtest	An iPod/iPhone application to test the speed of a connected wireless network
Fring	A multi-client instant messaging and Skype application for iPod/iPhone
eZimba	A photo editing application for iPod/iPhone
Air Sharing	An application for wireless sharing of files between an iPod/iPhone and a computer without requiring an iTunes sync
iTM MidiLab	A wireless MIDI remote control application for iPod/iPhone for controlling MIDI and audio software on a computer.

and collaborating on learning experiences. The main limitations of the iPhone for this project are its lack of video recording capability and lack of multitasking. Multitasking is especially important for using instant messaging, as the instant messaging application should be able to run 'in the background' while the user goes about other tasks on the device. The iPhone's lack of multitasking means that only one application can run at a time, limiting the usefulness of instant messaging.

Mobile Web 2.0 Facilitating Personal Learning Scenarios

YouTube

The YouTube application on the iPod and iPhone makes searching and viewing YouTube videos over a wireless connection simple. Students were encouraged to create YouTube video reflections of their course and performances and subscribe to each other's YouTube 'shows' in iTunes, and view them anywhere using their iPod/iPhone. In the process of doing this, both course lecturers discovered YouTube videos of some of their previous performances and MTV videos. One MTV video in particular that had been recorded in 1992 was found uploaded to YouTube, giving the lecturer's music a new lease of life and an object lesson of the potential of the medium for their students.

VODCasting

Participants were asked to regularly post to their Vox blogs short video recordings of themselves reviewing their thoughts on the use of the iPod/iPhone and later to provide reviews of music apps downloaded from the iTunes store to their iPod/iPhone. The VODCasts were recorded using the built-in Webcams and microphones of the iMacs in the Music lab, then uploaded to students' YouTube accounts, and finally they were embedded into the student's Vox blog posts. The VODCasts were fun and engaging and generated the most collaborative peer review of the project in the form of Vox blog comments. A compilation of some of these VODCasts can be found on YouTube at http://www.youtube.com/watch?v=IXUekj8c86k .

Communication

Students and staff were encouraged to use instant messaging (IM) on the iPod or iPhone as a way of establishing a context independent collaborative learning environment. Email and instant messaging were used on the iPod/iPhone for communication between students (for social activities and help with assignments), and between the students and the technology steward (asking for help with software and hardware issues), and between the students and course lecturers (for clarifying assessment requirements). Lecturers were reticent to engage with instant messaging as they had not appropriated it as a part of their lifestyles and have yet to be convinced that such communication is not merely "phatic" (as described by one lecturer) and requiring 24/7 commitment from the lecturers to answer student requests. However the use of instant messaging for communication with the technology steward was particularly useful for supporting the students, as the technology steward was based on a separate campus from the students and encouraged the students to contact him that way. An example chat session between the technology steward and a participating student is shown below (Figure 2). The student was using IM on their iPhone.

Student and Staff Performances

Notifications of student performance venues and times were posted to a student's blog, informing other students' in their Vox neighbourhood via email or RSS to their iPhones of these upcoming events. A second student videoed the student performing live with their band at the venue, and subsequently the video of the performance was uploaded and shared via the student's blog.

Staff members also used their Vox blogs to advertise their upcoming performances, and provide reviews of these performances, including uploading photos and video clips.

DISCUSSION

The mobile Web 2.0 trial represented a significant learning curve for most participants. Fig 3 below summaries the participants previous use of wireless technology and popular Web 2.0 tools. Virtually all participants were consumers of Web 2.0 content, but prior to the trial few had ever created and uploaded their own content to Web 2.0 sites. None had previously attempted mobile blogging. Cellphone ownership was almost ubiquitous, but no participants had previously owned an iPod touch or a 'smartphone'.

The innovative nature of the iPod Touch and the iPhone, coupled with the build-up of marketing hype surrounding the release of the iPhone in New Zealand, generated a lot of interest in the iPod/iPhone trial beyond the Contemporary Music course, both on and off campus, resulting in articles in the local newspaper and on the institutions Website. Screenshots of two media releases about the project as viewed on an iPhone can be found at http://flickr.com/photos/thomcochrane/2842046366/ and http://flickr.com/photos/thomcochrane/2842051990/. The novelty of the iPod Touch initially captured the imagination and attention of the participants, but later in the year

Figure 2. Example instant message chat session with technology steward and student

as the pressure of assessments mounted many participants interaction reduced.

Although students loved the iPod Touch as a focal point of their personal multimedia collections, for media playback, Web connectivity and messaging, there was limited buy-in from the majority of students for VOX blogging. This was due to several factors. Students participating in the trial volunteered from across the entire Diploma of Contemporary Music programme and were not necessarily in the same classes, therefore there was little cohesion within the group and a lack of a sense of a collaborative learning community. The trial was viewed as an optional extra to the curriculum, as an investigation of how the tools might be integrated into the course delivery and assessment in the future. Therefore there was no

summative assessment associated with the trial, and when the pressure of assignment deadlines approached engagement in the optional Vox blogging died away.

The lecturers were new to the concepts of Web 2.0 tools in education, and even more so regarding mobile Web 2.0. The lecturers therefore have taken significant time to understand how they could appropriate the WMDs and mobile Web 2.0 into the course assessment and their own pedagogical approaches. Instead, the Campuspack Blog tool within Blackboard was used by the lecturers as the official blogging tool for assessed activities in the course. This was a new activity for 2008, as a result of the Community of Practice in late 2007 involving the researcher, the programme director, and lecturers from various other programmes in the

Figure 3. Trial participants previous use of wireless technology and web 2.0

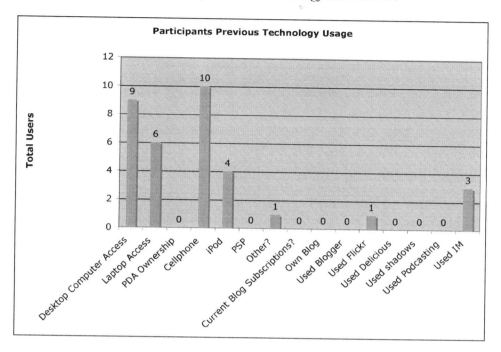

institution. The Blackboard Campuspack blog was used as an individual learning journal and virtual 'helpdesk' system rather than a collaborative social constructivist environment as was the aim of the Vox blogs. This and the fact that the Campuspack blog is not easily accessible via mobile devices led to very low student engagement in the official assessed Blackboard blogging activities. In comparison, those students (and staff) who used the Vox blog found it to be very mobile friendly, fun and generated a collaborative environment. Exploring how Vox mobile blogging can replace the Campuspack blogging activities will be explored with lecturers for 2009.

With the release of the iPhone 3G in New Zealand in July 2008 there was an opportunity to reinvigorate the project and motivate students and staff to engage in a more ubiquitously connected collaborative environment. To encourage the use of the Vox blogs, it was decided to offer the iPhone upgrade to students who met the following requirements:

To be eligible for an upgrade to the iPhone 3G you must fulfill the following over the next month (13 June to 13 July 2008, mid-year Semester break):

1. Regularly (at least two times per week) post to your VOX blog & comment on other students blog posts.
2. Upload a weekly PODCast (audio) or VODCast (video) recording to either your VOX collection or YouTube (1-2 minutes each). Listen/watch each others 'shows' and comment on them!

These posts and PODCasts/VODCasts should reflect on aspects relevant to your DipMus course - e.g. a critique of musical works, comments on local musicians/bands, reflections on your assignments, interviews with local musicians etc...

However, only five participants (3 students and 2 staff members) fulfilled these requirements. Therefore only five of the thirteen trial participants were upgraded to iPhones for semester two. This meant that the second half of the trial comprised of a mixed group of iPod Touch and iPhone users. The 'technology sessions' in semester two were targeted to be as relevant as possible to both groups of users, but inevitably the iPod Touch users felt left out and disengaged. Feedback from the end of the trial indicated that the iPhone users were more engaged and enthusiastic about the trial than the iPod Touch users, and the iPhone users satisfaction with the trial increased from their mid trial feedback.

A survey of how students were using the iPods/iPhones was taken during mid semester two (See Figure 4). Several of the last question categories were not applicable to the iPod or iPhone, as

Figure 4. Student usage of the iPod/iPhone for various activities

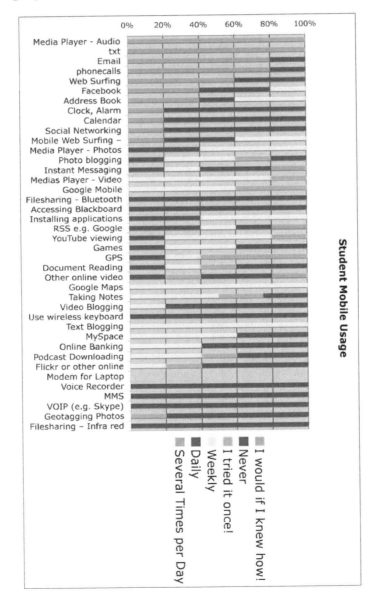

the survey was a generic one used across all the mobile Web 2.0 projects that the researcher has been involved in.

Figure 4 indicates that students used mainly the affordances of iPods/iPhones that aligned with their own personal learning, rather than directly relevant to the music course. The Students usage patterns are also reflected in their evaluations of their perceived most useful functions of mobile devices (see Figure 5). As Figure 5 indicates, some of these perceptions changed over the period of the trial as participants learned firsthand what worked and what didn't with the WMDs. Use of the iPhone brought an appreciation of the value of a built-in camera for mobile blogging and capturing learning events, and of the communication and collaboration facilitated by txt and voice capabilities (see fig 6). In comparison to other mobile Web 2.0 trials that the researcher has facilitated, the value assigned to accessing online course content on the iPod/iPhone was higher than for any other WMD used. This is a

reflection on the unique mobile Web experience that the iPod/iPhone provides. Course content was not a significant aspect of the trial, as the focus was on facilitating social constructivist environments with students (not staff) creating their own content and sharing and critiquing.

There was a high level of fun attached to the trial (see Figure 7), and most students were keen to see further integration of the WMD and mobile Web 2.0 into the rest of their course (see Figure 8). The drop-off in the enthusiasm for this after the second semester was a reflection on the relative disengagement of the remaining iPod users who where not upgraded to iPhones.

The following sections summarise example student and staff responses to the mid and end of trial surveys and focus groups.

Student Feedback

The benefits of mobility and context independence facilitated by the iPod Touch and iPhone were

Figure 5. Comparison of participants pre, mid and post trial evaluation of the most useful functions of mobile devices

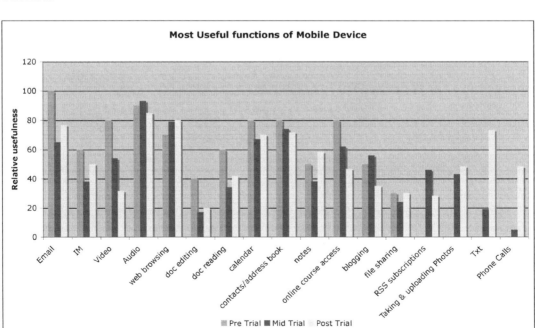

Figure 6. Comparison of participants evaluation of the most important features of mobile devices, mid and post trial

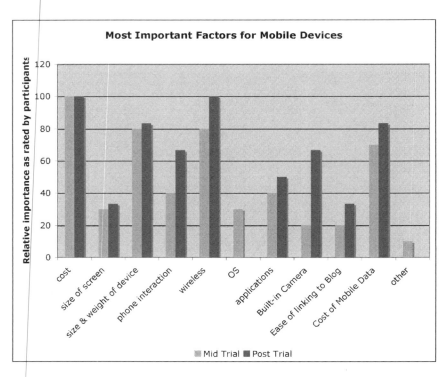

key themes identified by students, e.g. "When away from the classroom it was easy to keep up to date". "It was a good way to communicate with the other students. It was excellent that I could ask questions of lecturers when I needed to know something – it's a fast way of communicating." An example student YouTube VODCast (video cast) show can be seen at http://www.youtube.com/rimzcoop/. Other student feedback included:

No matter where I was I could use it, spare time having lunch, toilet, even in the classroom while the teacher wanted some information about a particular person. Makes a huge difference (Student 1).

I quite enjoyed the course because I learnt about so much more about today's modern technology. Now I have more understanding on what I can do with the WMD, how I can utilise the device for

communication and to gain access to information. All this was new for me. I enjoy learning about new technologies. Especially the new capabilities like chatting, blogging, surfing the net, and sending out multi emails. (Student 2).

I absolutely enjoyed the project. I gained knowledge of today's technology and how to incorporate that knowledge and understanding into today (Student 3).

By default the more motivated students became the iPhone users. They were differentiated from other students by their ability to take responsibility for their learning and ownership of developing a personal learning environment using the mobile Web 2.0 tools. These students identified a lack of 'community' as limiting the engagement with the Vox blogging and the uptake of the mobile Web 2.0 tools. This 'community' could be better achieved

Figure 7. Participant survey results

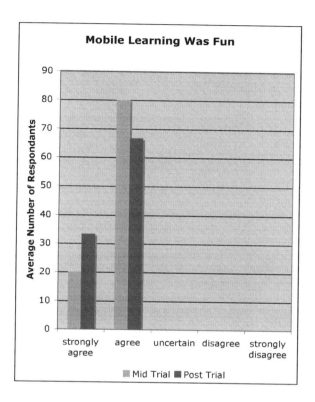

Figure 8. Participant survey results

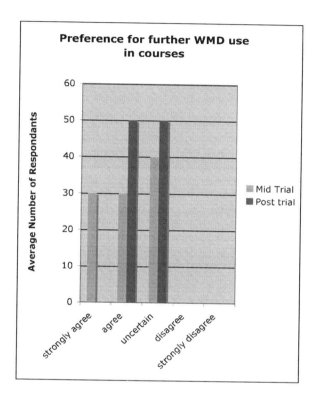

by locating the project within a specific class group of the programme, which would also provide an environment to 'scaffold' the less independent learners in the class via peer support.

Staff Feedback

Course lecturers were just as enthusiastic about the iPod Touch as the students, and they integrated the use of the device into their own personal daily routines. The main limitations identified by lecturers of the iPod Touch were its limited wireless connectivity (WiFi only), and getting used to the virtual keyboard for text entry.

The project is limited by wireless coverage available – but has great potential. It is beneficial being able to check/send email/blog while away from home. Instruction was good. Plethora of blogsites/

online communities was a little confusing – advantages of specific sites over others could have been emphasized more/explained a bit better. I would now be better able to integrate the WMD into assignments rather better. (Lecturer 1)

It's a brilliant piece of hardware, and styley, but I still struggle with the small virtual keyboard. It's great for students who need to communicate for group projects. I will be taking mine overseas with me! (Lecturer 2)

An example teacher YouTube VODCast (video cast) show about the project can be seen at http://www.youtube.com/ipodtrial/.

The academic staff were also asked to reflect on four questions related to the main research questions:

- What potential benefits do you see for mobile Web 2.0 to enhance teaching and learning?
- Have you (so far) seen increased engagement in the course from students when using this technology?
- What are the key issues for integrating this technology into your courses?
- In what ways has (or will) your teaching approach changed by using these tools?

Their answers to these questions are available on YouTube as VODCasts at http://www.youtube.com/thomcochrane. Their responses indicated that although they were enthusiastic about the personal use of the iPod/iPhone, they struggled to conceptualise the affordances of the devices for integration into the course curriculum. They did however agree that course integration of the tools was critical for the future. There was a perception among the lecturers that the Vox blogging was fun, but 'real' blogging within the course curriculum should be conducted using the Campuspack Blog tool within the institutional LMS, Blackboard. This is a key issue that will be addressed by the

formation of a Community of Practice between the end of the 2008 course and the start of the 2009 course to investigate ideas for course integration and appropriate assessment activities for 2009. The inability to see how to integrate the tools into the curriculum may merely be pragmatic (the lecturers need some new ideas, time for reflection and guidance), or it may be symptomatic of an ideological clash of pedagogical approaches. The project has focused upon facilitating a social constructivist environment, whereas the course lecturers appear to be more used to an instructivist, apprenticeship model of teaching and learning. Therefore this will form one of the core discussions of planning for 2009 projects.

Blog Analysis

Student and staff blogs provided a media-rich record of their engagement with the mobile Web 2.0 trial. Mobile blogging was initially slow to take-off, but increased dramatically with the introduction of the iPhone due to its anywhere anytime 3G connectivity (see Figure 9). Mobile blog posts and peer commenting both increased with the use

Figure 9. Comparison of average iPod and iPhone Vox posts

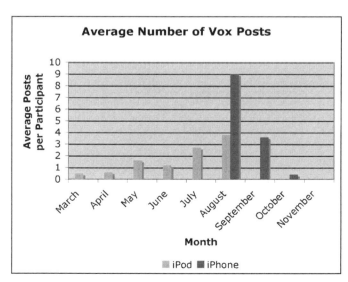

of the iPhone (see Figure 10). The iPhone thus better facilitated bridging learning contexts and creating personalized learning environments than the iPod Touch. However, the pressure of end of semester deadlines resulted in a decrease in the optional mobile blogging activity.

Figure 11 summarises the type and amount of media embedded into participants Vox blogs. The

numbers are somewhat deceptive in comparison between the iPod and iPhone timeframe, as the most active iPod media uploaders became the iPhone users, and the iPhone timeframe was shorter than that for the iPod use. Participants identified the lack of video recording capability of the iPhone as a significant limitation of the device.

Figure 10. Comparison of iPod and iPhone Vox mobile posts and comments

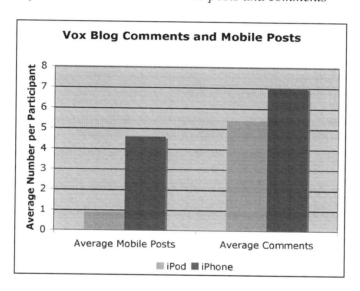

Figure 11. Comparison of total number of media elements used in Vox blogs

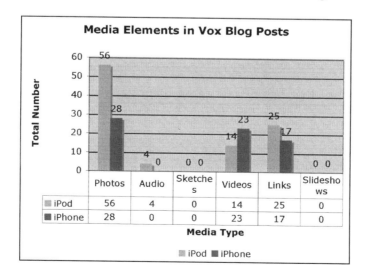

	Photos	Audio	Sketches	Videos	Links	Slideshows
iPod	56	4	0	14	25	0
iPhone	28	0	0	23	17	0

Key Issues

The trial has highlighted several key issues that are related to the research questions.

- What are the key factors in integrating Wireless Mobile Devices (WMDs) within tertiary education courses?

Carefully planned course integration including authentic assessment of the use of mobile Web 2.0 tools is needed.

Course lecturers need to appropriate the mobile Web 2.0 tools into their own daily routines and gain an understanding of the affordances of these tools for their pedagogical toolkits. This requires significant time for exploration of the affordances of the mobile Web 2.0 tools, and lecturer professional development, and should be factored into such projects.

- What challenges/advantages to established pedagogies do these disruptive technologies present?

Mobile Web 2.0 tools are disruptive devices that facilitate social constructivist pedagogies, and therefore disrupt instructivist pedagogies.

- To what extent can these WMDs be utilized to support learner interactivity, collaboration, communication, reflection and interest, and thus provide pedagogically rich learning environments that engage and motivate the learner?

Students are engaged by the use of these tools and will use them to enhance collaboration and communication, but to hold that engagement under the pressures of tertiary education requires integration into the course assessment strategies.

- To what extent can WMDs be used to harness the potential of current and emerging social constructivist eLearning tools?

The iPod Touch and the iPhone demonstrate a new level of integration between wireless mobile devices and Web 2.0 services. However, every wireless mobile device has strengths and weaknesses, the lack of video recording and multitasking of the iPhone is its key weaknesses in supporting mobile Web 2.0. These weaknesses can be addressed by 'jailbreaking' the iPhone to enable a wider range of affordances, including: video recording, video streaming, browsing and accessing the files on the iPhone without restrictions, and enabling sharing of the iPhones 3G internet connection with a laptop computer etc... These will be explored in mobile Web 2.0 projects in 2009.

This case study serves to illustrate several critical pedagogical success factors of mobile Web 2.0 integration within tertiary education:

- The level of pedagogical integration of the technology into the course criteria and assessment.
- The level of lecturer modelling of the pedagogical use of the tools.
- The use of regular formative feedback from both Lecturers and student peers.
- Appropriate choice of mobile devices and software.
- The importance of technological and pedagogical support.

Several of these critical success factors are also corroborated by studies such as the recent mobile learning projects at the University of Wollongong (J. Herrington et al., 2008), which were based upon the nine characteristics of authentic learning (A. Herrington & Herrington, 2006). The above critical success factors were identified across several mobile Web 2.0 projects during 2007 and 2008, of which the Diploma of Contemporary Music was one project. Each project was evaluated by:

- The level of student engagement and satisfaction achieved – as evidenced in evaluative surveys and focus group feedback.

- The level of moblogging (mobile blogging) achieved by students in the courses.
- Lecturer reflective feedback.

Plans for 2009

Everyone on the trial indicated that they found the iPod Touch effective for increasing communication, and would be willing to purchase their own iPod Touch. The current high cost of the iPhone is a deterrent to student purchases. Student blogging made slow progress without specific integration into the course in 2008. The main limitation of the iPod Touch were the reliance upon WiFi hotspots, and the slow speed of the Unitec WiFi network at Waitakere. The introduction of the iPhone 3G effectively solved this issue. The ubiquitous connectivity of the iPhone better facilitates personalised learning environments within and between multiple contexts. The project is continuing into 2009, and will aim for better course integration and wider use of the iPhone.

The iPod Touch and iPhone version 2.0+ software coupled with the opening of the iTunes application store has opened the potential of the iPod Touch and iPhone platform to a vast array of applications that are very relevant to the music industry and music education. The potential for using some of these available and emerging applications within the course is to be investigated.

Feedback and evaluation of the other five mobile Web 2.0 projects during 2008 demonstrated an enthusiastic response to continuing and developing these projects in 2009. Following this enthusiastic response from the students and lecturers, internal institutional funding was sought, and approved, for extending these small projects to a major large-scale mLearning project in 2009 involving the use of 250 smartphones, and 200 netbooks. In the 2009 Diploma of Contemporary Music programme, the iPods/iPhones will be integrated into the course delivery and assessment as part of a PODcast and VODcast sharing project with another similar course at another New Zealand

institution. This will include elements of peer critique and review recorded on their VOX blogs. The iPods will be used within the first year of the course, as part of the performance course. The iPhones will be used within the second year of the course, as part of the new technologies paper. This will facilitate a stronger sense of development of a learning community.

An sms text messaging system will be explored for use in the mobile Web 2.0 trials in 2009 as a communication and notification system operating as a plug-in from within the institutions learning management system.

The cost of prepay mobile data in New Zealand has dropped dramatically during the second half of 2008 and so options for sustainable funding of the iPhone and 3G data are better than they were in 2008.

Finally, plans for Lecturer professional development (using a community of practice model) in the technical and pedagogical underpinnings of mobile Web 2.0 to tackle the issues of course integration are underway in preparation for the beginning of semester one 2008.

CONCLUSION

The Diploma of Contemporary Music case study has served as an initial investigation of some of the potential of mobile Web 2.0 within the course. The trial highlighted the need for lecturer appropriation of the tools and identified the key issue of course integration including summative and formative assessment. Student engagement simply on the basis of using the 'coolest' phone or media player in the world is not sustainable when the pressures of course deadlines for assessments loom. The trial has set a sound basis from which to enhance the course for next year, and illustrates a potentially transferable model of implementation and support for mobile Web 2.0 projects. This model is further developed and illustrated across a variety of contexts via concurrent mobile Web

2.0 trials (Cochrane, 2008a, 2008b; Cochrane & Bateman, 2009). Now that course lecturers have experience with mobile Web 2.0 tools, they will be better equipped for developing new pedagogical approaches for future projects that facilitate the establishment of personal learning environments for students beyond the confines of the institutionally hosted learning management systems. In particular 2009 projects will investigate the use of MySpace, student created podcasts, and microblogging as authentic mobile learning environments within the context of music delivery, promotion and critique.

REFERENCES

Attwell, G. (2006). The wales-wide Web. What is a PLE? The future or just another buzz word? Retrieved 1 July, 2006, from http://www.know-net.com/writing/Weblogs/Graham_Attwell/entries/6521819364

Bijker, W., Hughes, T., & Pinch, T. (Eds.). (1987). Social construction of technological systems: New directions in the sociology and history of technology. Cambridge, MA: MIT Press.

Cochrane, T. (2007, October 16-19). Moving mobile mainstream: Using communities of practice to develop educational technology literacy in tertiary academics. Paper presented at the MLearn 2007 - Making the Connections 6th International Conference on Mobile Learning, Melbourne.

Cochrane, T. (2008a, October 8-10). Designing mobile learning environments: Mobile trials at unitec 2008. Paper presented at the MLearn08: The bridge from text to context, University of Wolverhampton, School of Computing and IT.

Cochrane, T. (2008b, December 1 - 4). Mobile Web2.0 the new frontier. Paper presented at the ASCILITE 2008, Deakin University, Melbourne, Australia.

Cochrane, T., & Bateman, R. (2009). Transforming pedagogy using mobile Web 2.0, IADIS International Conference on Mobile Learning 2009. Barcelona, Spain.

Cochrane, T., & Kligyte, G. (2007, June 11-14). Dummies2delight: Using communities of practice to develop educational technology literacy in tertiary academics. Paper presented at the JISC online conference: Innovating eLearning, JISC online conference.

Herrington, A., & Herrington, J. (Eds.). (2006). Authentic learning environments in higher education. Hershey, PA: Information Science Publishing.

Herrington, A., & Herrington, J. (2007). Authentic mobile learning in higher education. Paper presented at the AARE 2007 International Educational Research Conference, Fremantle, Australia.

Herrington, J., Mantei, J., Herrington, A., Olney, I., & Ferry, B. (2008, December 1 - 4). New technologies, new pedagogies: Mobile technologies and new ways of teaching and learning. Paper presented at the ASCILITE 2008, Deakin University, Melbourne, Australia.

Jafari, A., McGee, P., & Carmean, C. (2006). Managing courses, defining learning: What faculty, students, and administrators want. *EDUCAUSE Review*, (July/August): 50–70.

Kukulsa-Hulme, A., & Traxler, J. (2005). Mobile teaching and learning. In A. Kukulsa-Hulme & J. Traxler (Eds.), Mobile learning (pp. 25 - 44). Oxon, UK: Routledge.

Laurillard, D. (2001). Rethinking university teaching: A framework for the effective use of educational technology (2nd ed.). London: Routledge.

Laurillard, D. (2007). Pedagogical forms of mobile learning: Framing research questions. In N. Pachler (Ed.), Mobile learning: Towards a research agenda (Vol. 1, pp. 33-54). London: WLE Centre, Institute of Education.

Lave, J., & Wenger, E. (1991). Situated learning: Legitimate peripheral participation. Cambridge, UK: Cambridge University Press.

McLoughlin, C., & Lee, M. J. W. (2008). Future learning landscapes: Transforming pedagogy through social software. Innovate: Journal of Online Education, 4(5).

Mishra, P., Koehler, M. J., & Zhao, Y. (Eds.). (2007). Faculty development by design: Integrating technology in higher education. Charlotte, NC: Information Age Publishing.

O'Reilly, T. (2005). What is Web 2.0: Design patterns and business models for the next generation of software. Retrieved March, 2006, from http://www.oreillynet.com/pub/a/oreilly/tim/news/2005/09/30/what-is-Web-20.html

Sharples, M. (2000). Disruptive devices: Personal technologies and education. Retrieved June 27, 2006, from http://www.eee.bham.ac.uk/handler/ePapers/disruptive.pdf

Sharples, M. (2001). Disruptive devices: Mobile technology for conversational learning. *International Journal of Continuing Education and Lifelong Learning, 12*(5/6), 504–520. doi:10.1504/IJCEELL.2002.002148

Sharples, M. (2005). Learning as conversation: Transforming education in the mobile age. Paper presented at the Conference on Seeing, Understanding, Learning in the Mobile Age, Budapest, Hungary.

Sharples, M., Milrad, M., Sanchez, I. A., & Vavoula, G. (2007). Mobile learning: Small devices, big issues. In N. Balacheff, S. Ludvigsen, T. de Jong, A. Lazonder, S. Barnes & L. Montandon (Eds.), Technology enhanced learning: Principles and products (Vol. chapter 14, pp. 20).

Stead, G. (2006). Mobile technologies: Transforming the future of learning. Emerging Technologies for Learning. Retrieved 6 April, 2006, from http://www.becta.org.uk/corporate/publications/

Uden, L. (2007). Activity theory for designing mobile learning. *International Journal of Mobile Learning and Organisation, 1*(1), 81–102. doi:10.1504/IJMLO.2007.011190

Vygotsky, L. (1978). Mind in society. Cambridge, MA: Harvard University Press.

Wadsworth, Y. (1998). What is participatory action research? Retrieved May 3, 2002, from http://www.scu.edu.au/schools/gcm/ar/ari/p-ywadsworth98.html

Wali, E., Winters, N., & Oliver, M. (2008). Maintaining, changing and crossing contexts: An activity theoretic reinterpretation of mobile learning. ALT-J . *Research in Learning Technologies, 16*(1), 41–57.

Wenger, E., McDermott, R., & Snyder, W. (2002). Cultivating communities of practice: A guide to managing knowledge. Boston: Harvard Business School Press.

Wenger, E., White, N., Smith, J., & spa, K. R.-. (2005). Technology for communities. Retrieved July 14, 2006, from http://technologyforcommunities.com/

APPENDIX

Table 4. Wireless Mobile Study – end of trial questionnaire (DipLSD2007 Students)

QUESTION: (This is an anonymous questionnaire)	Your Answer: tick or circle most applicable answer/s, or write your answer in the space provided below.					
1. What is your Student ID number?						
2. What is your age?						
3. What is your gender?	Male	Female				
4. What has been your experience of group work facilitated by Blogs and RSS?	Very Good	Good	Not Bad	Neither Good nor Bad	Not Good	Terrible
6. It was easy to use the smartphone (Nokia N80)?	Strongly agree	Agree	Uncertain	Disagree	Strongly disagree	
7. This mobile learning experience was fun.	Strongly agree	Agree	Uncertain	Disagree	Strongly disagree	
8. Based on my experience during this trial, I would use a smartphone in other courses	Strongly agree	Agree	Uncertain	Disagree	Strongly disagree	
9. I would be willing to purchase my own smartphone?	Yes	No				
10. Where did you use the Smartphone? Circle all that apply.	At home At Unitec in class At Unitec not in class While Travelling On site while investigating or building your project Other (specify)					
11. In your opinion, does mobile learning increase the quality of learning?	Strongly agree	Agree	Uncertain	Disagree	Strongly disagree	

12. Mobile blogging helped create a sense of community (group work)?	Strongly agree	Agree	Uncertain	Disagree	Strongly disagree
13. Accessing your course blog was easy using the mobile device?	Strongly agree	Agree	Uncertain	Disagree	Strongly disagree
14. Mobile learning increases access to education?	Strongly agree	Agree	Uncertain	Disagree	Strongly disagree
15. Communication and feedback from the course lecturer/lecturer was made easier?	Strongly agree	Agree	Uncertain	Disagree	Strongly disagree
16. Mobile learning is convenient for communication with other students?	Strongly agree	Agree	Uncertain	Disagree	Strongly disagree
17. Rate the usefulness of the following applications using mobile devices? (0 = no use, 10 = extremely useful).	Email Instant Messaging Video Audio Web Browsing Document editing Document Reading Calendar Contacts/Addressbook Notes Accessing online course material Blogging File sharing RSS subscriptions Taking and uploading photos Txt Phone calls				
18. What factors would be most important in deciding upon mobile learning?	Cost of device Size of the screen Size & weight of the mobile device Phone integration Wireless capability The operating system: PocketPC, Palm OS, or Symbian Availability of installable applications A built-in camera Ease of linking to your Blog The cost of mobile data Other				

19. Do you have any other comments on the mobile project?	

Questions for Discussion

The main purpose of the focus group is to provide critical reflective feedback on the design and implementation of the learning activities and enhanced communication facilitated by the Wireless Mobile Device (WMD) used in the 'trial'. This feedback will provide valuable insights into the design of the following trial, and forms a critical reflective action research cycle of evaluation.

Focus Group Questions

- How would you rate the effectiveness of the WMD (Smartphone) for accessing your/your students' blogs?
- How user friendly was the interface of the WMD?
- How would you rate the effectiveness of the WMD for increasing communication:
- Between students
- Between Students and Lecturers/lecturers?
- How useful were the WMDs for accessing course content?
- Describe how the integration into the course of the WMDs may be improved.
- (For Lecturers) How would you rate the usefulness of the WMDs for your own teaching?
- What level of interactivity did the WMDs provide?
- What were the benefits of wireless connectivity?
- What were the support requirements for the WMDs?
- What other uses did you find for the WMD?
- In what situations would the WMDs be most effective?
- What do you think worked well, and what would you do differently another time?

Compilation of References

Absalom, M., & Marden Pais, M. (2004). Email Communication and Language Learning at University - an Australian Case Study. *Computer Assisted Language Learning*, *17*(3-4), 403–440. doi:10.1080/0958822042000319647

Acar, A. (2008). Antecedents and Consequences of Online Social Networking Behavior: The Case of Facebook. *Journal of Website Promotion*, *3*(1), 62–83. doi:10.1080/15533610802052654

Ackermann, E. (1996). Perspective-Taking and Object Construction. In Y. Kasai, & M. Resnick (Eds.), *Constructionism in Practice: Designing, Thinking and Learning in a Digital World* (pp. 25-35). Mahwah, NJ: Lawrence Erlbaum.

Ackermann, E. (2001) *Piaget's Constructivism, Papert's Constructionism: What's the difference?* Retrieved July 20, 2008, from http://learning.media.mit.edu/content/publications/EA.Piaget%20_%20Papert.pdf

Ackermann, E. (2004). Constructing knowledge and transforming the world. In M. Tokoro & L. Steels (Eds.) *A learning zone of one's own: Sharing representations and flow in collaborative learning environment* (pp. 15-37). Washington, DC: IOS Press.

Alberici, A. (2007). Una nuova popolazione universitaria. In A. Alberici (Ed.), *Adulti e Università. Sfide ed innovazioni nella formazione universitaria e continua.* Milano, Italy: Franco Angeli.

Alberici, A., Catarsi, C., Colapietro, V., & Loiodice, I. (2007). *Adulti e Università. Sfide ed innovazioni nella formazione universitaria e continua.* Milano, Italy: Franco Angeli.

Alessi, S. M., & Trollip, S. R. (2001). *Multimedia for learning: Methods and development,* (3rd ed.). Boston: Allyn & Bacon.

Alexander, B. (2006). Web 2.0: A New Wave of Innovation for Teaching and Learning? *EDUCAUSE Review*, *41*(2), 32–44.

Alexander, R. (2008). *Essays on Pedagogy.* Abingdon, UK: Routledge.

Alexander, S. (2001). E-learning developments and experiences. *Education and Training*, *43*(4/5), 240–248. doi:10.1108/00400910110399247

Amine, M. (2007). *My PLE/PKM.* Retrieved 11th September, 2008, from http://mohamedaminechatti.blogspot.com/2007/06/my-plepkm.html

Anderson, P. (2007). *What is Web2.0? Ideas, technologies and implications education.* Bristol, UK: Joint Information Systems Committee. Retrieved 28 October, 2008, from http://www.jisc.ac.uk/media/documents/techwatch/tsw0701.pdf

Ankolekar, A., Krötzsch, M., Tran, T., & Vr, D. (2007). *The Two Cultures - Mashing up Web 2.0 and the Semantic Web.* Retrieved May 18, 2008 from http://www.aifb.uni-karlsruhe.de/WBS/aan/resources/papers/www-07-tc.pdf

Annacontini, G. (2007). Adulti in rete: tecnologie didattiche e formazione universitaria. In A. Alberici (Ed.), *Adulti e Università. Sfide ed innovazioni nella formazione universitaria e continua.* Milano, Italy: Franco Angeli

Appleby, J., Samuels, P., & Treasure-Jones, T. (1997). Diagnosys - a knowledge-based diagnostic test of basic mathematical skills. *Computers & Education, 28*(2), 113–131. doi:10.1016/S0360-1315(97)00001-8

Association of Colleges. (2006). *Personalisation in electronic environments: A definition and check list.* (Briefing: AoC NILTA 15/06). London: Association of Colleges.

Association of Colleges. (2007). *Personalising further education: Developing a vision.* London: Association of Colleges.

Atkins, D., Seely Brown, J., & Hammond, A. L. (2007). *A review of the Open Educational Resource movement: achievements, challenges and new opportunities.* Report to the William and Flora Hewlett Foundation. Retrieved February 8, 2009 from http://www. hewlett.org/NR/rdonlyres/5D2E3386-3974-4314-8F67-5C2F22EC4F9B/0/AReviewoftheOpenEducationalResourcesOERMovement_BlogLink.pdf

Atkinson, T. (2000). *The Intuitive Practitioner: On the Value of Not Always Knowing What One Is Doing.* Buckingham, UK: Open University Press.

Attwell, G. (2005). What is the significance of Open Source Software for the education and training community? In M. Scotto, & G. Succi, (Eds.), *Proc. Of the First International Conference on Open Source Systems,* Genova, 11th-15th July 2005.

Attwell, G. (2006). Personal Learning Environments. *The Wales Wide Web.* Retrieved June 30, 2008, from http://www.knownet.com/writing/weblogs/Graham_Attwell/entries/6521819364

Attwell, G. (2006). The wales-wide web. What is a PLE? The future or just another buzz word? Retrieved 1 July, 2006, from http://www.knownet.com/writing/weblogs/Graham_Attwell/entries/6521819364

Attwell, G. (2007). The Personal Learning Environments - the future of eLearning? *eLearning Papers, 2*(1,). Retrieved November 21, 2008 from http://www.elearningpapers.eu/index.php?page=doc&doc_id=8553&doclng=6

Attwell, G. (2008). Personal Learning Environments – a new learning concept or a new learning system? In V. Homung-Prahauser, M. Luckman, & M. Kalz, (Ed.), *Selbstorganisiertes Lernen im Internet – Edumedia Proceeding.* Retrieved October 29, 2008, from http://edumedia.salzburgresearch.at/images/stories/4_EduMedia_Konferenz/Praesentationen/edumedia_proceeding.pdf

Attwell, G. (2008). *Social Software, Personal Learning Environments and the future of Education.* Keynote presentation at the Conference on Web 2.0, University of Minho, Braga, Portugal, October 10th. Retrieved October 23, 2008, from http://www.pontydysgu.org/wp-content/uploads/2008/09/portplesfin.doc

Ausubel, D. P. (1963). *The psychology of meaningful verbal learning.* New York: Grune and Stratton.

Avallone, F. (Ed.). (2006). *Tutor. Manuale teorico-pratico per migliorare l'efficacia dei sistemi formativi.* Milano, Italy: Guerini.

Awang, D. (2008, November). *PebblePad: Big Splashes or mini Ripples? Reflections on Electronic Portfolio Usage on a Blended Learning Course.* Paper presented at ECEL 2008, 7th European Conference on E-learning. Grecian Bay Hotel, Agia Napa, Cyprus.

Ayala, J. I. (2006). Electronic Portfolios for Whom? *EDUCAUSE Quarterly, 1,* 12–13.

Baker, M., & Lund, K. (1997). Promoting reflective interactions in a CSCL environment. *Journal of Computer Assisted Learning, 13*(3), 175–193. doi:10.1046/j.1365-2729.1997.00019.x

Baldi, S., Heier, H., & Stanzick, F. (2002). *Open Courseware vs. Open Source Software – A Critical Comparison.* ECIS 2002, Gdansk.

Baldwin, C. (2004). X4L review: final report. *JISC.* Retrieved October 29th 2008 from http://www.jisc.ac.uk/media/documents/programmes/x4l/Baldwin, 2004.pdf

Bandura, A. (1971). Vicarious and self-reinforcement processes. In R. Glaser (Ed.) *The nature of reinforcement* (pp. 228-278). New York: Academic.

Bandura, A. (1977). *Social Learning Theory*. New York: General Learning Press.

Bandura, A. (1989). Perceived self-efficacy in the exercise of personal agency. *The Psychologist: Bulletin of the British Psychological Society, 2*, 411–424.

Bannan-Ritland, B. (2003). The role of design in research: The integrative learning design framework. *Educational Researcher, 32*(1), 21–24. doi:10.3102/0013189X032001021

Barger, J. (1997). Robot Wisdom WebLog for December 1997, *Robot Wisdom WebLog*. Retrieved September 6, 2008 from http://www.robotwisdom.com/log1997m12.html

Bariso, B. (2004). *New technologies: Tools for Widening Participation in Lifelong Learning?* Unpublished doctoral dissertation, University of London, London.

Bariso, E. (2008, November). *ESOL for Work: Does it Work?* Paper presented at The AAACE 2008 Conference on the Future of Adult Education/Learning, Denver, CO.

Barnett, R. (2008). *A will to learn*. London: Open University Press.

Barney, D. (2008). *The Network Society*. Cambridge, UK: Polity Press Ltd.

Barr, R., & Tagg, J. (1995). From Teaching to Learning: A New Paradigm for Undergraduate Education. *Change Magazine, 2*(12), 8-12. Retrieved January 11, 2008, from www.cic.uiuc.edu/resources/deo/paradigm.html

Barton, R., & Haydn, T. (2006). Trainee Teachers' Views on What Helps Them to Use Information and Communication Technology Effectively in Their Subject Teaching. *Journal of Computer Assisted Learning, 22*(4), 257–272. doi:10.1111/j.1365-2729.2006.00175.x

Batson, T. (2002). The Electronic Portfolio Boom: What's It All About? *Syllabus, 16*(5), 14–17.

Bax, S. (2003). CALL - past, present and future. *System, 31*(1), 13–28. doi:10.1016/S0346-251X(02)00071-4

Becher, T., & Trowler, P. (2001). *Academic tribes and territories. Intellectual. enquiry and the cultures of disciplines*. Buckingham, UK: Open University Press.

Beck, J. C., & Wade, M. (2004). *Got game: How the gamer generation is reshaping business forever*. Cambridge, MA: Harvard Business School Press.

Beck, U. (1992). *Risk society towards a new modernity*. London: Sage.

Becker, K., Kehoe, J., & Tennent, B. (2007). Impact of personalised learning styles on online delivery and assessment. *Campus-Wide Information Systems, 24*(2), 105–119. doi:10.1108/10650740710742718

Becta (2008). *Harnessing technology: next generation learning 2008-14*. Retrieved February 8, 2009 from http://publications.becta.org.uk/display.cfm?resID=37348&page=1835

BECTA. (2006). *ICT and e-learning in Further Education*. Retrieved July 26, 2008, from http://partners.becta.org.uk/index.php?section=rh&catcode=_re_rp_ap_03&order=2&rid=13649

BECTA. (2007). *Personalising Learning: The Opportunities Offered by Technology*. Retrieved October 28, 2008, from http://feandskills.becta.org.uk/display.cfm?resID=31571

Beetham, H. (2005). *JISC report on e-portfolios in post-16 learning in the UK: Developments, issues and opportunities*. Retrieved October 20, 2008, from http://www.jisc.ac.uk/uploaded_documents/eportfolio_ped.doc

Beetham, H. (2007). An approach to learning activity design. In H. Beetham & R. Sharpe(Eds.), *Rethinking Pedagogy for a digital age: Designing and delivering for e-learning* (pp. 26-40). London: Routledge.

Beetham, H., & Sharpe, R. (Eds.). (2007). *Rethinking Pedagogy for a digital age*. Abingdon, UK: Routledge Falmer.

Beetham, H., & Strivens, J. (2005). *Current e-Portfolio developments in the 14-19, adult and continuing learning sectors*. Commissioned by the National Learning Network Transformation Board.

Bellon, T., & Oates, R. (2002). *Best practices in cyberspace. Motivating the online learner.* Harrisburg, PA: Technology-Mediated Learning Resource Center. Retrieved October 28, 2008, from http://168.144.129.112/Articles/Best%20Practices%20in%20Cyberspace.pdf

Bennett, S., Maton, K., & Kervin, L. (2008). The 'digital natives' debate: A critical review of the evidence. *British Journal of Educational Technology, 39*(5), 775–786. doi:10.1111/j.1467-8535.2007.00793.x

Berners-Lee, T., Handler, J., & Lassila, O. (2001). The Semantic Web. *Scientific American.* Retrieved September 23, 2008 from http://www.ryerson.ca/~dgrimsha/courses/cps720_02/resources/Scientific%20American%20The%20Semantic%20Web.htm

Biggs, J. (1998). Assessment and Classroom Learning: a role for summative assessment? *Assessment in Education: Principles . Policy & Practice, 5*(1), 103–110.

Biggs, J. B. (2003, 2nd Edition). *Teaching for Quality Learning at University.* Buckingham, UK: SRHE and Open University Press.

Biggs, J., & Tang, C. (2007). *Teaching for quality learning at university* (3rd ed.). Maidenhead, UK: Open University Press.

Bijker, W., Hughes, T., & Pinch, T. (Eds.). (1987). Social construction of technological systems: New directions in the sociology and history of technology. Cambridge, MA: MIT Press.

Bird, L. (2007). The 3C model for networked collaborative eLearning: a tool for novice designers. *IETI, 44*(2), 153–177.

Blake, A., & Doherty, I. (2008). An instructional design course for clinical educators: First iteration design research reflections. *Journal of Learning Design, 2*(2), 104–115.

Bloom, B. S. (1984). The 2 Sigma Problem: The Search for Methods of Group Instruction as Effective as One-to-One Tutoring. *Educational Researcher, 13*(6), 4–16.

Bloom, B. S., Krathwohl, D. R., & Masia, B. B. (1964). *Taxonomy of Educational Objectives: the Classification of Educational Goals. Handbook II: Affective Domain.* New York: McKay.

Boekaerts, M. (2003). How do students from different cultures motivate themselves for academic learning? In F. Salili & R. Hoosain (Eds.) *Research on Multicultural Education and International Perspectives: Vol. 3. Teaching, learning and motivation in a multi-cultural context.* (pp. 13-31). Greenwich, CT: Information Age Publishing.

Boekaerts, M., Pintrich, P. R., & Zeidner, M. (Eds.). (2000). *Handbook of self-regulation.* San Diego: Academic Press.

Boekarts, M. (1997). Self-regulated learning: a new concept embraced by researchers, policy makers, educators, teachers and students. *Learning and Instruction, 7*, 161–186. doi:10.1016/S0959-4752(96)00015-1

Boekarts, M. (1999). Self-regulated learning: where we are today. *International Journal of Educational Research, 31*, 445–475. doi:10.1016/S0883-0355(99)00014-2

Boje, D. M. (2001). *Narrative methods for organizational and communication research.* Thousand Oaks, CA: SAGE.

Bonaiuti, G. (2007). I learning object nella prospettiva dell'eLearning 2.0. In *Atti del IV congresso Sie-l.* Macerata: EUM.

Booth, D., Edwards, P., Gordon, N. A., Khait, A., & Taylor, I. (2004). Goal orientation in mathematics education for computer scientists and engineers. In L. Price (Ed.), *Undergraduate Mathematics Teaching Conference* (pp. 73 – 82). Birmingham, UK: Birmingham University Press.

Borkowski, J. G. (1996). Metacognition: theory or chapter heading? *Learning and Individual Differences, 8*, 391–402. doi:10.1016/S1041-6080(96)90025-4

Boud, D. (1995). Assessment and Learning: Contradictory or Complementary? In P. Knight (ed.) *Assessment for Learning in Higher Education* (35-48). London: Kogan Page.

Boud, D., & Falchikov, N. (Eds.). (2007). *Rethinking Assessment in HE*. Abingdon, UK: RoutledgeFalmer.

Boud, D., & Walker, D. (1998). Promoting reflection in professional courses: the challenge of context. *Studies in HE*, *23*(2), 91–206.

Boud, D., Keogh, R., & Walker, D. (1985). *Reflection: Turning experience into learning*. London: Kogan Page.

Bouffard, T., Boisvert, J., Vezeau, C., & Larouche, C. (1995). The impact of goal orientation on self-regulation and performance among college students. *The British Journal of Educational Psychology*, *65*(3), 317–329.

Bournemouth University. (2006). *Corporate Plan 2006 – 2012*. Retrieved 18 February, 2008, from http://www.bournemouth.ac.uk/about/introduction_to_bu/corporate_plan/downloads/corporate_plan.pdf

Bowles, J. (2006). Why CEOs Are Afraid Of Social Media. *Enterprise Web 2.0*. Retrieved October 16, 2008, from http://www.enterpriseweb2.com/?p=77

Boyatzis, R. E. (1998). *Transforming Qualitative Information: Thematic Analysis and Code Development*. Thousand Oaks, CA: Sage.

Boyer, E. (1998). Reinventing Undergraduate Education: a Blueprint for America's Research Universities. *Boyer Commission on Educating Undergraduates in the Research University*. Retrieved October 10, 2008, from http://naples.cc.sunysb.edu/Pres/boyer.nsf/

Boyle, T., & Cook, J. (2001). Towards a pedagogically sound basis for learning object portability and re-use. In G. Kennedy, M. Keppell, C. McNaught & T. Petrovic (Eds.) *Meeting at the Crossroads. Proceedings of the 18th Annual Conference of the Australian Society for Computers in Learning in Tertiary Education*, (pp. 101-109). Melbourne: Biomedical Multimedia Unit, The University of Melbourne. Retrieved August 18, 2008, from http://www.ascilite.org.au/conferences/melbourne01/pdf/papers/boylet.pdf

Bradley, C., Haynes, R., Cook, J., Boyle, T., & Smith, C. (2009). *Chapter 8 Design and Development of Multimedia Learning Objects for Mobile Phones*. In M. Ally (ed). *Mobile Learning: Transforming the Delivery of Education and Training*, Athabasca University Press.

Bradley, C., Haynes, R., Smith, C., Cook, J., & Boyle, T. (2007). *Multimedia Learning Objects for Mobiles*. Mobile Learning, 5-7 July 2007, Lisbon, Portugal.

Brandes, D., & Ginnes, P. (1996). *A Guide to Student-Centred*. Oxford, UK: Basil Blackwell.

Bransford, J., Brown, A., & Cocking, R. (2000). *How people learn: Brain, mind, experience and school: Expanded edition*. Washington, DC: National Academy Press.

Brayshaw, M., & Gordon, N. A. (2008). Inquiry based learning in computer science teaching in Higher Education. *Innovations in Teaching and Learning in Information and Computer Sciences*, *7*(1), 22–33.

Brett, P. (2006). Staff using an institution-wide VLE for blended e-learning. In J. O'Donoghue (Ed.) *Technology supported learning and teaching: a staff perspective* (pp 160-175). Heshey, PA: Idea Group Publishing.

Brew, A. (2001). *The nature of research: inquiry in academic contexts*. London: Routledge Falmer.

Brew, A. (2006). *Research and teaching: beyond the divide*. London: PalgraveMacmillan.

Brew, A. (2007). Research and teaching from the students' perspective. *International policies and practices for academic enquiry: An international colloquium*, Winchester, UK, April 19–21. Retrieved November 1, 2008, from http://portal-live.solent.ac.uk/university/rtconference/2007/resources/angela_brew.pdf

Briscoe, B., Odlyzko, A., & Tilly, B. (2006). Metcalfe's Law is Wrong. *Ieee Spectrum Online*. Retrieved February 22, 2009, from http://spectrum.ieee.org/jul06/4109

British Educational Research Association (BERA). (2009). Retrieved February 21, 2009, from http://www.bera.ac.uk

Brockbank, A., & McGill, I. (2007). *Facilitating Reflective Learning in Higher Education*. Maidenhead, UK: OU Press.

Brockbank, A., McGill, I., & Beech, N. (2002). *Reflective learning in practice*. Aldershot, UK: Gower.

Brown, G., Bull, J., & Pendlebury, M. (1997). *Assessing Student Learning in Higher Education*. London: Routledge.

Brown, J. S. (2000). *New Learning Environments for the 21st Century*. Retrieved 29 October, 2008, from http://www.johnseelybrown.com/newlearning.pdf

Brown, J. S. (2006). Growing up Digital: How the Web Changes the Work, Education and the Ways People Learn. *Change, 32*, March/April. Retrieved 29 October, 2008, from http://www.johnseelybrown.com/Growing_up_digital.pdf

Brown, R. E. (2001). The process of community building in distance learning classes. *Journal of Asynchronous Learning Networks, 5*(2). Retrieved 28 October, 2008, from http://www.sloan-c.org/publications/jaln/v5n2/v5n2_brown.asp

Brown, S., & Knight, P. (1994). *Assessing learners in higher education*. London: Kogan Page.

Bruce, C. S., Edwards, S., & Lupton, M. (2006). Six frames for information literacy education [Electronic Version]. *Italics, 5*. Retrieved August 8th 2008, from http://www.ics.heacademy.ac.uk/italics/vol5-1/pdf/six-frames_final%20_1_.pdf

Bruett, K. (2006). Why American business demands twenty-first century learning: An industry perspective. *New Directions for Youth Development*, (*2006*)110, 25–30. doi:10.1002/yd.163

Bruner, J. (1996). *The Culture of Education*. Cambridge, MA: Harvard University Press.

Bruner, J. S. (2006). The course of cognitive growth. In J. S. Bruner (Ed.), *In search of pedagogy, volume 1: The selected works of Jerome S. Bruner*. (pp. 67-89). Oxford, UK: Routledge.

Brush, T., & Saye, J. (2000). Implementation and evaluation of a student-centered learning unit: A case study. *Educational Technology Research and Development, 48*(3), 79–100. doi:10.1007/BF02319859

Brusilovsky, P. (1999). Adaptive and Intelligent Technologies for Web-based Education. *Künstliche Intelligenz, 4*, 19–25.

Brusilovsky, P. (2001). Adaptive Hypermedia. *User Modelling and User-Adapted Interaction*, 11(1-2), 87-110. Hingham, MA: Kluwer Academic Publishers.

Brusilovsky, P., Schwarz, E., & Weber, G. (1996). A Tool for Developing Hypermedia-Based ITS on WWW. In *Proceedings of Workshop "Architectures and Methods for Designing Cost-Effective and Reusable ITSs" at Third International Conference on Intelligent Tutoring Systems (ITS 1996)*, Montreal, Canada.

Bryan, C., & Clegg, K. (2006). *Innovative Assessment in HE*. Abingdon, UK: Routledge.

Bull, K., & Webb, L. (2007). E-portfolio as a tool for online collaborative group research and experiences of running a whole school module on PDP. In F. Deepwell, (Ed.), *ELATE (Enhancing Learning And Teaching Environments) Conference 07 – Internationalisation Conference Proceedings* (pp 95-96). Coventry, UK: Coventry University Press.

Burden, K., & Atkinson, S. (2008). Beyond content: Developing transferable learning designs with digital video archives. In J. Luca & E. R. Weippl (Eds.), *Ed-Media 2008 World Conference on Educational Multimedia, Hypermedia & Telecommunications* (pp. 4041-4050). Chesapeake, VA: AACE.

Burden, K., & Atkinson, S. (2008). The Transformative Potential of the DiAL-e Framework: Crossing Boundaries, Pushing Frontiers. *Where are you in the digital landscape? Proceedings ascilite, Melbourne, 2008.*

Burgess, R. (2007). *Beyond the honours degree classification: Burgess Group Final Report*. Retrieved August 15, 2008 from http://www.universitiesuk.ac.uk/Publications/Bookshop/Documents/Burgess_final.pdf

Burnett, F. H. (1909). *The Secret Garden*. New York: HarperCollins.

Burr, V. (2003). *Social Constructionism* (2nd Ed.). London: Routledge.

Cade, A. (2008) *Employable graduates for responsible employers*. Report to the Higher Education Academy Education for Sustainable Development. Retrieved February 2009, from http://www.heacademy.ac.uk/projects/detail/esd_employable_graduates

Calvani, A. (2005). Rete, comunità e conoscenza. *Costruire e gestire dinamiche collaborative*. Trento: Erickson.

Calvani, A., & Rotta, M. (2000). *Fare formazione in internet*. Trento: Erickson.

Calvani, A., Buonaiuti, G., Fini, A. & Ranieri, M. (2007). I Personal Learning Environment: una chiave di volta per il Lifelong Learning? *Atti del IV congresso* Sie-l. Macerata: EUM.

Cameron, L. (2003). *Metaphor in educational discourse*. London: Continuum.

Campbell, R. J., Robinson, W., Neelands, J., Hewston, R., & Mazzoli, L. (2007). Personalised learning: ambiguities in theory and practice. *British Journal of Educational Studies*, 55(2), 135–154. doi:10.1111/j.1467-8527.2007.00370.x

CareStandards (2000). Retrieved October 1, 2008 from Office of Public Sector Information http://www.opsi.gov.uk/acts/acts2000/ukpga_20000014_en_1

Caruso, J. B., & Salaway, G. (2007). *The ECAR Study of Undergraduate Students and Information Technology*. Boulder, CO: EDUCAUSE.

Castells, M. (2000). *The rise of the network society*. Oxford: Blackwell.

Catarsi, C. (2007). La formazione di terza generazione: necessaria rifinitura di un paradigma". In A. Alberici (Ed.), *Adulti e Università. Sfide ed innovazioni nella formazione universitaria e continua*. Milano, Italy: Franco Angeli.

Center for Support of Teaching and Learning. (2008). *Reflective practice*. Retrieved 13th September, 2008, from http://cstl.syr.edu/cstl2/home/Teaching%20Support/Teaching%20Practice/141000.htm

CETIS. (2008). *Portfolio interoperability prototyping*. Retrieved November 13, 2008, from http://wiki.cetis.ac.uk/Portfolio_interoperability_prototyping

Chappell, C., Rhodes, C., et al. (2003). *Reconstructing the Life Long learner: Pedagogy and identity in individual, organisational and social change*. London, RoutledgeFalmer.

Chatti, M. A., Jarke, M., & Frosch-Wilke, D. (2007). The future of e-learning: a shift to knowledge networking and social software. *International Journal of Knowledge and Learning*, 3(4/5), 404–420. doi:10.1504/IJKL.2007.016702

Chen, N-S., Ko, H-C., & Kinshuk, L, T. (2005). A model for synchronous learning using the internet. *Innovations in Education and Teaching International*, 42(2), 181–194. doi:10.1080/14703290500062599

Cheng, Y. C., & Tam, M. M. (1997). Multi-models of quality in education. *Quality Assurance in Education*, 5, 22–31. doi:10.1108/09684889710156558

Cheyne, J. A. (1989). *Serious Play from Peregrination to Cultural Change: A Bateson-Gadamer-Harris Hypothesis.* [online]. Retrieved January 23rd, 2007 from http://watarts.uwaterloo.ca/~acheyne/Misc/SeriousPlay.html

Chickering, A., & Ehrmann, S. C. (1996). Implementing the seven principles: technology as lever. *AAHE Bulletin*, October, 3-6. Retrieved January 7, 2008, from http://www.tltgroup.org/programs/seven.html

Clarke, C. (2003). *The future of higher education*. White Paper, HMSO.

Clarke, J., Dede, C., Ketelhut, D. J., & Nelson, B. (2006). A design based research strategy to promote scalability for educational innovations. *Educational Technology*, 46(3), 27–36.

Claxton, G. (1998). *Hare Brain, Tortoise Mind*. London: Fourth Estate.

Claxton, G. (1999). *Wise-Up*. London: Bloomsbury.

Coates, H. (2005). Leveraging LMSs to enhance campus-based student engagement. *EDUCAUSE Quarterly*, 1, 66–68.

Cochrane, T. (2007, October 16-19). Moving mobile mainstream: Using communities of practice to develop educational technology literacy in tertiary academics. Paper presented at the MLearn 2007 - Making the Connections 6th International Conference on Mobile Learning, Melbourne.

Cochrane, T. (2008, October 8-10). Designing mobile learning environments: Mobile trials at unitec 2008. Paper presented at the MLearn08: The bridge from text to context, University of Wolverhampton, School of Computing and IT.

Cochrane, T. (2008, December 1 - 4). Mobile web 2.0 the new frontier. Paper presented at the ASCILITE 2008, Deakin University, Melbourne, Australia.

Cochrane, T., & Bateman, R. (2009). Transforming pedagogy using mobile web 2.0, IADIS International Conference on Mobile Learning 2009. Barcelona, Spain.

Cochrane, T., & Kligyte, G. (2007, June 11-14). Dummies2delight: Using communities of practice to develop educational technology literacy in tertiary academics. Paper presented at the JISC online conference: Innovating eLearning, JISC online conference.

Colapietro, V. (2007). Studenti adulti all'università: il peso dell'esperienza. In A. Alberici (Ed.), *Adulti e Università. Sfide ed innovazioni nella formazione universitaria e continua*. Milano, Italy: Franco Angeli.

Cole, M. (2005). Putting Culture in the middle. In H. Daniels, (ed). *An Introduction to Vygotsky*, (2nd Ed.). Routledge: London.

Cole, R. (2008). Review of "Bad for Democracy," by Professor Dana D. Nelson. *Midwest Populist America*. Retrieved October 18, 2008, from http://www.midwest-populistamerica.com/articles/review-of-bad-for-democracy-by-professor-dana-d-nelson

Collins, A., Joseph, D., & Bielaczyc, K. (2004). Design research: Theoretical and methodological issues. *Journal of the Learning Sciences*, 13(1), 15–42. doi:10.1207/s15327809jls1301_2

Collis, B. (1998). New didactics for university instruction: Why and how. *Computers & Education*, 31(4), 373–395. doi:10.1016/S0360-1315(98)00040-2

Collis, B., & Moonen, J. (2001). *Flexible learning in a digital world: Experiences and expectations*. Kogan Page: London.

Colvin Clark, R., & Kwinn, A. (2007). *The New Virtual Classroom: Evidence-based Guidelines for Synchronous e-Learning*. San Francisco, CA: Pfeiffer.

CONEL. (2008). *3 Year Development Plan for Transforming E-Learning at CONEL*. London: CONEL.

Confederation Of British Industry. (2008). *CBI Launches New Higher Education Task Force*. Retrieved 28 October, 2008, from http://www.cbi.org.uk/ndbs/press.nsf/0363c1f07c6ca12a8025671c00381cc7/3f109c6775f30aec802574c6003a51ce?OpenDocument

Conlan, O., Hockemeyer, C., Wade, V., & Albert, D. (2002). Metadata Driven Approaches to Facilitate Adaptivity in Personalized eLearning systems. *Journal of Information Systems Education*, 1, 38–44.

Conole, G. (2005, December). *Designing for effective e-learning - feeding pedagogical research into practice*. Paper presented at the Higher Education Academy E-Learning symposium: pedagogy and practice, University of Southampton, Southampton, UK.

Conole, G. (2008). Listening to the learner voice: The ever changing landscape of technology use for language students. *ReCALL*, 20(2), 121–140. doi:10.1017/S0958344008000220

Conole, G. (2008). New schemas for mapping pedagogies and technologies. [Retrieved from http://www.ariadne.ac.uk/]. *Ariadne*, (July): 2008.

Conole, G. (forthcoming). Stepping over the edge: the implications of new technologies for education. In M. Lee & C. McLouglin (eds), *Web 2.0-based e-learning: applying social informatics for tertiary teaching*. Hershey, PA: ICI Global.

Conole, G. (forthcoming). Using Compendium as a tool to support the design of learning activities. In A. Okada,

S. Buckingham Shum, & T. Sherborne (Eds.), *Knowledge Cartography – software tools and mapping techniques.* Retrieved December 14, 2007, from http://kmi.open.ac.uk/projects/kc-book

Conole, G., de Laat, M., Dillon, T., & Darby, J. (2006). *JISC LXP: Student experiences of technology.* Draft final report. Retrieved February 25, 2009 from http://jisc.ac.uk/media/documents/programmes/elearningpedagogy/lxp_project_final_report_nov_06.pdf

Conole, G., de Laat, M., Dillon, T., & Darby, J. (2006). *LXP: Student experience of technologies.* Bristol, UK: Joint Information Systems Committee. Retrieved 28 October, 2008, from http://www.jisc.ac.uk/whatwedo/programmes/elearning_pedagogy/elp_learneroutcomes.aspx

Conole, G., De Laat, M., Dillon, T., & Darby, J. (2008, February). 'Disruptive technologies', 'pedagogical innovation': What's new? Findings from an in-depth study of students' use and perception of technology.' *Computers & Education, 50*(2), 511–524. doi:10.1016/j.compedu.2007.09.009

Cook, J. (2009). *The Digitally Literate Learner and the Appropriation of New Technologies and Media for Education.* Inaugural Lecture, Learning Technology Research Institute, London Metropolitan University, 3 February 2009. Retrieved February 4, 2009, from http://www.slideshare.net/johnnigelcook

Cook, J., Pachler, N., & Bradley, C. (2008). Bridging the Gap? Mobile Phones at the Interface between Informal and Formal Learning. *Journal of the Research Center for Educational Technology,* Spring. Retrieved September 23, 2008, from: http://www.rcetj.org/?type=ci&id

Cooren, F. (2000). *The organizing property of communication.* Amsterdam: John Benjamins.

Corner, F. (2002). What to teach? Qualitative research into fine art undergraduate programmes. In *Enhancing curricula: Exploring effective curricula practices in art, design and communication.* (pp. 144-160). Retrieved October 18, 2008, from http://www.arts.ac.uk/docs/cltad_2002corner.pdf

Coryell, E., & Chlup, T. (2007). Implementing E-Learning Components with Adult English Language Learners: Vital Factors Learned. *Computer Assisted Language Learning, 20*(3), 263–278. doi:10.1080/09588220701489333

Courtney, K., & Deane, M. (2006). Collaborating to Strengthen Students' Writing Skills. *Impressions: Newsletter of the Centre for the Study of Higher Education (CSHE), 1*(15). Coventry, UK: Coventry University. Retrieved November 5, 2008 from http://www.corporate.coventry.ac.uk/content/1/c6/01/49/14/CSHE%20Newsletter.pdf

Cousin, G. (2009). *Researching Learning in Higher Education: An Introduction to Contemporary Methods and Approaches.* London: Routledge.

Cowan, J. (2006), *On Becoming an Innovative University Teacher, 2nd Ed.* Maidenhead, UK: OU Press.

Cramb, M. (2008, July). *ESOL for Work Final Report.* Evaluation report submitted to CONEL, London.

Creanor, L., Trinder, K., Gowan, D., & Howells, C. (2006). *LEX: The Learner Experience of eLearning – Final project report.* Retrieved September 16, 2008, from http://www.jisc.ac.uk/elp_learneroutcomes

Creative Commons. (2002). Licenses Explained. Retrieved from http://creativecommons.org/learn/licenses/

Croker, K. (2008). Giving Feedback via audio files. *HEA Assessment SIG 5th June 2008 Meeting,* York, UK

Cross, J. (2008). From Content to Context. In V. Hornung-Prahauser, M. Luckman, & M. Kalz (Ed.). *Selbstorganisiertes Lernen im Internet – Edumedia Proceeding.* Retrieved October 29, 2008, from http://edumedia.salzburgresearch.at/images/stories/4_EduMedia_Konferenz/Praesentationen/edumedia_proceeding.pdf

Cross, P. (1981). *Adults as Learners: Increasing Participation in Lifelong Learning.* San Francisco, CA: Jossey-Bass Publishers.

Cusmai, M. (2007). L'allestimento di ambienti di apprendimento costruttivisti nella formazione blended. *Formazione e Cambiamento, 7*(48). Retrieved December 10, 2007, from http://db.formez.it/ArchivioNews.nsf/F&C

Czarniawska, B. (1997). *Narrating the organization: Dramas of institutional identity.* Chicago: University of Chicago Press.

Dabbagh, N., & Kitsantas, A. (2004). Supporting Self-Regulation in Student-Centered Web-Based Learning Environments. *International Journal on E-Learning, 3*(1), 40–47.

Dagdilelis, V. (2005). Integrating ICT in universities: Some actual problems and solutions. In S. Mishra & C. Ramesh (Eds.) *Interactive multimedia in education and training* (pp. 113–134). Hershey, PA: IGI Global.

Dalrymple, R., & Smith, P. (2008). The Patchwork Text: enabling discursive writing and reflective practice on a foundation module in work-based learning. *IETI, 45*(1), 47–54.

Daniel, J. S. (1996). *The mega-universities and knowledge media: technology strategies for higher education.* London: Kogan Page.

Davies, G. (2005). *Computer Assisted Language Learning: Where are we now and where are we going?* Retrieved March 11, 2007 http://www.camsoftpartners.co.uk/docs/UCALL_Keynote.htm#_Toc142650261

Davis, W., & Fulton, J. (1997). The Effects of professors' feedback on the growth of students' overall writing quality in two college freshman English courses. *EDRS Research Report.* Retrieved June 24, 2008, from http://www.eric.ed.gov/ERICDocs/data/ericdocs2sql/content_storage_01/0000019b/80/15/17/cb.pdf

DCSF. (2008). *Personalised Learning: a practical guide.* HMSO.

De Bra, P. (1997). Teaching through adaptive hypertext on the WWW. *International Journal of Educational Telecommunications, 3*, 163–180.

De Bra, P., Brusilovsky, P., & Houben, G.-J. (1999). Adaptive hypermedia: From systems to framework. *ACM Computing Surveys, 31*(4). doi:10.1145/345966.345996

Dearing, R. (1997). *Higher Education in the learning society.* London: Stationery Office.

Dede, C. (2007). Introduction: A Sea Change in Thinking, Knowing, Learning and Teaching. In G. Salaway., & J. Borreson Caruso (Eds.), *The ECAR Study of Undergraduate Students and Information Technology. ECAR: USA.* (pp. 19-26). Retrieved June 28, 2008, from http://net.educause.edu/ir/library/pdf/ers0706/rs/ers0706w.pdf

Delanty, G. (2001). *Challenging Knowledge: The University in the Knowledge Society.* Buckingham, UK: SRHE/OUP.

Delgado, D. (2007). *My Personal Learning Environment (PLE)* [blog posting]. Retrieved from http://eduspaces.net/davidds/weblog/193197.html

Demetrio, D. (2002). Cittadini in formazione. In Baratelli M. et al (Ed.), *F.A.Re. Formazione con gli adulti. Esperienze a confronto.* Milano: Franco Angeli.

Department for Children. Schools and Families. '*Every Child Matters*' on http://www.everychildmatters.gov.uk/ete/ retrieved November 21st 2008

Department for Education and Skills. (2004). *A national conversation about personalised learning.* Retrieved June 10, 2008, from http://www.innovation-unit.co.uk/images/stories/files/pdf/PersonalisedLearningBooklet.pdf

Department for Education and Skills. (2005). *Harnessing technology: Transforming learning and children's services.* Retrieved June 25, 2008, from http://www.dfes.gov.uk/publications/e-strategy/docs/e-strategy.pdf

Department for Education and Skills. (2006). *2020 Vision: Report of the teaching and learning in 2020 review group.* Retrieved September 19, 2008, from http://www.teachernet.gov.uk/_doc/10783/6856_DfES_Teaching_and_Learning.pdf

Department of Health. (2002). *Requirements for Social Work Training.* Retrieved October 1, 2008 from Department of Health http://www.dh.gov.uk/en/PublicationsandstatisticsPublications/PublicationsPolicyAndGuidance/DH_4007803

DfES. (2005). *Harnessing Technology Transforming Learning and Children's Services*. Retrieved March 19, 2007, http://www.dfes.gov.uk/publications/e-strategy/docs/e-strategy.pdf

DfES. (2006). *Personalising further education, developing a vision*. Department for Education and Skills white paper. Retrieved February 8, 2009 from http://www.dcsf.gov.uk/consultations/downloadableDocs/DfES%20Personalisation.pdf

DfES. (2006). *Education: Raising Skills, Improving Life Chances*. Retrieved January 8, 2008, from http://www.official-documents.gov.uk/document/cm67/6768/6768.pdf

DfES. (2006). *Personalising Further Education: Developing a Vision*. Retrieved February 20, 2008, from http://www.dfes.gov.uk/consultations/downloadableDocs/DfES%20Personalisation.pdf

DfES. (2006). *Five Year Strategy for Children and Learners: Putting people at the heart of public services*. Retrieved January 10, 2008, from http://www.dfes.gov.uk/publications/5yearstrategy/docs/DfES5Yearstrategy.pdf

DfES. (Department for Children, Schools and Families), (2008). *About Personalised Learning*. Retrieved October 1, 2008, from http://www.standards.dfes.gov.uk/personalisedlearning/about/

DiBiase, D. (with Zembal-Saul, C., Melander, G., Sabre, J., Schall, J., Howard, D., Spielvogel, E., Rademacher, H., Mathews, J., Burlingame, P., & Orndorff, R.). (2002). *Using ePortfolios at Penn State to enhance student learning. Status, prospects, and strategies*. College Park, PA: Education Institute, The Pennsylvania State University. Retrieved June 24, 2006, from: https://www.e-education.psu.portfolios/e-port_report.shtml

Dillenbourg, P. (1999). What do you mean by collaborative learning? In P. Dillenbourg (Ed) *Collaborative-learning: Cognitive and Computational Approaches* (pp.1-19). Oxford, UK: Elsevier.

Dillenbourg, P., Baker, M., Blaye, A., & O'Malley, C. (1995). The evolution of research on collaborative learn-

ing. In E. Spada & P. Reimann (eds.), *Learning in Humans and Machine: Towards an interdisciplinary learning science* (pp. 189-211). Oxford: Elsevier.

Dillenbourg, P., Baker, M., Blaye, A., & O'Malley, C. (1996). The evolution of research on collaborative learning. In E. Spada & P. Reiman (Eds) *Learning in Humans and Machine: Towards an interdisciplinary learning science* (pp. 189-211). Oxford, UK: Elsevier.

DIUS. (2008). *Adult Learning – Shaping the Way Ahead*. London: DIUS. Retrieved 28 October, 2008, from http://www.adultlearningconsultation.org.uk/userfiles/DIUS_adu_lea_bro_an_05.8.pdf

Dodgson, M., Gann, D., & Salter, A. (2005). *Think, Play, Do: Technology, Innovation, and Organization*. Oxford, UK: Oxford University Press.

Doherty, I., & Blake, A. (2007). Teaching instructional design principles to clinical educators: A design research approach. In C. Montgomerie & J. Seale (Eds.), *Ed-Media 2007 World Conference on Educational Multimedia, Hypermedia and Telecommunications* (pp. 2799-2804). Chesapeake, VA: AACE.

Donaghy, M., & Morss, K. (2007). An evaluation of a framework for facilitating and assessing physiotherapy students' reflection on practice. *Physiotherapy Theory and Practice*, *23*(2), 83–94. doi:10.1080/09593980701211952

Donnelly, R., & O'Rourke, K. C. (2007). What now? Evaluating eLearning CPD practice in Irish third-level education. *Journal of Further and Higher Education*, *31*(1), 31–40. doi:10.1080/03098770601167864

Downes, S. (2005). ELearning 2.0. *eLearn Magazine*, October 17, 2005. Retrieved September 23, 2008 from http://elearnmag.org/subpage.cfm?section=articles&article=29-1

Downes, S. (2006). Learning Networks and Connective Knowledge. *eLearn Magazine*, October 16, 2006. Retrieved September 23, 2008 from http://it.coe.uga.edu/itforum/paper92/paper92.html

Driscoll, M. P. (1994). *Psychology of learning for instruction*. Boston: Allyn and Bacon.

Dron, J. (2006). *Control and Constraint in ELearning: Choosing When to Choose*. Hershey, PA: IGI Global.

Ducates, C., & Lomicka, L. (2008). Adventures in the blogosphere: from blog readers to blog writers. *Computer Assisted Language Learning, 21*(1), 9–28. doi:10.1080/09588220701865474

ECAR. (2007). The ECAR study of undergraduate students and Information Technology. *Educause report, 6*. Retrieved from http://connect.educause.edu/library/abstract/TheECARStudyofUnderg/45075

Edinburgh University. (2007). *Guidelines for Using External Web 2.0 Services*. Retrieved November 13, 2008, from http://www.vp.is.ed.ac.uk/content/1/c4/12/45/GuidelinesForUsingExternalWeb2.0Services-20070823.pdf

Educational Development Services (EDS). (2008). Retrieved October 29, 2008, from http://www.bournemouth.ac.uk/eds/

Eijkman, H. (2008). Web 2.0 as a non-foundational network-centric learning space. *Campus-Wide Information Systems, 25*(2), 93–104. doi:10.1108/10650740810866567

Ellis, R. (1999). *Learning a second language through interaction*. Amsterdam: John Benjamins Publishing Company.

Ellison, N. B., Steinfield, C., & Lampe, C. (2007). The benefits of Facebook "friends:" Social capital and college students' use of online social network sites. *Journal of Computer-Mediated Communication, 12*, 1143–1168. doi:10.1111/j.1083-6101.2007.00367.x

Elton, L. (1996). Strategies to enhance Student motivation: A conceptual analysis. *Studies in Higher Education, 21*, 57–68. doi:10.1080/03075079612331381457

Elvers, G., Polzella, D., & Graetz, K. (2003). Procrastination in online courses: Performance and attitudinal differences. *Teaching of Psychology, 30*(2), 159–162. doi:10.1207/S15328023TOP3002_13

Ende, J. (1983). Feedback in clinical medical education. *Journal of the American Medical Association, 250*(6), 777–781. doi:10.1001/jama.250.6.777

Eraut, M. (1994). *Developing Professional Knowledge and Competence*. Abingdon, UK: The Falmer Press

Eraut, M., Alderton, J., Cole, C., & Senker, P. (1998). Learning from other people at work. In R. Harrison, F. Reeve, M. Cartwright, & R. Edwards. 2002 *Supporting Lifelong learning* (Vol. 1, pp. 127-145). Abingdon, UK: OUP / Routledge Falmer.

eRes, Innovative eLearning with e-Resources, (2008). Retrieved October 29, 2008, from http://www.bournemouth.ac.uk/eds/eres/

Eskow, S., & Trevitte, C. (2007). Reschooling Society and the Promise of e e-Learning: An Interview with Steve Eskow. *Innovate, 3*(6). Retrieved June 9, 2008 from http://www.innovateonline.info/index.php?view=article&id=502

European Commission. (2002). *European Report on Quality Indicators of Lifelong Learning*. Brussels: European Commission.

European Commission. (2008). *An updated strategic framework for European cooperation in education and training*. Communication from the Commission to the European Parliament, the Council, the European Economic and Social Committee and the Committee of the Regions. Retrieved February 8, 2009 from http://ec.europa.eu/education/lifelong-learning-policy/doc28_en.htm

Evans, M. (2005). *Killing Thinking: The Death of the Universities*. London: Continuum International Publishing Group Ltd.

Ewins, R. (2005). Who are you? Weblogs and Academic Identity. *Journal of E-Learning, 2*(4).

Facebook (n.d.). Retrieved from http://en-gb.facebook.com/

Ferdig, R., & Trammel, K. (2004). Content Delivery in the 'Blogosphere.' *T.H.E. Journal*, Feb 2004. Retrieved June 8, 2008 from http://www.thejournal.com/articles/16626/

Fiaidhi, J., & Mohammed, S. (2004). Design issues involved in using Learning Objects for Teaching a Programming Language within a Collaborative eLearning Environment. *International Journal of Instructional Technology and Distance Learning, 1*(3), 39–54. http://www.itdl.org/Journal/Mar_04/March-04.pdf Retrieved October 29th, 2008.

Field, S. (2006). *Personalised learning.* The Teacher Training Resource Bank. Retrieved October 6, 2008, from http://www.ttrb.ac.uk/viewarticle2.aspx?contentId=12406

Fini, A. (2008). ELearning 2.0. A case study on a growing community. *Journal of eLearning and Knowledge Society, 4*(3), 167 - 175.

Fini, A., & Vanni, L. (2004), Learning Objects e metadati. *I quaderni di Form@re*, n. 2. Trento: Erickson.

Fiocco, M. (2005). *'Glonacal' Contexts: Internationalisation Policy in the Australian Higher Education Sector and the Development of Pathway Programs.* Digital PhD, Murdoch University, Australia. Retrieved October 10, 2008 from https://wwwlib.murdoch.edu.au/adt/browse/view/adt-MU20060502.154739?PrintFriendly=1

Fisher, W. R. (1987). *Human communication as narration: Toward a philosophy of reason, value, and action.* Columbia, SC: University of South Carolina Press.

Fook, J., & Gardner, F. (2007). *Practising critical reflection: A resource handbook.* Maidenhead, UK: Open University Press.

Foucault, M. (1995). *Discipline and Punish.* New York: Vintage.

France, D., & Ribchester, C. (2008). Podcasts and feedback. In Salmon, G., & Edirisingha, P. (Eds.), *Podcasting for learning in universities.* Maidenhead, UK: Society for Research into Higher Education/Open University Press

Franklin, T., & van Harmelen, M. (2007). *Web 2.0 for content for learning and teaching in higher education.* Bristol, UK: Joint Information Systems Committee. Retrieved 28 October, 2008, from http://www.jisc.ac.uk/media/documents/programmes/digitalrepositories/web2-content-learning-and-teaching.pdf

Fraser, B. J. (1998). Science learning environments: Assessment, effects and determinants. In B.J. Fraser & K.G. Tobin (Eds.) *The international handbook of science education* (pp. 527-564). Dordrecht, The Netherlands: Kluwer.

Fraser, J. (2006). *Personalisation: customisation – is it enough?* Entry posted to EdTechUK, archived at http://fraser.typepad.com/edtechuk/2006/10/personalisation.html

Fraser, J. (2006, October 12th). *Personalisation: customization - is it enough* [blog post]. Retrieved February 8, 2009 from http://fraser.typepad.com/edtechuk/2006/10/personalisation.html

Fredriksson, U., & Hoskins, B. (2007). The development of learning to learn in a European context. *Curriculum Journal, 18*(2), 127–134. doi:10.1080/09585170701445921

Friedman Ben David, M., Davis, M. H., Harden, R. M., Howie, P. W., Ker, J., & Pippard, M. J. (2001). AMEE medical education guide no.24: Portfolios as a method of student assessment. *Medical Teacher, 23*(6), 535-551. Retrieved October 18, 2007, from http://dx.doi.org/10.1080/01421590120090952

Frigo, F. (1993). La formazione per le Piccole Imprese: le condizioni per lo sviluppo. Ruolo degli organismi e fabbisogni dei formatori. *Osservatorio ISFOL, 5,* 15–23.

Frigo, F. (2000). *La formazione continua in Italia: l'esperienza della legge 236/93.* Milano, Italy: Franco Angeli.

Funk, K. (2004). Brief or new: student learning portfolios: Balancing tradition with innovation. *Occupational Therapy in Health Care, 18*(1), 99–105. doi:10.1300/J003v18n01_10

Gaballo, V. (2007). Web 2.0 Educational eLearning and knowledge management in higher education. *Atti del IV congresso* Sie-l. Macerata, Italy: EUM.

Gabriel, Y. (2000). *Storytelling in organizations.* Oxford, UK: Oxford University Press.

Galusha, J. (1997). Barriers to learning in distance education. *Interpersonal Computing and Technology, 5*(4), 6–14. Retrieved 28 October, 2008, from http://www.emoderators.com/ipct-j/1997/n4/galusha.html

Gangadharbatla, H. (2008). Facebook me: Collective self-esteem, need to belong, and internet self-efficacy as predictors of the iGeneration's attitudes toward social networking sites. *Journal of Interactive Advertising, 8*(2). Retrieved 28 October, 2008, from http://www.jiad.org/article100

Gannon-Leary, P., & Fontainha, E. (2007). Communities of Practice and virtual learning communities: benefits, barriers and success factors. *eLearning Papers, 5*, September 2007. Retrieved October 16, 2008 from http://www.elearningeuropa.info

Gardner, H. (1983). *Frames of mind: The theory of multiple intelligences.* New York: Basic Books.

Gardner, H. (1993). *Multiple Intelligences.* New York: Basic Books.

Garrison, D. R., & Anderson, T. (2003). *E–Learning in the 21st century: A framework for research and practice.* London, UK: Routledge/Falmer.

Gauntlett, D. (2007). *Creative Explorations. New Approaches to Identities and Audiences.* London: Routledge.

Gauntlett, D., & Holzwarth, P. (2006). Creative and visual methods for exploring identities. *Visual Studies, 21*(01), 82–91. doi:10.1080/14725860600613261

Gebhard, J. (2005). Teacher Development through Exploration: Principles, Ways, and Examples. *TESL-EJ, 9*(2), 1-15. Retrieved June 28, 2008, from http://web.icu.ac.jp/lrb/vol_22/Kota%20LRB%20V22.pdf

Gee, J. (1996). *Social Linguistics and Literacies: Ideology in Discourses,* (2nd Ed.). London: Taylor & Francis.

Gee, J. P. (2003). *What Video Games Have to Teach Us About Learning and Literacy.* New York: Palgrave Macmillan.

Gibbons, H. S., & Wentworth, G. P. (2001). Andrological and Pedagogical Training Differences for Online Instructors. *Online Journal of Distance Learning Administration, 4*(3). Retrieved 28 October, 2008, from http://www.westga.edu/~distance/ojdla/fall43/gibbons_wentworth43.html

Gibbs, G. (1995). *Assessing Student Centred Courses.* Oxford, UK: Oxford Centre for Staff Learning and Development.

Gibbs, G., & Simpson, C. (2003). Measuring the response of students to assessment: the Assessment Experience Questionnaire. In [*th International Symposium Improving Students Learning: Theory, Research and Scholarship,* Hinckley, UK. Oxford, UK: Alden Press.]. *Proceedings of the, 2003*, 11.

Gibbs, G., & Simpson, C. (2004). Conditions under which assessment supports students' learning. *Learning and teaching in higher education, 1*, 3–31. Retrieved June 5, 2005, from http://www.glos.ac.uk/departments/clt/lathe/issue1/index.cfm

Giddens, A. (1990). *The Consequences of Modernity.* Cambridge, UK: Polity/Blackwell.

Giddens, A. (2000). *Runaway World: How Globalization is Reshaping Our Lives.* New York: Routledge.

Gilbert, C. (2006). *2020 Vision: Report of the teaching and learning in 2020 review group.* Nottingham, UK: Department for Education and Skills.

Giles, J. (2005, December 15). Special Report Internet encyclopaedias go head to head. *Nature, 438*, 900–901. doi:10.1038/438900a

Gillani, B. (2003). *Learning theories and the design of e-learning environments.* Lanham, MA: University Press of America Inc.

Giovannella, C. (2008). Learning 2.0? *Atti del V congresso Sie-l.* Macerata, Italy: EUM.

Glaser, B. G., & Strauss, A. (1967). Discovery of Grounded Theory. *Strategies for Qualitative Research.* Chicago: Aldine.

Goldin, S. (2008). Quoted in Technorati (2008) *State of the Blogosphere / 2008*. Retrieved Sept 18 2008 from http://technorati.com/blogging/state-of-the-blogosphere/

Goodfellow, R., & Lea, M. R. (2007). *Challenging E-learning in the University: a literacies perspective*. London: SRHE / OUP.

Goodyear, P. (2005). Educational design and networked learning: Patterns, pattern languages and design practice. *Australasian Journal of Educational Technology*, *21*(1), 82–101.

Goodyear, P. (2006). Technology and the articulation of vocational and academic interests: reflections on time space and e-learning. *Studies in Continuing Education*, *28*(2), 83–89. doi:10.1080/01580370600750973

Goodyear, P. M. (2001). Psychological foundations for networked learning. In C. Steeples & C. Jones (Eds.). *Networked learning: Perspectives and issues,* (pp 49-75). Berlin: Springer Verlag.

Gordon, N. A. (2005). Experiences of embedding information technology into discipline based teaching. *Innovations in Teaching and Learning in Information and Computer Sciences*, *4*, 1–9.

Gordon, N. A. (2005). The use of diagnostic software in teaching a mathematics module for computer science students. In H. Steed & U. O'Reilly (Eds), *Annual Conference of the Subject Centre for Information and Computer Sciences* (pp. 34 – 38). Ulster, UK: Higher Education Academy Subject Centre for Information and Computer Sciences.

Gordon, N. A. (2007). Issues in teaching IT within H.E. computing courses. In H. White (Ed.), *Annual Conference of the Subject Centre for Information and Computer Sciences* (pp. 131-134). Ulster, UK: Higher Education Academy Subject Centre for Information and Computer Sciences.

Gordon, N. A. (2008). Group work in Higher Education computing courses. In H. White (Ed.), *Annual Conference of the Subject Centre for Information and Computer Sciences* (pp. 35-39). Ulster, UK: Higher Education Academy Subject Centre for Information and Computer Sciences.

Grabinger, R. S., & Dunlop, J. C. (1996). Rich environments for active learning. *Association for Learning Technology Journal*, *3*(2), 5–34.

Graham, B. (1999). *Must See HTTP:// Sept 10, 1999*. Retrieved Feb 16 2009, http://www.bradlands.com/weblog/comments/september_10_1999/

Grant, P. (2006). Examining your practice: feedback as part of assessment. *National Middle School Association . Middle Ground*, *9*(3), 18–20.

Granter, B. (2008). Student Personal Learning and Social Homepages. *University of Sussex website*. Retrieved October 26, 2008, from http://sussex.ac.uk/splash

Greaves, L. (2006). *Developing Student Academic Competence: an investigation of curriculum designed to support progression and achievement*. TQEF Funded Project, Thames Valley University.

Greaves, L. (2007). Developing Student Academic Competence: the successes. *Faculty of Professional Studies Learning and Teaching Journal*, 4.

Greaves, L., & Hadzic, V. (2007). *Developing Student Academic Competence: a longitudinal investigation progression and achievement*. TQEF Funded Project, Thames Valley University.

Greaves, L., Bradley, C., & Cook, J. (2008). A Blended Learning Design to Support Student Learning. In *Proceedings of World Conference on Educational Multimedia, Hypermedia and Telecommunications* 2008 (pp. 4643-4651). Chesapeake, VA: AACE.

Green, H., Facer, K., Rudd, T., Dillon, P., & Humphreys, T. (2005). *Personalisation and digital technologies*. Bristol, UK: Futurelab. Retrieved February 5, 2009 from http://www.futurelab.org.uk/resources/documents/opening_education/Personalisation_report.pdf

Greene, J. (2002). Mixed-method evaluation: a way of democratically engaging with difference. *Evaluation Journal of Australasia*, *2*(2), 23–29.

Griffin, G., Coates, H., McInnis, C., & James, J. (2003). The development of an extended course experience questionnaire. *Quality in Higher Education*, *9*(3), 259–266. doi:10.1080/135383203200015111

Grimaldi, A., & Quaglino, G. P. (Eds.). (2004). *Tra orientamento e auto-orientamento tra formazione e autoformazione*. Roma: ISFOL

Grohmann, G., Kraemer, W., Milius, F., & Zimmermann, V. (2007). Modellbasiertes Curriculum-Design für Learning Management Systeme: Ein Integrationsansatz auf Basis von ARIS und IMS Learning Design. In A. Oberweis, et al. (Eds.), *Tagungsband 8. Internationale Konferenz Wirtschaftsinformatik "eOrganisation: Service-, Process-, Market Engineering"* (pp. 795-812). Karlsruhe, Germany.

Guldberg, H. (2004, July 21st). *Class divisions – who benefits from the 'personalised learning' strategy of dividing school pupils into sub-sets?* [blog posting]. Retrieved from http://www.spiked-online.co.uk/Articles/0000000CA60E.htm

Hall, C., Hall, E., & Cooper, L. (2007). A socio-emotional approach to building communities of learners online. In H. Spencer-Oatey (Ed.), *e-Learning initiatives in China: pedagogy, policy and culture* (pp. 79-93). Hong Kong: Hong Kong University Press.

Hall, G. E., & Hord, S. M. (2001). *Implementing Change: Patterns, principles and potholes*. Needham Heights, MA: Allyn & Bacon.

Hall, R. (in press, 2009). Towards a fusion of formal and informal learning environments: the impact of the read/write web. *Electronic Journal of eLearning*.

Hambleton, I. R., Foster, W. H., & Richardson, J. T. (1998). Improving student learning using the personalised system of instruction. *Higher Education*, *35*, 187–203. doi:10.1023/A:1003031601307

Hannafin, M. J., & Land, S. M. (1997). The foundations and assumptions of technology-enhanced student-centered learning environments. *Instructional Science*, *25*, 167–202. doi:10.1023/A:1002997414652

Hargreaves, D. (2008). *Personalising learning*. Retrieved October 28, 2008, from http://www.ssat-inet.net/whatwedo/personalisinglearning.aspx

Harper, B., Hedberg, J., & Wright, R. (2000). Who benefits from virtuality? *Computers & Education*, *34*(3-4), 163–176. doi:10.1016/S0360-1315(99)00043-3

Hartley, J., & Chesworth, K. (2000). Qualitative and quantitative methods in research on essay writing: no one way. *Journal of Further and Higher Education*, *24*, 15–24. doi:10.1080/030987700112282

Hartley, P. (2007). New technology and the modern university. In *Next Generation Environments, JISC*. Retrieved November 9, from http://www.jisc.ac.uk/media/documents/events/2007/04/next_gen_keynote.ppt

Harvey, L., & Knight, P. (1996). *Transforming Higher Education*. Buckingham, UK: SRHE/Open University Press.

Hauk, S. (2003). Understanding entering students via mathematical autobiography. Committee on the Undergraduate Program in Mathematics (Eds.), *Undergraduate Programs and Courses in the Mathematical Sciences* (pp. 79). Washington, DC: Mathematical Association of America.

HE Academy, (2006, February). *The UK Professional Standards Framework*. HEFCE, UUK.

HEA. Higher Education Academy, (2008). *ELearning Benchmarking Exercise*. Retrieved 20 February, 2008, from http://www.heacademy.ac.uk/ourwork/learning/elearning/benchmarking

HEA, Higher Education Academy, (2008). *Pathfinder*. Retrieved 20 February, 2008, from http://www.heacademy.ac.uk/ourwork/learning/elearning/Pathfinder

HEA, Higher Education Academy Evaluation and Dissemination Support Team. (2008). *Challenges and Realisations from the Higher Education Academy/JISC Benchmarking and Pathfinder Programme: An End of Programme Review*. HEA/JISC

Healey, M. & Jenkins, A. (2008, October). Developing students as researchers. *UC (University and College) Magazine*, 17-19.

Healey, M. (2005). Linking Research and Teaching to Benefit Student Learning. *Journal of Geography in Higher Education, 29*(2), 183–201. doi:10.1080/03098260500130387

Healey, M. (2005). Linking research and teaching exploring disciplinary spaces and the role of inquiry-based learning. In R. Barnett (Ed.), *Reshaping the university: new relationships between research, scholarship and teaching* (pp. 30-42). Maidenhead, UK: McGraw-Hill/Open University Press.

Health Professions Council. (2007). *Standards of proficiency: Radiographers*. Retrieved October 30, 2008, from http://www.hpc-uk.org/assets/documents/10000DBDStandards_of_Proficiency_Radiographers.pdf

HEFCE. (2006). *Strategy to support links between higher education and employers on skills and lifelong learning*. London, UK: HEFCE. Retrieved 28 October, 2008, from http://www.hefce.ac.uk/econsoc/employer/strat/Board_strategy_plus_annexes.doc

HEFCE. (2008). *Employer engagement*. London, UK: HEFCE. Retrieved 28 October, 2008, from http://www.hefce.ac.uk/econsoc/employer/

Helic, D. (2006). *A Didactics-Aware Approach to Management of Learning Scenarios in E-Learning Systems*. Graz, Austria: Graz University of Technology.

Henneberg, M. (1997). Peer review: the Holy Office of modern science. *naturalSCIENCE, 1*(2). Retrieved October 24, 2008, from http://naturalscience.com/ns/articles/01-02/ns_mh.html

Heron, J., & Reason, P. (2001). The Practice of Co-operative inquiry: Research "with" rather than "on" People. In P. Reason & H. Bradbury (Eds.), *Handbook of action Research: Participative inquiry and practice*. London: SAGE.

Herrington, A., & Herrington, J. (2007). Authentic mobile learning in higher education. Paper presented at the AARE 2007 International Educational Research Conference, Fremantle, Australia.

Herrington, A., & Herrington, J. (Eds.). (2006). Authentic learning environments in higher education. Hershey, PA: Information Science Publishing.

Herrington, J., Mantei, J., Herrington, A., Olney, I., & Ferry, B. (2008, December 1 - 4). New technologies, new pedagogies: Mobile technologies and new ways of teaching and learning. Paper presented at the ASCILITE 2008, Deakin University, Melbourne, Australia.

Herrington, J., Oliver, R., & Reeves, T. C. (2002). *Patterns of engagement in authentic online learning environments*. In A. Williamson, C. Gunn, A. Young & T. Clear (Eds.), *Ascilite 2002, Winds of Change in the Sea of Learning: Charting the Course of Digital Education* (pp. 279-286). Auckland, New Zealand: UNITEC Institute of Technology.

Higher Education Academy UK Centre for Legal Education. (2008). *Introduction to Developing Reflective Practice*. Retrieved June 14, 2008 from http://www.ukcle.ac.uk/resources/reflection/introduction.html

Higher Education Academy. website http://www.heacademy.ac.uk

Higher Education Funding Council for England (HEFCE). (2005). *HEFCE Strategy for ELearning*. Retrieved October 29, 2008, from http://www.hefce.ac.uk/pubs/hefce/2005/05_12/#exec

Hill, C. (2004). *Teaching Using Information and Learning Technologies in Further Education*. Exeter, UK: Learning Matters.

Hill, C. (2008) *Teaching with eLearning in the Lifelong Learning Sector*. Exeter, UK: Learning Matters.

Hills, J. M., Robertson, R., Walker, M. A., Adey, A., & Nixon, I. (2003). Bridging the gap between degree programme curricula and employability through implementation of work-related learning. *Teaching in Higher Education, 8*(2), 211–231. doi:10.1080/1356251032000052456

Hirst, T. (2008, December 23). *So what else are you doing at the moment?* [blog posting]. Retrieved February 9, 2009 from http://ouseful.wordpress.com/2008/12/23/so-what-else-are-you-doing-at-the-moment/

Hochschild, A. R. (1979). Emotion Work, Feeling Rules and Social Structure. *American Journal of Sociology, 85*(3), 551–575. doi:10.1086/227049

Hochswender, W., Martin, G., & Morino, T. (2006). *Il Budda nello specchio*. Milano: Esperia.

Hodges, L. (2008). Conflict on campus. *The Independent*, October 2, 2008, 2.

Hofmann, J. (2004). *Live and Online! Tips, Techniques, and Ready-to-Use Activities for the Virtual Classroom*. San Francisco, CA: Pfeiffer.

Hohl, H., Böcker, H.-D., & Gunzenhäuser, R. (1996). HYPADAPTER: An adaptive hypertext system for exploratory learning and programming. *User Modeling and User-Adapted Interaction, 6*(2-3), 131–155. doi:10.1007/BF00143965

Holley, D., Andrew, D., & Pheiffer, G. (2004). Exploring the usefulness of new technology with new students: a case study. *Investigations in university teaching and learning, 2*(1), Summer. JISC, (2007). *In their own words: Exploring the learner's perspective on e-learning*. Retrieved October 12, 2008 from http://www.jisc.ac.uk/intheirownwords

Holt, D., Smissen, I., & Segrave, S. (2006). *New students, new learning, new environments in higher education: Literacies in the digital age*. Paper presented at the 23rd Annual Ascilite Conference: Who's learning? Whose technology? Sydney, Australia.

Hopkins, D. (2006). Choice and voice in personalised learning. In *Personalised Learning: schooling for tomorrow*, (pp. 1-22). Paris: OECD publication, Centre for educational research and innovation. Retrieved February 5th, 2009 http://www.oecd.org/document/49/0,3343,en_2649_35845581_36168625_1_1_1_1,00.html

Horn, M. B., & Johnson, C. W. (2008). *How disruptive innovation will change the way the world learns*. New York: McGraw-Hill Professional.

Hughes, J. (2008). Exploring ePortfolios and weblogs as learning narratives in a community of new teachers. [JISTE]. *Journal of International Society for Teacher Education, 12*(1).

Huizinga, J. (1950). *Homo Ludens: A Study of the Play Element in Culture*. Boston: The Beacon Press.

Hutchins, H. (2003). Instructional immediacy and the seven principles: Strategies for facilitating online courses. *Online Journal of Distance Learning Administration, 6*(3).

Huxham, M. (2007). Fast and effective feedback: are model answers the answer? *Assessment & Evaluation in Higher Education, 32*(6), 601–611.

Illich, I. (1970). *Deschooling Society*. Retrieved October 20, 2008, from http://www.davidtinapple.com/illich/1970_deschooling.html.

Institute for Research on Learning. (2008). Retrieved October 10, 2008, http://portal.acm.org/citation.cfm?id=142750.142991

Ivanic, R. (1998). *Writing and Identity*. Amsterdam: John Benjamins.

Jafari, A., & Kaufman, C. (2006). *Handbook of Research on e-Portfolios*. Hershey, PA: Idea Group.

Jafari, A., McGee, P., & Carmean, C. (2006). Managing courses, defining learning: What faculty, students, and administrators want. *EDUCAUSE Review*, (July/August): 50–70.

James, B., & McInnes, D. (2001). Interdependent Academic Identities: Language and Learning Practitioners and the Subject who writes. Retrieved February 15, 2009 from http://learning.uow.edu.au/LAS2001/index.htm

Jaques, D., & Salmon, G. (2007). *Learning in Groups: a handbook for face-to-face and on-line environments*, (3rd Ed). London: Routledge.

Järvelä, S. (2006). Personalised Learning and Changing Conceptions of Childhood and Youth. In *Personalised Learning: schooling for tomorrow*, (pp. 35-52). Paris: OECD publication, Centre for educational research and innovation. Retrieved February 5th, 2009 http://www.oecd.org/document/49/0,3343,en_2649_35845581_36168625_1_1_1_1,00.html

Jasper, M. A., & Fulton, J. (2005). Marking criteria for assessing practice-based portfolios at master's level.

Nurse Education Today, 25, 377–389. doi:10.1016/j.nedt.2005.03.006

Jenkins, A., & Healey, M. (in press) Developing the student as a researcher through the curriculum. In C. Rust (ed.) *Improving Student Learning through the Curriculum*. Oxford: OCSLD.

Jenkins, A., Healey, M., & Zetter, R. (2007). *Linking Teaching and Research in Disciplines and Departments*. Retrieved 30 June 2008 from http://www.heacademy.ac.uk/ourwork/research/teaching

Jenny (2003). Eric Zorn Now Blogging on Chicago Tribune site. *The Shifted Librarian*. Retrieved October 20, 2008, from http://www.theshiftedlibrarian.com/2003/08/19.html#a4463

JISC Website. http://www.jisc.ac.uk, accessed September 2nd 2008

JISC. (2003). *Practical Exploitation of Linking Digital Libraries and VLEs*. Retrieved 29 October, 2008, from http://www.jisc.ac.uk/whatwedo/programmes/programme_divle/mle_divle_final_reports.aspx

JISC. (2007). *In Their Own Words: Exploring the Learner's Perspective on ELearning*, HEFCE

JISC. (2007). *Student expectations study*. Retrieved November 3, 2008, from http://www.jisc.ac.uk/media/documents/publications/studentexpectations.pdf

JISC. (2008). *At the cutting edge of educational technology*. Retrieved November 13, 2008, from http://www.jisc.ac.uk/news/stories/2008/02/labgroup.aspx

JISC. (2007). *Student Expectations Study*. Retrieved October 29, 2008, from http://www.jisc.ac.uk/publications/publications/studentexpectations

JISCInfoNet. (2008). *e-portfolios*. Retrieved June 24, 2008, from http://www.jiscinfonet.ac.uk/infokits/e-portfolios

Jochems, W., van Merriënboer, J., & Koper, R. (Eds.). (2004). *Integrated e-learning: Implications for pedagogy, technology and organization*. London: RoutledgeFalmer.

Joffe, H., & Yardley, L. (2004). Content and Thematic Analysis. In L. Yardley, & D. F. Marks (Eds), *Research Methods for Clinical and Health Psychology* (pp. 56-68). London: Sage.

Johanson, R. (1999). Rethinking the red ink: audio-feedback in the ESL writing classroom. *Texas Papers in Foreign Language Education, 4*(1), 31–38.

Johns, C. (1994). Guided reflection. In A. Palmer, S. Burns, & C. Bulman (Eds.), *Reflective practice in nursing: The growth of the professional practitioner* (pp. 110-129). Oxford, UK: Blackwell Scientific.

Johnson, M. (2004). *Personalised learning? An emperor's outfit?* London: Institute for Public Policy Research. Retrieved February 8, 2009 from https://www.ippr.org/uploadedFiles/research/projects/Education/Personalised%20Learning.pdf

Johnson, R. B., & Onwuegbuzie, A. J. (2004). Mixed Methods Research: A Research Paradigm Whose Time Has Come. *Educational Researcher, 33*(7), 14–26. doi:10.3102/0013189X033007014

Jonassen, D. H., & Land, S. M. (2000). *Theoretical Foundations of Learning Environment*. Mahwah, NJ: Lawrence Erlbaum Associates.

Jonassen, D., Davidson, M., Collins, M., Campbell, J., & Banna Haag, B. (1995). Constructivism and computer-mediated communication in distance education. *American Journal of Distance Education*. Retrieved February 9, 2009 from http://www.uni-oldenburg.de/zef/cde/media/readings/jonassen95.pdf, 9/2/09.

Kahn, P., & Baume, D. (Eds.). (2003). *A Guide to Staff and Educational Development*. London: SEDA /Kogan Page.

Kahn, P., Young, R., Grace, S., Pilkington, R., Rush, L., Tomkinson, B., & Willis, I. (2006). *The role and effectiveness of reflective practices in programmes for new academic staff: a grounded practitioner review of the research literature*. Manchester, UK: University of Manchester, The HE Academy.

Kakulska-Hulme, A., & Traxler, J. (2007).Designing for mobile and wireless learning. In H. Beetham & R. Sharpe (Eds.), *Rethinking Pedagogy for a digital age: Designing and delivering for e-learning* (pp.180-192). London: Routledge.

Kamel Boulos, M. N., & Wheeler, S. (2007). The emerging Web 2.0 social software: an enabling suite of sociable technologies in health and health care education. *Health Information and Libraries Journal, 24*(1), 2–23. doi:10.1111/j.1471-1842.2007.00701.x

Kane, P. (2005). *The play ethic: A manifesto for a different way of living*. London: Macmillan.

Karp, T. (2005). Unpacking the mysteries of change: mental modelling. *Journal of Change Management, 5*(1), 87–96. doi:10.1080/14697010500057573

Kay, J. (2001). Learner control. *User Modeling and User-Adapted Interaction, 11*, 111–127. doi:10.1023/A:1011194803800

Keegan, D. (1995). *Distance education technology for the new millennium: compressed video teaching* (ZIFF Papiere, Eric Document Reproduction Service No. ED 389 931). Hagen, Germany: Institute for Research into Distance Education.

Kelly, A. E. (2003). Research as design. *Educational Researcher, 32*(1), 3–4. doi:10.3102/0013189X032001003

Kelly, P., & Ryan, S. (1983). Using tutor tapes to support the distance learner. *International Council for Distance Education Bulletin, 3*, 1–18.

Kennedy, G., Judd, T. S., Churchward, A., Gray, K., & Krause, K. L. (2008). First year students' experiences with technology: are they really digital natives? *Australiasian Journal of Educational Technology, 24*(1), 108–122.

Kerr, B. (2007, February). *A Challenge to Connectivism*. Paper presented at the Online Connectivism Conference, University of Manitoba, Canada. Retrieved 28 October, 2008, from http://ltc.umanitoba.ca/wiki/Kerr_Presentation

Kieslinger, B., Fiedler, S., Wild, F., & Sobernig, S. (2006). iCamp: The Educational Web for Higher Education in an Enlarged Europe. In P. Cunningham & M. Cunningham (eds.), *Exploiting the Knowledge Economy: Issues, Applications, Case Studies* (pp. 1440-1448). Amsterdam: IOS Press.

Kiley, M., & Wisker, G. (2006, December). *Learning leaps and strides: when and in what ways do doctoral research students cross conceptual thresholds and achieve threshold concepts?* Paper presented at the Beyond boundaries: New Horizons for Research into Higher Education Conference, Brighton, England.

Kimble, C., Hildreth, P., & Wright, P. (2000). Communities of Practice: Going Virtual. In K.-P. Mehdi, (Ed.), *Knowledge Management and Business Model Innovation,* (pp. 220 - 234). London: Idea Group Publishing.

King, D., McGugan, S., & Bunyan, N. (2008). Does it make a difference? replacing text with audio feedback. *Practice and Evidence of Scholarship of Teaching and Learning in Higher Education, 3*(2), 145–163.

Kirschenbaum, H., & Henderson, L. V. (2002). The Interpersonal Relationship in the Facilitation of Learning. In *The Carl Rogers Reader*. London: Constable.

Kling, R. (2000). Learning About Information Technologies and Social Change: The Contribution of Social Informatics. *The Information Society, 16*(3), 217–232. doi:10.1080/01972240050133661

Kling, R., & Courtright, C. (2003). Group Behavior and Learning in Electronic Forums: A Sociotechnical Approach. *The Information Society, 19*(3), 221–235. doi:10.1080/01972240309465

Klug, R. (2002) *How to Keep a Spiritual Journal. A guide to journal keeping for inner growth and personal discovery*. Minneapolis, MN: Augsburg.

Knell, G. E. (2009). *Pockets of Potential: Using Mobile Technologies to Promote Children's Learning*, Joan Ganz Cooney Center. Retrieved January 10, 2009 from http://joanganzcooneycenter.org/publications/index.html

Knight, P. (2006). *The Effects of Post-graduate Certificates*. EPGC Project in collaboration with Open University, Management passed to Tony Brand at Anglia Ruskin in 2006.

Knight, P. (Ed.). (2004). *Assessment for Learning.* Abingdon,UK: SEDA/RoutledgeFalmer.

Knowles, M. (1989). *The Making of an Adult Educator.* San Francisco: Jossey Bass.

Knowles, M. S. (1975). *Self-Directed Learning. A guide for learners and teachers.* Englewood Cliffs, NJ: Prentice Hall.

Knowles, M. S. (1980). *The Modern Practice of Adult Education. From pedagogy to andragogy* (2nd ed.). Englewood Cliffs, NJ: Prentice Hall.

Knowles, M. S. (1992). Applying principles of adult learning in conference presentations. *Adult Learning, 4*(1), 11–14.

Knox, A. (2006). Why American business demands twenty-first century learning: A company perspective. *New Directions for Youth Development, (2006)*110, 31–37. doi:10.1002/yd.164

Knox, H., & Wyper, J. (2008). *Quality enhancement themes: The first year experience: Personalisation of the first year.* Retrieved June 20, 2008, from http://www.enhancementthemes.ac.uk/documents/firstyear/Personalisation%20-%20Final.pdf

Kolb, D. A. (1984). *Experiential learning: Experience as the source of learning and development.* Englewood Cliffs, NJ: Prentice-Hall.

Koper, R., Rusman, E., & Sloep, P. (2005). Effective Learning Networks. *Lifelong Learning in Europe, 1,* 18–27.

Kraemer, W., Milius, F., & Zimmermann, V. (2007). Von WINFO-Line zum Corporate Learning Management – Nachhaltiger Transfer wissenschaftlicher Konzepte in wettbewerbsfähige Produkte. *IM Information Management 20*(Special Edition), 50-67.

Kreber, C. (2004). An analysis of 2 models of reflection and their implications for educational development. *The International Journal for Academic Development, 9*(1), 29–49. doi:10.1080/1360144042000296044

Küchler, T., Pawlowski, J., & Zimmermann, V. (2008). Social Tagging and Open Content: A Concept for the Future of E-Learning and Knowledge Management? In Gaiser, B., Hampel, T., Panke, S. (Eds.), *Good Tags □ Bad Tags: Social Tagging in der Wissensorganisation,* Münster et al. (pp. 131-140).

Kuit, J. A., & Reay, G. (2001). Experiences of reflective teaching. *Active Learning in HE, 2*(2), 128–142. doi:10.1177/1469787401002002004

Kukulsa-Hulme, A., & Traxler, J. (2005). Mobile teaching and learning. In A. Kukulsa-Hulme & J. Traxler (Eds.), Mobile learning (pp. 25 - 44). Oxon, UK: Routledge.

Kukulska-Hulme, A., & Traxler, J. (2007). Designing for mobile and wireless learning. In H. Beetham & R. Sharpe (eds.), *Rethinking Pedagogy for a digital age* (pp.180-192). Abingdon, UK: Routledge Falmer

Kurhila, J. (2006). 'Unauthorized' Use of Social Software to Support Formal Higher Education. In T. C. Reeves, & S. F. Yamashita (Eds), *Proceedings of E-Learning 2006* (pp. 2602-2607). Chesapeake, VA: Association for the Advancement of Computing in Education.

Lakoff, G., & Johnson, M. (1999). *Philosophy in the Flesh.* New York: Basic Books.

Land, R., Meyer, J. H. F., & Smith, J. (Eds.). (2008). *Threshold Concepts within the Disciplines,* (pp. 59-74). Rotterdam: Sense.

Lathem, J., Gomadam, K., & Sheth, A. (2007). SA-REST and (S)mashups: Adding Semantics to RESTful Services. In *International Conference on Semantic Computing (ICSC 2007),* (pp. 469-476).

Latour, B. (2005). *Reassembling the Social: An Introduction to Actor-Network-Theory.* Oxford, UK: Oxford University Press.

Laurillard, D. (2001). Rethinking university teaching: A framework for the effective use of educational technology (2nd ed.). London: Routledge.

Laurillard, D. (2002). Rethinking teaching for the knowledge society. *EDUCAUSE Review, 17*(37), 16–25.

Laurillard, D. (2002). *Rethinking University Teaching: A Conversational Framework for the Effective Use of Learning Technologies,* (2nd Edition). London: Routledge.

Laurillard, D. (2006). E-learning in Higher Education. In P. Ashwin, (ed.), *Changing Higher Education: The Development of Learning and Teaching*. London: Routledge. Retrieved October 10, 2008, from http://www.bacs. uq.edu.au/CurriculumReview/DianaLaurillard.pdf

Laurillard, D. (2007). Pedagogical forms of mobile learning: Framing research questions. In N. Pachler (Ed.), Mobile learning: Towards a research agenda (Vol. 1, pp. 33-54). London: WLE Centre, Institute of Education.

Laurillard, D. (2007). *The Kaleidoscope scientific vision for research in technology enhanced learning*. Retrieved January 12, 2008, from http://telearn.noe-kaleidoscope. org/warehouse/Kaleidoscope-Scientific-Vision-v1.pdf

Laurillard, D. (2008). The teacher as action researcher: Using technology to capture pedagogic form. *Studies in Higher Education*, 33(2), 139–154. doi:10.1080/03075070801915908

Lave, J., & Wenger, E. (1991): *Situated learning: Legitimate peripheral participation*. Cambridge, UK: Cambridge University Press

Lave, J., & Wenger, E. (2002). Legitimate peripheral participation in communities of practice. In R. Harrison, F. Reeve, A. Hanson, J. Clarke, (Eds.) *Supporting Lifelong Learning Vol. 1 Perspectives on Learning*, (pp. 111-126). London: OUP/Routledge

Leadbeater, C. (2000). *Living on Thin Air. The new economy*. London: Penguin.

Leadbeater, C. (2004). *Learning about personalisation*. London: Demos.

Leadbeater, C. (2004). *Learning about personalisation: How can we put the learner at the heart of the education system?* Retrieved June 17, 2008, from http://www.demos. co.uk/files/learningaboutpersonalisation.pdf

Ledda, M. (2007). Personalised politics – how 'personalisation' devalues education and diminishes citizenship, blog posting 25th June 2007, http://www.culturewars.org. uk/2007-06/personalised.htm, last accessed 8/2/09.

Lee, G., Jolly, N., Kench, P., & Gelonesi, B. (2000). *Factors related to student satisfaction with university.*

Paper presented at the First year in Higher Education Conference: Creating futures for a new millennium, Brisbane, Australia.

Lee, K. (2000). *English Teachers' Barriers to the Use of Computer-assisted Language Learning*, Retrieved March 21, 2008, from http://iteslj.org/Articles/Lee-CALLbarriers.html

Lee, K. (2007). *ESL Teacher Professional Development & Curriculum Innovation: The Case of the Malaysian Smart School Project*. Unpublished doctoral dissertation, Lancaster University, UK.

Leijen, A., Lam, I., Wildschut, L., Simons, R.-J., & Admiraal, W. (2009). Streaming video to enhance students' reflection in dance education. *Computers & Education*, 52(1), 169–176. doi:10.1016/j.compedu.2008.07.010

Leitch, S. (2006). *Prosperity for all in the global economy - world class skills: Final Report*. Retrieved September 30, 2008 from HM Treasury http://www.hm-treasury. gov.uk/d/leitch_finalreport051206.pdf

Lemke, J. (1997). Cognition, context, and learning: A social semiotic perspective. In D. Kirshner & J. A. Whitson (Eds.), *Situated cognition: Social, semiotic, and psychological perspectives* (pp. 37-56). Mahwah, NJ: Erlbaum.

Leone, S. (2008). The use of new technologies in advanced Italian classes. In I. Olney, G. Lefoe, J. Mantei, & J. Herrington (Eds.), *Proceedings of the Second Emerging Technologies Conference 2008*, (pp. 120-129). Wollongong, Australia: University of Wollongong.

Leone, S. (2008). Lifelong learning and tertiary education in Italy. *The International Journal of Interdisciplinary Social Sciences*, 3(2), 7–14.

Leslie, S. (2009). *A collection of PLE diagrams*. Retrieved from http://edtechpost.wikispaces.com/PLE+Diagrams

Letschka, P., & Seddon, G. (2007). *See What I'm Saying?* Project report to Centre for Excellence in Learning & Teaching through Design. Retrieved September 18, 2008, from http://cetld.brighton.ac.uk/projects/ completed-projects/see-what-i-m-saying/see-what-i-m-saying-results

Levy, F., & Murnane, R. J. (2006). Why the changing American economy calls for twenty-first century learning: Answers to educators' questions. *New Directions for Youth Development, (2006)*110, 53–62. doi:10.1002/yd.167

Loewen, S., & Erlam, R. (2006). Corrective Feedback in the Chatroom: An Experimental. *Computer Assisted Language Learning, 19*(1), 1–14. doi:10.1080/09588220600803311

Loiodice, I. (2007). Formazione e orientamento degli adulti: il ruolo dell' università. In A. Alberici (Ed.), *Adulti e Università. Sfide ed innovazioni nella formazione universitaria e continua*. Milano: Franco Angeli.

Lord, F. (1980). *Applications of Item Response Theory to Practical Testing Problems*. Hillsdale, NJ: Erlbaum.

Loughran, J. J. (2002). Effective reflective practice: In search of meaning in learning about teaching. *Journal of Teacher Education, 53*(1), 33–43. doi:10.1177/0022487102053001004

Lubesky, R. (2006). The present and future of Personal Learning Environments (PLE). *Optusnet*. Retrieved June 14, 2008 from http://members.optusnet.com.au/rlubensky/2006/12/present-and-future-ofpersonal-learning.html

Luckin, R., Shurville, S., & Browne, T. (2007). Initiating e-learning by stealth, participation and consultation in a late majority institution. *Journal of Organisational Transformation and Social Change, 3*(3), 317–332. doi:10.1386/jots.3.3.317_1

Lueg, C. (2000). *Where is the Action in Virtual Communities of Practice? Proceedings of the Workshop Communication and Cooperation in Knowledge Communities*. Paper presented at the D-CSCW 2000 German Computer-Supported Cooperative Work Conference "Verteiltes Arbeiten - Arbeit der Zukunft", Munich, Germany.

Luft, J., & Ingham, H. (1955). The Johari window, a graphic model of interpersonal awareness. In *Proceedings of the western training laboratory in group development*. Los Angeles: UCLA

MacDonald, J. (2006). *Blended Learning and Online Tutoring: a Good Practice Guide*. Oxon, UK: Gower.

Manchester Metropolitan University. (2007). *The Shock Absorber Project*. Retrieved 28 October, 2008, from http://www.shockabsorber.mmu.ac.uk/

Marconato, G. (2003). Oltre l'eLearning. *Sviluppo & Organizzazione, 200*(12), 7–11.

Marcum, J. (2002). Beyond Visual Culture: The Challenge of Visual Ecology. *portal . Libraries and the Academy, 2*(2), 2189–2206.

Martin, J. (1982). Stories and scripts in organizational settings. In A. H. Hastrof & A. M. Isen (Eds.) *Cognitive social psychology*. New York: North Holland/ Elsevier.

Martin, M. (2007). *My personal learning environment* [blog posting]. Retrieved from http://michelemartin.typepad.com/thebambooprojectblog/2007/04/my_personal_lea.html

Mason, R., & Rennie, F. (2008). *E-Learning and Social Networking Handbook*. London: Routledge.

Mayer, R. (2003). The promise of multimedia learning: Using the same instructional design methods across different media. *Learning and Instruction, 13*(2), 125–139. doi:10.1016/S0959-4752(02)00016-6

Mayes, T., & de Freitas, S. (2007). Learning and e-learning: the role of theory. In H. Beetham & R. Sharpe (Eds.), *Rethinking Pedagogy for a digital age: Designing and delivering for e-learning* (pp. 13-25). London: Routledge.

McAndrew, P. (2006, October 26-27). *Motivations for OpenLearn: the Open University's Open Content Initiative*. OECD experts meeting on Open Educational Resources 2006, Barcelona, Spain. Available at http://kn.open.ac.uk/public/document.cfm?docid=8816

McConnell, D. (2000). *Implementing Computer Supported Cooperative Learning,* (2nd Ed.). London: Kogan Page.

McDowell, L., & Sambell, K. (1999). The experience of Innovative Assessment: Student Perspectives. In S.

Brown, & A. Glasner, (Eds.) *Assessment Matters in Higher Education* (pp. 71-82). Buckingham, UK: SRHE/Open University Press.

McGee, P., & Diaz, V. (2007). Wikis and Podcasts and Blogs! Oh, My! What Is a Faculty Member Supposed to Do? *EDUCAUSE Review, 42*(5), 28–41. Retrieved 28 October, 2008, from http://connect.educause.edu/Library/EDUCAUSE+Review/WikisandPodcastsand-BlogsO/44993

McInnis, C. (2003). *New Realities of the Student Experience: How should Universities respond?* The 25th Annual conference of the European Association for Institutional Research.

McKenney, S., Nieveen, N., & van den Akker, J. (2006). Design research from a curriculum perspective. In J. v. d. Akker, K. Gravemeijer, S. McKenney & N. Nieveen (Eds.), *Educational design research* (pp. 67-90). London: Routledge.

McKernan, J. (1992). *Curriculum Action Research.* London: Kogan Page.

McLoughlin, C., & Lee, M. (2008). The three P's of pedagogy for the networked society: personalization, participation and productivity. *International Journal of Teaching and Learning in Higher Education, 20*(1), 10–27.

McLoughlin, C., & Lee, M. J. W. (2007). Social software and participatory learning: Pedagogical choices with technology affordances in the web. In Atkinson, R.J., McBeath, C., Soong, S. K. A., Cheers, C. (Eds.), *24th Annual Conference of the Australasian Society for Computers in Learning in Tertiary Education, ICT: Providing Choices for Learners and Learning* (pp. 664-675). Singapore: Centre for Educational Development, Nanyang Technological University.

McLoughlin, C., & Lee, M. J. W. (2008). Future learning landscapes: Transforming pedagogy through social software. Innovate: Journal of Online Education, 4(5).

McMullen, M. (2003). Portfolios and assessment of competence: a review of the literature. *Journal of Advanced Nursing, 41*(3), 283–294. doi:10.1046/j.1365-2648.2003.02528.x

McNeely, B. (2005). *Using Technology as a Learning Tool, Not Just the Cool New Thing, Educating the Net Generation,* EDUCAUSE. Retrieved 29 October, 2008, from http://www.educause.edu/UsingTechnologyasaLearningTool%2CNotJusttheCoolNewThing/6060

McNiff, J. (1988). *Action Research: Principles and Practices.* London: Routledge.

McWilliam, E. (2008). Unlearning how to teach. *Innovations in Education and Teaching International, 45*(3), 263–269. doi:10.1080/14703290802176147

Meek, V. L. (2000). Diversity and marketisation of higher education: incompatible concepts? *Higher Education Policy, 13*(1), 23–39. doi:10.1016/S0952-8733(99)00030-6

Mergel, B. (1998). *Instructional design and learning theory.* Retrieved 14th June, 2007, from http://www.usask.ca/education/coursework/802papers/mergel/brenda.htm

Merholz, P. (1999). "Peterme.com". The Internet Archive. Archived from the original on 1999-10-13. Retrieved February 16, 2009 from http://web.archive.org/web/19991013021124/http://peterme.com/index.html

Metcalfe, B. (2006). Metcalfe's Law Recurses Down the Long Tail of Social Networking. *VCMike's Blog.* Retrieved February 22, 2009, from http://vcmike.wordpress.com/2006/08/18/metcalfe-social-networks/

Meyer, J. H. F., & Land, R. (2003). Threshold Concepts and Troublesome Knowledge (1). Linkages to Ways of Thinking and Practising within the disciplines. In C. Rust (Ed.), *Improving Student Learning – Ten Years On. 10th International Symposium, The Oxford Centre for Staff and Learning Development* (pp. 412-424). Oxford: OCSLD.

Meyer, J. H. F., & Land, R. (2003). Threshold concepts and troublesome knowledge (1): Linkages to ways of thinking and practising within the disciplines. In C. Rust (ed.) *Improving Student Learning - Ten Years On,* (pp 412-424). Oxford: OCSLD.

Meyer, J. H. F., & Land, R. (2005). Threshold concepts and troublesome knowledge (2): Epistemological considerations and a conceptual framework for teaching and learning. *Higher Education, 49*, 373–388. doi:10.1007/s10734-004-6779-5

Meyer, J. H. F., & Land, R. (2006). *Overcoming barriers to student understanding: Threshold concepts and troublesome knowledge.* London: Routledge/Falmer. *Module Information Directory* (n.d.). Coventry, UK: Coventry University. Retrieved November 5, 2008, from http://mid.coventry.ac.uk

Mezirow, J. (1978). Perspective Transformation. *Adult Education Quarterly, 28*(2), 100–110. doi:10.1177/074171367802800202

Mezirow, J. (1990). *Fostering critical reflection in adulthood: A guide to transformative and emancipatory learning.* San Francisco, CA: Jossey-Bass.

Micklewright, D. (2008). Podcasting as an alternative mode of assessment feedback. *Higher Education Academy Hospitality Leisure, Sport and Tourism Network Assessment Case Studies.* Retrieved October 26, 2008, from http://www.heacademy.ac.uk/assets/hlst/documents/case_studies/case129_-podcast_feedback.pdf

Middleton, A. (2008). Audio feedback: timely media interventions. In *Proceedings of The Third International Blended Learning Conference, "Enhancing the Student Experience,"* University of Hertfordshire, UK

Middleton, A., & Nortcliffe, A. L. (2008, in press). Understanding effective models of audio feedback. In Roy, R. (ed.), *Engineering Education.*

Miliband, D. (2004). *Personalised learning: Building a new relationship with schools.* Retrieved June 17, 2008, from http://publications.teachernet.gov.uk/eOrderingDownload/personalised-learning.pdf

Millband, D. (2006). "Personalised learning" New insights into fostering. In *Personalised Learning: schooling for tomorrow.* (23-34). Paris: OECD publication, Centre for educational research and innovation. Retrieved February, 5, 2009, from http://www.oecd.org/document/49/0,3343,en_2649_35845581_36168625_1_1_1_1,00.html

Mishra, P., Koehler, M. J., & Zhao, Y. (Eds.). (2007). Faculty development by design: Integrating technology in higher education. Charlotte, NC: Information Age Publishing.

Mödritscher, F., Neumann, G., García-Barrios, V. M., & Wild, F. (2008). A Web Application Mashup Approach for eLearning. In *Proceedings of the OpenACS and. LRN Conference,* (pp. 105-110).

Moon, J. (1999). *Reflection in learning and professional development: Theory and practice.* London: Kogan Page.

Moon, J. (2004). *A Handbook of Reflective and Experiential Learning.* London: Routledge.

Moon, J. (2004). *Reflection in Learning and Professional Development: theory and practice.* Oxon, UK: Routledge.

Moon, J. (2005). *Learning through reflection: Higher Education Academy guide for busy academics Number 4.* Retrieved June 23, 2008, from http://www.heacademy.ac.uk/resources/detail/id69_guide_for_busy_academics_no4_moon

Moon, J. (2006). *Learning Journals: A handbook for reflective practice and professional development.* London: Routledge.

Moore, G. (1999). *Crossing the chasm: Marketing and selling technology products to Mainstream customers,* (2nd Ed.). Oxford: Harper Business.

Moore, G. E. (1977). *Individualizing instructional feedback: a comparison of feedback modes in university classes.* Paper presented at the Annual International Conference for Individualized Instruction, West Lafayette, Indiana

Morrison, D. (2007). *The Benchmarking and Pathfinder Programme: a 'Basic Essentials Briefing."* Retrieved February 20, 2008, from http://elearning.heacademy.ac.uk/weblogs/Pathfinder/wp-content/uploads/2007/11/BenchPathfinderEssentialsBriefing.pdf

Motschnig-Pitrik, R., & Mallich, K. (2004). Effects of Person-Centered Attitudes on Professional and Social

Competence in a Blended Learning Paradigm. *Educational Technology & Society*, 7(4), 176–192.

Nadolski, R., Hummel, H., Van den Brink, H., Hoefakker, R., Slootmaker, A., Kurvers, H., et al. (2008). EMERGO: A methodology and toolkit for developing serious games in higher education. *Simulation & Gaming, 39*(3), 338-352. Retrieved August 22, 2008, from http://sag.sagepub.com/cgi/content/abstract/39/3/338.

Nair, C. S., & Fisher, D. L. (2001). Learning Environments and Student Attitudes to Science at the Senior Secondary and Tertiary levels. *Issues in Educational Research, 11*(2), 12–31.

National College for School Leadership. (2006). *An overview of the summary report findings.* Retrieved September 19, 2008, from http://www.ncsl.org.uk/media-579-61-personalised-learning-overview.pdf

New London Group. (1996). A pedagogy of multiliteracies: Designing social futures. *Harvard Educational Review, 66*(1), 60–92.

New Media Consortium (NMC), & the EDUCAUSE Learning Initiative (ELI), (2008). *2008 Horizon Report.* New Media Consortium.

Newland, B. (2003). Evaluating the Impact of a VLE on Learning and Teaching. In *Proceedings of World Conference on Educational Multimedia, Hypermedia and Telecommunications,* USA.

Newland, B. (2008). *eRes: Innovative eLearning with e-Resources.* Bournemouth, UK.

Newland, B., & Papaefthimiou, M. (2007). *Learning from the HEA ELearning Benchmarking Exercise.* Paper presented at the Blackboard European Conference, Nice.

Newland, B., Beard, J., Byles, L., Cheshir, K., Dale, P., & Callard, S. (2008a). *Bournemouth University Pathfinder Phase 1: The Pathfinder Journey.* Higher Education Academy. Retrieved October 29, 2008, from http://elearning.heacademy.ac.uk/weblogs/pathfinder/

NIACE. (2008). *Mobile Technology – the handheld choice.* Leicester, UK: NIACE. Retrieved 28 October, 2008, from http://www.niace.org.uk/mobiletechnology/

Nicol, D. (2008). Assessment as a driver for transformational change in HE. *HEA Education Subject Centre advanced learning and teaching in education (ESCalate) Newsletter* 10. Retrieved October 14, 2008, http://escalate.ac.uk/4451

Nicol, D. J., & Macfarlane-Dick, D. (2006). Formative assessment and self-regulated learning: a model and seven principles of good feedback practice. *Studies in Higher Education, 31*(2), 199–218. doi:10.1080/03075070600572090

Noam, E., Groebel, J., & Gerbarg, D. (2004). *Internet television.* London: Lawrence Erlbaum Associates.

Nolan, S. (2006). Building Magical Realms: Responses to Pervasive and Locative Technology. *Digital Creativity, 17*(3), 185–192. doi:10.1080/14626260600882489

Nonnecke, B., & Preece, J. (2001). *Why lurkers lurk.* AMCIS Conference, Boston, June. Retrieved May 21, 2008 http://snowhite.cis.uoguelph.ca/~nonnecke/research/whylurk.pdf

Nor, H. M. (2005). *Conditions facilitating the implementation of Information and Communication Technology (ICT) Integration in the Malaysia Smart School.* Unpublished doctoral dissertation, Universiti Putra Malaysia, Serdang, Selangor.

Nortcliffe, A. L., & Middleton, A. (2007). Audio feedback for the iPod generation. In *The Proceedings of the International Conference on Engineering Education 2007,* Coimbra, Portugal

Nortcliffe, A. L., & Middleton, A. (2008). Blending the engineer's learning environment through the use of audio. In *Proceeding of the Engineering Education 2008 Conference,* Loughborough, UK.

NSF task force on cyberlearning (2008). *Fostering learning in the networked world: learning opportunity and challenge. A 21st Century agenda for the National Science Foundation.* Report of the NSF task force on cyberlearning. Retrieved February 8, 2009 from http://www.nsf.gov/publications/pub_summ.jsp?ods_key=nsf08204

O'Brien, K. (2006). ePortfolios as Learning Construction Zones: Provost's Perspective. In A. Jafari & C. Kaufman (Eds.) *Handbook of Research on e-Portfolio*, (pp.75-82). Hershey, PA: Idea Group.

O'Donnell, A. M. (2006). The role of peers and group learning. In P. A. Alexander & P. H. Winne (Eds.), *Handbook of educational psychology* (pp. 781-802). Mahwah, NJ: Lawrence Erlbaum Associates.

O'Donoghue, J. (Ed.). (2006). *Technology supported learning and teaching: a staff perspective*. Heshey, PA: Idea Group Publishing.

O'Hear, S. (2005). *Seconds out, round two*. Retrieved September 18, 2008, from http://www.guardian.co.uk/education/2005/nov/15/elearning.technology3

O'Neill, G., & McMahon, T. (2005). Student–Centred Learning: What Does It Mean For Students And Lecturers? In O'Neill, G., & Moore, S., & McMullin, B. (Eds), *Emerging Issues in the Practice of University Learning and Teaching, Dublin: AISHE*. Dublin: University College Dublin.

O'Reilly, T. (2005). *What is web 2.0? Design patterns and business models for the next generation of software*. Retrieved 28 October, 2008, from http://www.oreillynet.com/pub/a/oreilly/tim/news/2005/09/30/what-is-web-20.html

OBHE. (2008). *Observatory on Borderless Higher Education*. Retrieved October 29, 2008, from http://www.obhe.ac.uk/

Oblinger, D. (2003). Boomers, Gen-Xers and Millennials, Understanding the New Students. *EDUCAUSE Review, July/August*.

Oblinger, D., & Oblinger, J. (2005). *Educating the Net Generation*. EDUCAUSE. Retrieved October 29, 2008, from http://www.educause.edu/EducatingtheNetGeneration/5989

OECD. (1998). *Redefining tertiary education*. Paris: OECD.

OECD. (2006). *Personalising education: Schooling for tomorrow*. OECD report. Paris: OECD. Retrieved February 5, from http://www.oecd.org/document/49/0,3343,en_2649_35845581_36168625_1_1_1_1,00.html

OECD. (2007). *Giving knowledge for free – the emergence of open educational resources, Centre for educational research and innovation*, Paris: OECD. Retrieved February 5, 2009 from http://www.oecd.org/dataoecd/35/7/38654317.pdf

Ofsted, (2008). *Transforming learning for student success: A good college with outstanding capacity to improve*. Retrieved December 8, 2008, from http://www.conel.ac.uk/docs/conel_ofsted_web_0.pdf

Oliver, R. (2001). Learning Objects: supporting flexible delivery of online learning. *18th ASCILITE conference proceedings*. Retrieved October 29th, 2008 from http://www.ascilite.org.au/conferences/melbourne01/pdf/papers/Oliver, 2001r.pdf

Ong, S. S., & Hawryszkiewycz, P. I. (2003). Towards personalised and collaborative learning management systems. In V. Devedzic, J. Spector, D. Sampson, Kinshuk (Eds.), *3rd IEEE International Conference on Advanced Learning Technologies* (ICALT'03). CA: IEEE Computer Society.

Orrell, J. (2006). Feedback on learning achievement: rhetoric and reality. *Teaching in Higher Education, 11*(4), 441–456. doi:10.1080/13562510600874235

Orsini-Jones, M. & Jones, D.E. (2007). Supporting Collaborative Grammar Learning via a VLE: a case study from Coventry University. *Arts and Humanities in Higher Education: an international journal of theory, research and practice, 6*(1), 90-106.

Orsini-Jones, M. (2008). Troublesome language knowledge: identifying threshold concepts in grammar learning. In R. Land, J. F. H. Meyer & J. Smith (Eds.), *Threshold Concepts within the Disciplines* (pp. 213-226). Rotterdam, The Netherlands: Sense.

Orsini-Jones, M., & Davidson, A. (1999). From reflective learners to reflective lecturers via WebCT. *Active Learning, 10*(1), 32–38.

Orsini-Jones, M., & De, M. (2007). Research-Led Curricular Innovation: Revisiting constructionism via e-portfolio shared assets and webfolios. *Coventry iPED Conference 2007: Researching Academic Futures,* September 10-12, (pp. 65-76). Retrieved November 10, 2008, from http://www.corporate.coventry.ac.uk/content/1/c6/02/15/41/iPED_2007_Proceedings.pdf

Orsini-Jones, M., & Sinclair, C. (2008). Helping students to GRASP the rules of grammar. In C. Rust (Ed.), *Improving Student Learning – For What?* (pp. 72-86). Proceeding of the 2007 15th International Symposium – The Oxford Centre for Staff and Learning Development. Oxford: OCSLD.

Orsini-Jones, M., Adley, D., Lamari, C., Maund, N., & Paruk, K. (2008). Integrating PDP (Personal Development Planning) and PebblePad into the curriculum – Students' perspectives. In F. Deepwell, (Ed.), *Proceedings of the ELATE (Enhancing Learning and Teaching Environments) Conference 2007: Internationalisation.* Coventry, UK: Coventry University. Retrieved November 9, 2008, from http://www.english.heacademy.ac.uk/explore/publications/casestudies/technology/eportfolio.php

Orsini-Jones, M., Kurowska, M., McTavish, A. M., & Mills, S. (2007). Personal Development Planning Perspectives from the Faculty of BES (Business, Environment and Society). *Proceedings of the Internationalisation – ELATE (Enhancing Learning and Teaching Environments) Conference,* 26-27 June, (pp. 65-72).

Paivio, A. (1986). *Mental representation: A dual coding approach.* New York: Oxford University Press.

Palloff, R. M., & Pratt, K. (1999). *Building learning communities in cyberspace: effective strategies for the online classroom.* San Francisco, CA: Jossey-Bass.

Paludan, J. P. (2006). Personalised learning in 2025. In *Personalised Learning: schooling for tomorrow,* (pp. 71-84). Paris: OECD publication. Retrieved February 5, 2009 from http://www.oecd.org/document/49/0,3343,en_2649_35845581_36168625_1_1_1_1,00.html

Panda, S., & Juwah, C. (2006). Professional Development of on-line facilitators in enhancing interactions and engagement: a framework. In C. Juwah (Ed.) *Interactions in online education: implications for theory and practice,* (pp. 207-227). Abingdon, UK: Routledge.

Papaefthimiou, M., & Newland, B. (2008) How Embedded is ELearning? Benchmarking ELearning in the UK HE Sector. In *Proceedings of World Conference on Educational Multimedia, Hypermedia and Telecommunications,* Vienna.

Papaefthimiou, M., Newland, B., & Callard, S. (2007). *Lessons Learnt from Implementing the Blackboard Content System.* Paper presented at the Blackboard European Conference, Nice.

Papert, S., & Harel, I. (1991). Situating Constructionism. In *Constructionism.* Norwood, NJ: Ablex Publishing Corporation.

Parchoma, G. (2008). *Adoption of technology enhanced learning in higher education: Influences of institutional policies and practices.* Saarbrücken, Germany: VDM Verlag Dr. Müller.

Parizotto-Ribeiro, R., & Hammond, N. (2005). *Does Aesthetics affect the users' perceptions of VLEs?* Paper presented at the meeting of the International Conference on Artificial Intelligence in Education. Workshop on motivation and affect in educational software, Amsterdam.

Patton, M. Q. (1986). *Utilisation-Focussed Evaluation.* Newbury Park, CA: Sage.

Patton, M. Q., (2002). *Qualitative Research and Evaluation Methods.* Thousand Oaks, CA: Sage.

Paulsen, M. F. (2003). Experiences with Learning Management Systems in 113 European Institutions. *Educational Technology & Society,* 6(4), 134–148.

PebbleLearning. (2008). *News.* Retrieved November 12, 2008, from http://www.pebblelearning.co.uk/news.asp

PebblePad – Pebble Learning (n.d.). Retrieved November 10, 2008, from www.pebblelearning.co.uk

Peel, D. (2005). Dual professionalism: facing the challenges of continuing professional development in the workplace? *Reflective Practice,* 6(1), 123–140. doi:10.1080/1462394042000326851

Perkins, D. (1999). The many faces of constructivism. *Educational Leadership, 57*(3), 6–11.

Perkins, D. (2006). Constructivism and troublesome knowledge. In J.H.F. Meyer & R. Land (Eds.), *Overcoming barriers to student understanding: Threshold concepts and troublesome knowledge* (pp. 33-47). London: RoutledgeFalmer.

Phipps, L., Cormier, D., & Stiles, M. (2008). Reflecting on the virtual learning systems – extinction or evolution? *Educational Developments, 9*(2), 1–4.

Phipps, L., Stiles, M., Cormier, (2008). Reflecting on the VL system – extinction or evolution. *Educational Developments, 9*(2), May.

Piaget, J. (1970). *Structuralism.* New York: Harper & Row.

Piaget, J. (Trans. P.A. Wells). (1982). *Psychology and Epistemology: Towards a Theory of Knowledge.* London: Penguin Books Ltd.

Pilkington, R. (2007). SEDA PDF – *A Tool for Supporting and Structuring Continuing Professional Development Frameworks.* London: SEDA Special 21 SEDA.

Pinnington, A. (1992). *Using video in training and education.* London: McGrawHill Training Series.

Pintrich, P. R. (2000). The role of goal orientation in self-regulated learning. In M. Boekaerts, P.R. Pintrich & M. Zeidner (Eds.), *Handbook of Self-regulation.* San Diego, CA: Academic Press.

Pintrich, P. R. (2004). A conceptual framework for assessing motivation and self-regulated learning in college students. *Educational Psychology Review, 16,* 385–407.

Pintrich, P., & Dr Groot, E. (1990). Motivational and self-regulated learning components of classroom academic performance. *Journal of Educational Psychology, 82*(1), 33–40. doi:10.1037/0022-0663.82.1.33

Plesser, A. (2006). Mainstream Media To Embrace Homegrown Video Uploads: New York Times Newspapers, Conde Nast and Others Take the Plunge. *Beet. TV.* Retrieved October 22, 2008, from http://www.beet. tv/2006/12/mainstream_medi.html.

Polanyi, M. (1967). *The Tacit Dimension.* New York: Anchor Books

Pollard, A. (2004). *Personalised learning – a commentary by the teaching and learning research programme.* Retrieved February 8, 2009 from http://www.tlrp.org/ documents/personalised_learning.pdf

Pollard, A., & James, M. (Eds.). (2004). *Personalised Learning: a commentary by the teaching and learning research programme.* Teaching and Learning Research programme. Swindon, UK: Economic and Social Research Council.

Powell, S., Tindal, I., & Millwood, R. (2008). *Personalised Learning and the Ultraversity Experience.* Inter-Disciplinary Inquiry-Based Learning Project, University of Bolton, Institute of Educational Cybernetics, Retrieved February 18, 2009, from http://idibl.bolton.ac.uk/resources/publications/Personalised%20Learning%20and%20 the%20Ultraversity%20Experience.pdf/view

Powers, A. (2004). An Evaluation of Four Place-Based Education Programs. *The Journal of Environmental Education, 35*(4), 17–32. doi:10.3200/JOEE.35.4.17-32

Prensky, M. (2000). *Digital Game-Based Learning.* New York: McGraw Hill.

Prensky, M. (2001). Digital natives, digital immigrants part 1. *Horizon, 9*(5), 1–6. doi:10.1108/10748120110424816

Pressey, S. L. (1926). A simple apparatus which gives tests and scores - and teaches. *School and Society, 23*(586), 373–376.

QAA. (2007). *Integrative assessment: Balancing assessment of and assessment for learning, guide number 2.* Gloucester, UK: QAA. Retrieved October 6, 2008, from http://www.enhancementthemes.ac.uk/documents/ IntegrativeAssessment/IABalancing.pdf

Qualifications and Curriculum Authority. (2005). *A review of GCE and GCSE coursework arrangements.* Retrieved October 5, 2008, from http://www.qca.org. uk/qca_10407.aspx

Qualifications and Curriculum Authority. (2006). *QCA announces changes to coursework*. Retrieved October 5, 2008, from http://www.qca.org.uk/qca_9678.aspx

Qualifications and Curriculum Authority. (2008). *The Diploma*. Retrieved October 20, 2008, from http://www.qca.org.uk/qca_5396.aspx

Queen Margaret University College. (2006). *QUELTA goals and aims: 2003-8: Quality enhancement of learning, teaching and assessment (revised spring 2006)*. Retrieved December 12, 2007, from http://www.qmu.ac.uk/quality/documents/QELTA%20Strategy%20revised%20June%202006.doc

Queen Margaret University. (2008). *New campus*. Retrieved November 13, 2008, from http://www.qmu.ac.uk/the_university/new_campus.htm

Race, P. (2001). *The lecturer's toolkit - A practical guide to learning, teaching and assessment* (2nd ed.). London: Kogan Page.

Race, P. (2004). *The Lecturer's Toolkit* (2nd Ed.). London: Routledge.

Ramírez Martinell, A. (2009). *Educational online video: Exploring the complex relationship between production, educational use and audience*. Unpublished PhD Thesis, Lancaster University, UK.

Ramírez Martinell, A., & Sime, J.-A. (2008, July). *Who is watching our Educational Videos anyway? An analysis of target audiences and their responses to different kinds of educational video*. Paper presented at the 8th International DIVERSE Conference, The Netherlands. Retrieved February 25, 2009 from http://www.inholland.nl/INHOLLANDCOM/Studying+at+INHOLLAND/Events/Diverse2008/Papers+abstracts+and+posters/Papers+abstracts+and+posters.htm

Ramírez Martinell, A., Sime, J.-A., & O'Donoghue, M. (2006). Design of a Constructivist Virtual Learning Environment composed by video summaries. In *Proceedings of the International EDUTEC 2006 conference: Education in Virtual Environments: Quality and Effectiveness in E-learning*. Tarragona, Spain: Rovira i Virgili University.

Ramsden, P. (2005). *Using Research on student learning to enhance educational quality, Deliberations*. Retrieved October 10, 2008 http://www.londonmet.ac.uk/deliberations/ocsld-publications/isltp-ramsden.cfm

Ranieri, M. (2005). *ELearning: modelli e strategie didattiche*. Trento, Italy: Erickson.

Ravensbourne College of Design and Communication. (2008). *Ravensbourne Learner Integration Project*. Retrieved 28 October, 2008, from http://confluence.rave.ac.uk/confluence/display/SCIRCLINR/Home

Ravenscroft, A., & Cook, J. (2007) New horizons in learning design. In H. Beetham & R. Sharpe (Eds.), *Rethinking Pedagogy for a digital age: Designing and delivering for e-learning* (pp. 207-218). London: Routledge.

Reardon, R., Hartley, C., & Lucas, S. (2007). Program Evaluation of E-Portfolios. *New Directions for Student Services, 119*, 83–97. doi:10.1002/ss.251

Reason, P. (2003). Pragmatist philosophy and action research: Readings and conversation with Richard Rorty. *Action Research, 1*, 103–123. doi:10.1177/14767503030011007

Reason, P., & Bradbury, H. (2001). Inquiry and Participation in Search of a World Worthy of Human Aspiration. In P. Reason & H. Bradbury (Eds.), *Handbook of action Research: Participative inquiry and practice* (pp. 1-14). London: SAGE.

Rees, C., Forbes, P., & Kubler, B. (2007). *Student employability profiles: A guide for higher education practitioners* (2nd ed.). Higher Education Academy. Retrieved October 24, 2008, from http://www.heacademy.ac.uk/assets/York/documents/ourwork/tla/employability_enterprise/student_employability_profiles_apr07.pdf

Reeves, T. C. (2000). *Enhancing the worth of instructional technology research through "design experiments" and other development research strategies*. Paper presented at session 41:29, of the Annual Meeting of the American Educational Research Association (pp.1-15).

Reeves, T. C. (2006). Design research from a technology perspective. In J. V. D. Akker, S. Gravemeijer, S. McKenny & N. Nieveen (Eds.), *Educational design research* (pp. 52-66). London: Routledge.

Reeves, T. C., Herrington, J., & Oliver, R. (2005). Design research: A socially responsible approach to instructional technology research in higher education. *Journal of Computing in Higher Education, 16*, 96–115. doi:10.1007/BF02961476

Reich, R. (1992). *The Work of Nations.* New York: Vintage Books.

Reimann, P. (2007). Communities of Practice. In Kinshuk, Pawlowski, J.M., Sampson, D. (Eds.), *Handbook on Information Technologies for Education and Training, 2nd Edition, International Handbook on Information Systems Series.* Berlin: Springer.

Reload (2006). *PLEX: Personal Learning Environment Download Page.* Reload. Retrieved March 31, 2008 from http://www.reload.ac.uk/plex/index.html

Ribchester, C., France, D., & Wakefield, K. (2008). *'It was just like a personal tutorial': Using podcasts to provide assessment feedback.* Paper presented at 'Transforming the student experience' Higher Education Academy Annual Conference, Harrogate, UK. Retrieved October 28, 2008, http://www.heacademy.ac.uk/assets/York/documents/events/conference/ 2008/Chris_Ribchester.doc

Rigutti, S., Paletti, G. & Morandini, A. (2008). Lifelong Learning eLearning 2.0: il contributo degli studi sull'usabilità. *Je-LKS - Journal of eLearning and Knowledge Society, 4*(1), 91-100.

Rogers, C. R. (1983). *Freedom to Learn for the 80's.* Columbus, OH: Charles E. Merrill Publishing.

Rogers, E. M. (1962). *Diffusion of Innovations.* New York: The Free Press.

Rollett, H., Lux, M., Strohmaier, M., Dösinger, G., & Tochtermann, K. (2007). The Web 2.0 way of learning with technologies. *International Journal of Learning Technology, 3*(1), 87–107. doi:10.1504/IJLT.2007.012368

Roos, J. (2006). *Thinking from Within: A Hands-on Strategy Practice.* New York: Palgrave Macmillan.

Roos, J., & Victor, B. (1998). In search of original strategies? How about some serious play? *Perspectives for Managers.* International Institute for Management Development, Lausanne.

Roos, J., & Victor, B. (1999). Towards a model of strategy making as serious play. *European Management Journal, 17*, 348–355. doi:10.1016/S0263-2373(99)00015-8

Roost, A. (2003). Writing intensive courses in theatre. *Theatre Topics, 13*(2), 225-233. Retrieved April 2008, from http://muse.jhu.edu/login?uri=/journals/theatre_topics/v013/13.2roost.html

Rotheram, B. (2007). Using an MP3 recorder to give feedback on student assignments. *Educational Developments, Staff and Educational Development Association,* 8.2, 7-10

Rourke, L., Anderson, T., Archer, W., & Garrison, D. R. (1999). Assessing social presence in asynchronous, text-based computer conferences. *Journal of Distance Education, 14*(3), 51–70.

Rust, C. (2001). A Briefing on the assessment of large groups. *LTSN Generic Centre.* Retrieved January 10, 2008, http://www.heacademy.ac.uk/resources/detail/ourwork/tla/assessment_series

Rust, C., Price, M., & O'Donovan, B. (2003). Improving students' learning by developing their understanding of assessment criteria and processes. *Assessment & Evaluation in Higher Education, 28*(2), 147–164. doi:10.1080/02602930301671

Sadler, D. (1989). Formative assessment and the design of instructional systems. *Instructional Science, 18*(2), 119–144. doi:10.1007/BF00117714

Salaway, G., & Caruso, J. B. (2008). *The ECAR Study of Undergraduate Students and Information Technology.* EDUCAUSE. Retrieved October 29, 2008, from http://net.educause.edu/ir/library/pdf/ers0808/rs/ers08081.pdf

Salmon, G. (2000). *E-moderating: The key to teaching and learning online.* London: Kogan Page.

Sampson, D., Karagiannidis, C., & Kinshuk, . (2002). Personalised Learning: Educational, Technological and

Standardisation Perspectives. *Interactive Educational Multimedia. Special Issue on Adaptive Educational Multimedia, 4,* 24–39.

Sampson, J. P., & Reardon, R. C, Peterson, G.W., & Lenz, J.L. (2004). *Career Counselling and Services: A cognitive Information Processing approach.* Pacific Grove, CA: Wadsworth-Brooks/Cole.

Samuels, P. (2008). Report on JISC Next Generation Environments Conference. *MSOR Connection, 7*(4), 26-29.

Sandoval, W. A. (2004). Developing learning theory by refining conjectures embodied in educational designs. *Educational Psychologist, 39*(4), 213–223. doi:10.1207/s15326985ep3904_3

Savin-Baden, M. (2008). *Learning Spaces: Creating opportunities for knowledge creation in academic life.* Maidenhead, UK:SRHE/OUP McGraw-Hill.

Scardamalia, M., & Bereiter, C. (2006). Knowledge building: Theory, pedagogy, and technology. In K. Sawyer (Ed.), *Cambridge Handbook of the Learning Sciences* (pp. 97-118). New York: Cambridge University Press.

Schapiro, S. A. (2003). From Andragogy to Collaborative Critical Pedagogy: Learning for Academic, Personal, and Social Empowerment in a Distance-Learning Ph.D. Program. *Journal of Transformative Education, 1*(2), 150-66. Retrieved 28 October, 2008, from http://jtd.sagepub.com/cgi/rapidpdf/1/2/150

Schön, D. A. (1983). *The Reflective Practitioner: How professionals think in action.* London: Temple Smith.

Schön, D. A. (1987). *Educating the reflective practitioner.* San Francisco: Jossey-Bass.

Schrage, M. (2000). *Serious Play: How the world's best companies simulate to innovate.* Cambridge, UK: Harvard Business School Press.

Schulmeister, R. (2002). *Grundlagen hypermedialer Lernsysteme.* München, Germany: Oldenbourg.

Schunk, D. H., & Pajares, F. (2002). The development of academic self-efficacy. In A. Wigfield & J. Eccles (Eds.), *Development of achievement motivation* (pp. 16-31). San Diego: Academic Press.

Scott, G. (2006). *Accessing the Student Voice: Using CEQuery to Identify What Retains Students and Promotes Engagement in Productive Learning in Australian Higher Education.* Canberra, Australia: Higher Education Innovation Program and the Collaboration and Structural Reform Fund, Department of Education, Science and Training.

Selwyn, N., & Gorard, S. (1999). Can Technology Really Widen Participation? *Adults Learning,* (February): 27–29.

Selwyn, N., Gorard, S., & Williams, S. (2002). "We are Guinea Pigs Really": Examining the Realities of ICT-Based Adult Learning. *Studies in the Education of Adults, 34*(1), 23–42.

Shang, F. (2007). An Exploratory Study of E-mail Application on FL Writing Performance. *Computer Assisted Language Learning, 20*(1), 79–96. doi:10.1080/09588220601118479

Sharples, M. (2000). Disruptive devices: Personal technologies and education. Retrieved June 27, 2006, from http://www.eee.bham.ac.uk/handler/ePapers/disruptive.pdf

Sharples, M. (2001). Disruptive devices: Mobile technology for conversational learning. *International Journal of Continuing Education and Lifelong Learning, 12*(5/6), 504–520. doi:10.1504/IJCEELL.2002.002148

Sharples, M. (2005). Learning as conversation: Transforming education in the mobile age. Paper presented at the Conference on Seeing, Understanding, Learning in the Mobile Age, Budapest, Hungary.

Sharples, M., Milrad, M., Sanchez, I. A., & Vavoula, G. (2007). Mobile learning: Small devices, big issues. In N. Balacheff, S. Ludvigsen, T. de Jong, A. Lazonder, S. Barnes & L. Montandon (Eds.), Technology enhanced learning: Principles and products (Vol. chapter 14, pp. 20).

Sharples, M., Taylor, J., & Vavoula, G. (2005). Towards a theory of mobile learning, in R. Andrews & C. Haythornthwaite (eds.) *The Sage Handbook of Elearning Research.* London: Sage, pp. 221-47.

Sharples, M., Taylor, J., & Vavoula, G. (2006). A Theory of Learning for the Mobile Age. In *The Sage Handbook of ELearning Research* (pp. 221-247). Retrieved October 7, 2008, from http://telearn.noe-kaleidoscope.org/openarchive/browse?resource=215_v1&back=%2Fstats%2Flast_week_popular_publications.php

Siemens, G. (2004). *Connectivism: A Learning Theory for the Digital Age.* Retrieved 28 October, 2008, from http://www.elearnspace.org/Articles/connectivism.htm

Siemens, G. (2004). Connectivism: A Learning Theory of the Digital Age. *Elearnspace.* Retrieved September 16, 2008, from http://wwwelearnspace.org/Articles/connectivism.htm

Siemens, G. (2004). *ePortfolios.* Retrieved November 9, 2007, from http://www.elearnspace.org/Articles/eportfolios.htm

Siemens, G. (2008). *elearnspace: everything elearning.* Retrieved 28 October, 2008, from http://www.elearnspace.org/

Siemens, G. (2008). *Learning and Knowing in Networks: Changing roles for Educators and Designer.* Retrieved October 10, 2008 from http://it.coe.uga.edu/itforum/Paper105/Siemens.pdf

Sime, J.-A., & Kemp, B. (2008). A 3D Multi-User Virtual Laboratory: Is Successful Implementation Enough? In J. Luca, & E. R. Weippl, (Eds.). *Proceedings of ED-MEDIA 2008: World Conference on Educational Multimedia, Hypermedia and Telecommunications* (pp. 3539-3547). Chesapeake, VA: AACE.

Simpson, O. (2002). *Supporting students in online, open, and distance learning.* London: Kogan Page.

Sinfield, S., Burns, T., & Holley, D. (2004). Outsiders looking in or insiders looking out? Widening participation in a post 1992 University. In J. Satterwaite, E. Atkinson,

& W. Martin, (Eds.), *The Disciplining of Education: new languages of power and resistance,* (pp. 137-152). Trentham, Stoke on Trent UK.

Sipple, S. (2007). Ideas in practice: developmental writers' attitudes toward audio and written feedback. *Journal of Developmental Education, 30*(3).

Siti Suria Salim & Sharifah Mohd. Nor. (2005). Teachers as Implementers of Change: The Smart School Experience. *International Journal of Learning, 12*(10), 197–204.

Smith, C., Bradley, C., Holley, D., Cook, J., & Haynes, R. (2007). Learning objects and blended learning designs for the net generation. In *Second International Blended Learning Conference, University of Hertfordshire,* June 14, 2007.

Smith, H., & Higgins, S. (2006). Opening classroom interaction: the importance of feedback. *Cambridge Journal of Education, 36*(4), 485–502. doi:10.1080/03057640601048357

Spiro, R. J., Feltovich, P. J., Jacobson, M. J., & Coulson, R. L. (1995). Cognitive flexibility, constructivism, and hypertext: Random access instruction for advanced knowledge acquisition in ill-structured domains. In L. P. Steffe & J. Gale (Eds.), *Constructivism in education* (pp. 85-107). Hillsdale, NJ: Erlbaum.

Sprey, J. A. (1997). Videoconferencing as a Communication Tool. *IEEE Transactions on Professional Communication, 40*(1), 41–47. doi:10.1109/47.557518

Staff and Educational Development Association website. www.seda.ac.uk

Stajkovic, A. D., & Luthans, F. (1998). Self-efficacy and work-related performances: A meta-analysis. *Psychological Bulletin, 124,* 240–261. doi:10.1037/0033-2909.124.2.240

Stead, G. (2006). Mobile technologies: Transforming the future of learning. Emerging Technologies for Learning. Retrieved 6 April, 2006, from http://www.becta.org.uk/corporate/publications/

Stefani, L., Clarke, J., & Littlejohn, A. (2000). Developing a Student Centred Approach to Reflective Learning. [United Kingdom: Routledge.]. *Innovations in Education and Teaching International, 37*(2), 163–171. doi:10.1080/13558000050034529

Stefani, L., Mason, R., & Pegler, C. (2007). *The educational potential of e-portfolios: Supporting personal development and reflective learning.* Abingdon, UK: Routledge.

Steffens, K. (2006). Self-Regulated Learning in Technology-Enhanced Learning Environments: lessons of a European peer review. *European Journal of Education, 41*(3/4), 353–379. doi:10.1111/j.1465-3435.2006.00271.x

Steffens, K., & Underwood, J. (2008). Self-regulated learning in a digital world. *Technology, Pedagogy and Education, 17*(3).

Stevenson, W. (1988). *The Play Theory of Mass Communication.* New Brunswick, NJ: Transaction Books.

Stewart, T. & Brown, M. (2008). Developing interactive scenarios: the value of good planning, whiteboards and table-based schemas. In *Proceedings of Ascilite 2008,* Melbourne. Retrieved February 9, 2009 from http://www.ascilite.org.au/conferences/melbourne08/procs/stewart.pdf

Stodel, J., Thompson, T., & Macdonald, C. (2006). Learners' Perspectives on What is Missing from Online Learning: Interpretations through the Community of Inquiry Framework. *International Review of Research on Open and Distance Learning, 7*(3). Retrieved 28 October, 2008, from http://www.irrodl.org/index.php/irrodl/article/view/325/743

Straub, R. (2008). Is the world open? *Global Focus, 2*(1). Retrieved October 22, 2008, from http://www.efmd.org

Strudler, N., & Wetzel, K. (2005). The diffusion of Electronic Portfolios in Teacher Education: Issues of Initiation and Implementation. *Journal of Research on Technology in Education, 37*(4), 411–433.

Sumner, N. (2006). *PebblePad ALT-N, (5).* Retrieved November 8, 2008, from http://newsletter.alt.ac.uk/e_article000611550.cfm?x=b11,0,w (Trafford, V. (2008). Conceptual Frameworks as a Threshold Concept in Doctorateness. In R. Land, J. F. H. Meyer & J. Smith (Eds.), *Threshold Concepts within the Disciplines* (pp. 273-288). Rotterdam: Sense.

Sun, L., & Williams, S. (2004). *An instructional design model for constructivist learning.* In L. Cantoni & C. McLoughlin (Eds.), Ed-Media 2007 World Conference on Educational Multimedia, Hypermedia and Telecommunications (pp. 2476-2486). Chesapeake, VA: AACE.

Swann, W. B., Jr. (1983). Self-verification: Bringing social reality into harmony with the self. In J. Suls & A. G. Greenwald (Eds.), *Psychological perspectives on the self* (pp. 33-66), Hillsdale, NJ: Erlbaum.

Swann, W. B., Jr., Chang-Schneider, C., & McClarty, K. (2007). *Do people's self-views matter? Self-concept and self-esteem in everyday life.* American Psychologist.

Takemoto, P. A. (1987). Exploring the educational potential of audio. *New Directions for Adult and Continuing Education,* (3): 19–28. doi:10.1002/ace.36719873405

Tapscott, P. (1997). *Growing Up Digital: the Rise of the Net Generation.* New York: McGraw Hill.

Taras, M. (2006). Do unto others or not: equity in feedback for undergraduates. *Assessment & Evaluation in Higher Education, 31*(3), 365–377. doi:10.1080/02602930500353038

Tashakkori, A., & Teddlie, C. (2003). *Handbook of Mixed Methods in Social and Behavioural Research.* Thousand Oaks, CA: Sage.

Taylor, J. C. (2001, April). *Fifth generation distance education.* Keynote address at International Council for Open and Distance Education, 20th world conference, Dusseldorf, Germany. Retrieved 28 October, 2008, from http://www.usq.edu.au/electpub/ejist/docs/old/vol4no1/2001docs/taylor.html

Taylor, J. R. (1993). *Rethinking the theory of organizational communication: How to read an organization.* Norwood, NJ: Ablex.

Taylor, P.G. (2000). Changing Expectation: Preparing students for flexible learning. *IETI 5*(2), November.

Taylor, W. (Ed.). (1984). Metaphors of Education. *Studies in education, new ser., 14*. London: Heinemann Educational Books for the Institute of Education University of London.

Teaster, P., & Blieszner, R. (1999). Promises and pitfalls of the interactive television approach to teaching adult development and aging. *Educational Gerontology, 25*(8), 741–754. doi:10.1080/036012799267477

Technorati (2008). *State of the Blogosphere / 2008*. Retrieved September 18, 2008 http://technorati.com/blogging/state-of-the-blogosphere/

Tennant, M. (2006). *Psychology and Adult Learning* (3rd Ed). Abingdon, UK: Routledge.

Terenzini, P., Cabrera, A., Colbeck, C., Parente, J., & Bjorklund, S. (2001). Collaborative learning vs. lecture/discussion: Students' reported learning gains . *Journal of Engineering Education, 90*(1), 123–130.

Tidwell, J. (2005). *Designing Interfaces: Patterns for Effective Interaction Design*. Sebastopol, CA: O'Reilly Media Inc.

TOPPS England (2004). *The National Occupational Standards for Social Work*. Retrieved October 1, 2008 from http://www.skillsforcare.net/view.asp?id=140

TOPPS England. (2000). *Modernising the Social Care Workforce*. Retrieved September 3, 2008 from www.topssengland.net/files/1%20MSCW%20training%20strategy%20FINAL.pdf

Tosh, D., & Werdmuller, B. (2004). *Creation of a learning landscape: weblogging and social networking in the context of ePortfolios*. Retrieved September 24, 2008 from http://elgg.net/bwerdmuller/files/61/179/Learning_landscape.pdf

Trentin, G. (2004). *Apprendimento in rete e condivisione delle conoscenze: ruolo, dinamiche e tecnologie delle comunità professionali online*. Milano, Italy: Franco Angeli.

Trentin, G. (2005). From "formal" to "informal" eLearning through knowledge management and sharing. *Journal of eLearning and Knowledge Society, 1*(2), 209-217.

Triggs, P., & John, P. (2004). From Transaction to Transformation: Information and Communication Technology, Professional Development and the Formation of Communities of Practice. *Journal of Computer Assisted Learning, 20*(6), 426–439. doi:10.1111/j.1365-2729.2004.00101.x

Trinder, K., Guiller, J., Margaryan, A., Littlejohn, A., & Nicol, D. (2008). *Learning from digital natives: bridging formal and informal learning (Final Report)*. York, UK: Higher Education Academy. Retrieved 28 October, 2008, from http://www.academy.gcal.ac.uk/ldn/LDNFinalReport.pdf

Trowler, P. (2007, September). *Disciplinary Differences and the Teaching-Research Nexus*. Keynote paper presented at the Researching Academic Futures: Emergent Pedagogies, Global Perspectives Leading Academic Learning, iPED (Inquiring Pedagogies) Conference. Coventry, UK: Coventry University Technocentre. Summary retrieved November 10, 2008, from http://www.corporate.coventry.ac.uk/content/1/c6/02/15/41/iPED_2007_Proceedings.pdf

Tusting, K., & Barton, D. (2006). *Models of adult learning: a literature review*. Leicester: NIACE.

UCL. (2009). *Information Behaviour of the Researcher of the Future. Executive Summary*. Ciber Briefing Paper for JISC and the British Library. Retrieved January 10, 2009 http://www.jisc.ac.uk/media/documents/programmes/reppres/gg_final_keynote_11012008.pdf

Uden, L. (2007). Activity theory for designing mobile learning. *International Journal of Mobile Learning and Organisation, 1*(1), 81–102. doi:10.1504/IJMLO.2007.011190

Ullrich, C., Borau, K., & Shen, R. (2008). Collaboration and Learning in the Social Web of the Future. In *Proceedings of the Conference on Integrated Design and Process Technology* (IDPT 2008).

Underwood, J., & Banyard, P. (2008). Managers', teachers', and learners' perceptions of personalised learning:

evidence from Impact 2007. *Technology, Pedagogy and Education, 17*(3), doi:10.1080/14759390802383850

UNESCO Institute for Education. (1999). *Glossary of Adult Learning in Europe*. Hamburg, Germany: UNESCO.

Van Harmelen, M. (2006). Personal Learning Environments. In *Proceedings of the IEEE International Conference on Advanced Learning Technologies (ICALT 2006)*, (pp. 815-816).

Van Harmelen, M. (2007). *Personal Learning Environments*. Retrieved December 23, 2008 http://octette. cs.man.ac.uk/jitt/index.php/Personal_Learning_Environments

Varisco, B. M. (2002). *Costruttivismo socio-culturale. Genesi filosofiche, sviluppi psico-pedagogici, applicazioni didattiche*. Roma: Carocci.

Vassileva, J. (2002). Motivating Participation in Peer to Peer Communities. In *Proceedings of the Workshop on Emergent Societies in the Agent World (ESAW 2002)*, (pp. 141-155).

Virilio, P. (2005). *The information bomb*. London: Verso.

Vitali, G. (2007). Relazione di gruppo e metacognizione in apprendimento nei modelli eLearning di terza generazione. *Atti del IV congresso* Sie-l. Macerata, Italy: EUM.

von Glasersfeld, E. (1998). *Il costruttivismo radicale. Una via per conoscere ed apprendere*. Roma: Società Stampa Sportiva.

Vuorikari, R. (2004). *Insight Special Report: Why Europe Needs Free and Open Source Software and Content in Schools*. Retrieved from http://ww.eun.org/ insight-pdf/special_reports/Why_Europe_needs_foss_ Insight_2004.pdf

Vygotsky, L. (1981). The instrumental method in psychology. In J. Wertsch. (Ed.), *The Concept of Activity in Soviet Psychology* (pp. 134-143). New York: Armond.

Vygotsky, L. S. (1962). *Thought and language*. Cambridge, MA: MIT Press.

Vygotsky, L. S. (1978). *Mind and society: The development of higher psychological processes*. Cambridge, MA: Harvard University Press.

Wadsworth, Y. (1998). What is participatory action research? Retrieved May 3, 2002, from http://www.scu. edu.au/schools/gcm/ar/ari/p-ywadsworth98.html

Wali, E., Winters, N., & Oliver, M. (2008). Maintaining, changing and crossing contexts: An activity theoretic reinterpretation of mobile learning. ALT-J . *Research in Learning Technologies, 16*(1), 41–57.

Wallis, J. (2004). Facilitating Scottish cultural publishing online. *Library Review, 53*(5), 265. doi:10.1108/00242530410538409

Walton, A.J., Weller, M. & Conole, G. (forthcoming). *SocialLearn – widening participation and sustainability of higher education, in EDEN book*.

Warschauer, M. (1996). Computer Assisted Language Learning: an Introduction. In S.Fotos (Ed.) *Multimedia language teaching* (pp. 3-20). Tokyo: Logos International.

Warschauer, M. (2004). Technological change and the future of CALL. In S. Fotos & C. Brown (Eds), *New Perspectives on CALL for Second and Foreign Language Classrooms* (pp. 15-25). Mahwah, NJ: Lawrence Erlbaum Associates.

Warschauer, M., & Ware, M. (2008). Learning, change, and power: Competing discourses of technology and literacy. In J. Coiro, M., Knobel, C. Lankshear, & D. J. Leu (Eds.), *Handbook of research on new literacies* (pp. 215-240). New York: Lawrence Erlbaum Associates.

Webb, L. (2006). Personal Development, Planning - Case Study from Graphic Design. *Impressions: Newsletter of the Centre for the Study of Higher Education (CSHE)1*, 8-9. Coventry, UK: Coventry University. Retrieved November 5, 2008 from http://www.corporate.coventry. ac.uk/content/1/c6/01/49/14/CSHE%20Newsletter.pdf

Webb, S. (2006). ICT Based Learning and Social Inclusion: the case of Adult Speakers of Other Languages. In D. Jary & R. Jones (Eds.), *Perspectives and Practice in*

Widening Participation in the Social Sciences C-SAP Monograph Series No 3. (pp.174–204). Birmingham, UK: University of Birmingham.

Wen, L. (2008). *Flexible Virtual Learning Environments: a Schema-Driven Approach using Semantic Web Concepts.* Unpublished doctoral dissertation, University of Hull, UK.

Wenger, E. (1998). *Communities of Practice. Learning, meaning and identity.* Cambridge, UK: Cambridge University Press.

Wenger, E., McDermott, R., & Snyder, W. (2002). Cultivating communities of practice: A guide to managing knowledge. Boston: Harvard Business School Press.

Wenger, E., White, N., Smith, J., & spa, K. R.-. (2005). Technology for communities. Retrieved July 14, 2006, from http://technologyforcommunities.com/

Whalley, J., Welch, T., & Williamson, L. (2006). E-Learning in FE. London: Continuum.

Whisnant, W. T., & Sullivan, J., C., & Slayton, S. L. (1992). The "old" new resource for education: Student age. *Community Service Catalyst, 22*(3), 7–11.

Wikipedia (2008). Anarcho-syndicalism. *Wikipedia.* Retrieved February 21, 2009, http://en.wikipedia.org/wiki/Anarcho-syndicalism

Wikipedia (2008). Open publishing. *Wikipedia.* Retrieved October 17, 2008, http://en.wikipedia.org/wiki/Open_publishing

Wikipedia (2008). Social media. *Wikipedia.* Retrieved February 21, 2009, http://en.wikipedia.org/wiki/Social_media

Wild, F., Modritscher, F., & Sigurdarson, S. (2008). Designing for Change: Mash-Up Personal Learning Environments. *eLearning Papers, 9,* July 2008. Retrieved October 16, 2008 from http://www.elearningeuropa.info

Williams, J. B., & Jacobs, J. (2004). Exploring the use of blogs as learning spaces in the higher education sector. *Australasian Journal of Communication Technology, 20*(2), 232–247.

Willison, J., & O'Regan, K. (2008). *The Research Skill Development Framework.* Retrieved November 1, 2008, from: http://www.adelaide.edu.au/clpd/rsd/

Willison, J., & Remenda, V. (2008, June). *Embedding Research Skills Development in Undergraduate Courses or Stuck in Blue-Sky Research in the Disciplines.* Paper presented at the second conference on Threshold Concepts: From Theory to Practice, Queen's University, Kingston, Ontario.

Wilson, S. (2005). *Future VLE – The Visual Vision.* Retrieved September 18, 2008 from http://www.cetis.ac.uk/members/scott/blogview?entry=20050125170206

Wilson, S. (2005). *The VLE of the Future.* Retrieved September 16, 2008, from http://zope.cetis.ac.uk/members/scott/blogview?entry=20050117150356

Wilson, S., et al. (2006). *Personal Learning Environments: Challenging the dominant design of educational systems.* Retrieved July 4, 2008, from http://dspace.learningnetworks.org/bitstream/1820/727/1/sw_ectel.pdf

Wilson, S., Liber, O., Beauvoir, P., Milligan, C., Johnson, M., & Sharples, P. (2006). Personal Learning Environments: Challenging the dominant design of educational systems. In *Proceedings of the first Joint International Workshop on Professional Learning, Competence Development and Knowledge Management (LOK MOL 2006 and L3NCD 2006),* (pp. 67-76).

Winne, P. H. (2001). Self-regulated learning viewed from models of information processing. In B. J. Zimmerman & D. H. Schunk (Eds.), *Self-regulated learning and academic achievement: Theoretical perspectives,* (pp. 153-189). Mahwah, NJ: Lawrence Erlbaum Associates.

Winnecott, D. (1971). *Playing and Reality.* London: Tavistock.

Winter, R. (2003). Contextualising the Patchwork text: addressing problems of coursework assessment in HE. *IETI, 40*(2), 112–122.

Wisker, G., Kiley, M., & Aiston, S. (2006). Making the learning leap: Research students crossing conceptual thresholds. In M. Kiley & G. Mullins (Eds.), *Quality in*

Postgraduate Research: Knowledge creation in testing times (pp. 195-201). Canberra, Australia: CEDAM, The Australian National University.

Wordpress (n.d.). Retrieved February 21, 2009, from http://wordpress.com/

Wright, C., & O'Neil, M. (2002). Service Quality in the Higher Education Sector: An Empirical Investigation of Students' Perceptions. *Higher Education Research & Development*, *21*(1), 23–39. doi:10.1080/07294360220124639

Ya'acob, A., Mohd Nor, N. F., & Azman, H. (2005). Implementation of the Malaysian Smart School: An Investigation of Teaching-learning Practices and Teacher-Student Readiness. *Internet Journal of e-Language Learning and Teaching, 2*(2) 16-25. Retrieved from http://www.eltrec.ukm.my/ijellt

Yancey, K. (2001). Introduction: Digitized student portfolios. In B. Cambridge (Ed.) *Electronic portfolios: Emerging practices in student, faculty and institutional learning*, (pp.15-30). Washington, DC: American Association for Higher Education.

Yang, Z., & Liu, Q. (2007). Research and development of web-based virtual online classroom. *Computers & Education*, *48*(2), 171–118. doi:10.1016/j.compedu.2004.12.007

Yorke, M., & Longden, B. (2004). *Retention and Student Success in HE*. Maidenhead, UK: SRHE, OUP, McGraw-Hill.

Young, P. (2000). 'I Might as well give up': self-esteem and mature students' feelings about feedback on assignments. *Journal of Further and Higher Education*, *24*(3), 409–418. doi:10.1080/030987700750022325

Yousif, H., et al. (2009). *SPLASH Blog*. Retrieved February 28, 2009, http://splashproject.blogspot.com/

Zeichner, K. (2001). Educational Action Research. In P. Reason & H. Bradbury (Eds.), *Handbook of action Research: Participative inquiry and practice* (pp. 273-282). London: SAGE.

Zimmerman, B. J. (1998). Academic studying and the development of personal skill: a self-regulatory perspective. *Educational Psychologist*, *33*, 73–86. doi:10.1207/s15326985ep3302&3_3

Zimmerman, B. J. (2000). Attaining self-regulation: a social cognitive perspective. In M. Boekarts, P.R. intrich & M. Zeidner (eds), *Handbook of Self-regulation*. San Diego, CA: Academic Press.

Zimmermann, V., & Faltin, N. (2006). Integration of Business Process Management Platforms and Learning Technologies: The PROLIX Process-oriented Learning Life Cycle. In *Proceedings eLearning 2006 Conference, Helsinki*.

Zuber-Skerritt, O. (1992). *Action research in higher education*. London: Kogan Page.

Zuber-Skerritt, O. (1996). *New Directions in Action Research*. London: Falmer Press.

About the Contributors

John O'Donoghue, University of Central Lancashire (UCLan), UK. John's background covers a range of educational experiences; teaching in a social priority area school, to postgraduate lecturing, advising and consultancy for both initial teaching training and education. He has held the position of Chair and President of the ALT. He holds the Chair in Learning Technology at the University of Central Lancashire as well as a visiting research fellowship in Australia. These roles embrace academic and pedagogical aspects of learning and teaching technologies, research, development, implementation and evaluation. His specialist area is technology use as a medium for student/ pupil services and delivery, learning, teaching and engagement. John sits on the JISC's Strategic Committee for Learning and Teaching as well as a number of JISC expert and advisory boards. He also is an executive committee member of ascilite – australiasian society for computers in learning in tertiary education. For many years an advocate of the 'global classroom', John has developed a number of active research links, including the development and application of computer technology within Russian schools, institutes and Universities. His visits to the former USSR and the CIS have been to instigate a collaborative study of the application of computer technology to enhance and enrich the wider curriculum. This cross cultural theme has enabled John to develop a number of trans national partnerships considering such aspects as distance based learning and teaching as well as cultural and infrastructural boundaries to the learner experience. He used these opportunities - together with his employment in local government - to develop and extend his research into information technology and the development and application from both an academic and a practical perspective. His current work is within a large Health faculty where he considers the strategic, practical and operational issues associated with the learning and teaching of staff and students. This extends to the traditional academic through to the professional clinician who is engaged in learning and teaching. Clearly John's emphasis will be located on utilising technology to support such engagements, but only where deemed appropriate, useful and an enhancement to the learning and teaching process. John is actively engaged with a major project focusing on the impediments to continuation and barriers to studying for the student new to university and study, particularly first generation students. He also works with a number of colleagues on the appropriate and timely feedback mechanisms for staff and students. John continues to write and publish extensively on the use and exploitation of the information in information technology. He sits on a number of review, editorial and programme committees and has edited books around technology supported learning and personalised learning. These both consider the way infrastructure, policies and culture affect eLearning intervention and include a number of case studies.

* * *

Simon Atkinson is a social scientist, educational developer and strategist with specialist interests in educational technologies. His research interests focus on tertiary educations strategic response to technology driven social change, the impact of technology-enabled communication on cultural interactions and the values of academe. Current work is developing reusable learning designs to maximize engagement with digitally rich resources (DiAL-e Framework). He has held a number of senior roles in higher education based eLearning as Strategic eLearning Advisor, College of Education, Massey University, New Zealand (2008-), Acting Director of the Learning & Teaching Support Unit, Head of Centre for Learning Development and Head of eLearning, at the University of Hull, United Kingdom (2003-2008). He was project officer for the UK Open University's Academic Professional Development Programme at the Institute of Educational Technology (2001-2003). Simon was a European TEMPUS visiting expert for the Croatian National eLearning Project – EQIBELT from 2005-2008. He presents on the web and in person on issues of foresight, planning and creative communications in higher education.

Elfneh Udessa Bariso is a Course Coordinator for English for Speakers of Other Languages (ESOL)/ Employability Skills Programme at the College of North East London (CONEL). Over the past twenty years, he has taught various courses including English, Research Methods, Distance, Open and Flexible Learning and Employability Skills at universities and colleges in Eritrea, Ethiopia and the UK. His PhD investigates the role of new technologies in widening participation in lifelong learning and related barriers. His current research activities focus on studying use of electronic resources to personalise learning and examining attitudes and motivation of unemployed low literacy adults to participation in learning and or employment.

Adam Blake began working in educational design and professional development in the latter half of the 1990s. He has managed projects for staff orientation to eLearning, learning management system development and implementation, creation of blended and fully-online courses, and implementation of eLearning initiatives across a range of university programmes. He facilitates the online course, 'ELearning & Clinical Education', as part of the University of Auckland's post-graduate programme in clinical education. Adam's research interests span learning design, knowledge visualisation, and professional development and change management for eLearning. He holds BCom and LLB degrees from the University of Auckland and a Masters in Educational Technology from the University of British Columbia.

Margo Blythman is the Director of Teaching and Learning at the London College of Communication, University of the Arts London. Her responsibilities include staff development, the quality of teaching and learning, tutorial systems and study support. She has published on such topics as retention, development strategies within higher education contexts and the development of student academic writing, particularly in the context of art and design. Recent projects include formative assessment in art and design, plagiarism in non-text based disciplines and the use of web 2.0 technology in professional development projects . Her academic interests also include the impact of quality assurance systems on the working lives of academic staff and micropolitics in UK higher education.

Kevin Burden has worked in a variety of different educational settings including schools and the university sector where he is currently responsible for post-graduate professional development (PPD) at The University of Hull. He works with teachers and other educators from across the region to explore their own professional learning through action research and other related methodologies. He is the programme director for the Advanced Certificate in Sustained Professional Development, a Teacher Development Agency (TDA) programme based in the work-place. Research interests are related to both professional learning of educators and the role and impact of new and emerging technologies. His interest in the emergence of new media forms and how they can be incorporated into teaching and learning is currently focused around the DiAL-e Framework.

Claire Bradley is a Research Fellow at the Learning Technology Research Institute. For the past 12 years she has worked on a number of prestigious funded UK and European research projects involved in mLearning, eLearning, online communities, multimedia and the general application and evaluation of digital technologies in teaching and learning. She has co-authored numerous journal articles and papers in these areas. In the past three years, in addition to conducting the internal evaluation of the use of learning objects for the RLO-CETL at LondonMet, Claire has developed significant expertise in evaluation methodologies for digital technologies; she is currently working on the evaluation of the pan- European Contsens project (http://www.londonmet.ac.uk/ltri/research/projects/contsens.htm).

Thomas Cochrane is an Academic Advisor (eLearning and Learning Technologies)with Unitec (March 2004 to present). His role at Unitec includes providing support for eLearning and learning technologies for Unitec teaching staff, and pushing the boundaries of educational technology for enhancing teaching and learning at Unitec. His research interests include mobile learning, web 2.0, and communities of practice. He is currently implementing mobile learning trials for his PhD thesis: "Mobilizing Learning: The potential impact of wireless mobile computing on teaching and learning in higher education in New Zealand". Harnessing the potential of social software tools (such as: Mobile Blogging, RSS, Instant Messaging, Moodle and Elgg…) using wireless mobile devices, such as: PDAs, laptops, and the new generation of mobile phones.

Gráinne Conole is Professor of ELearning in the Institute of Educational Technology at the Open University in the UK. Her research interests include the use, integration and evaluation of Information and Communication Technologies and eLearning and the impact of technologies on organisational change. Two of her current areas of interest are focusing on the evaluation of students' experiences of and perceptions of technologies and how learning design can help in creating more engaging learning activities and Open Educational Resources. Updates on current research and reflections on eLearning research generally can be found on her blog www.e4innovation.com. She has extensive research, development and project management experience across the educational and technical domains; funding sources have included the EU, HEFCE, ESRC, JISC and commercial sponsors). She serves on and chairs a number of national and international advisory boards, steering groups, committees and international conference programmes. She has published and presented over 300 conference proceedings, workshops and articles, including over 100 publications on a range of topics, including the use and evaluation of learning technologies. She is co-editor of the recently published RoutledgeFalmer book 'Contemporary perspectives on eLearning research'.

John Cook is Professor of Technology Enhanced Learning (TEL) at the Learning Technology Research Institute, London Metropolitan University. He has a cross-university role of ELearning Project Leader and sits on the University's small core planning group for Teaching, assessment, learning and TEL. John has over 14 years previous experience as a full-time lecturer at various HEIs. He has over 8 years project management experience, which includes AHRB, BECTA, HEFCE (CETL Manager 2005-2008) and EC work. Furthermore, John has been part of research and development grant proposals that have attracted £4 million in competitive external funding. In addition, he has published/presented around 200 refereed articles and invited talks in the area of TEL, having a specific interest in four related areas: informal learning, mobile learning, appropriation and ICT Leadership & Innovation. He was Chair/President of the Association for Learning Technology (2004-06).

Iain Doherty is Director of the Learning Technology Unit, Faculty Medical and Health Sciences, University of Auckland. In this role he is responsible for ensuring that the Learning Technology Unit meets the flexible and distance learning needs of the Faculty. Dr Doherty's research has focussed on enabling academics to effectively employ technologies in their teaching in order to facilitate student learning. The focus of this research has been the necessity of starting with pedagogically sound learning designs in order to use technologies effectively in teaching. Dr. Doherty is becoming increasingly interested in constructivist philosophies particularly in terms of the learner as a unique individual interpreting the world in terms of a particular mental and emotional disposition. He intends to concentrate on this subject area in order to develop a holistic understanding of the learning process.

Louise Frith is a Curriculum and Educational Developer at the University of Kent. Her particular areas of interest are, reflective learning, assessment, feedback and supporting students' writing. Louise delivers a wide variety of staff development sessions in areas such as supporting students' reflective learning, creating opportunities for formative feedback and assessing students' e-portfolios. Louise has published articles on PDP and the use of e-portfolios. She also regularly presents academic conferences on aspects teaching and learning. The following is a list of publications and conference presentations:

- LDHEN Symposium (2009). A Year in the Life of an E-portfolio Bournemouth
- LDHEN Symposium (2008). Embedding study skills into the curriculum. Bradford
- PDP-UK (Feb 2008). What to do with an e-portfolio? Issue 12
- PDP-UK (March 2007). Students Engagement with PDP at Kent. Issue 10
- LDHEN Symposium (2007). Students' engagement with PDP software. Bournemouth
- LDHEN Symposium (2006). Students' Views of Assessment. Liverpool

Simon Girdler is the Instructor on the Performing Arts Management degree and has 25 years of experience working in the Arts. He has held management positions at the Royal Opera House, Covent Garden, the Edinburgh International Festival, Universal Arts - Promoters and Producers, Suspect Culture Theatre company and was the Programmer of Scotland's Theatre Gateway, an Arts Council supported initiative to promote Scottish Theatre companies during the Edinburgh Festival Fringe. For the last 20 years he has been involved in training at a managerial level and currently he is examining ePortfolio and PDP as an essential part of management training within Performing Arts Management.

Neil Gordon is a lecturer in the Department of Computer Science at the University of Hull where he is Director of Taught Postgraduate Studies. Teaching duties range from first year core modules through to specialist masters' level computing courses. Following a joint undergraduate degree in computer science and mathematics, he pursued a PhD on Applied Mathematics. He worked on the U.K. Department for Education and Employment funded MathSkills discipline network, was on the advisory committee for the U.K. national Computer in Teaching Initiative (Mathematics) centre, and was chair of the 2003 international Undergraduate Mathematics Teaching Conference. His research interests include applications of mathematics to computer science problems – in particular applications of Finite geometry and mathematical modelling - and Computer algebra, as well Computer assisted learning including support for Peer Assessment. Recently he has been involved in work on Education for Sustainable Development.

Beth Granter. After completing her MA in Digital Media, Beth Granter worked at the University of Sussex on the Web Team as a Graduate Intern, then as a Project Developer, designing and managing the development of social networking community / mashup site, SPLASH – Student Personal Learning and Social Homepages. She currently works at a London advertising agency where she specialises in social media marketing and online communities. Beth writes a popular blog about social networking sites, feminism, art and user interfaces.

Lyn Greaves is a senior lecturer in the School of Business at Thames Valley University. Lyn was the first lecturer in Thames Valley University appointed as a University Teaching Fellow and for more than a decade she has consistently impacted on the development of teaching and learning. Her work has had a significant impact through a wide range of academic communities – from the student groups she teaches in the areas of Business, Tourism and Hospitality, to staff groups in Faculties across TVU who have been inspired by her. Externally, Lyn is notable for her contribution in a range of HEA Subject Centres, and in developmental areas of eLearning such as reuse of learning objects. Her work, individual and collaborative, has been widely researched and disseminated, drawing support from a range of internal and external funding bodies, including HEA and JISC. Most recently her interests have moved to the area of learning literacies for the digital age. Her work was recognised by the wider academic community in 2008 when she was made National Teaching Fellow by the Higher Education Academy.

Melanie Hall is a lecturer in Psychology at Staffordshire University, Stoke-on-Trent, UK. She is Level One Programme Tutor, with responsibility for the induction of all new students onto the range of Psychology awards. She is also e-mentoring co-ordinator for Psychology. Her research interests include eye witness testimony, psychology and the law, the implementation of psychological principles to eLearning and social networking, and the impact of technologies on individual and group cognition.

Richard Hall is the eLearning Co-ordinator for De Montfort University, Leicester, UK. He is responsible for the academic implementation of eLearning across the institution with the aim of enhancing the student learning experience. He is currently project managing: a Higher Education Academy co-funded project on transitions into higher education supported by social media, called CoTIL; and, a Joint Information Systems Committee-funded curriculum delivery project on supporting remote learners, called MoRSE. His research interests include the impact of new media on pedagogic practice, institutional change, and most importantly upon learner-empowerment and participation.

Jane Hislop qualified as a Physiotherapist from Queen's College Glasgow in 1991 and has worked as a senior physiotherapist in a range of clinical areas. In 1998, she completed an M.Sc in Community Health at Edinburgh University. In 2001, Jane commenced working as a lecturer in physiotherapy at Glasgow Caledonian University and in 2004 she completed a post graduate certificate in tertiary level teaching methods. While working at Glasgow Caledonian University, Jane developed an interest in the use of online teaching resources and had experience of developing materials using the online medium 'Blackboard'. In 2005, Jane went on to work as a lecturer in physiotherapy at Queen Margaret University, Edinburgh where she became the programme and admissions tutor for the MSc (Pre-registration) physiotherapy programme. Jane has had experience of introducing the ePortfolio system into teaching, learning and assessment within the MSc (pre-registration) programme. Jane is currently undertaking part-time PhD research into physical activity levels of preschool children in Lothian.

Debbie Holley is a Principal Lecturer in Learning and Teaching at London Metropolitan University Business School. Her teaching mainly focuses on professional courses leading to qualifications from the Chartered Institute of Purchasing & Supply and The Chartered Institute of Logistics & Transport. Since joining the University from Industry, she has become very interested in the use of technology to facilitate learning. Using a variety of multimedia objects within the WebCT/Blackboard environment she has successfully engaged students with blended learning. Part of the Reusable Learning Object Centre of Excellence for Teaching and Learning team, she is working with students to develop interactive learning materials. She was recently awarded a 3 year University Teaching Fellowship.

Lindesay Irvine studied for a degree in nursing at the then Queen Margaret College, following which she specialised in care of older people nursing. She was latterly Charge Nurse in the Royal Victoria Hospital in Edinburgh. On completion of her Masters in Nursing she was appointed as a lecturer at Queen Margaret University in 1992. She was programme leader for the BSc (Honours) Nursing degree for 15 years until 2008 and is now programme leader for the MSc Nursing degree. In 2008 she successfully completed her PhD which looked at older people's experiences of acute health care. She has extensive knowledge and experience of learning and teaching and runs the core module 'Education in Action' on the MSc Professional and Higher Education programme which focuses on reflection and its role in the learning environment. She works extensively with QMU's international collaborative programmes offered in Saudi Arabia, Egypt and Singapore.

Gordon Joyes is Associate Professor in eLearning at the University of Nottingham, UK and holds the Lord Dearing Award for Excellence in Teaching and Learning. He is an experienced online course developer and online tutor and course leader of an online Professional Doctorate in Teacher Education. Gordon is an accomplished director of international eLearning projects involving both research and innovation. Between 2004-9 he was project manager for five HEFCE funded eChina-UK projects and also Director the HEFCE funded V-ResORT project. From 2007-9 he was an eLearning expert consultant for the Joint Information Systems Committee (JISC) advising on policy and practice. He has a major research interest in the use of online tools for mediating learning and uses Activity Theory to underpin this work.

Tilman Küchler, born on January 21, 1963 is Director of Higher Education at imc Information Multimedia Communication AG and is responsible for the company's activities in schools and higher education. Tilman studied at the Universities of Tuebingen, Paris IV (Sorbonne), Washington and Guadalajara. He gained his doctorate at the University of Washington, Seattle. Before his current occupation, Tilman worked as lecturer at the University of Washington, consultant for structural and political questions in higher education at the Science Council of Cologne, as well as project manager at the CHE

Centrum for Higher Education Development in Guetersloh. Tilman is author of several publications in the areas of literature, philosophy, higher education development and learning technologies.

Sabrina Leone is a PhD student in ELearning at the Faculty of Engineering of the Università Politecnica delle Marche, Ancona, Italy. Her career has developed in the fields of education (secondary and tertiary teacher and consultant), business consultancy (quality systems designer and manager) and linguistic mediation. She has been involved in European special projects (Socrates programmes with Sweden, The Netherlands, Great Britain, Germany, Bulgaria, Lithuania, Estonia) and Italian ones (IG students, Business Laboratory for Italian University and Secondary School students). She has studied and worked abroad (Great Britain, France, Ireland, United States, Australia). She was appointed by the Italian Ministry of Foreign Affairs as a Lecturer in Italian Studies at the Faculty of Arts of the University of Wollongong (2006-2008).She has a honours degree in Foreign Languages (1988, I.U.L.M, Milan), one in Business Management (1998, University of Campobasso) and one in Sciences of Linguistic Mediation (2004, Scuola Superiore per Mediatori Linguistici, Florence). Her research interests are in lifelong learning, technology-enhanced learning environments, eLearning, cooperative learning, intercultural awareness.

Paul Lowe is the Course Director of the Masters programme in Photojournalism and Documentary Photography at the London College of Communication, University of the Arts London, where he developed and lead the validation team for the upgrading of the PG diploma to a full Masters in 2004. He was responsible for the development and launch of a new part time mode of the course delivered entirely online using web conferencing, blogs and the VLE, launched in 2008. Paul is an award-winning photographer, whose work is represented by Panos Pictures. He has covered breaking news the world over, including the fall of the Berlin Wall, Nelson Mandela's release, famine in Africa, the conflict in the former Yugoslavia and the destruction of Grozny. He is a consultant to the World Press Photo foundation in Amsterdam on online education of professional photojournalists in the majority world.

Steve Mackenzie works in the Postgraduate and Continuing Professional Development Office in the Faculty of Health and Life Sciences at De Montfort University, Leicester, UK. He is the team leader for the distance learning design team. The team support programme leaders in the design and implementation of distance learning resources and strategies. His research interests include the use of new media and technology for teaching and learning, in particular the use of online synchronous web conferencing applications and enhancing teacher skills in the areas of eLearning and new media through professional development.

Ruben Martin. Having obtained a professional social work qualification at Leicester University nearly 40 years ago, Ruben Martin initially worked as a Probation Officer. He had 4 years experience as a social work lecturer from 1979 – 1983 on a Certificate of Qualification in Social Work programme at Leicester Polytechnic. Moving to the Voluntary Sector he was for some years National Training Manager for the Salvation Army Social Services. He returned to lecturing on a Diploma in Social Work programme in 1995 and since 2003 has been a social work lecturer and tutor at the University of Kent. For the past 4 years he has been Director of Studies for the BA (Hons) Social Work programme.

Alberto Ramírez Martinell has a BSc. in computer engineering from the Universidad Nacional Autónoma de México; a BA in Humanities from the Universidad del Claustro de Sor Juana, Mexico; an MSc in Computer Science and Media from the Hochshchule Furtwangen, Germany and he is currently a full-time research student in the Department of Educational Research at Lancaster University. His postgraduate studies have been sponsored by the Mexican Council for Science and Technology (CONACyT). His research interests include educational broadcasting, design of video-enriched learning activities, student generated video, and design of technology enhanced learning environments. Alberto has presented his doctoral research in difference international conferences around Europe. He is a committee member of the DIVERSE Network (Developing Innovative visual educational resources for students everywhere), and the co-founder of Lancaster University Student Television (lutube.tv).

Patricie Mertova is currently a Research Fellow in the Centre for the Advancement of Learning and Teaching (CALT) and the Centre for Higher Education Quality (CHEQ) at Monash University, Australia. She has recently completed her PhD focusing on the academic voice in higher education quality. Her background is in the areas of linguistics, translation, cross-cultural communication and foreign languages. She also has research expertise in the areas of higher education and higher education quality.

Andrew Middleton is a Senior Lecturer in Creative Development and part of the Academic Innovation team in Sheffield Hallam University's Learning and Teaching Institute. He has been investigating the design and the potential application of digital audio by academics and students for about five years. As well as his ongoing research into audio feedback and the use of student audio notes, he has developed the concepts of Digital Audio Learning Objects and Media Intervention to demonstrate how such media can be used across the curriculum in a learner-centred paradigm. The mismatch between highly accessible digital media technology and institutional infrastructure is a new focus of investigation. Andrew presents the Learning, Teaching and Assessment in Higher Education podcast and is a leading member of the Podcasting for Pedagogic Purposes Special Interest Group in the UK.

Kate Morss was the founding Director of the Centre for Academic Practice (CAP) at Queen Margaret University, Edinburgh and joint programme leader for the MSc in Professional Education until September 2008. In that role, she and her team provided a wide portfolio of professional development opportunities in learning, teaching and research, including eLearning, as well as support for students through a learning advisory service. CAP has also been a leader in educational research and development within the university, and ePortfolios have been central to that work. Kate's own research interests and publications are in the area of professional practice and development, including reflective practice and evaluation of teaching.

Sue Murray is a researcher with the Centre for Academic Practice at Queen Margaret University and is currently involved in two studies, which are exploring different perspectives of the learner experience of ePortfolios. Her PhD, awarded in 2007, involved the development and evaluation of a web-based, interactive timetable for children with high-functioning autism. Her interests are in the areas of information management and eLearning and she has experience of lecturing in the field of Media and Communication. Sue recently completed a research activity with the Royal Bank of Scotland Centre for the Older Person's Agenda (QMU), for the Scottish Government, evaluating a digital inclusion project for a 50+ age group. She has presented at international conferences and has recently published on ePortfolios. Prior to returning to study, Sue was a state registered nurse (SRN).

Barbara Newland is National Teaching Fellow with over 16 years experience of supporting learning and teaching. She is Manager of Educational Development Services at Bournemouth University and previously she managed the Learning Technology Team at Durham University. Barbara was the Project Director of the HEA-funded Pathfinder project on Innovative -eLearning with E-resources (eRes) and the HEFCE-funded Accessibility in Learning Environments and Related Technologies (ALERT) project. She is a member of the Heads of eLearning Forum Steering Committee and previously Chair of the Association for Learning Technology Membership Committee. Barbara's current research interests focus on strategic educational developments, innovative use of e-resources in eLearning, threshold concepts and academic use of Web 2.0 technologies. Barbara publishes and presents at national and international conferences.

Stuart Nolan develops playful, performative methods for teaching and learning, change management, and innovation in the creative industries. As a NESTA Fellow he researched the role of the mysterious in learning, creativity and innovation, studying magic with Juan Tamariz, Paul Daniels, and with Eugene Burger and Jeff McBride of the Las Vegas Mystery School. Stuart has taught and developed courses in the new media and game design subject area at a number of European universities. He is currently a Curriculum Developer for the Centre for Excellence in Media Practice (Bournemouth Media School), a Media Development Professional for North West Vision & Media, and a board member of The Media Centre, Huddersfield. As an internationally respected authority on creativity and new media he has spoken at over 70 professional conferences in the past 10 years and has been a judge on both the BAFTA Interactive Awards and the Big Chip Awards.

Anne Nortcliffe is the Principal Lecturer in Engineering Department. Her research interests are educational pedagogical research to enhance student learning and assessment experience through the research and development of different methods of deployment of education technologies. In recent years the focus of her research has been in digital audio recording to enhance student learning experience through the distribution of audio lecture notes and audio feedback. As a result of this research Anne has been invited to contribute to a number of journals and book chapters with her co-author and fellow researcher Andrew Middleton in this subject area. Anne is also Teaching Fellow for Assessment for Faculty of Arts, Computing, Engineering and Science, actively involved in number of initiatives with staff and students in the Faculty and across Faculties to improve assessment and feedback experience for all students studying at Sheffield Hallam University.

Marina Orsini-Jones is a Principal Lecturer in the Department of English and Languages at Coventry University (UK) and has carried out research on the integration of eLearning into the languages curriculum for many years. In the 90s she developed student-centred multimedia software and published one of the first CD-ROMs that integrated the teaching of language and society in the higher education curriculum in the UK. She has published work on the impact that education technology can have on the undergraduate students' learning experience and is particularly interested in developing constructivist tasks that can enhance the development of students' critical multiliteracies. Marina is currently investigating both subject specific threshold concepts in languages and linguistics and more generic troublesome knowledge relating to academic and professional competences (e.g. undergraduate research skills). She is moreover exploring ways in which ePortfolios can facilitate and enhance personalised learning. Action research is her methodology of choice.

Samantha Osborne is the IT Manager at the School of Social Policy, Sociology and Social Research at the University of Kent. She is involved developing and encouraging the use of technology in the department and was responsible for the introduction of ePortfolios to the curriculum through several interdepartmental projects. Samantha has presented on her work at several conferences including the South East Education Consortium and the Telling Stories Conference and written for the LDHEN Symposium and Centre for Recording Achievement. Her current projects include linking Personal Development Planning with employability and the development of ePortfolio use for post-qualifying students. Prior to coming to work for Kent, she gained her Masters degree in Computer Science and has worked for a variety of organisations including the HM Prison Service and Pfizer Central Research.

Maria-Christiana Papaefthimiou. As eLearning Manager, a key part of Maria's work is to lead, promote and support the use of ICT and eLearning across the University of Reading. Her main interests include the pedagogical aspects of ICT use and how technology can be best deployed to enhance the quality of teaching and learning experience. She has been involved in a number of HEA/JISC national initiatives on eLearning and has presented to national and international conferences

Susi Peacock is a senior lecturer in eLearning at Queen Margaret University where she leads the implementation of technology enhanced learning. With her team, she is responsible for the deployment and support of e-systems such as the Virtual Learning Environment, ePortfolios, personal voting systems, online synchronous learning environments, online marking and smartboards. With a strong practitioner-focus, Susi works with academics across the institution to support the integration of eLearning into the curriculum to enhance the student experience. She provides numerous staff development activities for tutors and offers an online masters module in network technologies. She has presented extensively at international conferences and published on staff development and the student perspective on eLearning. For five years, she was editor of ALT-N and now regularly reviews for journals. She has several publications on ePortfolios and has worked with JISCinfoNet on developing a guide to using ePortfolios.

Ruth Pilkington is a principal lecturer in Professional Development and Higher Education in the School of Education and Social Science which she joined in January 2005. She began her career as a business linguist, moving to staff and education development as a result of managing two nationally funded projects in the UK. She assumed course leadership of the PG Certificate in Learning and Teaching in Higher Education at University of Central Lancashire in 2002 and has developed the M.Ed (Professional Practice in Education) there. Ruth has published on the subject of employability and professional development. Her current research focuses on the development of reflective professional learning for HE practice and assessment. In 2008, she received funding from JISC to develop professional learning materials for delivery online. She chaired the national Professional Development Framework Committee for the Staff and Educational Development Association (SEDA) from 2006-9 and is currently on SEDA Executive committee.

Alison Scott is a Lecturer in Radiography at Queen Margaret University with primary responsibilities for clinical and professional education. She has championed the introduction and implementation of ePortfolio for undergraduate radiography students in partnership with the team from the Centre for Academic Practice and is an active supporter of and contributor to the Virtual Learning Environment. Responsible for clinical practitioner education and development with regard to supervisory and assessment skills, she works in partnership with placement providers to ensure quality experiences for learners. Currently in the final stages of an MSc in Professional Education, her main interests are curriculum design and eLearning. Before joining the team at Queen Margaret University, she was Associate Directorate Manager in the Radiology Department of the Royal Hospital for Sick Children, Edinburgh.

Julie-Ann Sime is a lecturer in Educational Research in the Centre for Studies in Advanced Learning Technology at Lancaster University, UK, where she teaches on a professional doctorate in e-Research & Technology Enhanced Learning. With a background in psychology, computer science and artificial intelligence she adopts a multi-disciplinary approach to research into the design of interactive learning environments within professional development contexts in industry and higher education. She has been involved in 5 major research collaborations with European industry and with higher education partners to look at complex real-world problems. Julie-Ann is interested in how educational theory is put into practice, and how designers and educators can be supported in their working practice in adoption of new technologies.

Lindsay Smith is currently the Deputy Head of the School of Information Technology, Monash University, Australia. He is also the Chair of the Monash University Faculty of Information Technology's Undergraduate Programs' Committee, and Academic Progress Committee, the Chair of the Faculty Common Core Working Party, which oversees delivery a set of core IT skill units across all Monash campuses, including the international campuses, in South Africa and Malaysia. He has taught in Victorian secondary schools for 14 years, 2 years in Technical and Further Education and at Monash University for the last 20 years. In 2002, he was appointed as a Senior Lecturer at the Monash Berwick Campus. In 2001 awarded a Vice-Chancellor's Special Commendation for Excellence in Teaching.

Stan Stanier is manager of the Learning Technologies Group at the university of Brighton: the team responsible for studentcentral – the university's Shared Learning Environment. Studentcentral is a learning platform integrating the Blackboard Learning System with numerous other technologies including the university's student record system, online library and Community@Brighton - a university-wide social network that was shortlisted for the ISC/Times Higher award for Outstanding ICT Initiative of the Year 2007. Stan has worked in educational technologies for 20 years, from subject-specialist support and development to institutional implementations as well as advising on the development of the university's learning & teaching and information strategies.

Kim Styles is currently the Deputy Director of Teaching and Learning at Monash College, Melbourne, Australia. From 1990 until 2008, she was a lecturer and senior lecturer in Monash University's Faculty of Information Technology. She has taught a range of undergraduate and postgraduate subjects in programming, object-oriented modelling and information systems to on-campus and distance education students. Inspired by the challenges of the diverse learning needs of these groups, Kim has led several educational strategic initiatives in the Faculty using current education research and evidence of student needs to improve what happens in the classroom. In 2008, she was awarded the Monash University Individual Staff Excellence Award for Teaching.

Dirk Thißen, born on August 13, 1967 is Managing Director of IMC (UK) Learning Ltd and is responsible for the company's vision, strategic direction, and operational management in the UK market. Before that Dirk used to work as consultant and product manager for IMC. In these roles he was in charge of several LMS implementations at global enterprises and a product line of the company's LMS targeted at Corporate Universities. Dirk studied electrical engineering and economics at the RWTH Aachen University. He wrote his dissertation at the University of Hagen about methodologies for creating generic eContent frameworks for engineering subjects. Dirk is the author of several publications in the areas of learning solutions in businesses and universities.

Len Webster has expertise in educational policy, educational development, quality development and flexible learning. Currently he is the Educational Adviser in the Centre for the Advancement of Learning and Teaching (CALT) at Monash University, Australia. He previously was the director of an educational development unit in the Faculty of Law, Monash University, where he was the Faculty Quality Development Coordinator. He has also been a reviewer of the Australian University Quality Agency conference proceedings.

Volker Zimmermann is a member of the executive board. Volker, born on December 3, 1967, is co-founder of IMC Information Multimedia Communication AG. As a member of the board, he is responsible for innovation projects (new business), HRM and legal issues. He studied business administration, focusing on management informatics, HRM and organisation at the University of Saarland and at the University of California, San Diego (UCSD). He wrote his dissertation, which was awarded "summa cum laude", in 1998 at the Institute of Management Informatics (Head: Prof. Dr. Dr. h.c. mult. August-Wilhelm Scheer) of the Saarland University on the topic "Object-oriented business process management". Dr. Zimmermann is author of several books and of more than fifty publications, mostly in the area of learning solutions in businesses and universities. Since 2006 he has been a member of an expert commission of the EU on the future of "technology-based learning" in Europe. In 2007 he supported the German ministry for education and research (BMBF) in the question of more innovation in education through Web 2.0 in Germany.

Index